beauty therapy

THE FOUNDATIONS

Habia SERIES – RELATED TITLES

HAIRDRESSING

Student textbooks
Begin Hairdressing: The Official Guide to Level 1 1e *Martin Green*
Hairdressing – The Foundations: The Official Guide to Level 2 5e *Leo Palladino and Martin Green*
Professional Hairdressing: The Official Guide to Level 3 5e *Leo Palladino and Martin Green*
The Official Guide to the City & Guilds Certificate in Salon Services 1e *John Armstrong with Anita Crosland, Martin Green and Lorraine Nordmann*
The Colour Book: The Official Guide to Colour for NVQ Levels 2 & 3 1e *Tracey Lloyd with Christine McMillan-Bodell*
eXtensions: The Official Guide to Hair Extensions 1e *Theresa Bullock*
Salon Management 1e *Martin Green*
Men's Hairdressing: Traditional and Modern Barbering 2e *Maurice Lister*
African-Caribbean Hairdressing 2e *Sandra Gittens*
The World of Hair Colour 1e *Dr John Gray*

Professional Hairdressing titles
Trevor Sorbie: The Bridal Hair Book 1e *Trevor Sorbie and Jacki Wadeson*
The Art of Dressing Long Hair 1e *Guy Kremer and Jacki Wadeson*
Patrick Cameron: Dressing Long Hair 1e *Patrick Cameron and Jacki Wadeson*
Patrick Cameron: Dressing Long Hair 2 1e *Patrick Cameron and Jacki Wadeson*
Bridal Hair 1e *Pat Dixon and Jacki Wadeson*
Professional Men's Hairdressing: The Art of Cutting and Styling 1e *Guy Kremer and Jacki Wadeson*
Essensuals, the Next Generation Toni and Guy: Step by Step 1e *Sacha Mascolo, Christian Mascolo and Stuart Wesson*
Mahogany Hairdressing: Steps to Cutting, Colouring and Finishing Hair 1e *Martin Gannon and Richard Thompson*
Mahogany Hairdressing: Advanced Looks 1e *Martin Gannon and Richard Thompson*
The Total Look: The Style Guide for Hair and Make-Up Professionals 1e *Ian Mistlin*
Trevor Sorbie: Visions in Hair 1e *Trevor Sorbie, Kris Sorbie and Jacki Wadeson*
The Art of Hair Colouring 1e *David Adams and Jacki Wadeson*

BEAUTY THERAPY
Beauty Basics: The Official Guide to Level 1 2e *Lorraine Nordmann*
Beauty Therapy – The Foundations: The Official Guide to Level 2 4e *Lorraine Nordmann*
Professional Beauty Therapy: The Official Guide to Level 3 3e *Lorraine Nordmann*
The Official Guide to the City & Guilds Certificate in Salon Services 1e *John Armstrong with Anita Crosland, Martin Green and Lorraine Nordmann*
Encyclopedia of Hair Removal 1e *Gill Morris and Janice Brown*
The Complete Guide to Make-Up 1e *Suzanne Le Quesne*
The Complete Make-Up Artist 2e *Penny Delamar*
The Encyclopedia of Nails 2e *Jacqui Jefford and Anne Swain*
The Art of Nails: A Comprehensive Style Guide to Nail Treatments and Nail Art 1e *Jacqui Jefford*
Nail Artistry 1e *Jacqui Jefford, Sue Marsh and Anne Swain*
The Complete Nail Technician 2e *Marian Newman*
Manicure, Pedicure and Advanced Nail Techniques 1e *Elaine Almond*
The Official Guide to Body Massage 2e *Adele O'Keefe*
An Holistic Guide to Massage 1e *Tina Parsons*
Indian Head Massage 2e *Muriel Burnham-Airey and Adele O'Keefe*
Aromatherpy for the Beauty Therapist 1e *Valerie Ann Worwood*
An Holistic Guide to Reflexology 1e *Tina Parsons*
An Holistic Guide to Anatomy and Physiology 1e *Tina Parsons*
The Essential Guide to Holistic and Complementary Therapy 1e *Helen Beckmann and Suzanne Le Quesne*
The Spa Book 1e *Jane Crebbin-Bailey, Dr John Harcup and John Harrington*
Nutrition: A Practical Approach 1e *Suzanne Le Quesne*
Hands on Sports Therapy 1e *Keith Ward*

beauty therapy

THE FOUNDATIONS

THE OFFICIAL GUIDE TO NVQ/SVQ LEVEL 2

FOURTH EDITION

LORRAINE NORDMANN

 City & Guilds

 habia
standards · information · solutions

 THOMSON ™

Australia · Canada · Mexico · Singapore · Spain · United Kingdom · United States

THOMSON

Beauty Therapy – The Foundations, Fourth Edition
Lorraine Nordmann

Publishing Director
John Yates

Commissioning Editor
Melody Dawes

Development Editors
Lizzie Catford
Emily Gibson

Production Editor
Emily Gibson

Manufacturing Manager
Helen Mason

Marketing Manager
Leo Stanley

Typesetter
Meridian Colour Repro Ltd, Berkshire

Production Controller
Maeve Healy

Illustrations
Oxford Designers and Illustrators

Cover Design
Jackie Wrout, Land-Sky Ltd

Text Design
Design Deluxe Ltd, Bath, UK

Printer
Seng Lee Press, Singapore

First edition published 1995 by Macmillan.
Second edition published 1999 by Macmillan.
Third edition published 2004 by Thomson Learning.
This edition published 2007 by Thomson Learning.

British Library Cataloguing-in-Publication Data
A catalogue record for this book is available from the British Library

contents

acknowledgements

Activewise/Haslauer of Salzburg (www.activewise.co.uk)

Elaine Almond

American Express

Sameer Arain: professional photographer

BABTAC, the British Association of Beauty Therapy and Cosmetology

Ballets

Joanne Etherson at Beauty Express

Dr M.H. Beck

Dawn Harley at Becton, Dickinson and Company

Chubb Fire Ltd

Creative Nail/The Hyperion Group

Jane Critchley and Emma Tonkin: models at Spirit Health Club Beauty Salon, Haydock, Holiday Inn

Dale Sauna Ltd

Depilex/RVB

The Detox Box

Digi Nail Art – Digi Printers Ltd

Dream Workwear

Elisabeth Garcia, Elemis Ltd

Emma Kenny and Pam Linforth, Ellisons (www.ellisons.co.uk)

Floataway (www.floataway.co.uk)

Dr John Gray: *The World of Skin Care*

Habia, the Hair and Beauty Industry Authority

Helinova Ltd

HMSO (Her Majesty's Stationery Office)

HSE (Health and Safety Executive)

Nicola Hulbert: beauty therapist, New Woman, Westhoughton

Paul Gerrard, Jessica Nails/ The Natural Nail Company

Jacqui Jefford and Anne Swain with great appreciation for allowing us to reproduce images from their book: *The Encyclopedia of Nails*, 2nd ed. Jacqui Jefford, Sue Marsh and Anne Swain for allowing us to use an image from their book: *Nail Artistry*

Vicki Kennedy: salon owner and beauty therapist, New Woman, Westhoughton

Jonathan Knott

Pamela Linforth

Moom: Stick With Us Products

Millennium Nail Systems

NSI UK

Illustrations courtesy of Oxford Designers and Illustrators

Leah Park: beauty therapy lecturer and freelance make-up artist Lee@graduate-centre.com

Photographers: Anderson and Ian Littlewood; make-up artist: Jo Crowder; and illustrator: Pam Young

Precious Professional (Courtesy of Ellisons)

Kay Riding

Janine Rigby: beauty therapist

Hugh Rushton

Saks: Covent Garden

Joan Scott and Andrea Harrison: *Spa: The Official Guide to Spa Therapy at Levels 2 & 3*

Sally Smith at Original Additions (Salon System) Ltd

Sorisa

Spa Find International Ltd (www.spafindskincare.com)

Many thanks to Spirit Health Club, Haydock Holiday Inn Hotel, Lodge Lane, Newton-le-Willows for allowing us to reproduce their safety check sheets in Chapter 15. Contact: spirit.haydock@IChotelsgroup.com

Staff at Spirit Health Club, Holiday Inn Hotel, Lodge Lane, Newton-le-Willows: Stephen Ewing: club manager; Alan Cooke: lifestyle consultant; Helen Brough: beauty therapist; Stephen Helsby: lifestyle consultant; Nicola Shields: beauty therapist

Sukar: many thanks to Roger and Nagwa Stanforth of Nagwa Trading Co. Ltd for supplying the images of sugaring and strip sugar

Gail Proudman, S.P.M.U. Technical and Medical Tattooist for SurgiCare Ltd

Toria Law at Spangles/United Beauty Products Ltd

Unilever

With very grateful thanks to Caroline Morley at The Wellcome Photo Library

Elizabeth and Norman Whiteside

Lorraine Williamson

Dr A.L. Wright

8.1.9.18 Divas Ltd, Uckfield

foreword

I can scarcely believe that it has been ten years since I wrote the foreword for the second edition of Lorraine Nordmann's excellent book *Beauty Therapy – The Foundations: The Official Guide to Level 2*.

Since then, the beauty industry has grown from strength to strength, advancing in professionalism, technology and capability. UK standards are widely considered the best in the world and I am certain that Lorraine has played a huge role in pushing the development of beauty to the quality we now see. With her dedication, expertise and passion, she has helped make the industry the success it is today.

The fact that the fourth edition has now been published is testament to the popularity of her books and the depth and knowledge that they pass on to year after year of students. Her commitment to the development and introduction of innovative learning support and guidance is clearly reflected in her work.

Without a doubt, *Beauty Therapy – The Foundations, Fourth Edition*, is the most informative book to cover the Level 2 Beauty Therapy Standards as laid down by Habia.

Alan Goldsbro
Chief Executive Officer, Habia

note from the author

I am proud to present the fourth edition of *Beauty Therapy – The Foundations: The Official Guide to Level 2*.

The book builds on its previous educational strengths and retains its clear, concise presentation supporting you, the learner, as you progress through your beauty therapy qualification. However, as the industry continues to develop both in popularity and provision the revision to this edition aims to maintain a text that is fresh and current. This has enabled the inclusion of new features and more step-by-step images to inspire, motivate and challenge you to achieve your goals.

The text has been written to fully support the NVQ/SVQ Level 2 Beauty Therapy standards, as written by the Hairdressing and Beauty Industry Association (Habia). The chapter headings match the NVQ/SVQ titles and each NVQ/SVQ unit is broken into its outcomes for ease of reference.

I hope you will appreciate the revisions made to help you gain the practical skills, knowledge and understanding to make you a successful beauty therapist within the industry and be part of its future development.

Good luck in your beauty therapy career.

Lorraine Nordmann

introduction

AN INTRODUCTION TO NVQs/SVQs

National Vocational Qualifications (NVQs) and Scottish Vocational Qualifications (SVQs) are nationally recognised qualifications that have a common structure and design. They follow a similar format for all occupational and vocational sectors. The award of an NVQ/SVQ demonstrates that the person has the competence (sufficient skill and knowledge) to perform job roles/tasks effectively in their occupational area. An NVQ at Level 2 covers a wide range of varied work activities, some of which are complex and require that the candidate use their initiative and make independent decisions.

Each NVQ/SVQ is structured in the same way, and is made up of a number of units and elements.

The **unit** relates to a specific task or skill area of work. It is the smallest part of an award, which can be accredited separately.

The **outcome/s** describe/s in detail the skill and knowledge components of the unit.

An example from NVQ Level 2 Beauty Therapy is shown below.

The title of the unit is: **Unit BT 5 Provide eyelash and eyebrow treatments**.

The outcomes for the unit detail the practical skills and underpinning knowledge essential to provide eyelash and eyebrow treatments.

The *outcomes* which detail the *unit* components include:

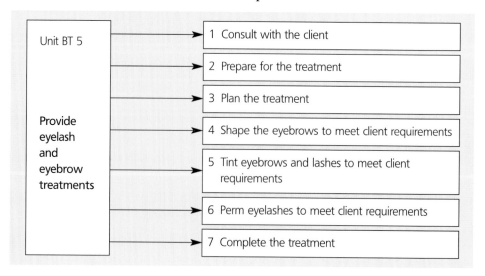

Units and outcomes

For each unit, when all competence requirements have been achieved, a unit of certification may be awarded, such as Unit BT5 Provide eyelash and eyebrow treatments.

Each NVQ/SVQ is made up of a specific number of units required for the occupational area. Some of the units are termed **mandatory** (compulsory) and some are termed **optional** (not compulsory).

Mandatory units must be competently achieved to gain the NVQ/SVQ award.

Optional units may be selected by the candidate to study in addition to the mandatory units.

The NVQ/SVQ will state the mandatory (compulsory) units required to achieve the qualification plus the number of optional units, which must be completed in order to achieve the full NVQ/SVQ award.

There are three training routes to achieve NVQ/SVQ Beauty Therapy Level 2:

1 Beauty Therapy General

2 Beauty Therapy Make-up

3 Nail Services

Whichever route you choose, you must achieve the mandatory units plus one optional unit from the selection of units provided.

The **core mandatory** units are fundamental, essential units to be achieved whichever route is chosen. These are as follows:

- G1 Ensure your own actions reduce risks to health and safety
- G6 Promote additional products or services to clients
- G8 Develop and maintain your effectiveness at work

Note that G4 Fulfil salon reception duties has been placed in the core section of the book, even though it is not actually mandatory. This is because it was felt that this is where lecturers would want to deliver this course content, as opposed to with the later, more practical units.

BEAUTY THERAPY NVQ/SVQ – LEVEL 2
NVQ/SVQ Qualification Structure

Candidates will need to achieve the 'core' mandatory units, plus the mandatory units from one of the two routes, and the specified number of optional units for that route.

'Core' Mandatory Units (all units must be achieved)

G1   Ensure your own actions reduce risks to health and safety

G6   Promote additional products or services to clients

G8   Develop and maintain your effectiveness at work

Beauty Therapy General (mandatory units)	Beauty Therapy Make-up (mandatory units)
BT4 Improve and maintain facial skin condition	BT4 Improve and maintain facial skin condition
BT5 Provide eyelash and eyebrow treatments	BT9 Provide make-up treatment
BT6 Remove hair using waxing techniques	BT10 Plan and promote make-up activities
BT7 Provide manicure treatment	BT11 Enhance the appearance of eyebrows and lashes
BT8 Provide pedicure treatment	
Plus one optional unit (see below)	*Plus* one optional unit (see below)

Optional Units (the relevant number of optional units must be achieved)

G4   Fulfil salon reception duties

BT5   Provide eyelash and eyebrow treatments

BT6   Remove hair using waxing techniques

BT7   Provide manicure treatment

BT8   Provide pedicure treatment

BT9   Provide make-up treatment

BT10 Plan and promote make-up activities

BT44 Extend and maintain nails

BT13 Provide nail art service

BT14 Pierce ears

BT15 Assist with spa treatments

Note: Where units are achieved as mandatory units in either of the two routes, these do not count as optional units as well.

NAIL SERVICES NVQ/SVQ – LEVEL 2
NVQ/SVQ Qualification Structure

Candidates will need to achieve all of the mandatory units and one optional unit

Mandatory Units (all units must be achieved)

G1 Ensure your own actions reduce risks to health and safety

G6 Promote additional products or services to clients

G8 Develop and maintain your effectiveness at work

BT7 Provide manicure treatment

BT8 Provide pedicure treatment

BT44 Extend and maintain nails

BT13 Provide nail art service

Optional Units

G4 Fulfil salon reception duties

BT4 Improve and maintain facial skin condition

BT5 Provide eyelash and eyebrow treatments

BT6 Remove hair using waxing techniques

BT9 Provide make-up treatment

BT10 Plan and promote make-up activities

BT14 Pierce ears

BT15 Assist with spa treatments

Performance criteria

The performance criteria lists the necessary actions that you must achieve to complete the task competently (demonstrating adequate practical skill and experience to the assessor).

The **performance criteria** requirements for BT5 Outcome 1 Consult with the client are listed below:

- using consultation techniques in a polite and friendly manner to determine the client's treatment plan
- discussing and agreeing the service and outcomes that are acceptable to your client and meets their needs
- maintaining the client's modesty and privacy at all times
- recognising contra-indications and taking the necessary action.

Range

Range statements are often identified for each outcome. The assessment range relates to the different conditions under which a skill must be competently demonstrated for the outcome.

For example the **range** assessment requirements for Unit BT5 outcome 5, Tint eyebrows and lashes to meet client requirements, are to cover all the hair colourings shown below:

- fair
- red
- dark
- white/grey

Range: Your performance must cover the following situations
a Fair
b Red
c Dark
d White/Grey

It is not sufficient to be able to only practically perform the task – you must understand why you are doing it, and be able to transfer your competence to a variety of situations. This is referred to as your *knowledge and understanding*. Further assessment of your knowledge and understanding of the skill, the knowledge specification, may be assessed through theoretical tasks such as written tests, assignments and oral questioning.

The **knowledge and understanding** requirements that you are required to know for **Unit BT5 Client consultation** are listed below:

- how to use effective communication and consultation techniques

- the reasons why it is important to encourage clients with contra-indications to seek medical advice
- the importance of, and reasons for, not naming specific contra-indications when referring clients to a general practitioner
- why it is important to maintain the client's modesty and privacy.

What often occurs is that the same knowledge and understanding may be necessary for similar units. This can be seen, for example, in the knowledge and understanding for **Organisational and Legal Requirements**. This duplication is necessary as some units may be studied and accredited as an individual skill, i.e. BT14 Pierce ears.

Where evidence has been achieved, this is cross-referenced (directed) in the portfolio (a file that holds your assessment evidence) to where the evidence can be found.

To achieve unit competence, all performance criteria, range, and knowledge and understanding requirements must have been met and evidence presented as necessary. Evidence is usually provided in your assessment book and portfolio.

Where there is evidence of previous experience and achievement, this may be presented to the assessor for consideration for accreditation. This is called Accreditation of Prior Learning (APL).

Beauty Therapy – The Foundations follows the Beauty Therapy NVQ/SVQ Level 2 format and covers both the practical and theoretical requirements for both the mandatory and optional units.

about the book

The book relates to the NVQ/SVQ Level 2 qualification structure and has been divided into three parts:

1 Core units
2 Anatomy and physiology
3 General beauty therapy units

CORE UNIT CHAPTERS

The core units relate to the three core mandatory units required for Beauty Therapy NVQ/SVQ Level 2, for both the Beauty Therapy general route and the Beauty Therapy make-up route.

The core unit chapters cover:

- G1 Ensure your own actions reduce risks to health and safety
- G6 Promote additional products or services to clients
- G8 Develop and maintain your effectiveness at work

Note that G4 Fulfil salon reception duties has been placed in the core section of the book, even though it is not actually mandatory. This is because it was felt that this is where lecturers would want to deliver this course content, as opposed to with the later, more practical units.

ANATOMY AND PHYSIOLOGY CHAPTER

Certain units have an anatomy and physiology knowledge requirement.

 Chapter 5 provides the essential knowledge, and also contains a useful reference chart that states the specific anatomy and physiology requirements to be studied for each unit. In addition, anatomy and physiology is discussed within the general beauty therapy units to aid understanding. Look for the key symbol in each chapter to remind you to check Chapter 5 for essential anatomy and physiology information.

GENERAL BEAUTY THERAPY

These chapters discuss the beauty therapy technical skills in the NVQ, including both the mandatory and optional units.

The general beauty therapy chapters cover the following units:

- G4 Fulfil salon reception duties – an essential skill requirement for some workplaces
- BT4 Improve and maintain facial skin condition
- BT5 Provide eyelash and eyebrow treatments
- BT6 Remove hair using waxing techniques
- BT7 Provide manicure treatment
- BT8 Provide pedicure treatment
- BT9 Provide make-up treatment – including BT10 Plan and promote make-up activities
- BT11 Enhance the appearance of eyebrows and lashes
- BT44 Extend and maintain nails
- BT13 Provide nail art service
- BT14 Pierce ears
- BT15 Assist with spa treatments

FEATURES WITHIN CHAPTERS

Common features appear within each chapter. An explanation for each is provided below:

Learning objectives

Learning objectives introduce each chapter and list the outcomes that make up the unit which must be achieved in order to be accredited with the NVQ/SVQ unit.

When you feel confident and competent with the skills/knowledge requirements you are ready to be assessed.

Learning objectives

This unit describes how to provide pedicure treatments for clients to improve the appearance and condition of the foot, nails and surrounding skin.

It describes the competencies to enable you to:

- **consult with the client**
- **prepare for the treatment**
- **plan the treatment**
- **improve the appearance of the natural nails and cuticles**
- **massage the foot and lower leg**
- **provide nail polishing treatments**
- **complete the treatment**

When providing manicure treatment it is important to use the skills you have learnt in the following core mandatory units:

Unit G1 – Ensure your own actions reduce risks to health and safety
Unit G6 – Promote additional products or services to clients
Unit G8 – Develop and maintain your effectiveness at work

Outcome charts

Outcome charts are provided in each chapter to summarise the skills/knowledge requirement for each outcome, with the title of the outcome and the unit in the left-hand box. These provide a useful checklist for you to refer to.

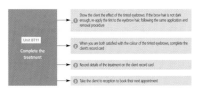

Unit BT11
Complete the treatment

1. Show the client the effect of the tinted eyebrows. If the brow hair is not dark enough, re-apply the tint to the eyebrow hair, following the same application and removal procedure
2. When you are both satisfied with the colour of the tinted eyebrows, complete the client's record card
3. Record details of the treatment on the client record card
4. Take the client to reception to book their next appointment

ACTIVITY

PPE Risk assessment
Carry out your own risk assessment. List the potentially hazardous substances handled in beauty therapy Level 2. Consider what protective clothing should be available.

HEALTH AND SAFETY

Cross-infection
Use a fresh cottonwool pad for each eyebrow to avoid cross-infection.

TIP

When you unpack a delivery, make sure that the product packaging is undamaged, to avoid possible personal injury from broken goods.

GLOSSARY OF KEY WORDS

Accident book a written record of any accident occurring in the workplace. Incidents in the accident book should be reviewed to see where improvements to safe working practice could be made.

Accident form a detailed report form to be completed following any accident in the workplace.

Antiseptic a chemical agent that prevents the multiplication of micro-organisms. It has a limited action and does not kill all micro-organisms.

Autoclave an effective method of sterilisation, suitable for small metal objects and beauty therapy tools, where water is boiled under increased pressure and temperatures reach 134°C.

Bacteria minute single-celled organisms of various shapes. Large numbers live on the skin's surface and are not harmful (non-pathogenic). Others, however, are harmful (pathogenic) and can cause skin diseases.

Contra-indication a problematic symptom that indicates that treatment may not proceed.

Control of Substances Hazardous to Health (COSHH) Regulations 2002 these regulations require employers to identify hazardous substances used in the workplace and state how they should be stored and handled.

Assessment of knowledge and understanding

You have now learnt about the health and safety responsibilities for everyone in the workplace. This will enable you to ensure your own actions reduce risks to health and safety.

To test your level of knowledge, answer the following short questions. These will prepare you for your summative (final) assessment.

Action to avoid health and safety risks

1 What are your main legal responsibilities under the Health and Safety at Work Act 1974?

2 Name four pieces of legislation relating to health and safety in the workplace.

3 What is the purpose of a salon health and safety policy? What sort of information does it include?

4 What is the importance of personal presentation in respect of your salon workplace policy?

5 Why is your personal conduct important to maintain the health and safety of yourself, colleagues and clients?

Activity boxes

Activity boxes feature within chapters and provide additional tasks for you to complete to assess and further your understanding of the unit content.

Health and safety boxes

In addition to the core chapter, G1 Ensure your own actions reduce risks to health and safety, health and safety boxes are provided in each chapter. They serve to draw your attention to related health and safety information for each technical skill.

Tip boxes

The author's experience is shared through tip boxes, which provide positive suggestions to improve your knowledge and skills for each unit.

Glossaries of key words

At the end of every chapter (except the anatomy and physiology chapter), you will find a useful glossary with all of the technical terms from that chapter clearly explained. There is also a summative glossary at the end of the book.

Assessment of knowledge and understanding

In addition to the activity boxes in each chapter, questions are provided at the end of each chapter. These questions relate to the specific essential knowledge and understanding requirements for the unit. You can use the questions to prepare you for oral and written assessments. Seek guidance from your supervisor/assessor if there are any areas that you are unsure of. Remember also to check the anatomy and physiology chapter, referring to the chart, to include revision in the related anatomy and physiology requirement as applicable.

Step-by-step and 'how to' photo sequences

Each chapter aims to demonstrate the featured practical skill using colour photographs to enhance your understanding.

Step by step: tinting the eyebrows

Equipment lists

To assist you preparing for each practical treatment an essential equipment list is provided, supported with images of treatment tools, materials and products required. These are also useful to provide to a Level 1 beauty therapist if assisting you to prepare the work area.

Client treatment record cards

Client treatment record cards are featured in each of the general beauty therapy units. They illustrate the information that you need to assess and gain from the client at consultation in order to establish client suitability and treatment aim. They also provide guidance on information that should be provided following treatment, including aftercare advice and the promotion of additional products and services.

Bold terms

The text highlights certain terms in bold lettering. These often denote important technical terms which are explained and that you must become familiar with to gain knowledge competence for the unit.

Summative glossary

There is a summative glossary at the back of the book, which explains all of the technical terms found within the book. This is in addition to the end-of-chapter glossaries.

core units

G1 Ensure your own actions reduce risks to health and safety

Learning objectives

This chapter covers health and safety duties and responsibilities for everyone in the workplace. It describes the competencies required to ensure that you:

- **identify the hazards and evaluate the risks in your workplace**
- **reduce the risks to health and safety in your workplace**

TAKING CARE OF ALL IN THE WORKPLACE

When working in a service industry, you are legally obliged to provide a **safe and hygienic environment**. This applies whether you are working in a hotel, a department store, a leisure centre or a private beauty salon, or operating a mobile beauty therapy service. You must pay careful attention to health and safety to minimise risk. Exactly the same is true when working in clients' homes: it is essential to follow the normal health and safety guidelines, just as you would when working in a salon.

This chapter is for everyone at work whatever their status: paid, unpaid, part time or full time.

Outcomes 1 and 2: Identify and reduce hazards and risks in your workplace

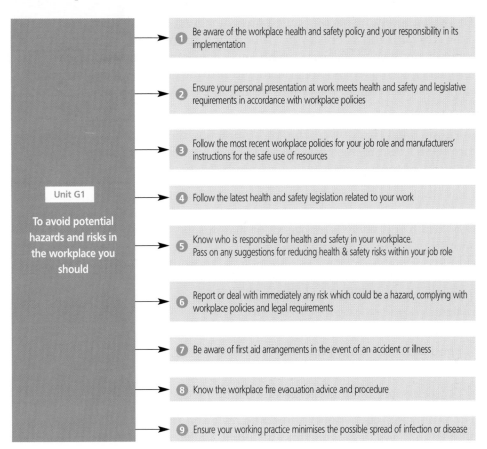

Unit G1

To avoid potential hazards and risks in the workplace you should

1. Be aware of the workplace health and safety policy and your responsibility in its implementation

2. Ensure your personal presentation at work meets health and safety and legislative requirements in accordance with workplace policies

3. Follow the most recent workplace policies for your job role and manufacturers' instructions for the safe use of resources

4. Follow the latest health and safety legislation related to your work

5. Know who is responsible for health and safety in your workplace. Pass on any suggestions for reducing health & safety risks within your job role

6. Report or deal with immediately any risk which could be a hazard, complying with workplace policies and legal requirements

7. Be aware of first aid arrangements in the event of an accident or illness

8. Know the workplace fire evacuation advice and procedure

9. Ensure your working practice minimises the possible spread of infection or disease

Legal responsibilities

If you cause harm to your client, or put them at risk, you will be held responsible and you will be liable to **prosecution**, with the possibility of being fined.

There is a good deal of **legislation** relating to health and safety. You will need to know about the laws relating to beauty therapy. Details are widely available, and you must be aware of your responsibilities and your rights. It is important that you obtain and read all relevant publications from your local Health and Safety Executive (HSE) offices. The HSE provides guidance and information on all aspects of health and safety legislation.

The Health and Safety at Work Act 1974

The **Health and Safety at Work Act 1974** is the main piece of legislation affecting these issues. It was developed from experience gained over 150 years, and now incorporates earlier legislation including the Offices, Shops and Railway Premises Act 1963 and the Fire Precautions Act 1971. It lays down the minimum standards of health, safety and welfare required in each area of the workplace – for example, it requires that business premises and equipment be safe and in good repair. It is the employer's legal

ACTIVITY

Health and safety information
Write to your local Health and Safety Executive (HSE) office to ask for a pack of relevant health and safety information or visit their websites: www.hse.gov.uk and www.hsedirect.gov.uk. Legislation relevant to business operation can also be found in the Health and Safety pack for salons.

ACTIVITY

Health and safety rules
Discuss the rules which you feel should appear in a salon's health and safety policy. The health and safety policy identifies how health and safety is managed for that business, who does what, when and why.

responsibility to implement the Act and to ensure, so far as is reasonably practicable, the health and safety at work of the people for whom they are responsible and those who may be affected by the work they do.

The HSE appoint inspectors called Environmental Health Officers (EHOs) to enforce health and safety law by visiting the workplace to check compliance is being met with all relevant health and safety legislation. Workplace Contact Officers (WCOs) are available to provide advice and guidance and gather relevant data in relation to health and safety and your business.

New businesses are required to register with their Local Authority Environmental Health Department, completing the relevant form – currently form **OSR1**. As the business develops it may be necessary to notify the Local Authority of further services that are available.

Each employer of more than five employees must formulate a written **health and safety policy** for their business. The health and safety policy identifies how health and safety is managed for that business, who does what, when and why. The policy must be issued and discussed with each employee and should outline their safety responsibilities. It should include items such as:

- details of the storage of chemical substances
- details of the stock cupboard or dispensary
- details and records of the checks made by a qualified electrician on specialist electrical equipment
- names and addresses of the keyholders
- escape routes and emergency evacuation procedures.

The health and safety policy should be reviewed regularly to ensure it meets all relevant legislation guidelines including updates. Regular health and safety checks should be made and procedures reviewed to ensure that safety is being satisfactorily maintained.

Employees must co-operate with their employer to provide a safe and healthy workplace. As soon as they observe any **hazard** (anything that can cause harm), this must be reported to the designated authority so that the problem can be put right. Hazards include:

- obstructions to corridors, stairways and fire exits (an obstruction is anything that blocks the traffic route in the salon work environment);
- spillages and breakages.

If there are fewer than five employees, appropriate health and safety arrangements and procedures should be in place. In 1992 European Union (EU) directives updated the legislation on health and safety management. Current legislation at the time of writing (2006) is outlined below.

The Management of Health and Safety at Work Regulations 1999

These require employers to make formal arrangements for maintaining and improving safe working conditions and practices. This includes training for employees to ensure competency and to monitor risk in the workplace (including product use), known as **risk assessment**. Employers with five or more employees need to record important risk assessment findings. Employers need to:

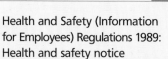

HEALTH AND SAFETY +

Health and Safety (Information for Employees) Regulations 1989: Health and safety notice
Every employer is obliged by law to display the health and safety law poster in the workplace. A leaflet is available called 'Your health and safety – a guide for workers'. Both poster and leaflets are available from the HSE.

HEALTH AND SAFETY +

Lone workers
If you are self employed and work alone, consider your safety. Guidance is provided in the information 'Working alone in safety – controlling the risks of solitary work' INDG73 (rev).

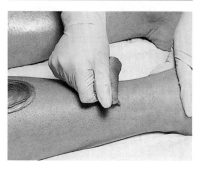

Ensure you follow health and safety guidelines when carrying out treatments such as removing hot wax

- identify potential hazards;
- assess the potential risks associated with the hazard;
- identify who is at risk from the hazard;
- identify how risk is to be minimised or eliminated;
- set up emergency procedures;
- train staff to identify and control risks;
- regularly review the risk assessment process.

The Personal Protective Equipment (PPE) at Work Regulations 1992

The **Personal Protective Equipment (PPE) at Work Regulations 1992** require managers to identify through a **risk assessment** those activities or processes which require special protective clothing or equipment to be worn. This clothing and equipment must then be made available, and must be suitable and in adequate supplies. Employees must wear the protective clothing and use the protective equipment provided, and make employers aware of any shortage so that supplies can be maintained.

PPE should be 'CE' marked – that it complies with the Personal Protective Equipment at Work Regulations, and satisfies basic safety requirements.

The Workplace (Health, Safety and Welfare) Regulations 1992

The **Workplace (Health, Safety and Welfare) Regulations 1992** require all at work to maintain a safe, healthy and secure working environment. The regulations include legal requirements in relation to the following aspects of the working environment:

- maintenance of the workplace and equipment;
- ventilation to ensure the air is changed regularly;
- working temperature;
- lighting;
- cleanliness and correct handling and disposal of waste materials;
- safe salon layout;
- falls and falling objects;
- windows, doors, gates and walls;
- safe floor and traffic routes;
- escalators and moving walkways;

HEALTH AND SAFETY

Protective equipment: gloves
If you are to come into contact with body tissue fluids or with chemicals, wear protective disposable surgical gloves. Latex gloves can cause allergic reactions and in some cases the development of asthma.

An alternative glove that provides adequate protection from contamination should be used, i.e. nitrile or PVC formulation.

ACTIVITY

PPE Risk assessment
Carry out your own risk assessment. List the potentially hazardous substances handled in beauty therapy level 2. Consider what protective clothing should be available.

HEALTH AND SAFETY

European directives
As a result of directives adopted in 1992 by the European Union, health and safety legislation has been updated.
1 Obtain a copy of the eight directives: *Workplace (Health, Safety & Welfare) Regulations 1992*.
2 Look through the publication, and make notes on any information relevant to you in the workplace.

TIP

Temperature and lighting
The salon temperature should be a minimum of 16°C within one hour of employees arriving for work. The salon should be well ventilated, or carbon dioxide levels will increase, which can cause nausea. Many substances used in the salon can become hazardous without adequate ventilation.

If the working environment is too warm this can cause heat stress, a condition that is recognised by the HSE.

Lighting should be adequate to ensure that treatments can be carried out safely and competently, with the minimum risk of accident.

- sanitary conveniences for staff and clients;
- washing facilities;
- drinking water;
- facilities for changing clothing;
- facilities for staff to rest and eat meals;
- fire exits and firefighting equipment.

Manual Handling Operations Regulations 1992

These regulations apply in all occupations where manual lifting occurs. The employer is required to carry out a risk assessment of all activities undertaken which involve manual lifting.

The risk assessment should provide evidence that the following have been considered:

- risk of injury;
- the manual movement involved in performing the activity;
- the physical constraint the load incurs;
- the environmental constraints imposed by the workplace;
- workers' individual capabilities;
- action taken in order to minimise potential risks.

Manual lifting and handling

Always take care of yourself when moving goods around the salon. Do not struggle or be impatient: get someone else to help. When **lifting**, lift from the knees, not the back. When **carrying**, balance weights evenly in both hands and carry the heaviest part nearest to your body.

Provision and Use of Work Equipment Regulations (PUWER) 1998

These regulations lay down the important health and safety controls on the provision and use of work equipment. They state the duties for employers and for users, including the self-employed. They affect both old and new

---

TIP ✓

Broken goods
When you unpack a delivery, make sure that the product packaging is undamaged, to avoid possible personal injury from broken goods.

---

left Lifting a box
centre Carrying several boxes
right Carrying equal weights in both hands

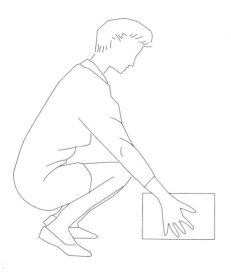

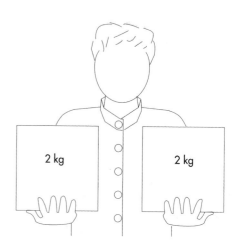

equipment. They identify the requirements in selecting suitable equipment and in maintaining it. They also discuss the information provided by equipment manufacturers, and instruction and training in the safe use of equipment. Specific regulations address the dangers and potential risks of injury that could occur during operation of the equipment.

Health and Safety (Display Screen Equipment) Regulations 1992

These regulations cover the use of display screen equipment and computer screens. They specify acceptable levels of radiation emissions from the screen and identify correct posture, seating position, permitted working heights and rest periods. Employers have a responsibility to comply with this regulation to ensure the welfare of their employees.

Control of Substances Hazardous to Health (COSHH) Regulations 2002

These regulations were designed to make employers consider the substances used in their workplace and assess the possible risks to health. Many substances that seem quite harmless can prove to be hazardous if used or stored incorrectly. Hazardous substances are anything that can harm your health.

Employers are responsible for assessing the risks from hazardous substances and controlling exposure to them to prevent ill health. Any hazardous substances identified must be formally recorded in writing, and given a hazard risk rating. Safety precaution procedures should then be implemented and training given to employees to ensure that the procedures are understood and will be followed correctly.

Hazardous substances are identified through the use of known symbols, examples of which are shown on page 10. Any substance in the workplace that is hazardous to health must be identified on the packaging and stored and handled correctly.

Hazardous substances may enter the body via:

- the eyes;
- the skin;
- the nose (**inhalation**);
- the mouth (**ingestion**).

Each beauty product supplier is legally required to make available guidelines on how materials should be used and stored, called material safety data sheets (MSDSs); these will be supplied on request.

ACTIVITY

Identifying hazards
Make a list of potential electrical hazards in the workplace e.g. damaged plugs. Who should these be reported to?

Correctly seated computer operator

ACTIVITY

COSHH assessments
Carry out a COSHH assessment on selected treatment products used in the salon. Consider manicures, nail extensions, waxing, and facial and eye treatments.

HEALTH AND SAFETY ✚

COSHH assessment
All hazardous substances must be identified when completing the risk assessment. This includes cleaning agents such as a wax equipment cleaner.

High-risk products should where possible be replaced with lower risk products.

COSHH assessment should be reviewed on a regular basis, and updated to include any new products.

TIP ✔

COSHH

A COSHH essential information document is available at www.coshh-essentials.org.uk. HSE publication, ISBN 0717627853 gives details on COSHH assessment.

HEALTH AND SAFETY ✚

Hazardous substances

Potentially hazardous substances include:

- aerosols
- disinfectants
- water treatment chemicals used in spa pools.

Six hazard symbols

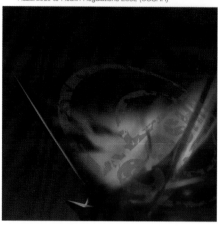

COSHH: A brief guide to the Regulations

What you need to know about the Control of Substances Hazardous to Health Regulations 2002 (COSHH)

COSHH Regulations, available from the HSE

C.O.S.H.H. CONTROL OF SUBSTANCES HAZARDOUS TO HEALTH

Health and Safety Information for the Beauty Salon and Beauty Therapist.

Compiled by The Sterex Academy

Contents:

50 x Product assessment record forms
1 x 'How to' fill in/use your product assessment record forms
1 x Daily/monthly/quarterly/annual Check List
1 x Ellisons Booklet COSHH and the Beauty Salon.

COSHH information, available from beauty suppliers

Cosmetic Products (Safety) Regulations 2004

This piece of legislation consolidates earlier regulations and incorporates current European directives. Part of consumer protection legislation, it requires that cosmetics and toiletries are safe in their formulation and are safe for use for their intended purpose as a cosmetic and comply with labelling requirements.

Electricity at Work Regulations 1989

These regulations state that every piece of electrical equipment in the workplace should be tested every 12 months by a qualified electrician. A written record of testing must be retained and made available for inspection. A list of all salon electrical equipment should be available with its unique serial number and date of purchase/disposal.

In addition to annual testing, a trained member of staff should regularly check all electrical equipment for safety. This is recommended every three months. Report to your supervisor if you see any of these potential hazards:

- exposed wires in flexes;
- cracked plugs or broken sockets;
- worn cables;
- overloaded sockets.

Although it is the responsibility of the employer to ensure all equipment is safe to use, it is also the responsibility of the employee to always check that equipment is safe before use, and to never use it if it is faulty.

Any pieces of equipment that appear faulty must immediately be checked and, if necessary, repaired before use. If faulty they must be labelled to ensure that they are not used by accident.

Accidents

Accidents in the workplace usually occur through negligence by employees or unsafe working conditions.

Any accidents occurring in the workplace must be recorded on a **report form**, and entered into an **accident book**. Incidents in the accident book should be reviewed regularly to see where improvements to working practice can be made. The report form requires more details than the accident book – you must note down:

- the date and time of the accident;
- the date of entry into the accident book;
- the name of the person or people involved;
- the accident details;
- the injuries sustained;
- the action taken;
- the signature of the person making the entry.

Breakages and spillages

Accidents can damage stock, resulting in breakage of containers and spillage of contents. Breakage of glass can cause cuts; spillages may cause somebody to slip and fall. Any breakages or spillages should therefore be dealt with immediately and in the correct way.

You must determine whether the spillage is a potential hazard to health, and what action is necessary. To whom should you report it? What equipment is required to remove the spillage? How should the materials be disposed of?

Always consider your COSHH data and check to see how the product should be handled and disposed of.

Reporting of Injuries, Diseases and Dangerous Occurrences Regulations (RIDDOR) 1995

RIDDOR requires the employer to notify the local enforcement officer, in writing, in cases where employees or trainees suffer personal injury at work. These include loss of sight, amputation, fracture and electric shock. When this occurrence results in death, major injury or more than 24 hours in hospital, it must be reported by telephone first, and followed by a written report within seven days. In all cases where personal injury occurs, an entry must be made in the workplace accident book. Where visitors to the work premises are injured this must be reported also. A record of any reportable injury, disease or dangerous occurrence must be kept for three years after the date it happened. This information assists the HSE in investigation of serious accidents.

First aid

The **Health and Safety (First Aid) Regulations 1981** state that workplaces must have first-aid provision. Employers must have appropriate and adequate first-aid arrangements in the event of an accident or illness occurring. It is recommended that at least one person holds an HSE-approved basic first-aid qualification.

ACTIVITY

Accidents

Discuss potential causes of accidents in the workplace. How could these accidents be prevented? Who would you report an accident or injury to in the workplace and when?

HEALTH AND SAFETY

Breakages and spillages

When dealing with hazardous breakages and spillages, the hands should always be protected with gloves. To avoid injury to others, broken glass should be put in a secure container prior to disposing of it in a waste bin.

HEALTH AND SAFETY

First aid

- This should only be given by a qualified first-aider.
- A first-aid certificate is only valid for three years after qualifying, it must be renewed. This may mean additional first-aid training.
- Know what action you can take within your responsibility in the event of an accident occurring.
- An accident book should be available to record details of any accident that has occurred.

TIP ✓

First Aid booklet
HSE guidance publicaton First Aid – ISBN 0717610705. This can be stored in the first aid box.

All employees should be informed of the first-aid procedures, including:

- where to locate the first-aid box;
- who is responsible for the maintenance of the first-aid box;
- which staff member to inform in the event of an accident or illness occurring;
- the staff member to inform in the event of an accident or emergency.

An adequately stocked first-aid box that complies with health and safety first-aid regulations should be available. This should contain as a minimum level of equipment:

- basic first-aid guidance leaflet (1);
- assorted sterile adhesive dressings (20);
- individually wrapped triangular bandages (6);
- safety pins (6);
- sterile eye pads, with attachments (2);
- medium-sized individually wrapped sterile unmedicated wound dressings, 10cm × 8cm (6);
- large individually wrapped sterile unmedicated wound dressings, 13cm × 9cm (2);
- extra-large sterile individually wrapped medicated wound dressings, 28cm × 17.5cm (3);
- individually wrapped medical wipes;
- antiseptic cream or liquid.

Where clean tap water is not readily available, sterile water should be stored in sealed containers for bathing eyes.

First-aid kits

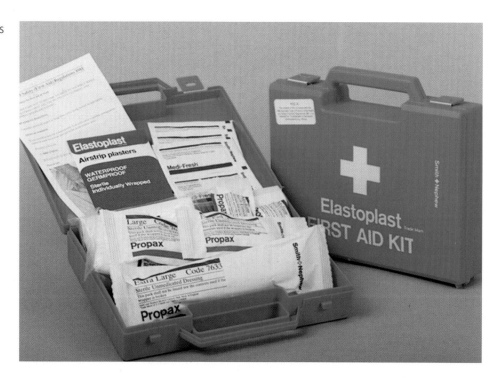

Further examples of first-aid procedures

Problem	Action to be taken
Casualty is not breathing	1 Place the casualty on their back. Open and clear their mouth. 2 Tilt head backwards to open airway (maintain this position throughout). Support the jaw. 3 Knee beside casualty, while keeping head backwards. Open mouth and pinch nose. 4 Open your mouth and take a deep breath. Seal mouth with yours and breathe firmly into it. Casualty's chest should rise. Remove your mouth and let their chest fall. If chest does not rise, check head is tilted sufficiently. Repeat at a rate of 10 times a minute until the casualty is breathing alone. 5 Place them in the recovery position.
Unconscious	Place into recovery position.
Severe bleeding	Control by direct pressure using fingers and thumb on the bleeding point. Apply a dressing. Raising the bleeding limb (unless it is broken) will reduce the flow of blood.
Suspected broken bones	Do not move the casualty unless they are in a position which exposes them to immediate danger.
Burns and scalds (due to heat)	Do not remove clothing sticking to the burns or scalds. Do not burst any blisters. If burns and scalds are small, flush them with plenty of clean, cool water before applying a sterilised dressing. If burns and scalds are large or deep, wash your hands, apply a dry sterilised dressing and send the casualty to hospital.
Burns (chemicals)	Avoid contaminating yourself with the chemical. Remove any contaminated clothing that is not stuck to skin. Flush with plenty of cool water for 10-15 minutes. Apply a sterilised dressing and send to hospital.
Foreign body in eye	Wash out eye with clean cool water. (A person with an eye injury should be sent to hospital with the eye covered with an eye pad.)
Chemicals in eye	Wash out the open eye continuously with clean, cool water for 10–15 minutes.
Electric shock	Don't touch the casualty until the current is switched off. If the current cannot be switched off, stand on some dry insulating material and use a wooden or plastic implement to free the casualty from the electrical source. If breathing has stopped start mouth-to-mouth breathing and continue until the casualty starts to breathe by themselves or until professional help arrives.
Gassing	Use suitable protective equipment. Move casualty to fresh air. If breathing has stopped start mouth-to-mouth breathing and continue until the casualty is breathing himself or until professional help arrives. Send to hospital with a note of the gas involved.
Minor injuries	Casualties with minor injuries of a nature they would normally attend to themselves may wash their hands and apply a small sterilised dressing from the first-aid box.

Disposal of waste

Waste should be disposed of in an enclosed waste bin fitted with a polythene bin liner, durable enough to resist tearing. The bin should be regularly disinfected in a well-ventilated area; wear protective gloves while doing this. Hazardous waste must be disposed of following the COSHH procedures and training by the employer.

Clinical (contaminated) waste is waste derived from human tissues, this includes blood and tissue fluids. **Clinical waste**, such as wax strips, should

Sharps container

be disposed of as recommended by the environment agency in accordance with the **Controlled Waste Regulations 1992**. Items which have been used to pierce the skin, such as disposable milia extractors, should be safely discarded in a disposable **sharps container**. Contact your local environmental health department to check on disposal arrangements.

Inspection and registration of premises

Inspectors from the HSE or your local authority enforce Health and Safety law. They visit the workplace to ensure compliance with government legislation is being met.

If the inspector identifies any area of danger, it is the responsibility of the employer to remove this danger within a designated period of time. The inspector issues an **improvement notice**. Failure to comply with the notice will lead to prosecution. The inspector also has the authority to *close* a business until they are satisfied that all danger to employees and public has been removed. Such closure involves the issuing of a **prohibition notice**.

Certain treatments carried out in beauty therapy, such as ear piercing, pose additional risk as they may produce blood and body tissue fluid. Inspection of the premises is necessary before such services can be offered to the public. The inspector will visit and observe that the guidelines listed in the **Local Government (Miscellaneous Provisions) Act 1982** relating to this area are being complied with. When the inspector is satisfied, a certificate of registration will be awarded.

ACTIVITY

Fire drill
Each workplace should have a fire drill regularly. This enables staff to practise so that they know what to do in the event of a real fire. What is the fire drill procedure for *your* workplace?

Fire

The **Fire Precautions Act 1971** states that all staff must be aware of and trained in fire and emergency evacuation procedures for their workplace. The **emergency exit route** will be the easiest route by which staff and clients can leave the building safely.

A **fire certificate** is a compulsory requirement of the Act if there are more than 20 employees, or more than 10 employees are on different floors at any one time.

HEALTH AND SAFETY

Fire!
If there is a fire, never use a lift. A fire quickly becomes out of control. You do not have very long to act!
   Fire drill notices should be visible to show people the emergency exit route.

The Fire Precautions (Workplace) Regulations 1997

These regulations ensure the safety of all present in the event of a fire. They require that every employer must carry out a risk assessment for the premises, under the **Management of Health and Safety Regulations 1999**.

- Any obstacles that may hinder fire evacuation should be identified as problem areas.
- Suitable fire detection equipment should be in place, such as a **smoke alarm** to forewarn you of a fire.
- A method to warn of a fire should be in place, this may be an automatic alarm or a trained employee shouting to raise the alarm.

- All escape routes should be clearly marked and free from obstacles.
- Fire-fighting equipment should be available and maintained, to be used only by those trained in its use.
- All employees should be trained in fire evacuation practice and procedures.
- Fire evacuation procedure should be reviewed regularly to account for changes to the staffing or premises. A fire drill should be carried out at least once a year to monitor evacuation procedures.

Fire-fighting equipment

Fire-fighting equipment must be available, located in a specified area. The equipment includes fire extinguishers, blankets, sand buckets and water hoses. Fire-fighting equipment should be used only when the cause of the fire has been identified – using the *wrong* extinguisher could make the fire worse.

There are four classifications of fires: class A, B, C and D. Symbols are used to identify these classifications and choice of fire extinguisher as shown below:

Class C Fire – Flammable gases such as methane and acetylene.

Class B Fire – Flammable liquids such as petrol, oil and paints.

Electrical hazard symbol – for extinguisher products safe on electrical fires.

Class A Fire – Carbonaceous materials such as paper and wood.

Fire extinguisher symbols

Class D Fires involve metals.

Never use fire-fighting equipment unless you are trained in its use.

Courtesy of Chubb Fire Ltd

Fire blankets

HEALTH AND SAFETY

Fire exits
Fire-exit doors must be clearly marked and remain unlocked during working hours, and be free from obstruction.

TIP

Fire extinguishers
Label colours and symbols indicate the use of particular fire extinguishers. Make sure you know the meaning of each of the colours and symbols.

Cause of fire and choice of fire extinguisher

Cause	Extinguisher type	Label colour
Electrical fire	Carbon dioxide (CO_2) extinguisher	Black
Solid material fire (paper, wood, etc.)	Water extinguisher	Red
Flammable liquids	Foam extinguisher	Cream/yellow
Electrical fire	Dry-powder extinguisher	Blue

Fire extinguishers

Fire extinguishers are available to tackle different types of fire. These should be located in a set place known to all employees. It is important that these are checked and maintained as required.

Fire blankets are used to smother a small, localised fire or if a person's clothing is on fire. **Sand** is used to soak up liquids if these are the source of the fire, and to smother the fire. **Water hoses** are used to extinguish large fires caused by paper materials and the like – buckets of water may be used to extinguish a small fire. *Turn off the electricity at the mains first!*

Never put yourself at risk – fires can spread quickly. Leave the building at once if in danger, and raise the alarm by telephoning the emergency services on the emergency telephone numbers, **999** or **112**.

ACTIVITY

Causes of fires
Can you think of several potential causes of fire in the salon? How could each of these be prevented?

Other emergencies

Other possible emergencies that could occur relate to fumes and flooding. Learn where the water and gas stopcocks are located. In the event of a gas leak or a flood, the stopcocks should be switched off and the appropriate emergency service contacted.

In the event of a bomb alert staff must be trained in the appropriate emergency procedures. This will involve recognition of a suspect package, how to deal with a bomb threat, evacuation of staff and clients and contacting the emergency services. Your local Crime Prevention Officer (CPO) will advise on bomb security.

Insurance

Public Liability Insurance protects employers and employees against the consequences of death or injury to a third party while on the premises. Professional indemnity insurance extends public liability insurance to cover named employees against claims.

Product and **Treatment Liability Insurance** is usually included with your public liability insurance, but should be checked with the insurance company. Product Liability Insurance covers you for risks which might occur as a result of the products you are using and/or selling.

Second, it is a legal requirement under the **Employer Liability (Compulsory Insurance) Act** that every employer must have **Employer's Liability Insurance**. This provides financial compensation to an employee should they be injured as a result of an accident in the workplace. This certificate must be displayed indicating that a policy of insurance has been obtained.

PERSONAL HEALTH, HYGIENE AND APPEARANCE

Your appearance enables the client to make an initial judgement about both you and the salon, so make sure that you create the correct impression! Employees in the workplace should always reflect the desired image of the profession that they work in.

Dream Workwear

Dream Workwear

Professional appearance

Assistant therapist

The assistant therapist qualified to Level 1 will be required to wear a clean protective overall as they will be preparing the working area for client treatments, and may be involved in preparing clients.

Beauty therapist

Due to the nature of many of the services offered, the beauty therapist must wear protective, hygienic clothing. The cotton overall is ideal; air can circulate, allowing perspiration to evaporate and discouraging body odour. The use of a colour such as white immediately shows the client that you are clean. A cotton overall may comprise a dress, a jumpsuit or a tunic top, with coordinating trousers. Overalls should be laundered regularly, and a fresh, clean overall worn each day.

Receptionist

If receptionists are employed solely to carry out reception duties, they may wear a different salon dress, complementary to those worn by the practising therapists. As the receptionists will not be as active, it may be appropriate for them to wear a smart jacket or cardigan. If on the other hand they are also carrying out services, the standard salon overall must be worn.

HEALTH AND SAFETY

Aprons and the Personal Protective Equipment (PPE) at Work Regulations 1992
For certain treatments, such as waxing, it is necessary to wear a protective apron over the overall. Assistant therapists may also wear an apron whilst preparing and cleaning the working area, to protect the overall and keep it clean.

General rules for employees

Make-up

Wear an attractive make-up, and use the correct skin-care cosmetics to suit your skin type. A healthy complexion will be a positive advertisement for your work.

ACTIVITY	

Personal appearance
1 Collect pictures from various suppliers of overalls. Select those that you feel would be most practical for an assistant therapist and for a Level 2 beauty therapist. Briefly describe why you feel these are the most suitable.
2 Design various hairstyles, or collect pictures from magazines, to show how the hair could be smartly worn by a therapist with medium-length to long hair.

Jewellery

Keep jewellery to a minimum, such as a wedding ring, a watch and small earrings.

Nails

Nails should be short, neatly manicured and free of nail polish unless the employee's main duties involve nail treatments or reception duties.

Artificial nails, if worn, must be short to avoid potential harm and ineffective treatment application when applying treatments to delicate areas such as the eye area during facial treatments.

Shoes

Wear flat, well-fitting, comfortable shoes that enclose the feet and which complement the overall. Flesh-coloured tights may be worn to protect the legs. Remember that you will be on your feet for most of the day!

Ethics

Beauty therapy has a **code of ethics**. This is a code of behaviour and expected standards for the professional beauty therapist to follow, which will uphold the reputation of the industry and ensure best working practice for the safety of the industry and members of the public. Beauty therapy professional bodies produce codes of practice for their members. A business may have its own code of practice. Although not a legal requirement, this code may be used in criminal proceedings as evidence of improper practice.

Diet, exercise and sleep

A beauty therapist requires stamina and energy. To achieve this you need to eat a healthy, well-balanced diet, take regular exercise and have adequate sleep.

ACTIVITY	

Staying healthy
Ask your tutor for guidelines before beginning this activity.
1 Write down all the foods and drinks that you most enjoy. Are they healthy? If you are unsure, ask your tutor.
2 How much exercise do you take weekly?
3 How much sleep do you regularly have each night?
4 Do you think you could improve your health and fitness levels?

CODE OF ETHICS

The BABTAC Code of Ethics is a statement of policies and principles to guide the professional conduct and behaviour of members.

PURPOSE – to set out core ethical principles and guidance of good practice for its members.

to maintain and promote high standards of professional treatment and behaviour by members towards BABTAC, clients, other professionals, other therapists, employers and employees.

to clarify expectations which the above may have.

to safeguard the public by ensuring professional practice.

to enable the public to have confidence in BABTAC as a professional body of practitioners.

In particular, professional behaviour should be observed towards the following bodies: BABTAC, clients, other professional bodies and their members, other therapists/members/colleagues, employers and employees.

1. Towards BABTAC

a)   By not bringing the profession as a whole into disrepute.

b)   By protecting collective morality.

Members should not professionally associate themselves with any person or premises which may be deemed to be unprofessional or disreputable, as such an association may put the good name of the therapist and of BABTAC at risk.

2. Towards clients (concerned with the individual therapist/client relationship)

a)   Appointments must be kept. If unforeseen circumstances arise every effort must be made to make the client aware of the treatment cancellation.

b)   Client confidentiality – personal information should be kept private and only used for the specific purpose for which it is given, namely, to enable the therapist to carry out a safe and effective treatment.

c)   Information concerning the client and views formed, must be kept confidential. The member should make every effort to ensure that this same level of confidence is upheld by receptionists and assistants where applicable.

d)   Client treatment details should remain confidential.

Possible exceptions are the following:

   i)   The clients knowledge and written consent are obtained.

   ii)   There is a necessity for the information to be given for example if the client is being referred on to another professional.

The exceptions are:

   i)   If the therapist is required by law to disclose the information.

   ii)   If the therapist considers it their duty for the protection of the public.

If a therapist is information of a criminal nature the member is advised to take legal advice.

e)   Members should respect the religious, spiritual, political and social views of clients.

f)   Client information should not be disclosed to a third party for gain.

g)   Treatment records must be kept.

Where applicable, members must comply with The Data Protection Act.

h)   Advertising – should not give guarantees or promises which cannot be kept and should comply with relevant legislation and the British Code of Advertising Practice where applicable.

i)   Members should work within the limits of their qualification and competence.

Qualifications should be displayed to enable clients to see areas of qualification/competence.

j)   Treatment prices should be displayed.

k)   Members should work towards the clients best interest at all times and should not financially or emotionally exploit clients.

l)   Proper moral conduct must always be maintained in the therapists/client relationship.

When treating members of the opposite sex it is particularly important that professional behaviour is maintained. It is recommended that another person should be within calling distance.

Members are reminded that they must comply with relevant legislation and bye-laws which may apply.

3. Towards other professional bodies and their members

a)   When carrying out therapeutic treatments medical diagnoses should not be made unless a member holds a qualification which covers such diagnoses.

b)   Members should communicate with the clients GP if it is appropriate, such as:

   i)   When a client is referred, even if the referral is informal.

   ii)   If the member wishes to cross refer with the clients GP.

   iii)   If the client is being treated by their GP, or has a condition which may affect or be affected by any treatments requested by the client.

Client permission must be obtained prior to any such communication and such communication should be professional.

c)   Members should not undermine the patients faith in another practitioner. (see also 4b).

4. Towards other therapists, colleagues and BABTAC members

Members should behave in a professional manner towards other therapists, whether or not they are BABTAC members.

a)   A member shall not criticise the work of fellow therapists and should act with discretion and professionalism if criticism of another therapist is communicated to them.

b)   When a member holds critical views of another therapists competence or behaviour, a professional approach should still apply. If approach to the therapist concerned is unsuccessful or unsuitable, notice should be brought to the governing body in an appropriate manner and with the necessary evidence.

c)   Members should note that unwarranted criticism of other therapists is unacceptable.

d)   Members shall assist other therapists professionally where possible.

e)   Members shall not knowingly solicit other members clients.

5. Towards an employer

a)   A member must act in good faith towards her employer and must not allow her personal interests and duty to conflict.

b)   A decision to change therapist must remain solely with the client and no attempt at persuasion should be made. An exception to this would be if the employer indicates that he or she wishes otherwise.

c)   A member must keep confidential all information concerning the employers business and not disclose it during employment or after the termination of that employment.

6. Towards employees

a)   A member must provide suitable working conditions.

b)   A member must not ask employees to carry out treatments beyond their qualifications or competence.

c)   A member should comply with relevant employment legislation and Health and Safety regulations.

d)   A member shall not emotionally or financially exploit employees.

A member shall be taken as encompassing all categories of membership as defined by rule number 1.

On membership ceasing, the former member shall not use any articles associated with BABTAC, or giving impression of membership, including the acronym, badges, certificate etc.

Members should have an understanding of the ethical requirements/principles on which these recommendations are based i.e. professionalism, courtesy, dignity, discretion, honesty and tact.

The association will in no way be precluded from considering and dealing with any form of professional misconduct which may be brought before them, although such misconduct may not directly appear to come within the scope or precise wording of any of the rules set out in the code.

Council has the power to adjudge as unethical any behaviour that adversely reflects upon the profession of beauty therapy, BABTAC, and/or its members.

If legal proceedings are being brought by any party, BABTAC will not make any ruling until legal proceedings are completed, and will not offer opinions or advice unless requested to do so by a legal representative.

Any breach of the code of ethics be referred to the disciplinary committee. When considering an ethical issue, in addition to following disciplinary procedure guidelines as laid down by BABTAC, the committee shall also bear in mind the following:

1.   Ethical issues are sensitive to the political, economic, social and historical contexts in which problems appear.

2.   The right of an action is judged by its outcome.

3.   The values that have shaped a given course of action.

4.   The rights of all affected parties must be respected.

5.   The actions should produce the greatest good for the greatest number of people.

6.   Decisions should be guided by fairness and equity as well as impartiality.

This code of ethics will be revised from time to time, as prevailing values and norms change.

BABTAC Code of Ethics

ACTIVITY

Code of ethics

As a professional beauty therapist it is important that you adhere to a code of ethical practice. You may wish to join a professional organisation, which will issue you with a copy of its agreed standards.

Posture

Posture is the way you hold yourself when standing, sitting and walking. *Correct* posture enables you to work longer without becoming tired; it prevents muscle fatigue and stiff joints; and it improves your appearance.

Good standing posture

If you are standing with good posture, this will describe you:

- head up, centrally balanced;
- shoulders slightly back, and relaxed;
- chest up and out;
- abdomen flat;

ACTIVITY

The importance of posture

1 Which treatments will be performed sitting, and which standing?

2 In what way do you feel your treatments would be affected if you were not sitting or standing correctly?

Good posture – standing

HEALTH AND SAFETY ✚

Repetitive strain injury (RSI)
If you do not follow correct postural positional requirements when performing treatments, muscles and ligaments may become overstretched and overused resulting in repetitive strain injury (RSI). This may result in you being unable to work in the short term, and potentially in the long term in the occupation!

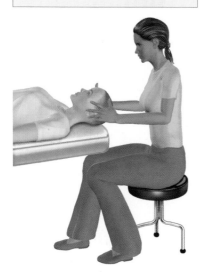

Good posture – sitting

- hips level;
- fingertips level;
- bottom in;
- knees level;
- feet slightly apart, and weight evenly distributed.

Good sitting posture

Sit on a suitable chair or stool with a good back support:

- sit with the lower back pressed against the chair back;
- keep the chest up and the shoulders back;
- distribute the body weight evenly along the thighs;
- keep the feet together, and flat on the floor;
- do not slouch or sit on the edge of your seat.

Personal hygiene

It is vital that you have a high standard of personal **hygiene**. You are going to be working in close proximity with people.

Bodily cleanliness is achieved through daily showering or bathing. This removes stale sweat, dirt and bacteria, which cause body odour. An anti-perspirant or deodorant may be applied to the underarm area to reduce perspiration and thus the smell of sweat. Clean underwear should be worn each day.

Hands

Your hands and everything you touch are covered with germs. Although most are harmless, some can cause ill health or disease. Wash your hands regularly, especially after you have been to the toilet and before eating food. You must also wash your hands before and after treating each client, and during treatment if necessary. Washing the hands before treating a client minimises the risk of cross-infection, and presents to the client a hygienic, professional, caring image.

Step by step: How to wash your hands

1 Wet your hands, wrists and forearms thoroughly using running water

2 Apply around 3ml to 5ml of liquid soap

3 Start the lathering up process, rubbing palm to palm

4 Interlock fingers and rub, ensuring a good lather

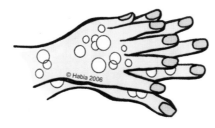

5 Rub right hand over back of left, then left over right hand

6 Rub with fingers locked in palm of hand ensuring fingertips are cleaned

7 Lock thumbs and rotate hands

8 Grasp thumb with hand and rotate, repeat with opposite thumb

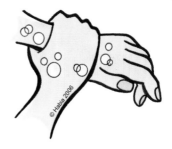

9 Rotate hand around wrist, repeat on opposite wrist

10 Rinse hands and wrists thoroughly using running water

11 Dry the hands and wrists thoroughly

12 Turn off the tap using a paper towel

13 Dispose of paper towel without touching any part of the waste bin

ACTIVITY

Hand hygiene
What further occasions can you think of when it will be necessary to wash your hands when treating a client?

HEALTH AND SAFETY

Soap and towels
Wash your hands with liquid soap from a sealed dispenser. This should take 10–20 seconds. Don't refill disposable soap dispensers when empty; if you do they will become a breeding ground for bacteria.
Disposable paper towels or warm-air hand dryers should be used to thoroughly dry the hands.

Feet

Keep your feet fresh and healthy by washing them daily and then drying them thoroughly. Deodorising foot powder may then be applied.

Teeth

Avoid bad breath by brushing your teeth at least twice daily and flossing the teeth frequently. Use breath fresheners and mouthwashes as required to freshen your breath. Visit the dentist regularly, to maintain healthy teeth and gums.

Hair

Your hair should be clean and tidy. Have your hair cut regularly to maintain its appearance, and shampoo and condition your hair as often as needed.

If your hair is long, wear it off the face, and taken to the crown of the head. Medium-length hair should be clipped back, away from the face, to prevent it falling forwards.

Hygiene in the workplace

Infections

Effective hygiene is necessary in the salon to prevent *cross-infection* and *secondary infection*. These can occur through poor practice, such as the use of implements that are not sterile. Infection can be recognised by red and inflamed skin, or the presence of pus.

Cross-infection occurs because some micro-organisms are contagious – they may be transferred through personal contact or by contact with an infected instrument that has not been disinfected or sterilised. **Secondary infection** can occur as a result of injury to the client during the treatment, or if the client already has an open cut, if bacteria penetrate the skin and cause infection. **Sterilisation** and **disinfection** procedures (below) are used to minimise or destroy the harmful micro-organisms which could cause infection – bacteria, viruses and fungi.

Infectious diseases that are contagious **contra-indicate** beauty treatment: they require medical attention. People with certain other skin disorders, even though these are not contagious, should likewise not be treated by the beauty therapist, as treatment might lead to secondary infection.

Sterilisation and disinfection

Sterilisation is the total destruction of all living micro-organisms in metal tools and equipment. **Disinfection** is the destruction of most living micro-organisms in non-metal tools, equipment and work areas. Sterilisation and disinfection techniques practised in the beauty salon involve the use of *physical* agents, such as radiation and heat; and *chemical* agents, such as antiseptics and disinfectants.

Radiation A quartz mercury-vapour lamp can be used as the source for **ultra-violet light**, which destroys micro-organisms. The object to be radiation sterilised must be turned regularly so that the UV light reaches all surfaces. (UV light has limited effectiveness, and cannot be relied upon for complete sterilisation.)

The UV lamp must be contained within a closed cabinet. This cabinet is an ideal place for storing sterilised objects.

Heat Dry and moist heat may both be used in sterilisation. One method is to use a dry **hot-air oven**. This is similar to a small oven, and heats to 150–180°C. It is seldom used in the salon.

More practical is a **glass-bead steriliser**. This is a small electrically heated unit that contains glass beads: these transfer heat to objects placed in contact with them. This method of sterilisation is suitable for small tools such as tweezers and scissors. All objects should be cleaned before placing in the glass-bead steriliser to remove surface dirt and debris.

An ultra-violet light cabinet

Water is boiled in an **autoclave** (similar to a pressure cooker): because of the increased pressure, the water reaches a temperature of 121–134°C. Autoclaving is the most effective method for sterilising objects in the salon.

An autoclave

Jefford and Swain,
The Encyclopedia of Nails

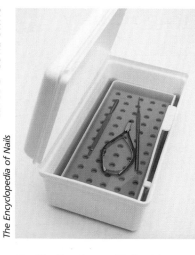

Ellisons

Sterilisation tray with liquid

Medi-Swabs (sterile tissues)

Disinfectants and antiseptics If an object *cannot* be sterilised, it should be placed in a chemical **disinfectant** solution. A disinfectant destroys most micro-organisms, but not all. Hypochlorite is a disinfectant – bleach is an example of a hypochlorite. Hypochlorite is suitable for cleanng work surfaces but is particularly corrosive and unsuitable for use with metals – use as directed by the manufacturer. Alcohol-impregnated wipes are a popular way to clean the skin using a disinfectant such as isopropyl alcohol.

An **antiseptic** prevents the multiplication of micro-organisms. It has a limited action, and does not kill all micro-organisms.

All sterilisation and disinfection techniques must be carried out safely and effectively:

1 Select the appropriate method of sterilisation or disinfection for the object. *Always* follow the manufacturer's guidelines on the use of the sterilising or disinfecting unit or agent.
2 Clean the object in clean water and detergent to remove dirt and grease. (Dirt left on the object may prevent effective sterilisation or disinfection.)
3 Dry it thoroughly with a clean, disposable paper towel.
4 Sterilise or disinfect the object, allowing sufficient time for the process to be completed.
5 Place tools that have been sterilised or disinfected in a clean, covered container.

Keep several sets of the tools you use regularly, so that you can carry out effective sterilisation and disinfection.

Workplace policies

Each workplace should have its own workplace policy identifying hygiene rules.

- *Health and safety* Follow the health and safety policies for the workplace.
- *Personal hygiene* Maintain a high standard of personal hygiene. Wash your hands with a detergent containing **chlorhexidine**.
- *Cuts on the hands* Always cover any cuts on your hands with a protective dressing.
- *Cross-infection* Take great care to avoid cross-infection in the salon. *Never* treat a client who has a contagious skin disease or disorder, or any other contra-indication.
- *Use hygienic tools* Never use an implement unless it has been effectively sterilised or disinfected, as appropriate.
- *Disposable products* Wherever possible, use disposable products.

- *Working surfaces* Disinfect all working surfaces (such as trolleys and couches) with a chlorine preparation, diluted to the manufacturer's instructions. Cover all working surfaces with clean, disposable paper tissue.
- *Gowns and towels* Clean gowns and towels must be provided for each client. Towels should be laundered at a temperature of 60°C.
- *Laundry* Dirty laundry should be placed in a covered container.
- *Waste*, including clinical waste and non-contaminated waste, must be disposed of following the COSHH procedures, guidelines provided by the Local Authority and training by the employer.
- *Waste* Put waste in a suitable container lined with a disposable waste bag. A yellow **sharps container** should be available for clinical waste contaminated with blood or tissue fluid.
- *Eating and drinking* Never eat or drink in the treatment area of the salon. Not only is it unprofessional, but harmful chemicals may also be ingested.
- *Smoking* Never smoke in the treatment area of the salon or other prohibited areas.
- *Drugs and alcohol* Never carry out treatments in the workplace under the influence of drugs or alcohol. Your competence will be affected putting both yourself, clients and possibly colleagues at risk.

SKIN DISEASES AND DISORDERS

The beauty therapist must be able to distinguish a healthy skin from one suffering from any skin disease or disorder. Certain skin disorders and diseases **contra-indicate** a beauty treatment: the treatment would expose the therapist and other clients to the risk of cross-infection. It is therefore vital that you are familiar with the skin diseases and disorders with which you may come into contact in the workplace. Relevant skin diseases and disorders are also discussed in each treatment chapter.

Bacterial infections

Bacteria are minute single-celled organisms of varied shapes. Large numbers of bacteria inhabit the surface of the skin and are harmless (**non-pathogenic**); indeed some play an important positive role in the health of the skin. Others, however, are harmful (**pathogenic**) and can cause skin diseases.

Impetigo

An inflammatory disease of the surface of the skin.

Infectious? Yes.

Appearance: Initially the skin appears red and is itchy. Small thin-walled blisters appear; these burst and form into crusts.

Site: The commonly affected areas are the nose, the mouth and the ears, but impetigo can occur on the scalp or the limbs.

Treatment: Medical – usually an antibiotic or an antibacterial ointment is prescribed.

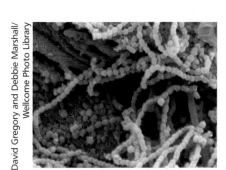

David Gregory and Debbie Marshall/ Wellcome Photo Library

Microscopic bacteria – Streptococcus bacteria on the tongue, computer-coloured red/pink

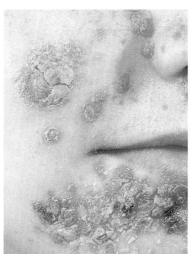

Dr M. H. Beck

Impetigo

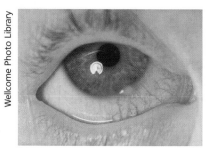

Conjunctivitis or pink eye

Wellcome Photo Library

Conjunctivitis or pink eye

Inflammation of the mucous membrane that covers the eye and lines the eyelids.

Infectious? Yes.

Appearance: The skin of the inner conjunctiva of the eye becomes inflamed, the eye becomes very red and sore, and pus may exude from the area.

Site: The eyes, either one or both, may be infected.

Treatment: Medical – usually an antibiotic lotion is prescribed.

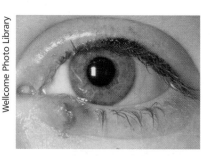

Hordeola or styes

Wellcome Photo Library

Hordeola or styes

Infection of the sebaceous glands of eyelash hair follicles.

Infectious? Yes.

Appearance: Small lumps containing pus.

Site: The inner rim of the eyelid.

Treatment: Medical – usually an antibiotic is prescribed.

Furuncles or boils

Red, painful lumps, extending deeply into the skin.

Infectious? Yes.

Appearance: A localised red lump occurs around a hair follicle; it then develops a core of pus. Scarring of the skin often remains after the boil has healed.

Site: The back of the neck, the ankles and the wrists.

Treatment: Medical.

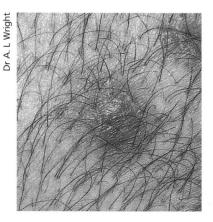

Boil

Dr A. L Wright

Carbuncles

Infection of numerous hair follicles.

Infectious? Yes.

Appearance: A hard, round abscess, larger than a boil, which oozes pus from several points upon its surface. Scarring often occurs after the carbuncle has healed.

Site: The back of the neck.

Treatment: Medical – usually involving incision, drainage of the pus, and a course of antibiotics.

Paronychia

Infection of the skin tissue surrounding the nail.

Infectious? Yes.

Appearance: Swelling, redness and pus in the cuticle and in the area of the nail wall.

Site: The cuticle and the skin surrounding the nail.

Treatment: Medical.

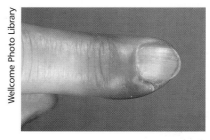

Wellcome Photo Library

Paronychia

Viral infections

Viruses are minute entities, too small to see even under an ordinary microscope. They are considered to be **parasites**, as they require living tissue in order to survive. Viruses invade healthy body cells and multiply within the cell: in due course the cell walls break down, liberating new viral particles to attack further cells, and thus the infection spreads.

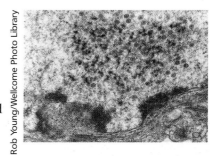

Rob Young/Wellcome Photo Library

Microscopic virus – herpes simplex virus particles (orange) in the nucleus of an epithelial cell

Herpes simplex

This is a recurring skin condition, appearing at times when the skin's resistance is lowered through ill health or stress. It may also be caused by exposure of the skin to extremes of temperature or to ultra-violet light.

Infectious? Yes.

Appearance: Inflammation of the skin occurs in localised areas. As well as being red, the skin becomes itchy and small vesicles appear. These are followed by a crust, which may crack and weep tissue fluid.

Site: The mucous membranes of the nose or lips; herpes can also occur on the skin generally.

Treatment: There is no specific treatment. A proprietary brand of anti-inflammatory antiseptic drying cream is usually prescribed.

Herpes zoster or shingles

In this painful disease, the virus attacks the sensory nerve endings. The virus is thought to lie dormant in the body and be triggered when the body's defences are at a low ebb.

Infectious? Yes.

Appearance: Redness of the skin occurs along the line of the affected nerves. Blisters develop and form crusts, leaving purplish-pink pigmentation.

Dr M. H. Beck

Herpes simplex

Site: Commonly the chest and the abdomen.

Treatment: Medical – usually including antibiotics. Any lasting pigmentation may be camouflaged with cosmetics.

Verrucae or warts

Small epidermal skin growths. Warts may be raised or flat, depending upon their position. There are several types of wart: plane, common and plantar.

Infectious? Yes.

Appearance: Warts vary in size, shape, texture and colour. Usually they have a rough surface and are raised. If the wart occurs on the sole of the foot it grows inwards, due to the pressure of body weight.

Site:
- plane wart: the fingers, either surface of the hand, or the knees;
- common wart: the face or hands;
- plantar wart: the sole of the foot.

Treatment: Medical – using acids, solid carbon dioxide, or electrocautery.

Infestations

Scabies or itch mites

A condition in which an animal parasite burrows beneath the skin and invades the hair follicles.

Infectious? Yes.

Appearance: At the onset, minute papules and wavy greyish lines appear, where dirt has entered the burrows. Secondary bacterial infection may occur as a result of scratching.

Site: Usually seen in warm areas of loose skin, such as the webs of the fingers and the creases of the elbows.

Treatment: Medical – an anti-scabetic lotion.

Pediculosis capitis or head lice

A condition in which small parasites infest scalp hair.

Infectious? Yes.

Appearance: The lice cling to the hair of the scalp. Eggs are laid, attached to the hair close to the skin. The lice bite the skin to draw nourishment from the blood; this creates irritation and itching of the skin, which may lead to secondary bacterial infection.

Site: The hair of the scalp.

Treatment: Medical – an appropriate lotion.

Pediculosis pubis

A condition in which small parasites infest body hair.

Infectious? Yes.

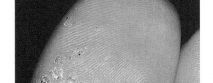

Dr A. L. Wright

Veruccae – plantar warts

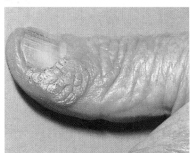

Dr M. H. Beck

A wart

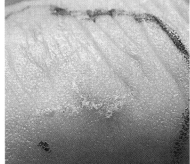

Dr M. H. Beck

A scabies burrow

Wellcome Photo Library

Pediculosis capitis or head lice clinging to the hair

Appearance: The lice cling to the hair of the body. Eggs are laid, attached to the hair close to the skin. The lice bite the skin to draw nourishment from the blood; this creates irritation and itching of the skin, which may lead to secondary bacterial infection.

Site: Pubic hair, eyebrows and eyelashes.

Treatment: Medical – an appropriate lotion.

Pediculosis corporis

A condition in which small parasites live and feed on body skin.

Infectious? Yes.

Appearance: The lice cling to the hair of the body. Eggs are laid, attached to the hair close to the skin. The lice bite the skin to draw nourishment from the blood; this creates irritation and itching of the skin, which may lead to secondary bacterial infection. Where body lice bite the skin, small red marks can be seen.

Site: Body hair.

Treatment: Medical – an appropriate lotion.

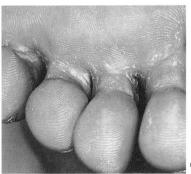

Microscopic fungi – Penicilliam mould producing spores, plus very close up view of spore fomulation

Fungal diseases

Fungi are microscopic plants. They are parasites, dependent upon a host for their existence. Fungal diseases of the skin feed off the waste products of the skin. Some fungi are found on the skin's surface; others attack the deeper tissues. Reproduction of fungi is by means of simple cell division or by the production of spores.

Tinea pedis or athlete's foot

A common fungal foot infection.

Infectious? Yes.

Appearance: Small blisters form, which later burst. The skin in the area can then become dry, giving a scaly appearance.

Site: The webs of skin between the toes.

Treatment: Thorough cleansing of the area. Medical application of fungicides.

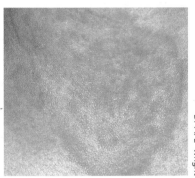

Tinea pedis

Tinea corporis or body ringworm

A fungal infection of the skin.

Infectious? Yes.

Appearance: Small scaly red patches, which spread outwards and then heal from the centre, leaving a ring.

Site: The trunk of the body, the limbs and the face.

Treatment: Medical – using a fungicidal cream, griseofluvin.

Tinea corporis or body ringworm

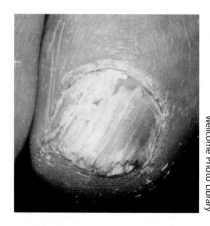

Tinea unguium

Tinea unguium

Ringworm infection of the nail plate.

Infectious? Yes.

Appearance: The nail plate is yellowish-grey. Eventually the nail plate becomes brittle and separates from the nail bed.

Site: The nail plates.

Treatment: Medical application of fungicides.

Sebaceous gland disorders

Milia

Keratinisation of the skin over the hair follicle occurs, causing sebum to accumulate in the hair follicle. This condition usually accompanies dry skin.

Infectious? No.

Appearance: Small, hard, pearly-white cysts.

Site: The upper face or close to the eyes.

Treatment: The milium may be removed by the beauty therapist or by a physician, depending on the location. A sterile needle is used to pierce the skin of the overlying cuticle and thereby free the milium.

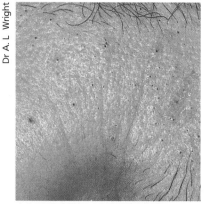

Comedones or blackheads

Comedones or blackheads

Excess sebum and keratinised cells block the mouth of the hair follicle.

Infectious? No.

Site: The face (the chin, nose and forehead), the upper back and chest.

Treatment: The area should be cleansed, and an electrical vapour treatment or other pre-heating treatment should be given to relax the mouth of the hair follicle; a sterile comedo extractor should then be used to remove the blockage. A regular cleansing treatment should be recommended by the beauty therapist to limit the production of comedones.

Seborrhoea

Excessive secretion of sebum from the sebaceous gland. This usually occurs during puberty, as a result of hormonal changes in the body.

Infectious? No.

Appearance: The follicle openings enlarge and excessive sebum is secreted. The skin appears coarse and oily; comedones, pustules and papules are present.

Site: The face and scalp. Seborrhoea may also affect the back and the chest.

Treatment: The area should be cleansed to remove excess oil. Medical treatment may be required – this would use locally applied creams.

Steatomas, sebaceous cysts or wens

Localised pockets or sacs of sebum, which form in hair follicles or under the sebaceous glands in the skin. The sebum becomes blocked, the sebaceous gland becomes distended, and a lump forms.

Infectious? No.

Appearance: Semi-globular in shape, either raised or flat, and hard or soft. The cysts are the same colour as the skin, or red if secondary bacterial infection occurs. A comedo can often be seen at the original mouth of the hair follicle.

Site: If the cyst appears on the upper eyelid, it is known as a **chalazion** or **meibomian cyst**.

Treatment: Medical – often a physician will remove the cyst under local anaesthetic.

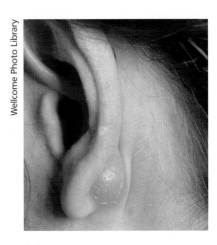

Wellcome Photo Library

Sebaceous cyst

Acne vulgaris

Hormone imbalance in the body at puberty influences the activity of the sebaceous gland, causing an increased production of sebum. The sebum may be retained within the sebaceous ducts, causing congestion and bacterial infection of the surrounding tissues.

Infectious? No.

Appearance: Inflammation of the skin, accompanied by comedones, pustules and papules.

Site: Commonly on the face, on the nose, the chin and the forehead. Acne may also occur on the chest and back.

Treatment: Medical – oral antibiotics may be prescribed, as well as medicated creams. With medical approval, regular salon treatments may be given to cleanse the skin deeply, and also to stimulate the blood circulation.

Dr M. H. Beck

Acne vulgaris

Rosacea

Excessive sebum secretion combined with a chronic inflammatory condition, caused by dilation of the blood capillaries.

Infectious? No.

Appearance: The skin becomes coarse, the pores enlarge, and the cheek and nose area become inflamed, sometimes swelling and producing a butterfly pattern. Blood circulation slows in the dilated capillaries, creating a purplish appearance.

Treatment: Medical – usually including antibiotics.

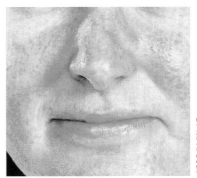

Dr M. H. Beck

Rosacea

Pigmentation disorders

Pigmentation of the skin varies according to the person's genetic characteristics. In general the darker the skin, the more pigment is present, but some abnormal changes in skin pigmentation can occur.

- **hyperpigmentation** – increased pigment production;
- **hypopigmentation** – loss of pigmentation in the skin.

TIP ✔

Hypopigmentation
Hypopigmentation may result from certain skin injuries, disorders or diseases.

Ephelides or freckles

Multiple small hyperpigmented areas of the skin. Exposure to ultra-violet light (as in sunlight) stimulates the production of melanin, intensifying their appearance.

Infectious? No.

Appearance: Small, flat, pigmented areas, darker than the surrounding skin.

Site: Commonly the nose and cheeks of fair-skinned people. Freckles may also occur on the shoulders, arms, hands and back.

Treatment: Freckles may be concealed with cosmetics if required. A sun block should be recommended, to prevent them intensifying in colour.

Lentigo (plural, lentigines)

Hyperpigmented areas of skin, slightly larger than freckles. Lentigo simplex occur in childhood. Actinic (solar) lentigines occur in middle age as a result of sun exposure.

Infectious? No.

Appearance: Brown, slightly raised, pigmented patches of skin, of variable size.

Site: The face, hands and shoulders.

Treatment: Application of cosmetic concealing products.

Chloasmata or liver spots

Hyperpigmentation in specific areas, stimulated by a skin irritant such as ultra-violet light, usually affecting women and darkly pigmented skins. The condition often occurs during pregnancy, and usually disappears soon after the birth of the baby. It may also occur as a result of taking oral contraceptive pills. The female hormone oestrogen is thought to stimulate melanin production.

Infectious? No.

Appearance: Flat, smooth, irregularly shaped, pigmented areas of skin, varying in colour from light tan to dark brown. Chloasmata are larger than ephelides, and of variable size.

Site: The back of the hands, the forearms, the upper part of the chest, the temples and the forehead.

Treatment: A barrier cream or a total sunblock will reduce the risk of the chloasmata increasing in size or number, and thereby becoming more apparent.

Dermatosis papulosa nigra

Often called flesh moles, these are characterised by multiple benign, small brown to black hyperpigmented papules, common among dark-skinned people.

Infectious? No.

Appearance: Raised pigmented markings resembling moles.

Site: Usually seen on the cheeks and forehead, although they may appear on the neck, upper chest and back.

Treatment: Medical by drug therapy or surgery.

Vitiligo or leucoderma

Patches of completely white skin which have lost their pigment, or which were never pigmented.

Infectious? No.

Appearance: Well defined patches of white skin, lacking pigment.

Site: The face, the neck, the hands, the lower abdomen, and the thighs. If vitiligo occurs over the eyebrows, the hairs in the area will also lose their pigment.

Treatment: Camouflage cosmetic concealer can be applied to give even skin colour; or skin-staining preparations can be used in the de-pigmented areas. Care must be taken when the skin is exposed to ultra-violet light, as the skin will not have the same protection in the areas lacking pigment.

Dr M. H. Beck

Vitiligo or leucoderma

Albinism

The skin is unable to produce the melanin pigment, and the skin, hair and eyes lack colour.

Infectious? No.

Appearance: The skin is usually very pale pink and the hair is white. The eyes also are pink, and extremely sensitive to light.

Site: The entire skin.

Treatment: There is no effective treatment. Maximum skin protection is necessary when the client is exposed to ultra-violet light, and sunglasses should be worn to protect the eyes.

Vascular naevi

There are two types of naevus of concern to beauty therapists: vascular and cellular. **Vascular naevi** are skin conditions in which small or large areas of skin pigmentation are caused by the permanent dilation of blood capillaries.

Erythema

An area of skin in which blood capillaries have dilated, due either to injury or inflammation.

Infectious? No.

Appearance: The skin appears red.

Site: Erythema may affect one area (locally) or all of the skin (generally).

Treatment: The cause of the inflammation should be identified. In the case of a skin allergy, the client must not be brought into contact with the irritant again. If the cause is unknown, refer the client to their physician.

Dilated capillaries

Capillaries near the surface of the skin that are permanently dilated.

Infectious? No.

Appearance: Small red visible blood capillaries.

Site: Areas where the skin is neglected, dry or fine, such as the cheek area.

Treatment: Dilated capillaries can be concealed using a green corrective camouflage cosmetic, or removed by a qualified electrologist using diathermy.

> **TIP** ✔
>
> **Vascular disorders**
> If there is a vascular skin disorder, avoid overstimulating the skin or the problem will become more noticeable and the treatment may even cause further damage.

Dr M. H. Beck

Spider naevus or stellate haemangiomas

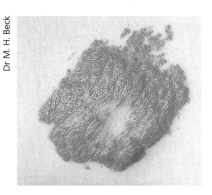

Naevus vasculosis or strawberry mark

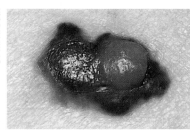

Malignant melanoma

Spider naevi or stellate haemangiomas

Dilated blood vessels, with smaller dilated capillaries radiating from them.

Infectious? No.

Appearance: Small red capillaries, radiating like a spider's legs from a central point.

Site: Commonly the cheek area, but may occur on the upper body, the arms and the neck. Spider naevi are usually caused by an injury to the skin.

Treatment: Spider naevi can be concealed using a camouflage cosmetic, or treated by a qualified electrologist with diathermy.

Dr M.H. Beck

Naevi vasculosis or strawberry marks

Red or purplish raised marks which appear on the skin at birth.

Infectious? No.

Appearance: Red or purplish lobed mark, of any size.

Site: Any area of the skin.

Treatment: About 60 per cent disappear by the age of 6 years. Treatment is not usually necessary; concealing cosmetics can be applied if desired.

Capillary naevi or port-wine stains

Large areas of dilated capillaries, which contrast noticeably with the surrounding areas.

Infectious? No.

Appearance: The naevus has a smooth, flat surface.

Site: Some 75 per cent occur on the head; they are probably formed at the foetal stage. Naevi may also be found on the neck and face.

Treatment: Camouflage cosmetic creams can be applied to disguise the area.

Cellular naevi or moles

Cellular naevi are skin conditions in which changes in the cells of the skin result in skin malformations.

Malignant melanomas or malignant moles

Rapidly-growing skin cancers, usually occurring in adults.

Infectious? No.

Appearance: Each melanoma commences as a bluish-black mole, which enlarges rapidly, darkening in colour and developing a halo of pigmentation around it. It later becomes raised, bleeds and ulcerates. Secondary growths will develop in internal organs if the melanoma is not treated.

Site: Usually the lower abdomen, legs or feet.

Treatment: Medical – *always* recommend that a client has any mole checked if it is changing in size, structure or colour, or if it becomes itchy or bleeds.

Junction naevi

Localised collections of naevoid cells that arise from the mass production locally of pigment-forming cells (melanocytes).

Infectious? No.

Appearance: In childhood junction naevi appear as smooth or slightly raised pigmented marks. They vary in colour from brown to black.

Site: Any area.

Treatment: None.

Dermal naevi

Localised collections of naevoid cells.

Infectious? No.

Appearance: About 1cm wide, dermal naevi appear smooth and dome-shaped. Their colour ranges from skin tone to dark brown. Frequently one or more hairs may grow from the naevus.

Site: Usually the face.

Treatment: None.

Hairy naevi

Moles exhibiting coarse hairs from their surface.

Infectious? No.

Appearance: Slightly raised moles, varying in size from 3cm to much larger. Colour ranges from fawn to dark brown.

Site: Anywhere on the skin.

Treatment: Hairy naevi may be surgically removed where possible, and this is often done for cosmetic reasons. Hair growing from a mole should be cut, not plucked: if plucked, the hair will become coarser and the growth of further hairs may be stimulated.

Skin disorders involving abnormal growth

Psoriasis

Patches of itchy, red, flaky skin, the cause of which is unknown.

Infectious? No. Secondary infection with bacteria can occur if the skin becomes broken and dirt enters the skin.

Appearance: Red patches of skin appear, covered in waxy, silvery scales. Bleeding will occur if the area is scratched and scales are removed.

Site: The elbows, the knees, the lower back and the scalp.

Treatment: There is no known treatment. Medication including steroid creams can bring relief to the symptoms.

TIP ✔

Naevi numbers and skin colour
Caucasian skin normally has up to four times as many naevi than black skin.

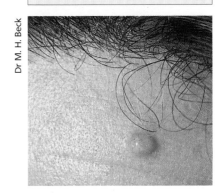

Benign naevus

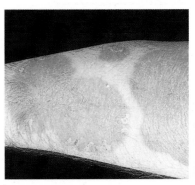

Psoriasis

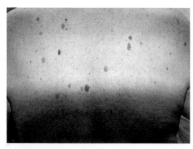

Seborrheic or senile warts

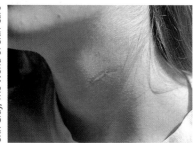

Verrucae filliformis or skin tags

Seborrheic or senile warts

Raised, pigmented, benign tumours occurring in middle age.

Infectious? No.

Appearance: Slightly raised, brown or black, rough patches of skin. Such warts can be confused with pigmented moles.

Site: The trunk, the scalp and the temples.

Treatment: Medical – the warts can be cauterised by a physician.

Verrucae filliformis or skin tags

These verrucae appear as threads projecting from the skin.

Infectious? No.

Appearance: Skin-coloured threads of skin 3–6mm long.

Site: Mainly seen on the neck and the eyelids, but may occur in other areas such as under the arms.

Treatment: Medical – cauterisation with diathermy, either by a physician or by a qualified electrologist.

Xanthomas

Small yellow growths appearing upon the surface of the skin.

Infectious? No.

Appearance: A yellow, flat or raised area of skin.

Site: The eyelids.

Treatment: Medical – the growth is thought to be connected with certain medical diseases, such as diabetes or high or low blood pressure; sometimes a low-fat diet can correct the condition.

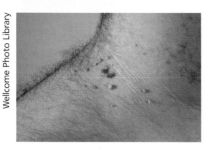

Keloids

Keloids

Keloids occur following skin injury and are overgrown abnormal scar tissue which spreads, characterised by excess deposits of collagen. To avoid skin discolouration the keloid must be protected from UV exposure.

Infectious? No.

Appearance: The skin tends to be red, raised and ridged

Site: Located over the site of a wound or other lesion.

Treatment: Medical by drug therapy or surgery.

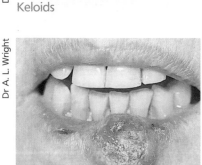

Squamous cell carcinoma

Malignant tumours

Squamous cell carcinomas or prickle-cell cancers

Malignant growths originating in the epidermis.

Infectious: No.

Appearance: When fully formed, the carcinoma appears as a raised area of skin.

Site: Anywhere on the skin.

Treatment: Medical – by radiation.

Basal cell carcinomas or rodent ulcers

Slow-growing malignant tumours, occurring in middle age.

Infectious? No.

Appearance: A small, shiny, waxy nodule with a depressed centre. The disease extends, with more nodules appearing on the border of the original ulcer.

Site: Usually the face.

Treatment: Medical.

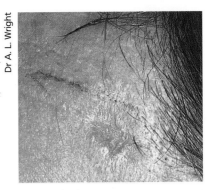

Dr A. L. Wright

Basal cell carcinoma

Skin allergies

The skin can protect itself to some degree from damage or invasion. **Mast cells** detect damage to the skin; if damage occurs, the mast cells burst, releasing the chemical **histamine** into the tissues. Histamine causes the blood capillaries to dilate, giving the reddening we call 'erythema'. The increased blood flow transports materials in the blood which tend to limit the damage and begin repair.

If the skin is sensitive to and becomes inflamed on contact with a particular substance, this substance is called an **allergen**. Allergens may be animal, chemical or vegetable substances, and they may be inhaled, eaten or absorbed following contact with the skin. An **allergic skin reaction** appears as irritation, itching and discomfort, with reddening and swelling (as with nettle rash). If the allergen is removed, the allergic reaction subsides.

Each individual has different tolerances to the various substances we encounter in daily life. What causes an allergic reaction in one individual may be perfectly harmless to another.

Here are just a few examples of allergens known to cause allergic skin reactions in some people:

- metal objects containing nickel;
- sticking plaster;
- rubber;
- lipstick containing eosin dye;
- nail polish containing formaldehyde resin;
- hair and eyelash dyes;
- lanolin, the skin moisturising agent;
- detergents that dry the skin;
- foods – well-known examples are peanuts, cow's milk, lobster, shellfish, and strawberries;
- plants such as tulips and chrysanthemums.

HEALTH AND SAFETY

Record any known allergies
When completing the client record card, always ask whether your client has any known allergies.

HEALTH AND SAFETY

Hypoallergenic products
The use of hypoallergenic products minimises the risk of skin contact with likely irritants.

HEALTH AND SAFETY

Allergies
You may suddenly become allergic to a substance that has previously been perfectly harmless. Equally, you may over time cease to be allergic to something.

HEALTH AND SAFETY

Infection following allergy
Following an allergic skin reaction in which the skin's surface has become itchy and broken, scratching may cause the skin to become infected with bacteria.

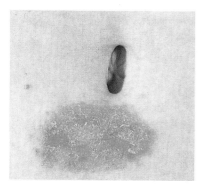

Allergic contact dermatitis –
nickel allergy

Dr M. H. Beck

Dermatitis

An inflammatory skin disorder in which the skin becomes red, itchy and swollen. There are two types of dermatitis. In *primary dermatitis* the skin is irritated by the action of a substance upon the skin, and this leads to skin inflammation. In *allergic contact dermatitis* the problem is caused by intolerance of the skin to a particular substance or group of substances. On exposure to the substance the skin quickly becomes irritated and an allergic reaction occurs.

Infectious? No.

Appearance: Reddening and swelling of the skin, with the possible appearance of blisters.

Site: If the skin reacts to a skin irritant outside the body, the reaction is localised. Repeated contact with the allergen will lead to a general hypersensitivity. If the irritant gains entry to the body it will be transported in the bloodstream and may cause a general allergic skin reaction.

Treatment: Barrier cream can be used to help avoid contact with the irritants. When an allergic dermatitis reaction occurs, however, the only 'cure' is the absolute avoidance of the substance. Steroid creams such as hydrocortisone are usually prescribed, to soothe the damaged skin and reduce the irritation.

Eczema

Inflammation of the skin caused by contact, internally or externally, with an irritant.

Infectious? No.

Appearance: Reddening of the skin, with swelling and blisters. The blisters leak tissue fluid which later hardens, forming scabs.

Site: The face, the neck and the skin, particularly at the inner creases of the elbows and behind the knees.

Treatment: Refer the client to their physician. Eczema may disappear if the source of irritation is identified and removed. Steroid cream may be prescribed by the physician, and special diets may help.

Dr M. H. Beck

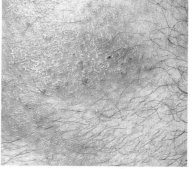

Dr A. L. Wright

Eczema

Urticaria (nettle rash) or hives

A minor skin disorder caused by contact with an allergen, either internally (food or drugs) or externally (for example, insect bites).

Infectious? No.

Appearance: Erythema with raised, round whitish skin weals. In some cases the lesions can cause intense burning or itching, a condition known as pruritis. Pruritis is a *symptom* of a disease (such as diabetes), not a disease itself.

Site: At the point of contact.

Treatment: Antihistamines may be prescribed to reduce the itching. The visible skin reaction usually disappears quickly, leaving no trace. Complete avoidance of the allergen 'cures' the problem.

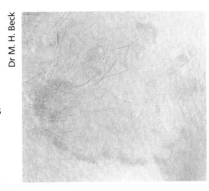

Dr M. H. Beck

Urticaria (nettle rash) or hives

GLOSSARY OF KEY WORDS

Accident book a written record of any accident occurring in the workplace. Incidents in the accident book should be reviewed to see where improvements to safe working practice could be made.

Accident form a detailed report form to be completed following any accident in the workplace.

Antiseptic a chemical agent that prevents the multiplication of micro-organisms. It has a limited action and does not kill all micro-organisms.

Autoclave an effective method of sterilisation, suitable for small metal objects and beauty therapy tools, where water is boiled under increased pressure and temperatures reach 134°C.

Bacteria minute single-celled organisms of various shapes. Large numbers live on the skin's surface and are not harmful (non-pathogenic). Others, however, are harmful (pathogenic) and can cause skin diseases.

Contra-indication a problematic symptom that indicates that treatment may not proceed.

Control of Substances Hazardous to Health (COSHH) Regulations 2002 these regulations require employers to identify hazardous substances used in the workplace and state how they should be stored and handled.

Controlled Waste Regulation 1992 categorises waste types. The Local Authority provides advice on how to dispose of waste types in compliance with the law.

Cosmetic Products (Safety) Regulations 2004 part of consumer protection legislation that requires that cosmetics and toiletries are safe in their formulation and are safe for use for their intended purpose as a cosmetic and comply with labelling requirements.

Cross-infection the transfer of contagious micro-organisms.

Disinfectant a chemical agent that destroys most micro-organisms when cleaning non-metallic tools, equipment and work areas.

Electricity at Work Regulations 1989 these regulations state that a qualified electrician should test every piece of equipment in the workplace every 12 months. It is the responsibility of the employer to keep record of the equipment tested and the date it was checked.

Employer's Liability (Compulsory Insurance) Act 1969 this provides financial compensation to an employee should they be injured as a result of an accident in the workplace. A certificate indicating that a policy of insurance has been obtained should be displayed.

Fire Precautions Act 1971 legislation that states that all staff must be familiar with and trained in fire and emergency evacuation procedures for their workplace.

Fire Precautions (Workplace) Regulations 1997 this legislation requires that every employer must carry out a risk assessment for the premises in relation to the fire evacuation practice and procedures, under the Management of Health and Safety Regulations 1999.

Fungi microscopic plants that are parasites. Fungal diseases of the skin feed off the waste products of the skin. They are found on the skin's surface or they can attack deeper tissues.

Hazard something with potential to cause harm.

Health and Safety at Work Act 1974 legislation that lays down the minimum standards of health, safety and welfare requirements in each workplace.

Health and Safety (Display Screen Equipment) Regulations 1992 these regulations cover the use of visual display units (VDUs) and computer screens. They specify acceptable levels of radiation emissions from the screen and identify correct posture, seating position, permitted working heights and rest periods.

Health and Safety (First Aid) Regulations 1981 legislation that states that workplaces must have first-aid provision. Employers must have appropriate and adequate first-aid arrangements in the event of an accident or illness.

Health and safety policy each employer of more than five employees must formulate a written health and safety policy issued to their employees outlining their health and safety responsibilities.

Infestation a condition where animal parasites invade and live off the host.

Legislation laws affecting the workplace in relation to treatments and services, systems and procedures, the premises, employers and employees.

Local Government (Miscellaneous Provisions) Act 1982 legislation that requires that salons offering any form of skin piercing be registered with the local health authority. This registration includes both the operators who will be carrying out the treatment and the workplace where the treatment will be carried out.

Management of Health and Safety at Work Regulations 1999 this legislation provides the employer with an approved code of practice for maintaining a safe, secure working environment.

Manual Handling Operations Regulations 1992 legislation that requires the employer to carry out a risk assessment of all activities undertaken which involve manual handling (lifting and moving objects).

Personal Protective Equipment (PPE) at Work Regulations 1992 this legislation requires managers to identify, through a risk assessment, those activities that require special protective equipment to be worn.

Posture the position of the body, which varies from person to person. Good posture is when the body is in alignment. Correct posture enables you to work longer without becoming tired. It prevents muscle fatigue, stiff joints and repetitive strain injury (RSI).

Provision and Use of Work Equipment Regulations (PUWER) 1998 these regulations lay down important health and safety controls on the provision and use of equipment.

Public Liability Insurance protects employers and employees against the consequences of death or injury to a third party while on the premises.

Reporting of Injuries, Diseases and Dangerous Occurrences Regulations (RIDDOR) 1995 this legislation requires the employer to notify the local enforcement officer in writing in cases where employers or trainees suffer personal injury at work.

Sanitisation the destruction of some, but not all, living micro-organisms when cleansing the skin.

Secondary infection bacterial penetration into the skin causing infection occurring as a result of injury to the client during the treatment, or if the client already has an open cut.

Skin allergy if the skin is sensitive to a particular substance an allergic skin reaction will occur. This is recognised by irritation, swelling and inflammation.

Sterilisation the total destruction of all micro-organisms in metal tools and equipment.

Viruses the smallest living bodies, too small to see under an ordinary microscope. They are considered to be *parasites*, as they require living tissue to survive. Viruses invade healthy body cells and multiply within the cell. Eventually the cell walls break down and the virus particles are freed to attack further cells.

Workplace (Health, Safety and Welfare Regulations) 1992 these regulations provide the employer with an approved code of practice for maintaining a safe, secure working environment.

Assessment of knowledge and understanding

You have now learnt about the health and safety responsibilities for everyone in the workplace. This will enable you to ensure your own actions reduce risks to health and safety.

To test your level of knowledge, answer the following short questions. These will prepare you for your summative (final) assessment.

Action to avoid health and safety risks

1 What are your main legal responsibilities under the Health and Safety at Work Act 1974?

2 Name four pieces of legislation relating to health and safety in the workplace.

3 What is the purpose of a salon health and safety policy? What sort of information does it include?

4 What is the importance of personal presentation in respect of your salon workplace policy?

5 Why is your personal conduct important to maintain the health and safety of yourself, colleagues and clients?

6 Why must regular health and safety checks be carried out in the workplace?

7 When completing a client's record card, you recognise that treatment is contra-indicated because the client has impetigo, an infectious skin disorder. What action do you take and why?

8 Effective sterilisation and disinfection methods prevent cross-infection and secondary infection. What do you understand by the following terms?
- sterilisation
- disinfection
- cross-infection
- secondary infection.

9 How should a large box be lifted from floor level to be placed on the work surface?

Dealing with significant risks in your workplace

1 What hazards may exist in the beauty therapy workplace?

2 Why must you always be aware of potential hazards?

3 In your role in the salon, what are the main risks that could occur, and what precautions do you take?

4 Whilst cleaning a wax heater you notice that the wires in the lead are exposed. What action should you take?

5 If you were unable to deal with a risk because it was outside of your responsibility, what action would you take?

6 What does the abbreviation COSHH stand for? Why is it important to follow the suppliers' and manufacturers' instructions for the safe use of materials and products?

7 When preparing a trolley for an eyelash tint, you drop and break a glass bottle of hydrogen peroxide. How would you deal with this spillage? How would you dispose of the broken glass?

Taking the right action in the event of danger

1 What is the procedure for dealing with an accident in the workplace?

2 What is a fire drill? What is the fire evacuation procedure in your salon? How often should this be carried out?

3 In the event of a real fire, after having safely evacuated the building, how would you contact the appropriate emergency service?

4 In reception, you discover a smoking bin, in which the fire has been caused by an un-extinguished cigarette. How should this fire be extinguished?

5 What action should be taken in the event of a bomb alert?

6 The air conditioning system in the salon has broken. Who should be contacted to deal with this? What is the potential risk of inadequate ventilation?

chapter 2

G4 Fulfil salon reception duties

Learning objectives

This chapter covers the skills required to ensure clients are greeted and dealt with efficiently through the salon reception. It describes the competencies to enable you to:

- **maintain the reception area**
- **attend to clients and enquiries**
- **make appointments for salon services**
- **handle payments from clients**

Salon reception

Saks Covent Garden

RECEPTION

Reception is a client's first and also final impression of the salon, whether this is on the telephone or in person when they visit. First impressions count, so ensure that the client gets the *right* impression!

Outcome 1: Maintain the reception area

G4

Maintain the reception area

1 Ensure that the reception area is clean and tidy at all times

2 Ensure that you have adequate equipment and materials at all times

4 Store client records confidentially

5 Ensure that retail displays are clean, well-stocked and appealing to the eye

6 Show good client care and hospitality

The design of the reception area

Location

Reception is usually situated at the front of a beauty salon; in a large department store, reception may be a cosmetic counter. It should be clean, uncluttered and inviting.

With a salon, the advantage of having reception at the front is that the window can be used to attract and capture the attention and interest of potential clients. Clients who are waiting in reception, however, may seek privacy, so the window should be attractively curtained and the seating should be situated away from the view of the main window if possible.

Size

The entrance to reception should be large enough for wheelchair access. There should be adequate seating, and an area in which to hang clients' coats.

It may be that small treatments, such as manicures including nail art, are carried out at reception. These treatments can then be seen by others, and may attract further clients.

Hospitality is important and shows the salon's commitment to client care. If the client arrives early or is likely to be delayed, offer magazines or refreshments such as coffee or water. Magazines should be renewed regularly. It is also a pleasant gesture to have boiled sweets on reception for the client to take.

Smoking

The smoking policy is determined by each salon. If smoking is allowed in reception, adequate ashtrays should be provided. These should be emptied and cleaned after each use.

Decoration

The reception area should be decorated tastefully, in keeping with the décor in the rest of the salon. Attractive posters promoting proprietary cosmetic ranges/services may be displayed on the walls. Framed certificates of the staff's professional qualifications can be displayed, as well as health-legislation registration certificates.

Equipment

The reception area should be uncluttered. The main equipment and furnishings required for an efficient reception include the following:

- *A reception desk* The size of the desk will depend on the size of the salon; some salons may have several receptionists. The desk should include shelves and drawers; some have an in-built lockable cash or security drawer. The desk should be at a convenient height for the client to write a cheque, etc. It should also be large enough to house the appointment book or computer (or both).
- *A comfortable chair* The receptionist's chair should provide adequate back support.
- *A computer* Computers are becoming more and more popular in the salon as they can perform many functions. They can be used to store data about clients, to keep appointment schedules, to carry out automatic stock control, and to record business details such as accounts and marketing information. They can also be programmed to recommend specific treatments on the basis of personal data about the client!
- *A calculator* This is used for simple financial calculations, especially if the salon does not have a computer.
- *Stationery* This should include price lists, gift vouchers, appointment cards and a receipt pad.
- *A notepad* This is for taking notes and recording messages.
- *An address and telephone book* This should hold all the frequently used telephone numbers.

> **TIP**
>
> Visitors to the salon may leave a business card, stating the name of the company, and the representative's name, address and telephone number. These cards should be filed by the receptionist for future reference.

HEALTH AND SAFETY

Ventilation
To avoid losing the custom of non-smoking clients, ensure that the air is fresh and the room adequately ventilated to remove the smell of stale tobacco.

TIP

Client attention
It is important to give the right amount of attention to all clients according to their specific requirements to ensure client satisfaction. This must always be considered in a busy situation where a client may be kept waiting.

HEALTH AND SAFETY

Eating and drinking
The receptionist and other employees should not eat or drink at reception, nor should they smoke.

TIP

Price lists
Some salons' price lists are in booklet form, detailing the treatments offered and explaining their benefits.

TIP

Electronic mail (e-mail)
E-mail is a more popular method of telecommunication today and requires a computer. E-mail can only be sent if the other person has a computer with this facility and an e-mail address.

- *A telephone and an answering machine* The answering machine allows clients to notify you, even when the salon is closed, of an appointment request, or an unavoidable change or cancellation: you can then re-schedule appointments as quickly as possible. If you are working on your own, the answering machine avoids interruptions during a treatment, yet without losing custom.

- *A fax* This may be available at reception. The fax is capable of transmitting text and image via a telephone line to another fax machine. This is useful when information needs to be passed on quickly.

- *Record cards* These confidential cards record the personal details of each client registered at the salon. They should be kept in alphabetical order in a filing cabinet or a card-index box, and should be ready for collection by the therapist when treating new or existing clients. See the general beauty therapy units of this book for complete unit specific examples of record cards. Each card records:
  - the client's name, address and telephone number;
  - any medical details;
  - any contra-indications (such as allergies and contra-actions);
  - treatment aims and outcomes;
  - a base on which to plan future treatments;
  - services received, products used and merchandise purchased.

- *Pens, pencils and an eraser* Make sure these stay at the desk!

- *A display cabinet* This may be used to store proprietary skin-care and cosmetic products, and any other merchandise sold by the salon.

A record card

BEAUTY WORKS

Date	Beauty therapist name	
Client name		Date of birth
Address		Postcode
Evening phone number	Day phone number	
Name of doctor	Doctor's address and phone number	

Related medical history (conditions that may restrict or prohibit treatment application)

Are you taking any medication (esp. antibiotics, steriods, the pill)

CONTRA-INDICATIONS REQUIRING MEDICAL REFERRAL
(Preventing facial treatment application)

CONTRA-INDICATIONS WHICH RESTRICT TREATMENT
(Treatment may require adaption)

- ☐ bacterial infection (e.g. impetigo)
- ☐ viral infection (e.g. herpes simplex)
- ☐ fungal infection (e.g. tinea corporis)
- ☐ eye infections (e.g. conjuncti...

- ☐ cuts and abrasians
- ☐ recent scar tissue
- ☐ skin allergies
- ☐ styes

- ☐ bruising and swelling
- ☐ eczema
- ☐ vitiligo
- ☐ hyper keratosis

ACTIVITY

Designing record cards
Design a card to be used to record the clients' requirements and the treatment details related to NVQ/SVQ Level 2 treatments.

Planning a reception area
Design a reception area, to scale, appropriate to a small or large beauty salon. Discuss the choice of wall and floor coverings, furnishings and equipment, and give the reasons for their selection. Consider clients' comfort, and health and safety.

Cleaning
In a large salon a cleaner may be employed to maintain the hygiene of the reception area. In a smaller salon this may be the responsibility of an apprentice, the receptionist or a therapist. Reception must be maintained to a high standard at all times.

Data Protection Act 1998

This legislation is designed to protect the client's privacy and confidentiality. It is necessary to ask the client questions before the treatment plan can be finalised.

The relevant information gathered on the client is confidential and should be stored in a secure area following client treatment. Inform the client that their personal details are being stored and will only be accessed by those individuals who are authorised to do so.

THE RECEPTIONIST

Outcome 2: Attend to clients and enquiries

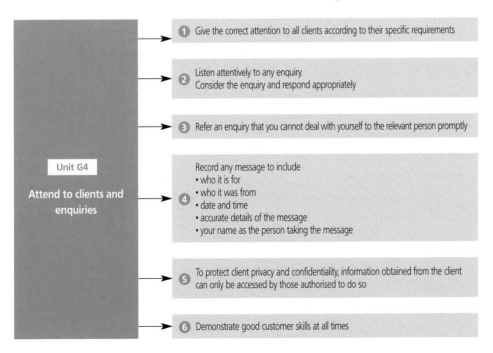

Courtesy 8.1.9.18 divas

A receptionist at work

TIP ✓

Name badges
It is a good idea for the receptionist to wear a badge indicating their name and position.

TIP ✓

Client care
If you are engaged on the telephone when a client arrives, look up and acknowledge their presence. This is positive body language, which makes the client feel welcome.

HEALTH AND SAFETY ✚

Fire drill
As the receptionist you should be familiar with the emergency procedure in case of fire.

TIP ✓

Opportunities for promoting products and services
Within your area of training and responsibility, bring to the attention of clients waiting in the reception area any new products, services or promotions.

Receiving clients

Receptionists should have a smart appearance and be able to communicate effectively and professionally, thereby creating the right impression.

The receptionists' duties include:

- maintaining the reception and retail area;
- looking after clients on arrival and departure;
- scheduling appointments;
- dealing with enquiries;
- dealing with complaints;
- telling the appropriate therapist that a client or visitor has arrived;
- assisting with retail sales;
- operating the payment point and handling payments.

The receptionist should know:

- the name of each member of staff, their role and their area of responsibility;
- the salon's hours of opening, and the days and times when each therapist is available;
- the range of services or products offered by the salon, and their cost;
- any booking treatment restrictions such as skin testing requirements;
- who to refer different types of enquiries to;
- the person in your salon to whom you should refer reception problems;
- any current discounts and special offers that the salon is promoting;
- the benefits of each treatment service and each retail product;
- the approximate time taken to complete each treatment;
- how to schedule follow-up treatments.

Qualities of a receptionist

All clients need to feel valued. The following **interpersonal skills** are essential in a receptionist:

- act positively and confidently;
- speak clearly;
- be friendly, and smile;
- look at the customer and maintain eye contact;
- good listening skills;
- be interested in everything that is going on around the reception area;
- give each client individual attention and respect.

ACTIVITY

Reception
Pair with a colleague and share your experiences of a well managed and a badly managed reception.

ACTIVITY

Non-verbal communication
In conversation you give signals that tell others whether you are listening or not.
1 What do you think the following signals indicate?
- A smile.
- Head tilted, and resting on one hand.
- Eyes looking around you.
- Eyes semi-closed.
- Head nodding.
- Fidgeting.
2 Can you think of further body signals that indicate whether you are interested or not?

ACTIVITY

Do's and don'ts
List *five* important do's and *five* don'ts for the receptionist. Think also of things that *should not* be discussed.

How to deal with a dissatisfied client

Occasionally a client may be dissatisfied and wish to complain. The receptionist is usually the first contact with the client (either face to face or through telephone contact) and may have to deal with dissatisfied, angry or awkward customers. Considerable skill is needed if you are to deal constructively with a potentially damaging situation.

Never become angry or awkward yourself. Always remain courteous and diplomatic, and communicate confidently and politely.

1 Listen to the client as they describe their problems, without making judgement. Do not make excuses, for yourself or for colleagues. Do not interrupt.

2 Ask questions to check that you have the full background details. Summarise the client's concerns to confirm this.

3 If possible, agree on a course of action, offering a solution if you can. Check that the client has agreed to the proposed course of action. It may be necessary to consult the salon supervisor before proposing a solution to the client: if you're not sure, always check first.

4 Log the complaint: the date, the time, the client's name, the nature of the complaint and the course of action agreed.

TIP

Behaviour breeds behaviour
If you behave calmly, the client will become less angry. If you become angry, the client will become even angrier!

ACTIVITY

Reception role-play
With colleagues, act out the following situations, which may occur when working as a receptionist. You may wish to video the role-plays for review and discussion later.
1 A client arrives very late for an appointment but insists that she be treated.
2 A client questions the bill.
3 A client comes in to complain about a treatment given previously. (Choose a particular service.)
Alternatively you may choose to do this as a written activity with a discussion of your answers.

APPOINTMENTS

Outcome 3: Make appointments for salon services

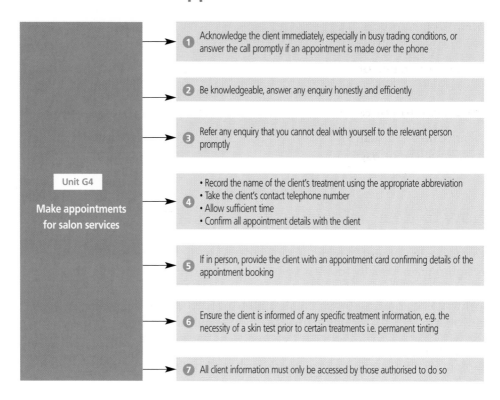

Unit G4

Make appointments for salon services

1. Acknowledge the client immediately, especially in busy trading conditions, or answer the call promptly if an appointment is made over the phone

2. Be knowledgeable, answer any enquiry honestly and efficiently

3. Refer any enquiry that you cannot deal with yourself to the relevant person promptly

4. • Record the name of the client's treatment using the appropriate abbreviation
   • Take the client's contact telephone number
   • Allow sufficient time
   • Confirm all appointment details with the client

5. If in person, provide the client with an appointment card confirming details of the appointment booking

6. Ensure the client is informed of any specific treatment information, e.g. the necessity of a skin test prior to certain treatments i.e. permanent tinting

7. All client information must only be accessed by those authorised to do so

Making correct entries in the **appointment book** or salon **computer** is one of the most important duties of the receptionist. As receptionist you must familiarise yourself with the salon's appointment system, column headings, treatment times and any abbreviations used.

Each therapist will usually have their name at the head of a column. Entries in columns must not be reallocated without the consent of the therapist or supervisor, unless they are absent.

HEALTH AND SAFETY

Health and Safety (Display Screen Equipment) Regulations 1992
These regulations cover the use of visual display units and computer screens. They specify acceptable levels of radiation emissions from the screen, and identify correct posture, seating position, permitted working heights and rest periods.

Bookings

When a client calls to make an appointment, record the client's name and the treatment they want. Allow adequate time to carry out the required service (as indicated in the following chapters). Take the client's telephone number in case the therapist falls ill or is unable to keep the appointment for some other reason. If the client requests a particular therapist, be sure to enter the client's name in the correct column.

The hours of the day are recorded along the left-hand side of the appointment page, divided into 15-minute intervals. You must know how long each treatment takes so that you can allow sufficient time for the therapist to carry out the treatment in a safe, competent, professional manner. If you don't allow sufficient time, the therapist will run late, and this will affect all later appointments. On the other hand, if you allow too much time, the therapist's time will be wasted and the salon's earnings will be less than they could be. Suggested times to be allowed for each service are given in the treatment chapters.

Ensure that you regularly check scheduled appointments and plan ahead where you can see any potential problem – put a strategy in place to rectify it. This may involve asking others to help you.

Confirm the name of the therapist who will be carrying out the treatment, the date and the time.

Finally, confirm or estimate the cost of the treatment to the client.

Treatments are usually recorded in an abbreviated form. All those who use the appointment page must be familiar with these abbreviations.

Treatment	Abbreviation	Treatment time allowed*
Cleanse and make-up	C/M/up	45 mins
Eyebrow shaping	E/B reshape or trim	15 mins
Eyebrow tint	EBT	10 mins
Eyelash tint	ELT	20 mins
Eyelash perm	ELP	45 mins
Manicure	Man	45 mins
Nail art	N/Art	5–10 mins per nail
Pedicure	Ped	45 mins
Leg wax: half	$1/2$ leg wax	30 mins
three-quarter	$3/4$ leg wax	30–40 mins
full	Full leg wax	50 mins
Bikini wax	B/wax	15 mins
Underarm wax	U/arm wax	15 mins
Arm wax	F/arm wax	30 mins
Eyebrow wax	E/B wax	15 mins
Ear pierce	E/P	15 mins
Facial	F	60 mins
False lashes	F/Lash	20 mins

*Treatment time does not include preparation for treatment and consultation

If an appointment book is used, write each entry neatly and accurately. It is preferable to write in pencil: appointments can be amended by erasing and rewriting, keeping the book clean and clear.

Appointment cards may be offered to the client, to confirm the client's appointment. The card should record the treatment, the date, the day and the time. The therapist's name may also be recorded.

Appointments may be made up to six weeks in advance. Often clients will book their next appointment whilst still at the salon. How far ahead the receptionist is able to book appointments will vary from salon to salon.

When the client arrives for their treatment, draw a line or checkmark through their name to indicate that they have arrived.

An appointment page

DAY SATURDAY		DATE 15th JANUARY	
THERAPIST	JAYNE	SUE	LIZ
9.00	Mrs Young		
9.15	½ leg wax	Jenny Iron	
9.30	Carol Green	ELT EBT	
9.45	F/ leg wax	trim	
10.00	B / wax		
10.15		Sandra Smith	Fiona Smith
10.30	Mrs Lord E/BWAX	C / M / UP	C / M / UP
10.45			Strip lash
11.00		Mrs Jones	
11.15		U/arm wax	
11.30		F/arm wax	Carol Brown
11.45	/ / /		E/F
12.00			
12.15			\
12.30	Nina Farrel	/ / /	
12.45	man .		
1.00	Ped.		
1.15		Sue Yip E/P	/ / /
1.30	½ leg wax	T. Scott	
1.45	\	3/4 leg wax	
2.00	Karen Davies	U/arm wax	
2.15	facial		
2.30			
2.45	\		Pat King
3.00			C / M / UP
3.15	Anna Wood		Man
3.30	Man .		
3.45	E/B Reshape		
4.00			

If the client cancels indicate this on the appointment page *immediately*, usually with a large C, placed through the booking. This enables another client to take the appointment.

If a client fails to arrive the abbreviation DNA (did not arrive) is usually written over the booking. The client's telephone number should then be used to see if a re-booking is required.

Some salons will have a policy to charge for a missed appointment.

Dealing with appointment problems

You are often required to use your initiative in helping colleagues and clients and be able to cope with the unexpected:

- clients arriving late for appointments;
- double bookings, with two clients requiring treatment at the same time;
- the arrival of unscheduled clients;
- staff absence with a column of appointments!

Effective teamwork can usually overcome any of these situations. Inform your colleague/supervisor of the problem and, dependent upon your experience, state what action needs to be taken or ask them to support you in identifying a solution. You must always:

- aim to accommodate clients;
- not disadvantage or compromise any clients in terms of quality of service;
- keep the client informed of what action is being taken;
- state how long any delay to treatment will be and if this is unsuitable offer an alternative future appointment.

ACTIVITY

How would you deal with the following reception problems?

- a client arriving late for a treatment;
- a double booking;
- the arrival of an unscheduled client.

SKIN SENSITIVITY (PATCH) TESTS

Before clients receive certain treatments it may be necessary to carry out **skin tests** to test skin sensitivity. The skin test is often carried out at reception, and the receptionist or NVQ/SVQ Level 1 therapist will be able to perform the test once they have been trained. Every client should undergo a skin test before a permanent tinting treatment to the eyelashes or eyebrows. Further tests may be necessary, depending on the sensitivity of the client, before treatments such as artificial eyelash treatment, eyelash perming, bleaching or wax depilation. Refer to the relevant chapters to familiarise yourself with the test required.

TELEPHONE CALLS: COMMUNICATION

In building new relationships, first impressions count. Good telephone technique can win clients; poor technique can lose them. Here are some guidelines for good technique:

TIP

Clients matter most
Don't regard the phone ringing as an interruption. Always remember that clients matter – it is they who ensure the success of your business!

ACTIVITY

Communicating with clients
Listen to experienced receptionists and notice how they communicate with clients.

ACTIVITY

Listening to yourself
A pleasant speaking voice is an asset. Do you think you could improve your speech or manner?
Record your voice as you answer a telephone enquiry, then play it back. How did you sound? This is how others hear you!

TIP

Personal calls
Check the salon's policy on personal calls. Usually they are permitted only in emergencies. This is so that staff are not distracted from clients, and to keep the telephone free for clients to make appointments.

ACTIVITY

What do you need to know?
Think of different questions that you might be asked as a receptionist. Then ask an experienced receptionist what the most common requests are.

TIP

Telephone services
Telephone directories, codebooks and guides to charges provide a great deal of useful information. Read them carefully to make yourself familiar with the telephone services that are available.

TIP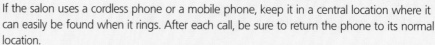

A client who has received a poor response to their telephone call may tell others about it.

TIP

If the salon uses a cordless phone or a mobile phone, keep it in a central location where it can easily be found when it rings. After each call, be sure to return the phone to its normal location.

- *Answer quickly* On average, a person may be willing to wait up to nine rings: try to respond to the call within six rings.
- Introduce yourself to build a rapport.
- *Be prepared* Have information and writing materials ready to hand. It should not normally be necessary to leave the caller waiting while you find something.
- *Be welcoming and attentive* Speak clearly, without mumbling, at the right speed. Pronounce your words clearly, and vary your tone. Sound interested, and never abrupt.

Remember: the caller may be a new client ringing several salons, and their decision whether to visit *your* salon may depend on your attitude and the way you respond to their call.

Here are some more ideas about good telephone technique:

- Smile – this will help you put across a warm, friendly response to the caller.
- Alter the pitch of your voice as you speak, to create interest.
- As you answer, give the standard greeting for the salon – for example: 'Good morning, Visage Beauty Salon, Susan speaking. How may I help you?'
- Listen attentively to the caller's questions or requests. You will be speaking to a variety of clients: you must respond appropriately and helpfully to each.
- Evaluate the information given by the caller, and be sure to respond to what they have said or asked.
- Use the client's name, if you know it; this personalises the call.
- In your mind, summarise the main requests from the call. Ask for further information if you need it.
- If you have an enquiry that you cannot deal with yourself, refer to the relevant person promptly for assistance. Tell the client what you are doing.
- At the end, repeat the main points of the conversation clearly to check that you and the client have understood each other.
- Close the call pleasantly – for example, 'Thank you for calling, Mrs Smith. Goodbye.'

If you receive a business call, or a call from a person seeking employment, always take the caller's name and telephone number. Your supervisor can then deal with the call as soon as they are free to do so.

Finding the right approach
What telephone manner should you adopt when dealing with people who are:

- angry?
- talkative?
- nervous?

Transferring calls

If you transfer a telephone call to another extension, explain to the caller what you are doing and thank them for waiting. If the extension to which you have transferred the call is not answered within nine rings, explain to the caller that you will ask the person concerned to ring back as soon as possible. Take the caller's name and telephone number.

Taking messages

Messages should be recorded on a memorandum ('memo') pad. Each message should record:

- who the message is for;
- who the message was from;
- the date and the time the message was received;
- accurate details of the message;
- the telephone number or address of the caller;
- the signature of the person who took the message.

When taking a message, repeat the details you have recorded so that the caller can check that you've got it right. Pass the message to the correct person as soon as possible.

A memo

TELEPHONE MESSAGE RECEIVED			
To	Angela	Date	10.7.07
From	Jenny Heron	Time	9:30 am
Number	273451	Taken by	Sandra

Please could you ring Jenny Heron regarding her appointment on Saturday.

THE PAYMENT POINT

Outcome 4: Handle payment from clients

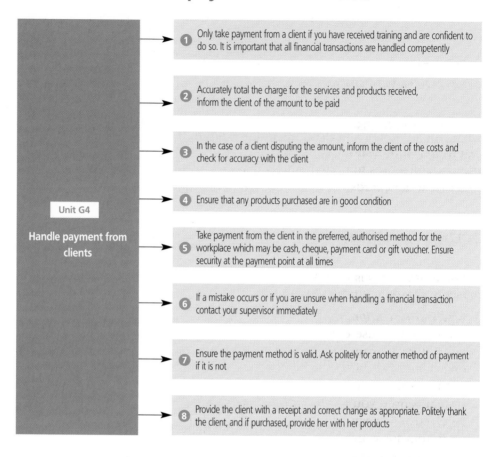

Unit G4

Handle payment from clients

1. Only take payment from a client if you have received training and are confident to do so. It is important that all financial transactions are handled competently

2. Accurately total the charge for the services and products received, inform the client of the amount to be paid

3. In the case of a client disputing the amount, inform the client of the costs and check for accuracy with the client

4. Ensure that any products purchased are in good condition

5. Take payment from the client in the preferred, authorised method for the workplace which may be cash, cheque, payment card or gift voucher. Ensure security at the payment point at all times

6. If a mistake occurs or if you are unsure when handling a financial transaction contact your supervisor immediately

7. Ensure the payment method is valid. Ask politely for another method of payment if it is not

8. Provide the client with a receipt and correct change as appropriate. Politely thank the client, and if purchased, provide her with her products

Every beauty therapy or cosmetic business will have a policy for handling cash and for operating the payment point.

It is important that you have received training and are confident to take payment in the client's preferred method, which may be cash (or cash equivalent, i.e. gift voucher), cheque or payment card.

Kinds of payment points

Manual tills

With **manual tills** a lockable drawer or box is used to store cash: this may form part of the reception desk. Each transaction must be recorded by hand.

At the end of the working day, record the total cash register in a book, to ensure that accurate accounts are kept. Records of petty cash must also be kept so that the final totals will balance.

Automatic tills

Modern electrical **automatic tills** use codes, one for each kind of treatment or retail sale. These are identified by keys on the till. Using these with each transaction makes it possible to analyse the salon's business each day or each week.

With each sale during the day a receipt is given to the client; the total is also recorded on the till's **audit roll**.

Automatic tills also provide **subtotals** of the amounts taken: these can be cross-checked against the amount in the till, to determine the daily **takings**:

- the **X reading** provides subtotals throughout the day, as required;
- the **Z reading** provides the overall figures at the end of the day.

Computerised cashdesks

Computerised cashdesks provide the same facilities as automatic tills, with additional features to help with the business's record-keeping, including client treatment cards and stock records.

Equipment and materials required

- *Calculator* This is useful in totalling large amounts of money or when using a manual till.
- *Credit-card equipment* If your business is authorised to accept credit cards you may use either an *imprinter* or *electronic terminal*. An imprinter is a manual system whereby the client's credit card is placed on a self-carbonating voucher within the machine and a manual sliding mechanism imprints the details of the card upon the voucher. If this system is used you require a supply of vouchers. Alternatively, where an electronic payment system is used a special till roll which provides a printout for yourself and a copy for the client is required.
- *A cash float* At the start of each day you need a small sum of money, comprising coins and perhaps a few notes, to provide change: this is

> **TIP** ✓
>
> **Tills**
> If there is too little change in the till, inform the relevant person. Running out of change would disrupt service and spoil the impression clients receive.

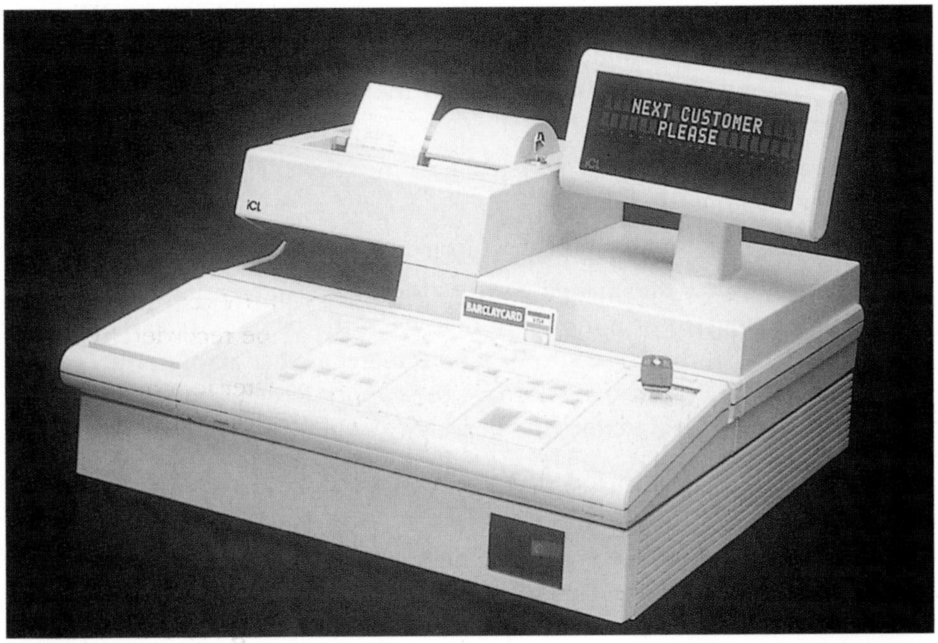

A computerised till

called the **float**. (At the end of the day there will be money surplus to the float: if no mistakes have been made, this should match the takings.)

- *A till roll* This records the sales and provides a receipt. Keep a spare to hand. If you're using a manual cash drawer, you'll need a **receipt book**.
- *An audit roll* The retailer's copy of the till roll.
- *A cash book* This is a record of income and expenditure, for a manual till.
- *Other stationery* A date stamp and a salon name stamp (for cheques), pens, pencils and an eraser, and a container to hold these.

Security at the payment point

Having placed money in the cash drawer and collected change as required, always close the cash drawer firmly – never leave it open. Do not leave the key in the drawer, or lying about reception unattended.

Some members of staff will be appointed to **authorise** cheques and credit-card payments; one of these should initial each cheque.

Errors may occur when handling cheques or when operating an electronic or computerised payment point. Don't panic! If you can't correct the error yourself, seek assistance – but don't leave the cash drawer unattended and open.

Methods of payment

Cash

When receiving payment by **cash**, follow this sequence:

1 Accurately total the charge for the services/products received. Inform the client of the amount to be paid.
2 Check that the money offered is **legal tender** – that is, money you will be able to pay into your bank. (Your salon will probably not accept foreign currency, for example.)
3 Place the customer's money on the till ledge until you have given change, or at least state to the customer verbally the sum of money that they have given you.
4 Aloud, count the change as you give it to the client. This will help avoid payment disputes.
5 Thank the client, and give them a receipt.
6 If a client disputes the change given as too little, ask how much money they are missing. Inform the client that when the takings are cashed at the end of the day if there is a surplus and it matches that amount they will be reimbursed. Ensure that you have the client's details so that you can inform them of the outcome the next day.

Cheques

Cheques are an alternative form of payment, and must be accompanied by a **cheque-guarantee card**. This has a spending limit, usually £100. Your salon may be willing to accept cheques for larger amounts if the client can

ACTIVITY

Fraud
Find out about your salon's policy in the case of fradulent monetary transactions, using either cash or cards. What actions should you take?

TIP

Forgeries
Hold notes to the light to check for forgeries. You should be able to see the watermark (picture of the Queen's head), the continuous metal strip that runs through the note and a hologram decal in the mid-left section of the note.
  An ultra-violet detector machine may also be used to check for forgeries.
  The police will often provide a list of forged note numbers to businesses to be aware of.

TIP

Cheques
A cheque is only valid for six months from the date on the cheque.

Beauty Bank
5 High Street
Telchester TR4 1PS

61–01–48

_____ 20 __

Beauty Bank plc, Telchester

Pay _____

ACCOUNT PAYEE

£

MS C E SMITH

Cheque No.   Branch Sort Code   Account No.   Transaction Code

⑈000877⑈ 60⑈0198⑈ 973116805⑈02

A cheque

show some other identification, such as a driving licence, but you must always check first with your supervisor.

When receiving payment by cheque, follow this sequence of checks:

1   the cheque must be correctly dated;

2   the cheque must be made payable to the salon (you may have a salon stamp for this);

3   the words and figures written on the cheque must match those in the box;

4   any errors or alterations must have been initialled by the client;

5   the signature on the back of the cheque card must match that on the cheque – compare these as the customer writes their signature on the cheque;

6   the bank's 'sort code' numbers on the cheque must match those on the card;

7   the date on the cheque card must be valid;

8   the value on the cheque must not exceed the cheque card limit;

9   the cheque card number must be recorded on the back of the cheque;

10   the cheque must be signed by the client.

Debit cards

Debit cards include Switch/Maestro, Connect and Solo. The card authorises immediate debit of the cash amount from the client's account. (This card may also be a cheque-guarantee card.) You cannot perform this kind of transaction unless your salon has an electronic terminal. The card processing company applies a fixed fee for each transaction made. Duplicated receipts are signed by the client; one copy is given to the client, the other kept by the salon.

Credit cards

Credit cards can be used only if your business has an arrangement with the relevant credit-card company. In this case the company will give the salon a credit limit (a **ceiling**), the maximum amount that may be accepted with the card. Any amount greater than this must be individually authorised by the credit-card company. (This is done by telephone at the time of transaction.)

A credit card

Swiping a card through an electronic terminal

Sharp

TIP ✓

Cards
If cards are accepted as a method of payment, those that are accepted by the business will usually be displayed at the payment point.

Electronic payment systems

An electronic computerised terminal may be used for payment by both credit and debit cards.

1 Check that the terminal display is in 'SALE' mode.

2 Confirm that a sale is to be made by pressing the YES button.

3 The terminal will request that you **swipe** the card. Do this, ensuring that the magnetic strip passes over the reader head and that you retain the card in your hand. In some cases the magnetic strip cannot be read by the swipe card reader: in this situation you will have to key the complete card number into the terminal manually. This does not necessarily mean that there is any reason for suspicion, but do look carefully at it for any signs that the card has been tampered with.

4 When prompted, enter the 'AMOUNT' using the keypad to input the purchases and total them. (If you make a mistake, you can clear the figures using the CLEAR button.)

5 Press ENTER, which will automatically connect the terminal to the credit card company. A message will indicate first 'DIALLING', and then 'CONNECTION MADE'.

6 Customer details are accessed automatically. After a few moments you should receive one of two messages. If the payment is authorised you will see 'AUTH CODE', and a code number will be printed on the receipt with the other purchase details. If the transaction is declined, you will see 'CARD NOT ACCEPTED'.

7 While holding the card, check the details and tear off the two-part receipt and ask the cardholder to sign in ballpoint pen, in the space provided. Alternatively the 'chip and pin' system may be used, where the client enters their personal pin number instead of signing their name. The transaction will be declined if the pin number is incorrect.

8 Where a signature is used, check the signature matches the signature on the card, and give the customer the top, signed copy, with the card.

9 Place the copies in the till. One copy is for the debit/credit card company, the other for your records.

When receiving payment by credit card, check these points:

1 the card logo is at the upper right corner on the front of the card;

2 the hologram should have a clear, sharp image and be in the centre right of the card;

3 the date on the credit card must be valid: if it is out of date ask for another form of payment;

4 the sex (Ms, Miss, Mrs, Mr, etc.) and the name of the customer must fit your client;

5 the cardholder's signature on the card must match the name on the front of the card;

6 the cardholder's account number should be embossed and across the width of the card;

7 the cardholder's account number must not be one of those on the credit-card company's warning list.

If you receive a card that is on a credit-card warning list, politely detain the customer, hold onto the card, and contact your supervisor, who will implement the salon's procedure. If the card is unsigned, do not allow the cardholder to sign the card unless you first get authorisation from the credit-card company's service provider. (The service provider's telephone number should be kept near the telephone.)

Credit card payment using an imprinter

1 Prepare the **sales voucher**, which comprises three copies.
2 Place the card in the transaction printer, with the front (embossed side) facing upwards.
3 Place the voucher over the card, and under the voucher guide.
4 Slide the handle from left to right, and back to its original position.
5 Remove the voucher and check that the recorded details are clear and on all copies of the voucher.
6 Complete the sales details on the appropriate credit-card voucher, using ballpoint pen so that the bottom copy is legible.
7 Ask the customer to sign the voucher. Check that the signature on the voucher matches that on the credit card.
8 Give the customer the top copy as a receipt, with their credit card.

A copy of the sales voucher is sent to the credit-card company; the third copy is kept by the salon.

Travellers' cheques

Travellers' cheques also may be acceptable, provided they are in particular currencies (usually sterling). Such cheques must be compared with the client's **passport** for validity.

A travellers' cheque

Charge cards

Some businesses accept **charge cards** such as American Express. These differ from credit cards in that the account holder must repay to the card company the complete amount spent each month.

A charge card

TIP

Advertisement vouchers
Sometimes the salon may publish other offers, such as a discount on producing a newspaper advertisement for the salon. The advertisement voucher is a form of payment, and must be collected.

TIP

Sale and Supply of Goods Act 1994
You have a duty to comply with the responsibilities of this Act, ensuring all products sold are of merchantable quality.

Gift vouchers

Gift vouchers are purchased from the salon as pre-payments for beauty therapy services or retail sales.

Check the following:

- There is usually a specific time period in which gift vouchers must be used. Check to see if this is the case and if they are still valid.
- Check the value of the voucher, and remember to request another form of payment if the cost of the treatment is higher than the voucher.

It is important that all financial transactions are handled competently. However busy you are always follow the guidelines for handling each method of payment.

If you are ever unsure when handling a financial transaction or make a mistake, inform your supervisor immediately. It may be that you have to be discreet when doing this, for example if a client has handed you a forged bank note!

A gift voucher

BEAUTY WORKS

3 Market Street
Whitely

Tel: 39473

This voucher entitles

....

to the value of £ ....

Signed:

Date:

Valid for six months from date of purchase

GLOSSARY OF KEY WORDS

Appointment arrangement made for a client to receive a service on a particular date and time.

Body language communication involving the body.

Charge card an alternative form of payment where the complete amount of credit spent must be repaid each month to the card company.

Cheque an alternative form of payment to that of using cash. A cheque must be accompanied by a cheque-guarantee card.

Communication the exchange of information and the establishment of understanding between people.

Credit card an alternative form of payment to that of using cash. These cards are held by those who have a credit account, where there is a pre-arranged borrowing limit. These can only be used if your business has an arrangement to deal with the relevant credit-card company.

Data Protection Act 1998 legislation designed to protect client privacy and confidentiality.

Debit card alternative method of payment where the card authorises immediate debit of the cash amount from the client's account.

Gift voucher a pre-payment method for beauty therapy services or retail sales.

Health and Safety (Display Screen Equipment) Regulations 1992 these regulations cover the use of visual display units (VDUs) and computer screens. They specify acceptable levels of radiation emissions from the screen and identify correct working posture, seating position, permitted working heights and rest periods.

Messages communication of information to another person in written or verbal form.

Non-verbal communication communicating using body language, i.e. using your eyes, face and body to transmit your feelings.

Reception the area where clients are received.

Receptionist person responsible for maintaining the reception area, scheduling appointments and handling payments.

Record cards confidential cards recording the personal details of each client registered at the business. This information may be stored electronically on the salon's computer.

Skin sensitivity (patch) test method used to assess skin tolerance/sensitivity to a particular substance or treatment.

Travellers' cheques alternative form of payment used when travelling abroad and must be compared with the client's passport.

Verbal communication occurs when you talk directly to another person, either face to face or over the telephone.

Assessment of knowledge and understanding

You have now learnt about the skills required to ensure clients are greeted and dealt with efficiently at the salon reception, to enable you to fulfil salon reception duties.

To test your level of knowledge, answer the following short questions. These will prepare you for your summative (final) assessment.

Maintain the reception area

1 What are the main duties of the salon receptionist?

2 Hospitality is important to show the salon's commitment to customer care. What examples of hospitality may be offered to clients at reception?

3 What equipment and materials do you need at the reception desk?

4 How should the reception be maintained?

5 What is a float? When must this be checked, and why?

6 Client records are often stored at reception. How should this information be used and stored to comply with the Data Protection Act 1998?

Attend to clients and enquiries

1 What interpersonal skills are essential in a receptionist?

2 How should clients be greeted on arrival?

3 What information should be sought by the receptionist from a visitor to the reception desk?

4 What are the important details to record when taking a message?

5 If as receptionist you were unable to give appropriate information to a client, what action should you take?

6 For what different reasons may people telephone the salon?

7 A client rings up to check the time of an appointment. What information do you need from them?

8 A client complains at reception about a leg wax treatment they have received. What questions should you ask? What action should you take?

Make appointments for salon services

1 A client telephones the salon, how should you:
   - answer the telephone and introduce yourself?
   - speak on the telephone?
   - seek information from the client?
   - finish the telephone conversation?

2 What are the common systems used in salons to make appointments?

3 Why is it necessary to confirm an appointment with a client verbally before they leave the salon?

4 A client wishes to make an appointment for an eyelash tint. What information is required from the client before making the appointment?

5 How long should you allow when making an appointment for the following treatments/services?

- full leg wax
- ear piercing
- nail art
- pedicure including a foot conditioning treatment
- full facial and eyelash tint.

Handle payment from clients

1 If you make an error when operating the till, why must you report this?

2 When taking cash from a client, what is the correct procedure to follow?

3 Why is it important to inspect the quality and condition of goods before payment is processed?

4 If you made a mistake in giving the client their change, how would you deal with this?

5 What would you check when receiving payment by cheque?

6 What is the procedure for receiving payment by credit card?

7 If a client has presented an invalid cheque card, what should you say to them?

8 If your salon accepts vouchers in exchange for salon treatment/services, how are these handled?

chapter 3

G6 Promote additional products or services to clients

Learning objectives

This chapter discusses ways to promote products and services to clients. It describes the competencies to enable you to:

- **identify additional products or services that are available**
- **inform clients about additional products or services**
- **gain client commitment to using additional products or services**

TIP

Positive promotion
The client's skin-care preparation needs to alter throughout the different seasons. As such, the client should be advised on products that are most suitable to maintain skin health and appearance. This gives you the opportunity to promote additional products and maintain client interest.

THE IMPORTANCE OF RETAIL SALES

When clients select a beauty therapy service or product they do so for one or a number of reasons. This may be:

- to improve their appearance, i.e. an eyelash tint or manicure;
- for a special occasion, i.e. make-up application;
- for therapeutic reasons, to receive a quality professional treatment in tranquil surroundings, i.e. a de-stress facial massage;
- to seek professional guidance on what would best suit their needs, i.e. skin-care advice;
- to maintain the benefits of a particular service they have received before, i.e. repeat booking for leg waxing service;
- to give a friend a service or product as a gift, i.e. a gift voucher.

Whatever the reason, you want the client to feel satisfied with their choice, enjoy their experience and tell others – thus promoting the business.

Retail sales are of considerable importance to the beauty salon: they are a simple way of greatly increasing the income without too much extra time and effort. Beauty therapy treatments are time-consuming and labour-intensive; selling a product in addition to providing the treatment will greatly increase the profitability.

Clients need to be regularly informed about what products and services the business is promoting. This will maintain their motivation and their experience of the salon or spa visit. In Chapter 1 we looked at the importance of creating an initial positive impression to the client. Staff knowledge of products and services is vital to ensure personal effectiveness and helps in gaining client loyalty.

If you have got it right the client will maintain their loyalty to you and this enables the business to grow. For example: a facial treatment might take one hour and cost the client £40. You might then sell the client a moisturiser costing £40, of which £10 might be clear profit. Supposing that you sold eight products each day, each yielding £10 profit. That would be a profit of £80 per day, or £400 per week, or £1600 each month – and thus, £19,200 profit over the whole year: a significant sum.

> **TIP** ✓
>
> **Client refreshments**
> Healthy light refreshments may be promoted as an additional retail opportunity.

POSITIVE PROMOTION

Outcome 1: Identify additional products or services that are available

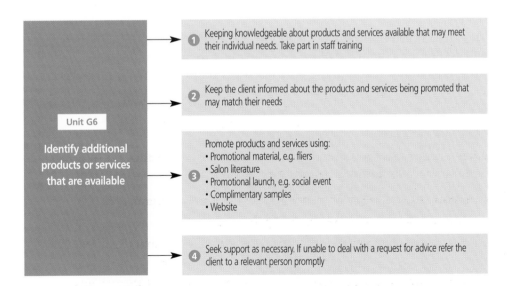

When promoting client products or services, find out first about their needs. Consider the following:

- What is the client's main priority? What would they like to achieve? This information will guide you on selecting and advising them of the most suitable product or service.
- Is a skin sensitivity (patch) test necessary before the service? Ensure there will be sufficient time to carry out any necessary tests when promoting a service.

> **HEALTH AND SAFETY**
>
> **Contra-indications**
> If the client has any contra-indication to the product, recommend they seek their doctor's approval before using it.

TIP ✓

Testers

Encourage your client to try the testers out. Make-up can look very different on the face compared with its appearance on the palette.

You can also take the opportunity to apply the product to show it at its best effect.

- Is the client allergic to any particular substance, contact with which should be avoided?

- Does the client have a skin disorder or nail disease which might contra-indicate use of a particular product? Contra-indications to products must always be noted and explained to the client.

- Is the client planning to use the product over cuts and abrasions? If so, is this safe?

- Find out what services the client has received before. Were they satisfied or disappointed in any way with them? If so, find out why.

- How much is the client used to spending on products? Ask about what they are presently using: this will give you an idea of the types of product they have experience with using, and the sort of prices they are used to paying.

Bearing in mind the client's needs, you can now guide them to the most suitable service or product. This is where your expertise and your product knowledge are so important: you can describe fully and accurately the features, functions and benefits of the services and products you can offer.

Selling products

The products themselves must be presented to the client in such a way that they seem both attractive and desirable: the presentation should encourage the client to purchase them. The packaging and the product should be clean and in good condition, and **testers** should be available wherever possible so that the client can try the product on themself before purchasing it.

The final choice of product is with the client, of course, but often the client will ask for a recommendation, for example if they cannot decide between two possibilities. It is in these circumstances that your ability to answer

A nail polish display

A nail polish product line poster

Men's nail product

technical questions fully, from a complete knowledge of the product, will help in closing the sale. Speaking with confidence and authority on the one product that will particularly suit the client's requirements may well persuade them to buy it.

Product suitability

If the client has not used the product or received the service before there is always a possibility of an allergic reaction.

If the client does not know what an **allergic reaction** is – or how to recognise an allergy – it is important that you describe it to them (red, itchy, flaking and even swollen skin). If they experience this sort of contra-action they should contact you immediately or in the case of product intolerance stop applying the product the client suspects is producing it.

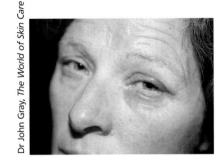

Dr John Gray, *The World of Skin Care*

Allergic reaction to a cosmetic product that has affected the eyes

---

HEALTH AND SAFETY ✚

Skin sensitivity (patch) tests

If the client has not tried a product before, or if there is doubt as to how their skin will react, a skin patch test must be carried out.

1 Select either the inner elbow or the area behind the ear.
2 Make sure the skin is clean.
3 Apply a little of the product, using a spatula.
4 Leave the area alone for 24 hours.
5 If there is no reaction after 24 hours, the client is not allergic to the product: they can go ahead and use it.
    If there has been any itching, soreness, erythema, or swelling in the area where the product has been applied, the client is allergic to it and should not use it.

TECHNIQUES IN SELLING

The first rule of selling is: *know your products*. This applies to all retail products and to all salon services.

Staff training

It is important that everybody is knowledgeable and able to answer the client's questions – this includes the receptionist who is often the first and last person the client comes into contact with. In conversation, especially during quieter periods, they have opportunities to discuss products and services informally.

Often product companies provide training either at the salon or at another venue. This is a great opportunity to update your knowledge and skills, which you will be able to share enthusiastically with your clientele. Often certificates to prove training are issued and these should be professionally displayed in the salon.

If not all staff can participate it is important that new information is passed on to them to make them effective in their jobs. Team meetings are a good opportunity to discuss salon policy and new products and promotions.

Information must be supplied for clients to read, and **displays** must be set up. Be aware of your **competitors** and their current advertising displays and campaigns.

Promoting products and services

When promoting products and services it is good to consider the following:

- Eye-catching promotional material (usually provided by the product supplier) displayed in the window will encourage new clients!
- Updated salon literature discussing benefits and costs may be provided.
- A promotional launch event, where clients can enjoy a social event and perhaps book services or buy products at discounted prices, may be held.
- Promotional packages may be presented.
- Samples may be given following a service.
- If you have a website you may wish to promote products and services on your homepage.

Know your products

Product usage must be discussed with clients, as necessary, and advice given on which product will best suit each of them. The only way to be able to do this is to memorise the complete range: all your products, including for example which skin types or treatment conditions each is for, what the active ingredients are, when and how each should be used, and its cost. Any questions asked must be answered with authority and confidence. Clients expect the staff in the beauty salon to be professionals, able to provide expert advice.

- Speak with confidence and enthusiasm.
- Avoid confusing technological words.
- Explain the benefits and personalise these, matching them to the needs of each client.

If the client requests advice on products or services that are outside of your responsibility refer them to the relevant colleague who has the expertise. You may have information literature you are able to provide to your client.

> **TIP** ✔
>
> **Product knowledge**
> Use the products yourself. It is always good to be able to speak from experience and shows your confidence in them.

ACTIVITY

Increasing product knowledge
With colleagues, discuss and note down the features, functions and benefits of a range of cosmetic products sold in your training establishment.

ACTIVITY

Learning the product range
Learn about and memorise the product range sold in the training establishment you attend.

Information to read

The **information** available to clients can start from the window display. Use the **window adverts** if supplied with product ranges, and include information that advertise the salon's treatments. Few salons use windows for product displays, but you could consider doing so.

Posters are supplied with good-quality product ranges, and most suppliers provide **information leaflets** for clients. Use the posters and **display cards** in the reception area; clients can then help themselves, and read about the products and their benefits. This will generate questions – and sales.

Product and retail displays

Two types of display can be used in the beauty salon. In the first, the display is there simply to be looked at, and seen as part of the decor. It should be attractive and artistically arranged, and can use dummy containers. It is not meant to be touched or sold from, so it can be behind glass or in a window display.

In the second, on the other hand, products are there to be sold. In this case products must be attractive but also accessible. The display should include testers so that clients can freely smell and touch. Each product must be clearly priced, and small signs placed beside the products or on the edge of the shelves to describe the selling points of each product.

This sort of active display must always be in the part of the salon where most people will see and walk past it – the area of 'highest traffic'. A large proportion of cosmetic and perfume sales are **impulse buys**. It is no accident that perfumery departments are beside the main entrances to department stores, or right beside access points such as escalators.

Product displays must always feature in the beauty treatment area. As the beauty therapist uses the products, she can discuss and recommend them for the client. If displays are there to see and to take from, the sale can be closed even before the client returns to reception. Although in theory clients can of course change their minds between the treatment area and actually paying, in practice once they have the product in their hands they will go on to buy it.

Displays

Most small salons will design and create their own displays using the counter **display packs** provided by the product companies. Some will have a professional **window dresser** to regularly change the window displays for the best effect.

Displays should be well stocked, with smart undamaged packaging. Eye-level displays are best and ideally should be accessible. Change the display regularly according to the promotion, for example UV skin protection products in summer.

Displays must be checked and cleaned regularly – in busy salons this will usually mean daily. A window display will need to be dusted, straightened,

HEALTH AND SAFETY

Maintaining hygiene
Spatulas must be used so customers do not put their fingers into the pots either when testing or during home use. (You may also like to sell spatulas for clients to use at home.)

ACTIVITY

Collecting information
Collect information leaflets from local salons and beauty product or perfume counters in department stores. Is this literature attractive? Will the presentation encourage sales?

Write to wholesalers and product companies for information about the display packs they supply with their products.

A range of men's skin-care
products for retail

Elemis Ltd.

and looked at from outside to make sure that it looks its best. The display
from which products are being sold will also need to be dusted, perhaps
wiped over (if testers have dripped), and straightened up. Testers need to be
checked to make sure they are not sticky and spilt, and that no one has left
dirty fingerprints on them.

ACTIVITY

Evaluating displays
Whenever you can, look at
displays and make a note of
neatness, cleanliness, availability,
pricing and information. Compare
the best with the worst.

ACTIVITY

Siting of displays
In your nearest large town, go into the big department stores and note where the cosmetic
and perfumery department displays are situated.

The range of products

It is not enough to stock just a few items and expect clients to fit in with the range you carry: different ranges must be available for each skin type, and a number of specialist products – such as eye gel or throat cream – that will suit all skin types. Make-up and nail polish should be attractive to all ages and types of customer. Sales must not be lost because of a lack of product range.

Information provided to the client should be accurate and not false or misleading. Legal action could follow in the case of non-compliance with consumer protection legislation.

A range of cosmetics

CONSUMER PROTECTION LEGISLATION

The salon has a legal obligation to implement and/or abide by the following legislation, designed to protect the rights of clients.

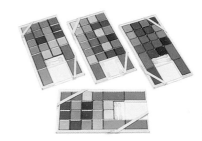

Make-up palettes available for retail

Consumer Protection Act 1987

This Act follows European Union (EU) directives to protect the customer from unsafe, defective services and products that do not reach safety standards. It also covers misleading price indications about goods or services available from a business. Dissatisfied clients may contact a number of organisations dealing with consumer protection for legal advice. If proven at fault the business may face legal action.

Consumer Safety Act 1978

This Act aims to reduce risk to consumers from potentially dangerous products.

Prices Act 1974

The price of products has to be displayed in order to prevent the buyer being misguided.

Trades Description Act 1968 and 1972

These Acts prohibit the use of false descriptions of goods and services provided by a business. Products must be clearly labelled. When retailing, the information supplied both in written and verbal form must always be accurate. The supplier must not:

- supply misleading information;
- describe products falsely;
- make false statements.

In addition they must not:

- make false comparisons between past and present services;
- offer products at what is said to be a 'reduced' price, unless they have previously been on sale at the full price quoted for a 28 day minimum;
- make misleading price comparisons.

Resale Prices Act 1964 and 1976

The manufacturer can supply a recommended price (MRRP), but the seller is not obliged to sell at the recommended price.

Sale and Supply of Goods Act 1994

Goods must be as described, of merchantable quality and fit for their intended purpose. The Act also covers the conditions under which customers can return goods.

Cosmetic Products (Safety) Regulations 2004

This piece of legislation consolidates earlier regulations and incorporates current European Union Directives. Part of consumer protection legislation, it requires that cosmetics and toiletries are safe in their formulation and are safe for use for their intended purpose as a cosmetic and comply with labelling requirements.

Data Protection Act 1998

Through communication with your client it is necessary to ask clients a series of questions before the treatment plan can be finalised. Client details are recorded on the client record card. This information is confidential and should be stored in a secure area. The client should understand the reason behind the questions asked of them. Confidential information on staff or clients should only be made available to persons to whom consent has been given.

Consumer Protection (Distance Selling) Regulations 2000

These regulations are derived from a European Union Directive and cover the supply of goods/services made between suppliers acting in a commercial capacity and consumers. They are concerned with purchases made by telephone, fax, internet, digital television and mail order, including catalogue shopping. Consumers must receive:

- Clear information on goods or services, including delivery arrangements and payment, suppliers' details and consumers' cancellation rights, which should be made available in writing.
- The consumer also has a seven working day cool-off period where they may cancel their purchase.

The Disability Discrimination Act 1996

Under the DDA from 1996 as a provider of goods, facilities and services your workplace has the duty to ensure that clients are not discriminated against on the grounds of disability. It is unlawful to use disability as a reason or justification to:

- refuse to provide a service;
- provide a service to a lesser standard;
- provide a service on worse terms;
- fail to make reasonable adjustments to the way services are provided.

From 2004 this includes failure to make reasonable adjustments to the physical features of service premises, to overcome physical barriers to access. Service can be denied to a disabled person if justified and if any other client would be treated in the same way. Your employer has a responsibility under the DDA to ensure that you receive adequate training to prevent discrimination in practice, and as such is responsible for your actions. Also they must make reasonable adjustments to the premises to facilitate access for disabled persons.

EQUAL OPPORTUNITIES POLICY

The Equal Opportunities Commission (EOC) states it is best practice for the workplace to have a written **equal opportunities policy**. This will include a statement of the commitment to equal opportunities by the employer and the details of structure for implementing the policy.

All employees should know this policy and it should be monitored regularly to review effectiveness.

Professional codes of practice

There is a code of behaviour and expected standards for the professional beauty therapist to follow, which will uphold the reputation of the industry and ensure best working practice for the safety of the industry and members of the public.

Beauty therapy professional bodies produce codes of practice for their members. Although not a legal requirement, this code may be used in criminal proceedings as evidence of improper practice. A business may have its own code of practice in relation to product and service promotion.

Insurance

Product and treatment liability insurance is usually included within public liability insurance, but should be checked with the insurance company. Product liability insurance covers risk, which might occur as a result of the products you are selling.

TIP ✔

Create your own selling opportunity

- If the client is having a manicure and has weak nails, you could recommend a course of nail treatments and an appropriate nail strengthener
- If the client is going away on holiday tell them about the special 'holiday treatment package promotion'
- If the client is having an eyelash tint, tell them how quick and simple an eyebrow wax is and the difference it can make!

ACTIVITY

Product and service promotion

Think of different services or products that your workplace offers that are not as popular as they once were. Consider a promotion you could offer to raise their profile.

INFORMING CLIENTS ABOUT ADDITIONAL PRODUCTS OR SERVICES

Outcome 2: Inform clients about additional products or services

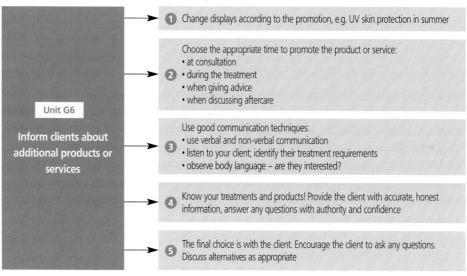

Unit G6

Inform clients about additional products or services

1. Change displays according to the promotion, e.g. UV skin protection in summer

2. Choose the appropriate time to promote the product or service:
   - at consultation
   - during the treatment
   - when giving advice
   - when discussing aftercare

3. Use good communication techniques:
   - use verbal and non-verbal communication
   - listen to your client; identify their treatment requirements
   - observe body language – are they interested?

4. Know your treatments and products! Provide the client with accurate, honest information, answer any questions with authority and confidence

5. The final choice is with the client. Encourage the client to ask any questions. Discuss alternatives as appropriate

Choose the most appropriate time to inform the client about additional products and services. If the client is receiving a treatment service this may be at the consultation, when you are getting to know the client, during the treatment when you have the opportunity to share advice, or when discussing aftercare. Here you will be able to reinforce the importance of further products and services to enhance the treatment benefits gained. This may be further use of products or services that the client has used before or those that are new to the client.

Outcome 3: Gain client commitment to using additional products or services

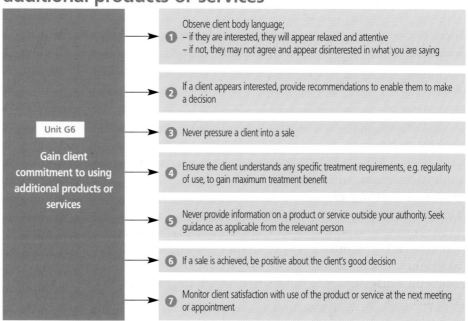

Unit G6

Gain client commitment to using additional products or services

1. Observe client body language;
   - if they are interested, they will appear relaxed and attentive
   - if not, they may not agree and appear disinterested in what you are saying

2. If a client appears interested, provide recommendations to enable them to make a decision

3. Never pressure a client into a sale

4. Ensure the client understands any specific treatment requirements, e.g. regularity of use, to gain maximum treatment benefit

5. Never provide information on a product or service outside your authority. Seek guidance as applicable from the relevant person

6. If a sale is achieved, be positive about the client's good decision

7. Monitor client satisfaction with use of the product or service at the next meeting or appointment

Communication

Communication with your client, both verbal and non-verbal, is important. Establish a rapport with your client and focus your attention fully on the client.

- Observe the client's body language: are they interested in what you are telling them? If the client is interested, they will agree with you and their body language will be relaxed yet attentive.

- Ensure that the client receives adequate attention in providing them with the products that they have agreed to purchase. Present the products to them and explain any specific requirements in their use in order to gain maximum benefit from their use.

- In the case of a service, make an appointment and provide the client with an appointment card and relevant literature relating to the service. If the client has made a decision to receive a service or purchase a product, you may find there is a delay in its availability. Ensure any delay is minimal. Do not be tempted to offer unsuitable alternatives, which are not as suited to the client's needs or treatment requirements. Inform the client honestly and realistically of their availability. In the case of a product you may be able to give the client a sample to use until the product is available.

- Record all sales on the client's record card. This is a useful reference point for the therapist and client to refer back to.

- If the client is not interested they will probably not agree, and will not appear to be interested in what you are saying. If this occurs go back to the beginning and suggest alternatives to attempt to regain their interest, but avoid pressuring the client.

- Ensure that the client has sufficient information to make a confident selection in their treatment or product choice.

- Give the client opportunity to ask questions and answer these confidently.

- Ensure the environment is conducive to the client feeling comfortable to ask questions.

- If a sale is achieved, be positive – smile, this will help to make the client feel they have made a good decision.

- Ask the client if there is anything else they need when closing the sale on the product. Confirm the size of product the client wishes to purchase, explaining any financial benefit to their selection.

> **TIP**
>
> **Effective stock control**
> It is important that you endeavour to always have retail stock available. It is disappointing for the client if they are unable to purchase a retail item and could potentially result in the loss of a sale – especially if they source an alternative.

Client suitability

Following the consultation, you may feel that the client is unsuitable for treatment. Tactfully explain to the client why this is. If it is for medical reasons, ask them to seek permission from their GP before the treatment is given. The expectations of some clients may be unrealistic. If this is the case, patiently and diplomatically explain why and aim to agree to a realistic treatment programme. Remember your legal duty under the **Health and Safety at Work Act 1974** to take reasonable care to avoid harm to yourself and others.

PRODUCT PROMOTION

Planning the demonstration

Demonstrating to an audience needs particularly careful planning if the demonstration is to achieve the maximum benefit. Everything required must be in place: the products, the means to apply them, and all the relevant literature to be given out to the audience or clients.

Consider all possibilities in your planning. What type of demonstration is required? Will you be working on one client, to demonstrate and sell a product, or demonstrating to a group? Is a range of products to be demonstrated, or just one item?

Single client

When demonstrating on a client have a mirror in front of them so that you can explain as you go along and the client can watch. They can then see the benefit of the product and learn how to use it at the same time. This is a simple but effective way to sell products.

A group

The presentation should include an introduction to the demonstrator and the product, the demonstration itself, and a conclusion with thanks to the audience and model. Written **promotional material** can be placed on the seats before the audience arrives, or handed out at an appropriate point during the demonstration; **samples** can be handed around the audience to try.

The demonstration itself must be clear, simple and not too long. The audience *must* be able to see what is being done and hear the commentary. Maximise the impact of the demonstration by giving the audience the opportunity to buy the product immediately.

If this is not possible – because the demonstration is in another room, away from the products or at another venue, such as at a women's club meeting – ensure that members of the audience leave with a **voucher** to exchange for the product. This should offer some incentive, such as a **discount**, to encourage potential buyers to make the effort to come to the salon and buy. Never sell the features and benefits to potential customers, creating the desire for the product, without also giving them the chance to buy it.

Questions must be accurate and detailed. You are the expert: show your knowledge. Do not ask the client what sort of skin they have – they are not the expert, and will probably give the wrong answer. Instead, ask more detailed questions, such as 'Does your skin feel tight?' (which may indicate dryness), or 'Do you have spots in a particular area?' (which may indicate an oily patch). Use open questions. These are questions that may not be answered with yes or no. Open questions usually start with *why, how, when, what* and *which*.

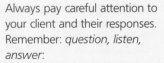

TIP

Demonstrations
An effective demonstration will always create sales. Have the product ready to sell, or give out vouchers to encourage clients to come to the counter.

TIP

Features and benefits
A *feature* is the product's specialist ingredients and the effects they can achieve.
  A *benefit* is what the client can expect from buying the product.

TIP

Always pay careful attention to your client and their responses. Remember: *question, listen, answer*:
● *Question* your client as to their needs.
● *Listen* to the answer.
● *Answer* with the relevant information.

Listening is a skill. Listen to your client; this will help you to identify their treatment requirements and personality. Always listen carefully to the answers your customer gives: do not talk over their answer or interrupt. Only when they have finished should you give a considered, informed reply. You may need to ask another question, or you may be able straightaway to direct them to the best product or service for their needs.

TARGETS

The setting of financial targets for the business and for individuals is important to enable analysis of overall performance. The salon owner must have an overall idea of productivity against the targets set. Targets may vary for different employees depending upon experience, length of service and workload.

Productivity

Levels of performance will take into account expected treatment services and retail product sales. Services are normally costed on the products used, including consumables such as cottonwool and tissues, and should include other hidden costs such as laundering of towels.

Productivity can be increased through:

- incentives;
- promotions;
- personal targets.

Poor levels of performance and productivity may indicate a need for additional training. Some companies provide rewards for employees who develop ideas for increased productivity and commission is one method of rewarding individuals who achieve and exceed targets.

Gaining client feedback

As a service industry, feedback from clients is important when measuring levels of service. It enables you to evaluate marketing methods, salon image and service.

Client feedback can be gathered in a variety of ways, both formally and informally.

Client questionnaires can be used at random to evaluate performance, for example following a promotion. The results should be analysed and appropriate action taken to improve areas of weakness, build on strengths and investigate potential areas of development.

Simply asking the client if they have enjoyed or been satisfied with the treatment received is another method of service evaluation.

GLOSSARY OF KEY WORDS

Body language communication involving the body.

Code of practice the expected standards and behaviour for the professional beauty therapist to follow, which will uphold the reputation of the industry and ensure best working practice for the industry and protect members of the public. Beauty therapy professional bodies produce codes of practice for their members. A business may have its own code of practice.

Communication the exchange of information and the establishment of understanding between people.

Consumer Protection Act 1987 this act follows European Union Directives to protect the customer from unsafe, defective services and products that do not reach safety standards.

Consumer Protection (Distance Selling) Regulations 2000 these regulations are derived from a European Union Directive and cover the supply of goods/services made between suppliers acting in a commercial capacity and consumers. They are concerned with purchases made by telephone, fax, internet, digital television and mail order.

Consumer Safety Act 1978 this act aims to reduce risks to consumers from potentially dangerous products.

Cosmetic Products (Safety) Regulations 2004 part of consumer protection legislation that requires cosmetics and toiletries be safe in their formulation and safe for use for their intended purpose as a cosmetic and comply with labelling requirements.

Data Protection Act 1998 legislation designed to protect client privacy and confidentiality.

Disability Discrimination Act 1995 implemented to prevent disabled persons being discriminated against during recruitment and employment. Employers have a responsibility to remove physical barriers and to adjust working conditions to prevent discrimination on the basis of having a disability.

Gift voucher a pre-payment method for beauty therapy services or retail sales.

Legislation laws affecting the workplace in relation to treatments and services, systems and procedures, the premises, employers and employees.

Prices Act 1974 this act states that the price of products has to be displayed in order to prevent the buyer being misguided.

Promotion ways of communicating products or services to clients to increase sales.

Resale Prices Act 1964 and 1976 this act states that the manufacturer can supply a recommended price (MRRP), but the seller is not obliged to sell at the recommended price.

Sales and Supply of Goods Act 1994 goods must be as described, of merchantable quality and fit for their intended purpose.

Target a goal or objective to achieve, usually set within a timescale.

Trades Description Act 1968 and 1972 legislation that states that information when selling products both in written and verbal form should be accurate.

Assessment of knowledge and understanding

You have now learnt about methods to promote sales of products and services to clients. This will enable you to promote additional products and services to clients, thus increasing salon income.

To test your level of knowledge, answer the following short questions. These will prepare you for your summative (final) assessment.

Identify additional products or services that are available

1 Why are retail sales important to the beauty salon?

2 Why is it important that you have a good knowledge about the products and services available in your salon?

3 How can you ensure that you are up to date with the beauty products and service you have on offer? Why is this important?

4 What are the opportunities that occur where you can promote a product or service? Think of examples from your experience.

Inform clients about additional products or services

1 Communication is important when selling. Why is it important to observe the client's body language?

2 As well as direct advice, what other ways can you make clients aware of the products and services available in your salon?

3 If the client required advice about a product or service on which you were not qualified to advise, what action would you take?

4 How must displays of retail stock be kept? Why is this important?

5 Clients have 'consumer rights'. Why is it important to give accurate information about products or services?

6 Name three pieces of legislation/regulations relating to the way products or services are delivered to clients which protect their legal rights.

Gain client commitment to using additional products and services

1 Why must the client's needs be ascertained before selling them products or services?

2 What are the benefits to the client of using additional products, as advised by the therapist?

3 Why is it important to stock a range of products?

4 How do you think speaking with confidence and authority on a product will influence the client?

5 Staff training is important to ensure that everybody is knowledgeable and able to advise clients on their questions. What other benefit does this have to the clients, employees and salon?

chapter 4

Develop and maintain your effectiveness at work

Learning objectives

This chapter covers the importance of taking personal responsibility to improve your performance at work. This also includes ensuring effective relationships are established with colleagues so as to make a positive contribution to the effectiveness of the business. It describes the competencies required to ensure that you:

- **improve your personal performance at work**
- **work effectively as part of a team**

WORKING RELATIONSHIPS

For any beauty therapy business to be a success requires the commitment of each employed individual to ensure quality at all levels and in all services.

For this to occur it is important both that you are effective in your job role and that you have positive **working relationships** with your colleagues and with clients.

Good working relationships in the workplace are essential. Each employee, whatever their role, is valuable as part of the team in ensuring the success of the business. All staff at **induction** should be told of the function of the business, and of their role in this. They should also be told about relevant **codes of conduct**.

Your workplace will have certain salon service standards with regard to appearance and behaviour whilst in the working environment.

Outcome 2: Work effectively as part of a team

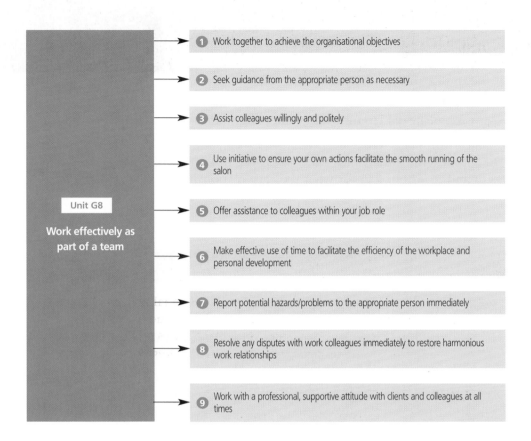

Unit G8

Work effectively as part of a team

1. Work together to achieve the organisational objectives

2. Seek guidance from the appropriate person as necessary

3. Assist colleagues willingly and politely

4. Use initiative to ensure your own actions facilitate the smooth running of the salon

5. Offer assistance to colleagues within your job role

6. Make effective use of time to facilitate the efficiency of the workplace and personal development

7. Report potential hazards/problems to the appropriate person immediately

8. Resolve any disputes with work colleagues immediately to restore harmonious work relationships

9. Work with a professional, supportive attitude with clients and colleagues at all times

General codes of conduct

- Have a smart, professional appearance at all times and follow the expected dress code – it creates an impression of the quality standard that can be expected.
- Always have high standards of personal hygiene.
- Never, eat, drink, chew gum or smoke in front of the client.
- Ensure that you follow your health and safety responsibilities, never putting yourself or anybody else at risk through your actions.
- Communicate clearly.
- Be polite and courteous at all times to both clients and colleagues.
- Never lose your temper, or swear in front of a client.
- Avoid controversial and personal topics of conversation.
- If you are unable to give the client information they need, quickly find somebody suitably qualified to assist.
- If there are any personal issues amongst staff or towards a client, do not let these show in front of a client. Settle the grievances (reasons for complaint) as soon as possible, to avoid job satisfaction and productivity being affected.

TIP

Image
A professional image creates confidence in clients, who learn to trust that they will be treated in a certain way – professionally and with respect.

TIP

Team meetings
The team should meet at least every two weeks to ensure that it remains focused on targets to be achieved and that communication within the team is effective.

Job roles and responsibilities

ACTIVITY

Roles and responsibilities
List the different roles and
responsibilities of personnel in
your workplace. Clients and
business callers may require this
information.

Each team member should have a **job description**. This details:

- the job title;
- the specific job role;
- the duties and responsibilities;
- the work location;
- any extra special circumstances affecting duties, such as attending salon promotional events.

The job description enables each employee to know what is expected of them and to whom and for what they are responsible.

Job description

Job description – Beauty Therapist

Location:	Based at salon as advised
Main purpose of job:	To ensure customer care is provided at all times To maintain a good standard of technical and client care, ensuring that up-to-date methods and techniques are used following the salon training practices and procedures
Responsible to:	Salon manager
Requirements:	To maintain the company's standards in respect of hairdressing/beauty services
	To ensure that all clients receive service of the best possible quality
	To advise clients on services and treatments
	To advise clients on products and aftercare
	To achieve designated performance targets
	To participate in self-development or to assist with the development of others
	To maintain company policy in respect of: • personal standards of health/hygiene • personal standards of appearance/conduct • operating safely whilst at work • public promotion • corporate image as laid out in employee handbook
	To carry out client consultation in accordance with company policy
	To maintain company security practices and procedures
	To assist your manager in the provision of salon resources
	To undertake additional tasks and duties required by your manager from time to time.

For reasons of safety and effectiveness it is important that you know what jobs and roles you are qualified to undertake.

A **contract of employment** is a written contract or statement given to an employee within two months of being employed. This contains details of the job description and employment including hours of work, holiday entitlement and length of notice requirements. It also identifies disciplinary rules and what disciplinary action will be applied when set rules or working conditions are broken. Ultimately this could lead to dismissal. Instant dismissal occurs where there is sufficient reason, for example, in cases such as theft or breach of health and safety practice that endangers others, termed as **gross misconduct**. Where an employee feels that they have been treated unfairly in their dismissal they may take this to an employment tribunal.

An efficient working environment

Support and guidance should be requested, but only when needed. It is important to use your initiative whenever possible whilst operating within your job role. When seeking support or guidance, any request should be courteously asked for at an appropriate time from the appropriate person, this may be the senior therapist, trainer or supervisor.

Any request for support or guidance should be responded to clearly and courteously.

Use your time effectively. Make a list of tasks you need to complete and prioritise them in importance. If you are not busy offer to help your colleagues.

Treatment times allowed for the beauty therapy services offered should be adhered to to ensure clients receive their treatment on time and potential profits are achieved.

Don't ignore problems – always report these to the relevant person.

> **TIP** ✓
>
> **Electronic communication**
> Check emails regularly if this is a form of communication within your business.

Treatment times

Treatment	Abbreviation	Treatment time allowed*
Cleanse and make-up	C/M/up	45 mins
Eyebrow shaping	E/B reshape or trim	15 mins
Eyebrow tint	EBT	10 mins
Eyelash tint	ELT	20 mins
Eyelash perm	ELP	45 mins
Manicure	Man	45 mins
Nail art	N/Art	5–10 mins per nail
Pedicure	Ped	45 mins
Leg wax: half	$^1/_2$ leg wax	30 mins
three-quarter	$^3/_4$ leg wax	30–40 mins
full	Full leg wax	50 mins
Bikini wax	B/wax	15 mins

Treatment	Abbreviation	Treatment time allowed*
Underarm wax	U/arm wax	15 mins
Arm wax	F/arm wax	30 mins
Eyebrow wax	E/B wax	15 mins
Ear pierce	E/P	15 mins
Facial	F	60 mins
False lashes	F/Lash	20 mins

*Treatment time does not include preparation for treatment and consultation

Punctuality

It is important to the efficient working of the salon that you are punctual for work. This ensures that you are composed, that clients are not kept waiting and that you are able to support other members of the team. You thereby minimise stress for yourself and for your colleagues.

Working under pressure

Sometimes you will be extremely busy and you may be feeling tired and weary. This is not the client's problem, however! Remain cheerful, courteous and helpful. You should also use your initiative in helping others, for example by preparing a colleague's work area when you are free and they are busy.

You must be able to cope with the unexpected:

- clients arriving late for appointments;
- clients' treatments overrunning the allocated treatment times;
- double bookings, with two clients requiring treatment at the same time;
- the arrival of unscheduled clients;
- changes to the bookings.

With effective teamwork such situations can usually be overcome.

ACTIVITY

Dealing with the unexpected
How would you deal with the unexpected situations listed opposite? With colleagues, discuss your experiences and record your ideas.

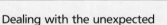

ACTIVITY

How good are we?
A questionnaire may be useful in monitoring client satisfaction. Questionnaires can be anonymous, and collected at a central point.
  Ask questions that are important to the team and the business. Collate the findings and use them to evaluate effectiveness and identify areas requiring development. Simple changes can make all the difference!

Absence from work

If a member of staff is absent from work, other staff will need to review the daily work schedule to minimise disruption. In the case of holiday cover this can be planned for, but if a staff member is absent unexpectedly, teamwork will be needed to get the work done.

When you learn that someone is to be absent, find out, if you can, for approximately how long. Then:

- Check the work schedule of the person who is absent.
- With authority to do so, reschedule clients, but without affecting the quality of the salon's service.
- Determine whether any clients' appointments can or must be cancelled, especially if there are double bookings or if the client must be treated specifically by the person who is away. Contact clients as soon as possible, so that they can reschedule their own time.

If you yourself are ill, to minimise disruption you must report your sickness as early as possible to the relevant person. You may be required to complete sickness forms.

Effective communication between staff

Personnel problems may occur if there are ineffective communication systems. Time should be made to hold regular staff meetings where any concerns can be shared. A staff meeting can also be an exciting opportunity to share ideas to improve the efficiency of the job role and to look together at ways of improving the business.

Positive relationships with colleagues

There can be no place in a customer care industry for poor working relationships. A great portion of your time is spent in the workplace alongside your colleagues, and if the environment becomes stressful this will affect your effectiveness. It will also be apparent to clients, and relationships between staff members should not trouble them. Disputes must be resolved immediately.

Grievances

It is important that you understand the salon's **staffing structure**. You need to know who is responsible for what, and who you should approach in various circumstances, for example if you felt that you were being treated unfairly. Any grievances should be reported to a supervisor, and you should familiarise yourself with the **grievance and appeals procedure**.

This includes what action to take if you:

- have a disagreement with a colleague that you cannot resolve
- feel you are being treated unfairly
- are being discriminated against
- are working outside the limitations of your job role.

The grievance and appeals procedure should ensure that the issue is fully investigated and appropriate action is taken or implemented. In some cases this will mean that disciplinary action against an individual is taken. For a team to work effectively problems should be addressed as soon as they arise and it is important that harmonious relationships are rebuilt.

Effective teamwork

An effective team member:

- knows who to report to for guidance;
- is supported in their job role by their supervisor and other colleagues;
- communicates freely;
- has targets to work towards that are regularly reviewed;
- is flexible and willing to change to meet organisational needs;
- operates in a supportive, friendly atmosphere;
- feels valued.

ACTIVITY

Teamwork

What personal characteristics do you need to work effectively in a team? From your own experience, discuss times when you have worked in a team. What was your role?

Ask a colleague: are you seen by others as a team player? If not, how can you develop the necessary skills?

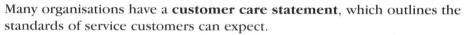

EFFECTIVE COMMUNICATION WITH CLIENTS

Customer care

Many organisations have a **customer care statement**, which outlines the standards of service customers can expect.

Clients want to enjoy their visits to the beauty salon and they are paying for a service. It is important that during each visit they are made to feel relaxed and comfortable.

ACTIVITY

Client care

Find out whether your organisation has a customer care statement. If so, how well do you do in providing that level of customer care? Monitor yourself against the statement, and ask colleagues for feedback.

Client care

Remember that each client has a different personality and different treatment needs, requiring an individual treatment approach.

A client can be made to feel intimidated, uncomfortable or ignored – and this can happen without your saying anything! Even without speaking you communicate with your eyes, your face and your body, transmitting some of your feelings. This is called **non-verbal communication**. How you look and how you behave in front of your clients is important.

Positive relationships with clients

ACTIVITY

Telephone calls

A telephone call is often the first contact the client has with the salon and is an important method of communication.

- How should the phone be answered?
- What should you confirm if the client requires an eyelash tint?
- What action would you take if there was not sufficient time for the appointment at the time requested?
- How would you handle a complaint about a service?

On meeting a client, always smile, make eye contact and greet her cheerfully – however bad your own day is! As you communicate you can:

- promote yourself, and gain the client's confidence in your professionalism and technical expertise;
- develop a professional relationship with the client;
- establish the client's needs;
- promote services and treatments.

Verbal communication occurs when you talk directly to another person, either face to face or over the telephone. Always speak clearly and precisely, and avoid slang. It is important to be a good listener: this will help you identify the client's treatment requirements and understand their personality. You can then guide the conversation appropriately.

Conversing with a client

Having developed a professional relationship with your client, centre the conversation on them, so that they feel special. Avoid interrupting the client whilst they are speaking, listen carefully and be patient. A nervous client may need to be reassured. Gain their confidence by being pleasant and cheerful without chattering constantly. When asking questions, don't interrogate your client. Never talk down to them, and avoid technical jargon – instead, use commonly understood words.

Certain technical information may not appear complicated, but if for example a client has bought several skin-care products it is important that they know how to use them safely and efficiently. Always check tactfully with the client to ensure that they have fully understood the information provided.

> **TIP**
>
> **Client care**
> Make notes on the client's record card of topics that interest them. You can introduce these topics in conversation next time the client receives a treatment, and they will be pleased that you have taken the trouble to remember.

> **TIP** ✔
>
> **Client confusion**
> If a client is confused about the information you have given them, identify which part is confusing.
>   Repeat the information clearly and logically to clarify your instructions, checking for understanding.
>   Always allow time for clients to consider your response and provide further explanation as necessary.
>   Confirm the client's understanding with them and ensure that they are now clear and satisfied.

Avoid all controversial topics, such as sex, religion and politics! When a relationship has been established, value it but be discreet – clients will often share confidences with you. Never pass judgement, and ensure that you deserve clients' trust by maintaining confidentiality.

Responding appropriately

It may be that the client requests information that you are unable to help with or which lies outside your responsibility. If this occurs politely inform them that you are not able or qualified to deal with their request but will get somebody else to assist. Always indicate how long this will take if it will not be immediately.

Keeping your client informed is reassuring and important to avoid dissatisfaction with the service provided.

> **TIP**
>
> **Using the correct title**
> It is important that a client is greeted appropriately according to their expectations.
>   Never use a client's first name unless invited to do so.

Non-verbal communication

Non-verbal communication is also referred to as **body language**. Interpreting body language is an important skill: learn to notice how the client is behaving, including their voice, their eyes, their body and their arm and hand movements. An instinctive 'feel' for customers' behaviour can be developed with experience.

Noticing client behaviour will help you to recognise the client's different needs and expectations. You must be able to adapt to these.

When approaching potential customers in a situation, such as a client who shows an interest in a product on a retail display, be aware that conflicting signals may be given. For example, a person may smile and nod as if interested but may, in fact, not be. On the other hand, if the customer makes the first approach then they obviously have an active interest already.

Initially the customer may be formal and may even have a stiff body posture and a reserved manner. As they become more interested, however, their posture will relax: they may begin to lean forward. It will become obvious at this stage that they are interested, and they then will go on to nod and agree, and to listen actively.

You must use your own body language to good effect. You must be relaxed but attentive, and listen actively – nodding and shaking your head, and smiling in agreement. Use relaxed, gentle hand movements: do not twitch or turn away from the customer.

If the customer is not agreeing with you, or is not interested, they may look bored, tap their fingers, fiddle with their shopping, look away, or even look at their watch. If these signs are evident, go back to the beginning and try to find out why they are not interested. This is important when selling. Perhaps they do not want the product you have recommended? Or perhaps it is too expensive? Suggest alternatives and see whether you can get their interest again.

When the customer has decided to buy, smile – help them to feel that they have made an excellent decision. They should leave feeling proud to have purchased the product.

Avoiding client dissatisfaction

Some dissatisfied clients will voice their dissatisfaction; others will remain silent and simply not return to the salon. This situation can often be prevented through good customer care and effective communication.

- Always ensure that the client has a thorough consultation before any new service. This should be carried out by a colleague with the appropriate technical expertise.
- Regularly check the client's satisfaction. If there is any concern, make the supervisor aware of this immediately.
- Inform the client of any disruption to service – do not leave them wondering what the problem may be. Politely inform them of the situation, for example 'I'm sorry but we are running ten minutes late – are you able to wait?' If your salon has the facilities, you may offer them a drink.

ACTIVITY

Evaluating customer care
Visit a local salon. Beforehand, think of questions you would like to ask in relation to treatments. Then evaluate the customer care and services you received. Were the staff:
- friendly?
- dressed smartly?
- knowledgeable?
- efficient and eager to assist you?
- helpful?

If you answered 'no' to any of these questions, discuss your reasons with your colleagues. What have you learnt from this experience?

- Inconvenience caused by disruption to service can usually be compensated in some way. It is important to resolve problems and keep clients satisfied.

Customer care is vital: clients provide the salon's income and your wages. The success of the business depends upon satisfied clients.

Complaints procedure

Unfortunately problems do sometimes arise in which the client cannot be appeased. A **complaints procedure** is a formal, standardised approach adopted by the organisation to handle any complaints. It should also be used to handle complaints of discrimination.

ACTIVITY

Handling customer complaints
List five complaints that might be made by a client. How would you handle each situation to ensure a positive outcome?

Dealing with client dissatisfaction

If a client is dissatisfied they may appear angry and complain or they may say nothing. However they react, remember that a dissatisfied client is bad for business.

You may be required to deal with an angry client:

- Stay calm and listen to the client's complaint.
- If you are unable to handle it refer it as quickly as possible to somebody who can. Inform the client of your actions at all times.
- Establish the facts and take appropriate action as laid down in your client complaints procedure.
- Always aim to repair the relationship, although at times this may not be possible.
- Not all clients are always genuine in their complaint – establish the facts and tactfully advise the client of the outcome.
- Always remain courteous, professional and create a positive impression.

Legal requirements

The salon has a legal obligation to implement legislation designed to protect client's rights.

Health and safety

Following the consultation you may feel that the client is unsuitable for treatment. Explain tactfully why this is and ask them to seek permission from their GP before the treatment is given. Some clients may have unrealistic expectations. If this is the case, tactfully explain why and aim to agree to a realistic treatment programme.

Remember your legal duty under the **Health and Safety at Work Act 1974** to take reasonable care to avoid harm to yourself and others. Never use equipment for which you do not have the professional expertise. As well as the obvious potential hazards, you would not have the expertise to adapt the treatment to suit the client's treatment needs, and you would not be able to provide the relevant treatment advice in order to obtain the optimum treatment results.

Data Protection Act 1998

Before treating your client it is necessary to ask them a series of questions so that a treatment plan can be finalised.

Client details are recorded on the client record card. This information is confidential and should be stored in a secure area. The client should understand the reason behind the questions asked of them.

Confidential information on staff or clients should only be made available to persons to whom consent has been given.

Equal opportunities

The United Kingdom has specific legislation on equality that outlaws discrimination, protecting employees. This legislation also covers the provision of goods and services.

The **Race Relations Act 1976** makes it unlawful to discriminate on the grounds of colour, race, nationality, ethnic or national origin. The **Commission for Racial Equality** has produced a code of conduct to eradicate racial discrimination.

The **Disability Discrimination Act (DDA) 1995** makes it unlawful to discriminate on the grounds of disability.

The **Sex Discrimination Act 1975 and 1985**, and the **Equal Pay Act 1970**, prevent discrimination or less favourable treatment of men or women on the basis of gender. This covers pay and conditions as well as promotion.

IMPROVING PERSONAL EFFECTIVENESS

In order to develop personally and to improve your skills professionally, it is important to set yourself targets against which you can measure your achievement.

To an employer it is important that you are *consistent*. You must always perform your skills to the highest standard, and present and promote a positive image of the industry and the organisation in which you are employed and which you represent.

Outcome 1: Improve your personal performance at work

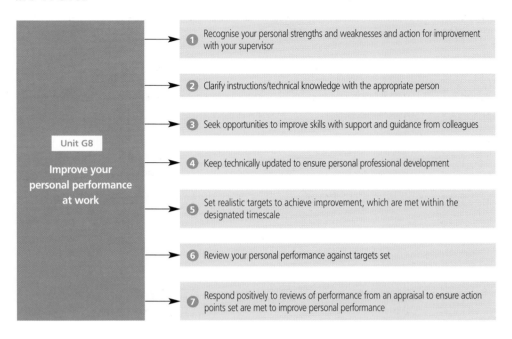

Unit G8	**1** Recognise your personal strengths and weaknesses and action for improvement with your supervisor
	2 Clarify instructions/technical knowledge with the appropriate person
Improve your personal performance at work	**3** Seek opportunities to improve skills with support and guidance from colleagues
	4 Keep technically updated to ensure personal professional development
	5 Set realistic targets to achieve improvement, which are met within the designated timescale
	6 Review your personal performance against targets set
	7 Respond positively to reviews of performance from an appraisal to ensure action points set are met to improve personal performance

Performance review or appraisal

Appraisal is a process whereby a supervisor identifies and discusses with individuals their strengths and weaknesses, and areas within their professional role that require further training and development. The job description is used as a key document during appraisal.

This may seem daunting, but it is an important and useful process. You can also use it to your advantage to:

- identify opportunities for further or specialist training;
- identify obstructions that are affecting progression;
- identify and amend any changes to your role;
- identify and focus on your achievements to date against targets set;
- make an action plan which will help you achieve your targets.

At the next appraisal the agreed objectives and targets set for the previous period are reviewed and the results measured. Additional accomplishments and contributions should also be looked at. A revised action plan will then be set for review at the next performance review or appraisal.

Targets

Targets to be achieved may be set by the employer either for individuals or for the team as a whole. These may review quality, efficiency and results. Computer systems are often able to provide relevant data about the salon.

> **TIP** ✔
>
> **Internal verification**
> When you are being assessed, all assessment is checked for validity using a process called *internal verification*. An appointed person titled *internal verifier* will investigate an appeal if it is thought by the candidate that the assessment decision outcome by the assessor was incorrect.

Performance Appraisal	
Name:	Jeanette Manners
Job Title:	Trainee beauty therapist
Date of Appraisal:	19 February 2007
Objectives:	To obtain competence within: Improving facial skin condition across the range.
Notes on Achievement:	Competence has been achieved for most facial skin condition range requirements.
Training Requirements:	Further training and practice is needed within the area of facial massage.
Any Other Comments on Performance by Appraiser:	Jeanette has achieved most of the objectives set out during the last appraisal.
Any Comments on the Appraisal by the Staff Member Appraised:	I feel that this has been a fair appraisal of my progress although I did not achieve all of my performance targets. J Manners
Action Plan:	- To achieve occupational competence across the range for facial skin condition. - To undergo training and practice in hair removal techniques. - To take assessment for hair removal.
Date of Next Appraisal:	20 October 2007

You should set your *own* targets, however, to monitor your effectiveness and performance. In training situations trainees undergo a programme which states:

- what training activities will take place and when;
- what tasks need to be performed;
- what standards are expected to be reached;
- when assessment should be expected;
- when a review of progress towards the agreed targets is to take place.

In the same way, you can set targets for yourself.

Personal effectiveness against targets set

Your ability to meet the expected standards is referred to as personal effectiveness.

Standards that you are assessed against include:

- The National Occupational Standards for Beauty Therapy
- Organisational Codes of Conduct

- Personal targets and their achievement, identified in appraisal and short- and long-term reviews

- Your productivity targets, i.e. with regard to technical and retail sales

If you meet the standards before the due target date, your trainer should be informed to review new targets for completion. This will ensure that you remain motivated in your work role and it will enable you to progress more quickly.

If personal targets are not being met it is important to identify the problem and constructive performance targets should be put in place to resolve unsatisfactory performance.

Your future personal objectives targets should be agreed with a date set for completion. At the next appraisal the agreed objectives and targets set for the previous period will be reviewed.

Being positive about negative feedback

Your appraisal may not always be a positive experience. It is important to be positive about recommendations to improve your performance and work towards achieving these. Not meeting targets may ultimately result in disciplinary procedure which may lead to dismissal. Your achievements of the productivity targets set leads to the financial effectiveness of the business.

> **TIP**
>
> **National Occupational Standards for Beauty Therapy**
> The NVQ/SVQ Level 2 Beauty Therapy qualification is used to plan your training needs and assessment requirements.
>   The National Occupational Standards are identified in the examination-awarding body's candidate logbook. They can also be obtained from the Hairdressing and Beauty Therapy Industry Authority (Habia). www.habia.org
>   An *individual learning plan*, negotiated with your assessor, sets short-term targets for completion and records valuable feedback on assessment completion and where there is a need for further training to meet the expected standards. This may be used when reviewing your personal performance.

Developing within the job role

There will be many opportunities to develop your skills and experience, and your understanding of your work:

- by attending trade seminars;

- by subscribing to professional trade magazines;

- by watching colleagues who have more advanced qualifications or experience;

- by developing your portfolio to include evidence and examples of experience gained;

- by using time effectively, and by practising – all tasks take time to master: the more you practise, the more skilled and efficient you will become.

> **TIP**
>
> **Job promotion**
> Internal promotion may require an employee to put in extra work, take on more responsibility or come up with new ideas.

> **TIP**
>
> **Continuous professional development (CPD)**
> Those involved in the training and assessment of candidates formally record activities undertaken to further develop their technical skills and expertise. This provides evidence of current, professional experience in the beauty therapy industry.

> **TIP**
>
> **Opportunities to improve technical skills and knowledge**
> Use your time effectively in the workplace; observe colleagues if you are not busy, ask questions, make opportunities to improve your knowledge and experience.

GLOSSARY OF KEY WORDS

Appraisal a process whereby a supervisor identifies and discusses with an individual their performance and achievements in their job role, against previously set targets.

Body language communication involving the body.

Code of conduct workplace service standards with regard to appearance and behaviour whilst in the working environment.

Complaint procedure a formal, standardised approach adopted by the organisation to handle any complaints.

Continuous Professional Development (CPD) activities undertaken to develop technical skill and expertise to ensure current, professional experience in the beauty industry is maintained.

Customer care statement defined customer service standards that are expected.

Equal opportunity non-discrimination on the basis of sex, race, disability, age, etc.

Grievance a cause for concern or complaint.

Job description written details of a person's specific work role, duties and responsibilities.

National Occupational Standards for Beauty Therapy Standards that set the relevant performance objectives, range statements and knowledge specifications to support performance. These can be obtained from the Hairdressing and Beauty Industry Authority (Habia) website: www.habia.org.uk.

Punctuality arriving at the correct time.

Target a goal or objective to achieve, usually set within a timescale.

Teamwork supportive work by a team.

Verbal communication occurs when you talk directly to another person either face to face or over the telephone.

Assessment of knowledge and understanding

You have now learnt about the importance of making a good impression and your part in building up the success of the business organisation. This includes the need for continuous professional development and the importance of good teamwork. This enables you to develop and maintain your effectiveness at work.

To test your level of knowledge, answer the following short questions. These will prepare you for your summative (final) assessment.

Salon roles, procedures and targets

1 It is necessary to ask a client a series of questions to finalise a treatment plan. Confidential information should only be available to persons to whom consent has been given. What is the name of the Act that implements this legislation?

2 List five important service standards to be followed with regard to appearance and behaviour whilst in the salon environment.

3 How can you make a client feel welcome?

4 Following the consultation you feel that the client is unsuitable for treatment. How would you handle this situation?

5 A client requests a service that you are not qualified to offer. They insist that they receive the treatment. You have seen other therapists carrying out the treatment before. What action should you take and why?

6 If a beauty therapist had an unprofessional attitude, how would this affect the reputation of the salon?

7 What could be a reason for client dissatisfaction? How could client dissatisfaction be avoided?

8 What steps need to be taken if a client makes a complaint?

9 If a client requested information that was outside your responsibility, how would you respond to ensure that dissatisfaction was avoided?

10 How will achievement of your training targets improve your personal performance?

11 Why is it important to have an awareness of and allocate the appropriate amount of time when booking and performing different beauty therapy services?

Improving your performance

1 All colleagues should be treated equally. The Equal Opportunities Commission (EOC), states that it is best practice to have a written Equal Opportunities Policy. What should this include?

2 Why are positive working relationships with your colleagues important?

3 If you have a dispute with a colleague why is it important that it is quickly resolved?

4 What are the main methods of communication?

5 Give three examples of positive body language.

6 Give three examples of negative body language.

7 A client arrives for a treatment to find that there has been a mistake with the booking and an appointment has not been made for them. What action should be taken?

8 Action points for your personal development are identified at performance review or appraisal. Why is it important to respond positively to reviews and feedback on your performance?

9 Why is it important to keep up to date with current trends, products and services in beauty therapy?

anatomy
and
physiology

chapter 5

Anatomy and physiology

As a beauty therapist it is important that you have a good understanding of anatomy and physiology, as many of your treatments aim to improve the particular functioning of systems of the body. For example a facial massage will improve blood and lymph circulation locally, as you massage the skin's surface, increase cellular renewal as you improve nutrition to the living cells, and remove dead skin cells. The result is healthier looking skin.

ANATOMY AND PHYSIOLOGY KNOWLEDGE REQUIREMENTS

It is necessary for you to know and understand anatomy and physiology as relevant to each beauty therapy unit. This may be assessed through oral questioning, written test or assignment. To guide you in your studies the essential anatomy and physiology you need to know and understand for each unit has been identified with a ✓ symbol. Look for the 🔑 to remind you to check back here for your essential anatomy and physiology knowledge!

 The beauty therapy units with an essential anatomy and physiology knowledge requirement are:

BT4 Improve and maintain facial skin condition

BT6 Remove hair using waxing techniques

BT7 Provide manicure treatment

BT8 Provide pedicure treatment

BT9 Provide make-up treatment

BT13 Provide nail art service

BT15 Assist with spa treatments

BT44 Extend and maintain nails

Anatomy and physiology knowledge and understanding is located in this unit, but it can also be found within each of the beauty therapy units where essential anatomy and physiology knowledge are identified as above.

Anatomy and physiology ✓ essential knowledge for unit

UNIT	BT4	BT6	BT7	BT8	BT9	BT13	BT15	BT44
Skin structure and function	✓	✓	✓	✓	✓	✓	✓	✓
Factors affecting skin condition	✓		✓	✓	✓		✓	✓
Structure of hair and types of hair growth		✓						
Hair growth cycle		✓						
Nail structure and function			✓	✓		✓		✓
Nail growth			✓	✓		✓		✓
Muscle groups in parts of the body, position, structure and function	✓		✓	✓				
Muscle tone	✓							
Bones in parts of the body, position, structure and function	✓		✓	✓				
Composition and function of blood and lymph	✓		✓	✓				
Blood flow and pulse rate			✓	✓			✓	
Central nervous system and autonomic system							✓	

THE SKIN

The structure and function of skin and the surrounding tissues

The skin varies in appearance according to our race, sex and age. It also alters from season to season and from year to year, and reflects our general health, lifestyle and diet.

At puberty the chemical substances (**hormones**) that control many of our bodies' activities become very active. Amongst other effects, this activity causes the skin to become more oily, and often blemishes appear on the skin's surface. Seven out of ten teenagers find that their skin becomes blemished with blackheads, inflamed angry spots and even scars at this time: a skin disorder called **acne vulgaris**.

During the twenties the skin should look its best; any hormonal imbalance that occurred at puberty should by now have stabilised. As we grow older, the skin ages too. In our late twenties and early thirties we will see fine lines appearing on the skin's surface, especially around the eyes where the skin is thinner and the skin gradually becomes drier.

At around the age of 40, hormone activity in the body becomes slower and the skin begins to lose its strength and elasticity. The skin becomes increasingly

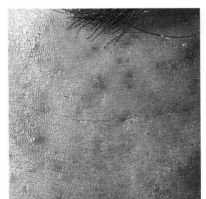

Acne vulgaris

Dr M. H. Beck

drier, and lines and wrinkles appear on the surface. In the late fifties brown patches of discoloured skin (**lentigines**) may appear: these are commonly seen at the temple region of the face and on the backs of the hands and are caused by ultra-violet light damage.

Fortunately help is at hand to care for the skin: there is an ever-increasing number of skin-care products from a vast and highly profitable cosmetics industry, and there are the skill and expertise of the qualified beauty therapist.

If it is your intention to become a qualified beauty professional, you need to learn about skin: its construction, its function, and how and why it is changed by both internal and external influences.

Cells

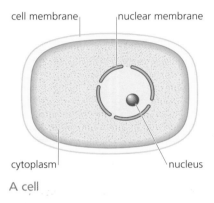

cell membrane
nuclear membrane
cytoplasm
nucleus

A cell

The human body consists of many trillions of microscopic **cells**. Each cell contains a chemical substance called **protoplasm**, which contains various specialised structures whose activities are essential to our health. If cells are unable to function properly, a disorder results.

Surrounding the cell is the **cell membrane**: this forms a boundary between the cell contents and their environment. The membrane has a porous surface which permits food to enter and waste materials to leave.

In the centre of the cell is the **nucleus**, which contains the **chromosomes**. On these are the **genes** we have inherited from our parents. The genes are ultimately responsible for cell reproduction and cell functioning.

The liquid within the cell membrane and surrounding the nucleus is called **cytoplasm**. Scattered throughout this are other small bodies, the **organelles** or 'little organs'; each has a specific function within the cell.

Cells in the body tend to specialise in carrying out particular functions. Groups of cells which share function, shape, size or structure are called **tissues**.

Tissues

If the tissues are damaged, for example if the skin is accidentally broken, the cells divide to repair the damage – called **regeneration**. The body is composed of four basic tissues. These are described below.

Types of tissue and general functions

Name of tissue	Examples	General functions
Epithelial	Epidermis	Forms surfaces and linings for protection

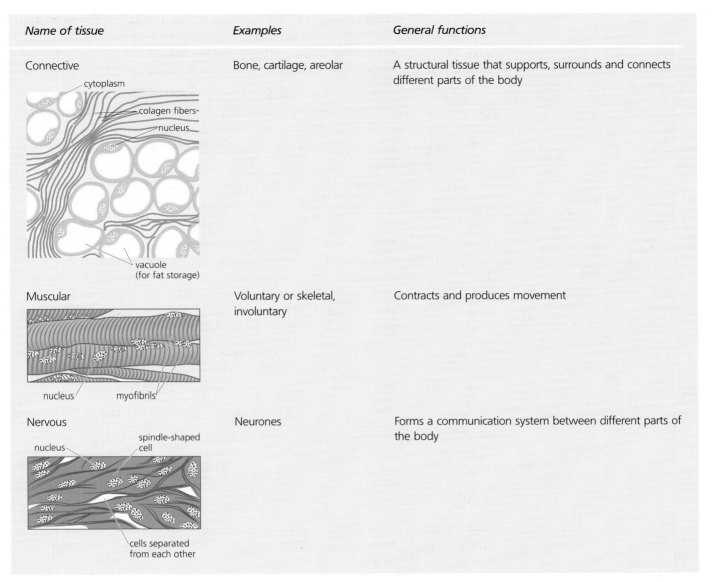

Name of tissue	Examples	General functions
Connective	Bone, cartilage, areolar	A structural tissue that supports, surrounds and connects different parts of the body
Muscular	Voluntary or skeletal, involuntary	Contracts and produces movement
Nervous	Neurones	Forms a communication system between different parts of the body

Tissues, may be grouped to form the larger functional and structural units we know as **organs**, such as the heart.

FUNCTIONS OF THE SKIN

The human skin is an organ – the largest of the body. It provides a tough, flexible covering, with many different important functions. The skin has many functions. The main functions are listed below.

Protection

The skin protects the body from potentially harmful substances and conditions.

HEALTH AND SAFETY

Skin protection
Although the skin is structured to avoid penetration of harmful substances by absorption, certain chemicals can be absorbed through the skin. Always protect the skin when using potentially harmful substances, and wear gloves when using harsh chemical cleaning agents.

- The outer surface is **bactericidal**, helping to prevent the multiplication of harmful micro-organisms. It also prevents the absorption of many substances (unless the surface is broken), because of the construction of the cells on its outer surface, which form a chemical and physical barrier.
- The skin cushions the underlying structures from physical injury.
- The skin provides a **waterproof coating**. Its natural oil, **sebum**, prevents the skin from losing vital water, and thus prevents skin dehydration.
- The skin contains a pigment called **melanin**. This absorbs harmful rays of ultra-violet light.

Heat regulation

Humans maintain a normal body temperature of 36.8–37°C. Body **temperature** is controlled in part by heat loss through the skin and by sweating. If the temperature of the body is increased by 0.25–0.5°C, the sweat glands secrete sweat to the skin's surface. The body is cooled by the loss of heat used to evaporate the sweat from the skin's surface. If the body becomes too warm there is an increase in blood flow into the blood capillaries in the skin. The blood capillaries widen (dilate) and heat is lost from the skin.

Excretion

Small amounts of certain **waste products**, such as urea, water and salt, are removed from the body in sweat by excretion through the surface of the skin.

Warning

The skin affords a warning system against outside invasion. **Redness** and **irritation** of the skin indicate that the skin is intolerant to something, either external or internal.

Sensitivity

The skin is a sensory organ and the sensations of **touch**, **pressure**, **pain**, **heat** and **cold** are identified by sensory nerves and receptors in the skin. It also allows us to recognise objects by their feel and shape.

Nutrition

The skin provides storage for **fat**, which provides an energy reserve. It is also responsible for producing a significant proportion of our **vitamin D**, which is created by a chemical action when sunlight is in contact with the skin.

Moisture control

The skin controls the movement of moisture from within the deeper layers of the skin.

THE STRUCTURE OF THE SKIN

If we looked within the skin using a microscope, we would be able to see two distinct layers: the **epidermis** and the **dermis**. Between these layers is a specialised layer which acts like a 'glue', sticking the two layers together: this is the **basement membrane**. If the epidermis and dermis become separated, body fluids fill the space, creating a **blister**.

Situated below the epidermis and dermis is a further layer, the **subcutaneous layer** or **fat layer**. The fat layer consists of cells containing fatty deposits, called adipose cells. The thickness of the subcutaneous layer varies according to the body area, and is, for example, very thin around the eyes.

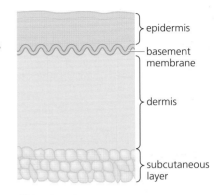

Skin structure

The fatty layer has a protective function and:

- acts as an insulator to conserve body heat;
- cushions muscles and bones below from injury;
- acts as an energy source, as excess fat is stored.

> **TIP** ✓
>
> **Liposuction**
> Liposuction is a cosmetic surgery treatment that involves the removal of fat cells by suction from any area of the body. Tiny incisions are made where the fat removal is required. Fat is then removed through a hollow surgical tube. The tube is moved around in the skin, breaking up the fat, which is then sucked out.
> A new treatment uses ultrasound waves applied to the skin's surface to liquefy fat. The fat is then naturally excreted from the body.

The epidermis

The epidermis is located directly above the dermis. It is composed of five layers, with the surface layer forming the outer skin – what we can see and touch. The main function of the epidermis is to protect the deeper living structures from invasion and harm from the external environment.

Nourishment of the epidermis, essential for growth, is received from a liquid called the **interstitial fluid**.

Each layer of the epidermis can be recognised by its shape and by the function of its cells. The main type of cell found in the epidermis is the **keratinocyte**, which produces the protein **keratin**. It is keratin that makes the skin tough and that reduces the passage of substances into or out of the body.

Over a period of about four weeks, cells move from the bottom layer of the epidermis to the top layer, the skin's surface, changing in shape and structure as they progress. The process of cellular change takes place in stages.

- *The cell is formed* – by division of an earlier cell.
- *The cell matures* – it changes structure and moves upwards and outwards.
- *The cell dies* – it moves upwards and becomes an empty shell, which is eventually shed.

> **TIP** ✓
>
> **The epidermis**
> The epidermis is the most significant layer of the skin with regard to the external application of skin-care cosmetics and make-up due to the effect on its appearance.

> **TIP** ✓
>
> **Did you know?**
> Every five days we shed a complete surface layer. About 80 per cent of household dust is composed of dead skin cells.

> **HEALTH AND SAFETY**
>
> **Psoriasis**
> With the skin disorder psoriasis, cell division occurs much more quickly, resulting in clusters of dead skin cells appearing on the skin's surface.

The layers of the epidermis

There are five layers or **stratum** that make-up the epidermis. The thickness of these layers varies over the body's surface. Each layer is found either in the germinative zone or keratinisation zone. This is illustrated and described below.

The layers of the epidermis

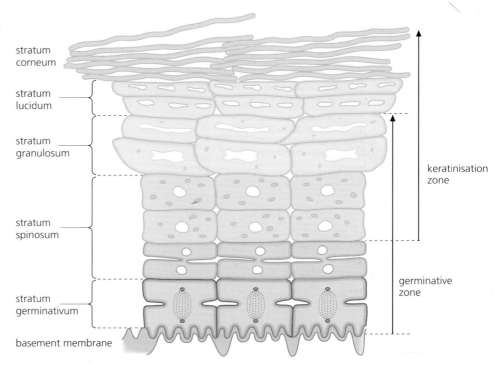

The germinative zone

In the **germinative zone** the cells of the epidermis layers are living cells. The germinative zone layers of the epidermis are the **stratum germinativum**, **stratum spinosum** and **stratum granulosum**.

Stratum germinativum   The **stratum germinativum**, or **basal layer**, is the lowermost layer of the epidermis. It is formed from a single layer of column-shaped cells joined to the basement membrane. These cells divide continuously and produce new epidermal cells (keratinocytes). This process of cell division is known as mitosis.

Stratum spinosum   The **stratum spinosum**, or **prickle-cell layer**, is formed from two to six rows of elongated cells; these have a surface of spiky spines which connect to surrounding cells. Each cell has a large nucleus and is filled with fluid.

Two other important cells are found in the germinative zone of the epidermis: langerhan cells and melanocyte cells.

Langerhan cells absorb and remove foreign bodies that enter the skin. They then move from the epidermis to the dermis below, and finally enter the lymph system (the body's waste-transport system).

Melanocyte cells produce the skin pigment **melanin**, which contributes to our skin colour. About one in every ten germinative cells is a melanocyte. Melanocytes are stimulated to produce melanin by ultra-violet rays, and their main function is to protect the other epidermal cells in this way from the harmful effects of ultra-violet.

The quantity and distribution of melanocytes differs according to race. In a white Caucasian person the melanin tends to be destroyed when it reaches the granular layer (see below). With stimulation from artificial or natural ultra-violet light, however, melanin will also be present in the upper epidermis.

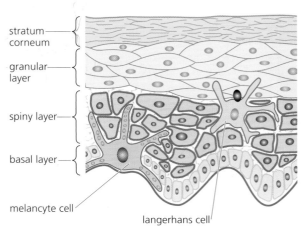

Melanocyte and langerhan cells in the skin

In contrast a black skin has melanin present in larger quantities throughout *all* the epidermal layers, a level of protection that has evolved to deal with bright ultra-violet light. This increased protection allows less ultra-violet to penetrate the dermis below, reducing the possibility of premature ageing from exposure to ultra-violet light. The more even quality and distribution of melanin also means that people with dark skins are less at risk of developing skin cancer.

Another pigment, **carotene**, which is yellowish, also occurs in epidermal cells. Its contribution to skin colour lessens in importance as the amount of melanin in the skin increases.

Skin colour also increases when the skin becomes warm. This is because the **blood capillaries** at the surface dilate, bringing blood nearer to the surface so that heat can be lost.

HEALTH AND SAFETY

Vitiligo
Lack of skin pigment is called *vitiligo* or *leucoderma*. It can occur with any skin colour, but is more obvious on dark skin. Avoid exposing such skin to ultra-violet light as it does not have melanin protection.

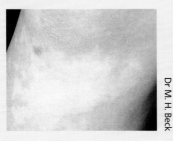

Dr M. H. Beck

TIP

Cosmetic sunscreens
Many hair and skin-care products and cosmetics, including lipsticks and mascaras, now contain *sunscreens*. This is because research has shown that ultra-violet exposure is the principal cause of skin ageing and can cause the hair to become dry.

Stratum granulosum   The **stratum granulosum**, or **granular layer**, is composed of one, two or three layers of cells that have become much flatter. The nucleus of the cell has begun to break up, creating what appear to be granules within the cell cytoplasm. These are known as **keratohyaline granules** and later form keratin. At this stage the cells form a new, combined layer.

HEALTH AND SAFETY

Sunburn
If the skin becomes red on exposure to sunlight, this indicates that the skin has been over-exposed to ultra-violet. It will often blister and shed itself.

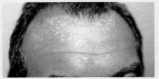

Dr John Gray, The World of Skin Care

TIP

Calluses

The skin will become much thicker in response to friction. A client with a manual occupation may therefore develop hard skin (calluses) on their hands. The skin condition can be treated with an *emollient* preparation, which will moisturise and soften the dry skin.

The keratinisation zone

The **keratinisation zone**, or **cornified zone**, is where the cells begin to die and where finally they will be shed from the skin. The cells at this stage become progressively flatter, and the cell cytoplasm is replaced with the hard protein keratin.

Stratum lucidum   The **stratum lucidum**, **clear layer** or **lucid layer**, is only seen in non-hairy areas of the skin such as the palms of the hands and the soles of the feet. The cells here lack a nucleus and are filled with a clear substance called **eledin** produced at a further stage of keratinisation.

Stratum corneum   The **stratum corneum**, **cornified** or **horny layer**, is formed from several layers of flattened, scale-like overlapping cells, composed mainly of keratin. These help to reflect ultra-violet light from the skin's surface; black skin, which evolved to withstand strong ultra-violet, has a thicker stratum corneum than does Caucasian skin.

It takes about three weeks for the epidermal cells to reach the stratum corneum from the stratum germinativum. The cells are then shed, a process called **desquamation**.

The dermis

The dermis is the inner portion of the skin, situated underneath the epidermis and composed of dense **connective tissue** containing other structures such as the lymphatic system, blood vessels and nerves. It is much thicker than the epidermis.

The skin

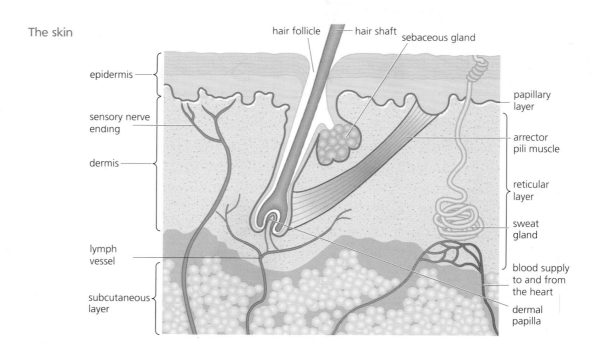

The papillary layer

Near the surface of the dermis are tiny projections called **papillae**; these contain both nerve endings and blood capillaries. This part of the dermis is known as the **papillary layer**, and it also supplies the upper epidermis with its nutrition.

The reticular layer

The dermis contains a network of protein fibres called the **reticular layer**. These fibres allow the skin to expand, to contract, and to perform intricate, supple movements.

This network is composed of two sorts of protein fibre: yellow **elastin** fibres and white **collagen** fibres. Elastin fibres give the skin its elasticity, and collagen fibres give it its strength. The fibres are produced by specialised cells called **fibroblasts**, and are held in a gel called the **ground substance**.

While this network is strong, the skin will appear youthful and firm. As the fibres harden and fragment, however, the network begins to collapse, losing its elasticity. The skin then begins to show visible signs of ageing.

A major cause of damage to this network is unprotected exposure of the skin to ultra-violet light and to weather. Sometimes, too, the skin loses its elasticity because of a sudden increase in body weight, for example at puberty or pregnancy. This results in the appearance of **stretch marks**, streaks of thin skin that is a different colour from the surrounding skin: on a white skin they appear as thin reddish streaks; on a black skin they appear slightly lighter than the surrounding skin. The lost elasticity cannot be restored.

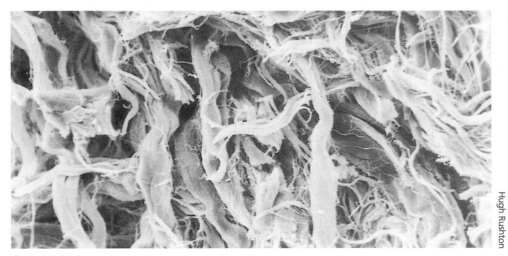

Collagen and elastin fibres

Hugh Rushton

Nerve endings

The dermis contains different types of sensory **nerve endings**, which register touch, pressure, pain and temperature. These send messages to the **central nervous system** and the **brain**, informing us about the outside world and what is happening on the skin's surface. The appearance of each of these nerve endings is quite varied.

TIP

Massage
Appropriate external massage movements can be used to increase the blood supply within the dermis, bringing extra nutrients and oxygen to the skin and to the underlying muscle. At the same time, the lymphatic circulation is increased, improving the removal of waste products that may have accumulated.

HEALTH AND SAFETY

Sunbathing
When sunbathing, always protect the skin with an appropriate protective sun-screen product, and always use an emollient after-sun preparation to minimise the cumulative effects of premature ageing, by rehydrating and soothing the skin.

TIP

Sensory nerve endings
Sensory nerve endings are most numerous in sensitive parts of the skin, such as the fingertips and the lips.

Sensory nerves

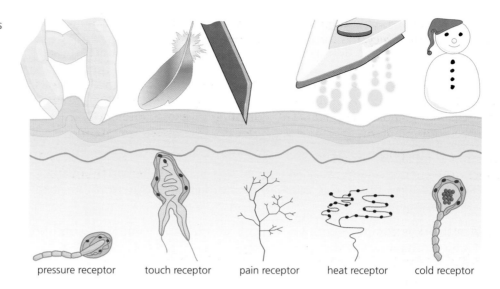

pressure receptor   touch receptor   pain receptor   heat receptor   cold receptor

Growth and repair   The body's blood system of arteries and veins continually brings blood to the capillary networks in the skin and takes it away again. The blood carries the nutrients and oxygen essential for the skin's health, maintenance and growth, and takes away waste products.

Defence   Within the dermis are the structures responsible for protecting the skin from harmful foreign bodies and irritants.

One set of cells, the **mast cells**, burst when stimulated during inflammation or allergic reactions, and release a chemical substance called **histamine**. This causes the blood vessels nearby to enlarge, thereby bringing more blood to the site of the irritation to limit skin damage and begin repair.

In the blood, and also in the lymph and the connective tissue, are another group of cells: the **macrophages** or 'big eaters'. These destroy micro-organisms and engulf dead cells and other unwanted particles. When necessary, they travel to an area where they are needed, for example the site of an infection. They form a role in the immune system that protects the body from disease-causing micro-organisms.

HEALTH AND SAFETY

Scars
When the surface has been broken, the skin at the site of the injury is replaced but may leave a scar. This initially appears red, due to the increased blood supply to the area, required while the skin heals. When healed, the redness will fade.

Waste products   Lymph vessels in the skin carry a fluid called **lymph**, a straw-coloured fluid similar in composition to blood plasma. Plasma is the liquid part of the blood that disperses from the blood capillaries into the tissue spaces. Lymph is composed of water, lymphocytes (a type of white blood cell that plays a key role in the immune system), oxygen, nutrients, hormones, salts and waste products. The waste products are eliminated and usable protein is recycled for further use by the body.

Control of functioning

Hormones are chemical messengers transported in the blood. They control the activity of many organs in the body, including the cells and glands in the skin. These include **melanosomes**, which produce skin pigment, and the **sweat glands** and **sebaceous glands**.

Hormone imbalance at different times of our life may disturb the normal functioning of these cells and structures, causing various **skin disorders**.

Skin appendages

Within the dermis are structures called **skin appendages**. These include:

- sweat glands;
- sebaceous glands;
- hair follicles, which produce hair;
- nails.

Sweat glands

Sweat glands or **sudoriferous glands** are composed of **epithelial tissue**, which extends from the epidermis into the dermis. These glands are found all over the body, but are particularly abundant on the palms of the hands and the soles of the feet. Their function is to regulate body temperature through the evaporation of sweat from the surface of the skin. Fluid loss and control of body temperature are important to prevent the body overheating, especially in hot, humid climates. For this reason, perhaps, sweat glands are larger and more abundant in black skins than white skins.

There are two types of sweat glands: *eccrine glands* and *apocrine glands*. **Eccrine glands** are simple sweat-producing glands, found over most of the body, appearing as tiny tubes (**ducts**). The eccrine glands are responsive to heat. These are straight in the epidermis, and coiled in the dermis. The duct opens directly onto the surface of the skin through an opening called a **pore**.

Eccrine glands continuously secrete small amounts of sweat, even when we appear not to be perspiring. In this way they maintain the body temperature at a constant 36.8°C.

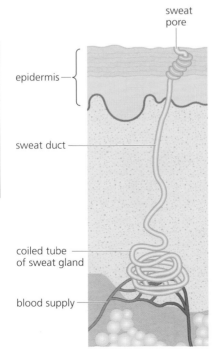

An eccrine sweat gland

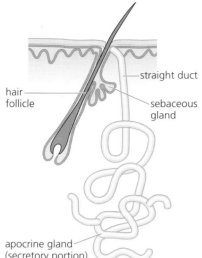

hair follicle

straight duct

sebaceous gland

apocrine gland (secretory portion)

Apocrine gland

ACTIVITY

Preventing body odour
Produce a checklist that should be followed daily to reduce the possibility of body odour.

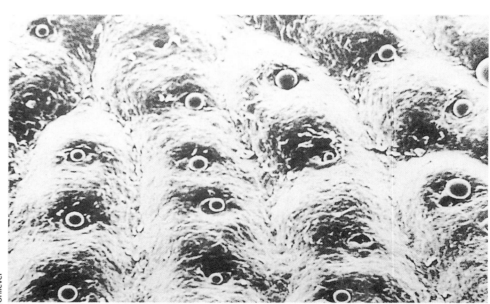

Sweat pores on the skin's surface

Unilever

Apocrine glands are found in the armpit, the nipples and the groin area. This kind of gland is larger than the eccrine gland, and is attached to a hair follicle. Apocrine glands are controlled by hormones, becoming active at puberty. They also increase in activity when we are excited, nervous or stressed. The fluid they secrete is thicker than that from the eccrine glands, and may contain urea, fats, sugars and small amounts of protein. Also present are traces of aromatic molecules called **pheromones,** which are thought to cause sexual attraction between individuals.

An unpleasant smell – **body odour** – develops when apocrine sweat is broken down by skin bacteria. Good habits of personal hygiene will prevent this.

Cosmetic perspiration control   To extend hygiene protection during the day, apply either a deodorant or an anti-perspirant. **Anti-perspirants** reduce the amount of sweat that reaches the skin's surface: they have an astringent action which closes the pores. **Deodorants** contain an active antiseptic ingredient which reduces the skin's bacterial activity, thereby reducing the risk of odour from stale sweat.

TIP

Anti-perspirants
The active ingredient in most anti-perspirant products is *aluminium chlorhydrate*. This is known to cause contact dermatitis in some people, especially if the skin has been damaged by recent removal of unwanted hair. Bear this in mind if you are performing an underarm depilatory wax treatment. (See the aftercare instructions, pages 295–6.)

Sebaceous glands

The **sebaceous gland** appears as a minute sac-like organ. Usually it is associated with the hair follicle with which it forms the **pilosebaceous unit**, but the two can appear independently.

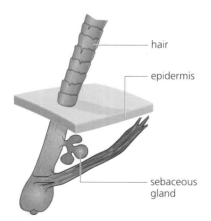

hair

epidermis

sebaceous gland

A sebaceous gland

Sebaceous glands are found all over the body, except on the palms of the hands and the soles of the feet. They are particularly numerous on the scalp, the forehead, and in the back and chest region. The cells of the glands decompose, producing the skin's natural oil, **sebum**. This empties directly into the hair follicle.

The activity of the sebaceous gland increases at puberty, when stimulated by the male hormone **androgen**. In adults, activity of the sebaceous gland gradually decreases again. Men secrete slightly more sebum than women; and on black skin the sebaceous glands are larger and more numerous than on white skin.

Sebum is composed of fatty acids and waxes. These have **bactericidal** and **fungicidal** properties, and so discourage the multiplication of micro-organisms on the surface of the skin. Sebum also reduces the evaporation of moisture from the skin, and so prevents the skin from drying out.

> **TIP**
>
> **Moisturisers**
> Cosmetic moisturisers mimic sebum in providing an oily covering for the skin's surface to reduce moisture loss.

> **HEALTH AND SAFETY** ✚
>
> **The lips**
> Sebaceous glands are not present on the surface of the lips. For this reason the lips should be protected with a lip emollient preparation to prevent them from becoming dry and chapped.

Acid mantle Sweat and sebum combine on the skin's surface, creating an acid film. This is known as the **acid mantle**, and discourages the growth of bacteria and fungi.

Acidity and alkalinity are measured by a number called the pH. An *acidic solution* has a pH of 0–7; a *neutral solution* has a pH of 7; and an *alkaline solution* has a pH of 7–14. The acid mantle of the skin has a pH of 5.5–5.6.

> **HEALTH AND SAFETY**
>
> **Using alkaline products**
> Because the skin has an acid pH, if alkaline products are used on it the acid mantle will be disturbed. It will take several hours for this protective film to be restored; during this time, the skin will be irritated and sensitive.

THE HAIR

The structure and function of hair and the surrounding tissues

A hair is a long, slender structure which grows out of, and is part of, the skin. Each hair is made up of dead skin cells, which contain the protein called keratin.

Hairs cover the whole body, except for the palms of the hands, the soles of the feet, the lips, and parts of the sex organs.

Hair has many functions:

- *scalp hair* insulates the head against cold, protects it from the sun, and cushions it against bumps;
- *eyebrows* cushion the browbone from bumps, and prevent sweat from running into the eyes;
- *eyelashes* help to prevent foreign particles entering the eyes;

TIP ✓

Did you know?
There are approximately 100,000 hairs on the scalp.

- *nostril hair* traps dust particles inhaled with the air;
- *ear hair* helps to protect the ear canal;
- *body hair* helps to provide an insulating cover (though this function is almost obsolete in humans), has a valuable sensory function, and is linked with the secretion of sebum onto the surface of the skin.

Hair also plays a role in social communication.

The structure of hair

Most hairs are made up of three layers of different types of epithelial cells: the *medulla*, the *cortex* and the *cuticle*.

The **medulla** is the central core of the hair. The cells of the medulla contain soft keratin, and sometimes some pigment granules. The medulla only exists in medium to coarser hair – there is usually no medulla in thinner hair.

TIP ✓

Did you know?
A strand of hair is stronger than an equivalent strand of nylon or copper.

The **cortex** is the thickest layer of the hair, and is made up of several layers of closely packed, elongated cells. These contain pigment granules and hard keratin.

It is the **pigment** in the cortex that gives hair its colour. When this pigment is no longer made, the hair appears white. As the proportion of white hairs rises, the hair seems to go 'grey'; in fact, however, each individual hair is either coloured as before, or white.

Cross-section of the hair

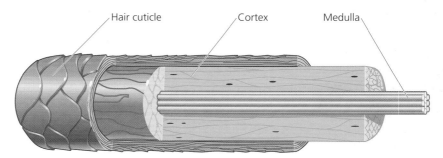

Hair cuticle   Cortex   Medulla

The **cuticle** is the protective outer layer of the hair, and is composed of a layer of thin, unpigmented, flat, scale-like cells. These contain hard keratin, and overlap each other from the base to the tip of the hair.

TIP ✓

Eyelash perm lotion and the eyelash/eyebrow tint mixed with hydrogen peroxide swells and penetrates the cuticle so that the products can enter the cortex. The coarser the hair the more resistant it is! Eyelash and eyebrow tints and perming make the permanent chemical changes to the hair's natural appearance in the cortex.

The parts of the hair and related skin

Each hair is recognised by three parts: the *root*, the *bulb* and the *shaft*:

- the **root** is the part of the hair that is in the follicle;
- the **bulb** is the enlarged base of the root;
- the **shaft** is the part of the hair that can be seen above the skin's surface.

ACTIVITY 🏃

The function of hair
Humans are not very hairy but their hairs sometimes stand on end! How do you know when this occurs? How does the appearance of skin change? What is the purpose of hair standing on end?

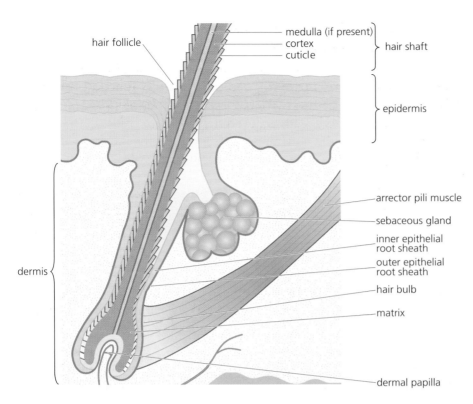

Cross-section of the skin, hair and hair follicle

Each hair grows out of a tube-like indentation in the epidermis, the **hair follicle**. The walls of the follicle are a continuation of the epidermal layer of the skin.

The **arrector pili muscle** is attached at an angle to the base of the follicle. Cold, aggression or fright stimulates this muscle to contract, pulling the follicle and the hair upright.

The **sebaceous gland** is attached to the upper part of the follicle; from it, a duct enters directly into the hair follicle. The gland produces an oily substance, **sebum**, which is secreted into the follicle. Sebum waterproofs, lubricates and softens the hair and the surface of the skin; it also protects the skin against bacterial and fungal infections. The contraction of the arrector pili muscle aids the secretion of sebum.

The **dermal papilla**, a connective tissue sheath, is surrounded by a hair bulb. It has an excellent blood supply, necessary for the growth of the hair. It is not itself part of the follicle, but a separate tiny organ which serves the follicle.

The **bulb** is the expanded base of the hair root. A gap at the base leads to a cavity inside, which houses the papilla. The bulb contains in its lower part the dividing cells that create the hair. The hair continues to develop as it passes through the regions of the upper bulb and the root.

The **matrix** is the name given to the lower part of the bulb, which comprises actively dividing cells from which the hair is formed.

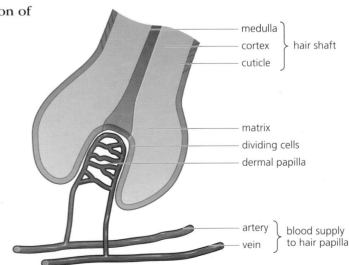

The hair bulb

The hair follicle The hair follicle extends into the dermis, and is made up of three sheaths: the *inner epithelial root sheath*, the *outer epithelial root sheath* and the surrounding *connective-tissue sheath*.

The **inner epithelial root sheath** grows from the bottom of the follicle at the papilla; both the hair and the inner root sheath grow upwards together. The inner surface of this sheath is covered with cuticle cells, in the same way as the outer surface of the hair: these cells lock together, anchoring the hair firmly in place. The inner root sheath ceases to grow when level with the sebaceous gland.

The **outer epithelial root sheath** forms the follicle wall. This does not grow up with the hair, but is stationary. It is a continuation of the growing layer of the epidermis of the skin.

The **connective-tissue sheath** surrounds both the follicle and the sebaceous gland, providing both a sensory supply and a blood supply. The connective-tissue sheath includes, and is a continuation of, the papilla.

The *shape* of the hairs is determined by the shape of the hair follicle – an angled or bent follicle will produce an oval or flat hair, whereas a straight follicle will produce a round hair. Flat hairs are curly, oval hairs are wavy, and round hairs are straight. As a general rule, during waxing curly hairs break off more easily than straight hairs.

> **TIP** ✓
>
> **Broken hairs**
> When hairs break off due to incorrect waxing technique, they will break at the level at which they are locked into the follicle by the cells of the inner root sheath.

Hair shapes

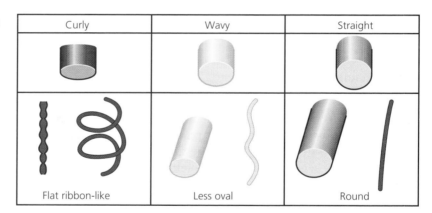

Curly	Wavy	Straight
Flat ribbon-like	Less oval	Round

> **TIP** ✓
>
> An angled follicle may cause the hair to be broken off at the angle during waxing, instead of being completely pulled out with its root. If this happens, broken hairs will appear at the skin's surface within a few days.
>
> By causing damage to the follicle and changing its shape, waxing can cause the regrowth of hairs to be frizzy or curled where previously the hairs have been straight.

The nerve supply The number, size and type of nerve endings associated with hair follicles is related to the size and type of follicle. The follicles of vellus hairs (see page 117) have the fewest nerve endings; those of terminal hairs have the most.

The nerve endings surrounding hair follicles respond mainly to rapid movements when the hair is moved. Nerve endings that respond to touch can also be found around the surface openings of some hair follicles, as well as just below the epidermis.

The three types of hair

There are three main types of hair: *lanugo*, *vellus* and *terminal*.

Lanugo hairs are found on the body prior to birth. They are fine and soft, do not have a medulla, and are often unpigmented. They grow from around the third to the fifth month of pregnancy, and are shed to be replaced by the secondary vellus hairs around the seventh to the eighth month of pregnancy. Lanugo hairs on the scalp, eyebrows and eyelashes are replaced by terminal hairs.

Vellus hairs are fine, downy and soft, and are found on the face and body. They are often unpigmented, rarely longer than 20mm, and do not have a medulla or a well-formed bulb. The base of these hairs is very close to the skin's surface. If stimulated, the shallow follicle of a vellus hair can grow downwards and become a follicle that produces terminal hairs.

Terminal hairs are longer and coarser than vellus hairs, and most are pigmented. They vary greatly in shape, in diameter and length, and in colour and texture. The follicles from which they grow are set deeply in the dermis and have well-defined bulbs. Terminal hair is the coarse hair of the scalp, eyebrows, eyelashes, pubic and underarm regions. It is also present on the face, chest and sometimes the back of males.

> **TIP** ✔
>
> **Waxing terminal hair**
> Some areas of the body – for example, the bikini line and underarm areas – often have terminal hairs with very deep follicles. When these hairs are removed, the resulting tissue damage may cause minor bleeding from the entrance of the follicle. Removal of these deep-seated hairs is obviously more uncomfortable than the removal of shallower hairs.

Hair growth

All hair has a cyclical pattern of growth, which can be divided into three phases: *anagen*, *catagen* and *telogen*.

Anagen is the actively growing stage of the hair – the follicle has re-formed; the hair bulb is developing, surrounding the life-giving dermal papilla; and a new hair forms, growing from the matrix in the bulb.

Catagen is the changing stage when the hair separates from the papilla. Over a few days it is carried by the movement of the inner root sheath, up the follicle to the base of the sebaceous gland. Here it stays until it either falls out or is pushed out by a new hair growing up behind it.

This stage can be very rapid, with a new hair growing straight away; or slower, with the papilla and the follicle below the sebaceous gland degenerating and entering a resting stage, telogen.

Telogen is a resting stage. Many hair follicles do not undergo this stage, but start to produce a new hair immediately. During resting phases, hairs may still be loosely inserted in the shallow follicles.

> **TIP** ✔
>
> A hair pulled out at the *anagen* stage will be surrounded by the inner and outer root sheaths and have a properly formed bulb.

> **TIP** ✔
>
> A hair pulled out at the *catagen* or *telogen* stage can be recognised by the brush-like appearance of the root.

The hair growth cycle

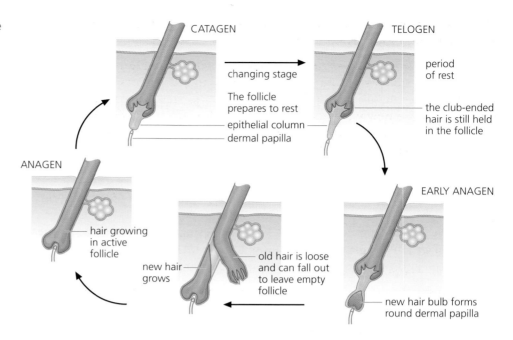

> **TIP** ✓
>
> Because of the cyclical nature of hair growth, the follicles are always at different stages of their growth cycle. When the hair is removed, therefore, the hair will not all grow back at the same time. For this reason, waxing can appear to reduce the quantity of hair growth. This is not so; given time, all the hair would regrow. Waxing is classed as a temporary means of hair removal.

Speed of growth

The anagen, catagen and telogen stages last for different lengths of time in different hair types and in different parts of the body:

- *scalp hair* grows for two to seven years, and has a resting stage of three to four months;
- *eyebrow* hair grows for one to two months, and has a resting stage of three to four months;
- *eyelashes* grow for three to six weeks, and have a resting stage of three to four months.

After a waxing treatment, body hair will take approximately six to eight weeks to return.

Because hair growth cycles are not all in synchronisation, we always have hair present at any given time. On the scalp, at any one time for example, 85 per cent of hairs may be in the anagen phase. This is why hair growth after waxing starts within a few days: what is seen is the appearance of hairs that were already developing in the follicle at the time of waxing.

> **TIP** ✓
>
> **Vellus hairs**
> Vellus hairs grow slowly and take two to three months to return after waxing. They can remain dormant in the follicle for six to eight months before shedding.

Types of hair growth

Hirsutism is a term used to describe a pattern of hair growth that is abnormal for that person's sex, such as when a woman's hair growth follows a man's hair-growth pattern.

Hypertrichosis is an abnormal growth of excess hair. It is usually due to abnormal conditions brought about by disease or injury.

Superfluous hair (excess hair) is perfectly normal at certain periods in a woman's life, such as during puberty or pregnancy. Terminal hairs formed at these times usually disappear once the normal hormonal balance has returned. Those newly formed during the menopause are often permanent unless treated with a permanent method of hair removal, such as electrical depilation or laser treatment.

Factors affecting the growth rate and quantity of hair

Hair does not always grow uniformly:

- *Time of day* Hair grows faster at night than during the day.
- *Weather* Hairs grow faster in warm weather than in cold.
- *Pregnancy* In women, hairs grow faster between the ages of 16 and 24, and (frequently) during mid-pregnancy.
- *Age* The rate of hair growth slows down with age. In women, however, facial hair growth continues to increase in old age, while trunk and limb hair increases into middle age and then decreases.
- *Colour* Hairs of different colour grow at different speeds – for example, coarse black hair grows more quickly than fine blonde hair.
- *Part of the body* Hair in different areas of the body grows at different rates, as do different types and thicknesses of hair. The weekly growth rate varies from approximately 1.5mm (fine hair) to 2.8mm (coarse hair), when actively growing.
- *Heredity* Members of a family may have inherited growth patterns, such as excess hair that starts to grow at puberty and increases until the age of 20–25.
- *Health and diet* Health and a varied, balanced diet are crucial in the rate of hair growth and appearance.
- *Stress* Emotional stress can cause a temporary hormonal imbalance within the body, which may lead to a temporary growth of excess hair.
- *Medical conditions* A sudden unexplained increase of body hair growth may indicate a more serious medical problem, such as malfunction of the ovaries; or result from the taking of certain drugs, such as corticosteroids.

The quantity as well as the type of hair present may vary with race:

- *People of Latin extraction* tend to possess heavier body, facial and scalp hair, which is relatively coarse and straight.
- *People of Eastern extraction* tend to possess very little or no body and facial hair growth, and usually their scalp hair growth is relatively coarse and straight.
- *People of Northern European and Caucasian extraction* tend to have light to medium body and facial hair growth, with their scalp hair growth being wavy, loosely curled or straight.
- *People of African-Caribbean extraction* tend to have little body and facial hair growth, but usually their scalp hair growth is relatively coarse and tightly curled.

HEALTH AND SAFETY

African-Caribbean clients
The body hair of African-Caribbean clients is prone to breaking during waxing, and to ingrowing after waxing. Skin damage can result in the loss of pigmentation (hypopigmentation).

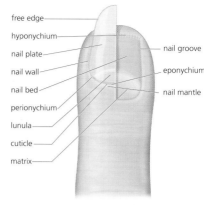

free edge
hyponychium
nail plate
nail wall
nail bed
perionychium
lunula
cuticle
matrix
nail groove
eponychium
nail mantle

The structure of the nail

nail plate

The nail plate

TIP ✓

Did you know?
Fingernails grow more quickly than toenails. Fingernails grow about 0.1mm each day (4cm per year), and grow faster in summer than in winter.

THE NAILS

The structure and function of the nail

Nails grow from the ends of the fingers and toes and serve as a form of protection. They also help when picking up small objects. Dark streaks caused by pigmentation are common on the nail plate of black-skinned clients. These tend to increase with age.

The nail plate

The **nail plate** is composed of compact translucent layers of keratinised epidermal cells: it is this that makes up the main body of the nail. The layers of cells are packed very closely together, with fat but very little moisture.

The nail gradually grows forward over the nail bed, until finally it becomes the free edge. The underside of the nail plate is grooved by longitudinal ridges and furrows, which help to keep it in place.

In normal health the plate curves in two directions:

- transversely – from side to side across the nail;
- longitudinally – from the base of the nail to the free edge.

There are no blood vessels or nerves in the nail plate: this is why the nails, like hair, can be cut without pain or bleeding. The pink colour of the nail plate derives from the blood vessels that pass beneath it – the nail bed.

Function: To protect the living nail bed of the fingers and toes.

The free edge

The **free edge** is the part of the nail that extends beyond the fingertip; this is the part that is filed. It appears white as there is no nail bed underneath.

Function: To protect the fingertip and the hyponychium (see page 121).

The matrix

The **matrix**, sometimes called the **nail root**, is the growing area of the nail. It is formed by the division of cells in this area, called mitosis, which is part of the stratum germinativum layer of the epidermis. It lies under the eponychium (see page 121), at the base of the nail, nearest to the body. The process of keratinisation takes place in the epidermal cells of the matrix, forming the hardened tissue of the nail plate.

Function: To produce new nail cells.

The nail bed

The **nail bed** is the portion of skin upon which the nail plate rests. It has a pattern of grooves and furrows corresponding to those found on the underside of the nail plate; these interlock, keeping the nail in place, but separate at the end of the nail to form the free edge. The nail bed is liberally supplied with blood vessels, which provide the nourishment necessary for continued growth; and sensory nerves, for protection.

Function: To supply nourishment and protection.

The nail mantle

The **nail mantle** is the layer of epidermis at the base of the nail, before the cuticle. It appears as a deep fold of skin.

Function: To protect the matrix from physical damage.

The lunula

The crescent-shaped **lunula** is located at the base of the nail, lying over the matrix. It is white, relative to the rest of the nail, and there are two theories to account for this:

- newly formed nail plates may be more opaque than mature nail plates;
- the lunula may indicate the extent of the underlying matrix – the matrix is thicker than the epidermis of the nail bed, and the capillaries beneath it would not show through as well.

Function: None.

The hyponychium

The **hyponychium** is part of the epidermis under the free edge of the nail.

Function: To protect the nail bed from infection.

The nail grooves

The **nail grooves** run alongside the edge of the nail plate.

Function: To guide and keep the nail plate growing forward.

The perionychium

The **perionychium** is the collective name given to the cuticle at the sides of the nail.

Function: To protect the nail.

The nail walls

The **nail walls** are the folds of skin overlapping the sides of the nails.

Function: To cushion and protect the nail plate and grooves from damage.

The eponychium

The **eponychium** is the extension of the cuticle at the base of the nail plate, under which the nail plate emerges from the matrix.

Function: To protect the matrix from infection.

ACTIVITY

Recognising nail structure
With a colleague, try to identify the structural parts of each other's nails. Write down both the parts that you can see and the parts that you cannot.

The cuticle

The **cuticle** is the overlapping epidermis around the base of the nail, developing from the stratum corneum. When in good condition, it is soft and loose.

Function: To protect the matrix from infection.

Nail growth

Cells divide in the matrix and the nail grows forward over the nail bed, guided by the nail grooves, until it reaches the end of the finger or toe, where it becomes the free edge. As they first emerge from the matrix the translucent cells are plump and soft, but they get harder and flatter as they move toward the free edge. The top two layers of the epidermis form the nail plate; the remaining three form the nail bed.

The nail plate is made up of a protein called keratin, and the hardening process that takes place in the nail cells is known as **keratinisation**.

The nail bed has a pattern of grooves and furrows corresponding to those found on the underside of the nail plate: the two surfaces interlock, holding the nail in place.

Fingernails grow at approximately twice the speed of toenails. It takes about six months for a fingernail to grow from cuticle to free edge, but about twelve months for a toenail to do so.

THE NERVOUS SYSTEM

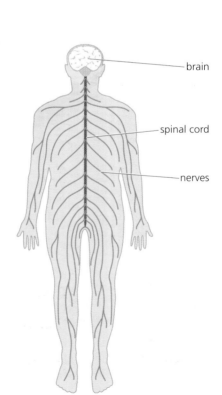

The nervous system transmits messages between the brain and other parts of the body. It controls everything that the body does with the endocrine system. The nervous system is made up of a network of nerve cells, called neurons. Nerve cells are long, narrow and delicate. They transmit messages to and from the central nervous system (CNS) in the form of impulses. Neurons are made up of a cell body containing a large central nucleus and bundles of nerve fibres.

The nervous system of the body has two main divisions:

1 the central nervous system;
2 the autonomic nervous system.

The central nervous system

The central nervous system (CNS) is composed of the brain and spinal cord. It co-ordinates the activities of the entire body.

The brain transmits impulses to all parts of the body in order to stimulate other organs to act and is protected by the bones of the cranium. The spinal cord extends downwards through the vertebral column and is protected by the bones (vertebrae) of the spinal column. The brain is composed of several parts, each of which performs special functions.

The central nervous system

Nerves

A nerve is a whitish bundle of fibres made up of neurons (nerve cells) in the body that transmits impulses of sensations between the brain or spinal cord and other parts of the body.

Kinds of nerves

There are two types of nerve: *sensory nerves* and *motor nerves*. Both are composed of white fibres enclosed in a sheath.

- **Sensory nerves** These receive information and relay it to the brain. They are found near to the skin's surface and respond to touch, pressure, temperature and pain.
- **Motor nerves** These are situated in muscle tissue and act on information received from the brain, causing a particular response, typically muscle movement.

All nerves emerge from the CNS. Sensory (receptor) nerves are linked to sensory receptors, while motor (effector) nerves end in a muscle or gland. Twelve pairs of cranial nerves emerge from the brain; thirty-one pairs of spinal nerves emerge from between the vertebrae of the spinal column.

Nerves of the face and neck

These nerves link the brain with the muscles of the head, face and neck.

Cranial nerves control muscles in the head and neck region, or carry nerve impulses from sense organs to the brain. Those of concern to the beauty therapist when performing a facial treatment are as follows:

- the 5th cranial nerve, or **trigeminal** controls the muscles involved in mastication (chewing) and passes on sensory information from the face such as the eyes;
- the 7th cranial nerve, or **facial** controls the muscles involved in facial expression;
- the 11th cranial nerve, or **accessory** controls muscles involved in moving the head, the sternocleido mastoid and trapezius muscle.

5th cranial nerve

This nerve carries messages to the brain from the sensory nerves of the skin, the teeth, the nose and the mouth. It also stimulates the motor nerve to create the chewing action when eating. The 5th cranial nerve has three branches:

- the **ophthalmic nerve** serves the tear glands, the skin of the forehead, and the upper cheeks;
- the **maxillary nerve** serves the upper jaw and the mouth;
- the **mandibular nerve** serves the lower jaw muscle, the teeth and the muscle involved with chewing.

HEALTH AND SAFETY

Nerve damage
Nerve cells do not reproduce; when damaged, only a limited repair occurs.

TIP

Massage
Appropriate massage manipulations, when applied to the skin, produce a stimulating or relaxing effect on nerves.

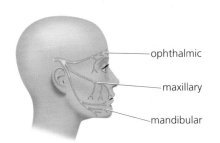

ophthalmic

maxillary

mandibular

5th cranial nerve

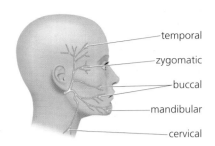

7th cranial nerve

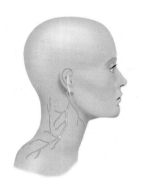

11th cranial nerve

7th cranial nerve

This nerve passes through the temporal bone and behind the ear, and then divides. It serves the ear muscle and the muscles of facial expression, the tongue and the palate.

The 7th cranial nerve has five branches:

- the **temporal nerve** serves the orbicularis oculi and the frontalis muscles;
- the **zygomatic nerve** serves the eye muscles;
- the **buccal nerve** serves the upper lip and the sides of the nose;
- the **mandibular nerve** serves the lower lip and the mentalis muscle of the chin;
- the **cervical nerve** serves the platysma muscle of the neck.

11th cranial nerve

This nerve serves the sternomastoid and trapezius muscles of the neck, and its function is to move the head and shoulders.

Nerve impulses

The CNS transmits instructions to organs through nerve impulses – tiny electrical signals – that pass along a neuron. Each nerve consists of a nerve cell and its parts, axons and dendrites. Axons carry nerve impulses away from the cell; dendrites carry impulses towards the cell.

When an impulse reaches the end of a nerve fibre, a chemical called a *neurotransmitter substance* is released. This chemical passes across a tiny gap called a *synapse* and is taken up by an adjacent neuron, generating an electrical impulse in the neuron.

> **TIP** ✔
>
> **Lifestyle factors affect the nervous system**
> *Caffeine* is a stimulant and will increase the release of the neurotransmitter chemical across the synapse between adjacent neurons.
> *Alcohol* is a sedative and will slow the release of the neurotransmitter chemical across the synapse between adjacent neurons.
> Can you think of other substances that affect the nervous system?

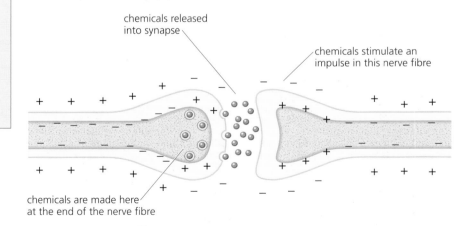

Passage of an impulse across a synapse

Neurons can stimulate muscles fibres to contract. The *motor point* is where a motor nerve enters a muscle. When stimulated by a motor nerve muscle contraction occurs.

The autonomic nervous system

The autonomic nervous system controls those body structures over which there is no conscious control – the involuntary activities. It regulates the functioning of organs such as the heart, the stomach, the lungs and the secretion of most glands. There are two divisions of the autonomic nervous system – the *sympathetic* and *parasympathetic nervous systems*.

Many organs receive a supply from each division. Fibres from one division stimulate the organ while fibres from the other division inhibit it, thus ensuring balance in the body.

The sympathetic nervous system is stimulated in periods of stress or danger and prepares the body for physical activity. Fibres of the sympathetic division increase blood flow by causing the heart to beat faster and the blood vessels in the muscles to widen. Activities that are not essential in this stressful situation are inhibited.

The parasympathetic nervous system is associated with resting and causes the blood flow to slow by causing the heart to beat slower and the blood vessels in the muscles to contract (go smaller). Fibres of this division stimulate digestion and absorption of food.

The nervous system therefore co-ordinates the activities of the body by responding to stimuli received by sense organs, including the nose, tongue, eyes, ears and skin.

TIP

Botox® botulinium toxin A
Botox® has developed as a cosmetic treatment from its previous use medically to treat eye spasms and disorders of the central nervous system. A purified protein called botulinum toxin A is injected into the face where it binds to the nerve endings, which prevent the release of the neurotransmitter substance that stimulates the muscle fibres to contract. The result is a paralysis of the muscle preventing expressions that may lead to visible expression lines on the face, such as frown lines.

TIP

Memory aid
The **s**ympathetic division is associated with **s**tress.
The **p**arasympathetic system is associated with **p**eace.

THE MUSCULAR SYSTEM

Muscles are responsible for the movement of body parts. Each is made up of a bundle of elastic fibres bound together in a sheath, the **fascia**. Muscular tissue contracts (shortens) and produces movement. Muscles never completely relax – there are always a few contracted fibres in every muscle. These make the muscles slightly tense and this tension is called muscle tone.

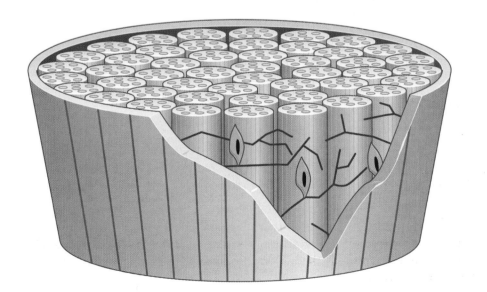

Muscle

Muscle tissue has the following properties:

- it has the ability to contract;
- it is extensible (when the extensor muscle in a joint contracts the corresponding flexor muscle will be stretched or lengthened);
- it is elastic – following contraction or extension it returns to its original length;
- it is responsive – it contracts in response to nerve stimulation.

A muscle is usually anchored by a strong tendon to one bone: the point of attachment is known as the muscle's **origin**. The muscle is likewise joined to a second bone: the attachment in this case is called the muscle's **insertion**. It is this second bone that is moved: the muscle contracts, pulling the two bones towards each other. (A different muscle, on the other side of the bone, has the contrary effect.) Not all muscles attach to bones, however: some insert into an adjacent muscle, or into the skin itself. The muscles with which we are concerned here are those of the face, the neck and the shoulders.

TIP ✓

Terminology for action

Flexor – bends a joint   *Extensor* – straightens a joint

If a muscle has 'flexor' or 'extensor' in front of the muscle name you will know what the action of the muscle is!

Abduction – 'move away'   *Adduction* – 'move towards'

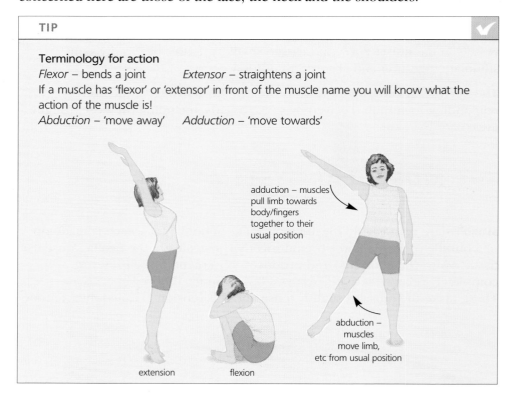

adduction – muscles pull limb towards body/fingers together to their usual position

abduction – muscles move limb, etc from usual position

extension   flexion

Facial muscles

Many of the muscles located in the face are very small and are attached to ('insert into') another small muscle or the facial skin. When the muscles contract, they pull the facial skin in a particular way; this creates facial expressions.

With age, the facial expressions that we make every day produce lines on the skin – frown lines. The amount of tension, or **tone**, also decreases with age. When performing facial massage, the aim is to improve the general tone of the facial muscles.

Anatomical terminology

Anatomical terminology is used to describe the location, function and description of a body part. It is useful to know these terms, as it will assist your anatomy understanding.

Anterior	Front (usually refers to front of the body)	Superficial	Near the surface
Posterior	Back (usually refers to the back of the body)	Superior	Above
Proximal	Nearest to	Inferior	Below
Medial	Middle	Plantar	Front surface
Distal	Furthest away	Dorsal	Back surface
Lateral	Side		

Muscles of facial expression

Muscle	Expression	Location	Action
Occipito frontalis	Surprise	The forehead	Raises the eyebrows, causes wrinkling across forehead
Corrugator	Frown	Between the eyebrows	Draws the eyebrows together
Orbicularis oculi	Winking	Surrounds the eyes	Closes the eyelid
Risorius	Smiling	Extends diagonally, from the corners of the mouth	Draws mouth corners outwards
Buccinator	Blowing	Inside the cheeks	Compresses the cheeks

Muscle	Expression	Location	Action
Zygomaticus, major and minor	Smiling, laughing	Extend diagonally upwards from the corners of the mouth	Lifts the corners of the mouth
Procerus	Distaste	Covers the bridge of the nose	Wrinkling of the skin over the bridge of the nose
Nasalis	Anger	Covers the front of the nose	Opens and closes the nasal openings
Quadratus labii superioris	Distaste	Surrounds the upper lip	Raises and draws back the upper lips and nostrils
Depressor labii	Sulking	Surrounds the lower lip	Depresses the lower lip and draws it slightly to one side
Orbicularis oris	Pout, kiss, doubt	Surrounds the mouth	Purses the lip (as in blowing), closes the mouth
Triangularis	Sadness	The corner of the lower lip extends over the chin	Draws down the mouth's corners
Mentalis	Doubt	Covers the front of the chin	Raises the lower lip, causing the chin to wrinkle

Muscle	Expression	Location	Action
Platysma 	Fear, horror	The sides of the neck and chin	Draws the mouth's corners downwards and backwards

platysma

ACTIVITY

Facial expressions
In front of a mirror, move the muscles of your face to create the expressions that you might form each day.

What expressions can you make? Which part or parts of the face are moving? Which facial muscles do you think have contracted to create these expressions?

TIP

Crow's feet
To avoid the premature formation of 'crow's feet':
- avoid squinting in bright sunlight – wear sunglasses
- have your eyes tested regularly
- if you use a visual display unit, ensure that you take regular breaks, and have a protective filter screen to remove glare.

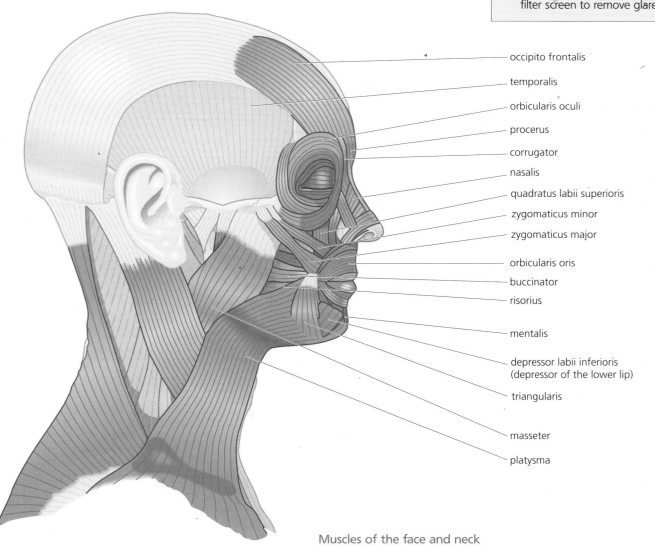

- occipito frontalis
- temporalis
- orbicularis oculi
- procerus
- corrugator
- nasalis
- quadratus labii superioris
- zygomaticus minor
- zygomaticus major
- orbicularis oris
- buccinator
- risorius
- mentalis
- depressor labii inferioris (depressor of the lower lip)
- triangularis
- masseter
- platysma

Muscles of the face and neck

Muscles of mastication

The muscles responsible for the movement of the lower jawbone (the **mandible**) when chewing are called the **muscles of mastication**.

Muscle	Location	Action
Masseter	The cheek area: extends from the zygomatic bone to the mandible	Clenches the teeth; closes and raises the lower jaw
Temporalis	Extends from the temple region at the side of the head to the mandible	Raises the jaw and draws it backwards, as in chewing

Muscles that move the head

Muscle	Location	Action
Sterno-cleido-mastoid	Runs from the sternum to the clavicle bone and the temporal bone	Flexes the neck; rotates and bows the head
Trapezius	A large triangular muscle, covering the back of the neck and the upper back	Draws the head backwards and allows movement at the shoulder
Occipitalis	Covers the back of the head	Draws scalp backwards

Muscles that move the head

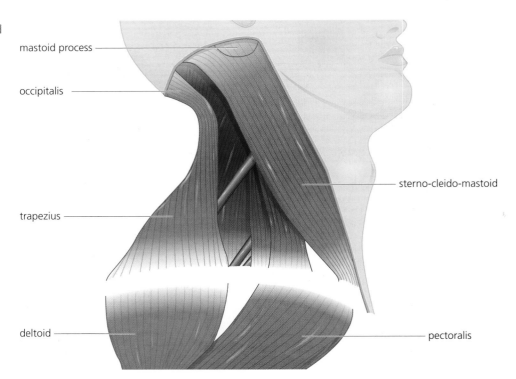

mastoid process

occipitalis

trapezius

deltoid

sterno-cleido-mastoid

pectoralis

Muscles of the upper body

When massaging the shoulder area you will cover the following muscles of the upper body.

Muscle	Location	Action
Pectoralis major	The front of the chest	Moves the arm towards the upper body
Deltoid	A thick triangular muscle, covering the shoulder	Takes the arm away from the side of the body

The muscles of the hand and arm

The hand and fingers are moved primarily by muscles and tendons in the forearm. These muscles contract, pulling the tendons, and thereby move the fingers much as a puppet is moved by strings.

The muscles that bend the wrist, drawing it towards the forearm, are **flexors**; other muscles, **extensors**, straighten the wrist and the hand.

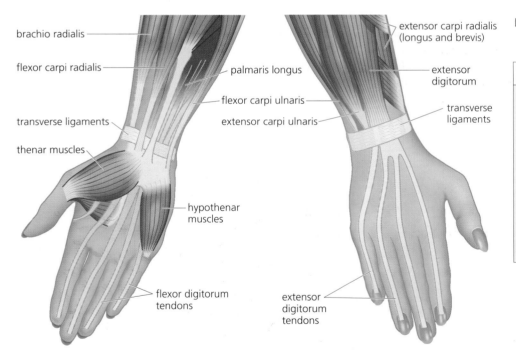

brachio radialis

flexor carpi radialis

palmaris longus

flexor carpi ulnaris

extensor carpi ulnaris

transverse ligaments

thenar muscles

hypothenar muscles

flexor digitorum tendons

extensor carpi radialis (longus and brevis)

extensor digitorum

transverse ligaments

extensor digitorum tendons

Muscles of the arm and hand

ACTIVITY

Observing the tendons
Tendons are made of strong connective tissue and attach muscle to bone. Hold your palm face upwards, with your sleeve pulled back so that you can see your forearm. Move the fingers individually towards the palm. Can you see the tendons moving?

Muscle	Location	Action
Brachio radialis	On the outer (thumb side) of the forearm	Flexes and turns the elbow
Flexor carpi radialis	Middle of the forearm	Muscle that flexes and abducts the wrist joint
Extensor carpi radialis (longus and brevis)	Thumb side of the forearm	Muscle that extends and straightens the wrist and hand

Muscle	Location	Action
Flexor carpi ulnaris	Front of the forearm	Muscle that flexes and adducts the wrist joint
Extensor carpi ulnaris	Back of the forearm	Extends and adducts the wrist
Palmaris longus	Middle of the front of the forearm	Flexes the wrist and hand
Hypothenar muscle	In the palm of the hand, below the little finger	Flexes the little finger and moves it outwards and inwards
Thenar muscle	In the palm of the hand, below the thumb	Flexes the thumb and moves it outwards and inwards
Flexor digitorum tendons	Front of fingers	Flexes the fingers when contracted
Extensor digitorum tendons	Back of fingers	Extends the fingers when contracted

The muscles of the foot and lower leg

The muscles of the foot work together to help move the body when walking and running. In a similar way to the movement of the hand, the foot is moved primarily by muscles in the lower leg; these pull on tendons, which in turn move the feet and toes.

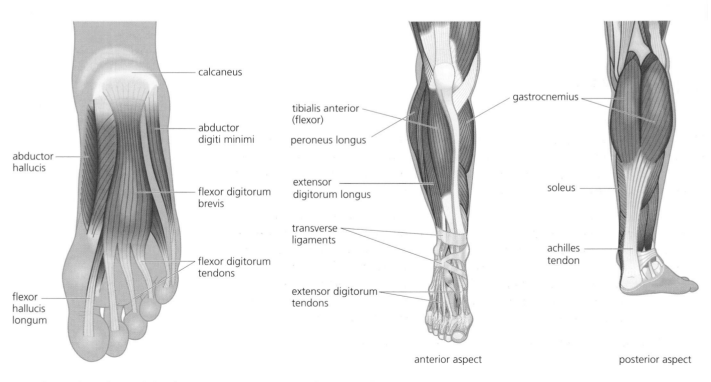

calcaneus

abductor digiti minimi

abductor hallucis

flexor digitorum brevis

flexor digitorum tendons

flexor hallucis longum

tibialis anterior (flexor)

peroneus longus

gastrocnemius

extensor digitorum longus

transverse ligaments

extensor digitorum tendons

soleus

achilles tendon

anterior aspect

posterior aspect

Muscles and tendons of the foot

Muscles of the lower leg

Muscle	Location	Action
Gastrocnemius	Calf of the leg, inserts through the achilles tendon into the heel	Flexes the lower leg; plantar flexes the foot (extends and points the toes down).
Tibialis anterior	Front of the lower leg	Inverts the foot; (turns sole inwards) dorsi flexes the foot (flexes and points the toes up); rotates foot outwards. Supports the medial longitudinal arch of the foot.
Soleus	Calf of the leg, situated below the gastrocnemius muscle. Inserts through the achilles tendon into the heel	Plantar flexes the foot.
Peroneus longus	Lateral side of the lower leg	Plantar flexes the foot and everts (turns sole outwards). Supports the foot arches.
Extensor digitorum longus	Lateral side of the front of the lower leg	Plantar flexes the foot and extends the toes.
Flexor digitorum longus	Front of lower leg to the toes	Dorsi flexes and inverts the foot. Supports the lateral longitudinal arch of the foot.
Achilles tendon	Attached to the soleus and gastrocnemius down to the heel	Raises the foot when related muscle contracts.
Extensor digitorum tendons	Tops of toes	Straightens the toes when related muscle contracts.
Flexor digitorum tendons	Underneath the toes	Bends the toes when related muscle contracts.

THE BONES

When carrying out a facial massage you will feel below your hands the underlying bones. **Bone** is the hardest structure in the body: it protects the underlying structures, gives shape to the body, and provides an attachment point for our muscles, thereby allowing movement.

The skeleton is made up of many bones. Each bone is connected to its neighbour by *connective tissue*, a structural tissue that supports, surrounds and links different parts of the body. Fibrous connective tissue is used for immovable joints such as those of the cranium. *Fibro-cartilage* is used for semi-immovable joints such as those between the bones of the vertebrae. The most common joints – *synovial joints* – are freely moveable and are loosely held together by a form of connective tissue called a *ligament*.

Bones have different shapes, according to their function.

Kinds of bones

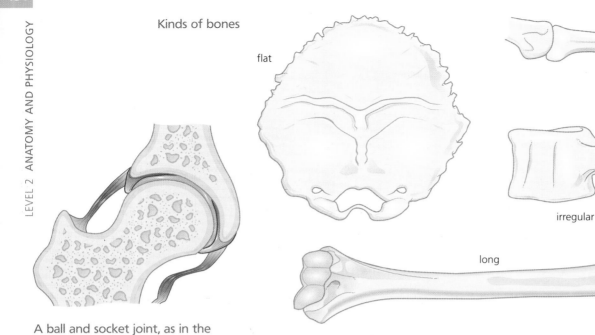

flat

short

irregular

long

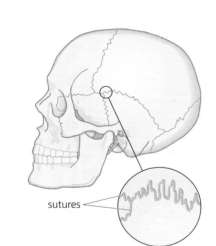

A ball and socket joint, as in the shoulder

sutures

Sutures

Bones of the head

The bones which form the head are collectively known as the **skull**. The skull can be divided into two parts, the face and the cranium, which together are made up of 22 bones:

- the 14 facial bones form the face;
- the eight cranial bones form the rest of the head.

As well as forming our facial features, the facial bones support other structures such as the eyes and the teeth. Some of these bones, such as the nasal bone, are made from **cartilage**, a softer tissue than bone.

The cranium surrounds and protects the brain. The bones are thin and slightly curved, and are held together by connective tissue. After childhood, the joints become immovable, and are called **sutures**.

Bones of the face

facial bones (14)

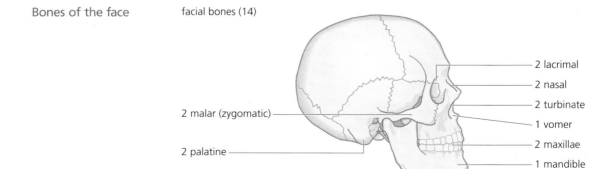

2 lacrimal
2 nasal
2 turbinate
1 vomer
2 maxillae
1 mandible

2 malar (zygomatic)

2 palatine

Facial bones

Bone	Number	Location	Function
Nasal	2	The nose	Form the bridge of the nose
Vomer	1	The nose	Forms the dividing bony wall of the nose
Palatine	2	The nose	Form the floor and wall of the nose and the roof of the mouth
Turbinate	2	The nose	Form the outer walls of the nose
Lacrimal	2	The eye sockets	Form the inner walls of the eye sockets; contain a small groove for the tear duct
Malar (zygomatic)	2	The cheek	Form the cheekbones
Maxillae	2	The upper jaw	Fused together, to form the upper jaw, which holds the upper teeth
Mandible	1	The lower jaw	The largest and strongest of the facial bones; holds the lower teeth

Cranial bones

Bone	Number	Location	Function
Occipital	1	The lower back of the cranium	Contains a large hole called the *foramen magnum*: through this pass the spinal cord, the nerves and blood vessels
Parietal	2	The sides of the cranium	Fused together to form the sides and top of the head (the 'crown')
Frontal	1	The forehead	Forms the forehead and the upper walls of the eye sockets
Temporal	2	The sides of the head	Provide two muscle attachment points: the mastoid process and the zygomatic process
Ethmoid	1	Between the eye sockets	Forms part of the nasal cavities
Sphenoid	1	The base of the cranium the back of the eye sockets	A bat-shaped bone that joins together all the bones of the cranium

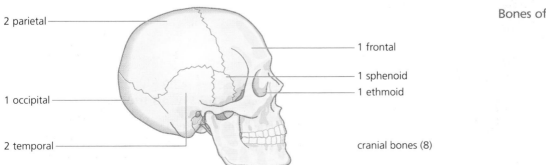

Bones of the cranium

2 parietal
1 occipital
2 temporal
1 frontal
1 sphenoid
1 ethmoid
cranial bones (8)

Bones of the neck, chest and shoulder

Bone	Number	Location	Function
Cervical vertebra	7	The neck	These vertebrae form the top of the spinal column: the *atlas* is the first vertebra, which supports the skull; the *axis* is the second vertebra, which allows rotation of the head
Hyoid	1	A U-shaped bone at the front of the neck	Supports the tongue
Clavicle	2	Slender long bones at the base of the neck	Commonly called the *collar bones,* these form a joint with the sternum and the scapula bones, allowing movement at the shoulder
Scapula	2	Triangular bones in the upper back	Commonly called the *shoulder blades*, the scapulae provide attachment for muscles which move the arms. The *shoulder girdle*, which allows movement at the shoulder, is composed of the clavicles and the scapulae
Humerus	2	The upper bones of the arms	Form ball-and-socket joints with the scapulae: these joints allow movement in any direction
Sternum	1	The breastbone	Protects the inner organs; provides a surface for muscle attachment and supports muscle movement

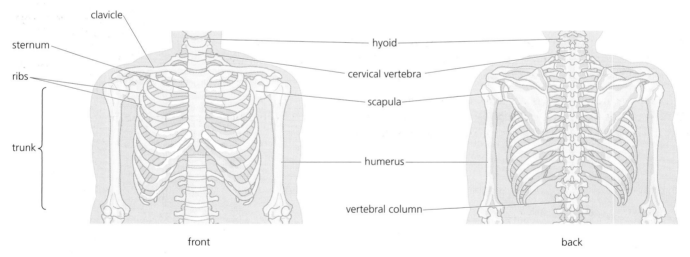

front   back

Bones of the neck, chest and shoulder

ACTIVITY

Identifying bones in the hand
Look very closely at your hand. Can you identify where the bones are? Try feeling the bones with your other hand. How many can you feel?

The hand and the forearm

The bones of the hand

The wrist consists of eight small **carpal** bones, which glide over one another to allow movement. This is called a **condyloid** or **gliding joint**.

There are then five **metacarpal** bones that make up the palm of the hand.

The fingers are made up of 14 individual bones called **phalanges** – two in each of the thumbs, and three in each of the fingers.

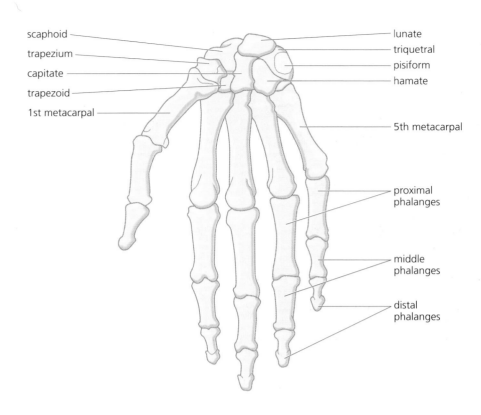

scaphoid
trapezium
capitate
trapezoid
1st metacarpal

lunate
triquetral
pisiform
hamate

5th metacarpal

proximal phalanges

middle phalanges

distal phalanges

Bones of the hand and wrist

The bones of the arm

The arm is made up of three long bones: the **humerus** is the bone of the upper arm, from the shoulder to the elbow; the **radius** and **ulna** lie side by side in the lower arm, from the elbow to the wrist.

Having two bones in the lower arm makes it easier for your wrist to rotate. This movement that causes the palm to face downwards is called **pronation**; the movement that causes it to face upwards is called **supination**.

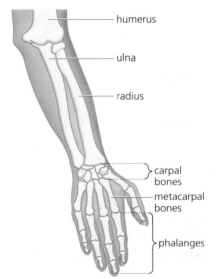

humerus

ulna

radius

carpal bones

metacarpal bones

phalanges

Bones of the arm

The foot and the lower leg

The bones of the foot

The foot is made up of seven **tarsal** (ankle) bones, five **metatarsal** (ball of foot) bones, and 14 **phalanges** (toes). These bones fit together to form arches, which help to support the foot and to absorb the impact when we walk, run and jump.

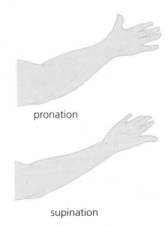

pronation

supination

Pronation and supination

Bones of the foot

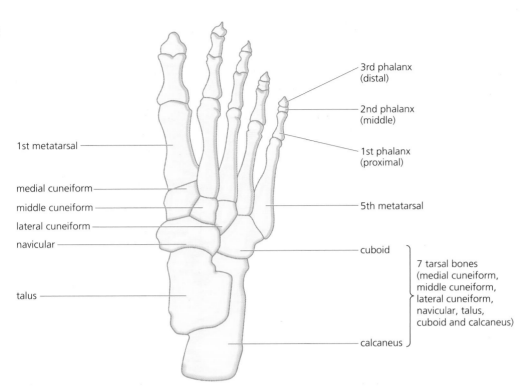

3rd phalanx
(distal)

2nd phalanx
(middle)

1st phalanx
(proximal)

1st metatarsal

medial cuneiform

middle cuneiform

lateral cuneiform

navicular

talus

5th metatarsal

cuboid

7 tarsal bones
(medial cuneiform,
middle cuneiform,
lateral cuneiform,
navicular, talus,
cuboid and calcaneus)

calcaneus

The arches of the foot

The **arches** of the foot are created by the formation of the bones and joints, and supported by ligaments. These arches support the weight of the body and help to preserve balance when we walk on even surfaces.

The longitudinal arch runs longitudinally from the calcaneus to the metatarsals. The arch on the inside aspect of the foot is the medial longitudinal arch, on the outside aspect it is the lateral longitudinal arch. The transverse arch lies perpendicular to this in the metatarsal area, as shown below.

> **TIP** ✔
>
> **Arches**
> Footprints made by bare feet show that only part of the foot touches the ground. Feet with reduced arches are referred to as 'flat feet', caused by weak ligaments and tendons

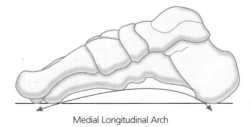

Medial Longitudinal Arch

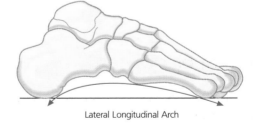

Lateral Longitudinal Arch

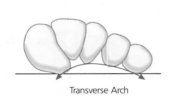

Transverse Arch

Arches of the foot

The bones of the lower leg

The lower leg is made up of two long bones, the **tibia** and the **fibula**. These bones have joints with the upper leg (at the knee) and with the foot (at the ankle). Having two bones in the lower leg – as with the forearm – allows a greater range of movement to be achieved at the ankle.

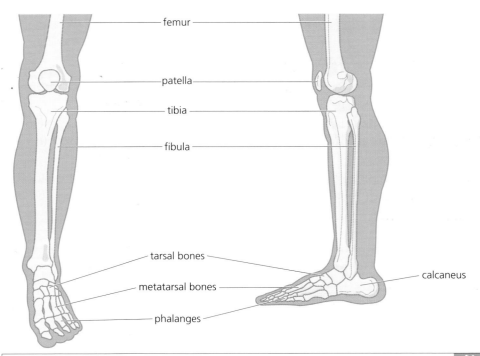

Bones of the lower leg

Bones of the lower leg

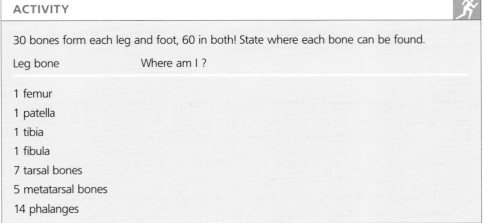

ACTIVITY

30 bones form each leg and foot, 60 in both! State where each bone can be found.

Leg bone	Where am I ?
1 femur	
1 patella	
1 tibia	
1 fibula	
7 tarsal bones	
5 metatarsal bones	
14 phalanges	

THE BLOOD

Composition and function of blood

A healthy muscle is activated by a nerve supply, which effects movement; the necessary oxygen and nutrients are brought by the blood.

Blood transports various substances around the body:

- It carries oxygen from our lungs, and nutrients from our digested food to supply energy – these allow the cells to develop and divide, and the muscles to function.

- It carries waste products and carbon dioxide away for elimination from the body.

- It carries various cells and substances which allow the body to prevent or fight disease.

TIP

Blood
Blood helps to maintain the body temperature at 36.8°C: varying blood flow near to the skin surface increases or diminishes heat loss.

The main constituents of blood

Blood consists of the following:

- **Plasma** A straw-coloured liquid: mainly water, with foods and carbon dioxide.
- **Red blood cells (erythrocytes)** These cells appear red because they contain **haemoglobin**; it is this that carries oxygen from the lungs to the body cells.
- **White blood cells (leucocytes)** There are several types of white blood cells: their main role is to protect the body, destroying foreign bodies and dead cells, and carrying away the debris (a process known as **phagocytosis**).
- **Platelets (thrombocytes)** When blood is exposed to air, as happens when the skin is injured, these cells bind together to form a clot.
- **Other chemicals** Hormones also are transported in the blood – 'chemical messengers' to target tissues.

The circulation

The circulation of blood is under the control of the **heart**, a muscular organ which pumps the blood around the body.

TIP

Pulse rate
The pumping of the blood under pressure through the carotid arteries can be felt as a pulse in the neck. Press gently on the neck just inside the position of the sternomastoid muscle.
   Pulse rate relates to the speed of the heartbeat. The strength of the pulse is affected by the pressure of the blood flow leaving the heart.
   Blood pressure increases during activity and decreases during rest.
   Relaxing treatments such as facial massage lower blood pressure.

Blood leaving the heart is carried in large, elastic tubes called **arteries**. The blood to the head arrives via the **carotid arteries**, which are connected via other main arteries to the heart. There are two main carotid arteries, one on each side of the neck.

These arteries divide into smaller branches, the *internal carotid* and the *external carotid*. The **internal carotid artery** passes the temporal bone and enters the head, taking blood to the brain. The **external carotid artery** stays outside the skull, and divides into branches:

- the **occipital branch** supplies the back of the head and the scalp;
- the **temporal branch** supplies the sides of the face, the head, the scalp and the skin;
- the **facial branch** supplies the muscles and tissues of the face.

These arteries also divide repeatedly, successive vessels becoming smaller and smaller until they form tiny blood **capillaries**. These vessels are just one cell

The blood supply to the head

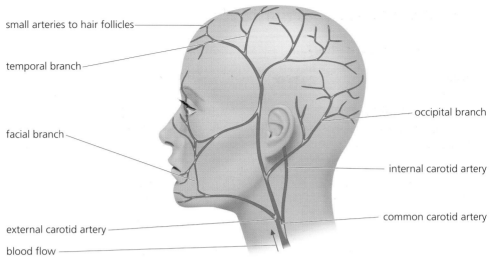

small arteries to hair follicles

temporal branch

facial branch

external carotid artery

blood flow

occipital branch

internal carotid artery

common carotid artery

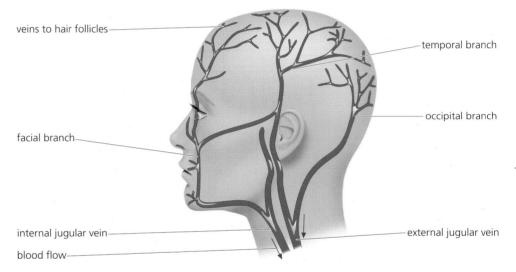

The blood supply from the head

veins to hair follicles

facial branch

internal jugular vein

blood flow

temporal branch

occipital branch

external jugular vein

thick, allowing substances carried in the blood to pass through them into the **tissue fluid** which bathes and nourishes the cells of the various body tissues.

The blood capillaries begin to join up again, forming first small vessels called **venules**, then larger vessels called **veins**. These return the blood to the heart.

Veins are less elastic than arteries, and are closer to the skin's surface. Along their course are **valves**, which prevent the backflow of blood.

The main veins are the external and internal jugular veins. The **internal jugular vein** and its main branch, the **facial vein**, carry blood from the face and head. The **external jugular vein** carries blood from the scalp and has two branches: the **occipital branch** and the **temporal branch**. The jugular veins join to enter the **subclavian vein**, which lies above the clavicle.

Blood returns to the heart, which pumps it to the lungs, where the red blood cells take on fresh oxygen, and where carbon dioxide is expelled from the blood. The blood returns to the heart, and begins its next journey round the body.

HEALTH AND SAFETY

Capillaries
The strength and elasticity of the capillary walls can be damaged, for example by a blow to the tissues.

The arteries of the arm and hand

The arm and hand are nourished by a system of arteries that carry oxygen-rich blood to the tissues. You can see the colour of the blood from the capillaries beneath the nail: it is these that give the nail bed its pink colour.

The brachial artery supplies blood to the upper arm. This branches into the ulnar and radial artery, which supplies the forearm and fingers. The radial and ulnar arteries are connected across the palm by a superficial and deep palmar arch. These arteries divide to form the metacarpal and digital arteries, which supply the palm and fingers.

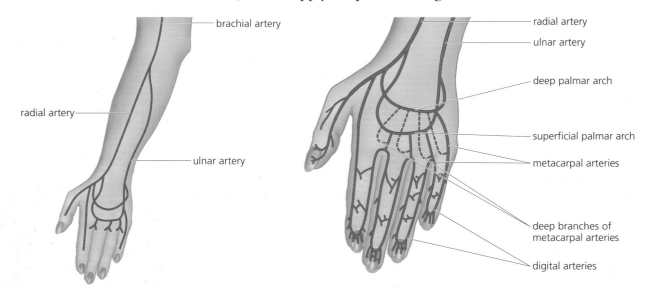

brachial artery

radial artery

ulnar artery

radial artery

ulnar artery

deep palmar arch

superficial palmar arch

metacarpal arteries

deep branches of metacarpal arteries

digital arteries

Arteries of the arm and hand

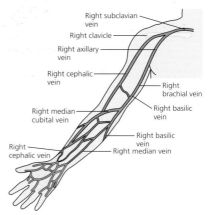

Right subclavian vein

Right clavicle

Right axillary vein

Right cephalic vein

Right brachial vein

Right basilic vein

Right median cubital vein

Right basilic vein

Right cephalic vein

Right median vein

Veins of the arms and hands

The veins of the arms and hands

Veins deliver deoxygenated blood back to the heart. Blood which has had oxygen removed appears blue. Veins often pass through muscles. Each time muscles contract, veins are squeezed and the blood is pushed along. Massage is particularly beneficial to help this process.

Blood in the digital veins drains blood from the fingers. The dorsal arch drains blood from the hands. The cephalic and basilic veins drain blood from the forearm.

The arteries of the foot and lower leg

The lower leg and feet are nourished by a system of arteries which bring blood to the tissues.

The anterior and tibial artery supplies blood to the lower leg and foot. The peroneal artery branches off the posterior tibial artery. At the ankle the anterior tibial artery becomes the dorsalis pedis artery. The posterior tibial artery divides at the ankle to form the medial and lateral plantar arteries. The plantar and dorsalis pedis arteries supply the digital arteries of the toes.

When it is cold, and when the circulation is poor, insufficient blood reaches the feet and they feel cold. Severe circulation problems in the feet may lead to **chilblains**.

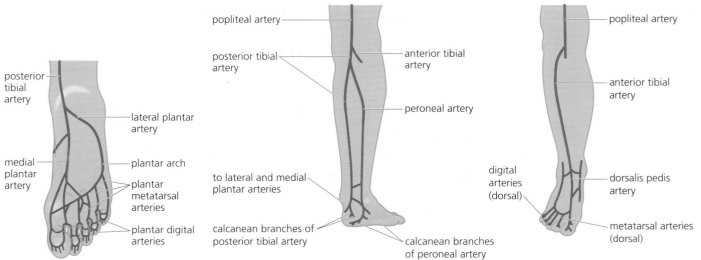

posterior
tibial
artery

lateral plantar
artery

medial
plantar
artery

plantar arch

plantar
metatarsal
arteries

plantar digital
arteries

Arteries of the foot

popliteal artery

posterior tibial
artery

anterior tibial
artery

peroneal artery

to lateral and medial
plantar arteries

calcanean branches of
posterior tibial artery

calcanean branches
of peroneal artery

Arteries of the lower leg

popliteal artery

anterior tibial
artery

digital
arteries
(dorsal)

dorsalis pedis
artery

metatarsal arteries
(dorsal)

The veins of the foot and lower leg

The digital veins from the toes drain into the plantar and dorsal venous arch. The dorsalis pedis veins drain to the saphenous vein. The following deep veins drain the lower leg: the posterior tibial vein at the back of the leg and the peroneal vein, and the anterior tibial vein at the front of the leg. The deep tibial veins join to form the popliteal vein.

THE LYMPHATIC SYSTEM

The **lymphatic system** is closely connected to the blood system, and can be considered as supplementing it. Its primary function is defensive: to remove bacteria and foreign materials, thereby preventing infection. It also drains away excess fluids for elimination from the body.

The lymphatic system consists of the fluid **lymph**, the **lymph vessels** and the **lymph nodes** (or glands). You may have experienced swelling of the lymph nodes in the neck when you have been ill.

Unlike the blood circulation, the lymphatic system has no muscular pump equivalent to the heart. Instead, the lymph moves through the vessels and around the body because of movements such as contractions of large muscles. Facial massage can play an important part in assisting this flow of lymph fluid, thereby encouraging the improved removal of the waste products transported in the lymph.

Lymph

Lymph is a straw-coloured fluid, derived from blood plasma, which has filtered through the walls of the capillaries. The composition of lymph is similar to that of blood, though less oxygen and fewer nutrients are available. In the spaces between the cells where there are no blood capillaries, lymph provides nourishment. It also carries **lymphocytes**

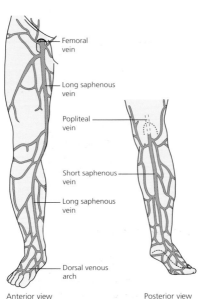

Femoral
vein

Long saphenous
vein

Popliteal
vein

Short saphenous
vein

Long saphenous
vein

Dorsal venous
arch

Anterior view

Posterior view

Veins of the foot and lower leg

(a type of white blood cell), which plays an important role in the immune system. They can destroy dangerous cells and disease causing bacteria and viruses directly.

Lymph travels only in one direction: from body tissues back towards the heart.

Lymph vessels

Lymph vessels often run very close to veins, forming an extensive network throughout the body. The lymph moves quite slowly, and there are valves along the lymph vessels to prevent backflow of the lymph.

The lymph vessels join to form larger lymph vessels, which eventually flow into one or other of two large lymphatic vessels: the **thoracic duct** (or **left lymphatic duct**) and the **right lymphatic duct**. The thoracic duct receives lymph from the left side of the head, neck, chest, abdomen and lower body; the right lymphatic duct receives lymph from the right side of the head and upper body.

Lymph vessels in the body

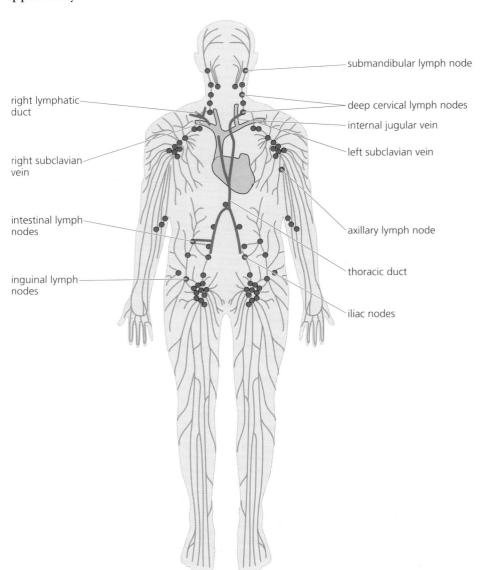

- submandibular lymph node
- right lymphatic duct
- deep cervical lymph nodes
- internal jugular vein
- right subclavian vein
- left subclavian vein
- intestinal lymph nodes
- axillary lymph node
- inguinal lymph nodes
- thoracic duct
- iliac nodes

These principal lymphatic vessels then empty their contents into a vein at the base of the neck, which in turn empties into the **vena cava**. The lymph is mixed into the venous blood as it is returned to the heart.

Lymph nodes

Lymph nodes or **glands** are tiny oval structures which filter the lymph, extracting poisons, pus and bacteria, and thus defending the body against infection by destroying harmful organisms. **Lymphocytes**, found in the lymph glands, are special cells which produce **antibodies** which enable us to resist invasion by micro-organisms.

When performing massage, the hands should be used to apply pressure to direct the lymph towards the nearest lymph node: this encourages the speedy removal of waste products. Various groups of lymph nodes drain the lymph of the head and neck.

Lymph nodes of the head

- The **buccal group** drains the eyelids, the nose and the skin of the face.
- The **mandibular group** drains the chin, the lips, the nose and the cheeks.
- The **mastoid group** drains the skin of the ear and the temple area.
- The **occipital group** drains the back of the scalp and the upper neck.
- The **submental group** drains the chin and the lower lip.
- The **parotid group** drains the nose, eyelids and ears.

Lymph nodes of the neck

- The **superficial cervical group** drains the back of the head and the neck.
- The **lower deep cervical group** drains the back area of the scalp and the neck.

Lymph nodes of the chest and arms

- The nodes of the armpit area drain various regions of the arms and chest.

> **TIP** ✓
>
> Frontal–Temporal–Parietal–Occipital–Mandible (mandibular)–Cervical
> Learn and remember these names of the main regions of the head and neck. Not only will this assist you in recalling the names and locations of the bones, it will also help you greatly with the names and locations of muscles, arteries, veins, nerves and lymph nodes.

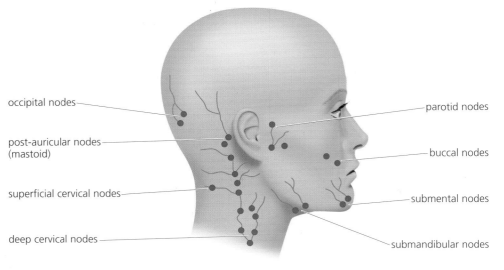

Lymph nodes of the head and neck

occipital nodes

post-auricular nodes (mastoid)

superficial cervical nodes

deep cervical nodes

parotid nodes

buccal nodes

submental nodes

submandibular nodes

Assessment of knowledge and understanding

You have now learnt about the related anatomy and physiology for the beauty therapy units with an essential knowledge requirement.

To test your level of knowledge, answer the following short questions. These will prepare you for your summative (final) assessment.

Skin structure and function

1 Referring to the cross section of the skin, name and briefly describe the function of the structures shown in 1–4.

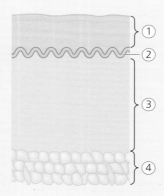

2 Name six functions of the skin.

3 Name the layers of the epidermis shown in 1–5. Which layer is continuously being shed?

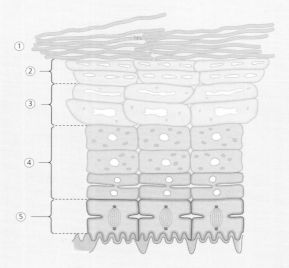

4 What are tissues? Name three types of body tissues.

5 Describe the structure of the dermis and label the illustration of the dermis shown below.

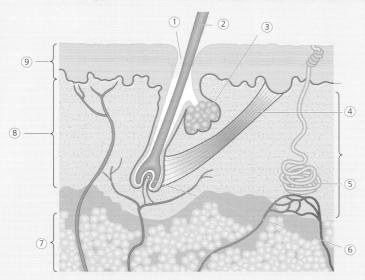

6 What is the function of the sensory nerves in the skin?

7 How is the temperature of the body regulated?

8 What gives the skin its colour? How does the skin become tanned on exposure to ultra-violet light?

9 Name two appendages of the skin and describe their function.

10 Name two protein fibres found in the reticular layer of the skin and describe their functions.

Structure of hair

1 Referring to the cross section of the hair follicle, briefly describe the name and function of each numbered area.

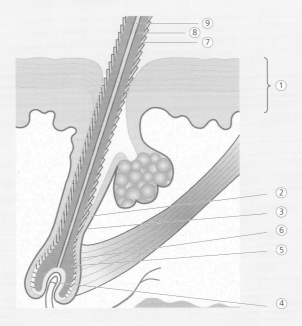

2 What is the soft downy hair on the face called?

3 What is coarse pigmented hair called?

4 What is the name of the protein found in skin cells?

5 What is the function of the dermal papilla in relation to the hair and the hair growth cycle?

Hair growth cycle

1 What are the different stages of the hair growth cycle called?

2 What happens to the hair at each stage?

3 What relevance has the hair growth cycle for a wax depilation treatment?

4 What is the difference in the time between the hair growth cycle anagen to telogen for scalp hair and eyebrow hair?

Nail structure and function

1 Referring to the cross section of the nail, briefly describe the name and function of each of the numbered areas.

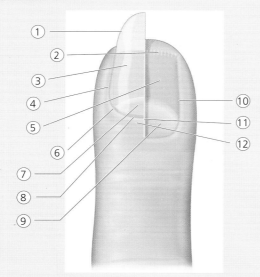

2 Why does the nail bed appear pink?

3 Why does the nail bed contain nerve endings?

Nail growth

1 In which part of the nail structure do the cells divide to form the nail?

2 As the nail cells grow forward they harden; what is this process called?

3 How long does it take for a fingernail to grow from cuticle to free edge?

4 When do nails grow faster – in summer or winter?

5 What is the difference in growth rate between fingernails and toenails?

6 Why does localised massage to the hand and foot encourage healthy nail growth?

7 What other factors affect nail growth?

Muscle groups in parts of the body, position structure and function

1 What happens when muscles contract?

2 What structure attaches a muscle to a bone?

3 On the diagram of the muscles of the face, name muscles 1–6. What are the actions of these muscles?

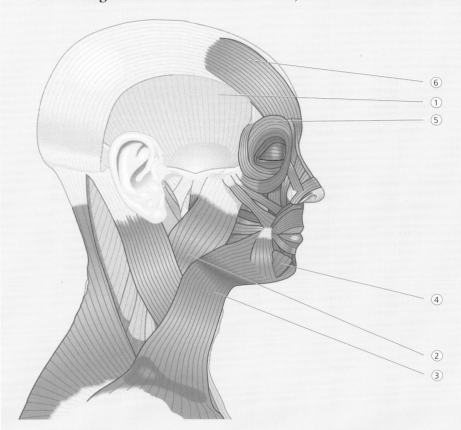

4 On the diagram of muscles that move the head and neck, name muscles 1–5. What are the actions of these muscles?

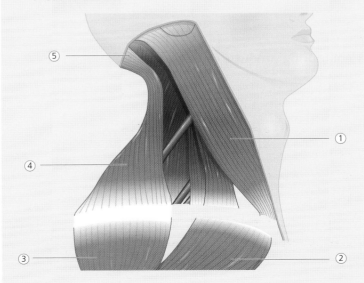

5 What is the collective name for the group of muscles that bend the wrist, drawing it towards the forearm?

6 What is the collective name for the group of muscles that straighten the wrist and the hand?

Muscle tone

1 What is muscle tone?

2 Name four properties of muscle tissue.

3 With age, the facial expressions that we make every day produce lines on the skin – frown lines. What happens to the tone of the muscles with age?

4 What effect does massage have on the tone of muscles?

Bones in parts of the body, position structure and function

1 What is the function of bone?

2 Bones have different shapes according to their function. Name three shapes of bones and where they are found.

3 What attaches bones to different parts of the body?

4 On the diagram of the cranium name the bones numbered 1–8.

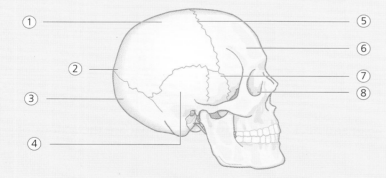

5 Name three facial bones to which you may apply contouring products during make-up.

6 Which of the bones form the:
   ● face
   ● cranium?

7 Name the bone or bones that form the
   ● forehead
   ● cheekbones
   ● jawbone.

8 On the diagram of the bones of the neck, chest and shoulder name the bones and their functions (items 1–7).

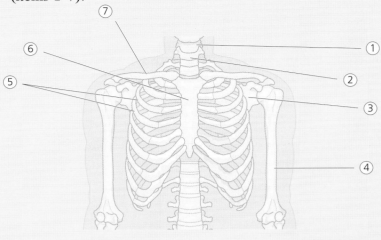

front

9 The wrist is made up of eight small carpal bones, which glide over one another to allow movement. Name them.

10 What type of joint is found in the wrist?

11 How do the fingers move?

12 Name and discuss the function of the arches of the foot.

13 Name the bones that form the ankle.

Composition and function of blood and lymph

1 What are the main constituents of blood?

2 What are the main constituents of lymph?

3 What does blood transport around the body?

4 What is the difference in function in the body between blood and lymph?

5 What is the function of lymph nodes or glands?

6 On the diagram of the head, name the lymph nodes numbered 1–5.

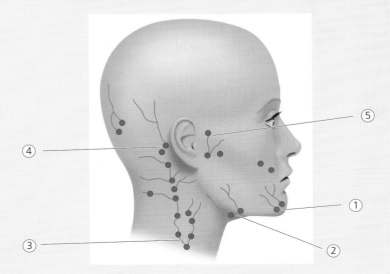

7 Blood helps to maintain body temperature. What is normal body temperature?

8 How does massage affect the circulation of lymph?

Blood flow and pulse rate

1 The circulation of the blood is under the control of the heart, which pumps blood around the body. On the illustration below label the arteries that transport blood to the head and veins that return blood from the head.

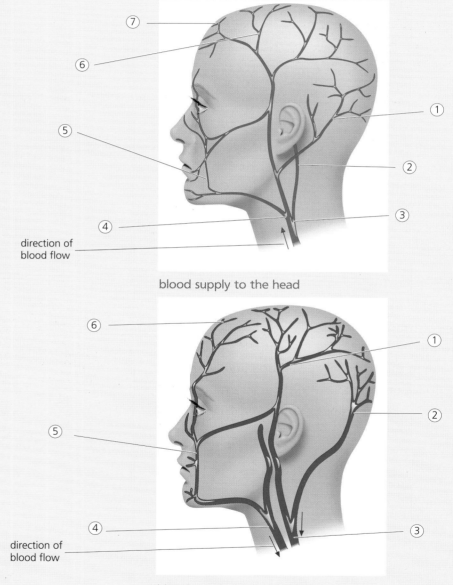

blood supply to the head

blood supply from the head

2 How does the pressure of blood leaving the heart affect pulse rate?

3 How does activity affect blood pressure?

4 How does massage affect blood flow and pulse rate?

Central nervous system and autonomic nervous system

1 The neurological system transmits messages between the brain and other parts of the body. There are two main divisions. What are they called?

2 What is the central nervous system composed of?

3 What is the difference between sensory nerves and motor nerves?

4 To what are the main sensory nerve endings in the skin receptive?

5 How do nerve impulses pass along nerve fibres?

6 How do nerves stimulate muscles to contract?

7 What is meant by the autonomic nervous system?

8 How many pairs of cranial nerves emerge from the brain?

9 Those of concern to the beauty therapist when performing facial massage are the 5th, 7th and 11th cranial nerves.
What is the function of the:
- 5th, known as trigeminal nerve
- 7th, known as the facial nerve
- 11th, known as the accessory nerve?

10 Name the main branches of the 7th cranial facial nerve, items 1–5 in the diagram.

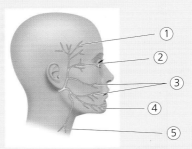

beauty
treatments

chapter 6

Improve and maintain facial skin condition

Learning objectives

This unit describes how to improve and maintain the facial skin condition using a variety of treatments.

It describes the competencies to enable you to:

- **consult with the client**
- **prepare for the treatment**
- **plan the treatment**
- **improve and maintain skin condition**
- **complete the treatment**

When providing facial treatments it is important to use the skills you have learnt in the following core mandatory units:

UNIT G1 Ensure your own actions reduce risks to health and safety

UNIT G6 Promote additional products or services to clients

UNIT G8 Develop and maintain your effectiveness at work

 Essential anatomy and physiology knowledge for this unit, BT4, is identified on the checklist in Chapter 5, page 101.

BASICS OF SKIN CARE

Nutrition

If the skin is to function efficiently, the skin must be cared for both internally and externally.

Internally, a nutritionally balanced diet is vital to the health and appearance of the skin. A number of skin allergies and disorders are in part the result of a poorly balanced diet, including highly processed food, alcohol and lack of essential nutrients.

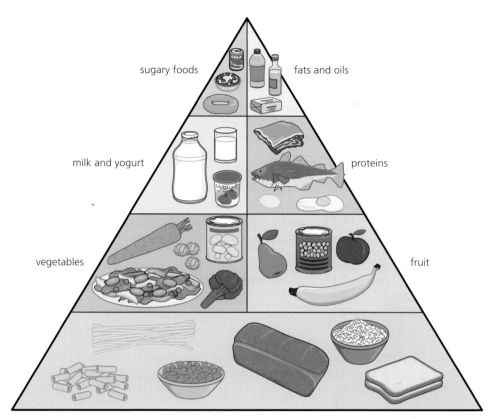

starches

Chart for a balanced diet

Foods contain the chemical substances we need for health and growth, the **nutrients**: a healthy diet contains all the essential nutrients. The nutrients are carried to the skin in the blood, where they nourish the cells in the processes of growth and repair.

There are six principal groups of nutrients.

Carbohydrates

Carbohydrates provide energy quickly. They are either simple sugars or starches that the body can turn into simple sugars.

Food sources: Carbohydrates are found in fruit, vegetables, milk, grains and honey.

Fats

Fats provide a concentrated source of energy, and are also used in carrying certain vitamins (see below) around the body. Fat is stored in the body around organs and muscles and under the skin. However, if too much fat is deposited under the skin, the elastic fibres there may be damaged by the expansion of the 'adipose' tissue. Fat is also used in the formation of sebum, the skin's natural lubricant.

Food sources: Although this is not always evident, fats are present in almost all foods, from plants and from animals.

TIP	

Five a day rule
Eat at least the recommended five servings of fruit and fresh vegetables every day. These foods provide vital vitamins and minerals that keep the skin healthy.
A serving is:

- 1 small glass of pure fruit juice;
- 3 heaped tablespoons of fruit salad;
- 4 heaped tablespoons of vegetables;
- 1 medium fruit (an orange);
- 2 small fruits (plums);
- 1 dessert bowl of salad.

Proteins

Proteins provide material for the growth and repair of body tissue, and are also a source of energy. Severe protein deficiency in children gives the skin a yellowish appearance, known as **jaundice**.

Food sources: Proteins are found in meat, fish, eggs, dairy products, grains and nuts.

Minerals

Minerals provide materials for growth and repair and for regulation of the body processes. The major minerals are calcium, iron, phosphorus, sulphur, sodium, potassium, chlorine and magnesium. Of these, the most important to the skin is iron. A pale, dry skin may indicate **anaemia**, caused by a shortage of iron.

Food sources: Fruit and vegetables; iron is found in liver, egg yolks and green vegetables.

Vitamins

Vitamins regulate the body's processes and contribute to its resistance to disease. Vitamins are divided into two groups, according to whether they are soluble in water or in fat:

- the fat-soluble vitamins are A, D, E and K;
- the water-soluble vitamins are B and C.

The vitamins most important to the condition of the skin are vitamins A, B_2, B_3, C and E.

Vitamin A Insufficient vitamin A in the diet leads to **hyperkeratinisation** (production of too much keratin). This causes blockages in the skin tissue. The skin becomes rough and dry, and eye disorders such as styes may occur.

Food sources: Vitamin A is found in red, yellow and green vegetables, and in egg yolk, butter and cheese.

Vitamin B_2 Vitamin B_2 (also called **riboflavin**) helps to break down other foodstuffs, releasing energy needed by cells to function efficiently. A deficiency of vitamin B_2 causes the skin at the corners of the mouth to crack.

Food sources: Vitamin B_2 is found in brewer's yeast, milk products, leafy vegetables, liver and whole grains.

Vitamin B_3 Vitamin B_3 (also called **niacin**) has the same function as vitamin B_2, but is also vital in the maintenance of the tissues of the skin.

Food sources: Vitamin B_3 is found in meat, brewer's yeast, nuts and seeds.

Vitamin C Vitamin C (also called **ascorbic acid**) maintains healthy skin and is important for the production of collagen. A lack of vitamin C causes the capillaries to become fragile, and haemorrhages of the skin, such as bruising, may occur. Severe deficiency results in **scurvy**.

Food sources: Vitamin C is found in fruit and vegetables.

Vitamin E   Vitamin E is found in most foods. It is an antioxidant and helps prevent premature skin ageing. It helps to rehydrate the skin, calm inflammation and help skin healing.

Food sources: Vitamin E is found in most foods. The richest sources are vegetable oils, cereal products, eggs and meat.

Water

Water forms about two-thirds of the body's weight, and is an important component both inside and outside the body cells. At least one litre of water should be drunk every day, to avoid dehydration of the body and the skin.

Food sources: Water is also a constituent of many foods, including fruits and vegetables.

Fibre

Fibre is not broken down into nutrients, but it is very important for effective digestion.

Food sources: Fibre is found in fruit, vegetables and cereals.

Threats to the skin

Internal

Alcohol   **Alcohol** deprives the body of its vitamin reserves, especially vitamins B and C, which are necessary for a healthy skin. Alcohol also tends to dehydrate the body, including the skin.

Caffeine   Coffee, tea, cocoa and soft fizzy drinks contain a mild stimulant drug called **caffeine**. In moderate doses, such as two or three cups of coffee per day, caffeine is safe. If you drink too much, however, caffeine can cause nervousness, interfere with digestion, block the absorption of vitamins and minerals, and spoil the appearance of the skin, stimulating skin ageing.

Drugs   **Drugs** are chemical substances that affect the way our body performs. When they enter the body they are transported throughout the body in the blood. Recreational drugs are taken because they cause a particular effect or sensation which may feel good initially. Long term, they are harmful and addictive. Most affect the blood pressure and heart rate and stimulants, for example, can cause sweating, shaking and headaches. Heroin, in the class of painkillers called *narcotics*, ravages the skin, causing chronic dryness and premature ageing.

Smoking   **Smoking** interferes with cell respiration and slows down the circulation. This makes it harder for nutrients to reach the skin cells and for waste products to be eliminated. Cigarette smoking also releases a chemical that destroys vitamin C. This interferes with the production of collagen, and thereby contributes to premature wrinkling. Nicotine is a **toxic** substance – a poison!

HEALTH AND SAFETY

Weight loss
If you lose weight too quickly, your skin will sag and wrinkle.

HEALTH AND SAFETY

Alcohol intake
Alcohol intake is measured in units – one unit is one centilitre of pure alcohol and is equivalent to:
- 1 single measure of spirits;
- ½ pint lager, beer or cider;
- 1 small glass of wine.

A maximum of four units a day are recommended for men and a maximum of three units for women.

TIP

Caffeine
Advise your clients to replace tea with herbal infusions and to drink decaffeinated coffee (in moderation) rather than regular coffee.

HEALTH AND SAFETY

Smoking
Smoking depletes the body of vital nutrients, preventing their absorption.

Medication   Certain **medicines** taken by mouth can cause skin dehydration, oedema – swelling of the tissues – (this may for example be caused by steroids) or irregular skin pigmentation (sometimes caused by the contraceptive pill). During the initial consultation with the client, find out whether they are taking any medication – and take this into account in your diagnosis and treatment plan.

Stress   **Stress** is shown in the face as tension lines where the facial muscles are tight. Because blood and lymph cannot circulate properly, this causes a 'sluggish' skin condition and poor facial nutrition. A person suffering from stress usually experiences disturbed sleep or sleeplessness (**insomnia**). Lack of sleep causes the skin to become dull and puffy, especially the tissue beneath the eyes, where dark circles also appear. Too *much* sleep also can cause the facial tissue to become puffy – because the circulation is less active, body fluids collect in the tissues.

If someone is suffering from stress, they may drink more tea, coffee or alcohol, or smoke more cigarettes: this too damages the skin.

Stress and anxiety are often the underlying cause of certain skin disorders. Some skin conditions, such as boils and styes, appear at times of stress; others, such as psoriasis and eczema, may become much worse. At the consultation, try to determine whether the client is suffering from stress: if they are, make sure that the salon treatments promote relaxation.

External

As well as looking after the skin from the *inside*, by diet, it needs care from the *outside* – it must be kept clean, and it must be nourished.

With normal physiological functioning, the skin becomes oily, and sweat is deposited on its surface. The skin's natural oil (**sebum**) can easily build up and block the natural openings, the hair **follicles** and **pores**: this may lead to infection. Facial cosmetics too affect the health of the skin; if not regularly removed, they may cause congestion. Skin-care treatments help to maintain and improve the functioning of the skin.

Ultra-violet light   Although recently **ultra-violet** (**UV**) has been identified as a hazard to skin, it also has some *positive* effects. One of these is its ability to stimulate the production of **vitamin D**, which is absorbed into the bloodstream and nourishes and helps to maintain bone tissue. Second, UV light activates the pigment **melanin** in the skin, and thereby creates a **tan**. Many people feel better when they have a tan, as it gives a healthy appearance.

Ultra-violet light is divided into different bands. The most important to skin tanning are UVA and UVB. **UVA** stimulates the melanin in the skin to produce a rapid tan, which does not last very long. UVA penetrates deep into the dermis where it can cause premature ageing of the skin. **Free radicals** – highly reactive molecules which cause skin cells to degenerate – are also formed. These molecules disrupt production of collagen and elastin, the fibres that give skin its strength and elasticity. Reduced elasticity leads to wrinkling.

UVB stimulates the production of vitamin D. Melanin activation by UVB produces a longer-lasting tan than that produced by UVA. UVB is partially absorbed by the atmosphere – it has a shorter wavelength than UVA – and

The effects of UV
To see evidence of the damaging effects of ultra-violet on the skin, compare the skin on the back of your hands to skin on parts of the body that are not normally covered.

only ten per cent reaches the dermis. UVB causes thickening of the stratum corneum layer, which reflects ultra-violet away from the skin's surface.

UVB causes **sunburn**: the skin becomes red as the cells are damaged, and the skin may blister. UVB is also implicated in skin cancers, especially malignant melanoma.

The relaxing, warming effect of the sun is caused by the **infra-red (IR)** light. This penetrates the skin to the subcutaneous layer and is thought to speed skin ageing and possibly to cause a cancer called squamous cell carcinoma. The tan is actually a sign of skin damage, therefore, and both UV and IR probably contribute to photo-ageing – the premature ageing of the skin by light.

Although black skin has a high melanin content, which absorbs more ultra-violet and allows less to reach the dermis, it is not fully protected against the UV and still requires additional protection.

Chemical skin protection, or sunscreens, are designed to absorb ultra-violet light (UVA and UVB), reducing the rate of skin ageing in all skin types. Various sunscreens are available, classified by numbers according to their sun-protection factor (SPF). This is the amount of protection that the sunscreen gives you from the sun. The application of the sunscreen extends your natural skin protection, allowing you to stay in the sun for longer without burning. For example, if normally you can be in the sun for ten minutes before the skin begins to go red, a sunscreen with an SPF of ten will allow you 10×10 minutes' – 100 minutes' – safe exposure in the sun.

Artificial UV light produced by sunbeds, used for cosmetic skin tanning, also causes premature ageing. Most sunbeds use concentrated UVA, which causes dermal tissue damage resulting in lines and wrinkles.

It may take years to see the effects of the dermal damage caused by unprotected UV exposure, but once they have occurred the effects are irreversible. UVA rays are present all year round, so to prevent premature ageing, cosmetic preparations containing sunscreens should be worn at all times.

Climate
Sebum, the skin's natural grease, provides an oily protective film over the surface of the skin that reduces evaporation. Despite this, unprotected exposure of the skin to the environment allows evaporation from the epidermis which results in a dry, dehydrated skin condition.

The climate has several effects on the skin:

- *Sebum production* When the skin is exposed to the cold, less sebum is produced. The skin has reduced protection, allowing moisture to evaporate.
- *Perspiration* In very hot weather more moisture is lost as **perspiration**: perspiration increases, to cool the skin and regulate the body's temperature.

Sunbathing
Never wear perfume, cosmetic products or deodorants when sunbathing, either in natural sunlight or in artificially produced (sun-canopy) ultra-violet. The chemicals in these products can sensitise the skin, causing an allergic skin reaction.

Pigmentation marks caused by repeated exposure to UV light eventually remain, even without the exposure to UV. Some clients dislike such marks, and you could advise them on camouflage make-up.

Ultra-violet can penetrate water to a depth of one metre, so even when swimming you need to wear a sunscreen. Special waterproof products are designed for this purpose.

To acquire a tan without the damaging effects of the sun or sunbeds, use a *fake tanning* preparation. This treatment is becoming popular in the beauty therapist's salon.

At the consultation, ask the client their occupation: this will guide you as to their likely skin-care requirements. The client who works outdoors, for example, will have different treatment needs from the one who works indoors.

- *Humidity* Moisture loss from the skin is also affected by the **humidity** (water content) of the surrounding air. In hot, dry weather humidity will be low, so water loss will be high. In temperate, damp conditions humidity will be high, so water loss will be low.

- *Extremes of temperature* Alternating heat and cold often leads to the formation of **broken capillaries**. These appear as fine red lines on Caucasian skin, and as discoloration on black skin.

- *Stratum corneum* The cells of the stratum corneum multiply with repeated unprotected exposure to the climate, as the body's natural defence.

The damaging effects caused by the climate can be reduced by using protective skin-care preparations such as moisturisers. These spread a layer of oil over the skin's surface, reducing evaporation.

Environmental stress and pollution
Further causes of moisture loss include harsh alkaline chemicals such as detergents and soaps – which remove sebum from the skin's surface – and air conditioning and central heating.

Environmental **pollutants** such as lead, mercury, cadmium and aluminium can accumulate in the body. One result is the formation of dangerous chemicals that attack proteins in the cells. Such pollutants find their way into food through polluted waters, rain and dust. To protect the body, always wash vegetables thoroughly, and eat a diet rich in vitamins C and E.

Air pollution, involving carbon from smoke, chemical discharges from factories, and fumes from car exhausts, should be removed from the skin by effective cleansing. Absorption of these pollutants is reduced by the application of moisturiser: this forms a barrier over the skin's surface.

Skin-care treatments

The beauty therapist has the professional expertise to help each client improve the appearance and condition of their skin by the application of appropriate cosmetic treatments and preparations. The facial skin services the beauty therapist offers include:

- consultation and skin analysis;
- skin cleansing;
- specialised skin-care treatments;
- manual massage of the face, neck and shoulders;
- the application of face masks or face packs;
- facial cosmetic make-up.

The beauty therapist cannot change the underlying skin type, which is genetically determined, but they can keep the physiological characteristics of each skin type in check.

SKIN TYPES

The basic structure of the skin does not vary from person to person, but the physiological functioning of its different features does; it is this that gives us **skin types**.

The first and most important part of a facial treatment is the correct diagnosis of the skin type. This is carried out at the beginning of each facial treatment. The beauty therapist must choose the correct skin-care products and facial treatments for the client's skin type. This assessment is called a **skin analysis**.

Basic types

There are four main skin types:

- normal;
- dry;
- oily (also known as greasy);
- combination.

Normal skin

Normal skin is often referred to as **balanced**, because it is neither too oily nor too dry. Because when young this skin type seldom has any problems, such as blemishes, it is often neglected. Neglect causes the skin to become dry, especially around the eyes, cheeks and neck, where the skin is thinner.

A normal skin type in adults is very rare. It has these characteristics:

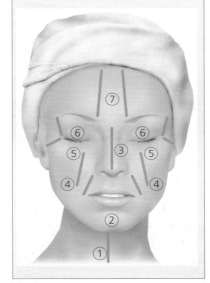

Normal skin

- the pore size is small or medium;
- the moisture content is good;
- the skin texture is even, neither too thick nor too thin;
- the colour is healthy (because of good blood circulation);
- the skin elasticity is good, when young;
- the skin feels firm to the touch;
- the skin pigmentation is even-coloured;
- the skin is usually free from blemishes.

Dry skin

Dr John Gray, *The World of Skin Care*

Dry skin is lacking in either sebum or moisture, or both. Because sebum limits moisture loss by evaporation from the skin, skin with insufficient sebum rapidly loses moisture. The resulting dry skin is often described as **dehydrated**.

Dry skin has these characteristics:

- the pores are small and tight;
- the moisture content is poor;
- the skin texture is coarse and thin, with patches of visibly flaking skin;
- there is a tendency towards sensitivity (broken capillaries often accompany this skin type);
- premature ageing is common, resulting in the appearance of wrinkles, seen especially around the eyes, mouth and neck;
- skin pigmentation may be uneven, and disorders such as ephelides (freckles) usually accompany this skin type;
- milia are often found around the cheek and eye area.

Dry skin

Oily skin

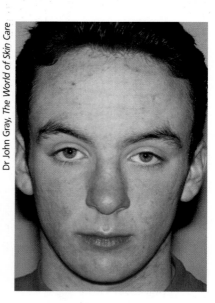

Dr John Gray, *The World of Skin Care*

In **oily skin** the sebaceous glands become very active at puberty, when stimulated by the male hormone **androgen**. An increase in sebum production often causes the appearance of skin blemishes. Sebaceous gland activity begins to decrease when the person is in their twenties.

Oily skin has these characteristics:

- the pores are enlarged;
- the moisture content is high;
- the skin is coarse and thick;
- the skin is sallow in colour, as a result of the excess sebum production, dead skin cells become embedded in the sebum, and the skin has sluggish blood and lymph circulation;
- the skin tone is good, due to the protective effect of the sebum;
- the skin is prone to shininess, due to excess sebum production;
- there may be uneven pigmentation;
- certain skin disorders may be apparent – comedones, pustules, papules, milia or sebaceous cysts.

Oily skin

Acne vulgaris and **seborrhoea** are skin disorders that occur when the skin becomes excessively oily due to the influence of hormones. Treatment of these skin disorders should be carried out to control sebum flow.

Combination skin

Combination skin is partly oily and partly dry. The oily parts are generally the chin, nose and forehead, known as the **T-zone**. The upper cheeks may show signs of oiliness, but the rest of the face and neck area is dry.

Combination skin is the most common skin type. It has these characteristics:

- the pores in the T-zone are enlarged, while in the cheek area they are small to medium;
- the moisture content is high in the oily areas, but poor in the dry areas;
- the skin is coarse and thick in the oily areas, but thin in the dry areas;
- the skin is sallow in the oily areas, but shows sensitivity and high colour in the dry areas;
- the skin tone is good in the oily areas, but poor in the dry areas;
- there is uneven pigmentation, usually seen as ephelides and lentigines;
- there may be blemishes such as pustules and comedones on the oily skin at the T-zone;
- milia and broken capillaries may appear in the dry areas, commonly on the cheeks and near the eyes.

Combination skin

Additional characteristics

Whilst looking closely at the skin, further skin characteristics may become obvious. The skin may be:

- sensitive;
- dehydrated;
- moist;
- oedematous (puffy).

Sensitive skin

Sensitive skin usually accompanies a dry skin type, but not always.

The characteristics of sensitive skin are these:

- the skin may show high colouring;
- there are usually broken capillaries in the cheek area;
- the skin feels warm to the touch;
- there is superficial flaking of the skin;
- the skin may show high colouring and tightness after skin cleansing, if it is sensitive to pressure.

In black skin, instead of the redness shown by Caucasian skin, irritation shows up as a darker patch.

Sensitive skin

Dr John Gray, *The World of Skin Care*

HEALTH AND SAFETY

Sensitive skin
Use hypoallergenic products – these do not contain any of the known common skin sensitisers.

Skin that is sensitive may also be allergic to certain substances.

Avoid lifestyle factors that can make sensitive skin worse. These include: alcohol, smoking, poor diet and stress.

> **TIP** ✔
>
> **Dehydrated skin**
> Encourage clients with dehydrated skin to drink six to eight glasses of water a day to replenish the moisture in the body.

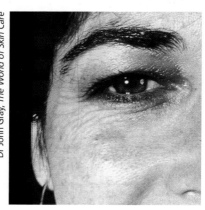

Dehydrated skin

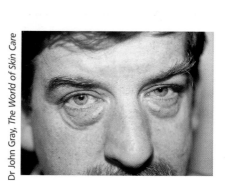

Oedematous (puffy) skin

> **TIP** ✔
>
> **Oedematous skin**
> Whilst completing the record card you may be able to recognise aspects of your client's lifestyle that probably contribute to the oedematous skin. If so, you can advise the client accordingly.

Allergic skin **Allergic skin** is irritated by external **allergens**, including chemicals in some cosmetics. The allergens inflame the skin and may damage its protective function. At the consultation, always try to discover whether the client has any allergies, and if so, to what.

The allergies of most concern to the beauty therapist are those caused by substances applied to the skin. The therapist must be aware of such substances and avoid their use. Contact with an allergen, especially if repeated, may cause skin disorders such as eczema or dermatitis (see pages 25–37, where skin diseases and disorders are dealt with in more detail).

Dehydrated skin

Dehydrated skin is skin that has lost water from the skin tissues. The condition can affect any skin type, but most commonly accompanies dry or combination skin types. The problem may be related to the client's general health. If they have recently been ill with a fever, for example, the skin will have lost fluid through sweating. If they are taking medication, this too may cause dehydration, as may drastic dieting. In many cases the dehydration is caused by working in an environment with a low humidity, or in one that is air-conditioned. You must try to discover the cause, and provide both corrective treatment and advice.

The characteristics of dehydrated skin are as follows:

- the skin has a fine orange-peel effect, caused by its lack of moisture;
- there is superficial flaking;
- fine, superficial lines are evident on the skin;
- broken capillaries are common.

Moist skin

Moist skin appears moist and feels damp: this is due to the over-secretion of sweat. The beauty therapist cannot correct this skin condition, which is often caused by some internal physiological disturbance such as a hormonal or metabolic imbalance.

Advise the client to use lightweight cleansing preparations. The client should avoid skin-toning preparations with a high alcohol content; these would stimulate the skin, causing yet further perspiration and skin sensitivity. They should avoid highly spiced food, and be aware that alcoholic or hot drinks will cause dilation of the skin capillaries, thereby increasing the skin's temperature.

Oedematous (puffy) skin

Oedematous skin is, and appears, swollen and puffy: this is because the tissues are retaining excess water. The condition may be caused by a medical disorder, or may be a side-effect of medication. Hot weather can cause temporary swelling of the tissues, as can local injury to the tissues. Poor blood circulation and lymphatic flow may cause puffy skin, too; this is often seen around the eyes. In this case the condition may benefit from gentle massage around the eye area. Tissue-fluid retention in the facial skin may be caused by an incorrect diet, such as one that includes too much salt or the drinking of too much alcohol, tea or coffee.

Unless you are quite sure about the cause of the oedema, always seek permission from your client's doctor before treating the skin.

The sex of the client

Men have a more acidic skin surface than females and the stratum corneum is thicker on males than females. However, males have coarse facial hair and shaving daily removes cells of the stratum corneum before they are ready to desquamate naturally. This can sensitise and dry the skin, especially if after-shave lotions with a high alcohol content are directly applied. A moisturiser should be applied to protect the skin.

The collagen content of the skin is different in men and women. Collagen and sebum production falls in menopausal women causing skin ageing. Skin does not appear to age as quickly in males as females because collagen and sebum production remain constant.

The main reason males choose to have a facial is for relaxation, to improve the appearance of the skin, and increasingly for the anti-ageing benefits.

The age of the skin

Having identified the skin type, the beauty therapist must classify the age of the skin.

Often the age of a client will relate to skin problems that are evident. A young client, for example, may have skin blemishes such as comedones, pustules and papules. These disorders are caused by overactivity of the sebaceous gland at puberty, when the body is developing its secondary sexual characteristics. It is at this time that acne vulgaris is most likely to occur, due to the hormonal imbalance. The skin of clients aged over 25 years, however, is generally termed **mature skin**.

The beauty therapist should also consider the client's skin tone and muscle tone in relation to their age. A young skin will probably have good skin tone, and the skin will be supple and elastic. This is because the collagen and elastin fibres in the skin are strong. Poor skin tone, on the other hand, is recognised by the appearance of facial lines and wrinkles.

A healthy young skin will also have good muscle tone, and the facial contours will appear firm. With poor muscle tone, the muscles becomes slack and loose.

Mature skin

The change in appearance of women's skin during ageing is closely related to the altered production of the hormones oestrogen, progesterone and androgen at the menopause.

Mature skin has the following characteristics:

- The skin becomes dry, as the sebaceous and sudoriferous glands become less active.
- The skin loses its elasticity as the elastin fibres harden, and wrinkles appear due to the cross-linking and hardening of collagen fibres.
- The epidermis grows more slowly and the skin appears thinner, becoming almost transparent in some areas such as around the eyes, where small veins and capillaries show through the skin.

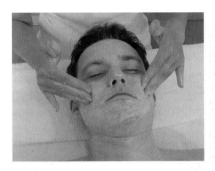

Male skin

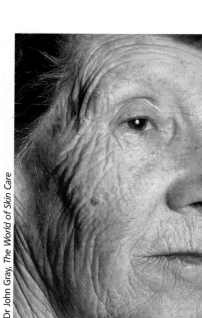

Dr John Gray, *The World of Skin Care*

Mature skin

ACTIVITY

The ageing process

Cut out photographs from magazines or newspapers showing men and women of different cultures and various ages.

1 Can you identify the visible characteristics of ageing?
2 Does ageing occur at the same rate in men and women and in different cultures?
3 Discuss your findings with your tutor.

- Broken capillaries appear, especially on the cheek area and around the nose.
- The facial contours become slack as muscle tone is reduced.
- The underlying bone structure becomes more obvious, as the fatty layer and the supportive tissue beneath the skin grow thinner.
- Blood circulation becomes poor, which interferes with skin nutrition, and the skin may appear sallow.
- Due to the decrease in metabolic rate, waste products are not removed so quickly, and this leads to puffiness of the skin.
- Patches of irregular pigmentation appear on the surface of the skin, such as lentigines and chloasmata.

The skin may also exhibit the following skin conditions, although these are not truly *characteristic* of an ageing skin:

- Dermal naevi may be enlarged.
- Sebhorrheic warts may appear on the epidermal layer of the skin.
- Verruca filiformis warts may increase in number.
- Hair growth on the upper lip or chin, or both, may become darker or coarser, due to hormonal imbalance in the body.
- Dark circles and puffiness may occur under the eyes.

Differences in skin

Although there is no difference between skin functions such as sweat and sebaceous gland activity in white and black skin, the amount of pigment, called *melanin*, varies, resulting in different skin and hair colour.

There are two forms of the melanin pigment: *eumelanin*, produced in black and brown skin colours, and *phaeomelanin*, found in lighter skins. Both forms of pigment can be present together but the amount of each can vary.

People who originate from hot countries and are nearer the equator have more melanin and a darker skin pigment. This is because the UV is very intense and the skin requires more protection. Those who originate from cooler countries have less melanin and a lighter skin pigment. The pigmentation of the skin is the result of millions of years of evolution.

African-Caribbean

The skin colour is dark and ranges in tone to almost black. This is because it has more melanin, which absorbs ultra-violet (UV) light. As black skin is exposed to UV light it becomes darker and darker. This causes hyperpigmentation – uneven patches of skin tone which are darker than the surrounding skin.

HEALTH AND SAFETY ✚

UV light and ageing

The ageing process is accelerated when the skin is regularly exposed to ultra-violet light.

TIP ✓

Skin appearance

As the surface of the skin reflects light and shows the skin colour, the therapist's aim is for the skin surface to be smooth and healthy. This is achieved by the removal of dead skin cells and ensuring it is adequately moisturised.

LEVEL 2 IMPROVE AND MAINTAIN FACIAL SKIN CONDITION (BT4)
Dr John Gray, The World of Skin Care

Care must be taken when dealing with blemishes on darker skins as scars may occur as the skin heals. The scars may become keloids, scarring that becomes enlarged and projects above the skin's surface. Even minor scratches may result in keloid formation.

Hyperpigmentation may also occur. It is more common in darker skinned people due to increased melanin. Hyperpigmentation most commonly occurs following skin inflammation, such as acne vulgaris. Keloids may become hyperpigmented if exposed to the sun in the early stages of their formation.

Vitiligo (loss of skin pigment) is a considerable problem when it occurs in dark skin, as it is very obvious. Cosmetics may be applied as a corrective technique.

Male clients may have a tendency towards *pseudo folliculitis*, an inflammatory skin disorder. This occurs as the hair is coarse and curly and has a tendency as it grows out of the skin to curl back and re-enter it, becoming ingrown. This foreign object in the skin becomes irritated and inflamed. Hyperpigmentation may also accompany this condition.

Dermatosis papulosis nigra, also called flesh moles, can occur. These are brown or black hyperpigmented markings, resembling moles, usually seen on the cheeks. Their cause is unknown but they are sometimes found to be hereditary. They also occur more frequently in women than men.

Hair colour is dark brown to black.

African-Caribbean skin

TIP ✓
Hyper and hypopigmentation can affect the skin of any race. Chloasma or liver spots are an example of hyperpigmentation and are commonly seen as dark brown marks on the backs of the hands. These occur as a result of skin damage caused by sun damage, skin trauma or hormonal imbalance. Freckles or ephelides are another example of hyperpigmentation. These become darker when the skin is exposed to the sun. Prescription creams containing hydroquinone bleach and laser treatment may be used to lighten the skin. However, care must be taken using hydroquinone bleach on black and Asian skin as hypopigmentation and skin allergy can occur. Increasing in popularity are botanical brightness which include the professional application of an exfoliant to remove the pigmented surface cells and serum.

Asian

The skin colour has a light to dark tone due to increased melanin, with yellow undertones. There is a tendency towards hyperpigmentation, appearing as dark patches of skin, and scarring can appear following skin inflammation. Dermatosis papulosis nigra can occur. In women there is a normal tendency towards superfluous facial hair.

Hair colour is dark brown to black.

Caucasian

The skin colour is pink. This skin has less melanin and so less defence in the presence of UV light; sun damage results in skin burning and premature ageing. Caucasian skin has a tendency to show freckles (ephelides), as a result of uneven melanin distribution in the skin.

Hair colour is usually fair, red or brown.

Dr John Gray, The World of Skin Care

Asian skin

8.1.9.18 Divas

Caucasian skin

Dr John Gray, *The World of Skin Care*

Oriental skin

TIP

Skin and UV light defence
Very dark skin offers up to 30 times more protection against the sun than lighter skin.

Oriental

The skin colour has more melanin present and has a yellowish tone. Oriental skin is usually oily and prone to hyperpigmentation. Blemishes should be treated with caution as hyperpigmentation and scarring could result due to increased levels of melanin. Female skin generally appears smooth and has little facial hair.

Hair colour is usually mid-brown to black.

PLAN AND PREPARE FOR SKIN-CARE TREATMENTS

Outcome 1: Consult with the client

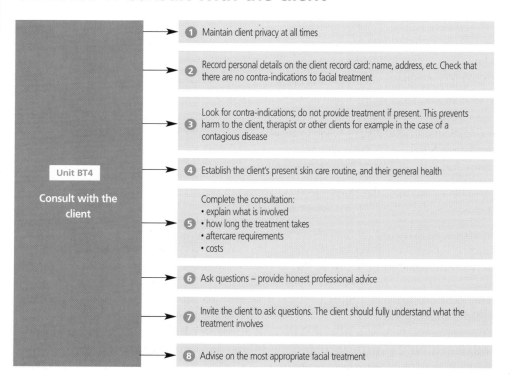

Unit BT4

Consult with the client

1. Maintain client privacy at all times

2. Record personal details on the client record card: name, address, etc. Check that there are no contra-indications to facial treatment

3. Look for contra-indications; do not provide treatment if present. This prevents harm to the client, therapist or other clients for example in the case of a contagious disease

4. Establish the client's present skin care routine, and their general health

5. Complete the consultation:
   - explain what is involved
   - how long the treatment takes
   - aftercare requirements
   - costs

6. Ask questions – provide honest professional advice

7. Invite the client to ask questions. The client should fully understand what the treatment involves

8. Advise on the most appropriate facial treatment

Reception

Before carrying out *any* facial treatments, the beauty therapist must consult with the client to determine their treatment needs and to discuss the services that are available. **Consultation** is a service that should be offered separately: there should be no pressure on the client to book a treatment following the consultation.

Making the appointment

When a new client telephones to make an appointment for a service, always allocate extra time for the consultation beforehand. Explain to the client how long they should allow for the appointment. For example, if a client is seeking a basic skin cleansing and mask treatment, allow 30 minutes; if they are a new client allow 45 minutes so that there is time for the consultation and filling in the record card. If it is necessary to remove facial blockages and to carry out other specialised treatments, allow 45 minutes to one hour. For a full facial treatment, allow one hour.

On arrival

When the client arrives for the treatment, the **record card** is completed. Record the client's personal details, such as their name and address. Check that there are no contra-indications to facial treatment.

The beauty therapist will add further information to the record card at the consultation and during treatment.

The consultation

In the privacy of the treatment cubicle, carry out the consultation. This takes place when the client first meets the therapist and again whenever a new treatment is to be carried out.

The consultation is the time when the beauty therapist can assess whether the client is actually suited to treatment. The therapist must look for contra-indications, and must give no treatment if there are any – this is to safeguard the therapist, the client and, in the case of a client with a contagious skin disorder, other clients who would be at risk of cross-infection.

Ask the client specific questions about their present skin-care routine and their general health.

The beauty therapist's knowledge of facial treatments and advice on skin care will instil confidence in the client. Explain what is involved with each treatment, how long it takes, the aftercare involved and any home care that is required. This will demonstrate your professional expertise.

The client is likely to ask which is the most suitable treatment for them, and you must advise them as to which would best meet their needs.

Make the client aware of the cost of the individual treatment – or treatment programme, if necessary – so that they can decide whether or not to undertake the financial commitment involved.

Invite the client to ask questions during the consultation. By the end, they should understand fully what the proposed treatment involves.

The client may receive the treatment immediately, following the consultation, or go away to consider the proposals.

During the consultation, details are noted on the client's record card. You can fill this in as you speak to them, without diverting your attention away from them.

TIP

Treatment timing
Full facial treatment: treatment time allow one hour.

HEALTH AND SAFETY

Consultation check
Check if a client has received any specialist electrical facials such as micro-dermabrasion or chemical peels. These treatments involve removing the surface epidermal cells from the skin, which may cause it to be sensitive. Ensure that you check at the consultation if the client has been receiving any specialised treatments for the facial skin, and if so what and when. Seek guidance as necessary from a senior therapist as to client suitability.

TIP

Never make assumptions about what the client can afford. Usually the client will indicate to you what they are prepared to spend.

TIP

Treatment modification
Examples of facial treatment modification include:
- altering the pressure or choice of manipulations during massage to suit the client's skin and muscle tone;
- altering the distance and application of steam to take into account skin sensitivity.

BEAUTY WORKS

Date	Therapist name	
Client name		Date of birth (identifying client age group)
Address		Postcode
Evening phone number	Day phone number	
Name of doctor	Doctor's address and phone number	
Related medical history (conditions that may restrict or prohibit treatment application)		
Are you taking any medication? (this may affect the appearance of the skin or skin sensitivity)		

CONTRA-INDICATIONS REQUIRING MEDICAL REFERRAL
(Preventing facial treatment application)

- ☐ bacterial infection (e.g. impetigo)
- ☐ viral infection (e.g. herpes simplex)
- ☐ fungal infection (e.g. tinea corporis)
- ☐ eye infections (e.g. conjunctivitis)
- ☐ watery eyes
- ☐ systemic medical condition
- ☐ severe skin condition

SKIN GROUP

- ☐ oily
- ☐ dry
- ☐ combination
- ☐ young
- ☐ mature

FACIAL PRODUCTS

- ☐ cleanser
- ☐ mask – non-setting
- ☐ toner
- ☐ massage medium
- ☐ eye cleanser
- ☐ moisturiser
- ☐ exfoliant
- ☐ specialist skin treatments (e.g. eye cream)
- ☐ mask – setting

MASSAGE MEDIUMS

- ☐ oil
- ☐ cream

CONTRA-INDICATIONS WHICH RESTRICT TREATMENT
(Treatment may require adaptation)

- ☐ cuts and abrasions
- ☐ bruising and swelling
- ☐ recent scar tissue
- ☐ eczema
- ☐ skin allergies
- ☐ vitiligo
- ☐ styes
- ☐ hyper keratosis
- ☐ watery eyes

SKIN CONDITION CHARACTERISTICS

- ☐ sensitive
- ☐ mature
- ☐ dehydrated
- ☐ milia
- ☐ broken capillaries
- ☐ comedones
- ☐ pustules
- ☐ papules
- ☐ open pores
- ☐ hyperpigmentation
- ☐ hypopigmentation
- ☐ dermatitis papulosa nigra
- ☐ keloids
- ☐ ingrowing hairs

Following skin analysis identify on the illustration below skin condition characteristics found and in which numbered area they appear.

EQUIPMENT AND MATERIALS

- ☐ magnifying light
- ☐ skin warming devices
- ☐ protective covering
- ☐ consumables

MASSAGE TECHNIQUES

- ☐ effleurage
- ☐ petrissage
- ☐ friction
- ☐ tapotement
- ☐ vibrations

Therapist signature (for reference)

Client signature (confirmation of details)

TREATMENT ADVICE

 Full facial treatment – *This treatment will take 60 minutes (1 hour)*

TREATMENT PLAN

Record relevant details of your treatment and advice provided for future reference.

Ensure the client's records are up to date, accurate and fully completed following treatment. Non-compliance may invalidate insurance.

DURING

Find out:

- what products the client is currently using to cleanse and care for the skin of the face and neck;
- how regularly the products are used;
- satisfaction with their current skin-care routine.

Explain:

- how the products used should be applied and removed.

Note:

- any adverse reaction, if any occur.

AFTER

Record:

- specific areas treated;
- any modification to treatment application that has occurred;
- what products have been used in the facial treatment;
- the effectiveness of treatment;
- any samples provided (review their success at the next appointment).

Advise on:

- product application and removal in order to gain maximum benefit from product use;
- use of make-up following facial treatment;
- recommended time intervals between treatments;
- the importance of a course of treatment to improve the skin condition.

RETAIL OPPORTUNITIES

Advise on:

- progression of the treatment plan for future appointments;
- products that would be suitable for the client to use at home to care for their skin;
- recommendations for further facial treatments;
- further products or services that you have recommended that the client may or may not have received before.

Note:

- any purchase made by the client.

EVALUATION

Record:

- comments on the client's satisfaction with the treatment;
- how you will progress the treatment to maintain and advance the treatment results in the future.

HEALTH AND SAFETY

Advise on:

- avoidance of activities or product application that may cause a contra-action;
- appropriate action to be taken in the event of an unwanted skin reaction.

Contra-indications

The consultation and skin analysis will draw your attention to any contra-indications or aspects that require special care and attention.

Remember that not all contra-indications are visible – a current bone fracture, for example, would not be. Refer to the checklist of contra-indications on the client's record card.

The following contra-indications are relevant to *all* facial treatments:

- *skin disorder*, such as acne vulgaris (unless medical approval has been sought and given);
- *skin disease*, such as impetigo;
- *bruising* in the area;
- *haemorrhage*, if recent – wait until the condition has healed;
- *operation* in the area, if recent – wait for six months;
- *fracture*, if recent – wait for six months;
- *furuncle* (boil);
- *inflammation or swelling* of the skin;
- *scar tissue*, if recent – wait for six months;
- *sebaceous cyst*;
- *eye disorder*, such as conjunctivitis.

Certain contra-indications restrict treatment; that is, the treatment may have to be adapted or delayed until the contra-indication has gone. For example, if eczema is present but the skin is not broken, the treatment can proceed but the area should be avoided as much as possible.

If the client has an allergy to an ingredient in the cosmetic preparations used, treatment cannot proceed until an alternative, non-allergenic product suited to the client is obtained. If the client has a stye, treatment cannot proceed. However, when the eye disorder has gone treatment may be carried out.

Refer to pages 25–37, where skin diseases and disorders are discussed in more detail.

ACTIVITY

Recognising contra-indications
Think of *six* skin disorders and *six* skin diseases. List them in a chart.
  Briefly describe how you would recognise each skin condition. Why would it be inappropriate to treat each?

HEALTH AND SAFETY

Herpes simplex (cold sore)
A small skin lesion due to herpes simplex may initially appear to be simply a pustule with a scab. At the consultation, always check whether the client knows if they suffer from any skin disease or disorder.

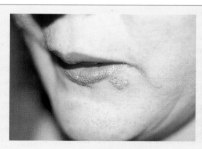

Dr John Gray,
The World of Skin Care

Outcome 2: Prepare for the treatment

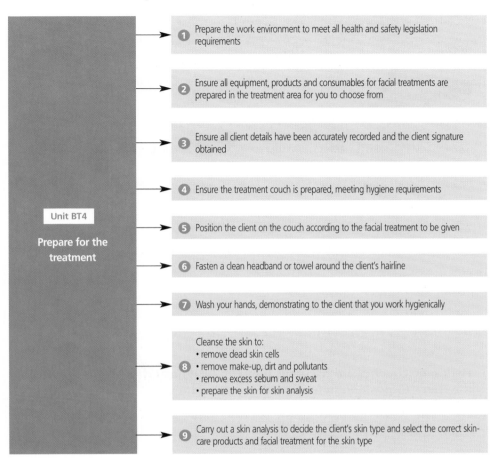

Unit BT4

Prepare for the treatment

1. Prepare the work environment to meet all health and safety legislation requirements

2. Ensure all equipment, products and consumables for facial treatments are prepared in the treatment area for you to choose from

3. Ensure all client details have been accurately recorded and the client signature obtained

4. Ensure the treatment couch is prepared, meeting hygiene requirements

5. Position the client on the couch according to the facial treatment to be given

6. Fasten a clean headband or towel around the client's hairline

7. Wash your hands, demonstrating to the client that you work hygienically

8. Cleanse the skin to:
   - remove dead skin cells
   - remove make-up, dirt and pollutants
   - remove excess sebum and sweat
   - prepare the skin for skin analysis

9. Carry out a skin analysis to decide the client's skin type and select the correct skin-care products and facial treatment for the skin type

Equipment and materials

Beauty salons differ in how much floor space is available and how much of that is allocated to each beauty service. There may be one or several facial-treatment cubicles. In the case of a salon having only one such cubicle, it is important that the range of facial services offered can all be delivered safely and hygienically.

If you are a mobile beauty therapist you will require a lightweight, durable beauty couch for facial treatments. These beds are also useful to have when carrying out demonstrations at a different location.

Basic equipment

Each treatment cubicle should have the following basic equipment:

- **Treatment couch or beauty chair**   The couch or chair should be covered with easy-to-clean upholstery: it must withstand daily cleaning with warm water and detergent. It must have an adjustable **back rest**, for the comfort of both the client and the therapist. If possible, purchase a couch that also has an adjustable **leg rest**, as this allows treatments such as pedicure to be carried out.

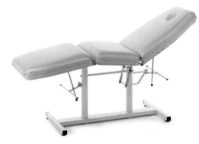

Sorisa

A treatment couch

Beauty Express Ltd.

Beauty Express Ltd.

Folding aluminium massage table

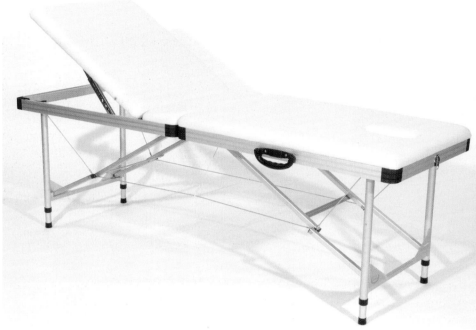

Folding aluminium massage table in treatment position

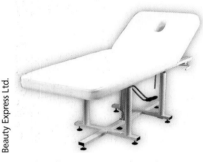

Beauty Express Ltd.

Hydraulic treatment couch

Hydraulic couches are useful as they can be adjusted in height to enable the client to position herself on the couch with ease.

A prepared facial trolley

- **Equipment trolley** The equipment trolley should be large enough to accommodate all the necessary equipment and products; trolleys are usually of a two- or three-shelf design. Like the chair or couch, the trolley should be made of a material that will withstand regular cleaning. Some models have restraining bars to prevent objects sliding off the trolley. Drawers are useful in storing tools and small consumables. The trolley should have securely fixed easy-glide castors.

- **Beauty stool** The stool should be covered in a fabric similar to that covering the treatment couch. It may or may not have a back rest; in some designs the back rest is removable. For the comfort of the therapist, it should be adjustable in height; to allow mobility, it should be mounted on castors.

- **Step-up stool** To assist clients as necessary to position themselves on the couch, have available a step-up stool.

- **Magnifying lamp** The magnifying lamp is available in three models: floor-standing, wall-mounted and trolley-mounted.

Beauty stools

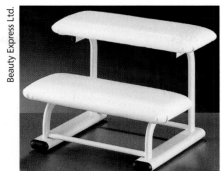

Step-up stool

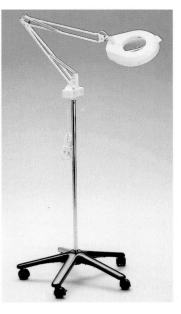

A magnifying lamp

- **Covered waste bin**   A covered waste bin should be placed unobtrusively within easy each. It should be lined with a disposable bin-liner. You should also have a 'sharps' box for the disposal of contaminated equipment.

Arrangements for the collection and disposal of contaminated waste should be made with your local environmental health office.

Preparing the cubicle

The following guidelines describe the basic preparation of the **facial treatment cubicle**. Further equipment and materials relevant to other beauty services are discussed within the appropriate chapters.

Covered waste bins

EQUIPMENT LIST

Headband A clean headband should be provided for each client. Use either a material headband or disposable. Disposable are useful as they can be discarded after the treatment

Skin-cleansing preparations The trolley should carry a display of facial skin-cleansing preparations to suit all skin types

Cottonwool There should be a plentiful supply of both damp and dry cottonwool, sufficient for the treatment to be carried out. *Dry* cottonwool should be stored in a covered container; *damp* cottonwool is usually placed in a clean bowl

Tissues Facial tissues should be large and of a high quality. They should be stored in a covered container

Waste bin A covered container for waste may be placed on the bottom shelf of the trolley or it can be put into the waste bin at once

Spatulas Several clean spatulas (preferably disposable) should be provided for each client. One should be used in tucking any stray hair beneath the headband. Others will be used in removing products from their containers

EQUIPMENT LIST *(continued)*

YOU WILL ALSO NEED:

Towel drapes There should be a large towel to cover the client's body, and a small hand towel to drape across the client's chest and shoulders

Trolley The surface of each shelf can be protected with a sheet of 500mm disposable bedroll

Towel A clean towel should be placed on the trolley for the therapist to wipe their hands on as necessary

Gown A clean gown should be provided for each client as necessary

Facial sponges or facial mitts are used to remove facial products from the skin during treatment. They are particularly useful when working on a male client where cottonwool would collect on coarse facial hair

Mirror A clean hand mirror should be available, for use in consulting with the client before, during and after their treatment

Container for jewellery A container may be provided in which the client can place their jewellery if they need to remove it prior to treatment – follow your salon procedures in respect of client possessions

TIP

Towel racks
Wall-mounted towel racks save storage space.

HEALTH AND SAFETY

Containers
Bottles and other containers should be clean and clearly labelled.

TIP

Disposable paper roll may be placed over the surface of the treatment couch if desired. This should be changed for each client.

TIP

It is bad practice to leave the client in order to fetch more cottonwool. It is also bad practice to prepare too much and be wasteful!

Pre-shaped cottonwool discs are ideal for facial treatments. Alternatively, cut high-quality cottonwool into squares (6cm × 6cm).

Preparing the client

By the time the client is shown through to the treatment cubicle, the record card will already have been partly filled in at reception. The card should be collected by the beauty therapist, who will add to it during and after the treatment.

HEALTH AND SAFETY

Poor health
If the client is in poor health, or is taking medication that affects their skin condition, it may not be possible to treat them until the medical condition has been treated by their general practitioner.

TIP

Compliance with the Data Protection Act 1998
Ensure all client records are stored securely, with only those staff who have the client's permission having access to them.

Outcome 3: Plan the treatment

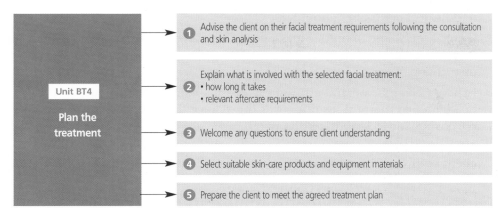

Following the consultation, the client's answers will indicate to the therapist what is required, and what is achievable, from a skin-care programme.

When finalising the most suitable treatment plan:

- explain what is involved in each treatment, how long it takes, and what aftercare and home care are required (if relevant);
- assess how much the client is willing to spend, and design a treatment programme within their budget.

This allows the client to:

- discover what the beauty therapist can offer;
- ask questions, and receive honest professional advice concerning the most appropriate choice of skin-care treatment;
- decide how much they are willing to spend.

The beauty therapist should ensure that the client fully understands what the proposed treatment involves.

ACTIVITY

Answering questions
You should be able to answer honestly, competently and tactfully any questions related to the beauty services you offer. Below are examples of the questions you may be asked at consultation.

- 'I have always used soap and water upon my face. Is this a satisfactory way to cleanse my face?'
- 'Why do I need to use a separate night cream as well as a day moisturiser?'
- 'How often should I have a facial?'
- 'I have extremely oily skin. Why do I need to wear a moisturiser?'
- 'What can I do to treat these fine lines around my eyes?'

What answers would you give? Think of further questions you might be asked with regard to skin care. An experienced beauty therapist will be able to advise you.

Prior to treatment

Depending on the treatment to be carried out, the client may need to remove some clothing. Offer them a **gown** to wear.

TIP

Client care
Always give clear instructions to your client. This will help to ensure that they are not embarrassed or uncomfortable at any time.

TIP

Headbands
Check that the headband is comfortable. A tight headband will cause tension and eventually a headache.

1 Position the client on the couch according to the treatment to be given. Cover the client with the large bath towel. If necessary, drape a small hand towel across her shoulders.

2 If facial, neck and shoulder massage is to be given, ask the client politely to remove her arms from her bra straps in preparation: this avoids disturbance later.

3 Fasten a clean headband around the client's hairline. Position the headband so that it does not cover the skin of the face. If using steam, cover the hair to stop it getting damp.

4 After preparing the client, wash your hands: this demonstrates to the client your concern to work hygienically.

Outcome 4: Improve and maintain skin condition

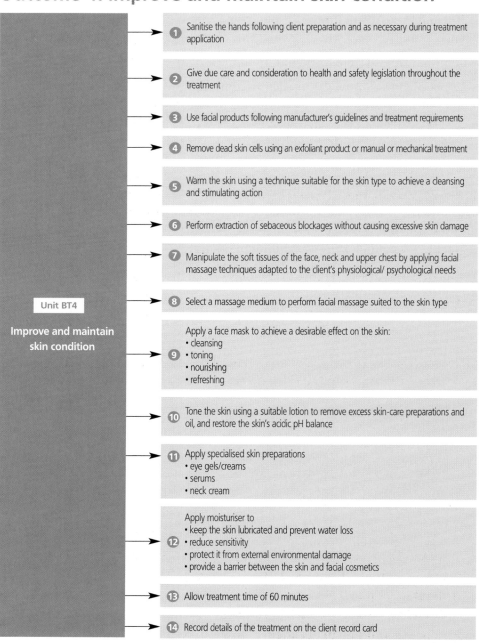

Unit BT4

Improve and maintain skin condition

1 Sanitise the hands following client preparation and as necessary during treatment application

2 Give due care and consideration to health and safety legislation throughout the treatment

3 Use facial products following manufacturer's guidelines and treatment requirements

4 Remove dead skin cells using an exfoliant product or manual or mechanical treatment

5 Warm the skin using a technique suitable for the skin type to achieve a cleansing and stimulating action

6 Perform extraction of sebaceous blockages without causing excessive skin damage

7 Manipulate the soft tissues of the face, neck and upper chest by applying facial massage techniques adapted to the client's physiological/ psychological needs

8 Select a massage medium to perform facial massage suited to the skin type

9 Apply a face mask to achieve a desirable effect on the skin:
• cleansing
• toning
• nourishing
• refreshing

10 Tone the skin using a suitable lotion to remove excess skin-care preparations and oil, and restore the skin's acidic pH balance

11 Apply specialised skin preparations
• eye gels/creams
• serums
• neck cream

12 Apply moisturiser to
• keep the skin lubricated and prevent water loss
• reduce sensitivity
• protect it from external environmental damage
• provide a barrier between the skin and facial cosmetics

13 Allow treatment time of 60 minutes

14 Record details of the treatment on the client record card

CLEANSING

Skin cleansing is essential in promoting and maintaining a healthy complexion. There are various cleansing preparations to choose from; basically their action is the same in each case:

- to gently exfoliate dead skin cells from the stratum corneum, exposing younger cells and improving the skin's appearance;
- to remove make-up, dirt and pollutants from the skin's surface, reducing the possibility of blemishes and skin irritation;
- to remove excess sweat and sebum from the skin's surface, reducing congestion of the skin and the subsequent formation of comedones and pustules;
- to prepare the skin for further treatments.

Cleansing preparations

A cleanser is required that will remove both oil-soluble and water-soluble substances. Oil is capable of dissolving grease; water will dissolve other substances. Usually, therefore, a cleanser is a combination of both oil and water.

Oil and water do not combine: if you simply mix the two together they separate again, with the oil floating on the top of the water. If the two substances are shaken together vigorously, however, one substance will break up and become suspended in the other. The result is known as an **emulsion**.

Emulsions are used in many cosmetic preparations. They are either:

- **oil-in-water** (O/W) – minute droplets of oil, surrounded by water;
- **water-in-oil** (W/O) – minute droplets of water, surrounded by oil.

To give the emulsion stability, and to stop it separating out again, an **emulsifier** is added.

Various cleansing preparations are available to the beauty therapist, with formulations designed to suit the different skin types. They include:

- cleansing milks;
- cleansing creams;
- cleansing lotions;
- facial foaming cleansers;
- cleansing bars;
- eye make-up removers.

Whichever cleanser is chosen, it should have the following qualities:

- it should cleanse the skin effectively, without causing irritation;
- it should remove all traces of make-up and grease;
- it should feel pleasant to use;
- it should be easy to remove from the skin;
- ideally, it should be pH-balanced.

TIP

Seasonal changes
Seasonal changes affect the skin. You may need to alter the client's basic skin-care routine through the year.

The pH scale

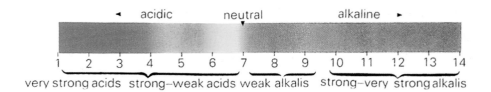

The **pH scale** is used to measure the **acidity** or **alkalinity** of a substance. Using a numbered scale of 1–14, acids have a pH less than 7; alkalis have a pH greater than 7. Substances with a pH of 7 are **neutral**.

ACTIVITY

Acidic or alkaline?
To discover whether a liquid product is acidic or alkaline, carry out a simple test using litmus paper. Litmus changes colour according to the pH:
● litmus paper turns *blue* if an *alkali* is present;
● litmus paper turns *red* if an *acid* is present.
Test the pH of various cleansing preparations.

The skin is naturally slightly acidic: it has an **acid mantle**. Alkalis strip the skin of its protective film of sebum, making it feel dry and taut. To avoid skin irritation it is preferable to use a product that matches the acid mantle, a product whose pH is 5.5–5.6.

HEALTH AND SAFETY

Sensitive skin
When treating a sensitive skin, choose a cleansing product that does not contain common known allergens such as mineral oil, alcohol or lanolin. Such products are usually referred to as *hypoallergenic* or *dermatologically tested*.

Cleansing milks

Cleansing milks are usually oil-in-water emulsions, with a relatively high proportion of water to oil, making the milk quite fluid in its consistency.

Cleansing milks have these specific treatment uses:

● treating dry skin that is prone to sensitivity;
● treating sensitive skin.

Cleansing creams

Cleansing creams have a relatively high proportion of oil to water, making the emulsion thicker and richer in its consistency than cleansing milks. The high oil content allows the product to be massaged over the skin surface without dragging the tissues. The cream is also more effective in removing grease and oil-based make-up from the skin.

Cleansing creams have these specific treatment uses:

● removing facial cosmetics;
● treating by deep cleansing massage;
● treating very dry skin.

Cleansing lotions

Cleansing lotions are solutions of detergents in water. They do not usually contain oil, and are therefore unsuitable for the removal of facial cosmetics.

Cleansing lotions have these specific treatment uses:

- cleansing a normal to combination skin type;
- treating oily skin (where a high oil content could aggravate the skin, causing yet further sebum production).

Medicated ingredients may be included in a cleansing formulation: these are only suitable for oily, congested, spotty skin types.

If the client has a mature, normal or combination skin, a cleansing lotion may not be effective because of the reduced oil content.

Facial foaming cleansers

Facial foaming cleansers usually contain a mild detergent which foams when mixed with water. Additional ingredients are selected for the treatment of different skin types. These cleansers are quick to use and afford a suitable alternative for the client who likes to cleanse their face with soap and water. If the client wears an oil-based make-up, advise them to use a cleansing cream first to remove make-up thoroughly before using this cleanser.

Facial foaming cleansers have a general application:

- treating most skin types except very dry or sensitive skin.

Cleansing bars

Although it is efficient as a cleanser, **soap** is usually considered unsuitable for use on the skin. It has an alkaline pH, which disturbs the skin's natural acidic pH balance. Soap strips the skin of its protective acid mantle, leaving insoluble salts on the skin's surface. The skin may be left feeling itchy, taut and sensitive.

Cleansing bars are a milder alternative to soap, and are specially formulated to match the skin's acidic pH of 5.5–5.6. They are less likely to dry out the skin.

Cleansing bars have this specific application:

- treating oily to normal skin that is not sensitive.

Eye make-up remover

Eye tissue is a lot finer than the skin on the rest of the face. It readily puffs if aggravated by oil-based cleansing preparations, and becomes very dry if harsh cleansing preparations are used.

To remove make-up from this area, use an **eye make-up remover**. This product cleanses the eyelid and lashes, gently emulsifying the make-up. It also conditions the delicate skin. Formulated as a lotion or a gel, it is designed to remove either water-based or oil-based products (or both) from the eye area.

Oily eye make-up removers have these specific treatment uses:

- treating clients who wear waterproof mascara;
- removing wax or oil-based eyeshadow.

TIP

Dry skin
If a client has very dry skin, advise them to avoid them use of tap water on the face – tap water contains salts and chlorine, which can dry the skin.

TIP

Male skin
Cleansing rinse-off formulations are very popular with male clients.

The use of a soft nylon bristle face brush is beneficial to use with a facial foaming cleanser or bar to prevent ingrowing hairs forming.

Non-oily eye make-up removers have these applications:

- treating clients with sensitive skin around the eyes;
- treating clients who wear contact lenses;
- treating clients who wear individual false eyelashes.

Cleansing treatment

There are two manual processes involved in the cleansing routine: the *superficial cleanse* and the *deep cleanse*.

The superficial cleanse uses lightweight cleansing preparations to emulsify surface make-up, dirt and grease. This is followed by the more thorough deep cleanse, in which a heavier cleansing cream is applied to the face. The high percentage of oil contained in the cream formulation allows the cream to be massaged over the skin's surface without evaporation of the product.

Step-by-step: Superficial cleansing

Each part of the face requires a special technique in the application and removal of the cleansing product. The face is cleansed in the following order:

- the eye tissue and lashes;
- the lips;
- the neck, chin, cheeks and forehead.

HEALTH AND SAFETY

Eye care
Never apply pressure over the eyeball when cleansing the eye area.

TIP

Unlike the muscles of the body, which attach to bones, most of the facial muscles are attached to the facial skin itself. You should therefore avoid stretching the skin unnecessarily – if you do, you may also stretch the facial muscles and contribute to premature ageing.

TIP

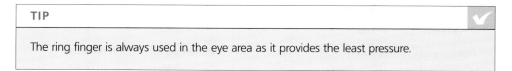

The ring finger is always used in the eye area as it provides the least pressure.

HEALTH AND SAFETY

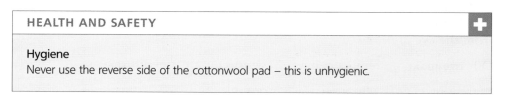

Hygiene
Never use the reverse side of the cottonwool pad – this is unhygienic.

Step-by-step: Superficial cleansing

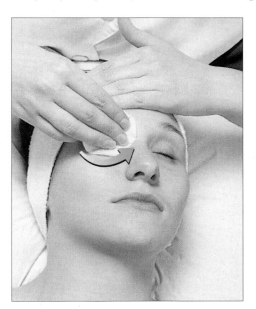

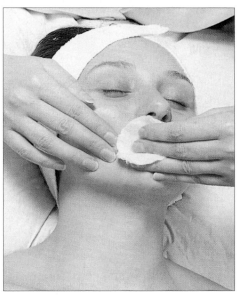

TIP

If there is any make-up left at the base of the lower lashes after eye cleansing, this may be removed with a cotton bud or a thin piece of clean cottonwool. Ask the client to look upwards, and gently draw the cottonwool along the base of the lower lashes, towards the nose. A cottonbud is useful for this task.

1 Wash your hands.

2 Cleanse the eye area, using a suitable eye make-up remover. Each eye is cleansed separately. Your non-working hand lifts and supports the eye tissue whilst the working hand applies the eye make-up remover.

If a water-based eye make-up remover is used, this is applied directly to a clean piece of cottonwool. Stroke down the length of the eyelashes, from base to points. Next, cleanse the eye tissue in a sweeping circle, outwards across the upper eyelid, circling beneath the lower lashes towards the nose. Repeat, regularly changing the cottonwool until the eye area and the cottonwool show clean.

Sometimes a cleansing milk is used to remove eye make-up. In this case, apply a little of the product to the back of one hand. The ring finger is then used to apply the cleansing milk to the lashes.

Use damp cottonwool to remove the emulsified product.

Repeat the cleansing process until the eye area is clean.

3 Cleanse the lips, preferably with a cleansing milk or lotion (as this readily emulsifies the oils or waxes contained in lipstick).

Apply a little of the product to the back of your non-working hand. Support the left side of the client's mouth with this hand. With the working hand, apply the product in small circular movements across the upper lip, from left to right; and then across the lower lip, from right to left.

Remove the cleanser from the lips. Support the corner of the mouth; using a clean damp piece of cottonwool wipe across the lips.

Repeat the cleansing process as necessary, until the lips and the cottonwool show clean.

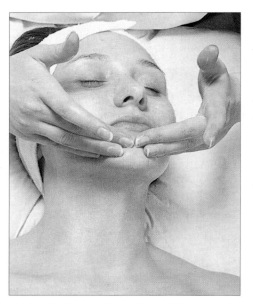

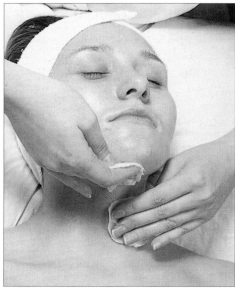

4 Select a cleansing milk or lotion to suit your client's skin type.

Pour the product into one hand – sufficient to cover the face and neck, and to massage gently over the surface of the skin. Massage the surface of the hands together: this warms the product (so that it isn't cold on the client's skin) and distributes it over your hands.

Clasp the fingers together at the base of the neck, and unlink them as you move up the neck.

Clasp the fingers together again at the chin, drawing the fingers outwards to the angle of the jawbone.

Stroke up the face, towards the forehead, with your fingertips pointing downwards and your palms in contact with the skin.

Using a series of light circular movements of your fingertips, gently massage the product into the skin, beginning at the base of the neck and finishing at the forehead.

5 Remove the cleanser thoroughly with clean damp cottonwool, facial sponges or facial mitts simultaneously stroking over the skin surface, upwards and outwards in a rolling motion. Repeat this process as necessary, using clean cottonwool each time.

Step-by-step: Deep cleansing

The deep cleanse involves a series of massage manipulations which reinforce the cleansing achieved with the cleansing product. Blood circulation is increased to the area; this has a warming effect on the skin, which relaxes the skin's natural openings, the hair follicles and pores. This aids the absorption of cleanser into the hair follicles and pores, where it can dissolve make-up and sebum.

There are various deep-cleansing sequences; all are acceptable if carried out in a safe, hygienic manner, and all can achieve the desired outcomes. Here is one sequence for deep cleansing.

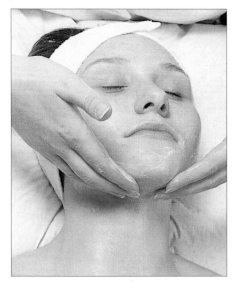

1 Select a cleansing medium to suit your client's skin type. The procedure for application is the same as that for the superficial cleanse.

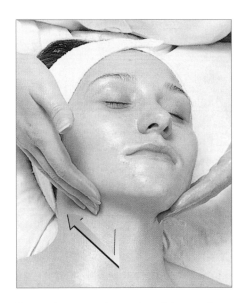

2 Stroke up either side of the neck, using your fingertips. At the chin, draw the fingers outwards to the angle of the jaw, and lightly stroke back down the neck to the starting position.

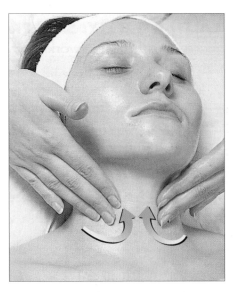

3 Apply small circular manipulations over the skin of the neck.

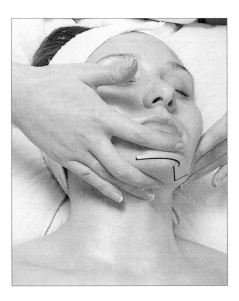

4 Draw the fingertips outwards to the angle of the jaw. Rest each index finger against the jawbone (you will be able to feel the lower teeth in the jaw). Place the middle finger beneath the jawbone. Move the right hand towards the chin where the index finger glides over the chin; return the fingers, beneath the jawbone, to the starting position. Repeat with the left hand.

Repeat step 4 *a further 5 times.*

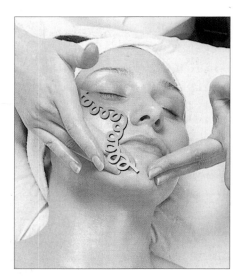

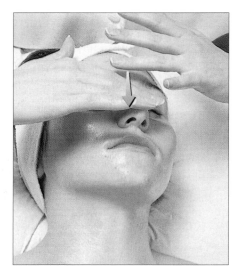

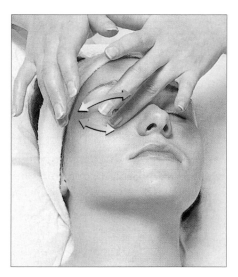

5 Apply small circular manipulations, commencing at the chin working up towards the nose, and finishing at the temples. Slide the fingers from the temples back to the chin, and repeat.

Repeat step 5 a further 5 times.

6 Position the ring finger of the right hand at the bridge of the nose. Perform a running movement, sliding the ring, middle and index fingers off the end of the nose. Repeat immediately with the left hand.

Repeat step 6 a further 5 times with each hand.

7 With the ring fingers, trace a circle around the eye orbits. Begin at the inner corner of the upper browbone; slide to the outer corners of the browbone, around and under the eyes, and return to the starting position.

Repeat step 7 a further 5 times.

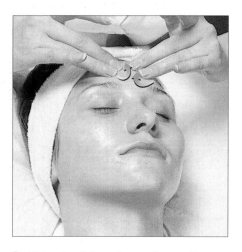

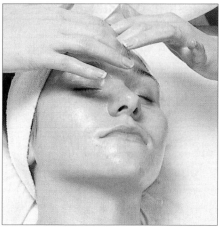

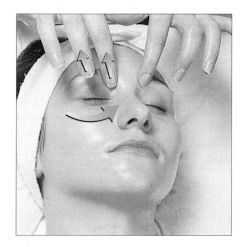

8 Using both hands, apply small circular manipulations across the forehead.

Repeat step 8 a further 5 times.

9 Open the index and middle fingers of each hand and perform a cross-cross stroking movement over the forehead.

10 Slide the index finger upwards slightly, lifting the inner eyebrow. Lift the centre of the eyebrow with the middle finger. Finally, lift the outer corner of the eyebrow with the ring finger. Slide the ring fingers around the outer corner and beneath the eye orbit.

Repeat step 10 a further 5 times.

11 With the pads of each hand, apply slight pressure at the temples. This indicates to the client that the cleansing sequence is complete.

12 Remove the cleansing cream from the skin, using damp cottonwool, facial sponges or facial mitts.

TIP ✓

Check that the brow hair and the skin beneath the chin are free of grease: it is easy to overlook some cleansing product in these areas.

TONING

After the skin has been cleansed it is then toned with an appropriate lotion.

Toning preparations

Toning lotions remove from the skin all traces of cleanser, grease and skin-care preparations. The toning lotion's main action is as follows.

- It produces a cooling effect on the skin when the water or alcohol in the toner evaporates from the skin's surface. (When a liquid evaporates it changes to a gas, which takes energy. In the case of toner, the energy is taken from the skin, which therefore feels cooler.)

- It creates a tightening effect on the skin, because of a chemical within the toner called an astringent. This causes the pores to close, thereby reducing the flow of sebum and sweat onto the skin's surface.

- It helps to restore the acidic pH balance of the skin. Milder skin toners have a pH 4.5–4.6; stronger astringents disturb the pH more severely, and may cause skin irritation and sensitivity.

There are three main types of toning lotions, the main difference being the amounts of alcohol they contain. They include:

- bracers and fresheners;
- tonics;
- astringents.

Skin bracers and fresheners

Skin bracers and **skin fresheners** are the mildest toning lotions: they contain little or no alcohol. They consist mainly of purified water, with floral extracts such as **rose water** for a mild toning effect.

Skin bracers and fresheners are recommended for:

- dry, delicate skin;
- sensitive skin;
- mature skin.

Skin tonics

Skin tonics are slightly stronger toning lotions. Many contain a little of some astringent agent such as witchhazel.

Skin toners are recommended for:

- normal skin.

Astringents

Astringents are the strongest toning lotions; they have a high proportion of alcohol. They may contain antiseptic ingredients such as **hexachlorophene**; these are for use on blemished skin, to promote skin healing.

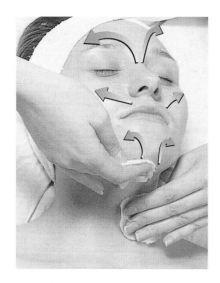

Toning

> **TIP** ✓
>
> **Toning lotions**
> *All* toning lotions have some astringent effect on the skin, but those that contain a relatively high alcohol content are actually marketed as astringents.
>
> Do not use toning lotions that contain more than 20 per cent alcohol on dry skin – they may cause skin irritation.
>
> Avoid the excessive use of astringent on oily skin – the astringent will make the skin dry, and it will then produce more sebum.

> **TIP** ✔
>
> **Combination skin**
> When applying toning lotion to a combination skin, you may need to apply different toning lotions to treat separate skin conditions.

> **TIP** ✔
>
> **Client care**
> Before facial application it is a good idea to spray the mist onto the back of the client's hand: this helps them to relax.

> **TIP** ✔
>
> For home use, advise the client to apply toning lotion using dampened cottonwool: this is more economical.

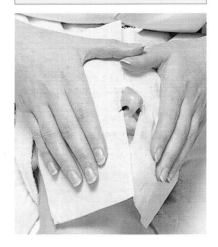

Blotting the skin

Astringents are recommended for:

- oily skin with no skin sensitivity;
- mild acne in young skin.

Application

Toning lotion may be applied in several ways. Whichever method you choose, it should leave the skin thoroughly clean and free of grease.

The most popular method of application is to apply the toner directly to two pieces of clean damp cottonwool, which are wiped gently upwards and outwards over the neck and face.

Alternatively, the toner may be applied under pressure as a fine spray, using a vaporiser. This produces a fine mist of the toning lotion over the skin. If using this method, always protect the eye tissue with cottonwool pads and hold the vaporiser about 30cm from the skin, directing the spray across the skin in a sweeping movement. This is preferable when treating a male client, where the cottonwool application technique would be unsuitable.

To produce a stimulating effect, the toning lotion can be applied to dampened cottonwool: hold this firmly at one corner, and gently tap it over the skin.

After applying toning lotion, immediately blot the skin dry with a soft facial tissue to prevent the toner evaporating from the skin's surface (which would stimulate the skin).

Blotting the skin

Make a small tear in the centre of a large facial tissue for the client's nose. Place the tissue over their face and neck, and mould it into position to absorb excess moisture.

> **HEALTH AND SAFETY**
>
> **Client comfort**
> To avoid claustrophobia and discomfort, tell the client before you start how and why facial blotting is carried out.

MOISTURISING

The skin depends on water to keep it soft, supple and resilient. Two-thirds of our body is composed of water and the skin is an important reservoir, containing about 20 per cent of the body's total water content. Most of the fluid is in the lower layers of the dermis, but it circulates to the top layer of the epidermis, where it evaporates.

The skin protects its water content in these ways:

- sebum keeps the skin lubricated, and reduces water loss from skin;
- the skin cells have **natural moisturising factors** (**NMFs**), a complex mix of substances which are able to fix moisture inside the cells;
- a 'cement' of fats (lipids) between the skin cells forms a watertight barrier.

The natural moisture level is constantly being disturbed. The application of a cosmetic **moisturiser** helps to maintain the natural oil and moisture balance by locking moisture into the tissues, offering protection and hydration.

The basic formulation of a moisturiser is oil and water to make an oil-in-water emulsion. The water content helps to return lost moisture to the surface layers; the oil content prevents moisture loss from the surface of the skin. Often a **humectant**, such as **glycerine** or **sorbitol**, is included: this attracts moisture to the skin from the surrounding air and stops the moisturiser from drying out. If a humectant is included, less oil is used in the formulation: this results in a lighter cream.

Moisturiser also has the following benefits:

- it protects the skin from external damage caused by the environment;
- it softens the skin and relieves skin tautness and sensitivity;
- it plumps the skin tissue with moisture, which minimises the appearance of fine lines;
- it provides a barrier between the skin and make-up cosmetics;
- it may contain additional ingredients which improve the condition of the skin (such as vitamin E, which has a humectant action and is an excellent skin conditioner);
- it may contain ultra-violet filters, which protect the skin against the age-accelerating sunlight.

Moisturisers are available for wear during the day or the night. These are available in different formulations, to treat all skin types and conditions.

Moisturisers for daytime use

Moisturising lotions

Moisturising lotions contain up to 85–90 per cent water and 10–15 per cent oil. They have a light, liquid formulation, and are ideal for use under make-up.

Moisturising lotions have these specific applications:

- oily skin;
- young combination skin;
- dehydrated skin;
- normal skin.

Moisturising creams

Moisturising creams contain up to 70–85 per cent water and 15–30 per cent oil. They have a thicker consistency, and cannot be poured.

TIP

Oily skin
Even oily skin requires a moisturiser. This skin can become dehydrated by the over-use of harsh cleansers and astringents.

TIP

Tinted moisturisers
If your client likes a natural look for the day, they may wish to wear a moisturiser that is tinted; this gives the skin a healthy appearance.

TIP

UV light
Even on an overcast day, as much as 80 per cent of the sun's age-accelerating UVA can penetrate the skin.

TIP

Antioxidant moisturisers
Antioxidant moisturisers protect against free-radical damage from UV exposure, cigarette smoke, pollution and stress.

TIP

Moisturising creams
Some clients dislike heavier cream, feeling that it is too heavy for their skin. Offer them a suitable moisturising lotion alternative.

Moisturising creams have these specific applications:

- mature skin;
- dry skin.

HEALTH AND SAFETY

Allergies
Hypoallergenic moisturisers are available for clients with sensitive skin. These are screened from all common sensitising ingredients, such as lanolin and perfume, and they also have soothing properties.

ACTIVITY

Moisturisers
Collect information on different moisturisers from various skin-care suppliers. You could visit local beauty salons, retail stores or beauty wholesale suppliers, or write to professional skin-care companies.

How to apply moisturiser

Moisturiser is applied after the final application of toning lotion. If the moisturiser is being applied before make-up, use a light formulation so that it does not interfere with the adherence of the foundation.

1 Remove some moisturiser from the jar, using a disposable spatula or disinfected plastic spatula. Place it on the back of the non-working hand, then take it on the fingertips of your working hand.

2 Apply the moisturiser in small dots to the neck, chin, cheeks, nose and forehead. Quickly and evenly spread it in a fine film over the face, using light upward and outward stroking movements.

3 Blot excess moisturiser from the skin using a facial tissue.

Applying moisturiser

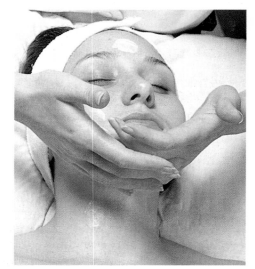

TIP

If the moisturiser is very fluid, apply it directly to the fingertips of the non-working hand – it would run if applied to the back of the hand.

Moisturisers for night-time use

Moisturisers are applied to the skin in the evening, after the skin has been cleansed, toned and blotted dry.

An emulsion **night cream** with a higher proportion of oil is the most effective for application in the evening: by this time the surrounding air is dry and warm, which encourages water loss from the skin; the oil seals the surface of the skin, preventing this water loss.

A small amount of **wax** (such as beeswax) may be included in the formulation: this improves the '*slip*' of the product, making it easier to apply and helping its skin-conditioning effect.

Specialist skin treatment products

In addition to basic skin-care products, specialist skin-care treatment products are available to target improvement for specific facial areas.

Throat creams

The neck can become dry as it is exposed to the weather, often without the protection of a moisturiser. As a client ages, the collagen molecules in the dermis become increasingly cross-linked; they are then unable to retain the same volume of water, and the skin loses its plump appearance.

The formulation for a **throat cream** is similar to that for a night cream; it also contains various skin conditioning supplements, such as collagen or vitamin E, which help maintain moisture in the stratum corneum.

Encourage your client to include the neck in their cleansing routine, applying facial moisturiser to the neck during the day and either a night cream or specially formulated throat cream in the evening. Recommend that they always apply the throat cream gently in an upward and outward direction, using their fingertips.

To improve the appearance of the neck, good posture is important. If the client is round-shouldered the head often drops forwards, putting strain on the muscles of the neck. This causes tension in the muscles, which become tight and painful. Correct the client's posture, and advise them to massage the neck when applying the throat cream to relieve tension.

> **TIP** ✔
>
> Advise the client against losing weight quickly, especially when older – the neck tissue can look loose and very wrinkled as the underlying fat is lost.

Eye creams

The eye tissue is very thin and readily becomes very dry, emphasising fine lines and wrinkles (**crow's feet**). Special care must be taken when applying products near this area: it contains a large number of **mast cells**, the cells that respond to contact with an irritant by causing an allergic reaction.

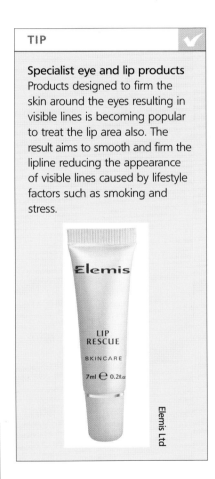

> **TIP** ✔
>
> **Specialist eye and lip products**
> Products designed to firm the skin around the eyes resulting in visible lines is becoming popular to treat the lip area also. The result aims to smooth and firm the lipline reducing the appearance of visible lines caused by lifestyle factors such as smoking and stress.

Elemis Ltd

ACTIVITY

Eye conditions
Think of different *non-medical eye* conditions for which a client might seek your advice. Discuss with colleagues the possible cause of these conditions, and what you could recommend to improve the appearance in each case.

Elemis Ltd

Ampoules

Eye cream is a fine cream formulated specifically for application to the eye area. A small quantity of the product is applied to the eye tissue using the ring finger of one hand, gently stroking around the eye, inwards and towards the nose. Support the eye tissue with the other hand. Do not apply the product too near to the inner eyelid or you will cause irritation to the eye.

Eye gel

Eye gel is usually applied in the morning: it has a cooling, soothing, slightly astringent effect. (This is caused partly by the evaporation of the water in the gel, and partly by the inclusion of plant extracts such as **cornflower** or **camomile**.)

Eye gel is recommended for all clients, but especially for those suffering with slightly puffy eye tissue. It may also be applied following a facial treatment, to normalise the pH of the skin.

Eye gel may be applied with a light tapping motion, using the pads of the fingers. This will mildly stimulate the lymphatic circulation in the area and help to reduce any slight swelling.

Ampoule treatment

Serums are chemicals used to revitalise the skin. They are supplied in **ampoules**, sealed glass or plastic phials which prevent the content from evaporating and losing their effectiveness. Serums are usually applied for 7–28 days as a skin-tonic course for the treatment of different skin types and conditions.

Blemished skin-care preparations

Professional products are available for the client to apply specifically to blemishes such as pistules and papules. Benzoyl peroxide is an example of a product ingredient that dries and promotes healing of skin blemishes. The skin care aims to purify the skin whilst keeping it hydrated.

Warming the skin

Steam is the ideal means of producing the required warming effect on the skin to achieve both cleansing and stimulation. Skin warming is often incorporated into a facial treatment after the manual cleansing, so as to stimulate the skin and make it more receptive to subsequent treatments.

The effects are these:

- the pores are opened;
- locally the blood circulation and the lymphatic circulation are stimulated;
- the surface cells of the epidermis are softened, which helps desquamation;
- sebaceous gland activity is improved, which benefits a dry, mature skin type;
- skin colour is improved.

Steam is provided by an electric **vapour unit**. In this, distilled water is heated electrically until it boils to create steam.

The resulting steam is applied as a fine mist over the facial area. As the steam settles upon the skin it is absorbed by the surface epidermal cells. These cells are softened and can be gently loosened with an exfoliation treatment.

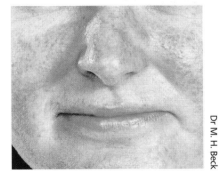

A vapour unit

Sorisa

HEALTH AND SAFETY

Vapour application
Keep the vapour directed away from the client's face until a visible jet of steam can be seen. To avoid skin sensitisation, consider carefully where to position the steam so as to ensure even heat distribution.

HEALTH AND SAFETY

Safe use and care of the vapour unit
- Always follow manufacturers instructions on correct usage.
- Have the unit tested annually by a qualified electrician to ensure its safety in compliance with the Electricity at Work Regulations 1989.
- Always use distilled water to avoid limescale build-up in the heating element.
- Never fill the water vessel past the recommended level or 'spitting' could occur, where hot droplets of water are ejected and could burn the client's skin.
- Never use the equipment if the water vessel is below the recommended level or the heating element could be damaged. Most units have a cut out feature so that the machine switches off if this occurs.
- Never leave the lead trailing across an area where somebody could trip and fall.

TIP

Heat the water in the vapour unit in advance of its application. This usually takes about 12 minutes. This will avoid an unnecessary delay in the facial routine waiting for the water to heat! Ensure that the couch is correctly positioned before treatment when using steam, to allow the vapour unit to be positioned at the correct distance from the client's skin.

Rosacea

Dr M. H. Beck

Contra-indications

Although the treatment is suitable for most clients, do not use steam if you discover that the client has any of the following:

- *Respiratory problems*, such as asthma or a cold.
- *Vascular skin disorders* – these would be aggravated by the heating action and increased blood circulation.
- *Claustrophobia* – fear of enclosure or confined space.
- *Excessively dilated capillaries*.
- *Skin with reduced sensitivity*.
- *Diabetes*, unless the client's GP has given permission.
- *Rosacea – a vascular skin disorder*, where excess sebum production combined with a chronic inflammatory condition is caused by dilation of the blood capillaries. The skin becomes coarse, the pores enlarge, and the cheek and nose become inflamed.
- *Dilated capillaries*, where capillaries near the surface of the skin are permanently dilated.

Dilated capillaries

Dr John Gray, *The World of Skin Care*

Applying steam to the back

Application

Explain to the client:

- how long the treatment is to be applied for;
- the sensations that will be experienced;
- the physical effect on the skin.

The duration of the application and the distance differ according to the skin type.

The client should be positioned in a semi-reclined position for facial application.

Before applying steam, protect the client's eyes with damp cottonwool. Areas of delicate skin should be protected with damp cottonwool and if necessary a barrier cream.

The distance between the vapour outlet and the client's skin to be treated should be approximately 30–35cm. The application time will depend on the treatment effect and the type of skin that is being treated. Generally allow:

- 10 minutes for the face;
- 15 minutes for the body.

Ensure that an even flow of steam covers all the area being treated; reposition as necessary.

If you are using ozone, this is applied following the steam application for the final few minutes, as directed by the manufacturer. The steam will change in appearance to a bluish-white cloud.

After applying steam vapour, blot the skin dry with a soft facial tissue and proceed to remove any blockages.

At the end of the treatment, turn off the machine and unplug it. Check that you have tidied away the trailing lead so that there is no risk of it causing an accident.

ACTIVITY

Vapour units
Collect literature on different vapour units. Compare their efficiencies and features. Which would be the best buy? Consider:
- Is the unit transportable, for marketing demonstrations?
- Is it height-adjustable, to suit the height of the treatment couch?
- Is it easy to clean?
- If floor-standing, does it move easily?
- Does it allow the addition of aromatic oils?
- Has it safety features to prevent overheating or the vessel running dry?

Contra-actions

Contra-actions to steaming include the following:

- *over-stimulation of the skin*, caused by incorrect application distance and duration of the steam;
- *scalding*, caused by spitting from a faulty steam jet or by the vessel being over-filled;
- *discomfort*, caused by the steam being too near the skin, leading to breathing difficulties, or by the treatment being applied for too long.

Towel steaming

Towel steaming is an alternative to steaming which can be used if an electrical vapour unit is not available to achieve the same beneficial effects. Several clean small towels are required: these are heated in a bowl of clean hot water, or specialised unit, and are then applied to the face. The towels must not be too hot to handle or you could burn the client's skin.

Application Seat the client in a semi-reclined position. Neatly fold a small clean towel and immerse it in very warm water. Wring it out quickly and, standing behind the client, transfer it to her face – with the towel folded in half, place it over the lower half of the face, directly under the client's lower lip; then unfold it to cover the upper face, leaving the mouth and nostrils uncovered.

Press the towel gently against the face for two minutes; during this time the towel will begin to cool. Remove the towel and replace it with another heated towel. Continue in this way, heating and replacing the towels, for approximately ten minutes.

After towel steaming, blot the skin dry with a soft facial tissue and proceed to remove any blockages.

Towel steaming

Towel heater

HEALTH AND SAFETY +

Treatment programme
If the client suffers from severe congestion, do not attempt to carry out all the removals in one session. This would sensitise the skin, making it appear very red, and would be most uncomfortable for the client. Instead they should visit the salon weekly for you to clear the skin gradually as part of an overall treatment programme.

TIP ✔

Aromatic oils
Provided that you have received instruction in the use of aromatic oils, and provided that the client has no contra-indications to them, you may add oils to the water.

REMOVING SKIN BLOCKAGES

After the skin has been cleansed, you may wish to remove minor skin blemishes such as comedones (blackheads) and milia (whiteheads). It is preferable to warm the tissues first: this softens the skin and relaxes the openings of the skin that are blocked.

HEALTH AND SAFETY +

Skin blockages
Do not attempt to remove larger skin blockages such as sebaceous cysts – these should be treated by a general practitioner.

Equipment and materials

You will need the following equipment and materials:

Sterilisation and disinfection

You must put the disposable milium extractor in a 'sharps' container. All waste material from this treatment (such as facial tissues and gloves) should be disposed of in an identified waste container, as directed by your local health authority.

After use the stainless steel comedone extractor should be cleaned with an alcohol preparation and then sterilised in an autoclave.

Wear disposable gloves whilst carrying out the treatment.

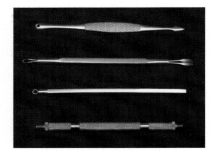

Comedone extractors

Treatment

Comedone removal

Using the loop end of the extractor tool, apply gentle pressure around the comedone. The comedone should leave the skin, apparent as a plug. You may need to apply gentle pressure with your fingers at the sides of the comedone to ensure that it is effectively removed; when doing this, wrap a tissue around the pads of the index fingers.

Contra-actions:

- Skin bruising could occur if too much pressure is applied.
- Capillary damage could result if too much force is used when squeezing the comedone. The surrounding blood capillaries can rupture, causing permanent skin damage.

Milium extraction

Hold the point of the extractor tool parallel with the skin's surface, and *superficially* pierce the epidermis. This makes an opening through which the sebaceous matter can pass to the skin's surface. Using either the comedone extractor or tissue wrapped around the index fingers, apply gentle pressure. A mild antiseptic soothing lotion applied after extraction will help the skin to heal.

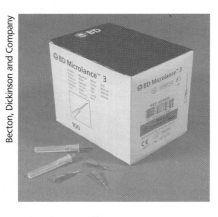

Becton, Dickinson and Company

Microlance milia extractors

HEALTH AND SAFETY

Client comfort
- Never obstruct the client's nostrils when removing a comedone from the nose area.
- Never apply pressure on the soft cartilage of the nose.

HEALTH AND SAFETY

Avoiding infection
Ensure that *all* contents of the skin blockage are removed, or infection may occur.

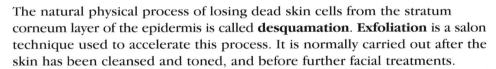

Milium extraction

EXFOLIATION

The natural physical process of losing dead skin cells from the stratum corneum layer of the epidermis is called **desquamation**. **Exfoliation** is a salon technique used to accelerate this process. It is normally carried out after the skin has been cleansed and toned, and before further facial treatments.

Exfoliation has the following benefits:

- dead skin cells, grease and debris are removed from the surface of the skin;
- fresh new cells are exposed, improving the appearance of the skin;
- skin preparations such as moisturising lotions are more easily absorbed;
- the blood circulation in the area is mildly stimulated, bringing more oxygen and nutrients to the skin cells and improving the skin colour.
- hyperpigmentation is improved in appearance by the removal of the pigmented surface skin cells.

Contra-indications

Exfoliation is beneficial for most skin types; however, avoid application if the client has the following:

- highly sensitive skin;
- a vascular skin disorder such as telangiectases or damaged broken veins in the area of treatment application;
- pustular, blemished skin.

ACTIVITY

Exfoliants
Apply an exfoliant to the back of your own – or a colleague's – hand or arm. Compare the appearance and the feeling of the skin before and after application.

This technique produces a particularly marked effect on black skin, as it reduces the greyish appearance of the skin. (This is due to the skin having a thicker stratum corneum.)

TIP

Exfoliation
Exfoliation should be strongly recommended for the mature client. The removal of the surface dead cells has a rejuvenating effect on the skin's appearance.

Teenagers regenerate external skin cells every 14 days. This increases to 30–40 days as a client reaches their forties.

TIP

Male skin
A man who shaves, exfoliates every day, as shaving removes the top layer of skin. You can recommend that he also uses a cosmetic exfoliating product on areas such as the nose and forehead. If a male client suffers from pseudo folliculitis, recommend an electric shave rather than a wet shave, which tends to make this disorder worse.

Exfoliants

Various exfoliants are available; they may be of chemical or vegetable origin. Alternatively, mechanical exfoliation may be used.

Biochemical skin peel

Natural acids (alpha-hydroxy acids – AHAs), derived from fruits, sugar cane and milk, are applied to the skin as a face mask. The natural acids dissolve dead surface cells and stimulate circulation in the underlying skin. These masks are available to suit all skin types.

AHAs may be combined with enzymes derived from fruits such as papaya (papain) to help remove surface dead skin to achieve maximum effect.

When you apply this type of face mask, warn the client that there will be a stinging sensation and then a tightening effect as the mask sets.

Pore grains

Pore grains are the most popular exfoliants: a base of cream or liquid containing tiny spheres of polished plastic or crushed nuts is gently massaged over the skin's surface.

Clay exfoliants

Gentler **clay exfoliants** have a clay base which is applied like a face mask. As it dries, the clay absorbs dead skin cells and sebum. The mask is then gently stroked away, using the pads of the fingers. A mask style exfoliant is more suitable for a blemished skin accompanying an oily skin type.

HEALTH AND SAFETY

Exfoliants
Avoid exfoliating products that contain sharp grains of nut shells: these can scrape, split and damage the epidermis. Before purchasing, test the exfoliating product on the back of your own hand to feel its action.

Mechanical exfoliation

Mechanical exfoliation, or 'facial brushing', softens and cleanses the skin. Dead skin cells and excess sebum are removed as the soft hair bristles rotate over the skin's surface. The rotary action also increases the cleansing action of exfoliation.

If steam is applied before mechanical exfoliation, this will soften the dead skin cells, and **skin peeling cream** may be applied: together these will maximise the result of exfoliation.

Be careful to avoid over-stimulation, and over exfoliation resulting in sensitising the skin's surface, or disturbing the skin's natural protective qualities. Permanent sensitisation could result from incorrect exfoliation techniques or over-exfoliation.

Mechanical exfoliation

TIP ✔

Steaming
Steaming before exfoliation softens the outer skin cells, making them easier to remove.

Step-by-step: Exfoliation treatment

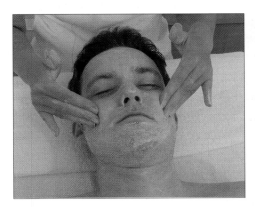

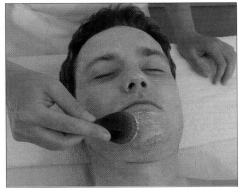

1 Facial exfoliant is applied manually to the skin following cleansing and steaming to warm and soften the skin. A cream exfoliant containing hydroxy acids is applied, which removes dead skin cells and stimulates skin renewal. Warn the client a mild stinging sensation may be experienced, but will disappear quickly upon removal.

2 A soft facial brush may be used in a rotary action to further enhance the effectiveness of the exfoliant to remove areas of dead skin and sebum. A client may purchase the brush to use as part of their homecare programme.

Advice on home use

The client can be advised to use exfoliants at home as a specialised cleansing treatment after normal cleansing and toning. Exfoliants should be applied once a week for all skin types except oily, for which it may be applied twice a week.

Advise the client to massage the product gently over the skin using their fingertips. Application should always be upwards and outwards. The application and removal technique will differ according to the exfoliant product type.

After application, any product residue should be thoroughly rinsed from the face using clean, tepid water. The client may then apply a face mask or tone the skin and apply a nourishing skin moisturiser.

A UV sunblock should be used to protect the skin to avoid skin damage.

TIP

Body exfoliants
Point out to clients that exfoliants designed for use on the *body* are unsuitable for use on the *face* – their action is not as gentle.

TIP

Retail opportunity
To encourage sales of this skin-care product, demonstrate the product on the back of one of the client's hands. They will be amazed when they compare the appearance of their hands.

HEALTH AND SAFETY +

Exfoliants
- Tell the client how the skin should look after exfoliation treatment. The skin's colour should be *slightly* heightened; but too vigorous a massage application may cause the formation of broken capillaries.
- Tell the client to avoid contact with the delicate eye tissue.
- A client with a pustular skin should not use exfoliant products – they would probably cause discomfort, and any lesions present might burst.

MASK TREATMENT

The **face mask** is a skin-cleansing preparation which may contain a variety of different ingredients selected to have a deep cleansing, toning, nourishing or refreshing effect on the skin. The mask achieves this through the following actions:

- if it contains *absorbent* materials, dead skin cells, sebum and debris will adhere to it when it is removed;
- if it contains *astringent* ingredients, the pores and the skin will tighten;
- if it contains *emollient* ingredients, the skin will be softened and nourished;
- if it contains *soothing* ingredients, the skin can be desensitised to reduce skin irritation.

Mask preparations

There are basically two types of mask: setting and non-setting.

Setting masks

Setting masks are applied in a thin layer over the skin and then allowed to dry. The mask need not necessarily set solid – a solid mask can become uncomfortable, and be difficult to remove.

Setting masks come in these varieties:

- clay packs;
- peel-off masks – gel, latex or paraffin wax;
- thermal masks.

Clay masks The **clay mask** absorbs sebum and debris from the skin surface, leaving it cleansed. It can also stimulate or soothe the skin, according to the ingredients chosen. Various clay powders are available – select from these according to the physiological effects you require:

- **Calamine** A light pink powder which soothes surface blood capillaries. *Uses in treatment*: for sensitive or delicate skin.
- **Magnesium carbonate** A very light, white powder which creates a temporary astringent and toning effect. *Use in treatment*: for open pores on dry and normal skins.
- **Kaolin** A cream-coloured powder which has a very stimulating effect on the skin's surface capillaries, thereby helping the skin to remove impurities and waste products. *Use in treatment*: for congested, oily skin.
- **Fuller's earth** A green, heavy clay powder. It has a very stimulating effect, such that the skin will show slight reddening. It also produces a whitening, brightening effect. *Use in treatment*: for oily skin with a sluggish circulation. Due to its strong effect, it is *not* suitable for a client with sensitive skin.
- **Flowers of sulphur** A light, yellow clay powder, which has a drying action on pustules and papules. *Use in treatment*: applied only to specific blemishes (pustules).

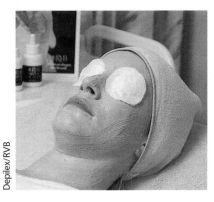

Depilex/RVB

A setting face mask

To activate these masks it is necessary to add a liquid – an **active lotion** – which turns the powder to a liquid paste. Active lotions are selected according to the skin type of the client and the mask to be used; they reinforce the action of the mask.

- **Rose water and orange-flower water** These are very popular; they have a very mild stimulating and toning effect.
- **Witchhazel** This has a soothing effect on blemished skin; it is also an astringent and is suitable for use on oily skin.
- **Distilled water** This is used on highly sensitive skins.
- **Almond oil** This is mildly stimulating. Because it is an oil, it does not allow the mask to dry: it is therefore recommended for highly sensitive skin or dehydrated skin.
- **Glycerol** A humectant, which prevents the mask drying and is suitable for dry, mature skin.

Clay masks have the disadvantage when treating a black skin that they tend on removal to leave streaks of white residue. Choose a mask that does not have this effect.

The mask should be kept in place for about 10–15 minutes.

ACTIVITY

Choosing face masks
Which clay powder and which active lotion would you mix for clients with the following skin types?
1 A mature, sensitive skin type.
2 A young, normal skin type.
3 A combination skin type: cheeks, neck area dry; forehead, nose and chin area oily.

Peel-off masks **Peel-off masks** may be made from gel, latex or paraffin wax. Because perspiration cannot escape from the skin's surface, moisture is forced into the stratum corneum. The mask also insulates the skin, causing an increase in temperature.

The **gel mask** is either a suspension of biological ingredients, such as starches, gums or gelatin, or a mixture of synthetic non-biological resin ingredients. The mask is applied over the skin; on contact with the skin it begins to dry. When dry it is peeled off the face in one piece. *Uses in treatment*: depending on the biological ingredients added, the gel mask can be used to treat all skin types. (If the client has excessive facial hair, such as at the sides of the face, this mask may cause discomfort on removal. To avoid this place a lubricant under the mask, or use a different sort of mask.)

The **latex mask** is an emulsion of latex and water: when applied to the skin, the water evaporates to leave a rubber film over the face. This produces a rise in temperature, thereby stimulating the skin. In alternative peel-off masks, latex is replaced by a synthetic resin emulsion such as **polyvinyl acetate** (PVA) resin. *Uses in treatment*: latex masks tighten the skin temporarily, and are suitable for mature skin; they can also be used with dry skin.

The **paraffin-wax mask** is stimulating in its action. The paraffin wax is blended with petroleum jelly or acetyl alcohol which improve its spreading properties. The wax is heated to approximately 37°C and is then applied to the skin as a liquid. It sets on contact, so speed is essential if the mask is to be effective. The wax mask is loosened at the sides and removed in one piece after 15–20 minutes. *Use in treatment*: the paraffin-wax mask is suitable for dry skin. Because of its stimulating action, it is unsuitable for oily skin or highly sensitive skin.

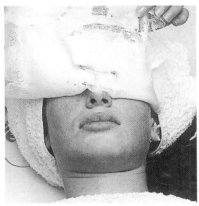

Helinova Ltd

Removal of paraffin-wax mask

HEALTH AND SAFETY

Client comfort
Before applying the wax to the client's skin always test the temperature of the wax on your own inner wrist.

HEALTH AND SAFETY

Contra-indications

Do not use thermal masks on a client with a circulatory disorder or one who has lost tactile sensation.

A non-setting mask for male skin

TIP

Gauze masks

Ensure that you position the gauze correctly so that the nose and eye holes are properly placed.

HEALTH AND SAFETY

Allergies

When using biological masks, always check first whether the client has any food allergies.

HEALTH AND SAFETY

Natural masks

Because natural masks are prepared from natural foods, they must be prepared *immediately* before use – they very quickly deteriorate.

Thermal masks The **thermal mask** contains various minerals. The ingredients are mixed and applied to the face and neck, avoiding the mouth and eye tissue. The mask warms on contact with the skin: this causes the pores to enlarge, thereby cleansing the skin. As the mask cools it sets, and the pores constrict slightly. The mask is removed from the face in one piece. *Uses in treatment*: thermal masks have a stimulating, cleansing action, suitable for a normal skin or for a congested, oily skin with open pores.

Non-setting masks

Some **non-setting masks** stay soft on application; others become firm, but they do not tighten like a setting mask. For this reason they do not tone the skin as effectively as setting masks. Non-setting masks include:

- warm oil;
- natural masks – fruit, plant and herbal;
- cream.

Warm-oil masks A plant oil, typically **olive oil** or **almond oil**, is warmed and then applied to the skin. It softens the skin and helps to restore the skin's natural moisture balance. *Uses in treatment*: warm-oil masks are recommended for mature skin and dry or dehydrated skin.

Gauze masks A **gauze mask** is cut to cover the face and neck, with holes for the eyes, nostrils and lips. This is then soaked in warm oil. A dampened cottonwool eye pad is placed over each eye. The gauze is then placed over the face and neck. It is usually left in place for 10–20 minutes.

Natural masks **Natural masks** are made from natural ingredients rich in vitamins and minerals. Fresh **fruit** and **vegetables** have a mildly astringent and stimulating effect. Usually the fruit is crushed to a pulp and placed between layers of gauze, which are laid over the face.

Honey is used for its toning, tightening, antiseptic and hydrating effect. **Egg white** has a tightening effect and is said to clear impurities from the skin. **Avocados** have a nourishing effect; **bananas** soften the skin, and are used for sensitive skins.

HEALTH AND SAFETY

Acidic fruit

Lemon and grapefruit are generally considered too acidic for use on the face.

ACTIVITY

Creating natural masks

Create some masks, listing the ingredients to suit each of the following skin types:
- dry;
- oily;
- mature, with superficial wrinkling;
- sensitive.

If possible, arrange to carry out one of the masks on a suitable client in the workplace. Evaluate the natural face mask. Consider: cost, preparation, application, removal and effectiveness. Remember to ask your client for *their* opinion!

Cream masks **Cream masks** are pre-prepared for you. They have a softening and moisturising effect on the skin. Each mask contains various biological extracts or chemical substances to treat different skin types or conditions. Instructions will be provided with the mask, stating how the product is to be used professionally.

These masks are popular in the beauty salon: they often complement a particular facial treatment range used by the salon, and they are available for retail sale to clients.

Contra-indications

The contra-indications to general skin care apply also to face-mask application. In addition, observe the following:

- *Allergies* Check whether your client knows if they have allergies. If so, avoid all contact with known allergens.
- *Claustrophobia* Do not use a setting mask on a particularly nervous client. Some clients feel claustrophobic under its tightening effect.
- *Sensitive skins* Do not use stimulating masks on clients with highly sensitive skin.

Equipment and materials

When applying masks you will need the following equipment and materials:

> **TIP** ✓
>
> Place a clean facial tissue under the edge of the headband at the forehead, so that it overlaps the headband. This will protect the headband from staining.

EQUIPMENT LIST

 Dampened clean cottonwool

 Facial tissues (white) to blot the skin dry after applying toner following mask removal

 Face-mask ingredients

 Cottonwool eye pads (2) pre-shaped, round and dampened

 Protective headband (clean)

 Gauze used in applying certain masks

 Scissors to cut cottonwool eye pads (if cottonwool discs are not used)

 Clean spatulas (several) to mix individual masks (if required)

 Waste bin (covered and lined) for waste consumables

EQUIPMENT LIST *(continued)*

YOU WILL ALSO NEED:

Disposable tissue roll   such as bedroll

Towels (2)   freshly laundered for each client

Flat mask brushes (3)   disinfected

Trolley   to display all facial treatment products to be used in the facial treatment

Client's record card   to record all the details relevant to the client's treatment

Facial toning lotions (a selection)   to suit various types of skin

Sterilised mask-removal sponges (2)   for use when removing the mask using clean warm water

Large bowl   to hold warm water during removal of the mask

Lukewarm water   if required for mask removal

Moisturisers (a range)   to suit different skin types for use after mask removal

Hand mirror (clean)   to show the client their skin following the facial treatment

---

TIP

Brushes
When purchasing mask brushes, note that a plastic-handled brush is preferable to one with a painted wooden handle – the painted one would be likely to peel on immersion in water, which spoils the professional image!

TIP

Ensure that you have plenty of dampened cottonwool – it is used to apply toner to the skin before mask application, to remove the mask or mask residue left on the skin, and to apply toner to the skin after mask removal.

Ideally, buy cottonwool discs to use for the eye pads. This will reduce preparation time and ensure an evenly shaped protective shield for the eye area.

TIP

Eye treatments
Many eye make-up removers are also eye treatments. If your workplace uses a commercial product in this way apply it to the dampened eye pads used during mask treatment. This may also assist your retail sales, as the client may wish to buy some for home use.

Sterilisation and disinfection

After applying the mask, clean the mask brush thoroughly in warm water and detergent. Next, place it in a chemical disinfecting agent; rinse it in clean water; allow it to dry; and then store it in the ultra-violet cabinet.

When you use a paraffin-wax mask, remove as much mask residue as possible from the brush, then place the brush in boiling water to completely remove all the wax. Disinfect the brush as usual before use.

If you use sponges to remove the mask, place them in warm water and detergent. After rinsing them in clean water, place them ready for disinfection in an autoclave. (With repeated disinfection, sponges will begin to break up.)

A large high-quality cottonwool disc may be purchased to use in mask removal.

HEALTH AND SAFETY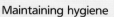

Maintaining hygiene
You need several mask brushes and mask sponges to allow effective disinfection of the tools, and so that you can provide freshly disinfected tools for each client.

Preparing the cubicle

Check that you have all the materials you need to carry out the treatment. You may like to place a paper roll at the head of the couch, underneath the client's head, to collect any mask residue on mask removal.

The head of the couch should be flat or slightly elevated. Don't have it in a semi-reclined position during the mask application, as some masks are liquid in consistency and may run into the client's eyes and behind their neck.

Treatment

Preparing the client

For maximum effect, the mask must be applied on a clean, grease-free surface. If the mask application follows a facial massage, ensure that the massage medium has been thoroughly removed.

Select the appropriate mask ingredients to treat the skin type and the facial conditions that require attention.

How to apply and remove the mask

The mask is usually applied as the *final* facial treatment, because of its cleansing, refining and soothing effects upon the skin. The methods of preparation, application and removal are different for the various face-mask types, so the guidelines below are a general outline of effective treatment technique.

1 Having determined the client's treatment requirements, select the appropriate mask ingredients. If you use a commercial mask, always read the manufacturer's instructions first.

2 Discuss the treatment procedure with the client. Tell him:
- what the mask will feel like on application;
- what sensation, if any, he will experience;
- how long the mask will be left on the skin.

Generally the mask will be left in place for 10–20 minutes, but the exact time depends on the type and effect required.

3 Prepare the mask ingredients for application.

4 Using the sterilised mask brush or spatula, begin to apply the mask. The usual sequence of mask application is neck, chin, cheeks, nose and forehead.

If you are using more than one mask to treat different skin conditions, apply first the one that will need to be on longest.

Apply the mask quickly and evenly so that it has maximum effect on the whole face. Don't apply it too thickly; as well as making mask removal difficult, this is wasteful as only the part that is in contact with the skin has any effect.

Keep the mask clear of the nostrils, the lips, the eyebrows and the hairline.

5 To relax the client, apply cottonwool eye pads dampened with clean water.

TIP

Paraffin wax
If you are using paraffin wax, remember to heat it in advance.

HEALTH AND SAFETY

Allergies
When using a commercial mask, try to find out *exactly* what it contains, so that you don't apply a sensitising ingredient to an allergic skin type.

HEALTH AND SAFETY

Client comfort
It is important to check that your client is comfortable whilst the mask is on their face. (They will suffer discomfort if their skin is intolerant to a particular mask.)

TIP

Don't mix the mask with the mask brush – if you do, the solid contents will tend to collect in the bristles, the mask won't be mixed effectively, and the brush won't spread the mask evenly.

HEALTH AND SAFETY

Setting masks
When using a setting mask, ensure that the mask is evenly applied or it will dry unevenly.

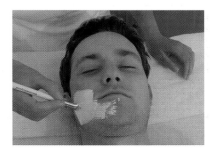

Applying the mask

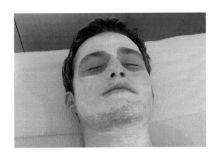

Leaving the mask for the recommended time

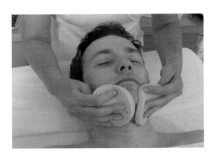

Removing the mask

TIP ✔

Mask removal
When using water to remove a mask you may need to renew the water as you work.

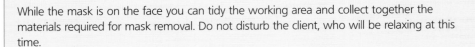

TIP ✔

While the mask is on the face you can tidy the working area and collect together the materials required for mask removal. Do not disturb the client, who will be relaxing at this time.

6 Leave the mask for the recommended time or according to the effect required. Take account also of the sensitivity of the skin and your client's comfort.

7 Wash your hands.

8 When the mask is ready for removal, remove the eyepads.
  Explain to the client that you are going to remove the mask. Briefly describe the process, according to whether this is a setting or a non-setting mask.
  Remove the mask. Mask sponges, if used, should be damp, not wet, so that water doesn't run into the client's eyes, nose or mouth.

9 When the mask has been completely removed, apply the appropriate toning lotion using dampened cottonwool. Blot the skin dry with a facial tissue.

10 Apply an appropriate moisturiser to the skin.

11 Remove the headband, and tidy the client's hair.

12 With a mirror, show the client their skin. Evaluate the treatment.

13 Record the results on their record card.

Contra-actions

Before you apply the mask, explain to the client what the action of the mask will feel like on the skin. This will enable them to identify any undesirable skin reaction, evident to them as skin irritation – a burning sensation.

Ask the client initially whether they are comfortable: this will give them the opportunity to tell you if they are experiencing any discomfort. Should there be a contra-action to the mask, remove the mask immediately and apply a soothing skin-care product.

If on removal of the mask you can see that there has been an unwanted skin reaction (that is, if you see inflammation), apply a soothing skin-care product. In either case, note the skin reaction on the record card, and choose a different mask next time.

Advice on home use

The client may be given a sample of the face mask for use at home. Explain to them the procedure for application and removal, so that they achieve maximum benefit from the mask. Encourage them to apply a mask once or twice a week depending on their skin type, to dislodge dead skin cells and to cleanse and stimulate the skin.

Advise the client not to apply the mask directly before a special occasion, in case it causes blemishes, as sometimes happens.

The skin should be toned and moisturised after removing the mask.

FACIAL MASSAGE

Manual massage is the external manipulation, using the hands, of the soft tissues of the face, neck and upper chest. Massage can improve the appearance of the skin and promote a sensation of stimulation or relaxation.

Each massage performed is adapted to the client's physiological and psychological needs. The skin's physiological needs are observed during the skin analysis; the client's psychological needs are usually discovered during the consultation.

The benefits of the facial massage include the following:

- Dead epidermal cells are loosened and shed. This improves the appearance of the skin, exposing fresh, younger cells.
- The muscles receive an improved supply of oxygenated blood, essential for cell growth. The tone and strength of the muscles are improved, firming the facial contour.
- The increased blood circulation in the area warms the tissues. This induces a feeling of relaxation, which is particularly beneficial when treating tense muscles.
- As the blood capillaries dilate and bring blood to the skin's surface, the skin colour improves.
- The lymphatic circulation and the venous blood circulation increase. These changes speed up the removal of waste products and toxins, and tend therefore to purify the skin. The removal of excess lymph improves the appearance of a puffy oedematous skin (provided that this does not require medical treatment).
- The increased temperature of the skin relaxes the pores and follicles. This aids the absorption of the massage product, which in turn softens the skin.
- Sensory nerves can be soothed or stimulated, depending on the massage manipulations selected.
- Massage stimulates the sebaceous and sudoriferous glands and increases the production of sebum and sweat. This increase helps to maintain the skin's natural oil and moisture balance.

Facial massage

Depilex/RVB

Reception

Facial massage is carried out as required, usually once every four to six weeks. Before the facial massage is given, the skin is cleansed; afterwards it is usual to apply a cleansing face mask, which absorbs any excess grease from the skin.

When booking a client for this treatment, allow one hour. The facial massage itself should take approximately 20 minutes, but this may vary according to the client's skin type.

Warn the client that the skin may appear slightly red and blotchy after treatment, due to the increase in blood circulation to the area: this reaction will normally subside after four to six hours.

> **ACTIVITY**
>
> **Planning a massage**
> How will observations from the skin analysis and the client consultation influence the facial massage treatment?

TIP

Client care

The headband can spoil the hair, and the massage medium may enter the hairline. Recommend that the client does not style their hair directly before the facial treatment.

Because of the stimulating effect on the skin recommend to the client that they receive this service when they do not have to apply any cosmetic products directly afterwards.

Sometimes the skin develops small blemishes after facial massage; this is due to its cleansing action. If the client is preparing for a special occasion, therefore, such as a wedding, make the appointment for at least five days in advance.

Massage manipulations

The facial massage is based on a series of classic massage movements, each with different effects. There are four basic groups of massage movements:

- effleurage;
- petrissage;
- percussion (also known as tapotement);
- vibrations.

The therapist can adapt the way each of these movements is applied, according to the needs of the client. Either the *speed of application* or the *depth of pressure* can be altered.

Effleurage

Effleurage is a stroking movement, used to begin the massage, as a link manipulation, and to complete the massage sequence. This manipulation is light, has an even pressure, and is applied in a rhythmical, continuous manner to induce relaxation.

The pressure of application varies according to the underlying structures and the tissue type, but it must *never* be unduly heavy.

Effleurage has these effects:

- desquamation is increased;
- arterial blood circulation is increased, bringing fresh nutrients to the area;
- venous circulation is improved, aiding the removal of congestion from the veins;

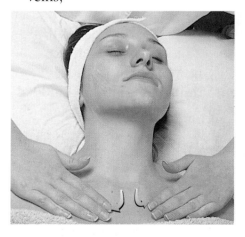

Effleurage

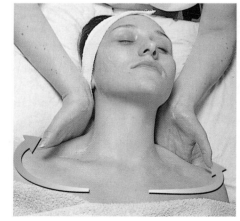

Effleurage

- lymphatic circulation is increased, improving the absorption of waste products;
- the underlying muscle fibres are relaxed.

Uses in treatment: to relax tight, contracted muscles.

Petrissage

Petrissage involves a series of movements in which the tissues are lifted away from the underlying structures and compressed. Pressure is intermittent, and should be light yet firm.

Petrissage has these effects:

- improvement of muscle tone, through the compression and relaxation of muscle fibres;
- improvement in blood and lymph circulation, as the application of pressure causes the vessels to empty and fill;
- increased activity of the sebaceous gland, due to the stimulation.

Movements include picking up, kneading, knuckling, pinching, rolling, frictions, and scissoring.

Uses in treatment: to stimulate a sluggish circulation; to increase sebaceous gland and sudoriferous gland activity, when treating a dry skin condition.

> **TIP**
>
> **Neck and shoulders**
> Pressure may be increased when working on larger muscles in the neck or shoulders.

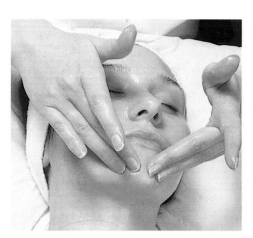

Petrissage

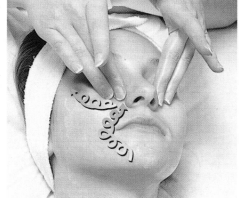

Petrissage

Percussion

Percussion, also known as **tapotement**, is performed in a brisk, stimulating manner. Rhythm is important as the fingers are continually breaking contact with the skin; irritation could occur if the movement were performed incorrectly.

Percussion has these effects:

- a fast vascular reaction because of the skin's nervous response to the stimulus – this reaction, erythema, has a stimulating effect;

> **TIP**
>
> **Stimulation**
> When a stimulating massage is required, incorporate more petrissage and tapotement into the massage sequence.

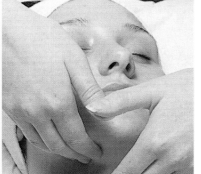

Percussion (tapotement)

- increased blood supply, which nourishes the tissues;
- improvement in muscle and skin tone in the area.

Movements include clapping and tapping. In facial massage, only light tapping should be used.

Uses in treatment: to tone areas of loose, crepey skin around the jaw or eyes.

HEALTH AND SAFETY
Contra-indications Do not apply percussion over highly sensitive or vascular skin conditions to avoid excessively increasing blood circulation in the area and over-stimulating the skin.

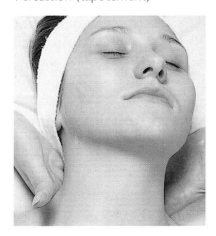

Vibrations

Vibrations

Vibrations are applied on the nerve centre. They are produced by a rapid contraction and relaxation of the muscles of the therapist's arm, resulting in a fine trembling movement.

Vibration has these effects:

- stimulation of the nerves, inducing a feeling of wellbeing;
- gentle stimulation of the skin.

Movements include *static* vibrations, in which the pads of the fingers are placed on the nerve, and the vibratory effect created by the therapist's arms and hands is applied in one position; and *running* vibrations, in which the vibratory effect is applied along a nerve path.

Uses in treatment: to stimulate a sensitive skin in order to improve the skin's functioning without irritating the surface blood capillaries.

TIP
It is important to maintain good posture during facial massage. If you slouch, you will experience muscle fatigue and long-term postural problems!

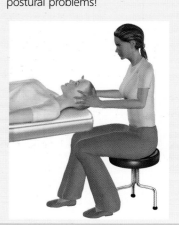

Equipment and materials

The massage is carried out using a **massage medium** which acts as a lubricant. A massage cream or oil may be used; these are slightly penetrating, and soften the skin. Choose a product that contains ingredients to suit the client's skin type and the age of the skin.

Whichever product you choose, it should provide sufficient slip whilst allowing you to control the massage movements.

ACTIVITY
Choosing a massage medium Compare two professional skin-care ranges. Look at: 1 the choice of facial-massage preparations; 2 the ingredients used in their formulation, and the effects claimed.

Step-by-step massage treatment

There are many different massage sequences, but each uses one or all of the massage manipulations discussed above. What follows is a basic sequence for facial massage.

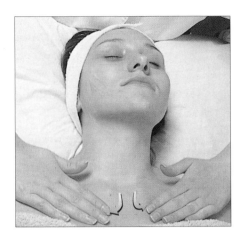
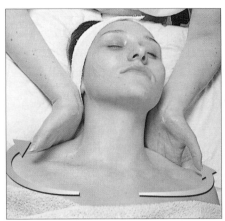
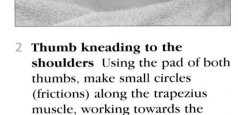

1 Effleurage to the neck and shoulders Slide the hands down the neck, across the pectoral muscles around the deltoid muscle, and across the trapezius muscle. Slide the hands up the back of the neck to the base of the skull.
Repeat step 1 a further 5 times.

2 Thumb kneading to the shoulders Using the pad of both thumbs, make small circles (frictions) along the trapezius muscle, working towards the spinal vertebrae.
Apply each movement 3 times; then repeat the sequence (step 2) a further 2 times.

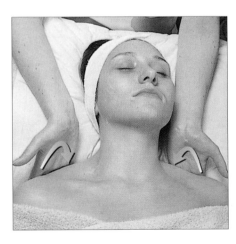
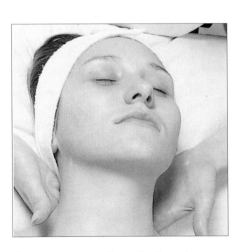
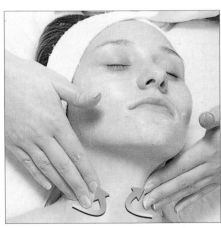

3 Finger kneading to the shoulders Position the fingers of each hand behind the deltoid, and make large rotary movements along the trapezius.
Apply each rotary movement 3 times; repeat the sequence (step 3) a further 2 times.

4 Vibrations Place the hands, cupped, at the base of the neck: perform running vibrations up the neck to the occipital bone.
Repeat step 4 a further 6 times.

5 Circular massage to the neck Perform small circular movements over the platysma and the sternomastoid muscle at the neck.

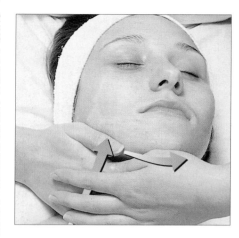

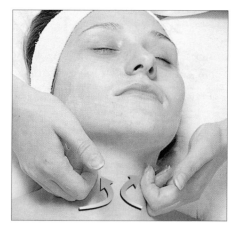

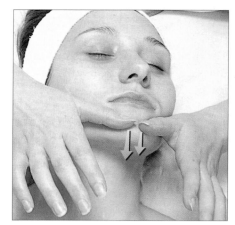

6 **Hands cupped to the neck**
Cup your hands together. Place the hands at the left side of the neck, above the clavicle. Slide the hands up the side of the neck, across the jawline, and down the right side of the neck; then reverse.

Repeat step 6 a further 2 times.

HEALTH AND SAFETY

The trachea
Never apply pressure when working on the neck over the trachea.

7 **Knuckling to the neck** Make a loose fist: rotate the knuckles up and down the neck area.

Repeat step 7 to cover, a further 2 times.

HEALTH AND SAFETY

Sensitive skin
Do not use knuckling on sensitive skin to avoid over-stimulation.

8 **Up and under** Place the thumbs on the centre of the chin, and the index and middle fingers under the mandible. Slide the thumbs firmly over the chin. Bring the index finger onto the chin, and place the middle finger under the mandible forming a V shape. Slide along the jawline to the ear. Replace the index finger with the thumb, and return along the jaw to the chin.

Repeat step 8 a further 5 times.

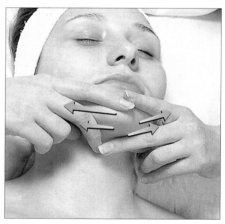

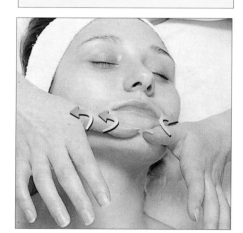

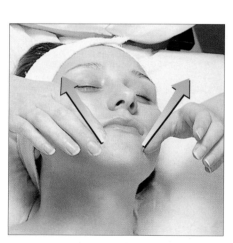

8 continued

9 **Circling to the mandible** Place the thumbs one above the other on the chin, and proceed with circular kneading along the jawline towards the ear. Reverse and repeat.

Repeat step 9 a further 2 times.

10 **Flick-ups** Place the thumbs at the corners of the mouth. Lift the orbicularis oris muscle, with a flicking action of the thumbs.

Repeat step 10 a further 5 times.

HEALTH AND SAFETY

The lips
Do not flick the lips. Position the thumbs 5mm from the corner of the mouth to avoid this.

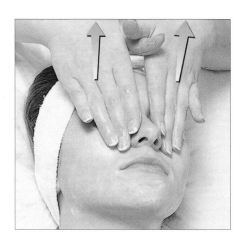

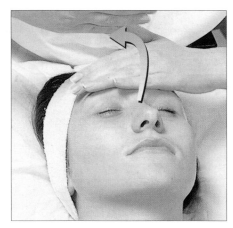

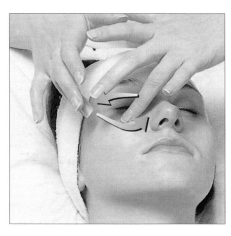

11 **Half face brace** Clasp the fingers under the chin; turn the hands so that the fingers point towards the sternum. Unclasp, and slide the hands up the face towards the forehead.

Repeat step **11** *a further 2 times.*

12 **Lifting the eyebrows** Place the right hand on the forehead at the left temple, and stroke upwards from the eyebrow to the hairline. Repeat the movement with the left hand. Alternate each hand; repeat the movement across the forehead.

Repeat step **12** *a further 2 times.*

13 **Inner and outer eye circles** Using the ring finger, *gently* draw 3 outer circles and 3 inner circles on each eye, following the fibre direction of the orbicularis oculi muscle.

Repeat step **13** *a further 2 times.*

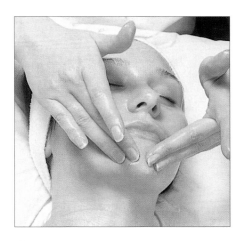

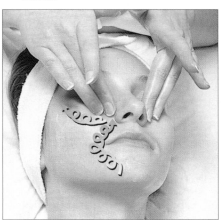

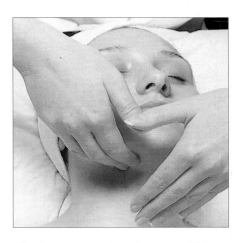

15 **Circling to the chin, the nose and the temples** Apply circular kneading to the chin, the nose and the temples. Return to the starting position.

Repeat step **15** *a further 2 times.*

16 **Thumb kneading under the cheeks** Place the thumbs under the zygomatic bones. Carry out a circular kneading over the muscles in the cheek area.

Repeat step **16** *a further 5 times.*

17 **Tapping under the mandible** Tap the tissue under the mandible, using the fingers of both hands. Work from the left side of the jaw to the right; then reverse.

Repeat step **17** *a further 5 times.*

TIP ✔

Massage medium
If the skin appears to drag during massage, stop and apply more massage medium. If you keep going you may cause skin irritation or discomfort.

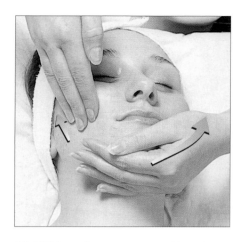

18 Lifting the masseter Cup the hands. Using the hands alternately, lift the masseter muscle.

Repeat step 18 a further 5 times.

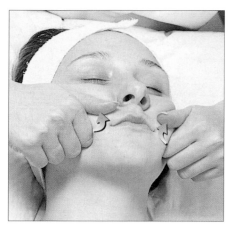

19 Rolling and pinching Using a deep rolling movement, draw the muscles of the cheek area towards the thumb in a rolling and pinching movement.

Repeat step 19 a further 5 times.

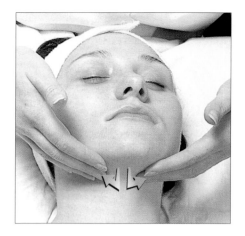

20 Lifting the mandible Place the pads of the fingers underneath the mandible and pivot diagonally. Lifting the tissues work towards the ear.

Repeat step 20 a further 2 times.

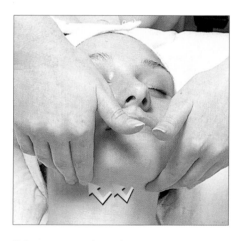

20 continued

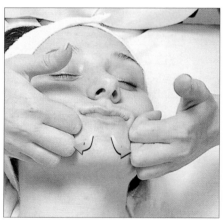

21 Knuckling along the jawline Knuckle along the jawline and over the cheek area.

Repeat step 21 a further 2 times.

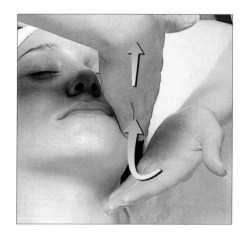

22 Upwards tapping on the face Using both hands, gently slap along the jawline from ear to ear, lifting the muscles.

Repeat step 22 a further 5 times.

TIP	

During the facial massage, the client's face should relax. If there are evident signs of tension, such as vertical furrows between the eyebrows, check that the client is warm and comfortable.

ACTIVITY	

Hand and wrist mobility exercises
Devise *ten* exercises to increase the strength and mobility of your hands and wrists.

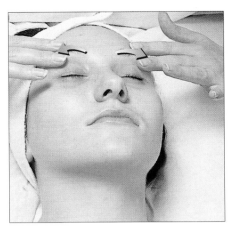
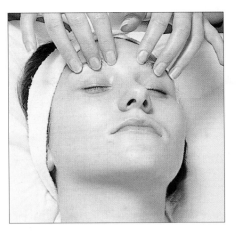
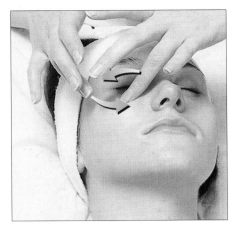

24 Scissor movement to the forehead Open the index and middle fingers to make a V shape at the outer corner of each eyebrow. Open and close the fingers in a scissor action towards the inner eyebrow.
Repeat step 24 a further 2 times.

25 Tapotement movement around the eyes Using the pads of the fingers, tap gently around the eye area.
Repeat step 25 a further 2 times.

26 Eye circling Repeat step 13, 3 times.

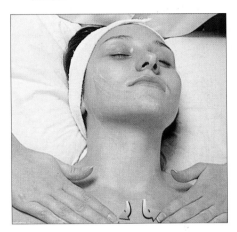

27 Effleurage Repeat step 1.

> **TIP**
>
> **Practise**
> When learning the facial massage you need to practise. Practise the movements on a styrofoam headblock with facial features, or mannequin head as used in hairdressing, to perfect the manipulations. If these are unavailable, practise each manipulation on your knee – this will increase the agility and strength of your fingers and wrists.

After the massage

After the facial massage, remove the massage medium thoroughly using clean, damp cottonwool. Check thoroughly that all product has been removed.

Apply toner to remove traces of oil, leaving the skin grease-free. Finally, blot the skin dry.

You may then proceed with further skin treatments, such as a face mask, or simply apply an appropriate moisturiser to conclude the treatment.

Advice on homecare

Encourage your client to use massage movements when applying emollient skin-care products. Show them how to perform such movements correctly.

Facial exercises may be given to the client to practise at home. These should be carried out at least four times per week.

> **TIP**
>
> Massage medium can easily be overlooked in the following areas: the eyebrows; the base of the nostrils; under the chin; in the creases of the neck; behind the ear and on the shoulders.

> **ACTIVITY**
>
> **Massage at home**
> Design a simple massage routine that a client could be taught to use at home.
> Which type of manipulation is involved in each movement in your sequence? What effect do you wish to achieve by incorporating it?

ACTIVITY

Facial exercises at home
Think of *ten* facial exercises that you could teach a client, to improve the muscle tone of the face and neck.

Teach these to a client after carrying out a facial massage treatment. At a later stage, evaluate the exercises and discuss with them their effectiveness.

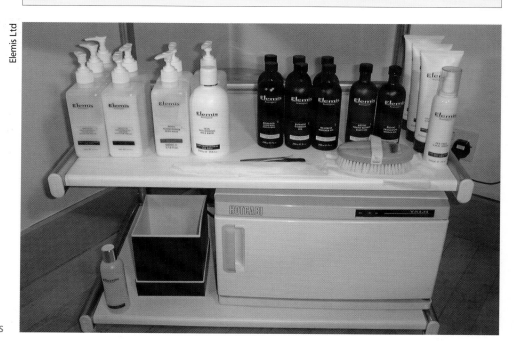

Elemis Ltd

Facial treatment preparations

SPECIALIST FACIAL TREATMENT

Specialist treatments should be offered to your client when there is a specific need or if they feel they would like to benefit from such a treatment. Specialist training in these advanced techniques is usually offered by the main product companies.

Step-by-step: Specialist facial

The model for this specialist facial treatment is a mature client with dry, dehydrated skin with areas of sensitivity. One hour and 15 minutes was allowed for this facial.

The following facial treatment will:

- stimulate the blood circulation;
- aid with the removal of toxins and waste products;
- have a skin cleansing action;
- remove dead skin cells (desquamation);
- improve the moisture content of the skin;
- firm skin tone.

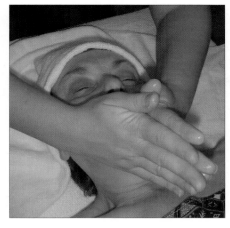

1 Cleansing the eye area

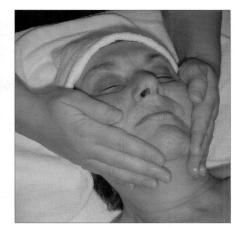

2 Application of facial cleanser.

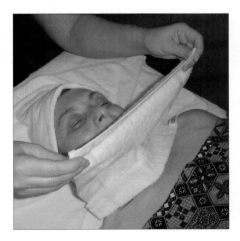

3 The cleanser is selected to rehydrate the skin.

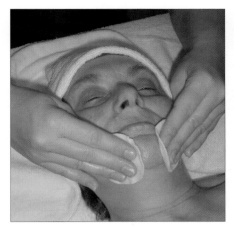

4 Removal of facial cleanser using dampened cottonwool in an upwards and outwards direction.

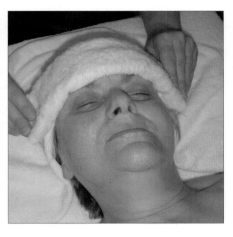

5 Application of a hot towel, infused with lavender oil, to the face. This will have a skin-cleansing action causing the pores to open. It also has therapeutic relaxation properties, as the client inhales the lavender oil.

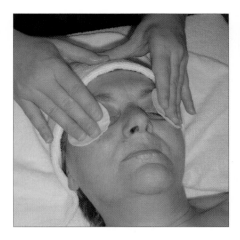

6 Removal of the hot towel.

7 Facial massage movements are applied to the shoulders and face. Eastern massage techniques are included to rebalance the mind and body.

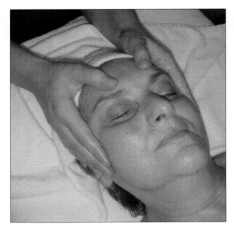

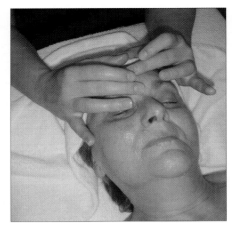

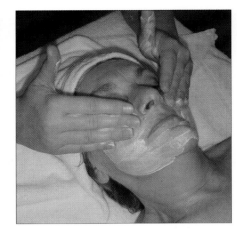

8 Pressure is applied to different points on the meridians or energy pathways based upon shiatsu massage – an ancient Eastern massage technique.

9 Application of a non-setting exfoliant cream mask.

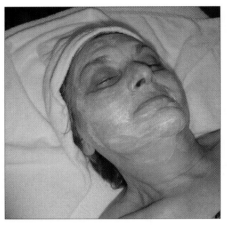

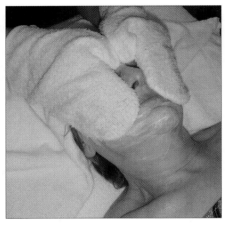

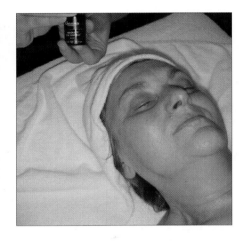

10 This mask will gently remove dead skin cells.

11 Exfoliant removal using warm, damp towelling mitts.

12 Application of an eye serum eye-mask to relax and strengthen the delicate skin tissue around the eye.

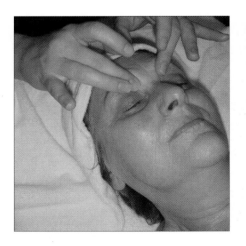

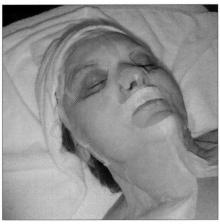

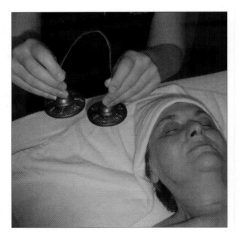

13 A specialised lifting massage is applied to increase cellular renewal around the eyes.

14 A Japanese silk cream mask is contoured to the face and neck, feeling like a second skin.

15 The treatment concludes with the skin being toned and moisturised and the client being gently awakened with Japanese chimes. The treatment will give both psychological and physiological benefits.

AFTERCARE AND ADVICE

Outcome 5: Complete the treatment

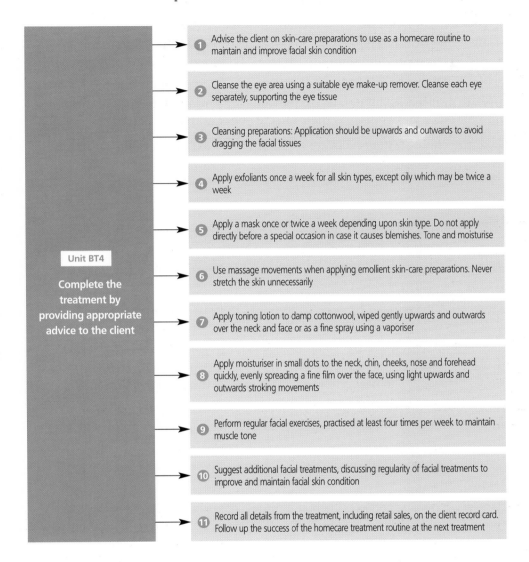

Unit BT4

Complete the treatment by providing appropriate advice to the client

1. Advise the client on skin-care preparations to use as a homecare routine to maintain and improve facial skin condition

2. Cleanse the eye area using a suitable eye make-up remover. Cleanse each eye separately, supporting the eye tissue

3. Cleansing preparations: Application should be upwards and outwards to avoid dragging the facial tissues

4. Apply exfoliants once a week for all skin types, except oily which may be twice a week

5. Apply a mask once or twice a week depending upon skin type. Do not apply directly before a special occasion in case it causes blemishes. Tone and moisturise

6. Use massage movements when applying emollient skin-care preparations. Never stretch the skin unnecessarily

7. Apply toning lotion to damp cottonwool, wiped gently upwards and outwards over the neck and face or as a fine spray using a vaporiser

8. Apply moisturiser in small dots to the neck, chin, cheeks, nose and forehead quickly, evenly spreading a fine film over the face, using light upwards and outwards stroking movements

9. Perform regular facial exercises, practised at least four times per week to maintain muscle tone

10. Suggest additional facial treatments, discussing regularity of facial treatments to improve and maintain facial skin condition

11. Record all details from the treatment, including retail sales, on the client record card. Follow up the success of the homecare treatment routine at the next treatment

Aftercare and advice is discussed throughout the chapter in relation to each of the facial treatment procedures.

At the conclusion of your facial treatment ensure that you have covered the following in your aftercare advice:

- explained what products have been used in the facial treatment and why;
- advised what products would be suitable for the client to use at home to gain maximum benefit from the treatment;
- advised on product application and removal, again in order to gain maximum benefit from their use;
- provided contra-action advice, action to be taken in the event of an unwanted skin reaction;

- discussed the use of make-up following treatment (only eye and lip make-up should be worn directly after a facial treatment; allow up to eight hours before make-up application to avoid congestion of the stimulated, cleansed skin);
- explained the recommended time intervals between treatments;
- provide guidance on what further treatments you would recommend to maintain or improve further the facial skin condition;
- discussed if product samples are to be provided, when and how they are to be used.

Update and record all details on the client record card, including products purchased. You can discuss their effectiveness at the next facial treatment.

Take the client to the reception to book their next appointment if required.

GLOSSARY OF KEY WORDS

Acid mantle the combination of sweat and sebum on the skin's surface, creating an acid film. The acid mantle is protective and discourages the growth of bacteria and fungi. The pH scale is used to measure the acidity or alkalinity of a substance using a numbered scale. The skin's pH is acid 5.5–5.6.

Aftercare advice recommended advice given to the client following treatment to continue the benefits of the treatment.

Antioxidant properties of some foods that maintain the health of the skin fighting the damaging effects of free radicals (unstable molecules which can cause skin cells to degenerate) in the body. Antioxidant ingredients are increasingly being included in skin-care preparations to neutralise free radicals or repel them from the skin.

Cleanser a skin-care preparation that removes dead skin cells, excess sweat and sebum, make-up and dirt from the skin's surface to maintain a healthy skin complexion. These are formulated to treat the different skin types, skin characteristics and facial areas.

Comedone removal facial techniques used to extract comedones (blackheads) from the skin. A small tool called a comedone extractor is used for this purpose.

Consultation assessment of client's needs using different assessment techniques, including questioning and natural observation.

Contra-action an unwanted reaction occurring during or after treatment application.

Contra-indication a problematic symptom which indicates that the treatment may not proceed or may restrict treatment application. Contra-indications identified for facial treatments are discussed in more detail in Chapter 1.

Effleurage a stroking massage manipulation used to begin the massage, as a link manipulation, and to complete the massage sequence. Applied in a rhythmic, continuous manner, it induces relaxation.

Erythema reddening of the skin cause by increased blood circulation to the area.

Exfoliant a treatment used to remove excess dead skin cells from the surface of the skin, which has a skin cleansing, cell rejuvenating action. This process can be achieved using a specialised cosmetic, or mechanically by using facial equipment where a brush is rotated over the skin's surface.

Facial a treatment to improve the appearance, condition and functioning of the skin and underlying structures.

Hyperpigmentation increased pigment production.

Hypopigmentation loss of pigmentation.

Mask a skin-cleansing treatment preparation applied to the skin, which may contain different ingredients. It can have a deep cleansing, toning, nourishing or refreshing effect. It may be applied to the face, hands and feet.

Massage manipulation of the soft tissues of the body, producing heat and stimulating the muscular, circulatory and nervous systems.

Massage manipulations movements which are selected and applied according to the desired effect, and which may be stimulating, relaxing or toning. Massage manipulations include effleurage, petrissage, percussion (also known as tapotement) and vibrations.

Milum extraction facial technique used to extract milia (whiteheads) from the skin. A small tool called a milia extractor is used for this purpose, which superficially pierces the epidermis, allowing effective removal of the milia.

Moisturiser a skin-care preparation whose formulation of oil and water helps maintain the skin's natural moisture by locking moisture into the skin, offering protection and hydration. The formulation is selected to suit the sin type, facial characteristics and facial area.

Muscle tone the normal degree of tension in healthy muscle.

Nutrition the process of nourishment derived from food, required for the body's growth, energy, repair and production.

Oedema extra fluid in an area, causing swelling.

Petrissage a massage manipulation in which the tissues are lifted away from the underlying structures and compressed. Petrissage improves muscle tone by the compression and relaxation of the muscle fibres.

Pigment the skin's and hair's colour, called melanin. The amount of pigment varies for each client, resulting in different skin/hair colour.

Skin analysis assessment of the client's skin type and condition.

Skin characteristics whilst looking at the skin type, additional characteristics may be seen. These include skin that may be sensitive, dehydrated, moist or oedematous (puffy).

Skin tone the strength and elasticity of the skin.

Skin type the different physiological functioning of each person's skin dictates their skin type. There are four main skin types normal (balanced), dry (lacking in oil), oily (excessive oil) and combination (a mixture of two skin types, e.g., dry and oily).

Specialist skin-care treatment products additional skin-care preparations available to target improvement. These products include eye gels, throat creams and ampoule treatments.

Steam treatment a warming effect created by boiling water, which is then vapourised and used on the skin to achieve both cleansing and stimulation.

Tapotement also known as percussion. A massage manipulation that is used for its general toning and stimulating effect.

Toning lotion a skin-care preparation formulated to treat the different skin types and facial characteristics. It is applied to remove all traces of cleanser from the skin. It produces a cooling effect on the skin and has a skin-tightening effect.

Towel steaming an alternative to facial steaming using an electrical vapour unit. Small, clean facial towels are heated in a bowl of warm water or specialised heater, before application to the face to warm, cleanse and stimulate the skin.

Treatment plan after the consultation, suitable treatment objectives are established to treat the client's conditions and needs.

Vapour unit an electrical appliance that heats water to produce steam, which is applied to the skin of the face and neck, to warm, cleanse and stimulate the skin.

Vibrations massage manipulations applied on the nerve centre. They stimulate the nerves to induce a feeling of wellbeing and to provide gentle stimulation of the skin.

Assessment of knowledge and understanding

You have now learnt about the different products and treatments that you can apply to the skin of the face and neck. This will enable you to improve and maintain facial skin condition.

To test your level of knowledge, answer the following short questions. These will prepare you for your summative (final) assessment.

 Anatomy and physiology questions required for this unit are found on pages 146–53.

Consult with the client

1 What details should be recorded on the client's record card?

2 At the consultation you notice the client has herpes simplex. What action do you take?

3 At the consultation a client asks you your advice about a small lump on her skin that occasionally bleeds. What advice do you give her?

4 How do you identify a client's skin type and treatment requirements?

5 How should all client records be stored to comply with the Data Protection Act 1998?

Prepare for the treatment

1 How can you ensure that the client will be relaxed during the facial treatment?

2 How can you ensure that you and the client are correctly positioned for the facial treatment to avoid discomfort?

3 It may be necessary when preparing for the facial treatment to dispense products for use in the treatment. Why should these be dispensed in amounts according to your needs?

4 Taking into account health and safety requirements, how should you prepare yourself for treatment?

5 What do you understand by the terms disinfection and sterilisation?

6 How can you ensure that skin-care products and equipment are used hygienically?

Plan the treatment

1 How long would you allow to complete a facial treatment?

2 Why is it important that the facial treatment is given in the allocated time?

3 Design a facial treatment, lasting one hour, for a client with oily skin. Describe:
   - the aim of the facial treatment;
   - the facial treatment products you are going to use;
   - when and how you will apply them;
   - the different stages of the facial and how long each stage will last;
   - any specialised treatments or products you are going to use;
   - aftercare advice which should be given to maintain the skin condition. Consider also what products the client should be recommended to use at home.

4 Why is it important to keep accurate records of the client's treatment?

5 How does the natural ageing process affect the skin? What characteristics would you expect to see?

6 What would be your treatment aim, and how would you adapt facial massage application, for a client with mature skin?

7 How would you select and apply skin care products for a client with an allergic skin type?

Improve and maintain the client's skin condition

1 When would you use a skin warming treatment such as facial steaming?

2 What is the purpose of the following skin care products?
- cleanser
- toning lotion
- exfoliant
- moisturiser
- face mask
- eye gel.

3 State three beneficial effects of facial massage on the skin.

4 What is the name given to the excessive erythema that can occur during a facial? What could be the cause of this?

5 What products should not be used immediately after a facial?

6 Why is the client's lifestyle an important consideration when analysing the condition of their skin?

Complete the treatment by providing appropriate advice to the client

1 What skin-care products would you recommend that a client use as part of their home care routine?

2 How would you explain to the client the correct application – and where relevant, removal of the following products for home use?
- cleansing milk
- cream exfoliant
- toning lotion
- non-setting face mask
- eye cream
- night cream.

3 What details should be recorded on the client record card following facial skin-care treatment?

4 What improvements to lifestyle can benefit the client's skin?

5 How often would you recommend a full facial treatment?

6 A client may visit the salon for a mini-facial. What would this usually consist of, and why would you recommend this additional service?

chapter 7

BT11 ## Enhance the appearance of eyebrows and lashes

BT5 ## Provide eyelash and eyebrow treatments

Learning objectives

These units describe how to enhance and improve the appearance of the client's eyebrows and lashes using the practical skills of brow shaping, lash and brow tinting, and eyelash perming.

Unit BT11 is mandatory for the BT make-up route.
Unit BT5 is mandatory for the BT general route.

This chapter describes the competencies to enable you to:

- **consult with the client**
- **prepare for the treatment**
- **plan the treatment**
- **shape the eyebrows to meet the client's requirements**
- **tint the eyebrows and lashes to meet the client's requirements**
- **perm eyelashes to meet the client's requirements**
- **complete the treatment**

It also covers the knowledge requirements for BT11 Enhance the appearance of eyebrows and lashes. False eyelash application is found on pages 410–21.

When providing eyebrow and lash treatments it is important to use the skills you have learnt in the following core mandatory units:

UNIT G1 Ensure your own actions reduce risks to health and safety

UNIT G6 Promote additional products or services to clients

UNIT G8 Develop and maintain your effectiveness at work

EYEBROW HAIR REMOVAL

The eyebrows, situated above the bony eye orbits of the face, help to protect the eyes from moisture and dust, and to cushion the skin from physical injury. Misshapen bushy brows give an untidy appearance to the face; but when correctly shaped, the brows give balance to the facial features and enhance the eyes – the most expressive feature of the face.

Outcome 1: Consult with the client – Shaping the eyebrows

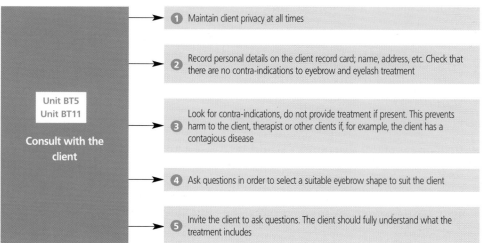

Unit BT5
Unit BT11

Consult with the client

1. Maintain client privacy at all times

2. Record personal details on the client record card; name, address, etc. Check that there are no contra-indications to eyebrow and eyelash treatment

3. Look for contra-indications, do not provide treatment if present. This prevents harm to the client, therapist or other clients if, for example, the client has a contagious disease

4. Ask questions in order to select a suitable eyebrow shape to suit the client

5. Invite the client to ask questions. The client should fully understand what the treatment includes

Reception

Eyebrow shaping is offered in the salon as either an **eyebrow reshape** or an **eyebrow trim** – the former involves removing eyebrow hair to create a new shape, the latter involves removing only a few stray hairs in order to maintain the existing shape. When making an appointment it is usual to allow 15 minutes for each service.

It is wise to have a designated time between treatments so that there is no confusion between the two services. For example, under two weeks could be regarded as a trim, and over two weeks as a reshape.

If the client has thick, heavy brows, or if they do not have their brows shaped regularly, they should be encouraged to have them shaped gradually over a period of weeks, until the desired shape is achieved. This will allow the client to become accustomed to the new shape and will minimise any discomfort.

Eyebrow shaping may be carried out as an independent treatment, or combined with other treatments such as permanent tinting of the brows. In the latter case, the brows should be tinted before shaping, to avoid the tint coming into contact with the open follicle and perhaps causing an allergic reaction.

Before brow-shaping treatment commences, carry out a consultation. Discuss the shape and the effect that might be achieved. Consider such factors as age, the natural shape of the brow, and fashion.

TIP

Positive promotion
Whilst the client is having their eyebrows shaped, you have an ideal opportunity to discuss further possible treatments, such as an eyebrow tint.

TIP

Communication
At the consultation, identify any peculiarities such as bald patches or scarring in the brow area to avoid any confusion or concern later.

Eyebrow tweezers

If a client wears contact lenses, these ideally must be removed before treatment commences, as the eyes may water during treatment.

Contra-indications

When a client attends for an eyebrow shaping treatment, the therapist should always check that there are no contra-indications that might prevent treatment.

If whilst completing the record card or on visual inspection of the skin the client is found to have any of the following in the eye area, eyebrow shaping treatment must not be carried out:

- *Hypersensitive skin* – the skin could become excessively red and swollen.
- *Any eye disorder*, such as those described in the chart below.
- *Inflammation or swelling*; the cause may be medical.
- *Skin disease*.
- *Skin disorder*, such as psoriasis or eczema.
- *Bruising* – client discomfort could be caused and the condition made worse.
- *Cuts or abrasions* – secondary infection could occur.
- *Scar tissue under six months old* – the skin lacks elasticity.

The following chart will help you to identify some eye disorders that contra-indicate eyebrow-shaping treatments.

Name	Description
Conjunctivitis or pink eye	Infectious bacterial infection. Inflammation of the mucous membrane that covers the eye and lines the eyelid. The skin of the inner conjunctiva of the eye becomes inflamed, the eye becomes very red, itchy and sore, and pus may exude from the eye area.
Stye or hordeola	Infectious bacterial infection. Infection of the sebaceous glands of the eyelash hair follicles. Small lumps appear on the inner rim of the eyelid containing pus.

Wellcome Photo Library

Wellcome Photo Library

Name	Description
Watery eye or epiphora	The eye over-secretes tears, which would normally drain into the nasal cavity.
Blepharitis	Inflammation of the eyelid caused by infection or an allergic reaction.
Cyst	Localised pocket of sebum, which forms in the hair follicle or under the sebaceous glands in the skin. Semi-globular in shape, either raised or flat, and hard or soft. The cysts are the same colour as skin, or red if bacterial infection occurs. A cyst appearing on the upper eyelid is known as a **chalazion** or **meibomian cyst.**
Fibroma	Benign tumour (non malignant). Harmless skin-coloured growths. They may appear as a 'thread' of skin on the eyelids growing between the eyelashes. Chemical treatments such as tinting and perming should be avoided to avoid skin irritation. Refer the client to their GP.

(Images: Wellcome Photo Library)

If you are unsure about the wisdom of proceeding with treatment – for example, if there is an undiagnosed lump in the area – ask your client to seek medical approval first.

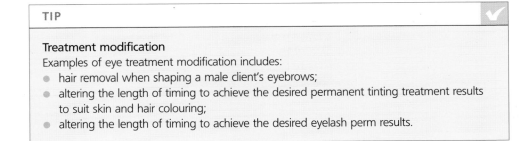

TIP ✔

Treatment modification
Examples of eye treatment modification includes:
- hair removal when shaping a male client's eyebrows;
- altering the length of timing to achieve the desired permanent tinting treatment results to suit skin and hair colouring;
- altering the length of timing to achieve the desired eyelash perm results.

BEAUTY WORKS

Date	Therapist name	
Client name		Date of birth (identifying client age group)
Address		Postcode

Evening phone number   Day phone number

Name of doctor   Doctor's address and phone number

Related medical history (conditions that may restrict or prohibit treatment application)

Are you taking any medication? (this may affect the condition of the skin or skin sensitivity)

CONTRA-INDICATIONS REQUIRING MEDICAL REFERRAL
(Preventing eye treatment application)

☐ severe skin conditions
☐ eye infections (e.g. conjunctivitis, styes)
☐ eye disease

EYE TREATMENT

☐ shaping eyebrows
☐ tinting eyebrow hair
☐ tinting eyelashes
☐ eyelash perming
☐ false eyelashes

BROW SHAPE WORK TECHNIQUES

☐ brow shape selected following measurement of the client's natural brow and eye for brow shaping treatment
☐ opening of the pores
☐ keeping the skin taut
☐ removal of hairs in the direction of hair growth
☐ protection of the eye
☐ hair removed to complement the shape and proportions of clients natural brow, in relation to facial features and shape

CONTRA-INDICATIONS WHICH RESTRICT TREATMENT
(Treatment may require adaptation)

☐ inflammation of the skin
☐ recent scar tissue
☐ eye disorders
☐ skin allergies
☐ bruising

TINTING WORK TECHNIQUES

☐ skin test carried out
☐ tint colour selection suited to client's colouring characteristics
☐ timing, development and removal of tint adapted according to client's natural colouring characteristics
☐ manufacturer's instructions complied with

COLOURING CHARACTERISTIC

☐ fair   ☐ red   ☐ dark   ☐ white/grey

EYELASH PERMING

☐ skin test carried out
☐ rod size selected to suit client's lash length and effect to be achieved
☐ treatment application timed in accordance with previous treatment history
☐ manufacturer's instructions complied with

FALSE EYELASHES

☐ skin test carried out
☐ colour and length of lash type selected to meet agreed treatment requirement and effect to be achieved
☐ individual lash
☐ strip lash
☐ manufacturer's instructions complied with

Therapist signature (for reference)

Client signature (confirmation of details)

BEAUTY WORKS *(continued)*

TREATMENT ADVICE

Eyebrow shape – *allow 15 minutes*
Eyebrow tint – *allow 10 minutes*
Eyelash tint – *allow 15 minutes*
Eyebrow shape and eyelash tint – *allow 30 minutes*

Eyebrow tint, shape and lash tint – *allow 30 minutes*
Eyelash perm – *allow 45 minutes**
*Eyelash perm timing may differ according to the system used. Always follow the manufacturer's instructions.

TREATMENT PLAN

Record relevant details of your treatment and advice provided for future reference.
Ensure the client's records are up to date, accurate and fully completed following treatment. Non-compliance may invalidate insurance.

DURING

Find out:

- what products the client is currently using to cleanse and care for the skin of the eye area;
- satisfaction with these products.

Explain:

- how the different eye products should be applied and removed.

Note:

- any adverse reaction, if any occur.

AFTER

Record:

- results of treatment;
- any modification to treatment application that has occurred;
- what products have been used in the eyelash/eyebrow treatment;
- the effectiveness of treatment;
- any samples provided (review their success at the next appointment).

Advise on:

- product application and removal in order to gain maximum benefit from product use;
- use of aftercare products following eye treatment;
- use of skin-care/make-up products following eye treatment;
- maintenance procedures;
- recommended time intervals between treatments.

RETAIL OPPORTUNITIES

Advise on:

- progression of the treatment plan for future appointments;
- products that would be suitable for the client to use at home to care for the eye area;
- recommendations for further treatments;
- further products or services that the client may or may not have received before.

Note:

- any purchase made by the client.

EVALUATION

Record:

- comments on the client's satisfaction with the treatment;
- if poor results are achieved, the reasons why;
- how you may alter the treatment plan to achieve the required treatment results in the future, if applicable.

HEALTH AND SAFETY

Advise on:

- how to care for the area following treatment to avoid an unwanted reaction;
- avoidance of any activities or product application that may cause a contra-action;
- appropriate action to be taken in the event of an unwanted skin or eye irritation.

Outcome 2: Prepare for the treatment

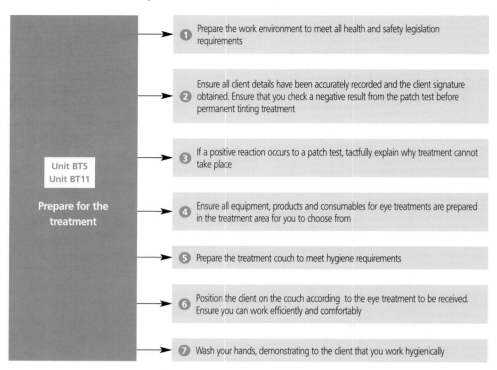

Unit BT5
Unit BT11

Prepare for the treatment

1 Prepare the work environment to meet all health and safety legislation requirements

2 Ensure all client details have been accurately recorded and the client signature obtained. Ensure that you check a negative result from the patch test before permanent tinting treatment

3 If a positive reaction occurs to a patch test, tactfully explain why treatment cannot take place

4 Ensure all equipment, products and consumables for eye treatments are prepared in the treatment area for you to choose from

5 Prepare the treatment couch to meet hygiene requirements

6 Position the client on the couch according to the eye treatment to be received. Ensure you can work efficiently and comfortably

7 Wash your hands, demonstrating to the client that you work hygienically

Equipment and materials

There are two sorts of tweezers. **Automatic tweezers** are designed to remove the bulk of excess hair; they have a spring-loaded action. **Manual tweezers** are used to remove stray hairs, and to accentuate the brow shape where more accurate care is required. They are available with various ends; which you use is a matter of personal preference, but slanted ends are generally considered to be the best for eyebrow shaping.

Although many therapists may complete an eyebrow shaping using only one of these – automatic or manual tweezers – it is important to be skilled in the use of both these tools.

> **TIP**
>
> **Tweezers**
> When purchasing tweezers, make sure that the ends meet accurately so they will grasp the hair effectively.

Automatic tweezers

> **HEALTH AND SAFETY**
>
> **Maintaining hygiene**
> Several pairs of tweezers must be purchased (perhaps five), due to the length of time required for sterilisation. Buy good-quality stainless-steel tweezers: cheaper metals rust after repeated sterilisation.

Disposable mascara wands are ideal for brushing the hairs during brow shaping.

To carry out eyebrow shaping, you will need the following equipment and materials:

EQUIPMENT LIST

 Couch or beauty chair with sit-up and lie-down positions and an easy-to-clean surface

 Dry cottonwool stored in a covered jar

 Surgical spirit for cleansing the tweezers before sterilisation

 Tweezers (sterilised) – both automatic and manual

 Scissors for trimming long hairs

 Disposable vinyl or rubber gloves

 Disposable spatulas

 Facial tissues (white) – for blotting the skin dry and for stretching the skin during hair removal

YOU WILL ALSO NEED:

Disposable tissue – such as bedroll

Towels (2) – freshly laundered for each client

Eyebrow pencil – used to mark the skin when measuring brow length

Pencil sharpener (stainless steel) – suitable for use in the autoclave

Antiseptic cleansing solution – for use on the skin

Soothing lotion or cream – with healing and antiseptic properties, for the skin of the face

Damp cottonwool – prepared for each client

Hand mirror (clean) – used when discussing the brow shaping requirements and the finished result

Client record card – confidential card recording details of each client registered at the salon

Trolley – on which to place everything

Light magnifier (cold)

Sterilisation and disinfection

Sterilise tweezers at an appropriate time during the working day. Ensure that you always have sterile tweezers ready for use with each client. After they have been sterilised in the autoclave, the tweezers should be stored in the ultra-violet cabinet.

A fresh disinfectant solution may be used to store a spare pair of tweezers while carrying out an eyebrow treatment. This solution is usually dispensed into a small container stored on the trolley. (Spare tweezers are necessary in case you should accidentally drop the other tweezers during the treatment.)

Disposable gloves may be worn for protection during the eyebrow shaping treatment – the therapist may come into contact with tissue fluids from the client's skin.

As the waste from the treatment may contain body fluids and pose a health threat, it must be collected and disposed of carefully, in accordance with the local health officer's rules and regulations.

Preparing the cubicle

Before the client is shown through to the cubicle, it should be checked to ensure that the required equipment and materials are available and the area is clean and tidy.

The plastic-covered couch should be clean, having been thoroughly washed with hot soapy water, or wiped thoroughly with surgical spirit or a professional, alcohol-based cleaner. The couch or chair should be protected with a long strip of disposable paper bedroll or a freshly laundered sheet and bath towel. A small towel should be placed neatly at the head of the couch – for hygiene and protection during treatment, this will be draped across the client's chest. The tissue will need changing and the towels should be freshly laundered for each client.

The couch or beauty chair should be flat or slightly elevated.

Planning the treatment

Factors to be considered

Before shaping the brows you must consider the following factors.

The natural shape of the brow   The natural brow follows the line of the eye socket. This varies greatly between clients, and affects what is achievable.

If the client has been shaping their own brows, it may be necessary to let them grow for a short period before shaping them professionally. If the brows are very thin or very thick, it may take several sessions before the desired shape is achieved.

If the brows have been plucked over a long period of time, they may not grow back successfully; this should be discussed with the client. In such instances, temporary eyebrow pencil or matt powder eyeshadow may be used to achieve the desired effect. Temporary brow colour is useful to apply when growing hairs into a new browshape, to create a defined browshape.

Fashion   Each season sees new fashion trends, which also affect eye make-up and eyebrow shapes. This should be considered before using any form of permanent hair removal to shape the brows.

TIP

Permanent brow colouring
By permanently tinting brow hair before shaping you will colour any finer lighter hairs, which will then form part of the brow.

Applying temporary brow colour

TIP

Temporary brow colour
A sharpened eyebrow pencil should be used to simulate brow hairs – apply feathery strokes using the pencil point. To create a natural effect, two different pencil colours may be used, for example brown and grey.

Male eyebrow shaping
Men may require a result that emphasises their natural brow shape. This generally requires removing hair:

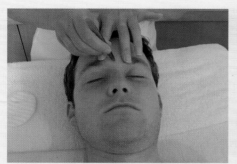 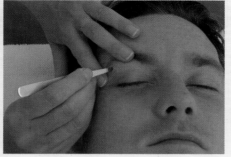

From the area between the brows where the brow hairs may meet. This brow hair if not removed can give the client a stern look.

Underneath the lower outer brow which will open up the eye area. This brow hair if not removed can create a hooded effect to the eyelid.

The age of the client The brow hair of older clients may include a few coarse, long, discoloured white or grey hairs. These may be removed provided that this does not alter the brow line or leave bald patches.

In general, thick eyebrows make the client look older, by creating a hooded appearance; and thin eyebrows will make the client look severe. Ideally the brows should therefore be shaped to a medium thickness.

The natural growth pattern The shape and effect that the client requests may be made impossible by the pattern of the natural growth of the hair, which is genetically determined. When shaping the brows of the Oriental client, for example, you will notice that the eyebrow hair grows in a downward direction. To create an arch it may be necessary to trim the hairs, using a small, sterile pair of sharp nail scissors. Alternatively, you may remove the outer eyebrow length and use a cosmetic pencil to create a new brow-line. Use your professional judgement to advise the client.

Choosing an eyebrow shape

The eyebrows should be in balance with the rest of the facial features: the right brow shape for each client will depend on her facial proportions and her natural brow shape.

There is no single ideal brow shape; different brow shapes are shown on the right and overleaf.

Oblique eyebrow

Arched eyebrow

Angular eyebrow

Straight eyebrow

Rounded eyebrow

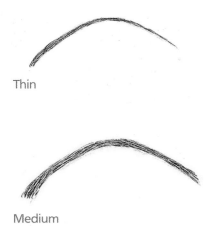

Thin

Medium

Thick

> **TIP** ✔
>
> **False eyebrows**
> These are ideal for disguising any bald areas in the natural eyebrow hair.

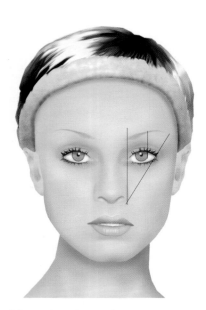

Measuring the eyebrow

What is achievable?

Obviously not all of these brow shapes are achievable for every client, but the skilful application to the eyebrows of temporary cosmetic colour can create the illusion of the desired brow shape.

The quantity of brow hair removed during shaping produces a thin, medium or thick final shape, as illustrated opposite and on the following page. Other approaches, too, may be used:

- *Semi-permanent make-up,* also referred to as micro-pigmentation, can be used to add colour permanently to the brows, for example to disguise a bald patch.
- *Hair transplants* are already available in the USA for the client with sparse eyebrows.
- *False individual eyebrow hairs* are applied in the same way as individual false eyelashes.

> **TIP** ✔
>
> **Semi-permanent make-up**
> Suspended pigment particles in a liquid base are inserted into the outer skin using a disposable needle. Many of the popular dyes are based on plant extracts.
>   The effect gradually fades, lasting up to three years.
>
> Before   After
> Courtesy Gail Proudman, SurgiCare Ltd.

Ideally, the distance between the two eyebrows should be the width of one eye. If this is not the case, the illusion may be created by removing hairs or by applying temporary brow colour to create this effect.

Wide-set eyes can be made to appear closer together by extending the brow-line beyond the inside corner of the eye; close-set eyes can be made to look further apart by widening the distance between them.

How to measure the eyebrows to decide length

In order to determine the correct length of the client's eyebrows, there are three main guidelines:

1 Place an orange stick or spatula beside the nose and the inside corner of the eye. This is usually in line with the tear duct. Any hairs that grow between the eyes and beyond this point should be removed. If the client

has a very broad nose, however, this guide is inappropriate: tweezing would commence near the middle of the brow. In this instance, use the tear duct at the inside corner of the eye as a guide.

2 Place an orange stick or spatula in a line from the base of the nose (to the side of the nostril) to the outer corner of the eye. Any hairs that grow beyond this point should be removed.

3 Place an orange stick or spatula in a vertical line from the centre of the eyelid. This is where the highest point of the arch should be.

Initially these guidelines will be needed to ensure that the correct length and brow shape are achieved, but the experienced therapist will recognise the corrective work to be carried out without the need for measuring.

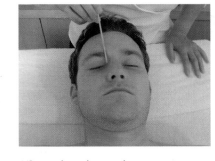

Measuring the eyebrow:
The inner eye

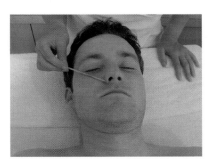

Measuring the eyebrow:
The outer eye

ACTIVITY

Correcting brow shapes (1)
You cannot change the bone structure of the facial features without cosmetic surgery, but brow shaping can create the illusion of improved facial balance and proportion. Discuss why each of the brow shapes below would complement the accompanying face shape.

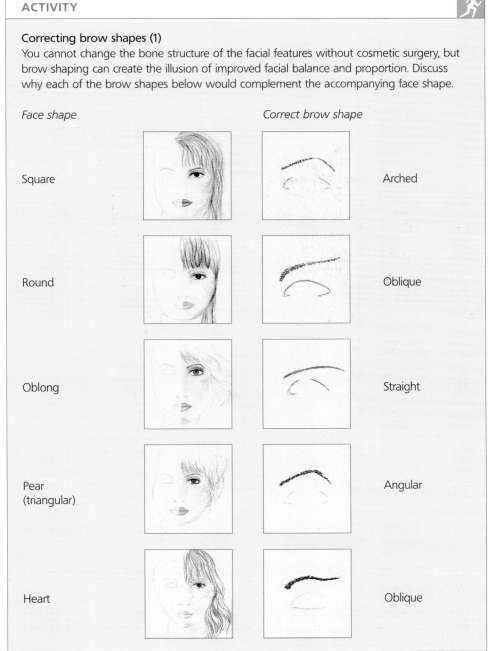

Face shape	Correct brow shape
Square	Arched
Round	Oblique
Oblong	Straight
Pear (triangular)	Angular
Heart	Oblique

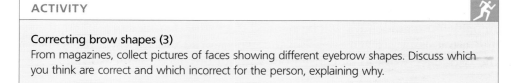

ACTIVITY

Correcting brow shapes (2)
How would you correct the following eye shapes?
● wide-set
● close-set

ACTIVITY

Correcting brow shapes (3)
From magazines, collect pictures of faces showing different eyebrow shapes. Discuss which you think are correct and which incorrect for the person, explaining why.

Outcome 3: Plan the treatment

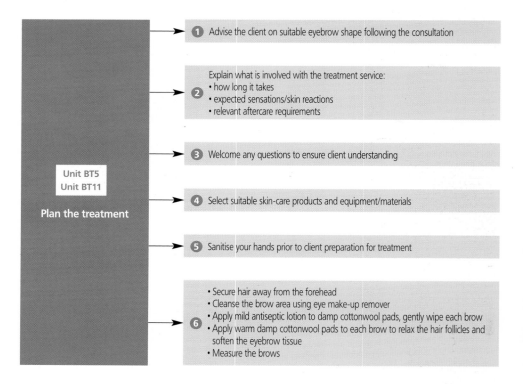

Unit BT5
Unit BT11

Plan the treatment

1. Advise the client on suitable eyebrow shape following the consultation

2. Explain what is involved with the treatment service:
   • how long it takes
   • expected sensations/skin reactions
   • relevant aftercare requirements

3. Welcome any questions to ensure client understanding

4. Select suitable skin-care products and equipment/materials

5. Sanitise your hands prior to client preparation for treatment

6. • Secure hair away from the forehead
   • Cleanse the brow area using eye make-up remover
   • Apply mild antiseptic lotion to damp cottonwool pads, gently wipe each brow
   • Apply warm damp cottonwool pads to each brow to relax the hair follicles and soften the eyebrow tissue
   • Measure the brows

Preparing the client

The client should be shown through to the cubicle after the record card has been completed.

Consult the record card and check the area for any contra-indications to treatment.

Outcome 4: Shape the eyebrows to meet client's requirements

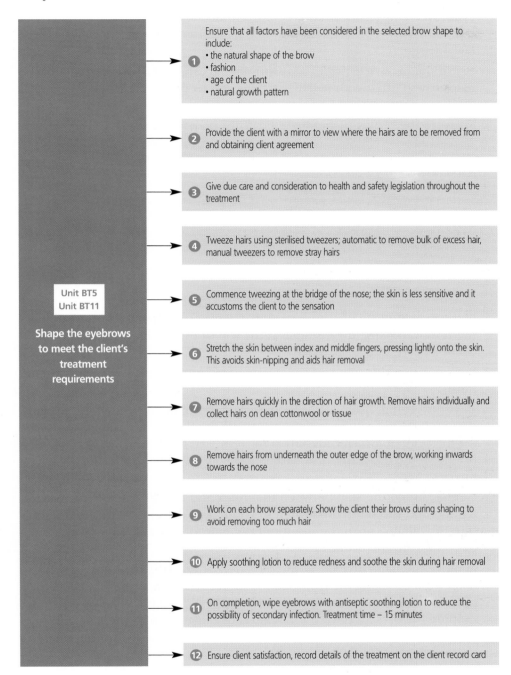

Unit BT5
Unit BT11

Shape the eyebrows to meet the client's treatment requirements

1. Ensure that all factors have been considered in the selected brow shape to include:
   • the natural shape of the brow
   • fashion
   • age of the client
   • natural growth pattern

2. Provide the client with a mirror to view where the hairs are to be removed from and obtaining client agreement

3. Give due care and consideration to health and safety legislation throughout the treatment

4. Tweeze hairs using sterilised tweezers; automatic to remove bulk of excess hair, manual tweezers to remove stray hairs

5. Commence tweezing at the bridge of the nose; the skin is less sensitive and it accustoms the client to the sensation

6. Stretch the skin between index and middle fingers, pressing lightly onto the skin. This avoids skin-nipping and aids hair removal

7. Remove hairs quickly in the direction of hair growth. Remove hairs individually and collect hairs on clean cottonwool or tissue

8. Remove hairs from underneath the outer edge of the brow, working inwards towards the nose

9. Work on each brow separately. Show the client their brows during shaping to avoid removing too much hair

10. Apply soothing lotion to reduce redness and soothe the skin during hair removal

11. On completion, wipe eyebrows with antiseptic soothing lotion to reduce the possibility of secondary infection. Treatment time – 15 minutes

12. Ensure client satisfaction, record details of the treatment on the client record card

How to shape the eyebrows

1 Position the cold-light magnifying lamp to give maximum visibility of the area.

2 Position the client on the couch.

3 Wash your hands.

HEALTH AND SAFETY

Cross-infection
Use a fresh cottonwool pad for each eyebrow to avoid cross-infection.

4 Working from behind the client, cleanse the eyebrow area, using a lightweight cleansing lotion or eye make-up remover. Apply a mild antiseptic lotion to two damp cottonwool pads, then gently wipe each eyebrow. (This removes all grease from the area, so that the tweezers will not slip.) The brow area should then be blotted dry, using a clean, folded facial tissue.

5 Brush the brow hair with the disposable brush, first *against* the natural hair growth, then with it. This enables you to define the brow shape and to observe the natural line.

6 Measure the brows (using the guidelines on pages 236–7).

TIP

It is often stated that before beginning shaping, the brows should be prepared with warm, damp cottonwool pads, to relax the hair follicles and soften the eyebrow tissue, thus making hair removal easier. During treatment, however, you will be wiping over the area with an antiseptic lotion, which has a cooling, soothing and tightening effect on the skin, so this preparation is ineffectual.

7 Place a clean piece of cottonwool in a convenient position for collecting the removed hairs, for instance at the top of the couch next to the client's head.

8 Put on disposable gloves, as you may come into contact with body tissue fluid.

9 Begin tweezing, using a sterilised pair of automatic tweezers. These are designed to remove hairs quickly and efficiently, and are therefore used for the bulk of the hair identified for removal. It is usual to start at the bridge of the nose: the skin here is less sensitive than under the brow line.

TIP

Occasionally clients start sneezing when you tweeze hairs at the bridge of the nose. If this happens, leave this area till last.

10 Gently stretch the skin between the index and middle fingers, pressing lightly onto the skin. This will help you to avoid accidentally nipping the skin; it will also open the mouth of the hair follicle and minimise discomfort to the client.

11 Remove the hairs quickly, in the direction of growth. This prevents the hairs from breaking off at the skin's surface. Hair breakage can be seen to have occurred if a stubbly regrowth appears one or two days after shaping. Incorrect removal may also cause distortion of the hair follicle, or result in the hair becoming trapped under the skin as it starts to regrow (*ingrowing hair* – see page 294).

   Hairs should be removed individually, and the tweezers should be wiped regularly on the pad of clean cottonwool used to collect the removed hairs.

12 Remove the hairs from underneath the outer edge of the brow, working inwards towards the nose. It is advisable to work on each brow alternately. This ensures that the brows are evenly shaped; it also reduces prolonged discomfort in any one area during shaping. Hairs should ideally be removed only from *below* the brow, otherwise the natural line may be lost. It is sometimes necessary, however, to remove the odd stray hair growing *above* the natural line.

TIP

Twenty per cent of hairs are not visible above the skin's surface at any one time. Explain this to the client so that they understand why stray hairs may appear shortly after treatment.

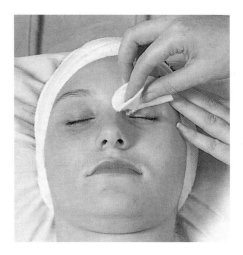

Cleansing the eyebrow

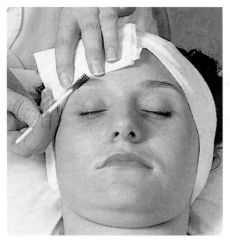

Brushing the eyebrow

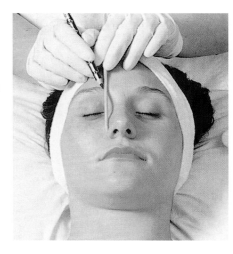

Measuring the eyebrow: The inner eye

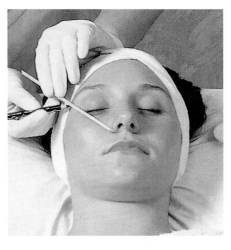

Measuring the eyebrow: The outer eye

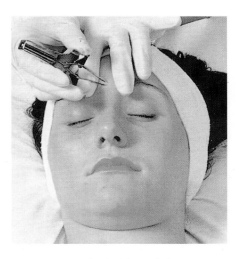

Tweezing at the bridge of the nose, using automatic tweezers

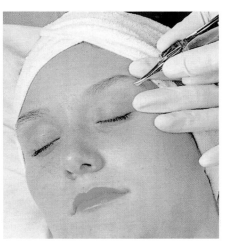

Tweezing at the outer corner of the eyebrow

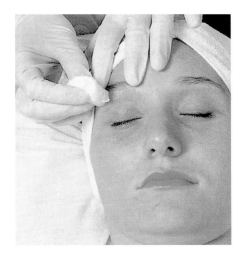

Applying antiseptic and soothing lotion

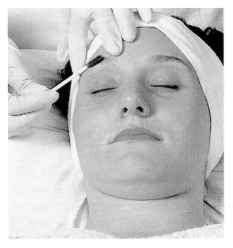

Brushing the eyebrow into shape

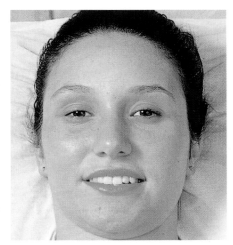

The completed eyebrows after shaping

During shaping, show the client her brows and avoid removing too much hair.

13 At regular intervals during shaping, brush the brows to check their shape. Apply antiseptic lotion to a clean, dampened cottonwool pad, and wipe this gently over the eyebrow tissue to reduce sensitivity and to sanitise the area.

14 When the bulk of excess hair has been removed, manual tweezers may be used to take away any stray hairs and to define the line. Long hairs may be trimmed with scissors if necessary. Any discoloured, coarse, long, curly or wavy hairs may be removed, as long as this does not alter the line or leave a bald patch.

15 On completion of brow shaping, wipe the eyebrows with the antiseptic soothing lotion, applied with clean, damp cottonwool. Apply a mild antiseptic cream to the area, using clean, dry cottonwool, to reduce the possibility of infection.

Outcome 7: Complete the treatment

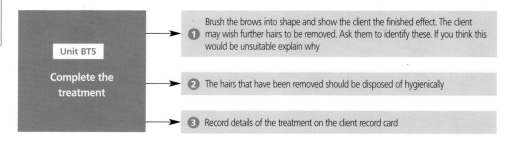

Unit BT5	
Complete the treatment	① Brush the brows into shape and show the client the finished effect. The client may wish further hairs to be removed. Ask them to identify these. If you think this would be unsuitable explain why
	② The hairs that have been removed should be disposed of hygienically
	③ Record details of the treatment on the client record card

Contra-actions

Erythema is considered to be a contra-action to the treatment: it is recognised as a marked reddening of the skin seen over the whole area or specifically around one damaged follicle. It is usually accompanied by minor swelling of the area. If this occurs the therapist must try to reduce the redness by applying a soothing antiseptic lotion or cream to the area. In extreme cases it may be necessary to apply ice. Record details of any contra-action on the client's record card.

If the reddening reduces in response to your corrective action, you may decide in future to remove only a few stray hairs at each eyebrow-shaping treatment, to minimise the risk of this reaction recurring.

Aftercare and advice

Advise the client not to wear eye make-up for at least eight hours following the eyebrow-shaping treatment. The hair follicle has been damaged where the hair has been torn out: it will be susceptible to infection unless the area is cared for whilst it heals. It should not be necessary for the client to continue using antiseptic lotion at home, but they should be advised to carry out these instructions if discomfort or continued reddening occurs:

1 Cleanse the eyebrow area using a mild antiseptic lotion or witchhazel, applied with a small piece of clean, dampened cottonwool.

2 Apply an antiseptic soothing lotion or cream with clean, dry cottonwool.

3 Gently remove excess antiseptic lotion or cream using a clean, soft facial tissue.

4 Repeat as necessary, approximately every four hours. *If the reddening does not subside in the next 24 hours, contact the salon.*

5 Eye make-up may be worn as soon as the redness has gone – usually after eight hours.

HEALTH AND SAFETY

Avoiding infection
If excess antiseptic lotion or cream is left on the area, this may attract small particles of dust, which could cause infection.

PERMANENT EYELASH AND EYEBROW TINTING

The hair of the eyelashes and eyebrows protects the eyes from moisture and dust, but the lashes and brows also give definition to the eye. Many clients, especially those with fair lashes and brows, feel that without the use of eye cosmetics their eyes lack this definition.

Further definition of the brow and lash hair can be created if a permanent dye is applied to them. Most clients will benefit from tinting because the tips and the bases of these hairs are usually lighter than the body of the hairs, causing the hairs to appear shorter than they actually are. Tinting the length of the lash or brow hair makes it appear longer and bolder, yet the effect created looks natural.

Because the skin around the eye area is very thin and sensitive, dyes designed for permanently tinting the hair in this area have been specially formulated to avoid any eye or tissue reactions. *The application of any other dye materials in this area is dangerous, and may even lead to blindness.*

Permanent tints are available in different forms, including jelly, liquid and cream tints. The most popular and acceptable permanent tinting product is the cream tint: this is thicker, so it does not run into the eye and it is easy to control during mixing, application and removal.

Several colours of permanent tint are available, including brown, grey, blue and black.

If the shade you want is not available, you can vary the shade of available tints by leaving the dye on the hair for different lengths of time, or by mixing different colours together. For example, to produce a navy blue colour; leave the tint to process for 3–5 minutes. If left to process for ten minutes, the same tint will produce a raven blue-black colour.

The development of colour

Two products are essential for the permanent tinting treatment:

- professional **eyelash** or **eyebrow tint**;
- **hydrogen peroxide** (H_2O_2).

HEALTH AND SAFETY

Permanent tinting
Always use a tint that is permitted for use under EU regulations and complies with The Cosmetic Products (Safety) Regulations 2003. If you use any other tint your insurance may be invalid.

TIP

Blue tint
When a client requests a blue eyelash tint, make clear that this will not produce an 'electric blue' fashion colour.

HEALTH AND SAFETY

Peroxide strength
Do not use a higher strength than 10-volume or 3% hydrogen peroxide. If you do, skin irritation or minor skin burning may occur.

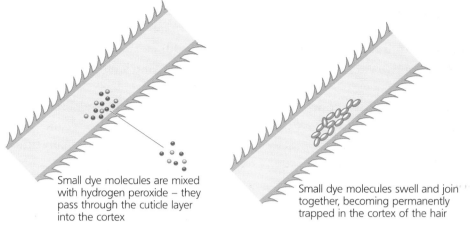

Small dye molecules are mixed with hydrogen peroxide – they pass through the cuticle layer into the cortex

Small dye molecules swell and join together, becoming permanently trapped in the cortex of the hair

Permanent hair colouring

The tint contains small molecules of permanent dye called **toluenediamine**. These need to be 'activated' before their colouring effect becomes permanent: this is achieved by the addition of hydrogen peroxide. The peroxide is said to **develop** the colour of the tint.

Chemically, hydrogen peroxide is an **oxidant**, a chemical that contains available oxygen atoms and encourages certain chemical reactions – in this case, tinting.

The hydrogen peroxide container will state either its volume or its percentage strength. To activate the tint and for safe use around the eye area, a 3% or 10-volume strength peroxide is used.

When you add the hydrogen peroxide to the tint, the small dye molecules together form large molecules, which remain trapped in the cortex of the hair. The hair is thus permanently coloured, but in time, as it continues to grow, the new hair will show the natural colour.

Outcome 1: Consult with the client

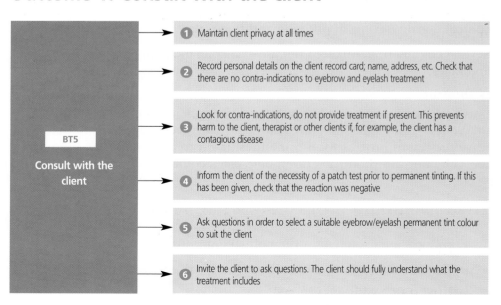

BT5

Consult with the client

1 Maintain client privacy at all times

2 Record personal details on the client record card; name, address, etc. Check that there are no contra-indications to eyebrow and eyelash treatment

3 Look for contra-indications, do not provide treatment if present. This prevents harm to the client, therapist or other clients if, for example, the client has a contagious disease

4 Inform the client of the necessity of a patch test prior to permanent tinting. If this has been given, check that the reaction was negative

5 Ask questions in order to select a suitable eyebrow/eyelash permanent tint colour to suit the client

6 Invite the client to ask questions. The client should fully understand what the treatment includes

Reception

When making an appointment for this service, allow 5 minutes for a skin test, 10 minutes for an eyebrow tint, and 20 minutes for an eyelash tint. When the client is booking a treatment, ask them:

- to visit the salon 24 hours before the appointment, for a skin test;
- if they wear contact lenses, to bring their lens container so that they can place the lenses in it during the tinting treatment.

On average, a client will need their lashes tinted every six weeks, or sooner if for example they take a holiday in a climate where sun bleaches them. Eyebrow tinting, on the other hand, should be repeated when the client feels it to be necessary, perhaps every four weeks, as eyebrows seem to lose colour intensity more quickly than lash hair.

Skin sensitivity (patch) test

Some clients are sensitive to the tint, and produce an allergic reaction immediately on contact with it; others may become allergic later. For this you therefore need to carry out a skin sensitivity test before each lash- or brow-tinting treatment. (The skin sensitivity (patch) test, a hypersensitivity test, or a predisposition test – see page 53.) This test should be given either on the inside of the elbow or behind the ear.

Two responses to the skin sensitivity test are possible – positive and negative:

- a *positive* result is recognised by irritation, swelling or inflammation of the skin – if this occurs, do not proceed with the treatment;
- a *negative* result produces no skin reaction – in this case you may proceed with the treatment.

Contra-indications

When a client attends for an eyelash or brow tinting treatment, the therapist should always check that there are no contra-indications that might prevent treatment.

After completing the record card and inspecting the eye area, if you have found any of the following in the eye area, do not proceed with the tinting treatment:

- *Inflammation or swelling* – the cause may be medical.
- *Skin disease*.
- *Skin disorder*, such as psoriasis or eczema.
- *Cuts and abrasions* – secondary infection and irritation of the skin could occur.
- *Hypersensitive skin* – the skin could become excessively red and swollen.
- *Any eye disorders*, such as conjunctivitis, blepharitis, styes or hordeola, watery eye, or cysts.
- *A positive (allergic) reaction* to the skin sensitivity test.
- *Contact lenses* (unless removed).

TIP

It is acceptable for the salon receptionist – provided that they have been trained to do so – to carry out the skin test.

ACTIVITY

Eyelash and eyebrow tinting
List reasons why clients would benefit from this service. Discuss the reasons with your tutor.

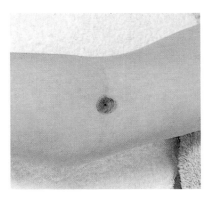

A skin sensitivity (patch) test

ACTIVITY

Allergic reactions
With colleagues, discuss the possible implications of ignoring a positive reaction to the skin test

A particularly nervous client would also be contra-indicated:

- it would be difficult for them to keep their eyes closed for 10 minutes;
- they might panic as the tint was applied, creating the possibility of tint entering the eye;
- they might blink frequently, making preparation of the eye area and application of the tint both difficult and hazardous.

Equipment and materials

To carry out the tinting you will need the following equipment and materials.

EQUIPMENT LIST

 Beauty Express Ltd. Coloured tints (a selection)   Disposable brushes (2)

YOU WILL ALSO NEED:

Couch or beauty chair – with sit-up and lie-down positions and an easy-to-clean surface

Trolley – on which to display everything

Towels (medium-sized) – freshly laundered for each client

Headband (clean) – to protect long hair or bleached hair from the tint

Cleansing milk – used to remove make-up from the eye area

Eye make-up remover (non-oily)

Hydrogen peroxide (10-volume/3%)

Petroleum jelly – to protect the the skin and prevent skin staining

Damp cottonwool – for cleansing the eye area and for lash and brow tint removal

Eyeshields (commercial) – to prevent skin staining during eyelash tinting

Facial tissues (white) – for blotting the eye area dry

Disposable spatulas – for removing the petroleum jelly from its container

Non-metallic bowl – for mixing the permanent tint (note that some metals cause immediate release of the oxygen from the hydrogen peroxide, causing ineffective processing of the tint)

Skin stain remover – to remove any accidental staining

Collodion ('new skin') – used to cover the tint when carrying out the skin sensitivity (patch) test

Bowl (clean) – to hold dampened cottonwool

Swing-top bin – lined with a disposable bin-liner, for waste

Hand mirror (clean) – to show the client the results

Client record card – confidential card recording the details of each client registered at the salon

TIP

The brows or lash hair to be tinted must be grease-free – the grease would be a barrier to the tint.

TIP

Lipbrushes
Disposable lipbrushes can be used to apply the petroleum jelly and permanent tint.

HEALTH AND SAFETY

Applicator brushes
Because it is impossible to sterilise applicator brushes effectively, use disposable brushes for the application of petroleum jelly and permanent tint.

Sterilisation and disinfection

It is necessary to use disposable applicator brushes for the application of the petroleum jelly and the permanent tint because it is impossible to disinfect brushes effectively.

Preparing the cubicle

Before the client is shown through to the cubicle, it should be checked to ensure that the required equipment and materials are available and the area is clean and tidy.

Clean and protect the couch or beauty chair (as for eyebrow-shaping treatment page 234). The couch or chair should be flat or slightly elevated.

The cubicle should be adequately lit to ensure that treatment can be given, safely, but avoid bright lighting that could cause eye irritation.

Outcome 3: Planning the treatment

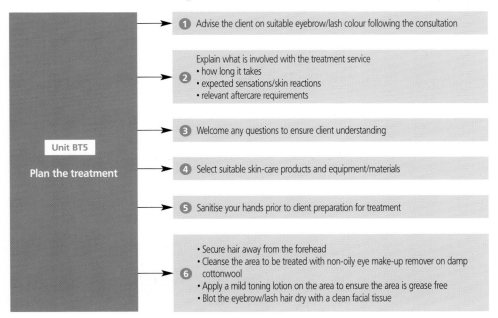

Unit BT5

Plan the treatment

1. Advise the client on suitable eyebrow/lash colour following the consultation

2. Explain what is involved with the treatment service
   • how long it takes
   • expected sensations/skin reactions
   • relevant aftercare requirements

3. Welcome any questions to ensure client understanding

4. Select suitable skin-care products and equipment/materials

5. Sanitise your hands prior to client preparation for treatment

6. • Secure hair away from the forehead
   • Cleanse the area to be treated with non-oily eye make-up remover on damp cottonwool
   • Apply a mild toning lotion on the area to ensure the area is grease free
   • Blot the eyebrow/lash hair dry with a clean facial tissue

For the eyelashes and eyebrows, select a colour that complements the client's hair and skin colours, her age and her usual eye cosmetics. Always discuss the choice of colour carefully with the client to discover her preference. You may ask certain questions in order to help you in your selection:

- 'What colour mascara do you normally wear?'
- 'How dark would you like your eyelashes/eyebrows?'
- 'Do you normally wear eyebrow pencil? What colour?'

TIP	✓
When selecting and using permanent tint for a white-haired client, note that the hair is very often resistant to colour.	

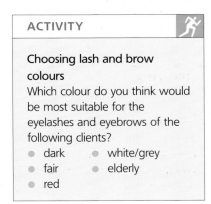

ACTIVITY	🏃

Choosing lash and brow colours
Which colour do you think would be most suitable for the eyelashes and eyebrows of the following clients?
- dark
- white/grey
- fair
- elderly
- red

Outcome 5: Tint eyebrows and lashes to meet client requirements

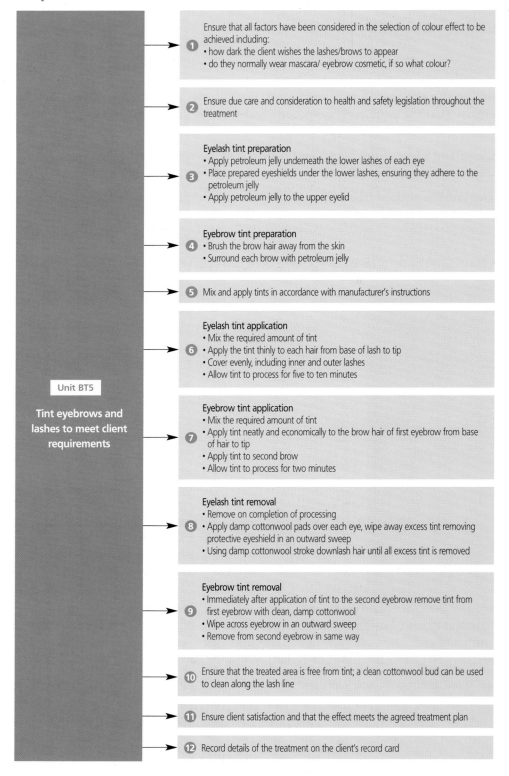

Unit BT5

Tint eyebrows and lashes to meet client requirements

1 Ensure that all factors have been considered in the selection of colour effect to be achieved including:
- how dark the client wishes the lashes/brows to appear
- do they normally wear mascara/ eyebrow cosmetic, if so what colour?

2 Ensure due care and consideration to health and safety legislation throughout the treatment

3 **Eyelash tint preparation**
- Apply petroleum jelly underneath the lower lashes of each eye
- Place prepared eyeshields under the lower lashes, ensuring they adhere to the petroleum jelly
- Apply petroleum jelly to the upper eyelid

4 **Eyebrow tint preparation**
- Brush the brow hair away from the skin
- Surround each brow with petroleum jelly

5 Mix and apply tints in accordance with manufacturer's instructions

6 **Eyelash tint application**
- Mix the required amount of tint
- Apply the tint thinly to each hair from base of lash to tip
- Cover evenly, including inner and outer lashes
- Allow tint to process for five to ten minutes

7 **Eyebrow tint application**
- Mix the required amount of tint
- Apply tint neatly and economically to the brow hair of first eyebrow from base of hair to tip
- Apply tint to second brow
- Allow tint to process for two minutes

8 **Eyelash tint removal**
- Remove on completion of processing
- Apply damp cottonwool pads over each eye, wipe away excess tint removing protective eyeshield in an outward sweep
- Using damp cottonwool stroke downlash hair until all excess tint is removed

9 **Eyebrow tint removal**
- Immediately after application of tint to the second eyebrow remove tint from first eyebrow with clean, damp cottonwool
- Wipe across eyebrow in an outward sweep
- Remove from second eyebrow in same way

10 Ensure that the treated area is free from tint; a clean cottonwool bud can be used to clean along the lash line

11 Ensure client satisfaction and that the effect meets the agreed treatment plan

12 Record details of the treatment on the client's record card

How to prepare the client

The client should be shown through to the cubicle after the record card has been completed.

1 Position the client comfortably, in a flat or slightly elevated position. If she is wearing contact lenses, these must be removed.

2 Drape a towel across the client's chest and shoulders, and protect her hair with a clean headband.

3 Wash your hands, which assures the client that the treatment is beginning in a hygienic and professional manner.

4 Consult the client's record card, then check the area for any visible contra-indications or abnormalities before proceeding.

5 Cleanse the area to be treated with a cleansing milk to dissolve facial make-up. Then use a non-oily eye make-up remover to remove eye products: apply this with clean, damp cottonwool.

6 To ensure that the area is thoroughly clean and grease-free, apply a mild toning lotion, stroked over the lash or brow hair.

7 Blot the eyelashes or eyebrows dry with a clean facial tissue. This ensures that the tint is not diluted, and also prevents the tint from being carried into the eye.

8 Prepare the pre-shaped eyeshields by applying petroleum jelly to the inner surface of each eyeshield (the surface that comes into contact with the skin).

9 Ensure that the light is not shining directly into the client's eyes. If it were, the eyes might water, carrying the tint into the eye or down the face (causing skin staining).

10 Finally, check that the client is comfortable before beginning tint application.

Cleansing the eye

TIP

Make sure that work surfaces are protected with disposable coverings, to prevent permanent staining following spillages.

How to tint the eyelashes

1 Remove some petroleum jelly from its container, using a new disposable spatula.

2 Working from behind the client, ask the client to open her eyes and to look upwards towards you. Using a disposable brush, apply petroleum jelly underneath the lower lashes of one eye, ensuring that it extends at the outer corner of the eye. (This is in case the client's eyes water slightly during treatment, which might otherwise lead to skin staining.) The petroleum jelly must not come into contact with the lash hair, where it would create a barrier to the tint.

3 Place the prepared eyeshield on the skin under the lower lashes, ensuring that it adheres to the petroleum jelly and fits 'snugly' to the base of the lower lashes.

4 Repeat the above process for the other eye.

5 Ask the client to close her eyes gently. Instruct her not to open them again until you advise her to do so, in about ten minutes' time.

6 Apply petroleum jelly to the upper eyelid, in a line on the skin at the base of the lashes.

7 Considering the length and density of the clients eyelashes, mix the required amount of tint with 10-volume (3%) hydrogen peroxide. As a guide, a 5mm length of tint from the tube, mixed with two or three drops of hydrogen peroxide, is usually sufficient. Mix the products to a smooth cream in the tinting bowl, using the disposable brush. Always re-cap bottles and tubes tightly after use, to avoid deterioration of materials.

HEALTH AND SAFETY +

Maintaining hygiene
Do not use the same spatula in the container again, or you might contaminate the product.

TIP

Client care
Speak to your client as you apply the eyelash tint. Check that they are comfortable and understand what you are doing. Remember: the eyes are very sensitive and will water readily.

8 Wipe excess tint off the brush onto the inside of the bowl. Apply the tint thinly to each hair. Work from the base of the lash to the tip, ensuring that each hair is evenly covered. Press down gently with the applicator to ensure that the lower lashes also are covered. The few inner and outer lashes should also be covered, down to the base.

9 Allow the tint to process, for approximately five to ten minutes from the completion of application. Discard any unused mixture as soon as the tint has been applied.

10 On completion of processing, remove the eyelash tint by applying clean, damp cottonwool pads over each eye, wiping away most of the tint and removing the protective eyeshield in one movement, an outward sweep. Using fresh dampened cottonwool pads, gently stroke down the lashes from roots to tips, until all excess tint has been removed. With a sweeping action on each eye and using one cottonwool pad, wipe from the side to the middle against the lash growth, whilst the other hand supports the eye tissue. *All tint must be thoroughly removed before the client opens her eyes*.

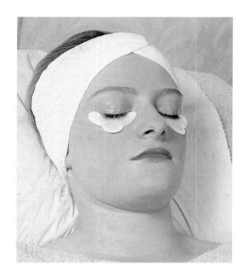

Eyeshields

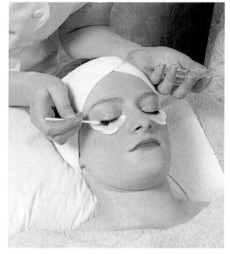

Applying the tint

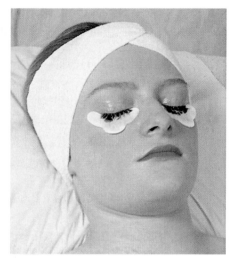

Processing the tint

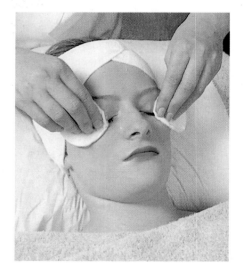

Removing the tint

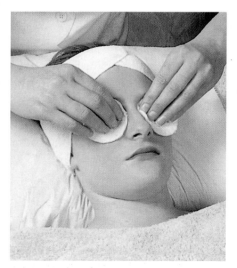

Soothing the eyes

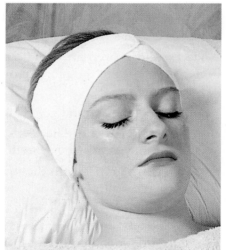

The completed eyelash tint

11 Ask the client to open her eyes. If removal has been correctly carried out, the lashes and their bases will be free from tint. (While training, if any tint remains at the base of the lashes after the eyes have been opened, ask the client to close her eyes again and finish the removal process using clean, damp cottonwool.) Check that every lash has been tinted, especially the base of each lash and the inner and outer corner lashes.

12 Once you are satisfied that all tint has been removed, place a cool, damp cottonwool pad over each eye for two to three minutes to soothe the eye tissue.

HEALTH AND SAFETY

Using tints
Always read the manufacturer's instructions carefully before using a permanent tint.

Outcome 7: Complete the treatment

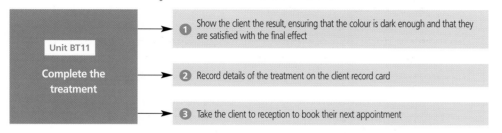

Unit BT11

Complete the treatment

1. Show the client the result, ensuring that the colour is dark enough and that they are satisfied with the final effect
2. Record details of the treatment on the client record card
3. Take the client to reception to book their next appointment

Step by step: tinting the eyebrows

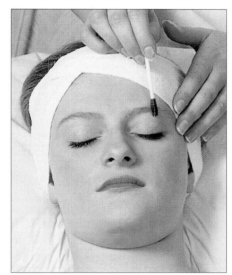

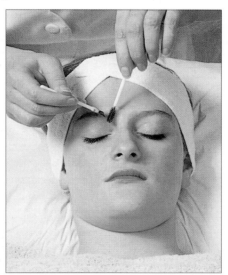

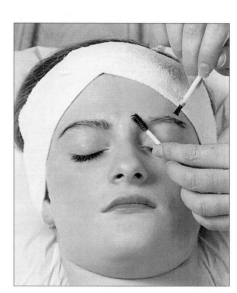

1 Remove some petroleum jelly from its container, using a new disposable spatula.

2 Brush the brow hair away from the skin, using a disposable brow brush (as shown in the picture).

3 Using a disposable brush, surround each eyebrow with petroleum jelly, as close as possible to the brow hair (to avoid skin staining).

4 Mix approximately 5mm of the chosen tint colour with two or three drops of 10-volume (3%) hydrogen peroxide in a tinting bowl. Ensure that the tint is mixed thoroughly to a creamy consistency.

5 Wipe excess tint off the brush onto the inside of the tinting bowl. Apply the tint neatly and economically to the brow hair of the first eyebrow; ensuring that the brow hairs, from the base to the tips, are evenly covered (as shown in the picture).

6 Apply the tint to the second eyebrow; following the same procedure.

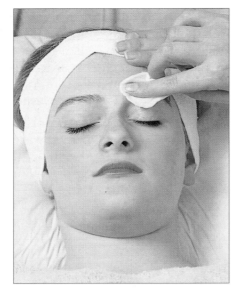

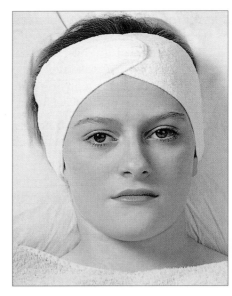

7 Immediately after application of the tint to the second eyebrow, remove the tint from the first eyebrow. Use a clean dampened cottonwool pad. Place it on the eyebrow, then wipe it across the eyebrow in an outward sweep, removing the excess tint. Ensure that all traces of excess tint have been removed, to prevent skin staining.

Never leave tint on the eyebrows for longer than two minutes. Eyebrow hair colour develops much more quickly than lash hair.

8 Remove the tint from the second eyebrow in the same way.

9 The completed effect, showing both eyelash and eyebrow tint

HEALTH AND SAFETY

Skin stains
If skin staining accidentally occurs, use a professional skin stain remover designed for this purpose. Afterwards, use plenty of clean, dampened cottonwool pads to avoid skin irritation.

ACTIVITY

Explaining poor results
What reasons can you think of to explain why a permanent tint applied to the eyelashes or eyebrows has not coloured the hair successfully? Discuss your answers with your tutor.

Outcome 7: Complete the treatment

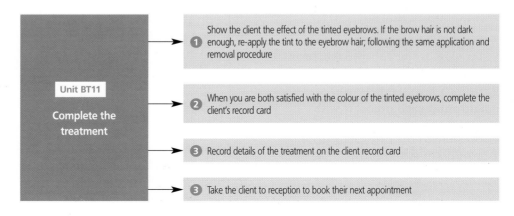

Unit BT11

Complete the treatment

1 Show the client the effect of the tinted eyebrows. If the brow hair is not dark enough, re-apply the tint to the eyebrow hair; following the same application and removal procedure

2 When you are both satisfied with the colour of the tinted eyebrows, complete the client's record card

3 Record details of the treatment on the client record card

3 Take the client to reception to book their next appointment

> **TIP** ✓
>
> The effect of tinting depends on the natural colour:
> - *Blonde hair* develops colour rapidly – if the tint is left on the eyebrow too long, a harsh appearance will be created.
> - *Red/grey hair* is more resistant to the tint, and developing will take a little longer – allow 15 minutes' processing time when tinting lash hair.
> - *Dark hair* requires tinting to increase the intensity of the natural eyebrow colour, giving a glossy, conditioned appearance.

Contra-actions

If the client complains of discomfort during the treatment, tint may have entered the eye. Take the following action:

1 Remove the tint immediately from the eye area, using clean, damp cottonwool pads in an outward sweep.

2 When you are satisfied that all excess tint has been removed (that is, when the cottonwool shows clean), carefully flush the eye with clean water. Repeat the rinsing process until discomfort has been relieved.

3 Apply a cool compress to cool and soothe the eye area.

If there is a noticeable sensitivity of the eye tissue after eyebrow or eyelash tinting, recommend that the client does not receive the treatment again. Record this on her record card.

> **TIP** ✓
>
> **Contra-action to product**
> Source an alternative manufacturer. The client may not be allergic to all products if the cause of the contra-action is allergy.

EYELASH PERMING

Eyelash perming entails permanently curling the lashes, which enhances the appearance of the eyes. The lashes immediately appear longer, which suits most clients. The treatment also suits:

- short sparse lashes, to make them appear longer and denser;
- downward-slanting eyes, as the eyes appear lifted when the outer lashes are curled;
- special occasions and holidays;
- clients who are unable to wear eye make-up at work;
- a natural effect to enhance the eyes.

The effect lasts as long as the hair growth cycle of the eyelashes.

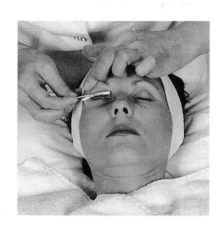

Eyelash perming

The development of curl

Hair maintains its shape and strength by chemical cross bonds in the cortex (the thickest layer of the hair) called **disulphide bonds** (two sulphur bonds joined together). In the perm **processing** stage, these bonds must be broken to alter the shape of the hair. When the perm solution is applied to the hair the chemical cross bonds are broken by the addition of hydrogen and the hair is softened. The hair then assumes the shape of the rod that it is curved around.

This shape is made permanent by the application of the fixing/neutralising lotion. This stops the action of the perm lotion. This stage is called the **neutralising** stage, where the chemical cross bonds in the cortex are reformed by adding oxygen (known as oxidation) and removing the hydrogen. This stage is completed before the rods are removed. On removal of the rods the eyelash hair assumes its new shape.

Wella

Disulphide bonds

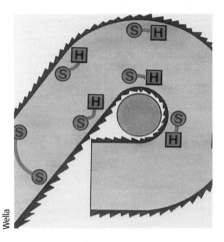

Wella

Processing stage: breaking existing disulphide bonds by the addition of hydrogen

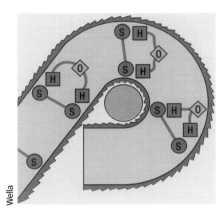

Wella

Oxidation: forming new disulphide bonds

Outcome 1: Consult with the client

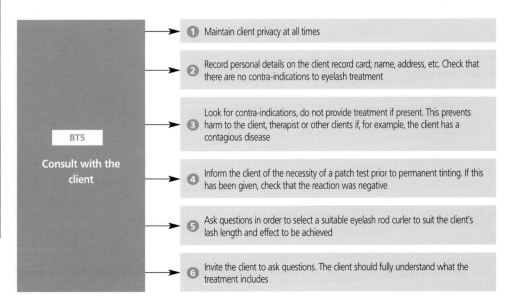

BT5

Consult with the client

1. Maintain client privacy at all times

2. Record personal details on the client record card; name, address, etc. Check that there are no contra-indications to eyelash treatment

3. Look for contra-indications, do not provide treatment if present. This prevents harm to the client, therapist or other clients if, for example, the client has a contagious disease

4. Inform the client of the necessity of a patch test prior to permanent tinting. If this has been given, check that the reaction was negative

5. Ask questions in order to select a suitable eyelash rod curler to suit the client's lash length and effect to be achieved

6. Invite the client to ask questions. The client should fully understand what the treatment includes

Reception

When making an appointment for this service, recommend that the client has a skin test. Ask them to visit the salon for this 24 hours before the appointment.

If they wear contact lenses, ask them to bring the lens container so that they can place the lenses in it during the perming treatment.

Advise the client that the treatment requires that they keep their eyes closed for a long time. Some clients may find this uncomfortable, and may choose not to have the treatment.

The client should not have an eyelash tint immediately before perming, as the colour of the lashes will be lightened by the treatment process. However, tinting is effective *following* eyelash perming and should be promoted. Allow a minimum of 24 hours following the eyelash perming service before tinting.

On average, a client will need their eyelashes permed every two to three months. Treatment takes approximately 45 minutes.

Contra-indications

If whilst completing the record card or on visual inspection of the skin, the client is found to have any of the following in the eye area, do not proceed with the eyelash perming treatment:

- *Inflammation or swelling* – the cause may be medical.
- *Skin disease*.
- *Skin disorder*, such as psoriasis or eczema.
- *Cuts and abrasions* – skin irritation or secondary infection could occur.
- *Hypersensitive skin* – the skin could become excessively red and swollen.
- *Any eye disorder*, such as conjunctivitis, blepharitis, styes or hordeola, epiphora or watery eye, or cysts.
- *Positive (allergic) reaction* to the skin sensitivity test.
- *Contact lenses* – unless removed.
- *Considerable nervousness* – a particularly nervous client may make application, fixing and removal hazardous.

> **TIP** ✔
>
> Permanent curling is not advisable if:
> - the lashes are naturally curly;
> - the lashes are very short and sparse;
> - the lashes are fragile.

> **HEALTH AND SAFETY** ✚
>
> **Allergies**
> Some perming lotions contain lanolin. If using such lotions, ask the client before application whether they are allergic to lanolin.

Outcome 2: Prepare for the treatment

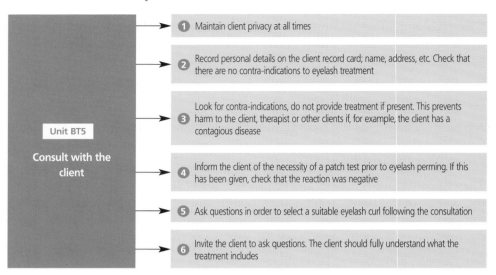

Unit BT5	
Consult with the client	**1** Maintain client privacy at all times
	2 Record personal details on the client record card; name, address, etc. Check that there are no contra-indications to eyelash treatment
	3 Look for contra-indications, do not provide treatment if present. This prevents harm to the client, therapist or other clients if, for example, the client has a contagious disease
	4 Inform the client of the necessity of a patch test prior to eyelash perming. If this has been given, check that the reaction was negative
	5 Ask questions in order to select a suitable eyelash curl following the consultation
	6 Invite the client to ask questions. The client should fully understand what the treatment includes

Skin sensitivity (patch) test

Some clients may be sensitive to the perm solution, and may produce an allergic reaction immediately on contact with it; others may become allergic later. For this reason, a skin sensitivity (patch) test must be carried out before *each* eyelash perming treatment. This is essential not just for new clients, but also if there has been a lengthy interval since the last eyelash perming service.

1. Apply a small amount of perm solution to the inside of one elbow or behind the ear, and a small amount of fixing lotion to the other.

2. Test the client's tolerance to the adhesive by applying a small amount of the adhesive to the inside of the elbow or behind the ear. Avoid immediate contact with clothing.

3. Advise the client how to recognise a positive skin reaction: skin reddening, itching and swelling. Advise them to apply a soothing agent if this occurs and to notify you. This reaction can then be recorded on the client's record card.

TIP ✓

Positive promotion

To maximise revenue and to enhance the client's treatment, offer the client another service while the lashes are being permed. Suitable treatments include a manicure or hand treatment.

Equipment and materials

To carry out the perming you will need the following equipment and materials:

EQUIPMENT LIST

 Couch or beauty chair with sit-up and lie-down positions and an easy-to-clean surface
Trolley on which to place everything

 Eyelash perm rods (a selection of different sizes) – small curlers are used for fine hair, larger curlers for thicker, longer hair

 Disposable brushes to apply the perm lotion and fixing lotion

 Headband (clean) – to protect the hair

 Eyelash adhesive to secure the lashes to the curlers

 Damp cottonwool for cleansing the eye area and to remove excess products

 Eye make-up remover (non-oily)

 Disposable wooden cocktail or orange sticks to secure the natural lashes to the curlers

 Swing-top bin lined with a disposable bin-liner, for waste

YOU WILL ALSO NEED:

Towels (medium-sized) – freshly laundered for each client

Mild perm solution (usually 6% thioglycollate) – especially designed for use in the eye area (this solution curls the lash into the desired new shape)

Fixing/neutralising lotion – sodium bromate (this makes the new curl permanent)

Lint-free pads – to remove the perm and fixing lotion

Bowls (two, clean) – to hold damp cottonwool or lint-free pads

Moisturising agent – to facilitate removal of the curlers

Timer – to accurately time the 'curling' and 'fixing' processes

Hand mirror (clean) – to show the client the results

Client record card – confidential card recording the details of each client registered at the salon

Perm lotions

TIP

Perm lotions for the eye area are usually of *gel* formulation: this makes the lotion easy to control. Bear this in mind when selecting this product. The bottles are small to reduce the risk of oxidation, which would make the lotion ineffective.

Sterilisation and disinfection

Ideally, applicators used for the perming chemical agents should be disposable. Alternatively, several brushes must be available to allow effective disinfection between clients.

Preparing the cubicle

Before the client is shown through to the cubicle it should be checked to ensure that the required equipment and materials are available and the area is clean and tidy.

The couch or beauty chair should be flat or slightly elevated. Clean and protect the couch or chair as for eyebrow-shaping treatment (page 234).

The cubicle should be adequately lit to ensure that the treatment can be given safely, but avoid bright lighting which might cause eye irritation.

Outcome 3: Plan the treatment

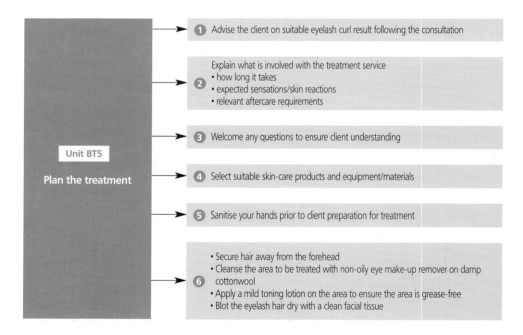

Unit BT5

Plan the treatment

1. Advise the client on suitable eyelash curl result following the consultation

2. Explain what is involved with the treatment service
   • how long it takes
   • expected sensations/skin reactions
   • relevant aftercare requirements

3. Welcome any questions to ensure client understanding

4. Select suitable skin-care products and equipment/materials

5. Sanitise your hands prior to client preparation for treatment

6. • Secure hair away from the forehead
   • Cleanse the area to be treated with non-oily eye make-up remover on damp cottonwool
   • Apply a mild toning lotion on the area to ensure the area is grease-free
   • Blot the eyelash hair dry with a clean facial tissue

Outcome 6: Perm eyelashes to meet client's requirements

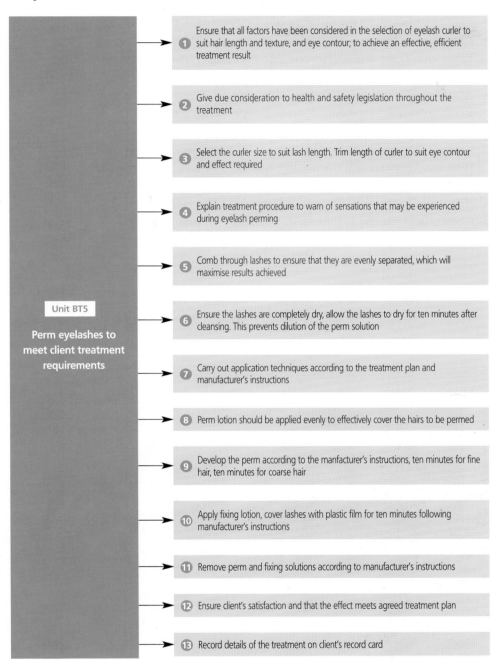

Unit BT5

Perm eyelashes to meet client treatment requirements

1. Ensure that all factors have been considered in the selection of eyelash curler to suit hair length and texture, and eye contour; to achieve an effective, efficient treatment result

2. Give due consideration to health and safety legislation throughout the treatment

3. Select the curler size to suit lash length. Trim length of curler to suit eye contour and effect required

4. Explain treatment procedure to warn of sensations that may be experienced during eyelash perming

5. Comb through lashes to ensure that they are evenly separated, which will maximise results achieved

6. Ensure the lashes are completely dry, allow the lashes to dry for ten minutes after cleansing. This prevents dilution of the perm solution

7. Carry out application techniques according to the treatment plan and manufacturer's instructions

8. Perm lotion should be applied evenly to effectively cover the hairs to be permed

9. Develop the perm according to the manfacturer's instructions, ten minutes for fine hair, ten minutes for coarse hair

10. Apply fixing lotion, cover lashes with plastic film for ten minutes following manufacturer's instructions

11. Remove perm and fixing solutions according to manufacturer's instructions

12. Ensure client's satisfaction and that the effect meets agreed treatment plan

13. Record details of the treatment on client's record card

Preparing the client

The client should be shown through to the cubicle after the record card has been completed.

1 Position the client comfortably, in a flat or slightly elevated position. If they wear contact lenses, these must be removed.

2 Drape a towel across the client's chest and shoulders, and protect their hair with a clean headband.

3 Wash your hands. This assures the client that the treatment is beginning in a hygienic and professional manner.

4 Consult the client's record card, then check the area for any visible contra-indications or abnormalities before proceeding.

5 Cleanse the surrounding eye area with a cleansing milk to dissolve facial make-up. Then use a non-oily eye make-up remover to remove eye products: apply this with clean, damp cottonwool.

6 Blot the eyelashes dry with a clean facial tissue. This ensures that the perm lotion is not diluted, and also prevents the perm lotion being carried into the eye.

7 Explain the procedure to the client and tell them about the sensations they may experience during eyelash perming. Warn them that they will need to keep their eyes closed for a long period. Some clients may find this difficult, while others will enjoy this as a time of relaxation!

8 Comb through the lashes to ensure they are evenly separated and dry. This will optimise the results.

> **TIP**
>
> A protective damp cottonwool pad may be placed over the lower lashes to form a barrier to the perm lotion, when it is being applied to the upper lashes.

> **TIP**
>
> Avoid overhandling the curler as this will affect the natural adhesion of the curler to the skin.

Step by step: Perming the eyelashes

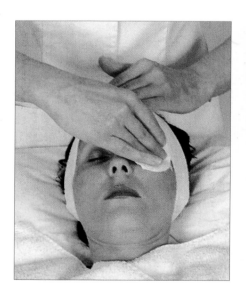

1 Cleanse the eye area

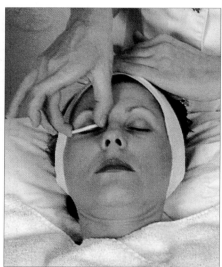

2 Select the correct size of curler for the client's lash length. Bend it so that it fits the contour of the eye. If the curler is too long it may be trimmed.

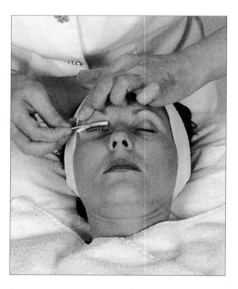

3 Place the curler at the base of the upper lashes, near the inner tear duct. Gently curl the natural lashes around the curler, using the disposable stick. Ensure that the lashes do not overlap each other and are straight or the ends will be 'crooked', spoiling the overall effect and appearance.

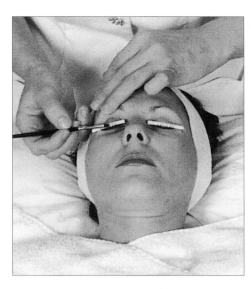

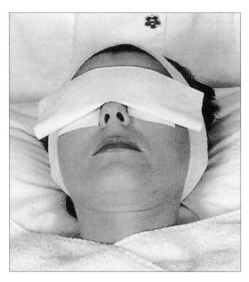

4 When you are satisfied that the lashes are straight and that the client is comfortable, apply the perm lotion evenly to the upper lashes, using a disposable brush.

5 Cover the lashes with plastic film (clear wrap) or dry lint-free pads. This creates warmth which aids the perming process. Allow:
- 7–10 minutes for fine or previously tinted hair;
- 10 minutes for coarse hair.
Follow manufacturer's guidance on timing as this may vary.

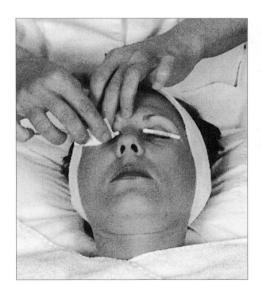

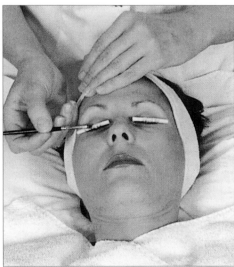

6 Remove the perm lotion using dry lint-free pads, gently blotting the lashes.

7 Apply the fixing/neutralising lotion with a clean disposable brush.

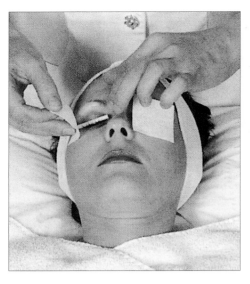

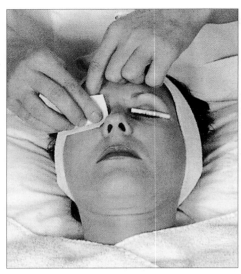

8 Cover the lashes with plastic film (clear wrap) or dry lint-free pads for 10 minutes.

9 Gently remove the fixing/neutralising lotion from the lashes, using dry lint-free pads.

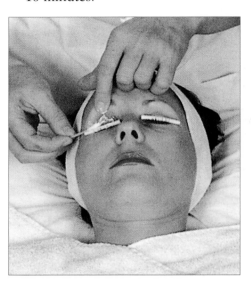

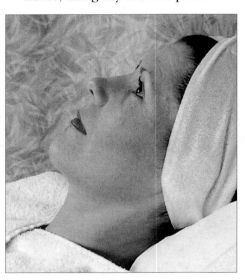

10 When all fixing/neutralising lotion has been thoroughly removed, gently remove each curler, rolling downwards. A moisturising agent may be applied with a cotton bud to the lashes to aid the removal of the curlers. Warn the client that she will feel a gentle pulling movement as the curlers are removed. Wipe excess product from the lashes with damp, clean cottonwool. Brush gently through the lashes to define their shape and appearance.

11 The completed effect

TIP ✔

If necessary, apply non-permanent eyelash adhesive using a fine wooden or plastic cocktail stick to secure the lashes to the curler and to keep them even and straight so that the lower and upper lashes do not stick together.

Outcome 7: Complete the treatment

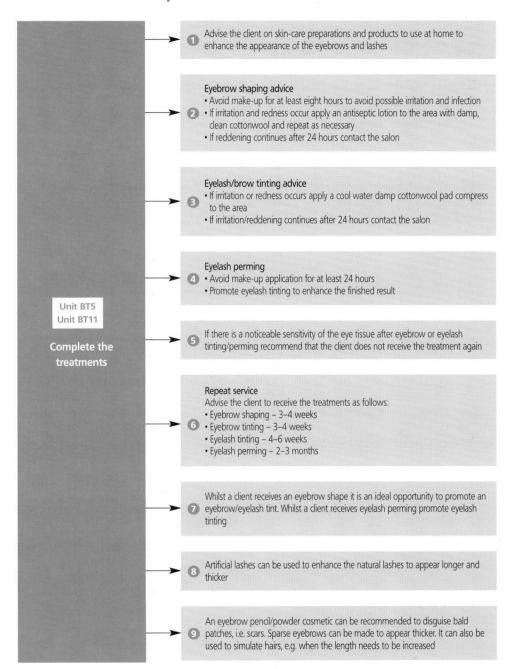

**Unit BT5
Unit BT11**

Complete the treatments

① Advise the client on skin-care preparations and products to use at home to enhance the appearance of the eyebrows and lashes

② Eyebrow shaping advice
• Avoid make-up for at least eight hours to avoid possible irritation and infection
• If irritation and redness occur apply an antiseptic lotion to the area with damp, clean cottonwool and repeat as necessary
• If reddening continues after 24 hours contact the salon

③ Eyelash/brow tinting advice
• If irritation or redness occurs apply a cool water damp cottonwool pad compress to the area
• If irritation/reddening continues after 24 hours contact the salon

④ Eyelash perming
• Avoid make-up application for at least 24 hours
• Promote eyelash tinting to enhance the finished result

⑤ If there is a noticeable sensitivity of the eye tissue after eyebrow or eyelash tinting/perming recommend that the client does not receive the treatment again

⑥ Repeat service
Advise the client to receive the treatments as follows:
• Eyebrow shaping – 3–4 weeks
• Eyebrow tinting – 3–4 weeks
• Eyelash tinting – 4–6 weeks
• Eyelash perming – 2–3 months

⑦ Whilst a client receives an eyebrow shape it is an ideal opportunity to promote an eyebrow/eyelash tint. Whilst a client receives eyelash perming promote eyelash tinting

⑧ Artificial lashes can be used to enhance the natural lashes to appear longer and thicker

⑨ An eyebrow pencil/powder cosmetic can be recommended to disguise bald patches, i.e. scars. Sparse eyebrows can be made to appear thicker. It can also be used to simulate hairs, e.g. when the length needs to be increased

How to complete the treatment

1 Show the client the effect of their permed eyelashes.

2 When you are both satisfied with the result, complete the client's record card.

3 Record details of the treatment on the client record card.

4 Take the client to reception to book their next appointment.

Contra-actions

If the client complains of discomfort during the treatment, perm lotion may have entered the eye. Take the following action:

1 Remove the perm lotion immediately from the eye area, using clean, damp cottonwool. Remove the perm rod, using the moisturising agent if necessary to facilitate removal.

2 Carefully flush the eye with clean water. Repeat the rinsing process until discomfort has been relieved.

3 Apply a cool compress to soothe the eye area.

If there is noticeable sensitivity of the eye tissue after eyelash perming treatment, recommend that the client does not receive the treatment again. Record this on their record card.

HEALTH AND SAFETY ✚

Protective disposable gloves
Disposable gloves may be worn to reduce the risk of chemical contact with the skin.

Undesirable perm results	Possible cause	Preventative action
Hooked end	Incorrect positioning of the point of the eyelash hair around the curler.	Ensure that the point of the eyelash is corrected if it appears crooked before application of the perm lotion. Use eyelash adhesive to secure hair into the desired position.
Poor curl result	Incorrect preparation of the lashes; oil present on the lashes. Eyelashes too damp before perm lotion application. Uneven application of the perm/fixing/ neutralising lotion. Incorrect curler size for the hair.	Ensure that the lashes are clean and excess moisture removed before perm lotion application. Ensure that the lashes are brushed through to separate the ends before curler application. Be methodical in application of perm/fixing/ neutralising lotions to ensure effective curl result. Select the correct curler size for the lash length and coarseness of the hair.
	Insufficient timing of the chemical process of perming/neutralising or both.	Use a reliable timing device to ensure accuracy of the timing process.
Hairs pointing in different directions	Incorrect placing of the eyelash hair along the eyelash curler.	Ensure the hairs are evenly placed and secured along the eyelash curler.
Vertical not curled	This tends to occur on short lashes where the small curlers have been selected and the perm lotion has been applied to the majority of the length of the hair. From the base of the lashes the hair stands vertically.	Ensure correct application of the perm lotion.
Too curled	Curler too small for the eyelash length.	Ensure that the correct curler is chosen for the lash length and thickness.

Aftercare and advice

Advise your client not to apply make-up for at least 24 hours. Similarly, they should not receive any other eye treatments for at least 24 hours.

Subsequently, however, eyelash tinting will enhance the effect of the newly permed lashes, so you can promote this service to the client.

GLOSSARY OF KEY WORDS

Aftercare advice recommended advice given to the client following treatment to continue the benefits of the treatment.

Blepharitis inflammation of the eyelid caused by an infection or an allergic reaction.

Conjunctivitis a bacterial infection. Inflammation of the mucous membrane that covers the eye and lines the eyelid. The skin of the inner conjunctiva of the eye becomes inflamed, the eye becomes very red, itchy and sore, and pus may exude from the eye area.

Consultation assessment of client's needs using different assessment techniques, including questioning and natural observation.

Contra-action an unwanted reaction occurring during or after treatment application.

Contra-indication a problematic symptom that indicates that the treatment may not proceed.

Cortex the thickest layer of the hair structure.

Cyst localised pocket of sebum that forms in the hair follicle or under the sebaceous glands in the skin. Semi-globular in shape, either raised or flat, and hard or soft. Cysts are the same colour as the skin, or red if bacterial infection occurs.

Disulphide bonds two chemical sulphur bonds joined together forming a chemical bond in the cortex of the hair.

Eyebrow shaping involves the removal of eyebrow hair to create a new shape (reshape) or to remove stray hairs to maintain the existing brow shape (trim). Small metal tools, called tweezers, are use to remove the hairs.

Eyelash adhesive an adhesive used during perming eyelash treatment to secure the eye lashes to the curlers.

Eyelash and eyebrow tinting definition of the brow and lash hair, achieved by the application of a permanent dye especially formulated for use around the delicate eye area.

Eyelash curlers small flexible rods around which the natural eyelashes are curled during eyelash perming treatment.

Eyelash perming a chemical treatment applied to the eyelashes to permanently curl the lashes, which enhances the appearance of the eyes.

Fixing/neutralising lotion usually containing sodium bromate, which makes the curl produced during eyelash perming permanent.

Hair a long slender structure that grows out of, and is part of, the skin. Each hair is made up of dead skin cells, which contain the protein called keratin.

Hair follicle an appendage (structure) in the skin formed from epidermal tissue. Cells move up the hair follicle from the bottom (the hair bulb), changing in structure to form the hair.

Hydrogen peroxide (H_2O_2) an *oxidant*, a chemical that contains available oxygen atoms and encourages chemical reactions.

Perm solution usually contains 6% thioglycollate, which when applied to the eyelash hair softens and curls the hair into its new shape.

Positive skin sensitivity test an allergic reaction to the skin test. The skin appears red, swollen and feels itchy.

Skin sensitivity (patch) test method used to assess skin tolerance/sensitivity to a substance or treatment.

Stye bacterial infection. Infection of the sebaceous glands of the eyelash hair follicles. Small lumps appear on the inner rim of the eyelid and contain pus.

Thioglycollate the active ingredient in perm solution.

Toluenediamine small molecules of permanent dye used in tinting treatment.

Treatment plan after the consultation, suitable treatment objectives are established to treat the client's conditions and needs.

Tweezers small metal tools used to remove body hair by pulling it from the bottom of the hair follicle (small opening in the skin where the hair grows from). There are two types: *automatic* – designed to remove the bulk of the hair and *manual* – designed to remove the stray hairs.

Watery eye over-secretion of tears from the eyes, which would normally drain into the nasal cavity.

Assessment of knowledge and understanding

You have now learnt about the different eye treatments available to treat the lashes and the eyebrows. These skills will enable you to enhance the appearance of the eyebrows and lashes.

To test your level of knowledge, answer the following short questions. These will prepare you for your summative (final) assessment.

Consult with the client

1 How should all client records be stored to comply with the Data Protection Act 1998?

2 Good communication is important. Why is it important to have a thorough consultation before you commence the treatment?

3 If the client is having an eyelash/brow tint why is it important to check the results of the skin test before you proceed?

4 Why is a skin sensitivity test needed before every tinting treatment?

5 What eye disorders would contra-indicate treatment?

6 What factors should you consider when deciding the correct eyebrow shape for a client?

7 How can you determine the length of a client's eyebrows that will best suit their facial features?

8 How do you select the colour when carrying out a permanent tinting treatment?

9 What details should be recorded on the client's record card?

10 Why is it important to keep a record of the treatment carried out?

Prepare for the treatment

1 What are the acceptable methods of sterilisation for tweezers?

2 How would you prepare the treatment area to ensure general client comfort during treatment application?

3 How should the client be positioned for the eye treatment to avoid discomfort and ensure effective treatment application?

4 How should the brows be prepared to minimise discomfort and the risk of infection, before shaping commences?

5 How should the lash and brow area be prepared to avoid skin staining and to ensure effective tinting?

Client consultation

1 When observing the area for eye treatments, what conditions would contra-indicate treatment?

2 A client complains that her previous eyelash perm had been too curly. What will you need to ask and how will you adapt your treatment to ensure client satisfaction this time?

3 At consultation you notice that a client has what you think is conjunctivitis. What action should you take?

Prepare for treatment

1 Why is it important that the eye treatment is given in the allocated time?

2 It is important to select the correct and most suitable equipment and materials for the treatment. When would you use the following?
- automatic tweezers
- manual tweezers.

Plan the treatment

1 Why is it important to discuss the treatment plan with the client before treatment commences?

2 If the client wished to have their fair brows tinted, but had a positive reaction to the skin test, what could you recommend as an alternative?

Shape the eyebrows to meet the client's treatment requirements

1 How long would you allocate to carry out an eyebrow shaping treatment?

2 How can you ensure that hairs are removed at their root?

3 What factors should you consider in your approach to eyebrow shaping with the following clients?
- a client with excessively thick eyebrows who requests a thin eyebrow shape
- a client who has close-set eyes
- a client with a round face
- a client who has a few stray long, coarse hairs
- a client with sensitive skin.

4 How should consumables used during a brow shape be disposed of?

5 What hygiene and safety precautions should be followed when performing an eyebrow shape?

6 Give two examples of contra-actions that may occur following eyebrow shaping.

7 What action would you take if a skin contra-action occurred following eyebrow shaping?

Tint the eyebrows and lashes to meet the client's treatment requirements

1 How long would you allocate to carry out an eyelash and eyebrow tint?

2 Why is the quantity of tint applied to the area important in relation both to efficiency and the final result?

3 How would permanent tinting be performed when treating the following:
- a very nervous client, to ensure a safe, efficient eyelash tinting treatment
- a client who requires an eyebrow shape and an eyebrow tint. In which order should these treatments be given and why?

4 What is the difference in processing time between a brow tint and an eyelash tint?

5 How long would you allow the tint to process when treating a client with:
- blonde hair
- grey hair
- red hair
- dark hair?

6 If a client complained of irritation during an eyelash tinting treatment, what action would you take?

7 How would a contra-action to permanent tint be recognised?

Perm eyelashes to meet client requirements

1 How can you ensure the eyelashes are securely attached to the curler?

2 Why should crossing the eyelashes be avoided when fixing the hair to the curler?

3 Why are the bottom lashes often protected with a protective shield during perm lotion application to the upper lashes?

4 How will timing following perm lotion application vary according to hair texture, colouring and previous treatment of the eyelashes, including perming and tinting?

5 What lotion is applied to fix the hair into its new curled shape?

6 How are the curlers removed following neutralising/fixing procedure?

7 How often would you recommend a client has their eyelashes permed?

Complete the treatment

1 Why is a soothing antiseptic lotion applied following an eyebrow shaping treatment?

2 What aftercare advice should be given to a client following an eyebrow shaping treatment?

3 What aftercare advice should be given to a client following a permanent tinting treatment?

4 When would you recommend that a client returns to the salon for an eyebrow trim, following an eyebrow shape?

5 When would you recommend that the client returned to the salon for a permanent tinting treatment:
- for the eyelashes
- for the eyebrows?

6 What other eye treatment service would enhance the effect of eyelash perming?

chapter 8

BT6 Remove hair using waxing techniques

Learning objectives

This unit describes how to remove facial and body hair using temporary methods, including waxing and sugaring hair removal products.

It describes the competencies to enable you to:

- **consult with the client**
- **prepare for the treatment**
- **plan the treatment**
- **remove unwanted hair**
- **complete the treatment**

When providing temporary hair removal using wax it is important to use the skills you have learnt in the following core mandatory units:

UNIT G1 Ensure your own actions reduce risks to health and safety

UNIT G6 Promote additional products or services to clients

UNIT G8 Develop and maintain your effectiveness at work

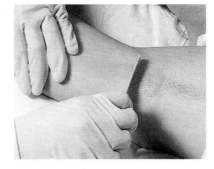

Hair removal

 Essential anatomy and physiology knowledge requirements for this unit, BT6, are identified on the checklist in Chapter 5, page 101.

HAIR REMOVAL METHODS

Hair removal is a popular treatment in the beauty salon, where both temporary and permanent methods of removal are usually available. Temporary removal must be repeated regularly, as the removed hair will regrow. With permanent methods, the client needs to visit the salon regularly to have the hair removed; thereafter, the part of the hair responsible for its growth has been destroyed and the hair will not grow again.

ACTIVITY

Hair removal
Make short notes on the suitability and effectiveness of the different methods of hair removal.

Temporary methods of hair removal

Depilatory waxing

Depilatory waxing, using a warm, hot or cold wax, involves applying wax to the treatment area and embedding the hairs in it. When the wax is removed from the area, the hairs are removed also, at their roots. They grow again in approximately four weeks.

Plucking

Plucking or **tweezing** uses a pair of tweezers to remove the hair. These grasp the hair near the surface of the skin, and the hair is then plucked in the direction of growth, again removing it at its root. The hair grows again in approximately four weeks.

Due to the sensitive nature of the eye tissue, tweezing is often considered the most suitable choice for temporary hair removal from eyebrows.

Threading

Threading involves the use of a thread of twisted cotton, which is rolled over the area from which the hair is to be removed: the hairs catch in the cotton, and are pulled out. This skill is frequently practised by people of Asian or Mediterranean origin.

Permanent methods of hair removal

Galvanic electrolysis, **electrical epilation** and the **blend epilation technique** are all techniques that use an electrical current. The current is passed to the hair root via a fine needle inserted into the hair follicle. The current destroys the hair root, preventing hair regrowth.

Laser hair removal

Laser energy is passed through the epidermis of the skin, which stops the activity of the hair follicle creating hair growth through a process called *photothermolysis*. The melanin pigment that provides hair colour absorbs the laser energy that is converted to heat, which at a sufficient temperature destroys the part of the hair follicle where the cells divide to create the hair.

A course of laser treatment is required. Treatment length will depend on the coarseness of the hair type and the size of the hair follicle. The treatment is most effective when the hair is in the anagen (growth) stage of the hair growth cycle. Subsequent treatments therefore target hairs in their anagen stage of growth until all hairs cease to grow.

The client needs to understand that the hair will never grow back if effectively treated with any of the above permanent methods. This is an important consideration when treating the brow hair, as the desired shape and thickness of the brows change frequently under the influence of fashion.

HEALTH AND SAFETY

Laser hair removal
Registration with the National Care Standards Commission (NCSC) is a requirement to practise laser hair removal.

Other methods of hair removal

There are other methods of hair removal that the client may have used at home previously.

- *Cutting the hairs with scissors* Scissors are used to trim the hair close to the skin's surface.
- *Shaving* A razor blade is stroked over the skin, against the natural hair growth. This removes the hair at the skin's surface.
- *Depilatory cream* A strong alkaline chemical cream containing ammonium thioglycollate is applied to the hair, and removed after five to ten minutes: the hair will have been dissolved at the skin's surface.
- *Abrasive mitt* An abrasive glove is rubbed against the skin and the hair is broken off at the skin's surface.

PLAN AND PREPARE FOR WAX DEPILATION TREATMENT

Wax depilation involves using wax to remove hair temporarily from the face and body. Waxing removes both the visible hair and the root, so the regrowth is of completely new hairs with soft, fine-tapered tips. It will take four to six weeks before the client requires the service again.

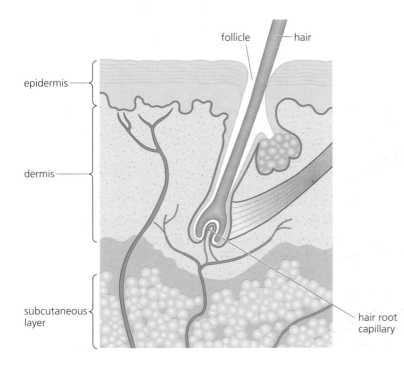

The hair in its follicle

Cross-section of the skin showing a hair in the hair follicle. Waxing removes the entire hair, the visible hair above the skin's surface and the part that cannot be seen in the hair follicle.

Outcome 1: Consult with the client

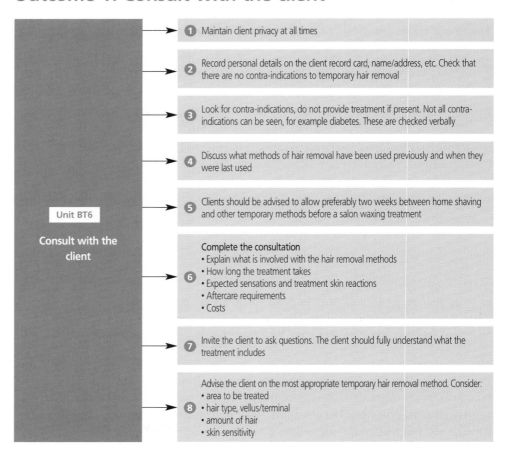

Unit BT6

Consult with the client

1. Maintain client privacy at all times

2. Record personal details on the client record card, name/address, etc. Check that there are no contra-indications to temporary hair removal

3. Look for contra-indications, do not provide treatment if present. Not all contra-indications can be seen, for example diabetes. These are checked verbally

4. Discuss what methods of hair removal have been used previously and when they were last used

5. Clients should be advised to allow preferably two weeks between home shaving and other temporary methods before a salon waxing treatment

6. **Complete the consultation**
   - Explain what is involved with the hair removal methods
   - How long the treatment takes
   - Expected sensations and treatment skin reactions
   - Aftercare requirements
   - Costs

7. Invite the client to ask questions. The client should fully understand what the treatment includes

8. Advise the client on the most appropriate temporary hair removal method. Consider:
   - area to be treated
   - hair type, vellus/terminal
   - amount of hair
   - skin sensitivity

Reception

When the client is booking their treatment they should be asked whether they have had a wax treatment before in the salon. If they have not, a small area of waxing should be carried out as a **patch test**, to ensure that the client is not sensitive to the technique or allergic to any of the products used. If the patch test causes an unwanted reaction within 48 hours, then the treatment must not be undertaken. Unwanted reactions include redness, irritation and swelling.

Advise the client not to apply any lotions or oils to the area on the day of the treatment – these could prevent the adhesion of the wax to the hairs being removed. Ask them also to allow at least one week, and preferably two, between any home shaving or other depilatory treatment and a salon waxing treatment. This is to let the hairs grow to a length sufficient to be waxed.

When a client makes an appointment for a wax depilation treatment, the receptionist should advise the client how long the treatment will take.

It is important to complete treatment in the time allowed in order to be efficient in treatment application and to ensure the appointment schedule runs smoothly and clients are not kept waiting.

Treatment	Warm waxing (minutes)	Hot waxing (minutes)	Sugaring (minutes)
Half leg	30	30	20–30
Half leg and bikini	30	45	45–50
Full leg	50	60	55
Full leg and bikini	60	60–75	60–75
Bikini	15	15	15–20
Underarm	15	15	15
Half arm	15	15–20	15–20
Full arm	30	20–30	20–30
Top lip	5	5–10	5–10
Chin and throat	10	20	15–20
Top lip and chin	15	15–20	15–20
Eyebrows	15	10–15	10–15

Allow a four- to six-week interval between successive wax depilation appointments. The times to be allowed for wax treatments are as shown in the table.

Consultation

A consultation must be performed for all clients who have not received the treatment service before or are new clients to you. Explain what is involved with the method of hair removal technique to be used, the expected sensations, treatment reactions and aftercare requirements.

It is a good idea to discuss the hair growth cycle with the client using a visual aid. This will help the client to understand that hairs that grow through following hair removal were at a different stage of the hair growth cycle and were below the skin's surface at the time of the treatment. It also is beneficial to support the need for regular intervals between waxing appointments as hairs will be at a similar hair growth pattern.

Immediately following hair removal, the skin becomes slightly red around the follicle where the hair has been removed. There may also be slight swelling of the skin in the area. This will soon disappear following treatment but this will vary according to skin sensitivity and hair strength and the quantity of hair that has been removed.

Invite the client to ask questions. It is important that they understand fully what the treatment includes.

> **TIP** ✔
>
> Here are some useful explanatory phrases: 'It's a bit like ripping a plaster off, and taking the hairs with it. It isn't so bad, or so many people wouldn't have it done time and time again!'

> **TIP** ✔
>
> **Histamine reaction**
> Damage to the skin that occurs during a waxing treatment causing cells called *mast cells* to burst in the skin releasing a chemical substance called *histamine*. Histamine is released into the tissues causing the blood capillaries to dilate, giving the redness called *erythema*. The increased blood flow limits damage and begins repair.

The hair growth cycle

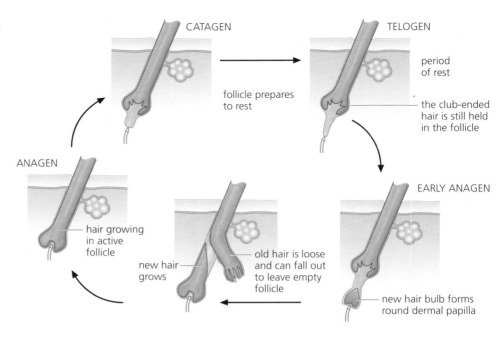

Contra-indications

When a client attends for a wax depilation treatment, the therapist should always check that there are no contra-indications that might prevent treatment.

If the client has any of the following, wax depilation must not be carried out:

- *Skin disorders*, such as severe eczema or psoriasis.
- *Eye disorders*, such as conjunctivitis when treating the face.
- *Swellings* – the cause may be medical.
- *Diabetes* – a client with this condition is vulnerable to infection as they have slow skin healing.
- *Defective circulation* – poor skin healing may occur.
- *Recent scar tissue (under six months old)* – the skin lacks elasticity.
- *Fractures or sprains* – discomfort may occur.
- *Phlebitis* – an inflammatory condition of the vein.
- *Retin-A, Tetracycline medication*, as the skin is more sensitive and prone to skin irritation.
- *Loss of skin sensation* – the client would be unable to identify if the wax was too hot.

TIP

Waxing a client with a recent well-established suntan may cause the loose sun-damaged epidermis to peel and be lost, along with the hair. Inform the client of this at consultation.

HEALTH AND SAFETY

Diabetes
Clients who have the medical condition diabetes should be treated with care. This is because diabetics generally have poor circulation and are slow to heal. As there is some tissue damage to the skin during wax depilation when the hair is removed from the follicle, secondary infection could occur. Approval to treat should be obtained by the client from their GP before temporary hair removal treatment.

TIP

Precaution if there is a restrictive contra-indication present
If there is a hairy mole or small abrasion you may apply petroleum jelly to avoid wax adherence.

Further contra-indications that prevent waxing treatment

Name	Description
Bruising _Wellcome Photo Library_	Injury to an area causes blood to leak from damaged blood vessels. Bruises may swell, appearing dark purple or blue at first and then turn, brown, green or yellow as they fade.
Folliculitis _Wellcome Photo Library_	A bacterial infection where pustules develop in the skin tissue around the hair follicle.
Severe varicose veins _Wellcome Photo Library_	Veins are vessels that carry blood away from the body tissues and back to the heart. Veins have valves to prevent backflow as they carry blood under low blood pressure back towards the heart. If valves become weak and their elasticity is lost, it becomes a _varicose vein_. The area appears knotted, swollen and bluish-purple in colour.

Certain contra-indications restrict treatment application. This may mean that the treatment has to be adapted for the client. For example, in the case of a small, localised bruise the area could be avoided.

Other contra-indications that restrict treatment include:

- _Cuts_ – secondary infection could occur.
- _Mild skin disorders_, such as psoriasis or eczema.
- _Abrasions_ – secondary infection could occur.
- _Self tan_ – waxing will remove the surface skin cells and the chemically tanned skin.
- _Bruises_ – client discomfort may be caused and the condition made worse.
- _Sunburn_ – the skin is damaged due to acute over exposure to the sun.
- _Varicose veins_ (non-severe) – avoid the area.

TIP ✔

If there is any bruising on the client's legs, tactfully draw their attention to these bruises, or they might later think that the treatment has caused them.

Further contra-indications that restrict waxing treatment

Name	Description
Heat rash *Wellcome Photo Library*	A reaction to heat exposure where the sweat ducts become blocked and sweat escapes into the epidermis. Red pimples occur and the skin becomes itchy.
Warts *Dr M. H. Beck*	Small epidermal skin growths. Warts may be raised or flat, depending upon their position. Usually they have a rough surface and are raised.
Hairy moles *Wellcome Photo Library*	Moles exhibiting coarse hairs from their surface. Hair growing from a mole may be cut, not plucked: if plucked, the hairs will become coarser and the growth of the hairs further stimulated.
Skin tags *Wellcome Photo Library*	Skin-coloured threads of skin three to six mm long, projecting from the skin's surface. Skin tags often occur under the arms.

After the record card has been completed, the client should be asked to read the list of contra-indications and sign to state that they are not suffering from any of the problems stated.

The therapist must not carry out a wax treatment immediately after a heat treatment, such as a sauna, or steam or ultra-violet treatments, as the heat-sensitised tissues may be irritated by the wax treatment.

If you are unsure if treatment may commence, refer the client to their General Practitioner for permission to treat. A copy of the GP's letter on receipt should be kept with the client's record card. If the treatment cannot be carried out for any reason, always explain why, without naming a contra-indication, as you are not qualified to do so. Clients will respect your professional advice.

BEAUTY WORKS

Date	Therapist name

Client name	Date of birth (identifying client age group)

Address	Postcode

Evening phone number	Day phone number

Name of doctor	Doctor's address and phone number

Related medical history (conditions that may restrict or prohibit treatment application)

Are you taking any medication? (this may affect the sensitivity and skin reaction following treatment)

CONTRA-INDICATIONS REQUIRING MEDICAL REFERRAL
(Preventing hair removal treatment)

- ☐ bacterial infection (e.g. impetigo, conjunctivitis)
- ☐ viral infection (e.g. herpes simplex/warts)
- ☐ fungal infection (e.g. tinea corporis)
- ☐ severe skin conditions
- ☐ diabetes
- ☐ severe varicose veins
- ☐ phlebitis

TEST CONDUCTED

- ☐ self
- ☐ client

WAX PRODUCTS

- ☐ hot wax
- ☐ warm wax – spatula method
- ☐ warm wax – roller system
- ☐ strip sugar
- ☐ sugar paste

WORK TECHNIQUES

- ☐ keep the skin taut during application and removal
- ☐ speed of product removal
- ☐ direction and angle of removal
- ☐ ongoing wax product temperature checks

CONTRA-INDICATIONS WHICH RESTRICT TREATMENT
(Treatment may require adaptation)

- ☐ cuts and abrasions
- ☐ bruising and swelling
- ☐ self tan
- ☐ skin disorders
- ☐ heat rash
- ☐ sunburn
- ☐ warts or hairy moles
- ☐ mild eczema/psoriasis

AREAS TREATED FOR HAIR REMOVAL

- ☐ eyebrows
- ☐ face
- ☐ legs
- ☐ underarm
- ☐ bikini line
- ☐ arm

Therapist signature (for reference)

Client signature (confirmation of details)

BEAUTY WORKS *(continued)*

TREATMENT ADVICE*

Half leg wax – *allow 30 minutes*
Full leg wax – *allow 50 minutes*
Bikini wax – *allow 15 minutes*
Underarm wax – *allow 15 minutes*
Half arm wax – *allow 15 minutes*
Full arm wax – *allow 30 minutes*

Eyebrow wax – *allow 15 minutes*
Facial wax top lip or chin – *allow 10 minutes*
　　　　　top lip and chin – *allow 15 minutes*

*Waxing timings may differ according to the system used.
Always allow slightly longer when using hot wax.

TREATMENT PLAN

Record relevant details of your treatment and advice provided for future reference.
Ensure the client's records are up to date, accurate and fully completed following treatment. Non-compliance may invalidate insurance.

DURING

Monitor:

- client's reaction to treatment to confirm suitability.

Note:

- any adverse reaction, if any occur.

AFTER

Record:

- results of treatment;
- any modification to treatment application that has occurred;
- what products have been used in the wax removal treatment;
- the effectiveness of treatment;
- any samples provided (review their success at the next appointment).

Advise on:

- use of aftercare products following wax removal treatment;
- use of skin-care products following wax removal treatment;
- maintenance procedures;
- the recommended time intervals between treatments.

RETAIL OPPORTUNITIES

Advise on:

- products that would be suitable for the client to use at home to care for and maintain the treatment area (these include body exfoliation and moisturising skin-care products);
- recommendations for further treatments;
- further products or services that the client may or may not have received before.

Note:

- any purchase made by the client.

EVALUATION

Record:

- comments on the client's satisfaction with the treatment;
- if poor results are achieved, the reasons why;
- how you may alter the treatment plan to achieve the required treatment results in the future, if applicable.

HEALTH AND SAFETY

Advise on:

- how to care for the area following treatment to avoid an unwanted reaction;
- avoidance of any activities or product application that may cause a contra-action;
- appropriate action to be taken in the event of an unwanted skin or eye irritation.

> **TIP**
>
> Examples of waxing treatment modification include:
> - hair removal around contra-indications that restrict treatment (such as hairy moles and skin tags);
> - altering the choice of wax to suit skin sensitivity and hair type.

> **HEALTH AND SAFETY**
>
> Client record card
> The client record card should be updated signed and dated at every visit and stored securely in compliance with the Data Protection Act 1998. Non-compliance may invalidate insurance.

Clients under 16 years of age must be accompanied by a parent/guardian who will be required to sign a consent form for treatment to proceed.

Outcome 2: Prepare for the treatment

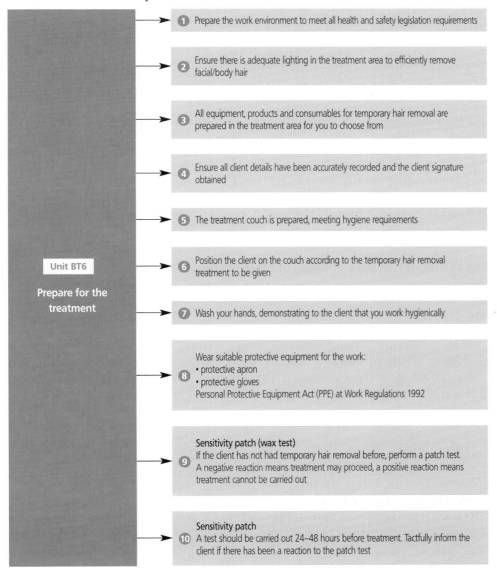

Unit BT6

Prepare for the treatment

1. Prepare the work environment to meet all health and safety legislation requirements

2. Ensure there is adequate lighting in the treatment area to efficiently remove facial/body hair

3. All equipment, products and consumables for temporary hair removal are prepared in the treatment area for you to choose from

4. Ensure all client details have been accurately recorded and the client signature obtained

5. The treatment couch is prepared, meeting hygiene requirements

6. Position the client on the couch according to the temporary hair removal treatment to be given

7. Wash your hands, demonstrating to the client that you work hygienically

8. Wear suitable protective equipment for the work:
   - protective apron
   - protective gloves
   Personal Protective Equipment Act (PPE) at Work Regulations 1992

9. Sensitivity patch (wax test)
   If the client has not had temporary hair removal before, perform a patch test. A negative reaction means treatment may proceed, a positive reaction means treatment cannot be carried out

10. Sensitivity patch
    A test should be carried out 24–48 hours before treatment. Tactfully inform the client if there has been a reaction to the patch test

Salon system wax

Salon system hot wax (discs)

A wax depilation trolley

ACTIVITY

Methods of hair removal

Other methods of temporary hair removal include the professional use of threading; and the home use of plucking, cold wax, ready-waxed strips, sugaring, electrical devices, chemical depilatory creams, shaving and pumice powder. Find out how each method works and assess its effectiveness. Are any of them potentially hazardous?

Equipment and materials

Types of wax

Warm wax   **Warm wax** first became available in 1975 and is now the market leader for hair removal. It is clean and easy to use; and because it is disposed of afterwards it is also hygienic. Finally, it is very economical.

Warm wax is used at a low temperature, around 43°C, so there is little risk of skin burning, and in less sensitive areas the wax can be re-applied once or even twice if necessary.

Warm wax does not set but remains soft at body temperature. It adheres efficiently to hairs and is quick to use; treatment is relatively pain-free. It can remove even very short hairs (2.5 mm) from legs, arms, underarms, the bikini line, the torso, the face and the neck.

Warm waxes are frequently made of mixtures of glucose syrup and zinc oxide. Honey (fructose syrup) can be used instead of glucose syrup, and this type is often called **honey wax**.

Hot wax   **Hot wax** takes longer to heat than warm wax, and is relatively slow to use, taking approximately double the time of a warm waxing.

As hot wax is used at quite a high temperature, 50°C, extra care must be taken to avoid accidental burns. Because of this risk, hot wax cannot be re-applied to already treated areas.

Hot wax cools on contact with the skin. It contracts around the hair shaft, gripping it firmly. This makes it ideal for use on stronger, short hairs.

Hot waxes for hair removal need to be a blend of waxes and resins so that they stay reasonably flexible when cool. **Beeswax** is a desirable ingredient, and often comprises 25–60 per cent of the finished product. **Cetiol**, **azulene** and **vitamin E** are often added to wax preparations to soothe the skin and minimise possible skin reactions.

Cold wax   **Cold wax** is used cold straight from its container (although some do in fact need gentle heating). It is spread with a clean spatula, and removed using a cellophane, muslin or paper strip. This product was designed for home use by the public, and is not generally seen in salons.

Cold waxes are often natural rubber solutions in a volatile solvent. The solvent evaporates from the skin to leave a rubber film with the hairs embedded in it; this is pulled off and thrown away. The adhesion between the rubber and the hair is not sufficient for strong terminal hair or short hair growth.

ACTIVITY

Wax heaters

Look in current beauty magazines for the different types of wax heater, including roll-ons. Try to see demonstrations of them working. Discuss size, cleaning, safety, hygiene and any other points that you think are important. Which heater would you choose, and why?

Sugar wax   There are two methods of sugar wax hair removal – *sugar paste* and *strip sugar*.

Sugar paste is applied to the skin, using the hands, in the direction of hair growth. The hairs embed in the wax, which is then removed swiftly against hair growth, removing the hairs.

Strip sugar is similar in application and removal to warm wax and requires a wax removal strip to remove the wax, against hair growth. Sugar wax has pure sugar as the main ingredient, plus other natural ingredients such as lemon.

A wax depilation heater

WARM WAXING

HEALTH AND SAFETY

Personal Protective Equipment Act (PPE) at Work Regulations 1992
Waxing is a treatment where there is a risk of contamination and cross-infection, therefore protective equipment such as gloves should be available and worn.

Sugar wax

Equipment and materials

EQUIPMENT LIST

 Couch with sit-up and lie-down positions and an easy-to-clean surface **Trolley** to hold all the necessary equipment and materials

 Cottonwool pads for cleaning equipment and the client's skin

 Tweezers for removing stray hairs

 Disposable wooden spatulas – a selection of differing sizes, for use on different body areas

 Facial tissues (white) for blotting skin dry and protecting the client's underwear

 Single-use disposable rubber/vinyl gloves to ensure a high standard of hygiene and to reduce the possibility of contamination

 Wax-removal strips (bonded-fibre) thick enough that the wax does not soak through, but flexible enough for ease of work. These strips should be cut to size and placed ready in a container

 Anti-bacterial skin cleanser (also known as pre-wax lotion) or professional antiseptic wipes

 Bin (swing-top) lined with a disposable bin-liner

EQUIPMENT LIST

YOU WILL ALSO NEED:

Wax heater – with a thermostatic control, a lid and a central bar

Disposable tissue roll – such as bedroll

Protective plastic couch cover

Talcum powder – to absorb body perspiration and to facilitate hair removal

Disposable panties – these may be provided when carrying out bikini waxing

Surgical spirit – or a commercial cleaner designed for cleaning equipment

Towels (medium-sized) – for draping around the client

Small scissors (curved) – for trimming over-long hairs

Disinfecting solution – in which to immerse small metal implements following sterilisation in the autoclave

Wax – see below

After-wax lotion – with soothing, healing and antiseptic qualities

Mirror (clean) – for facial waxing

Apron – to protect workwear from spillages

Client record card – confidential card recording details of each client registered at the salon

List of contra-indications – to discuss with client prior to treatment

Aftercare leaflets – recommended advice for the client to refer to following treatment

---

TIP

After-wax lotion
After-wax lotions reduce redness and promote skin healing. They contain ingredients such as tea tree, aloe vera, azulene and witchhazel. These are an ideal retail product to recommend to your client to ensure effective skin healing.

HEALTH AND SAFETY

Avoiding cross-infection
Never filter hot wax after use: it cannot be used again as it will be contaminated with skin cells, tissue fluid, and perhaps even blood.

HEALTH AND SAFETY

Contaminated waste
Any wax waste that contains bodily fluids should be bagged separately from other regular waste and special arrangements made for its disposal.

When choosing a wax, select one with the following qualities:

- Warm wax should have a low melting temperature – the wax should be liquid at body temperature (37°C), and very runny at around 43°C.
- It should be easy to remove from equipment.
- It should be able to remove short, strong hairs (25mm).
- It should have a pleasant fragrance or no smell.
- It should not stick to the skin, but only to the hair.

Sterilisation and disinfection

Disposable waste from waxing may have body fluids on it: potentially it is a health risk. It must be handled, collected and disposed of according to the local environmental health regulations. It is a requirement to wear disposable gloves whilst carrying out bikini and underarm wax treatments, to protect yourself from body fluids and the client from contamination.

Wash your hands regularly with anti-bacterial soap, before and after preparing the work area and before application of the disposable gloves. This shows the client that you have a high standard of hygiene.

An apron should be worn to protect workwear from wax spillage.

All metal tools should be sterilised in the autoclave before use. This includes tweezers and scissors.

ACTIVITY

Maintaining hygiene
Spreading wax on the client and dipping the used spatula back into the tub creates the possibility of cross-infection between clients. How can cross-infection be avoided, with this method and the use of roll-on wax applicators?

Preparing the cubicle

To enable the hairs to be removed effectively the treatment area should be well lit and warm as the client must be made as comfortable as possible when performing the treatment. If the client is cold the follicles will restrict, making hair removal more difficult.

Before the client is shown through, the cubicle and its contents should be checked to ensure that they are clean and tidy. The bins should have been emptied since the previous client.

Check the trolley to ensure that you have all that you need for carrying out the treatment, and that the wax is of a suitable consistency, i.e. ready for application.

The plastic-covered couch should be clean, having previously been washed with hot soapy water and wiped thoroughly with a disinfectant which is bactericidal, fungicidal and virucidal. The use of an additional heavy-duty plastic sheet is recommended: this is easier to wipe than the couch, and can be replaced if damaged.

The couch should then be covered and protected with a long strip of paper-tissue bedroll. Place a towel neatly on the couch, ready to protect the client's clothing and to cover them when they have undressed. The tissue should be disposed of after use, and the towel freshly laundered for each client.

The couch should be in the sit-up position, unless the client is only having their bikini line or underarm areas waxed, in which case it should be flat.

HEALTH AND SAFETY

Couch covers
If the salon chooses to use stretch-towelling couch covers or additional towels to provide extra comfort, these must be provided clean for each client and laundered in hot soapy water after use.

Outcome 3: Plan the treatment

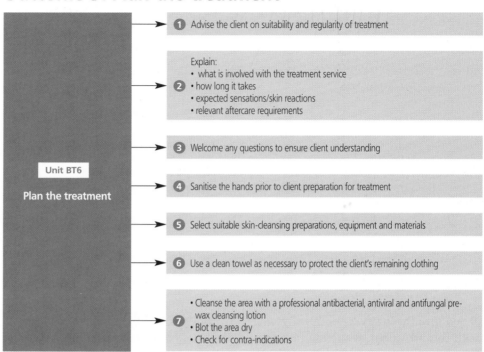

Unit BT6

Plan the treatment

1. Advise the client on suitability and regularity of treatment

2. Explain:
   - what is involved with the treatment service
   - how long it takes
   - expected sensations/skin reactions
   - relevant aftercare requirements

3. Welcome any questions to ensure client understanding

4. Sanitise the hands prior to client preparation for treatment

5. Select suitable skin-cleansing preparations, equipment and materials

6. Use a clean towel as necessary to protect the client's remaining clothing

7.
   - Cleanse the area with a professional antibacterial, antiviral and antifungal pre-wax cleansing lotion
   - Blot the area dry
   - Check for contra-indications

Preparing the client

Following the consultation an appropriate treatment plan will be confirmed with the client. Their understanding of the treatment is important to ensure that their needs are met and that they will not be disappointed.

The client should be shown through to the treatment cubicle, and asked to remove specific items of clothing as necessary so that the treatment may be carried out.

If it is the first time the client has had the treatment, explain to them that the treatment can be uncomfortable, but it is quick and any discomfort experienced is tolerable.

Be efficient and quick, so that the client does not have to wait. Try to get the client talking about something pleasant, such as a holiday, to take their mind off the treatment. Throughout the treatment, reassure them, praising them in order to motivate them to continue with the treatments. Do try to be sympathetic to your client's feelings, and provide support and encouragement when necessary. Waxing, although a necessity for many people, is not a particularly pleasant or relaxing treatment.

How to prepare the client for treatment

1. Use a towel to protect the client's remaining clothing.
2. Wipe the area to be waxed with a professional antiseptic pre-wax cleansing lotion on cottonwool. Blot the area dry with tissues before applying the wax. While wiping the skin, look for contra-indications.
3. Record any bruising on the record card to avoid potential problems later.

TIP

Client records
In accordance with the **Data Protection Act 1998**, confidential information on clients should only be made available to persons to whom consent has been given. All client records should be stored securely, and be available to refer to at any time as required. They must be kept for up to three years.

ACTIVITY

Ensuring client comfort
Imagine that you are a client who has never had a waxing treatment before. You are shown through to a cubicle and left to 'Get yourself ready, please.' How would you feel? What would you do? What clothing would you think it necessary to remove for each area of waxing?

4 If the client's skin is very greasy (they may for example have applied oil before coming to the salon), cleanse it using an astringent lotion such as witchhazel. Talcum powder may be applied lightly to the area to facilitate hair removal.

5 Immediately before starting the treatment, wash your hands.

6 Perform a **thermal sensitivity test**: before applying the wax, check its temperature. Test the wax on yourself first, to ensure that it's not too warm; then try a little on a small visible area of the client (such as the inside of the ankle) before spreading it on other areas.

Outcome 4: Remove unwanted hair

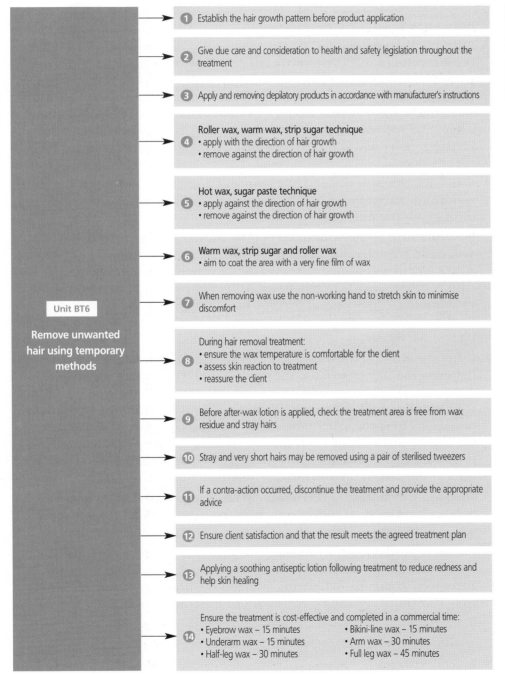

Unit BT6
Remove unwanted hair using temporary methods

1 Establish the hair growth pattern before product application

2 Give due care and consideration to health and safety legislation throughout the treatment

3 Apply and removing depilatory products in accordance with manufacturer's instructions

4 Roller wax, warm wax, strip sugar technique
• apply with the direction of hair growth
• remove against the direction of hair growth

5 Hot wax, sugar paste technique
• apply against the direction of hair growth
• remove against the direction of hair growth

6 Warm wax, strip sugar and roller wax
• aim to coat the area with a very fine film of wax

7 When removing wax use the non-working hand to stretch skin to minimise discomfort

8 During hair removal treatment:
• ensure the wax temperature is comfortable for the client
• assess skin reaction to treatment
• reassure the client

9 Before after-wax lotion is applied, check the treatment area is free from wax residue and stray hairs

10 Stray and very short hairs may be removed using a pair of sterilised tweezers

11 If a contra-action occurred, discontinue the treatment and provide the appropriate advice

12 Ensure client satisfaction and that the result meets the agreed treatment plan

13 Applying a soothing antiseptic lotion following treatment to reduce redness and help skin healing

14 Ensure the treatment is cost-effective and completed in a commercial time:
• Eyebrow wax – 15 minutes
• Underarm wax – 15 minutes
• Half-leg wax – 30 minutes
• Bikini-line wax – 15 minutes
• Arm wax – 30 minutes
• Full leg wax – 45 minutes

TIP

Trimming hair
Trim long hair before waxing to avoid unnecessary client discomfort and to enable the hair growth direction to be more easily viewed.

Skin disorders such as skin tags can be hidden if the hair is too long.

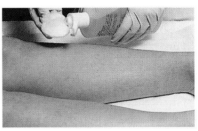

Cleansing the skin of the lower leg

TIP

A woman's pain threshold is at its lowest immediately before and during her period. The hormones which stimulate the regrowth of hair are also at their most active during this period. For these two reasons, avoid wax depilation at this time if possible.

TIP

An angled follicle may cause the hair to be broken off at the angle during waxing, instead of being completely pulled out with its root. If this happens, broken hairs will appear at the skin's surface within a few days.

By causing damage to the follicle and changing its shape, waxing can cause the regrowth of hairs to be frizzy or curled where previously they were straight.

TIP

The thinner the wax, the easier the treatment is to carry out and the better the result. Also, less wax and fewer strips are used.

TIP

Wax spilt on carpets can be removed by placing fabric waxing strips or brown paper over the spill, and running a warm iron over them. Test on a small bit of your carpet first, to make sure the carpet won't melt.

TIP

To take the sting out of the removal, immediately place a hand or finger over the depilated area.

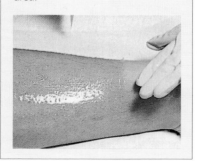

General techniques

Warm waxing has a few basic rules which must be followed to ensure a good result.

1. Observe the direction of hair growth. Warm wax must always be *applied with* the direction of hair growth, and *removed against* the direction of growth. This ensures both maximum adhesion between the hair, the strip and the wax, and that the hair will be pulled back on itself in the follicle and thus removed complete with its bulb.

2. Dip the spatula into the wax. Remove the excess on the sides and tip by wiping the spatula against the metal bar or the sides of the tub. Place the strip under the spatula while transferring it to the client: this will control dripping and improve your technique.

3. Place the spatula onto the skin at a 90° angle, and push the wax along in the direction of the hair growth. Do not allow the spatula to fall forward past 45°. The objective is to coat the area with a very thin film of wax. Quite a large area can be spread with each sweep of the spatula, as warm wax does not set. Do not attempt to smooth out or go over areas on which wax has already been spread, however, as the wax will have become cooler and will not move again, but will drag painfully on the client's skin.

4. Fold back 20mm at the end of a strip and grip the flap with the thumb widthways across the strip. The flap should provide a wax-free handle throughout the treatment.

5. Place the strip at the bottom end of the wax-covered area, and make a firm bond between the wax and the strip by pressing firmly along the strip's length and width, following the direction of hair growth. If the strip is placed anywhere but at the *bottom* of a waxed area, the hairs at the bottom of the strip will become tangled together and held in the wax on the area below the strip: the removal of the strip will then be far more painful for the client.

6. Using the non-working hand, stretch the skin to minimise discomfort. Gripping the flap tightly, use the working hand to remove the strip against the direction of hair growth. Use a firm, steady pull. Make sure that the strip is pulled back on itself, close to the skin. (To obtain the correct angle of pull, stand at the side of the client, facing them.) Maintain this same horizontal angle of pull until the last bit of the strip has left the skin: *do not pull the strip upwards at the end of the pull*, as this would break the hairs at the end of the strip and be very painful.

7. The strip may be used many times; in fact it works best when some wax builds up on its surface. When there is too much wax on the surface it will stop picking up more: throw it away and start with a new one.

8. Do not repeatedly spread and remove wax over one area. In particular, wax should not be spread and removed more than twice on sensitive areas such as the bikini line, the face and the underarms. Any remaining stray hairs must instead be removed using sterilised tweezers.

Different temperatures

Summer heat and winter cold can each give rise to problems with the wax treatment. In summer, the wax stays too warm on the body, becoming sticky and difficult to work with, and tending to leave a sticky residue on the treated areas. In winter, the client's legs may be cold, causing the wax to set too quickly as you spread it, so that it becomes too thick. This prevents the efficient removal of both the wax and the hair growth.

To some extent these problems can be overcome by using thicker waxes with higher melting points in the summer, and thinner waxes with lower melting points in the winter.

How to provide a half-leg treatment

The areas of the body where warm-wax hair removal is most frequently used are the lower legs. This is often referred to simply as a **half-leg treatment**. A 'pair of half legs' should take 20–30 minutes to treat, and use no more than two or three strips.

1 Prior to the treatment, the area to be waxed should be cleansed as previously described.

2 Sit the client on the upraised couch, with both legs straight out in front of her.

3 Spread the wax on the *front* of the leg further away from you. Use three sweeps of the spatula: each sweep should go from just below the knee to the end of hair growth at the ankle.

   Repeat this pattern of spreading on the leg nearer to you. (By spreading the further leg first, you will not have to lean over an already waxed area.)

4 Starting with the nearer leg, remove the wax using the strip. Start at the ankle and work upwards towards the knees.

   Repeat for the other leg.

5 Ask the client to bend her legs to one side. Beginning again with the further leg, spread wax on one *side* of the leg, from the knee to the ankle, using two sweeps of the spatula.

   Repeat for the nearer leg.

6 Starting with the nearer leg, remove the wax from the bottom upwards.

   Repeat for the other leg.

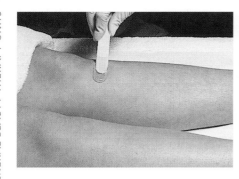

Applying warm wax to the lower leg

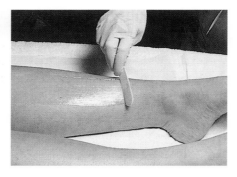

Spreading on wax (to show the angle of the spatula)

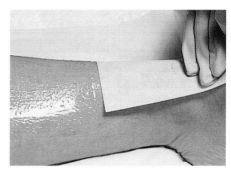

Applying a strip

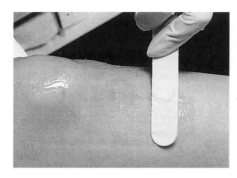

Applying warm wax to the knee

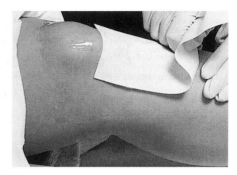

Removing the wax strip from the knee

7 Repeat steps **5** and **6** for the other side of the legs.

8 Bend one knee. Spread the wax from just above the knee, downwards.

9 Remove this wax from the bottom upwards, remembering that strips cannot pull around corners effectively. To keep the angle of the pull horizontal, remove wax below the knee first, then that above the knee.

10 Repeat steps **8** and **9** for the other knee.

11 Lower the back rest and ask the client to turn over.

12 On the *back* of the legs, the direction of hair growth is not from the top to the bottom but sweeping at an angle, from the outside to the inside of the calf muscle.

Starting with the further leg, spread wax following the direction of the natural hair growth.

Repeat for the nearer leg.

13 Starting with the nearer leg, remove the wax against the direction of the natural hair growth.

Repeat for the other leg.

14 Finally, apply after-wax lotion to clean cottonwool and apply this to the back of the client's legs. As you apply the lotion, check for hairs left behind: if there are any, remove them using tweezers.

Ask the client to turn over, and repeat application on the front of the legs. Remove any excess using a tissue.

TIP ✔

The most common fault seen in half-leg waxing is trying to take too big an area at once over the calf muscle and not supporting the surrounding tissues adequately. This will result in a painful treatment for the client.

Toes

Clients frequently request that their toes be waxed in conjunction with a half leg or full-leg treatment. When doing this, follow the normal guidelines for waxing, but be aware that hair may grow in many directions. Cut strips into small pieces to effectively remove hair.

Full-leg treatment

A **full-leg wax** should take 40–50 minutes and four to six strips should be sufficient.

When doing a full-leg wax, follow the same sequence of working as with the half leg. On the thighs, observe the direction of hair growth carefully, as the hair grows in different directions. It is best not to spread wax on too large an area at once, or you may forget the direction of growth. Each direction of hair growth should be treated as a separate area. It is of prime importance that you support the skin on the thighs as you remove the strip – the tissues in this area can bruise very easily. The two essential factors in preventing bruising, pain and hair breakage are:

- the correct angle of pull;
- adequate support for the tissues.

How to provide a bikini-line treatment

A **bikini-line treatment** takes 10–15 minutes, and requires a new strip for each section to ensure effective hair removal from this delicate area.

1 Treat one side at a time. It is best if the client lies flat, as the skin's tissues are then pulled tighter, but the treatment can be carried out in a semi-reclining position if the client prefers. Bend the client's knee out to the side, and put her foot flat against the knee of the other leg. This is sometimes referred to as the **figure-four position**.

2 Tuck a protective tissue along and under the lower edge of the client's briefs. Raise this edge and agree with the client where she wants the final line to be. Hold the briefs slightly beyond this line, and ask the client to place her hand on top of the protective tissue to hold everything in place. This leaves you with both hands free, one to pull the strip and one to support the skin.

3 Cleanse and dry the areas to be waxed.

4 Using sterilised scissors, trim both the hair to be waxed and the adjacent hairs down to about 5–12 mm in length. This is essential to avoid tangling, pulling and pain, and to prevent wax going onto hair that you do not want to remove.

5 Spread and remove the wax in two or three separate and distinct areas, the number depending on the directions of hair growth.

6 Use half of the strip length to remove the wax. Do not cover the whole area and tear it off at once! As soon as an area is completed, apply after-wax lotion. If necessary, use a clean tissue to remove excess lotion.

TIP

Wax spills
If you spill wax on the couch cover, immediately place a quarter-width facial-sized piece of strip on top of the spill. This prevents the wax from damaging the client's clothing when they move.

TIP

When a client books for a bikini-line wax, ask them when they come for the treatment to wear an old pair of high-cut panties.

TIP

Intimate waxing
Intimate waxing is a range of waxing techniques which remove pubic and/or anal body hair. This is an advanced waxing service covered in NVQ/SVQ Level 3 and differs from the requirements of a bikini waxing service.

HEALTH AND SAFETY

Bruising
Bruising is neither normal nor acceptable, but a sign of faulty technique.

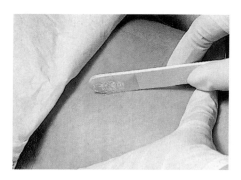

Applying warm wax to the bikini line

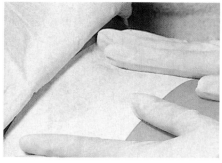

Applying a strip (showing the support of the skin area)

Removing the wax strip

7 With both legs straight out in front on the couch, place a protective tissue along the top edge of the client's briefs, against the abdomen. Lower the briefs as necessary to expose just the hair to be removed – check this with your client. Usually the direction of hair growth here sweeps in from the sides and then up to the navel.

8 Trim the hair as before.

9 Apply and remove the wax in small sections, carefully observing hair growth. On completion, apply after-wax lotion.

How to provide an underarm treatment

An underarm treatment should take 5–15 minutes and two strips, one for each underarm.

1 With her bra still on, ask your client to lie flat on her back with her hands behind her head, elbows flat on the couch.

2 Cleanse both underarms with pre-wax lotion on clean cottonwool; blot with a tissue.

3 Place a protective tissue under the edge of the bra cup on the side away from you. Ask the client to bring her opposite arm down and over, and to pull the breast away from the underarm being waxed and across towards the middle of her chest. This pulls the tissues tight, making the treatment a lot more comfortable for her; it also leaves you with both hands free, one to pull and one to support.

4 Underarm hair usually grows in two main directions. Observe the directions of hair growth, then apply and remove the wax separately for each small area.

5 Apply after-wax lotion to the treated area. Check for stray hairs; remove these with sterile tweezers.

6 Blot any excess cream with a clean tissue.

> **TIP**
>
> **Perspiration**
> If certain types of water-soluble waxes are being used, perspiration may cause problems: it may prevent the wax from gripping the hair. Bear this in mind when selecting the wax to use on areas liable to perspiration such as the underarm and the top lip.

> **TIP** ✔
>
> Both bikini-line and underarm waxing can be uncomfortable, especially if the hair growth is thick – always bear this in mind when carrying out the treatment. Some slight bleeding can be expected as the hairs in this area are very strong and have deep roots. Any waste contaminated by blood must be disposed of hygienically in a sealed bag.

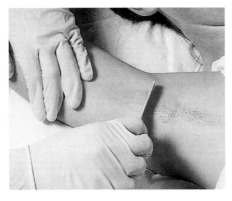
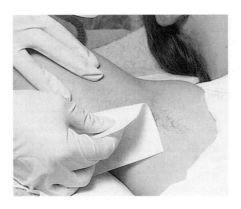
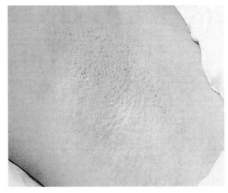

Applying warm wax to the underarm (showing support)

Removing the wax strip

The completed area

Step-by-step: Arm treatment

Depilation in this area should take 10–15 minutes for a **half-arm treatment** and 20–30 minutes for a **full-arm treatment**. Half the length of the strip should be used.

Arms are usually waxed with the client in the sitting position, with their general clothing protected with a towel. Sleeve edges can be protected with tucked-in tissues; ideally, though, upper outer clothing should be removed.

The roundness of the arm means that in order to effect a horizontal pull the work must be done in short lengths. Other than this, follow the general rules for waxing.

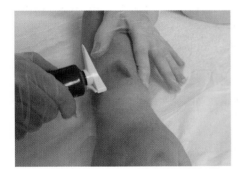
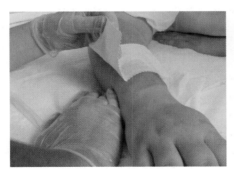
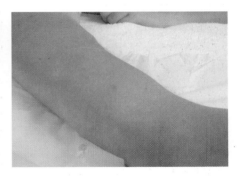

1 Wax applied in the direction of hair growth using disposable applicator warm-wax technique.

2 Wax is removed against hair growth, ensuring that the skin is held taut to minimise discomfort and ensure effective hair removal.

3 Mild erythema of the skin following hair removal. Check the area from all angles to ensure all hairs have been removed.

Step-by-step: Face treatment

The **face treatment** must always be approached with extra care as facial skin is more sensitive than skin elsewhere on the body. Faulty technique can result in the top layer of skin being removed. (If this happens, a scab will form after about a day and the mark will take days to heal and fade completely.)

> **TIP**
>
> Previously bleached hair tends when waxed to break off at skin level. Clients should be told not to bleach facial hair if it is to be waxed.

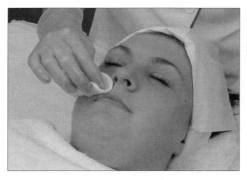

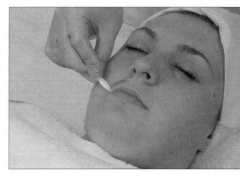

1 The client should be in a semi-reclining position, with her head supported and a clean towel draped across her shoulders to protect her clothing. A clean headband can be used to keep the hair away from the face.

2 Cleanse and wipe over the area using an antiseptic cleansing lotion. Blot it dry with a tissue.

3 Application of warm wax to the upper lip using a disposable applicator, paying close attention to the direction of natural hair growth. Hair removal is only required to the outer upper lip area. You might need to spread one-half of the top lip with wax; remove this in three or four narrow strips; repeat the process on the other half; and finally treat the central section immediately under the nose.

HEALTH AND SAFETY ✚

Surgical spirit
Surgical spirit is too harsh for use on the face.

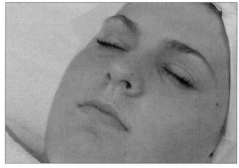

4 Removal of wax against hair growth. The area is held taut to minimise discomfort and ensure effective hair removal.

5 The completed area, free from superflous hair.

A **top-lip wax** should take approximately 5 minutes, a **chin and throat wax** approximately 10 minutes, and a **lip and chin wax** approximately 15 minutes. A removal strip of no more than one-eighth normal size should be used on the face. Do not allow wax to build up on the facial wax strips – such a build-up could lead to skin removal. Use a new strip for each area.

HEALTH AND SAFETY

The lips
The lips are extremely sensitive. To avoid possible irritation, do not allow the wax to come into contact with them.

How to provide an eyebrow treatment

Eyebrows, as a part of the face, are treated accordingly (see above). An **eyebrow wax** should take approximately 10–15 minutes.

1 Study the eyebrows and decide upon their final shape and proportions.

2 Brush the eyebrows and separate the unwanted hair from the line of the other hairs.

3 Using a small spatula, apply a thin film of wax to the unwanted hairs in a small area. Remove the wax using a clean strip. Repeat in different areas, using a clean strip each time, until all the unwanted hairs have been removed.

4 Apply a soothing antiseptic cream and use sterile tweezers to remove any stray hairs.

HEALTH AND SAFETY

Health and safety
When performing an eyebrow wax, eyebrow hair that does not need to be removed may be protected with petroleum jelly.

Cottonwool pads may be placed over the eyes to protect the eye and eyelashes from accidental wax spillage.

TIP

Other areas of the neck and face can be treated by wax depilation – for example to tidy up a haircut at the neckline, or to remove sideburns – provided that you follow the general guidelines for facial treatments.

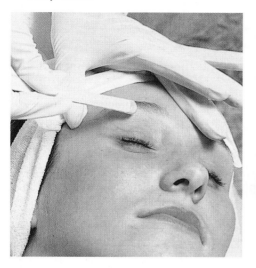

Applying warm wax to an eyebrow

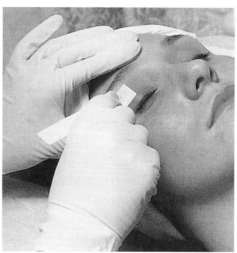

Removing the wax strip

HEALTH AND SAFETY

Sensitisation
Under no circumstances should wax be applied to facial hair, underarm hair or bikini-line hair more than twice during any one treatment. If after this any hairs remain, they must be removed with tweezers. The delicate skin in these areas readily becomes sensitised.

Regrowth

Because of the cyclical nature of hair growth and the fact that follicles will be at different stages of their growth cycle when the hair is removed, the hair will not all grow back at the same time. Waxing can therefore appear to reduce the *quantity* of hair growth. This is not so, however, and the hair will all grow back eventually: waxing is therefore classed as a temporary form of hair removal.

Nevertheless, certain bodily changes (such as ageing), when *combined* with waxing, can result in permanent hair removal. This effect is so erratic and unpredictable, though, that waxing cannot reliably be sold as a permanent method of hair removal.

Contra-actions

Four contra-actions are quite common with waxing:

- ingrowing hairs;
- removal of skin;
- burns – both wax and friction burns;
- erythema – increased blood flow to the skin, giving a slight redness.

Ingrowing hairs

Ingrowing hairs can arise in three ways:

- *Over-reaction to damage* An excessive reaction by the skin and the follicle to the 'damage' produced by depilation may cause extra cornified cells to be made. These may block the surface of the follicle, causing the newly growing hair to turn around and grow inwards.
- *Overtight clothing* If after the treatment the client wears clothing that is too tight, this too can block the follicle.
- *Dry skin* Likewise dry skin can cause blockage of the follicle.

Ingrowing hairs can usually be recognised to be one or other of three types:

- *A hair growing along beneath the surface of the skin* Identify the tip (the pointed end); then pierce the tissues over the root end with a sterile needle. Free the tip and leave it in place so that the follicle can heal around it.
- *A coiled ingrowing hair* This looks like a small black spot or dome on the skin. If this is gently squeezed and rolled between the fingertips, using a tissue, it will release the coiled ingrowing hair and some hardened sebum. If the hair does not fall out, it should be left in place (as above).
- *An infected ingrowth* If the trapped sebum or hair starts to decay, either of the two preceding forms can become infected or begin to display an immune response. The area first becomes red (irritation); then an infected white dome-shaped pustule develops. Release the trapped tissue (as above), and cover the affected area – which may bleed, or leak tissue fluid – with a sterile non-allergenic dressing.

Skin removal

If the upper, dead, protective cornified layer of the skin is accidentally removed during a treatment – leaving the granular layer of the living, germinative layer exposed – the skin should be treated as if it has been burnt. Cool the area immediately by applying cold-water compresses for 10 minutes. Dry it carefully; then apply a dry, non-fluffy dressing to protect the area from infection. The dressing should be worn for three to four days, and the area then left open to the air. (Antiseptic cream by itself should be used only when the injury is very minor.) Medical attention should be sought if necessary.

Burns

A burn should be treated as 'skin removal' (page 294). If blisters form, they should not be broken – they help prevent the entry of infection into the wound. Medical attention should be sought.

Erythema

Erythema is a visible redness, accompanied by an increase in warmth on the surface of the skin. It derives from increased blood flow through the capillaries near the surface of the skin, caused by the histamine reaction after waxing (page 37). Ask the client to follow the recommended aftercare advice.

Outcome 5: Complete the treatment

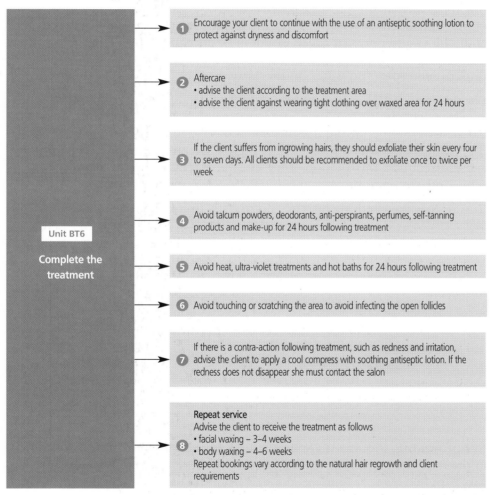

Unit BT6

Complete the treatment

1. Encourage your client to continue with the use of an antiseptic soothing lotion to protect against dryness and discomfort

2. Aftercare
   • advise the client according to the treatment area
   • advise the client against wearing tight clothing over waxed area for 24 hours

3. If the client suffers from ingrowing hairs, they should exfoliate their skin every four to seven days. All clients should be recommended to exfoliate once to twice per week

4. Avoid talcum powders, deodorants, anti-perspirants, perfumes, self-tanning products and make-up for 24 hours following treatment

5. Avoid heat, ultra-violet treatments and hot baths for 24 hours following treatment

6. Avoid touching or scratching the area to avoid infecting the open follicles

7. If there is a contra-action following treatment, such as redness and irritation, advise the client to apply a cool compress with soothing antiseptic lotion. If the redness does not disappear she must contact the salon

8. Repeat service
   Advise the client to receive the treatment as follows
   • facial waxing – 3–4 weeks
   • body waxing – 4–6 weeks
   Repeat bookings vary according to the natural hair regrowth and client requirements

Aftercare and advice

An **after-wax antiseptic, soothing lotion** should be applied, using clean cottonwool, at the end of the treatment. This breaks down any wax residue, helps to guard against infection and irritation, and takes away any feelings of discomfort. Encourage your client to continue with the use of such a lotion

> **TIP** ✔
>
> **After-wax lotion**
> Before after-wax lotion is applied ensure that the treatment area is free of waxing product and hair and check that the finished result is to the client's satisfaction.

at home for a few days: it will protect against dryness, discomfort and ingrowing hairs.

Advise the client against wearing any tight clothing (such as tights or hosiery) over the waxed areas for the 24 hours following a treatment. Such clothing could lead to irritation and ingrowing hairs.

If the client suffers from ingrowing hairs, they should **exfoliate** their skin every four to seven days, starting two or three days after the treatment. Exfoliation prevents the build-up of dead skin cells on the surface of the skin; these would otherwise block the exit from the follicle and cause a growing hair to turn back on itself and grow inwards. Ingrowing hairs should be freed and, if possible, left in place so that the follicle exit will re-form around the hair's shaft. Demonstrate to the client the correct use and benefits of the exfoliant product.

Advise the client that for the 24 hours following their treatment they should not apply any talcum powders, deodorants, anti-perspirants, perfumes, self-tanning products or make-up over the treated areas. Any of these products could block the pores or cause irritation or allergy reactions on the temporarily sensitised area. During this time she must use only plain, unperfumed soap and water on the treated area.

For the same 24-hour period they should preferably avoid exercise, especially swimming, and not apply heat or ultra-violet treatments – hot baths, for example, or the use of a sunbed or sauna – as these would add to the heat generated in the skin following the treatment and would probably cause discomfort or irritation. They must also refrain from touching or scratching the area, so as to avoid infecting the open follicles.

Ensure that the client records are up to date, accurate and complete.

TIP

Aftercare leaflets should contain this information: as best prractice these can be given to the client at the end of the treatment to remind them what to do at home.

HOT WAXING

In **hot waxing**, the wax is applied at a higher temperature. The hairs embed in the wax and are gripped tightly as the wax cools and contracts. When the wax is pulled away, it removes the hair from the base of the follicle.

Equipment and materials

The equipment and materials required for hot waxing are the same as for warm waxing (pages 281–93), except that:

- *a wax heater* suitable for hot wax should be selected;
- *wax-removal strips* are not necessary;

TIP

When selecting a wax, choose one that does not go brittle when cool. Wax sold as small bars is preferable as this melts quickly.

- *pre-wax oil* may be applied to the skin before wax application to make wax removal easier.

Some people prefer to apply the hot wax with disposable brushes rather than spatulas, but either can be used.

How to carry out the treatment

1 Ensure that the area to be waxed is clean and grease-free.

2 Apply a small amount of talc against the direction of hair growth. This will make the hairs stand on end and stick more firmly into the wax.

3 Keep the same order of work as for warm waxing.

4 Apply wax in strips approximately 5cm wide and 10cm long, with about 5cm distance between the strips.

5 Carefully observe the direction of hair growth and the size of the area to be waxed.

6 Test the heat of the wax on the inside of the wrist.

TIP

Wax temperature

If the wax is *not hot enough* when it is applied, it will not contract effectively around the hair and will therefore not grip it properly. This may result in poor depilation and possible hair breakage.

If on the other hand the wax is allowed to *overheat*, it may cause burns. Also, the quality of the wax will deteriorate and the wax will become brittle as it cools.

---

7 Using either a disposable spatula or a brush, apply a layer of wax about 5cm × 10cm *against* the direction of hair growth. Apply a second layer *with* the direction of growth; and a third layer *against* the direction of growth. (If two or three strips are applied at the same time, you can work faster.)

Keep the edges of the wax thicker than the middle, to make it easier to remove. Overlap the lower edge by about 2cm onto a hair-free area: this makes it less painful later, when you lift the edge to make a lip to pull.

Curl up the lower end of the wax to make a lip, and press and mould the wax firmly onto the skin.

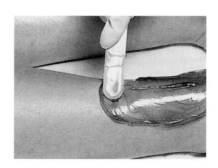

Applying hot wax to the lower leg

8 Leave the wax for a minute or so to cool. The wax has to cool sufficiently to grip the hairs, but not so much that the wax becomes brittle and breaks on removal. As it sets, it starts to lose its gloss: it should be removed when this happens and while it is still pliable.

9 Support the area below the wax, grasp the lip, and tear the wax off the skin *against* the direction of hair growth in one movement (as with warm-wax removal). Immediately press or firmly stroke the area with your hand: this takes away some of the discomfort.

10 Check the area for any remaining wax and any stray hairs. Remove using tweezers. (Second applications are not advisable when using hot wax, because of the risk of burning.)

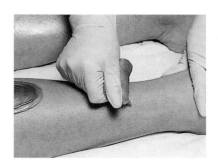

Removing the hot wax

If this general application technique is followed, any area of the body can be depilated – use the same order of work as for warm waxing: observe the direction of hair growth and take into account the body area; use smaller strips in smaller areas; support the skin; and use the correct angle of pull for removal.

Aftercare and contra-actions

The contra-actions and aftercare are the same as for warm waxing (pages 294–6).

SUGARING AND STRIP SUGAR

Sugaring is an ancient and popular method for hair removal. The superfluous hairs become embedded in a pliable organic paste of sugar, lemon and water. The sugar paste is then removed from the skin's surface, against the hair's growth, leaving the skin hair-free.

Sugaring may be applied using a paste formulation removed with the hands, referred to as sugar paste, or in a formulation similar to warm wax, removed with material strips, referred to as **strip sugar**. Sugaring is effective on fine hair growth, and as it contains no chemicals or additives this method is unlikely to cause skin allergy.

Reception

Re-book the client for sugaring hair removal every four to six weeks, dependent upon the hair growth rate and area. For effective hair removal, the hairs must be at least 2mm long.

Equipment and materials

The equipment and materials required for sugaring are the same as for warm waxing (pages 281–93), except for the following differences.

Sugar paste

- *Wax heater (with a thermostatic control)* or *microwave* – to heat the paste.
- *Sugaring paste* – either soft or hard, depending on your personal preference and the temperature of the working environment: hard paste is a better choice in warmer temperatures and when working on coarser hair.
- *Talc (purified)*.
- *Bowl of clean water* – to remove the sugar paste from the hands, reducing stickiness.

Strip sugar

- *Wax heater (with a thermostatic control)* – to heat the strip sugar.
- *Strip sugar.*

- *Talc (purified)*.
- *Disposable wooden spatulas* – a selection of differing sizes, for use on different body areas.
- *Wax-removal strips (bonded-fibre)* – thick enough that the wax does not soak through, but flexible enough for easy working.
- *Disposable surgical gloves*.

Sterilisation and disinfection

As sugar paste is water-soluble, it is easily cleaned from any surface. However, the wax heater containing the sugar wax must be regularly disinfected.

Step-by-step: Preparing the client

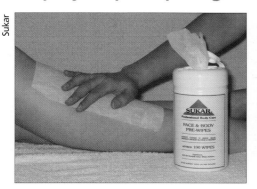

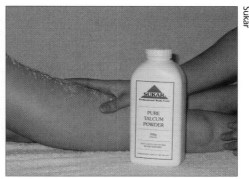

1 Cleanse the area to be treated, using an antiseptic cleansing tissue. Blot the skin dry.

2 Apply talc to cover the area: this prevents the sugar from sticking to the skin.

How to provide a sugar paste treatment

The sugar paste adheres to the hair and not to the skin, which allows the sugar to be reapplied to a treatment area. Technique is important and it takes practice and experience to become skilled.

1 Heat the sugar gently, to soften it.

2 Apply the sugar paste to the skin by hand. Select the amount used according to the treatment area. Draw the paste over the treatment area *in the direction* of the hair growth, embedding the hair in the paste.

3 Remove it quickly *against* the hair growth.

4 If necessary, reapply the paste to the area to remove further hairs. Continue this process until no hair remains.

5 After use, discard the paste as it will be contaminated with excess hair and dead skin cells: this affects the ease of paste removal, and presents a risk of cross-infection.

6 To complete the treatment, a cooling treatment spray may be applied to the area, followed by a soothing cream.

7 Record details of the treatment on the client's record card.

> **TIP** ✔
>
> Sugar wax – both strip and paste – may be heated in a microwave to soften it. Check guidelines set by the microwave manufacturer on power and timing.

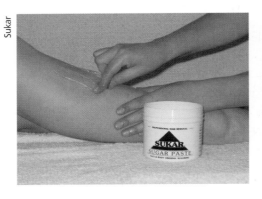

Applying and removing sugar paste

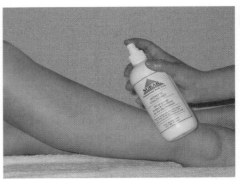

Applying a cooling spray

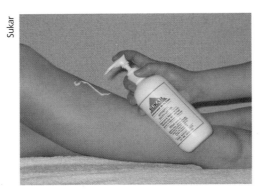

Applying a soothing cream

How to provide a strip sugar treatment

This is similar in application and removal to warm wax.

1 The wax is gently heated until it is fluid.
2 Apply the wax using a spatula *in the direction of* the hair growth to cover the treatment area.
3 Remove the wax *against* the hair growth using a clean strip.
4 To complete the treatment, a cooling treatment spray may be applied to the area, followed by a soothing cream.
5 Record details of the treatment on the client's record card.

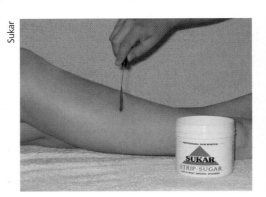

Applying strip sugar

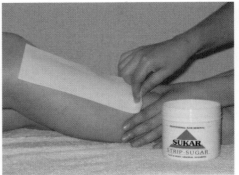

Removing strip sugar

Contra-action

General waxing contra-actions should be considered (see pages 294–5), as well as:

- *Ingrowing hairs* – caused by incorrect removal technique when using sugaring, or a build-up of dead skin cells over the hair follicle opening.
- *Discomfort* – caused by the wax being too hard, affecting application and efficient removal.
- *Burning*, of the client or the therapist – caused by the sugar paste or the strip sugar being too hot.

Aftercare and advice

General post-waxing advice should be offered (see pages 295–6). Appropriate aftercare retail products may be recommended such as an exfoliating body mitt, or antiseptic moisturising lotion to promote skin healing.

DISPOSABLE APPLICATOR ROLLER WAXING SYSTEMS

This is a hygienic method, using **disposable applicators** that are new for each client. A disposable applicator head screws onto the wax applicator tube in place of a cap. This reduces the possible risk of contamination through cross-infection. The method is less messy, as the wax is contained in the tube and is not exposed until application.

Each tube of wax as needed is heated to working temperature, which minimises the risk of burning.

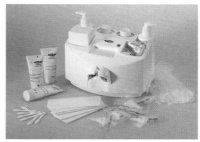

Starter kit

Step-by-step: Waxing the legs

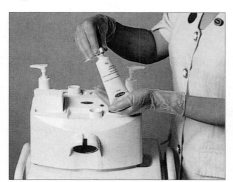

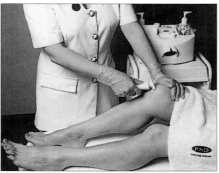

1 Follow general waxing preparation guidelines for the treatment area (see page 283). Remove the disposable applicator from the right-hand heating and storage compartment.

2 Remove the cap from the tube of wax. Attach the applicator head to the tube.

3 Release the applicator by lifting the lever upwards. Squeeze until a small amount of wax appears on the front of the applicator, then apply the wax. Hold the applicator at a 45° angle to the leg, and glide it smoothly down the leg.

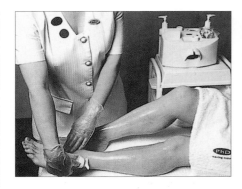

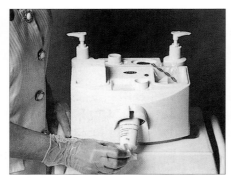

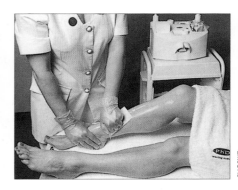

4 Apply a thin film of wax to the front of both legs, then press down the closing device on the applicator to stop wax flow.

5 Wipe any wax residue from the front of the applicator and return the tube to heat.

6 Remove wax from the leg, starting at the ankle and working towards the knee. Support the skin with one hand, and firmly stretch it against the removal of the wax. Continue application and removal to the sides and back of the legs.

7 When treatment is complete, apply antiseptic soothing lotion (shown). Record details of the treatment on the client's record card.

8 Remove the applicator from the tube, replacing the cap and returning the tube to the heater. Dispose of the applicator head.

Aftercare and advice

Follow the general aftercare and advice guidelines on pages 295–6.

LIGHTENING HAIR

Bleaching lightens the hair and is an effective way to disguise pigmented facial and body hair that the client finds unacceptable. The effect lasts up to four weeks.

The bleaching products, usually powder and cream, are mixed together and are immediately applied directly to the area to be lightened.

Reception

The client should receive the bleaching treatment every three to four weeks. Allow 15–30 minutes when booking this service, according to the client's treatment requirements.

HEALTH AND SAFETY ✚

Bleaching materials
Store the bleach materials in a cool environment away from direct sunlight and other heat sources.

Avoid contact with the eyes. In the case of contact, rinse the eyes thoroughly with water until sensitivity subsides.

Wear protective gloves when dealing with any spillages.

Treatment should not follow any preheating treatment such as facial steaming, as the pores would be open, which could cause skin irritation.

Skin tests

1 Mix a small amount of the product, as directed by the manufacturer.

2 Apply a little of this to the inner arm, approximately 25mm square. If there is an allergic reaction, remove the bleach product immediately.

3 After 10–15 minutes, remove the product using cool water applied with cottonwool.

4 Check the area over the next 24 hours to assess skin tolerance. Redness, itchiness and swelling indicate a positive (allergic) reaction.

5 Note the test result on the client's record card.

Contra-indications

After completing the record card and inspecting the area, if you have found any of the following do not proceed with the bleaching treatment:

- *hypersensitive skin*;
- *dry, sensitive skin*;
- *cuts and abrasions* in the area;
- *skin disorder or disease*;
- *positive reaction (allergy)* to a skin test;
- *skin erythema*.

HEALTH AND SAFETY

Hydrogen peroxide
Hydrogen peroxide is a strong skin irritant. Perform a skin test if the client has a possible skin sensitivity. Remember that clients can become allergic or sensitive to ingredients that have previously been satisfactory.

TIP

Ensure the bleach does not come into contact with the client's clothes – these too could be bleached!

Equipment and materials

EQUIPMENT LIST

Couch – with sit-up and lie-down positions and an easy-to-clean surface

Trolley – to hold all the necessary equipment and materials

Bleach powder and cream hydrogen peroxide – in facial and body cosmetic formulations

Cleansing cosmetic preparations – to cleanse the area to be lightened

Barrier cream – to protect the surrounding areas

Damp cottonwool – to remove cleansing preparations and excess bleach from the skin and hair

Bowl (clean) – to hold the clean cottonwool

Facial tissues (white) – for blotting skin dry

Headband (clean) – to protect the scalp hair when performing facial bleaching

Towels (medium-sized) – to protect the client's clothing

Non-metallic mixing dish – metal would speed the decomposition of the product

Disposable spatula – for mixing and application

Mirror (clear) – for facial bleaching to show the client the effect produced for acceptability

Soothing lotion – to apply to the skin following bleaching

Disposable surgical gloves – to protect your hands

Swing-top bin – lined with a disposable bin-liner, for waste

Client's record card

Sterilisation and disinfection

Use disposable equipment where possible to avoid cross-infection. Wear protective gloves during application and removal of the bleach, to protect your hands from possible chemical contact.

Preparing the cubicle

Before the client is shown through to the cubicle, check to ensure that the required equipment and materials are available and the area is clean and tidy.

The couch or chair should be protected with a long strip of disposable tissue-paper bedroll, or a freshly laundered bedsheet and a bath towel. A small towel should be placed neatly at the head of the couch, ready to be draped across the client for protection. The paper tissue will need replacing and the towels laundered for each client.

Preparing the client

How to lighten facial hair

1 Protect the client's clothing with clean towels. A headband should be worn to protect the client's hair. Drape a small towel across her chest.

2 Cleanse and tone the area. Blot the skin dry with a clean facial tissue. Ensure that the area is free of grease, which would form a barrier to the hair-lightening products.

3 For facial bleaching, the client should be slightly elevated.

How to lighten body hair

1 Protect the client's clothing in the area with clean towels or disposable paper tissue.

2 Cleanse the area thoroughly, with a cleansing agent and clean cottonwool, to remove dead skin cells and any body oils or cosmetic lotions. Blot the skin dry with a clean facial tissue.

3 Position the client comfortably, in a position in which you are able to treat the area easily.

Lightening the hair

How to lighten facial hair

1 Place the required amount of powder and cream in a non-metallic dish, following the manufacturer's instructions. Mix well to a smooth opaque cream.

2 Using a clean, disinfected spatula, apply the bleach to the area. Cover the hair evenly.

3 Time the application accurately, taking into account:
- hair coarseness and pigmentation;
- skin type and tolerance.

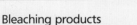

TIP

The lightening process will vary according to the coarseness and colour of the client's hair. You should always consider this.

TIP

Advise the client that the part of the *skin* treated will be lightened slightly also. As this affects only the surface dead skin cells of the epidermis, the effect is temporary – usually 12–24 hours.

HEALTH AND SAFETY

Bleaching products
Always mix the ingredients according to manufacturer's instructions.
A barrier cream may be applied to protect the surrounding area from the bleaching products.

HEALTH AND SAFETY

Bleach
Never spread the bleach onto other surrounding areas unnecessarily.

4 If necessary – e.g. if the hair is very dark – apply the bleach a second time.

5 When the hair is sufficiently bleached, remove the bleaching products thoroughly, using a spatula and dampened cottonwool.

6 Dry the area with a facial tissue and apply an unperfumed moisturising agent.

7 Show the client the finished result in the mirror.

8 Discard the bleach and clean the mixing container.

9 Record the treatment details on the client's record card.

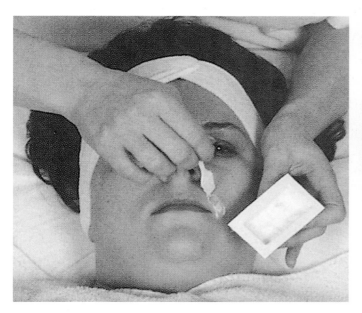

Applying bleach to the upper lip

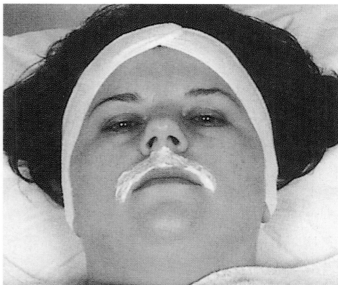

Processing

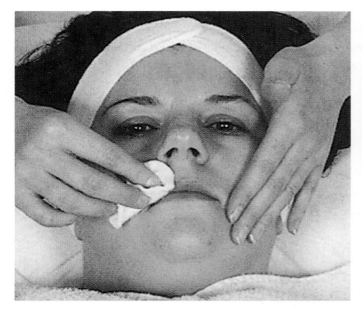

Removing the bleach

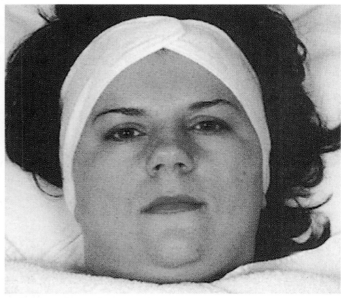

The finished result

How to lighten eyebrows

1 The brows lighten very quickly. Lighten the brows to complement the colour of the client's scalp hair.

2 Show the client the finished result in the mirror.

3 Discard the bleach and clean the mixing container.

4 Record the treatment details on the client's record card.

HEALTH AND SAFETY

Eye care
Take great care to avoid the bleach mixture entering the eyes or sensitising the delicate eye tissue.

How to lighten body hair: arms and legs

1 Mix sufficient bleach for one arm or one leg.

2 Allow the bleach to process, for approximately 15 minutes. If the hair is not sufficiently lightened, mix and apply the product for approximately a further 10 minutes.

3 Remove the mixture.

4 Mix new bleach and apply this to the other limb. Process and remove.

5 Discard the bleach and clean the mixing container.

6 Record the treatment details on the client's record card.

Contra-actions

- *Irritation* – caused by skin intolerance. If irritation occurs, wash off the bleaching product immediately with clean water and apply a suitable soothing product. If irritation continues, obtain medical attention.

- *Erythema or skin burn* – caused by over-exposure to the bleaching agents, or using bleaching agents at an incorrect strength for the body part.

HEALTH AND SAFETY

Ultra-violet light
On areas that have been previously bleached, ultraviolet light may cause a reaction and hyperpigmentation in the skin.

Aftercare and advice

A moisturising, soothing agent should be applied following treatment. For the next 24 hours the client should avoid possible sensitisers such as perfumed products and ultra-violet light.

GLOSSARY OF KEY WORDS

Aftercare advice recommendations given to the client following treatment to continue the benefits of the treatment.

After-wax lotion a product applied to the skin following hair removal to reduce redness and promote skin healing.

Anagen the active stage of the hair growth cycle.

Burn injury to the skin caused by excess heat; the skin appears red and may blister.

Catagen the stage of the hair growth cycle where the hair becomes detached from its source of nourishment, the dermal papilla, and stops growing.

Cold wax a wax used straight from its container or lightly heated. Cold waxes are often natural rubber substances in a volatile solvent. The solvent evaporates to leave a rubber film with the hairs embedded in it; this is removed with a wax removal strip.

Consultation assessment of client's needs using different assessment techniques, including questioning and natural observation.

Contra-action an unwanted reaction occurring during or after treatment application.

Contra-indication a problematic symptom which indicates that the treatment may not proceed.

Dermal papilla an organ that provides the hair with blood, necessary for hair growth.

Electrical current hair removal techniques (galvanic electrolysis, electrical epilation and blend epilation) permanent hair removal techniques that use an electrical current. The current is passed to the hair root via a fine needle inserted into the hair follicle. The current destroys the hair root, preventing hair regrowth.

Erythema reddening of the skin, caused by increased blood circulation to the area.

Folliculitis a bacterial infection where pustules develop in the skin tissue around the hair follicle.

Hair a long slender structure that grows out of, and is part of, the skin. Each hair is made up of dead skin cells, which contain the protein called keratin.

Hair follicle an appendage (structure) in the skin formed from epidermal tissue. Cells move up the hair follicle from the bottom (the hair bulb), changing in structure to form the hair.

Hair growth cycle the cyclical pattern of hair growth, which can be divided into three phases: anagen, catagen and telogen.

Hairy moles moles exhibiting coarse hairs from their surface.

Heat rash a reaction to heat exposure where the sweat ducts become blocked and sweat escapes into the epidermis. Red pimples occur and the skin becomes itchy.

Histamine a chemical released when the skin comes into contact with a substance that it is allergic to. Cells called 'mast cells' burst, releasing histamine into the tissues. This causes the blood capillaries to dilate, which increases blood flow to limit skin damage and begin repair.

Hot wax a system of wax depilation used to remove hair from the skin. Hot wax cools and sets on contact with the skin. They are a blend of waxes, such as beeswax and resins, which keep the wax flexible. Soothing ingredients are often included to avoid skin irritation.

Ingrowing hair a build-up of skin occurs over the hair follicle, causing the hair to grow under the skin.

Keratin a protein produced by cells in the epidermis called keratinocytes. Keratin makes the skin tough and reduces the passage of substances into our bodies. Each hair contains keratin.

Laser hair removal a technique of permanent hair removal. Laser energy is passed through the skin which stops the activity of the hair follicle creating hair growth through a process called *photothermolysis*.

Melanin a pigment in the skin and the hair that contributes to the skin/hair colour.

Patch test a.k.a. skin test a method used to assess skin tolerance to substances.

Photothermolysis an effect created when using a laser for hair removal. The melanin pigment that provides hair colour absorbs the laser energy, which is converted to heat, and at a sufficient temperature destroys the part of the hair follicle where the cells divide to create the hair.

Pre-wax lotion an antibacterial skin cleanser to clean the skin before wax application.

Roller wax a warm wax used to remove hair from the skin. The wax is contained in a cartridge container with a disposable applicator, which rolls the wax onto the skin's surface. The applicator is renewed for each client.

Skin removal accidental removal of the upper, dead, protective cornified layer of the skin, leaving the granular layer exposed.

Skin tags skin-coloured threads of skin three to six mm long, projecting from the skin's surface.

Skin test *see patch test*.

Strip sugar a system of wax depilation similar to the warm-wax technique, used to remove hair from the skin. Made from sugar, lemons and water, the sugar wax is applied to the skin, and is then removed using a wax removal strip.

Sugar paste a system of wax depilation. An organic paste made from sugar, lemons and water is used to embed the hair, which is then removed by the paste from the skin.

Sugaring an ancient popular method of hair removal using organic substances, sugar and lemon.

Telogen the resting stage of the hair growth cycle where the hair is finally shed.

Terminal hair deep-rooted, thick, coarse, pigmented hair found on the scalp, underarms, pubic region, eyelashes and brows.

Thermal sensitivity test a test performed before wax application to check that the temperature of the wax is not too warm. The wax is tested by the therapist on themself, usually on the inner wrist, and then on the client on a small visible area such as the inside of the ankle.

Treatment plan after the consultation, suitable treatment objectives are established to treat the client's conditions and needs.

Varicose veins veins whose valves have become weak and lost their elasticity. The area appears knotted, swollen and bluish/purple in colour.

Vellus hair hair which is fine, downy and soft; found on the face and body.

Warm wax a system of wax depilation. Warm wax remains soft at body temperatures. It is frequently made of mixtures of glucose syrup and zinc oxide. Honey can be used instead of glucose syrup; this is referred to as honey wax.

Wax depilation the temporary removal of excess hair from a body part using wax.

Assessment of knowledge and understanding

You have now learnt about the different temporary hair removal and lightening methods available for the face and body. This knowledge will enable you to remove hair using temporary methods with waxing and sugaring techniques.

To test your level of knowledge, answer the following short questions. These will prepare you for your summative (final) assessment. Anatomy and physiology questions required for this unit are found on pages 146–53.

Consult with the client

1 To reassure the client, how would you explain to them the treatment sensation and expected post-treatment skin reaction?

2 It is necessary to check the hair growth before hair removal. How long should hair growth be before wax/sugar depilation can be carried out?

3 A client complains that on their previous treatment (which was their first), stubbly hairs appeared the following week. What could have been the cause?

4 When observing the area for hair removal, what conditions would contra-indicate treatment?

5 Why is diabetes normally regarded as a contra-indication to temporary hair removal methods?

Prepare for the treatment

1 What hygiene legislation should be followed in relation to wax and sugar depilation?

2 What hygiene precautions should be taken when completing wax depilation? Consider:
   - the therapist's safety
   - care of the client.

3 What is the recommended temperature of wax when using:
   - hot wax
   - warm wax – spatula method
   - warm wax – roller method
   - strip sugar?

4 What additional precautions should be taken to ensure that the wax is used at a comfortable temperature?

5 How should the area to be treated for wax depilation be prepared to ensure effective hair removal?

6 How would you position the client for temporary hair removal in the following areas:
   - bikini wax
   - underarm wax
   - chin wax?

Plan the treatment

1 It is important to select the most suitable method to remove the hair type. From the following temporary hair removal methods – warm wax, hot wax, strip sugar and sugar paste – identify which you would select for:
   - the face
   - the underarm
   - the bikini

- the legs
- the eyebrows

2 It is necessary to consider the direction of hair growth for the hair removal technique chosen. Why is this?

3 Considering the body part to be treated, why is it important to consider the client's privacy and modesty?

4 Why is preparation of the area important in terms of lighting, heating and client comfort?

5 In compliance with your responsibilities under health and safety legislation, when should personal protective equipment be worn? Which Health and Safety Act does this come under?

6 Certain ingredients may cause an allergic reaction; therefore it is important that you know what the product contains. What are the main ingredients in:
- warm wax
- strip sugar

Remove unwanted hair

1 How do hot wax and warm wax differ in relation to:
- application
- removal

2 How does warm wax applied with a roller differ from that applied with a spatula in terms of:
- application
- removal

3 Which contra-indications restrict treatment, meaning that the treatment may proceed, but the area contra-indicated must be avoided?

4 What would be three undesirable post-treatment skin reactions? How could these be avoided?

5 Why is it important to position yourself and the client correctly, (whilst considering their comfort) for hair removal?

6 How should contaminated waste be disposed of?

Complete the treatment

1 What aftercare instructions should be given to the client following wax depilation treatment for both the face and body?

2 If your client suffers from ingrowing hairs, what advice would you give them that could possibly prevent them reoccurring?

3 When would you book a client to return for the following repeat depilation treatments, and how long would you allow for each area:
- eyebrow
- full leg
- bikini
- underarm
- arm

BT7 Provide manicure treatment

Essential anatomy and physiology knowledge requirements for this unit, BT7, are identified on the checklist chart in Chapter 5, page 101.

THE PURPOSE OF A MANICURE

The word **manicure** is derived from the Latin words *manus*, meaning 'hand', and *cura*, meaning 'care'. A manicure therefore cares for the hands for the following reasons:

- to improve the hands' appearance;
- to keep the nails smooth;
- to keep the cuticles attractive and healthy;
- to keep the skin soft.

ACTIVITY

Making appointments
What questions could the receptionist ask when booking a client for manicure in order to make the business run more efficiently? Write down your answers.

PREPARING FOR THE MANICURE

Outcome 1: Consult with the client

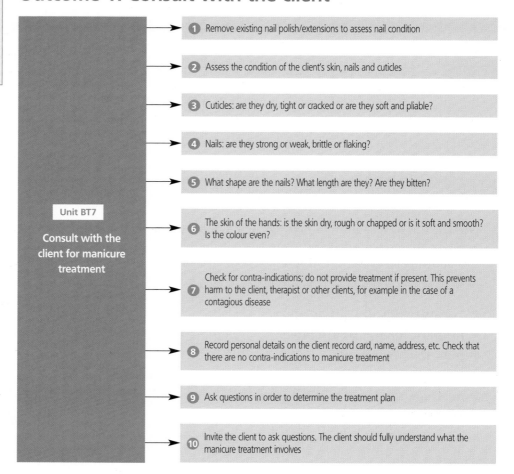

Unit BT7

Consult with the client for manicure treatment

1. Remove existing nail polish/extensions to assess nail condition

2. Assess the condition of the client's skin, nails and cuticles

3. Cuticles: are they dry, tight or cracked or are they soft and pliable?

4. Nails: are they strong or weak, brittle or flaking?

5. What shape are the nails? What length are they? Are they bitten?

6. The skin of the hands: is the skin dry, rough or chapped or is it soft and smooth? Is the colour even?

7. Check for contra-indications; do not provide treatment if present. This prevents harm to the client, therapist or other clients, for example in the case of a contagious disease

8. Record personal details on the client record card, name, address, etc. Check that there are no contra-indications to manicure treatment

9. Ask questions in order to determine the treatment plan

10. Invite the client to ask questions. The client should fully understand what the manicure treatment involves

Reception

When a client makes an appointment for a manicure treatment, the receptionist should ask a few simple questions that will save time when they arrive for treatment.

- Do they require nail polish? With drying time, this part of the treatment can last up to 20 minutes, so the appropriate length of time needs to be booked out in the appointment book.

- Are any nails damaged or in need of repair? Again extra time will need to be allowed for this work.

- Do they require any services in addition to the nail treatment, such as paraffin wax or warm oil? Allow extra time accordingly.

- Has the client had artificial nails applied previously which require removal? Allow approximately 20 minutes for this process.

Allow 45 minutes for a manicure.

Allow up to one hour for a specialist hand-nail treatment.

BEAUTY WORKS

Date	Therapist name	

Client name		Date of birth (identifying client age group)
Address		Postcode

Evening phone number	Day phone number

Name of doctor	Doctor's address and phone number

Related medical history (conditions that may restrict or prohibit treatment application)

Are you taking any medication? (this may affect the sensitivity of the skin to the treatment)

CONTRA-INDICATIONS REQUIRING MEDICAL REFERRAL
(Preventing manicure treatment application)

☐ bacterial infections (e.g. paronychia)
☐ viral infections (e.g. plane warts)
☐ fungal infections (e.g. tinea unguium)
☐ severe nail separation
☐ severe eczema and psoriasis
☐ severe bruising

EQUIPMENT AND MATERIALS

☐ nail and skin treatment tools
☐ abrasives (e.g. buffing cream)
☐ cuticle softeners
☐ nail and skin products
☐ nail conditioners (e.g. cuticle cream)
☐ skin conditioners (e.g. hand cream)
☐ nail, skin and cuticle corrective treatments (e.g. paraffin wax)
☐ consumables

HAND AND NAIL TREATMENTS

☐ warm oil
☐ hand mask
☐ paraffin wax
☐ thermal mitts
☐ exfoliators

NAIL FINISH

☐ light colour
☐ dark colour
☐ french manicure
☐ buffing

CONTRA-INDICATIONS WHICH RESTRICT TREATMENT
(Treatment may require adaptation)

☐ minor nail separation
☐ minor eczema and psoriasis
☐ recent scar tissue
☐ severely bitten nails
☐ severely damaged nails
☐ broken bones
☐ minor cuts or abrasions
☐ minor bruising or swelling

COURSE OF TREATMENT

	Date	Date	Date
☐ improvement of skin condition products used	——	——	——
☐ improvement of nail condition products used	——	——	——

NAIL, CUTICLE AND SKIN CONDITION

Nails	Cuticle	Skin
☐ normal	☐ dry	☐ dry
☐ brittle	☐ split	☐ hard
☐ dry	☐ overgrown	
☐ weak		
☐ ridged		

MASSAGE MEDIUMS

☐ creams
☐ oils

Therapist signature (for reference)

Client signature (confirmation of details)

TREATMENT ADVICE

Manicure – *allow 45 minutes*
Specialised hand/nail treatment – *allow up to 60 minutes*

TREATMENT PLAN

Record relevant details of your treatment and advice provided for future reference.

Ensure the client's records are up to date, accurate and fully completed following treatment. Non-compliance may invalidate insurance.

DURING

Discuss:

- details that may influence the client's nail condition, such as their occupation;
- the products the client is currently using to care for the skin of the hands and nails, and the regularity of their use;
- the client's satisfaction with these products;
- relevant manicure procedures (e.g., how to file the nails correctly).

Note:

- any adverse reaction, if any occur.

AFTER

Record:

- results of treatment;
- any modification to treatment application that has occurred;
- what products have been used in the manicure treatment;
- the effectiveness of treatment;
- any samples provided (review their success at the next appointment).

Advise on:

- product application in order to gain maximum benefit from product use;
- specialised products following manicure treatment for homecare use;
- general hand/nail care and maintenance;
- the recommended time intervals between treatments;
- the importance of a course of treatment to improve nail/skin conditions.

RETAIL OPPORTUNITIES

Advise on:

- progression of the treatment plan for future appointments;
- products that would be suitable for the client to use at home to care for the skin of the hands and nails;
- recommendations for further treatments;
- further products or services that the client may or may not have received before.

Note:

- any purchase made by the client.

EVALUATION

Record:

- comments on the client's satisfaction with the treatment;
- if poor results are achieved, the reasons why;
- how you may alter the treatment plan to achieve the required treatment results in the future, if applicable.

HEALTH AND SAFETY

Advise on:

- appropriate action to be taken in the event of an unwanted skin or nail reaction.

Examples of manicure treatment modification includes:
- depth of massage pressure when applying hand and arm massage and choice of massage movements applied;
- choice of massage medium when client has excessively hairy arms;
- choice of nail polish product to improve the nail condition and appearance.

TIP

Artificial nails

If the client has had several new sets of artificial nails applied this will damage the natural nail.

The nail plate may be thin, ridges may appear upon the nail plate and the removal technique, using acetone, will cause dehydration. All of these effects will need to be discussed with your client at consultation and an appropriate treatment plan discussed.

HEALTH AND SAFETY

You are not qualified to diagnose, this is the job of the GP.
Therefore if you are unsure about any nail or skin condition present refer the client to their GP.

TIP

Removal of artificial nails

These are removed using a solvent containing acetone that softens the product, allowing removal from the natural nail. However, it is particularly drying to the natural nail which will later require rehydrating.

Procedure

Remove any nail polish, trim any excess length using clippers.

Soak the nails in acetone for approximately 20 minutes, until the product has thoroughly softened.

Remove the softened product with an orange stick.

Wash the hands and nails thoroughly to remove acetone.

Continue with manicure treatment.

Skin and nail disorders of the hands

When a client attends for a manicure treatment, the therapist should always look at the client's skin and nails to check that no infection or disease is present which might contra-indicate treatment. These include bacterial, fungal and viral infections. These are described in more detail in Chapter 1, where contra-indications are illustrated and discussed.

Contra-indications

The following disorders contra-indicate manicure treatment. If you suspect the client has any disorder from the chart below, do not attempt a diagnosis, but refer the client to their GP.

Disorder	Appearance
Broken bones 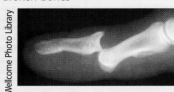	Injury resulting in a broken bone can often not be seen; confirm at consultation that there is no known injury in the treatment area
Cuts or abrasions in the hands 	Broken skin Any cut or abrasion could lead to secondary infection and the area should not be treated until healed
Paronychia 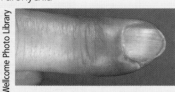	Infectious bacterial infection Swelling, redness and pus appears in the cuticle area of the nail wall
Severe eczema of the nail 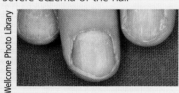	Inflammation of the skin occurs. Differing changes to the nail may occur, including the appearance of ridges, pitting, onycholysis or nail thickening (hypertrophy)
Severe eczema of the skin 	Inflammation of the skin caused by contact internally or externally, with an irritant Reddening of the skin occurs with swelling and blistering; the blisters leak tissue fluid, which later hardens and forms scabs
Severe nail separation (onycholysis) 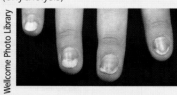	Lifting of the nail plate from the nail bed, may be caused by trauma or infection to the nail or surrounding area; where separation has occurred this appears as a greyish-white area on the nail as the pink undertone of the nail bed does not show
Severe psoriasis of the nail 	An inflammatory condition where there is an increased production of cells in the upper part of the skin Pitting occurs on the surface of the nail plate Separation (onycholysis) may also occur

Wellcome Photo Library

Wellcome Photo Library

Wellcome Photo Library

Wellcome Photo Library

Dr A.L. Wright

Wellcome Photo Library

Wellcome Photo Library

Disorder	Appearance
Severe psoriasis of the skin Dr M.H. Beck	Red patches of skin appear, covered in waxy, silvery scales Bleeding will occur if the area is scratched and the scales are removed The cause is unknown
Tinea unguium Wellcome Photo Library	Fungal infection of the fingernails The nail plate is yellowish-grey. Eventually the nail plate becomes brittle and separates from the nail bed
Verrucae or warts Dr M.H. Beck	A viral infection Small epidermal skin growths. Warts may be raised or flat depending upon their position Warts vary in size, shape, texture and colour. Usually they have a rough surface and are raised Plane wart – found on the surface of the hand

Below is a list of common disorders that may be seen on the hands. Not all of these contra-indicate treatment.

Disorder	Cause	Appearance	Salon treatment	Homecare advice
Blue nail Wellcome Photo Library	Poor blood circulation in the area Heart disease	The nail bed does not appear a healthy pink colour but has a blue tinge	Permission to treat to be received from the client's GP Regular manicure, including hand treatment to improve circulation	General manicure advice Hand exercises and massage to improve circulation
Bruised nails Dr A.L. Wright	Trauma to the nail (e.g. trapping it in a door); severe damage can result in loss of the nail	Part of the nail plate may appear blue or black where bleeding has occurred on the new bed	Although this disorder does not contra-indicate treatment, it is advisable to postpone manicuring the nails until the condition is no longer painful Nail polish may be used to disguise the damaged nail	Be careful with the hands and nails Seek medical advice if swelling is present or if pain persists
Eggshell nail Wellcome Photo Library	Illness	Thin, fragile, white nail plate, curving under at the free edge	Permission to treat to be received from the client's GP Regular manicure	General manicure advice Strengthening base coats

Disorder	Cause	Appearance	Salon treatment	Home-care advice
Hangnail	Biting the skin around the nails Cracking of a dry skin or cuticle condition	Epidermis around the nail plate cracks and a small piece of skin protrudes between the nail plate and the nail wall, sometimes accompanied by redness and swelling: this condition can become extremely painful	Warm-oil treatments to soften the skin and cuticles Remove the protrusion of dead skin with cuticle nippers: do not cut into live tissue	Regular use of a rich handcream Wear rubber gloves when cleaning and washing up Wear warm gloves in cold weather Ensure a balanced diet
Leuconychia	Trauma to the nail plate or matrix, due to pressure or hitting with a hard object Air pockets form between the nail plate and nail bed	White spots or marks on the nail plate: will grow out with the nail	General manicure treatment Coloured nail polish application will disguise their appearance until the damaged area disappears as it grows towards the free edge	Be careful with the hands Wear protective gloves when doing housework or gardening Do not use the nails as tools!
Longitudinal ridges in the nail plate (corrugated nails)	Illness Damage to the matrix Age, associated with the ageing process	Grooves in the nail plate running along the length of the nail from the cuticle to the free edge: may affect one or all nails	Abrasive buffing paste applied to smooth out the ridges Use of a ridge-filling base coat prior to nail polish application	General manicure advice Use of a ridge-filling base coat polish Ensure a balanced diet
Minor nail separation (onycholysis)	Lifting of the nail plate from its bed Can accompany a medical condition such as eczema or psoriasis or a fungal infection in the area	Where separation has occurred this appears as a greyish-white area as the pink undertone of the nail bed does not show through the nail plate	It is advisable to postpone manicuring for this nail until the condition is corrected Refer the client to their GP to confirm cause	Be careful to avoid infection of the nail bed Protect the nail with a protective dressing
Onychophagy	Excessive nail-biting	Very little nail plate; bulbous skin at the fingertip; nail walls often red and swollen, due to biting of the skin surrounding the nails	Regular weekly manicures Cuticle treatment to maximise the visible nail-plate area Nail conditioning treatments to prevent dry cuticles and hangnails	Bitter-tasting preparations painted onto the nail plate Wear gloves to avoid biting in bed
Onychorrhexis	Using harsh detergents without wearing gloves Poor diet Not wearing gloves in cold weather	Split, flaking nails	Warm-oil manicures on a weekly basis	Regular use of a rich handcream Always wear rubber gloves when cleaning or washing up Always wear warm gloves in cold weather Ensure a balanced diet Prescribe nail base coat to protect split, flaking nails

Dr A.L. Wright

Dr A.L. Wright

Dr A.L. Wright

Wellcome Photo Library

Dr A.L. Wright

Dr A.L. Wright

Disorder	Cause	Appearance	Salon treatment	Home-care advice
Pitting	Eczema Psoriasis	Pitting resembling small irregular pin pricks appear on the nail plate	Refer the client to their GP for permission to treat if required Regular manicure with gentle buffing	General manicure advice Ridge-filling base coat polish
Pterygium	Neglect of the nails	Overgrown thickened cuticles, often tightly adhered to the nail plate: if left untreated, this may lead to splitting of the cuticle and subsequent infection	Warm-oil or paraffin wax treatments weekly Once softened, remove excess cuticle with cuticle nippers If overgrown cuticle is excessive, refer client to their GP	Regular use of a rich cuticle cream Wear rubber gloves when cleaning and washing up Gently push back the cuticles with a soft towel when softened, e.g. after bathing
Transverse furrows in the nail plate (Beau's lines)	Temporary arrested development of the nail in the matrix, due to illness or trauma of the nail	Groove in the nail plate, often on all nails simultaneously, running from side to side: this will grow out with the nail	Regular manicure until normal cells replace the damaged cells	General manicure advice Ensure a balanced diet

Wellcome Photo Library

Dr A.L. Wright

Dr A.L. Wright

Consultation

Before carrying out a manicure treatment, it is necessary to assess the condition of the client's skin, nails and cuticles. This is done in order that the most appropriate equipment and products may be chosen. Also, by correctly assessing and analysing the client's hand condition and writing this on their record card, you will be able to see over a period of time how the condition is progressing.

The parts to assess are these:

- *The cuticles* Are they dry, tight or cracked, or are they soft and pliable?
- *The nails* Are they strong or weak, brittle or flaking? Are they discoloured or stained? What shape are they – square, round, oval? Are they long or short? Are they bitten?
- *The hands* Is the skin dry, rough or chapped, or is it soft and smooth? Is the colour even?

Whilst assessing the client's hands or feet for treatment, you should also be looking for any *contra-indications* to treatment.

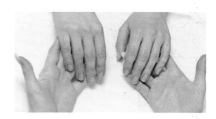

Assessing the hands

ACTIVITY

Assessing the hands
Look closely at your own hands. Assess their condition and make notes about everything you see.

Then assess the hands of a colleague. How do they differ from your own?

Complete a record card and record the condition of the nails and adjacent skin. Design a suitable treatment plan for your client.

Outcome 2: Prepare for the manicure treatment

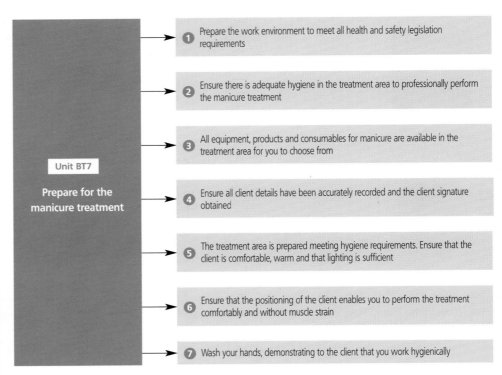

Unit BT7

Prepare for the manicure treatment

1. Prepare the work environment to meet all health and safety legislation requirements

2. Ensure there is adequate hygiene in the treatment area to professionally perform the manicure treatment

3. All equipment, products and consumables for manicure are available in the treatment area for you to choose from

4. Ensure all client details have been accurately recorded and the client signature obtained

5. The treatment area is prepared meeting hygiene requirements. Ensure that the client is comfortable, warm and that lighting is sufficient

6. Ensure that the positioning of the client enables you to perform the treatment comfortably and without muscle strain

7. Wash your hands, demonstrating to the client that you work hygienically

A manicure station

Equipment and materials

Before beginning the manicure, check that you have the necessary equipment and materials to hand.

EQUIPMENT LIST

 Manicure table or trolley on which to place everything

 Emery boards used to shape the new free edge

 Orange sticks tipped at either end with cottonwool. (Orange sticks should be disposed of after each client, as they cannot be effectively sterilised.) Used to remove products from containers, to ease the cuticle back and clean under the free edge

 Hand cream or oil to massage the skin of the hand and arm

Base coat to prevent nail staining and improve the appearance of the nail
Coloured nail polish a selection for the client to choose from
Top coat to provide shine and strength to the nail polish. Reduces peeling and chipping and increases durability of the nail polish

 Nail polish remover to remove nail polish and excess nail care and skin-care preparations

 Hoof stick to gently push back the cuticles, when softened

 Cuticle nippers to remove excess cuticle and dead, torn skin surrounding the nail

 Nail scissors to shorten nail length

EQUIPMENT LIST

  Cuticle remover used to soften the skin cells and cuticle before treatment

 Cottonwool to remove nail polish and excess nail treatment products used

Tissues to protect clean clothing in the area, etc

 Cuticle oil or cream used to condition the skin of the cuticle; especially beneficial for dry nails

YOU WILL ALSO NEED:

Medium-sized towels (3) to dry the skin, nails, etc

Small bowls (3) lined with tissues

A finger bowl to place the hand into a nail cleansing agent

Cuticle knife to remove excess eponychium from the nail plate

Buffers to improve nail shine, stimulate blood circulation and remove surface ridges when used with a buffing paste

Buffing paste used to reduce the appearance of ridges on the nail plate surface

Disinfecting solution for all surfaces

Antiseptic to cleanse the skin

Four-sided buffer to impart shine and improve nail appearance

Client record card confidential record card recording the details of each client registered at the salon

Nail polish drier an aerosol or oil preparation applied to speed the drying process of nail polish

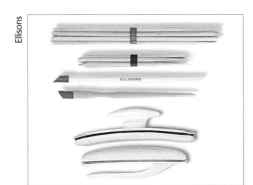

Hoof sticks and buffers to improve nail shine, stimulate blood circulation and remove surface ridges (when used with a buffing paste)

Buffing paste to remove the appearance of ridges on the nail plate surface

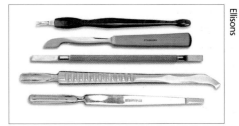

Cuticle knives to remove excess eponychium from the nail plate

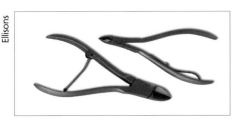

Cuticle nippers to remove excess cuticle and dead, torn skin surrounding the nail

Scissors to shorten nail length

Products used in manicure and pedicure treatments

Product	Ingredients	Use
Nail polish remover	Acetone or ethyl acetate – solvent Perfume Colour Oil – emollient to reduce drying effect of solvent	To remove nail polish To remove grease from the nail plate prior to applying polish
Hand lotion/oil	Vegetable oils (e.g. almond oil) Perfume Emulsifying agents (e.g. beeswax or gum tragacanth) Emollients (e.g. glycerine or lanolin) Preservatives	To soften the skin and cuticles To provide slip during hand massage
Nail bleach	Citric acid or hydrogen peroxide – bleaches the nail Glycerine – emollient Water	To whiten stained nails and the surrounding skin
Nail polish	Formaldehyde – film-forming plastic resin, improving adherence and flexibility Solvent – to create a suitable consistency to apply, and dries at a controlled rate Colour pigments – create nail polish colour Resin – improve adhesion of polish to nail plate and flexibility Toluene – solvent which dissolves ingredients in nail polish Nitrocellulose – film-forming plastic, holds colour Plasticisers – to provide flexibility after the polish has dried, reducing chipping Pearlised particles – creates a pearlised effect	To colour nail plates To provide some protection
Cuticle cream	Emollients (e.g. lanolin or glycerine) Perfume Colour	To soften the cuticles
Cuticle oil	Oils such as lanolin – emollient	To condition the nail and surrounding skin
Nail strengthener	Formaldehyde – film-forming plastic resin	To strengthen weak nails
Cuticle remover	Potassium hydroxide – a caustic alkali Glycerine – a humectant added to reduce the drying effect on the nail plate	To soften the skin of the cuticles
Buffing paste	Perfume Colour Abrasive particles (e.g. pumice, talc or silica) to remove surface cells	To shine the nail plate (used with a buffer)
Nail polish drier	Mineral oil – assists drying Oleric acid or silicone – lubricant	Increases the speed at which the polish hardens
Nail polish solvent	Ethyl acetate – thins nail polish consistency Toluene – solvent which dissolves	Thins nail polish that has thickened, restoring consistency

TIP ✔

UV stabilisers
UV stabilisers are additives which prevent the polish changing colour on exposure to UV sunlight.

TIP ✔

Pearlised polishes
Pearlised polishes are created by the addition of sparkling, reflective particles such as mica, a synthetic product.

Sterilisation and disinfection

Hygiene must be maintained in a number of ways:

- ensure that tools and equipment are clean and sterile before use;
- disinfect work surfaces regularly;
- use disposable products wherever possible;
- always follow hygienic working practices;
- maintain a high standard of personal hygiene.

Manicure and pedicure tools and equipment can be sterilised or disinfected by the following methods:

Tool/Equipment	Method	Term used
Cuticle knife	Autoclave	Sterilisation
Cuticle nippers	Autoclave	Sterilisation
Orange stick	Throw away after use	Disposable
Callus file	Autoclave	Sterilisation
	Chemical (e.g. disinfectant)	Disinfection
Bowl	Chemical (e.g. disinfectant)	Disinfection
Emery board	Throw away after use	Disposable
Buffer	Wipe handle with surgical spirit or disinfectant	Disinfection
	Wash buffing cloth in hot (60°C) soapy water	Cleansed
Towel	Wash in hot soapy water (60°C)	Cleansed
Spatula	Throw away after use	Disposable
Nail clippers	Autoclave	Sterilisation
Scissors	Autoclave	Sterilisation
Hoof stick	Immerse in chemical (e.g. disinfectant)	Disinfection
Trolley	Wipe with chemical (e.g. disinfectant)	Disinfection

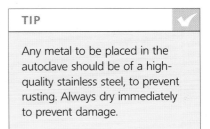

TIP ✔

Any metal to be placed in the autoclave should be of a high-quality stainless steel, to prevent rusting. Always dry immediately to prevent damage.

HEALTH AND SAFETY ➕

Sterilising sprays
You can buy sterilising sprays to sterilise the surface of the tools that the chemical agent comes into contact with.

Use in a well-ventilated area and avoid contact with flame and excessive heat.

Preparing the working area

Ensure that all manicure tools and equipment are clean, sterilised and disinfected, as appropriate, and that all necessary materials are neatly organised on the trolley.

Keeping the working area tidy promotes an organised and professional image, and prevents time being wasted as you try to find materials.

Place a towel over the work surface, then fold another towel into a pad and place it in the middle of the work surface. The pad helps to support the client's forearm during treatment. Place the third towel over the pad, with more of the towel on the manicurist's side – this is used to dry the client's hands during treatment.

A tissue or disposable manicure mat should then be placed on top of the towels, to catch any nail clippings or filings. This can be thrown away later, avoiding irritation to the client from filings.

Preparing the client

Ensure that the client is warm and comfortable when preparing them for a manicure.

Lighting must be efficient to avoid eyestrain and to allow the treatment to be performed competently.

Offer the client a lightweight gown to cover their clothing. This will prevent damage to their clothes from accidental spillage of products during treatment. Ask them to remove any jewellery from the area to be treated, to prevent the jewellery being damaged by creams and to avoid obstructing massage movements. Put the jewellery in a tissue-lined bowl where the client can see it. Ensure that the client is seated at the correct height, and close enough to the manicurist to avoid having to lean forward.

When the client is comfortably seated, wash your hands – preferably in view of the client, who will then observe hygienic procedures being carried out. This will assure them that they are receiving a professional treatment.

Consult the client's record card, and begin the treatment.

The Natural Nail Company/Jessica Nails

Client receiving a manicure

Outcome 3: Plan the manicure treatment

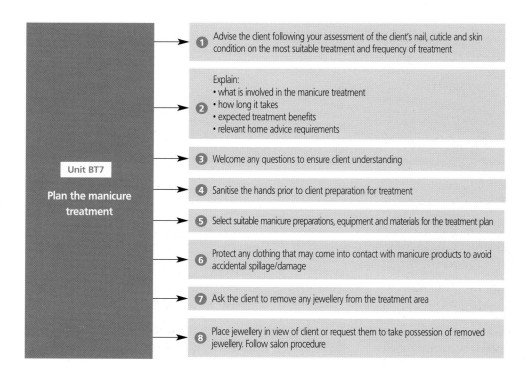

Unit BT7

Plan the manicure treatment

1. Advise the client following your assessment of the client's nail, cuticle and skin condition on the most suitable treatment and frequency of treatment

2. Explain:
   • what is involved in the manicure treatment
   • how long it takes
   • expected treatment benefits
   • relevant home advice requirements

3. Welcome any questions to ensure client understanding

4. Sanitise the hands prior to client preparation for treatment

5. Select suitable manicure preparations, equipment and materials for the treatment plan

6. Protect any clothing that may come into contact with manicure products to avoid accidental spillage/damage

7. Ask the client to remove any jewellery from the treatment area

8. Place jewellery in view of client or request them to take possession of removed jewellery. Follow salon procedure

Treatment plan

After analysing the client's nails and adjacent skin, a treatment plan should be considered and agreed with the client. In order to correct nail problems the client should attend the salon weekly. They should also be advised of the appropriate treatment preparations to use at home, so as to support the salon treatment. Specialist nail treatments to use will depend upon the nail condition; they include:

- **Nail strengthener** This is used on brittle, damaged nails, to strengthen, condition and protect them against breaking, splitting or peeling.
- **Ridge filler** This is used on nails with ridges to provide a more even surface, creating a bond between the base coat and polish, allowing a smoother application of polish.
- **Nail oil** This contains ingredients to rehydrate the nail and soften the cuticle.
- **Cuticle creams** These nourish the skin and restore the condition of the cuticle.
- **Specialist hand and nail treatments** These may also be recommended within the manicure treatment to improve the appearance of the skin texture and cuticle condition and provide a number of physiological benefits. These may be offered each time the client has a manicure treatment to maintain the condition of the nails and hands.

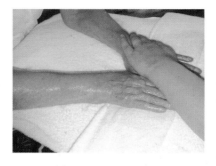

Warm oil application

Solar oil

PROVIDING MANICURE TREATMENTS

Outcome 4: Improve the appearance and condition of the natural nail and cuticle

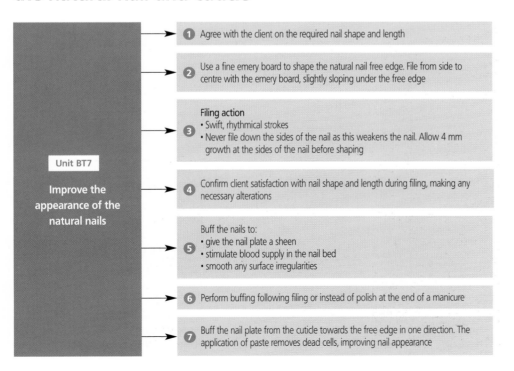

Unit BT7

Improve the appearance of the natural nails

1. Agree with the client on the required nail shape and length

2. Use a fine emery board to shape the natural nail free edge. File from side to centre with the emery board, slightly sloping under the free edge

3. **Filing action**
   - Swift, rhythmical strokes
   - Never file down the sides of the nail as this weakens the nail. Allow 4 mm growth at the sides of the nail before shaping

4. Confirm client satisfaction with nail shape and length during filing, making any necessary alterations

5. Buff the nails to:
   - give the nail plate a sheen
   - stimulate blood supply in the nail bed
   - smooth any surface irregularities

6. Perform buffing following filing or instead of polish at the end of a manicure

7. Buff the nail plate from the cuticle towards the free edge in one direction. The application of paste removes dead cells, improving nail appearance

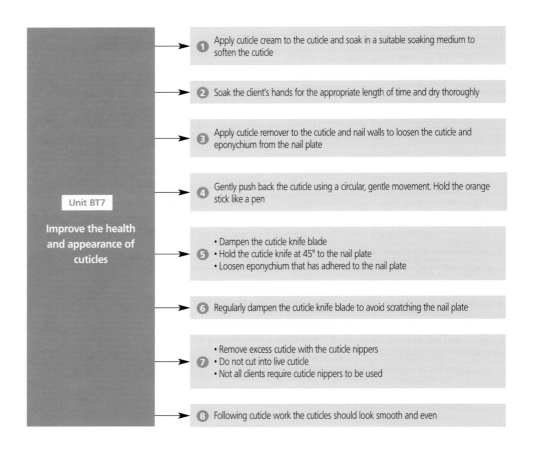

Unit BT7

Improve the health and appearance of cuticles

1. Apply cuticle cream to the cuticle and soak in a suitable soaking medium to soften the cuticle

2. Soak the client's hands for the appropriate length of time and dry thoroughly

3. Apply cuticle remover to the cuticle and nail walls to loosen the cuticle and eponychium from the nail plate

4. Gently push back the cuticle using a circular, gentle movement. Hold the orange stick like a pen

5. • Dampen the cuticle knife blade
   • Hold the cuticle knife at 45° to the nail plate
   • Loosen eponychium that has adhered to the nail plate

6. Regularly dampen the cuticle knife blade to avoid scratching the nail plate

7. • Remove excess cuticle with the cuticle nippers
   • Do not cut into live cuticle
   • Not all clients require cuticle nippers to be used

8. Following cuticle work the cuticles should look smooth and even

Step by step: Manicure procedure

This procedure briefly shows the stages in the manicure. Each step is discussed in detail later in the chapter.

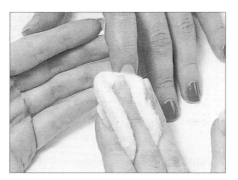

1 Remove any existing nail polish with nail polish remover, using fresh cottonwool for each hand.

2 File the nails of the left hand.

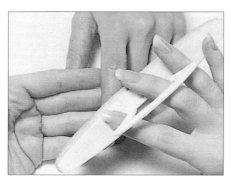

3 Buff the nails of the left hand.

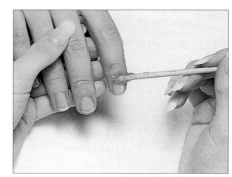

4 Apply cuticle cream.

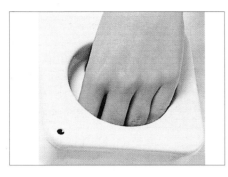

5 Place the left hand in a manicure bowl containing warm water and a little antiseptic liquid soap. Repeat steps 2 and 3 for the right hand. Remove the left hand from the manicure bowl and dry with a towel. Place the right hand into the manicure bowl.

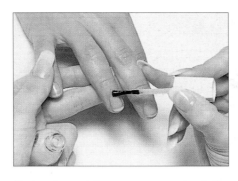

6 Apply cuticle remover to the left hand.

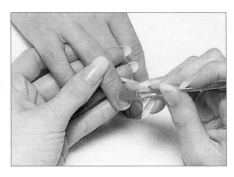

7 Push back the cuticle with a cottonwool-tipped orange stick or hoof stick.

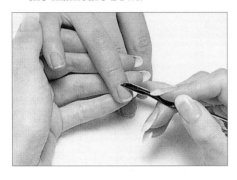

8 Remove excess cuticle with nippers, and excess eponychium with a knife. Wipe the nails with cottonwool to remove the cuticle remover.

9 Apply cuticle oil and massage it in with your thumbs. Repeat steps 6–9 for the right hand. Apply massage routine to both hands and forearms. Remove grease from the nail plate with a cottonwool pad soaked in nail polish remover.

10 The client may find it convenient to pay for her treatment at this stage, to avoid smudging her polish later. Also, if jewellery has been removed ask her to replace it to avoid damage to the polish after application.

11 Apply the polish: base coat (once); polish (twice); and top coat (once). If a pearlised polish is used a top coat is not required and a third coat of polish may be applied. If the client doesn't want polish, buff to a shine with paste or use a four-sided buffer.

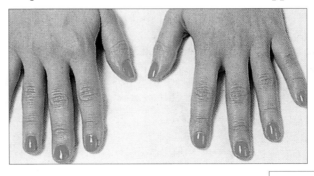

12 The completed manicure

TIP

Keep the client's jewellery in full view throughout the treatment, so that they don't forget it when they leave.

A selection of files

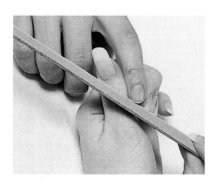

Filing

Filing

The part of the nail that is filed is the free edge. When filing the natural nail, use a fine emery board. Very often emery boards have different degrees of coarseness on either side, indicated by different colours. Use the darker, rougher side to remove excess length, and the lighter, smoother side for shaping and removing rough edges. A flexible emery board is preferable to a stiff one as it generates less friction.

Always file the nails from the side to the centre, with the emery board sloping slightly under the free edge. Use swift, rhythmical strokes. Avoid a sawing action – this would generate friction and might cause the free edge to split.

Never file completely down the sides of the nail, as strength is required here to balance the free edge. Always allow about 4mm of nail growth to remain at the sides of the nail.

TIP ✔

Nail shapes
When filing the nails ensure that the finished appearance complements the client's nail/hand.
    If the fingers are long and thin, select a rounded/square shape and keep the nail length short.
    If the fingers are short and fat, the nails should be filed into an oval shape and the nail length should be longer to elongate the fingers.

Cutting the nails

Where it is necessary to reduce nail length, it is more efficient to do so by cutting the nail free edge. This is performed using nail scissors, which have been sterilised before use on each client. Support the nail wall with one hand on the free edge being cut. This minimises client discomfort. Dispose of the trimmed nail plate hygienically.

Nail shapes

Oval   The ideal nail shape is oval. This is the shape that offers the most strength to the free edge.

Square   A recent trend from America is to have the free edge square. The client should be informed, however, that if they have severe corners on the nails they will be more likely to catch and break them.

Pointed   One nail shape that should never be recommended is the pointed nail. This leaves the nail tip very weak and likely to break.

Squoval   A combination of oval and square nail shape. The nail is filed to a square finish at the free edge and is then gently curved at the corners.

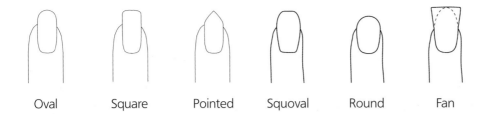

Oval   Square   Pointed   Squoval   Round   Fan

Round   The free edge is rounded and is an ideal shape for short nails. This style is popular with male clients.

Fan   The nail becomes broader as it grows towards the free edge, appearing as a fan shape. The wider sides of the nail at the free edge should be shaped to achieve an oval shape.

Buffing

In manicure, **buffing** is used for these reasons:

- to give the nail plate a sheen;
- to stimulate the blood supply in the nail bed, increasing nourishment and encouraging strong, healthy nail growth;
- to smooth any surface irregularities.

A **buffer** should have a handle made of plastic and a replaceable convex pad covered with chamois or soft leather. **Buffing paste** is the cream used to help smooth out surface irregularities, and thereby give the nail a shine. It contains abrasive particles such as pumice, talc or kaolin.

The **four-sided buffer**: this is shaped like a thick emery board and has four types of surface, ranging from slightly abrasive to very smooth. It can be used to bring the nail to a shine without the need for buffing paste. It cannot be effectively sterilised, however, and must therefore be discarded after use on one client.

Buffing is carried out after filing to stimulate healthy nail growth and before the nails are soaked in the finger bowl. It could also be used instead of polish at the end of the manicure, or as a nail finish. It is popular when performing a male manicure treatment as an alternative finish to nail polish application.

If it is being used, **buffing paste** is applied by taking a small amount out of the pot with a clean orange stick and applying this to each nail plate. With the fingertip, use downward strokes from the cuticle to the free edge to spread the paste without getting it under the cuticle (which would cause irritation). With the buffer held loosely in the hand, buff in one direction only from the base of the nail to the free edge, using smooth, firm, regular strokes. Use approximately six strokes per nail.

Cuticle work

Cuticle work is carried out to keep the cuticle area attractive and also to prevent cuticles from adhering to the nail plate, which could lead to splitting of the cuticle as the nail grows forward, and subsequently to infection of the area.

Buffing

HEALTH AND SAFETY

If you accidentally cut the skin causing bleeding at the cuticle area, protect you hands with disposable gloves and wipe the skin with an antiseptic wipe. Any waste is classed as clinical waste and should be disposed of in a sealed bag in accordance with the **Environmental Act 1990**.

Pushing back cuticles

Using a cuticle knife

Using cuticle nippers

An oil wax heater

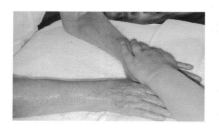

Warm oil application

The work is carried out after soaking the nails in warm soapy water. This step loosens dirty particles from the free edge and softens the skin in the cuticle area.

How to provide cuticle work

1 Take the fingers from the soapy water and pat them dry with a soft towel.

2 Apply cuticle remover to the cuticle and nail walls, using the applicator brush. (**Cuticle remover** is a slightly caustic solution that helps soften and loosen the cuticles and the eponychium from the nail plate.)

3 Gently push back the cuticle with a cottonwool-tipped orange stick or hoofstick. This is tipped with cottonwool to avoid splinters from the wood, and also so that the cottonwool may be replaced if necessary.) Use a gentle, circular motion to push back the cuticle, holding the orange stick like a pen.

4 Hold the cuticle knife at 45° to the nail plate and stroke it in one direction only, gently loosening any eponychium that has adhered to the nail plate: do not scratch it backwards and forwards. The cuticle knife should have a fine-ground flat blade which can be resharpened when necessary. Dampen it regularly in the manicure bowl to prevent scratches occurring on the nail plate.

5 Hold the nippers comfortably in the palm of the hand, with the thumb resting just above the blades – this gives firm control over what can be a dangerous instrument. Use the cuticle nippers to remove any loose or torn pieces of cuticle, and to trim excess dead cuticle. *Do not cut into live cuticle*: if you do, it will bleed profusely and will be very uncomfortable for the client. Not every client will require the use of cuticle nippers – use them only when needed. (Cuticle nippers should have finely ground cutting blades to give a clean cut and to avoid tearing the cuticle.)

> **HEALTH AND SAFETY** ✚
>
> Hygiene
> Use a fresh orange stick for each part of the manicure treatment, and when working on different hands, to prevent cross-infection.

HAND AND NAIL TREATMENTS

In addition to a manicure, further treatments may be added as appropriate. Here are some examples.

Warm-oil treatment

Warm-oil treatment involves gently heating a small amount of vegetable oil (such as almond oil) and soaking the cuticles in it for ten minutes. This nourishes the nail plate, softens the cuticles and the surrounding skin, and is an excellent treatment for clients with dry, cracked cuticles.

Warm oil may also be applied to the skin of the hand and forearm to improve skin texture, colour and blood circulation in the area.

Exfoliating treatment

Exfoliating treatment is carried out as part of the massage routine. The massage is performed as usual, using a mildly abrasive cream. It may be applied prior to hand and arm massage also to expose new cells and aid the absorption of the massage oil/cream. This treatment offers the following benefits:

- the removal of dead skin cells;
- improvement of the skin texture;
- improvement of the skin colour;
- increased blood circulation.

The abrasive particles must be thoroughly removed with hot, damp towels before continuing with the rest of the manicure.

An exfoliating treatment

Hand treatment mask

An appropriate **treatment mask** may be applied, according to the client's treatment requirements. This may be either stimulating and rejuvenating, or moisturising. The hands may be placed inside warm mittens or hand gloves for ten minutes to enable the mask to penetrate the epidermis. The mask is then removed, and followed with treatment massage cream.

A hand treatment mask

Paraffin wax treatment

The wax is heated in a special bath to a temperature of 50–55°C. It is then applied to the hands with a brush and left to set for 10–15 minutes. This offers the following benefits:

- the heating effect stimulates the blood circulation;
- eases discomfort of arthritic and rheumatic conditions;
- softens the skin; improving the appearance and condition of the nails and dry skin.

After use the wax is disposed of.

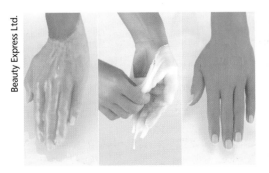

Paraffin wax application and removal   Paraffin wax resources

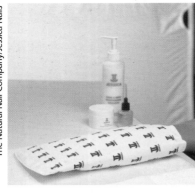

The Natural Nail Company/Jessica Nails

Thermal mitts

Thermal mitts

These are electrically heated gloves in which the hands are placed for approximately 15 minutes.

They are usually used following the application of a treatment within the manicure routine. The hands are prepared by wrapping them in a plastic protective covering.

The treatment has the following benefits:

- decreases joint stiffness in the case of a client suffering from arthritis;
- improves the condition of dry skin of the cuticles and hands by increasing the absorption of moisturising products;
- improves skin colour and blood circulation.

ACTIVITY

Researching treatments
Research other types of hand and nail treatments. Write down the details of your research, and try out the treatments on clients.

Step by step: Specialist hand and arm treatment

Specialist treatments should be offered to your client when there is a specific treatment need or if they feel they would like to benefit from such a treatment.

Specialist training in these advanced techniques is usually offered by major product companies.

The model for this specialist hand and arm treatment is a mature client who suffers from the medical condition rheumatoid arthritis where the joints become inflamed and painful.

The following hand and arm treatment will:

- stimulate the blood circulation;
- have a skin cleansing action;
- remove dead skin cells (desquamation);
- improve the moisture content of the skin;
- minimise discomfort caused by an arthritic, rheumatic condition.

Your treatments should be adapted the meet the treatment objectives for the client.

Allow 30 minutes for this specialist hand and arm treatment.

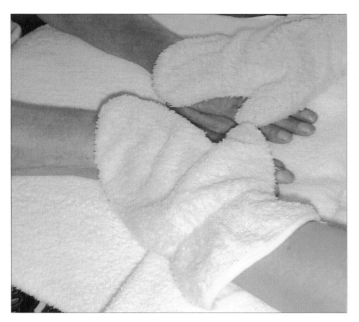

1 The hands and arms are cleansed using warm towelling mitts infused with lime oil for its therapeutic, refreshing and energising properties.

2 The hands are exfoliated to remove all dead skin cells and brighten the skin. A salt-based preparation with emollient, skin-softening ingredients is applied to the skin of each hand and is rubbed gently over the skin's surface.

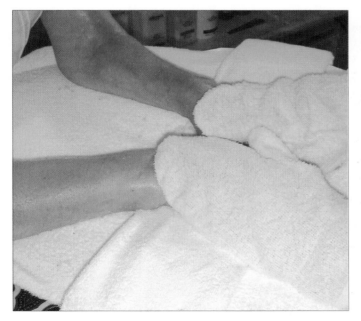

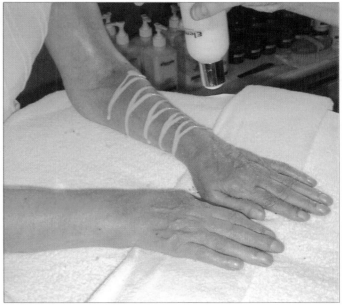

3 Towelling mitts are used to remove the exfoliating treatment. These have been steamed and are warm when used.

4 A skin-nourishing milk lotion is applied to each arm using a 'drizzling' technique. The milk is particularly beneficial for dry, sensitive skin.

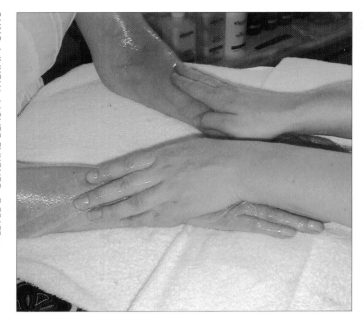

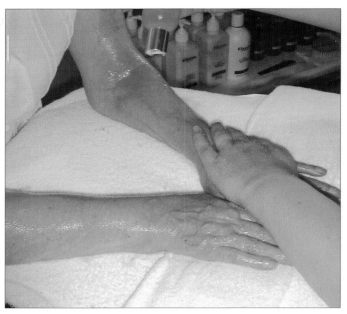

5 Massage movements are applied using effleurage and petrissage massage manipulations.

6 A further skin treatment product warm oil is applied and massaged into the skin. This will act as a treatment mask for the skin.

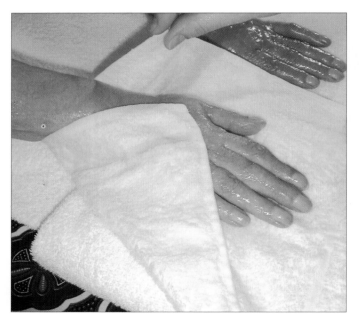

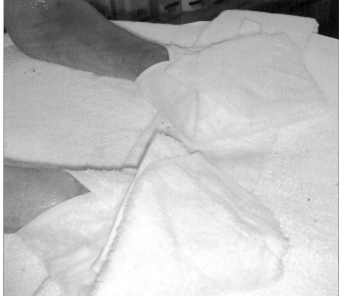

7 The hands are then placed in steamed towels and encased in a plastic bag and dry towelling mitten for 10–15 minutes. Remove mittens and continue with nail polish application if desired.

HAND AND FOREARM MASSAGE

Outcome 5: Massage the hand and forearm

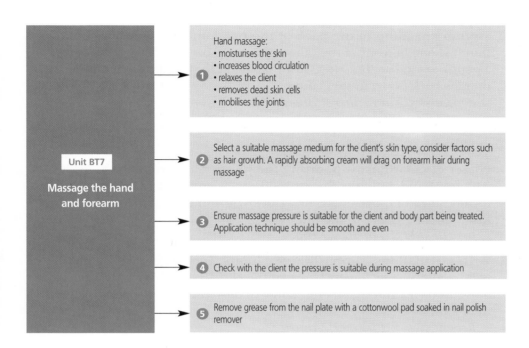

Unit BT7

Massage the hand and forearm

① Hand massage:
• moisturises the skin
• increases blood circulation
• relaxes the client
• removes dead skin cells
• mobilises the joints

② Select a suitable massage medium for the client's skin type, consider factors such as hair growth. A rapidly absorbing cream will drag on forearm hair during massage

③ Ensure massage pressure is suitable for the client and body part being treated. Application technique should be smooth and even

④ Check with the client the pressure is suitable during massage application

⑤ Remove grease from the nail plate with a cottonwool pad soaked in nail polish remover

Hand massage is generally carried out near the end of the manicure treatment, just prior to nail polish application. It can also be carried out on its own if the client wants the effects of the massage but does not need or want treatment to their nails.

The massage incorporates classic massage movements, each with different effects:

- **Effleurage** – a stroking movement, used to begin the massage as a link manipulation, and to complete the massage sequence.
- **Petrissage** – movements including *kneading* where the tissues are lifted away from the underlying structures and compressed. Pressure is intermittent, and should be light yet firm.

The therapist can adapt the massage application according to the needs of the client. Either the *speed of application* or *depth of pressure* can be altered.

The reasons for offering a hand massage during a manicure are as follows:

- to moisturise the skin with hand cream;
- to increase blood circulation to the lower arm and hand;
- to help maintain joint mobility;
- to ease discomfort from arthritis or rheumatism;
- to relax the client;
- to help remove any dead skin cells (desquamation).

> **TIP** ✔
>
> **Positive promotion**
> Hand massage can be included during a facial whilst the mask is applied, maximising treatment benefits and client relaxation. It also gives you the opportunity to promote another treatment product or service to the client.

How to provide hand and forearm massage

1 **Effleurage to the whole hand and forearm** Use long sweeping strokes from the hand to the elbow, moving on both the outer and the inner sides of the forearm.
   Repeat step 1 *a further 5 times.*

2 **Thumb kneading to the back of the hand and the forearm** Use the thumbs, one in front of the other, and move backwards and forwards in a gently sawing action. Move from the hand to the elbow, then slide the thumbs back down to the hands.
   Repeat step 2 *a further 2 times.*

3 **Thumb kneading to the palm and the inner forearm** Use the same movements as in step 2.

4 **Finger circulations, supporting the joints** Supporting the knuckles with one hand, hold the fingers individually and gently take each through its full range of movements, first clockwise and then anticlockwise. Move from the little finger to the thumb.
   Repeat step 4 *a further 2 times.*

5 **Wrist circulations, supporting the joints** Support the wrist with one hand and put your fingers between the client's, gently grasping her hand. Move the wrist through its full range of movement, first clockwise and then anticlockwise.
   Repeat step 5 *a further 2 times.*

6 **Effleurage to the whole hand and forearm** Use the same movement as in step 1.
   Repeat step 6 *a further 5 times*

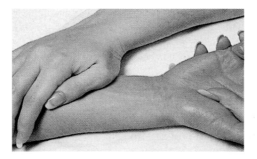

Effleurage to the hand and forearm

Thumb kneading to the back of the hand

Thumb kneading to the palm

Finger circulations

NAIL POLISH APPLICATION

Outcome 6: Provide nail polishing treatments

Unit BT7

Provide nail polishing treatment

1. Nail polish is applied to:
   • adorn the nail
   • disguise stained nails
   • add temporary strength
   • co-ordinate with clothes/accessories

2. Do not apply polish if the client has an allergy to nail polish. Certain cosmetic ingredients are known to cause allergic reactions

3. Select a nail polish formulation suited to the client's nail condition and length

4. Generally, short nails should be painted with pale polishes

5. Ensure the nail plate is grease-free. Apply a suitable base coat suited to the client's needs

6. Apply nail polish according to manufacturer's instructions and the effect to be achieved. The final effect should be a smooth, even surface

7. No nail polish should appear on the cuticle or nail wall. Remove any nail polish on these areas with a clean orange stick and nail polish remover

8. A nail 'fast-drying' product may be applied to reduce the time taken for nail polish to dry

Nail polish is used to coat the nail plate for a number of reasons:

- to adorn the nail;
- to disguise stained nails;
- to add temporary strength to weak nails;
- to improve the condition or appearance of the natural nail;
- to coordinate with clothes or make-up;
- to create designs and effects, called 'nail art'.

Nail art

Before nail polish is applied, the client's hand jewellery may be replaced, to avoid smudging afterwards.

Styles of polish application

- **Traditional application** This style is the one most commonly requested by clients: the entire nail plate is covered with polish.
- **French application** This style involves painting the nail plate of the nail bed pink or pale beige, and the free edge white.
- **Free lunula application** This style involves applying polish over the whole nail plate except the area of the lunula.

> **TIP** ✓
>
> **Fast-drying products**
> A nail 'fast-drying' product may be applied to reduce the time taken for the polish to dry.

> **TIP** ✓
>
> **Choosing colours**
> For short nails, select a pale, neutral colour. Darker, more dramatic colours suit healthy, long nails, especially on clients with darker skin tones.

> **TIP** ✓
>
> **Essential nail polish qualities**
> Nail polish should:
> - adhere to the nail plate and be flexible to resist peeling and chipping;
> - have good durability on exposure to water, detergents and other chemicals it may come into contact with;
> - not stain the nail plate;
> - flow freely onto the nail plate and be easy to apply.

Cream polish

- **Application to give the appearance of longer nails** This style creates an optical illusion that the nails are longer than they really are. The whole nail plate is painted, leaving a slightly larger gap than usual along the nail walls.

Reasons for peeling and chipping nail polish

Chipping may be explained by any of the following:

- The nail polish was not thick enough because of over-thinning with solvent.
- No base coat was used.
- Grease was left on the nail plate prior to painting.
- The nail plate is flaking.
- The polish was dried too quickly by artificial means.

Peeling polish may have the following explanations:

- No top coat was used.
- Successive coats were not allowed to dry between applications.
- The nail polish was too thick, due to evaporation of the solvent.
- Grease was left on the nail plate prior to painting.

Nail polish storage

Nail polish should be stored in a cool, dark place, to avoid separation and fading. The caps and the rims of bottles *must* be kept clean, not only for appearance but also to ensure that the bottle is airtight.

If polish does thicken, **solvent** may be added to restore the correct consistency. This should be done 20 minutes prior to use to ensure an even consistency.

Types of polish

- **Cream** This has a matt finish, and requires a top coat application to give a sheen.
- **Pearlised** This has a frosted, shimmery appearance due to the addition of natural fish scales or synthetic ingredients such as bismuth oxychloride.
- **Base coat** This protects the nail from staining by a strong-coloured nail polish; it also gives a good grip to polish, and smooths out minor surface irregularities. Many base coats are formulated using ingredients to treat different nail problems such as weak, brittle, peeling or ridged nails.
- **Top coat** This gives a sheen to cream polish, and adds longer wear as it helps to prevent chipping.

Contra-indications to nail polish

Do not apply polish in these circumstances:

- if there are diseases and disorders of the nail plate and surrounding skin;
- if the client is allergic to nail polish.

In addition, crystalline nail polish should not be applied to excessively ridged nails as it may appear to exaggerate the problem. Short or bitten nails should be painted only with pale polishes, to avoid attracting attention.

Step by step: Base coat application

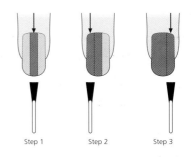

Step 1   Step 2   Step 3

Nail polish application

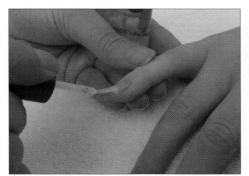 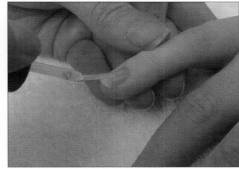

1 After ensuring that the nail plate is free from grease, start with the thumb and apply three brush strokes down the length of the nail from the cuticle to the free edge, beginning in the centre, then down either side close to the nail wall.

Take care to avoid touching the cuticle or the nail wall. If flooding occurs, remove the polish immediately with an orange stick and polish remover.

2 Apply one base coat, two coats of coloured polish and one top coat. Top coat is required only after using cream polish; pearl polish does not need a top coat.

MANICURE FOR A MALE CLIENT

A man's hands differ slightly from a woman's so some adaptations to the basic manicure are necessary if the treatment is to be effective:

- File the nails to a shorter length.
- Usually coloured nail polish is omitted.
- Shape the nails square rather than oval.
- Buff the nails with paste, if a shine is required.
- Use unperfumed lotion for massage.
- Use a lotion or an oil rather than cream for massage, to avoid dragging body hair.
- Use deeper movements during hand and arm massage.

ACTIVITY

Comparing hands
Carefully look at and touch a man's hands, then look at and touch those of a woman. Write down as many differences as you can.

From your observations, can you think of any further adaptations that may be necessary in manicuring a man's hands?

Step by step: Male manicure

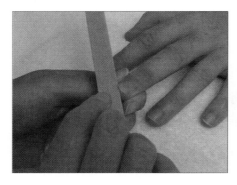

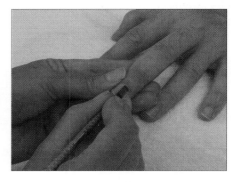

1 File the nails to a shorter length. The nails are usually filed to a square shape rather than oval.

2 Improve the appearance of the cuticles. Push back the cuticles gently.

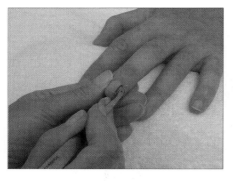

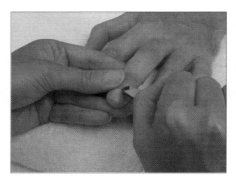

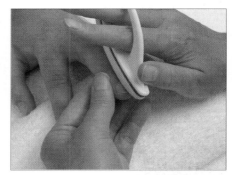

3 A cuticle knife is used to remove the excess eponychium from the cuticle area. Remember to keep the blade dampened to avoid scratches to the nail plate.

4 Remove excess cuticle using cuticle nippers.

5 Buff the nails to improve blood circulation to the nail bed, giving a healthy appearance to the nail. Buff the nails with a buffing paste if a shine is required.

Step by step: Hand and arm massage

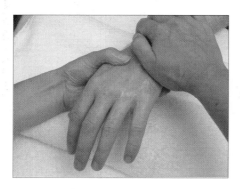

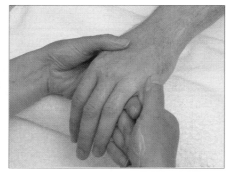

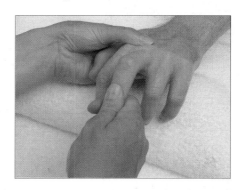

1 Effleurage to the hand and forearm. This movement starts and concludes the hand and arm massage. Use long, sweeping strokes from the hand to the elbow, moving on both the outer and inner sides of the forearm.

2 Finger twists movement. Gently apply a rotary petrissage movement to each finger.

3 Finger resistance movement. Move each finger backwards through its range of movement to exercise the joints.

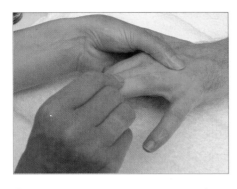

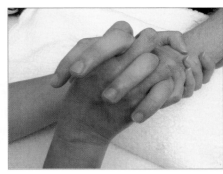

4 Finger rotary movement. Circle each finger in a rotary movement clockwise and then anti-clockwise. Move the little finger to the thumb.

5 Thumbs kneading movement to the palm of the hand.

6 Wrist circulations movement, supporting the joints. Support the wrist with one hand and put your fingers between the client's, gently grasping their hand. Move the wrist through its full range of movement, first clockwise and then anti-clockwise.

COMPLETING THE MANICURE TREATMENT

Outcome 7: Complete the manicure treatment

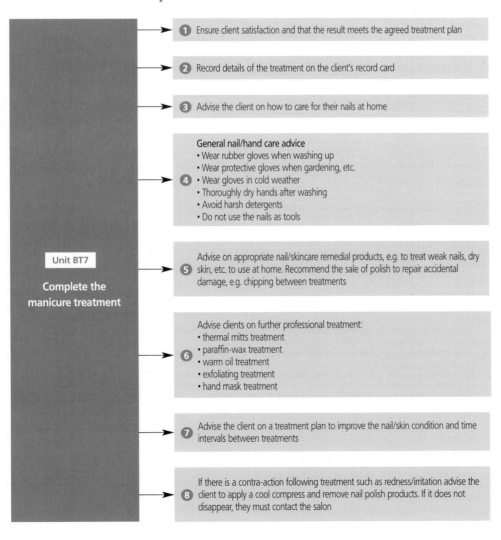

Unit BT7

Complete the manicure treatment

1 Ensure client satisfaction and that the result meets the agreed treatment plan

2 Record details of the treatment on the client's record card

3 Advise the client on how to care for their nails at home

4 General nail/hand care advice
- Wear rubber gloves when washing up
- Wear protective gloves when gardening, etc.
- Wear gloves in cold weather
- Thoroughly dry hands after washing
- Avoid harsh detergents
- Do not use the nails as tools

5 Advise on appropriate nail/skincare remedial products, e.g. to treat weak nails, dry skin, etc. to use at home. Recommend the sale of polish to repair accidental damage, e.g. chipping between treatments

6 Advise clients on further professional treatment:
- thermal mitts treatment
- paraffin-wax treatment
- warm oil treatment
- exfoliating treatment
- hand mask treatment

7 Advise the client on a treatment plan to improve the nail/skin condition and time intervals between treatments

8 If there is a contra-action following treatment such as redness/irritation advise the client to apply a cool compress and remove nail polish products. If it does not disappear, they must contact the salon

The Natural Nail Company/Jessica Nails

A range of retail products

Client with an allergic reaction that has affected the face

Contra-actions

Certain cosmetic ingredients are known to cause allergic reactions in some people.

The client – or the manicurist – may at some time develop an allergy to a manicure product that has been successfully used previously. This could be for a number of reasons, including new medication being taken or illness.

The symptoms of an allergic reaction could be as follows:

- redness of the skin (erythema);
- swelling;
- itching;
- raised blisters.

The symptoms do not necessarily appear on the hands. In the case of nail polish allergy, the symptoms often show up on the face, which the hands are continually touching.

In the case of an allergic reaction:

- Remove the offending product immediately, using water or, in the case of polish, solvent.
- If symptoms persist, seek medical advice.

Always record any allergies on the client's record card, so that the offending product may be avoided in future.

Aftercare and advice

It is important when carrying out a manicure that the client knows how to care for their nails at home. It is your duty as a therapist to ensure that the correct aftercare advice is given. If it isn't, the client may unwittingly undo all the good work you have done during the treatment.

When giving aftercare advice you have a good opportunity to recommend retail products, such as nail treatment polish or hand cream, thereby enhancing retail sales and the salon's profit.

Aftercare advice will differ slightly for each client, according to individual needs, but generally it will be as follows:

- Wear rubber gloves when washing up.
- Wear protective gloves when gardening or doing housework.
- Always wear gloves in cold weather.
- Dry the hands thoroughly after washing, and apply handcream.
- Avoid harsh soaps when washing hands.
- Advise the client on how to file their nails.
- Do not use the fingernails as tools (for instance, to prise lids off tins).
- Advise on appropriate nail/skin-care products to remedy the problems present, i.e dry skin, weak nails.

The Natural Nail Company/Jessica Nails

JESSICA

A range of treatment products

- Advise the client on what other professional treatments you could recommend.
- Advise the client on a treatment plan to improve the nail/skin condition and the time intervals recommended between each treatment.

It is also advisable to tell the client what to do in the event of a contra-action.

ACTIVITY

Designing an aftercare leaflet
Devise an aftercare leaflet for clients, advising a suitable homecare routine.
It is good practice to provide the client with an aftercare leaflet following treatment.

Exercises for the hands

Hand exercises play an important role in the homecare advice given to clients, for the following reasons:

- They keep the joints supple, allowing greater movement.
- Circulation is increased, encouraging healthy nail and skin growth.
- Good circulation helps to prevent cold hands.
- Exercises keep the client interested in their hands, and so more likely to keep regular salon appointments.

Exercise routine

1 Rub the palms together, back and forth, until warm.
2 Make a tight fist with each hand, then slowly stretch out all the fingers as far as possible.
   Repeat step 2 a further 3 times.
3 With the fingers extended, rotate the wrists slowly in large clockwise circles.
   Repeat step 3 a further 3 times.
4 With the fingers extended, rotate the wrists slowly in large anticlockwise circles.
   Repeat step 4 a further 3 times.
5 Play an imaginary piano vigorously with the fingers for ten seconds.
6 With the hands together as if praying, gently widen the fingers as far as possible, then relax.
   Repeat step 6 a further 3 times.

Hand exercises

GLOSSARY OF KEY WORDS

Aftercare advice recommendations given to the client following treatment to continue the benefits of the treatment.

Base coat a nail polish product applied to protect the natural nail and prevent staining from coloured nail polish.

Bevelling a nail filing technique used at the free edge of the nail to ensure it is smooth.

Blue nail nail condition where the nail bed has a blue tinge rather than a healthy pink colour due to poor blood circulation in the area.

Bruised nail nail condition where the nail appears blue/black in colour where bleeding has occurred on the nail bed following injury.

Buffer a manicure tool with a handle made of plastic and a pad with a replaceable cover, used on the nail to give a sheen, increased blood supply to the area and, if used with the gritty cream buffing paste, to help smooth out nail surface irregularities.

Consultation assessment of client's needs using different assessment techniques, including questioning and natural observation.

Contra-action an unwanted reaction occurring during or after treatment application.

Contra-indication a problematic symptom that indicates that the treatment may not proceed.

Cuticle cream or oil a cosmetic preparation used to condition the skin of the cuticle.

Cuticle knife a metal tool used on the nail to remove excess *eponychium* (the extension of the skin of the cuticle at the base of the nail).

Cuticle remover a cosmetic preparation used to soften and loosen the skin cells and cuticle from the nail.

Eczema of the nail inflammation of the skin, causing changes to the nail including ridges, pitting, nail separation and nail thickening.

Effleurage a stroking massage movement, used to begin the massage, as a link manipulation and to complete the massage sequence.

Eggshell nail nail condition where thin, fragile white nails curve under at the free edge.

Emery board a nail file used to shape the free edge of the nail.

Exfoliant a mild abrasive cream applied and massaged over the skin's surface to remove dead skin cells and improve the appearance and texture of the skin.

Hand cream/oil a cosmetic mixture of waxes and oils applied to soften the skin of the hands and cuticles.

Hangnail nail condition where small pieces of epidermal skin protrude between the nail plate and nail wall, accompanying a dry cuticle condition.

Hoof stick a nail tool used to gently push back the softened cuticles.

Leuconychia nail condition where white spots or marks appear on the nail plate.

Longitudinal ridges nail condition where grooves appear in the nail plate, running along the length of the nail from the cuticle to the free edge.

Manicure a treatment to care for and improve the condition and appearance of the hands and nails.

Mask a treatment mask applied to the skin of the hands to treat and improve the condition of the skin. This may include properties to stimulate, rejuvenate and moisturise.

Nail polish a clear or coloured nail product that adds colour/protection to the nail. Cream polish has a matt finish and requires a top coat application. Pearlised polish produces a frosted, shimmery appearance and top coat is not required.

Nail polish drier an aerosol or oil preparation applied following nail polish application to increase the speed at which the polish hardens.

Nail polish remover a solvent used to remove nail polish and grease from the nails prior to applying polish.

Nail polish solvent used to thin nail polish and restore its consistency.

Nail strengthener a nail polish product that strengthens the nail plate, which has a tendency to split.

Onycholysis nail condition where the nail plate separates from the nail bed.

Onychopagy nail condition where a person bites their nails excessively.

Onychorrhexis nail condition where the person has split, flaking nails.

Orange stick a disposable wooden tool used around the cuticle and free edge of the nail and to apply products to the nail.

Paronychia bacterial infection where swelling, redness and pus appears in the cuticle area of the nail wall.

Paraffin wax paraffin wax is heated and applied to the skin of the hands to provide a warming effect. This improves skin functioning, aids the absorption of treatment products and is beneficial to ease the discomfort of arthritic and rheumatic conditions.

Petrissage massage movements, including *kneading*, where the tissues are lifted away from the underlying structures and compressed. Pressure is intermittent, and should be light yet firm.

Psoriasis of the nail an inflammatory condition where there is an increased production of cells in the upper part of the skin. Pitting occurs on the surface of the nail.

Pterygium nail condition where the cuticle is thickened and overgrown.

Ridge-filler a nail product used on ridged nails that improves the nail's appearance and provide a more even surface.

Scissors nail tools used to shorten the length of the nail before filing.

Thermal mitts electrically heated gloves in which the hands are placed following the application of a skin treatment product such as a mask. The heat aids the absorption of the product and improves skin functioning.

Tinea unguium fungal infection of the nails. The nail is yellowish-grey in colour.

Top coat a nail polish product applied over another nail polish to provide additional strength and durability to the finish.

Transverse furrows nail condition where grooves appear on the nail, running from side to side.

Treatment plan after the consultation suitable treatment objectives are established to treat the client's conditions and needs.

Verrucae or wart a viral infection where small epidermal skin growths appear, either raised or flat depending upon their location, and have a rough surface.

Warm oil treatment involves gently heating a small amount of treatment oil and soaking the nails and cuticles in it to nourish the nails and soften the cuticles and surrounding skin.

Assessment of knowledge and understanding

You have now learnt about the different manicure treatments available to improve the condition of the hands, nails and surrounding skin. These skills will enable you to professionally provide manicure treatment.

 To test your level of knowledge, answer the following short questions. These will prepare you for your summative (final) assessment.

Additional anatomy and physiology questions required for this unit are found on pages 146–8.

Anatomy and physiology

1 How many bones form the hand? Name them.

2 Name the bones of the forearm.

3 Name the main arteries of the arm and hand.

4 Name two muscles of the hand.

5 What are the group of muscles called that bend the wrist, drawing it towards the forearm?

Consult with the client

1 Communication is important. Give three examples of good communication techniques.

2 Why should the manicurist consult the client's record card prior to treatment?

3 Why is it important to assess the condition of the client's hands and nails before treatment commences?

4 Why is it important to discuss and agree the treatment service and outcomes with your client at consultation?

5 Name three contra-indications observed at consultation that would prevent treatment being carried out.

Prepare for the treatment

1 Personal appearance is important to make a good impression. Give three examples of good personal appearance relevant to the manicurist and to organisational requirements.

2 How can cross-infection be avoided when performing a manicure treatment? Give examples of three preventative measures.

3 Why is it important that the client is warm and comfortable when having a manicure?

4 Why is good lighting important?

Plan the treatment

1 Why would you choose to include the following hand and nail treatments in your treatment plan?
- paraffin-wax therapy
- hand mask
- warm oil
- thermal mitts
- exfoliators.

2 Why are several treatments often necessary to improve the condition of the nails and skin to their full potential?

3 Why is it important to complete your treatment plan in the allocated time?

4 What is the commercially acceptable time for a manicure?

Improve the appearance of the natural nails

1 How can buffing improve the appearance of the natural nails?

2 How would you recognise each of the following, and what could you recommend to improve the appearance and condition?
- weak nails
- dry nails
- brittle nails
- ridged nails
- dry cuticles
- overgrown cuticles
- dry skin
- hard skin.

Improve the health and appearance of the cuticles and surrounding skin

1 Which manicure tools are used to improve the appearance of the cuticles?

2 Describe how a cuticle knife should be used in order to avoid damage to the surface nail plate and cuticle.

3 If used incorrectly cuticle remover can cause drying of the cuticle. Explain how this could occur.

4 What products used on the cuticles help to prevent them from drying and splitting?

Massage the hand and forearm

1 What are the differences in formulation and treatment benefits for the massage mediums:
- cream
- oil.

2 How would you adapt your hand and arm massage technique when treating a male client?

3 What are the terms used for the different types of massage applied in a manicure?

4 State four benefits of hand and arm massage.

5 What would be the benefit of massaging cream into the hands at home?

Provide nail polishing treatments

1 What is the difference between a base coat and a top coat in terms of purpose and application technique?

2 What is the nail polish application technique for a 'French manicure'?

3 If a client had badly bitten nails, what type and colour of polish would you suggest that they tried?

4 When would the appearance of the client's natural nails be unsuitable for the application of a dark nail polish?

5 Which nail polish product would reduce the appearance of ridges on the nail plate?

6 If a client has their nails polished professionally, what would be the recommended time interval between treatments?

7 Why is it a good idea to retail the nail polish colours used within the treatment?

Complete the treatment

1 What general advice should be given to a client on maintaining the condition and appearance of their nails following a manicure?

2 Why is it important to advise the client to avoid a sawing action when filing the nails?

3 What aftercare advice would you give to a client with very dry hands and cuticles?

4 List three retail products that you could recommend to a manicure client.

5 For each of the clients below, suggest a treatment routine. Detail the treatment plan to include: cause of the condition, aims of the treatment, products used, treatments recommended, relevant retail sales and homecare advice.
   - a hairdresser with very soft, weak, stained nails
   - an engineer with a bruised nail, overgrown cuticles and cracked skin on the fingers
   - a teenager who has badly bitten nails
   - an elderly client with strong, ridged nails and dry skin on the hands.

chapter 10

BT8 Provide pedicure treatment

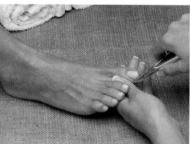

Courtesy Creative Nail Design

Pedicure treatment to improve condition of the feet

Essential anatomy and physiology knowledge requirements for this unit, BT8, are identified on the checklist chart in Chapter 5, page 101.

THE PURPOSE OF A PEDICURE

The word **pedicure** is derived from the Latin word *pedis*, meaning 'foot' and *cura*, meaning 'care'. The treatment is very similar to manicure except that it is carried out on the feet instead of the hands. A pedicure is carried out for many reasons:

- to improve the appearance of the foot;
- to reduce the amount of hard skin;
- to relax tired, aching feet;
- to keep the nails smooth and healthy.

PREPARING FOR THE PEDICURE

Outcome 1: Consult with the client

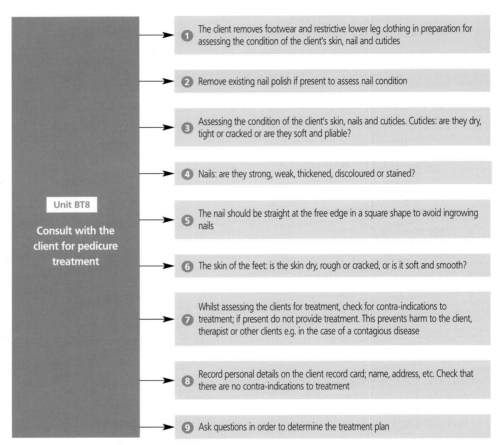

Unit BT8

Consult with the client for pedicure treatment

① The client removes footwear and restrictive lower leg clothing in preparation for assessing the condition of the client's skin, nail and cuticles

② Remove existing nail polish if present to assess nail condition

③ Assessing the condition of the client's skin, nails and cuticles. Cuticles: are they dry, tight or cracked or are they soft and pliable?

④ Nails: are they strong, weak, thickened, discoloured or stained?

⑤ The nail should be straight at the free edge in a square shape to avoid ingrowing nails

⑥ The skin of the feet: is the skin dry, rough or cracked, or is it soft and smooth?

⑦ Whilst assessing the clients for treatment, check for contra-indications to treatment; if present do not provide treatment. This prevents harm to the client, therapist or other clients e.g. in the case of a contagious disease

⑧ Record personal details on the client record card; name, address, etc. Check that there are no contra-indications to treatment

⑨ Ask questions in order to determine the treatment plan

Ellisons

Pedicure equipment

Reception

When a client makes an appointment for a pedicure treatment, the receptionist should advise the client how long the treatment will take. This will include sufficient time for the nail polish to dry before replacing footwear.

Ask the client whether they are currently receiving treatment from a chiropodist for conditions such as verrucas or athlete's foot. These would contra-indicate treatment: the receptionist should advise the client to wait until the condition has cleared.

Allow 45 minutes for a pedicure.

Allow up to $1\frac{1}{2}$ hours for a specialist foot treatment.

BEAUTY WORKS

Date	Therapist name

Client name	Date of birth (identifying client age group)
Address	Postcode

Evening phone number	Day phone number

Name of doctor	Doctor's address and phone number

Related medical history (conditions that may restrict or prohibit treatment application)

Are you taking any medication? (this may affect the sensitivity of the skin to the treatment)

CONTRA-INDICATIONS REQUIRING MEDICAL REFERRAL
(Preventing pedicure treatment application)

☐ bacterial infections (e.g. paronychia)
☐ viral infections (e.g. plantar warts)
☐ fungal infections (e.g. tinea unguium, tinea pedis)
☐ severe toenail separation
☐ severe eczema and psoriasis
☐ severe bruising
☐ diabetes

EQUIPMENT AND MATERIALS

☐ toenail and skin treatment tools
☐ abrasives (e.g. buffing paste)
☐ cuticle softeners
☐ toenail and skin products
☐ toenail conditioners (e.g. cuticle cream)
☐ skin conditioners (e.g. hand cream)
☐ toenail, skin and cuticle corrective treatments (e.g. paraffin wax)
☐ consumables

FEET AND TOENAIL TREATMENTS

☐ heat treatments
☐ skin conditioners
☐ paraffin wax
☐ foot masks
☐ thermal boots
☐ exfoliators

TOENAIL FINISH

☐ light colour
☐ dark colour
☐ French manicure

CONTRA-INDICATIONS WHICH RESTRICT TREATMENT
(Treatment may require adaptation)

☐ mild toenail separation
☐ minor eczema and psoriasis
☐ recent scar tissue
☐ severely damaged toenails
☐ broken bones
☐ minor cuts or abrasions
☐ minor bruising or swelling

COURSE OF TREATMENT

	Date	Date	Date
☐ improvement of skin condition	——	——	——
products used			
☐ improvement of toenail condition	——	——	——
products used			

TOENAIL, CUTICLE AND SKIN CONDITION

toenails	cuticle	skin
☐ normal	☐ dry	☐ dry
☐ brittle	☐ split	☐ hard
☐ dry	☐ overgrown	
☐ weak		
☐ ridged		

MASSAGE MEDIUMS

☐ creams
☐ oils

Therapist signature (for reference)

Client signature (confirmation of details)

TREATMENT ADVICE

 Pedicure – *allow 45 minutes*
Specialised foot/nail treatment – *allow up to 60 minutes*

TREATMENT PLAN

Record relevant details of your treatment and advice provided for future reference.

Ensure the client's records are up to date, accurate and fully completed following treatment. Non-compliance may invalidate insurance.

DURING

Discuss:

- details that may influence the client's toenail condition, such as the client's occupation;
- the products the client is currently using to care for the skin of the feet and toenails;
- the client's satisfaction with these products;
- relevant pedicure procedures (e.g., how to file the toenails correctly).

Note:

- any adverse reaction, if any occur.

AFTER

Record:

- results of treatment;
- any modification to treatment application that has occurred;
- what products have been used in the pedicure treatment;
- the effectiveness of treatment;
- any samples provided (review their success at the next appointment).

Advise on:

- product application in order to gain maximum benefit from product use;
- specialised products following pedicure treatment for homecare use;
- general foot/toenail care and maintenance;
- the recommended time intervals between treatments;
- the importance of a course of treatment to improve toenail/skin conditions.

RETAIL OPPORTUNITIES

Advise on:

- progression of the treatment plan for future appointments;
- products that would be suitable for the client to use at home to care for the skin of the feet and toenails;
- recommendations for further treatments;
- further products or services that the client may or may not have received before.

Note:

- any purchase made by the client.

EVALUATION

Record:

- comments on the client's satisfaction with the treatment;
- if poor results are achieved, the reasons why;
- how you may alter the treatment plan to achieve the required treatment results in the future, if applicable.

HEALTH AND SAFETY

Advise on:

- appropriate action to be taken in the event of an unwanted skin or nail reaction.

Examples of pedicure treatment modification includes:

- depth of massage pressure when applying foot and leg massage and choice of massage movements applied;
- choice of massage medium when client has excessively hairy legs.

Skin and nail disorders of the feet

Contra-indications

When a client attends for a pedicure treatment, the therapist should always look at the client's skin and nails to check that no infection or disease is present which might contra-indicate treatment.

These include bacterial, fungal and viral infections, which are described in more detail in Chapter 1, where contra-indications are illustrated and discussed.

The following disorders contra-indicate pedicure treatment. If you suspect the client has any disorder from the chart below, do not attempt a diagnosis, but refer the client to their GP or a chiropodist.

The role of the chiropodist
A chiropodist is a person who is trained and qualified to treat minor foot complaints.
Refer the treatment of non-cosmetic foot conditions to a chiropodist, e.g. conditions such as excessive hard skin.

Disorder	Appearance
Broken bones 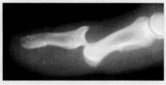	Injury, resulting in a broken bone can often not be seen. Confirm at consultation that there is no known injury in the treatment area
Cuts or abrasions on the feet 	Broken skin Any cut or abrasion could lead to secondary infection and the area should not be treated until healed
Diabetes	If a client has diabetes they are vulnerable to infection as they have slow skin healing. This could be problematic if the skin was accidentally broken during a pedicure treatment Permission must be obtained from the client's GP before treatment can be received
Ingrowing toe nail 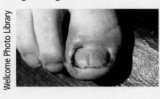	The sides of the nail penetrates the nail wall: redness, inflammation and pus may be present, depending on the severity of the condition The client should be referred to chiropodist for appropriate treatment To prevent ingrowing toe nails clients should be advised to cut the toenails straight across, and not too short

Disorder	Appearance
Paronychia 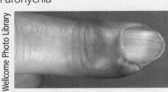 Wellcome Photo Library	Infectious bacterial infection Swelling, redness and pus appears in the cuticle area of the nail wall
Scabies or itch mites  Dr M. H. Beck	An infestation of the skin by an animal parasite. The animal parasite burrows beneath the skin and invades the hair follicles Papules and wavy greyish lines appear, where dirt enters the burrows Secondary bacterial infection may occur as a result of scratching
Severe eczema of the nail 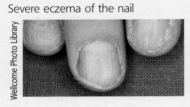 Wellcome Photo Library	Inflammation of the skin occurs. Differing changes to the nail may occur including the appearance of ridges, pitting, onycholysis and nail thickening (hypertrophy)
Severe eczema of the skin  Dr A.L. Wright	Inflammation of the skin caused by contact internally or externally, with an irritant Reddening of the skin occurs with swelling and blistering. The blisters leak tissue fluid which later hardens forming scabs
Severe nail separation (onycholysis) 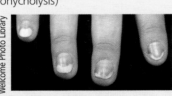 Wellcome Photo Library	Lifting of the nail plate from the nail bed, may be caused by trauma or infection to the nail or surrounding area. Where separation has occurred this appears as a greyish-white area on the nail as the pink undertone of the nail bed does not show
Severe psoriasis of the nail  Wellcome Photo Library	An inflammatory condition where there is an increased production of cells in the upper part of the skin Pitting occurs on the surface of the nail plate Separation (onycholysis) may also occur
Severe psoriasis of the skin 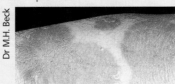 Dr M.H. Beck	Red patches of skin appear, covered in waxy, silvery scales. Bleeding will occur if the area is scratched and the scales are removed The cause is unknown

Disorder	Appearance
Tinea corporis (body ringworm)	Fungal infection of the skin, which may occur on the limbs. Small scaly red patches, which spread outwards and then heal from the centre, leaving a ring
Tinea pedis (athletes' foot)	Fungal infection of the foot occurring in the webs of the skin between the toes. Small blisters form, which later burst. The skin in the area can become dry, with a scaly appearance
Tinea unguium	Fungal infection of the toenails. The nail plate is yellowish-grey. Eventually the nail plate becomes brittle and separates from the nail bed
Verrucae or warts on the feet	A viral infection. Small epidermal skin growths. Warts occurring on the sole of the foot grow inwards, due to the pressure of body weight. Warts vary in size, shape, texture and colour. Usually they have a rough surface and are raised. Plantar wart – found on the sole of the foot

Below is a list of common disorders that may be seen on the feet. Not all of these contra-indicate treatment.

Disorder	Cause	Appearance	Salon treatment	Homecare advice
Blue nail	Poor blood circulation in the area. Heart disease	The nail bed does not appear a healthy pink colour but has a blue tinge	Permission to treat to be received from the client's GP. Regular pedicure including foot treatment to improve circulation	General pedicure advice. Foot exercises and massage to improve circulation
Bunions	Long-term wear of ill-fitting shoes, especially those with high heels or pointed toe areas. A weakness in the arches of the feet	The large joint at the base of the big toe protrudes, forcing the big toe inwards towards the other toes	None – refer the client to a chiropodist if the bunion is painful; gentle massage may help to ease any pain or discomfort	Try to keep pressure off the affected area

Disorder	Cause	Appearance	Salon treatment	Homecare advice
Calluses Dr A.L. Wright	Incorrect footwear	Thick, yellowish, hardened patches of skin, usually found on prominent areas of the foot such as the heel and the ball of toe: may be painful	Use a rasp or pumice stone gently to remove any build-up of hard skin: painful calluses should be treated by a chiropodist	Ensure that shoes fit correctly Avoid standing for long periods Alternate style of footwear regularly Keep the skin of the foot moisturised with a specialised skin conditioner for the feet Use a pumice stone regularly to remove excess
Chilblains	Poor blood supply to the hands and feet, aggravated in cold weather	Fingers and toes may be red, blue or purple in colour; the client may complain of painful or itchy areas	Regular manicures or pedicures, with special attention paid to massage which will help to improve the circulation	Keep affected areas warm and dry Avoid tight footwear, which might restrict the circulation If the condition is severe, seek medical advice
Corns Dr A.L. Wright	Incorrect footwear (corns are often found on toes which have been squeezed together by tight shoes)	Similar to calluses except that the affected area is smaller and more compact; corns often look white, and may be extremely painful	Small corns may be treated in the same way as a callus, but if the client has large or painful corns she should be treated by a chiropodist	Ensure that shoes fit correctly Avoid standing for long periods Alternate style of footwear regularly
Pitting Wellcome Photo Library	Eczema Psoriasis	Pitting, resembling small, irregular pin pricks, appear on the nail plate	Refer the client to their GP for permission to treat if required Regular pedicure with gentle buffing	General pedicure advice Ridge-filling base coat polish

Consultation

Before carrying out a pedicure treatment, it is necessary to assess the condition of the client's skin, nails and cuticles. This is done in order that the most appropriate equipment and products may be chosen. Also, by correctly assessing and analysing the client's foot condition and writing this on their record card, you will be able to see over a period of time how the condition is progressing.

The parts to assess are these:

- *The cuticles* Are they dry, tight, cracked or overgrown, or are they soft and pliable?

- *The nails* Are they strong or weak, thickened, discoloured or stained? Sometimes this may indicate a nail disorder. The nails of the foot should be filed straight across into a square shape. Shaping the nails at the corners can cause ingrowing toenails.
- *The skin* Is the skin dry, rough or cracked, or is it soft and smooth? Is the colour even? Also check the skin between the toes.

Outcome 2: Prepare for the treatment

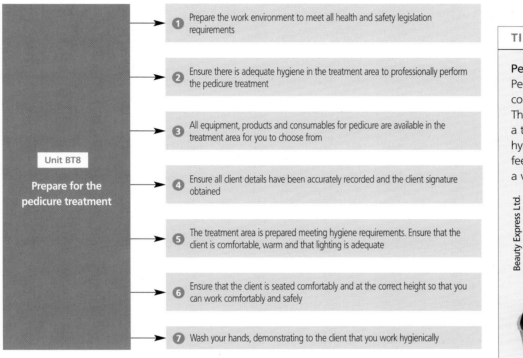

Unit BT8

Prepare for the pedicure treatment

1. Prepare the work environment to meet all health and safety legislation requirements

2. Ensure there is adequate hygiene in the treatment area to professionally perform the pedicure treatment

3. All equipment, products and consumables for pedicure are available in the treatment area for you to choose from

4. Ensure all client details have been accurately recorded and the client signature obtained

5. The treatment area is prepared meeting hygiene requirements. Ensure that the client is comfortable, warm and that lighting is adequate

6. Ensure that the client is seated comfortably and at the correct height so that you can work comfortably and safely

7. Wash your hands, demonstrating to the client that you work hygienically

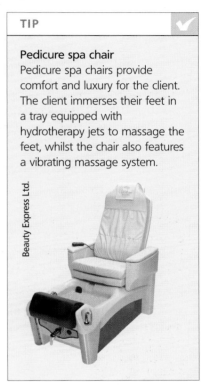

TIP ✔

Pedicure spa chair
Pedicure spa chairs provide comfort and luxury for the client. The client immerses their feet in a tray equipped with hydrotherapy jets to massage the feet, whilst the chair also features a vibrating massage system.

Beauty Express Ltd.

Equipment and materials

EQUIPMENT LIST

Dry cottonwool to remove nail polish and excess nail preparations

Nail polish remover to remove nail polish and excess nail care and skin-care preparations

Scissors or toenail clippers to shorten nail length

Emery boards to shorten and shape the nail free edge

Cuticle oil used to condition the skin of the cuticle; especially beneficial for dry cuticles

Cuticle remover used to soften the skin cells and the cuticle before treatment

Cuticle nippers to remove excess cuticle and dead, torn skin surrounding the nail

EQUIPMENT LIST

Hoof stick or cuticle pusher to gently push back the softened cuticles

Foot rasp or exfoliating scrub to remove excess dead skin from the foot

Massage lotion or oil to massage the skin of the foot and lower leg

Base coat provides an even surface to improve nail polish application and prevent skin staining
Coloured nail polish a selection for the client to choose from
Top coat to provide shine to nail polish. Adds strength and reduces peeling and chipping and increases durability of the polish

Tissues to protect client's clothing in the area, etc

YOU WILL ALSO NEED:

Pedicure bowl (1) to soak and cleanse the foot; or foot spa, to soak, cleanse, revitalise and refresh the skin by stimulation of the blood and circulation

Small towels (5) to protect and dry the client's skin

Small bowls (3) for storage

Disinfecting fluid solution

Antiseptic to cleanse and sanitise the clean skin. Specialised hygiene sprays are available for this purpose

Cuticle knife to remove excess eponychium from the nail plate

Client's record card to record the client's personal details and products used

Nail polish drier an aerosol preparation applied to speed the drying process of nail polish

Toe separators used to keep the toes separated during nail polish application. Alternatively, disposable items such as cottonwool or tissues may be used for this purpose, as they are more hygienic

Disposable footwear optional: enabling the client to move without smudging the nail polish application

Disposable footwear

Beauty Express Ltd.

TIP

Foot spa
Foot spas help to relax the feet by a combination of massage provided by an integral vibration feature, aeration of the water, creating a bubbling effect, and heating of the water.

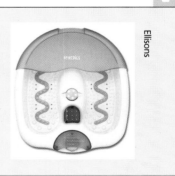

Ellisons

Ensure that the client is warm and comfortable when preparing for the pedicure. Client privacy and modesty should also be considered. Not all clients would be happy to be on view while receiving the treatment. Ensure that lighting is efficient to avoid eye strain and to enable the treatment to be performed competently.

Products used in pedicure treatments

Product	Ingredients	Use
Nail polish remover	Acetone or ethyl acetate – solvent Perfume Colour Oil – emollient to reduce the drying effect of solvent	To remove nail polish To remove grease from the nail plate prior to polishing
Foot lotion/oil	Vegetable oils (e.g. almond oil) Perfume Emulsifying agents (e.g. beeswax or gum tragacanth) Emollients (e.g. glycerine or lanolin) Preservatives	To soften the skin and cuticles To provide slip during foot massage
Nail bleach	Citric acid or hydrogen peroxide – bleaches the nail Glycerine – emollient Water	To whiten stained nails and the surrounding skin
Nail polish	Formaldehyde – film-forming plastic resin, improving adherence and flexibility Solvent – to create a suitable consistency to apply and dries at a controlled rate Colour pigments – creates nail polish colour Resin – improves adhesion of polish to nail plate and flexibility Toluene – solvent that dissolves ingredients in nail polish Nitrocellulose – film forming plastic, holds colour Plasticisers – to provide flexibility after the polish has dried, reducing chipping Pearlised particles – creates a pearlised effect	To colour nail plates To provide some protection
Cuticle cream	Emollients (e.g. lanolin or glycerine) Perfume Colour	To soften the cuticles
Cuticle oil	Oils such as lanolin – emollient	To condition the nail and surrounding skin
Nail strengthener	Formaldehyde – film-forming plastic	To strengthen weak nails
Cuticle remover	Potassium hydroxide – a caustic alkali Glycerine – a humectant added to reduce the drying effect on the nail plate	To soften the skin of the cuticles
Buffing paste	Perfume Colour Abrasive particles (e.g. pumice, talc or silica) – to remove surface cells	To shine the nail plate (used with a buffer)
Nail polish drier	Mineral oil – assists drying Oleric acid or silicone – lubricant	Increases the speed at which the polish hardens
Nail polish solvent	Ethyl acetate – thins nail polish consistency Toluene – solvent that dissolves nail polish	Thins nail polish that has thickened
Exfoliating scrub	Abrasive ingredients such as pumice, sea salt, detergent, water and water-soluble ingredients, added moisturisers, refreshing agents, e.g. peppermint oil	To remove dead skin cells, cleanse the skin, condition, soften and refresh the skin, improving blood circulation in the area

Preparing the working area

All metal instruments should be sterilised in the autoclave prior to use. Non-metal instruments should be disinfected by immersing them in a suitable disinfecting fluid. Prepare the equipment neatly on a trolley so that everything you need is to hand and the client need not be disturbed during treatment.

Place a towel on the floor between you and the client. The foot bowl or foot spa containing warm, soapy water should be placed on this towel.

Towels should be placed on your lap: one is for protection, the other is for drying the client's feet. Keep the other towels close by for wrapping the client's feet.

When cutting the client's nails and removing hard skin, disposable tissue should be placed on your lap and then removed before continuing treatment.

Preparing the client

Ensure that the client has a comfortable chair at the correct height, so that you can work comfortably and the client can enjoy the treatment without strain to the muscles and joints of the leg.

Before treatment begins, ask the client to remove their tights or socks, and any clothing that might restrict their lower leg movement, such as jeans or trousers. Cover their upper legs with a clean towel or provide a gown. This will help them to be more comfortable and allow you to work without restriction.

The Natural Nail Company/Jessica Nails

Client receiving a pedicure

Outcome 3: Plan the treatment

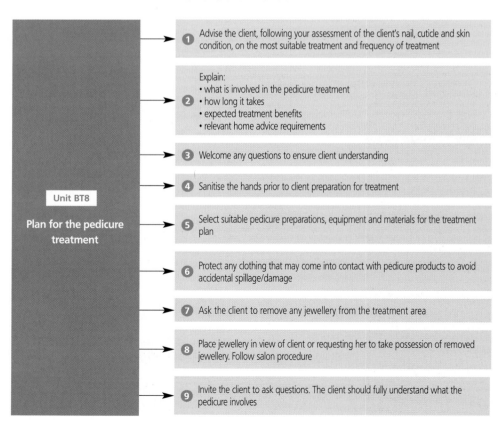

Unit BT8

Plan for the pedicure treatment

1. Advise the client, following your assessment of the client's nail, cuticle and skin condition, on the most suitable treatment and frequency of treatment

2. Explain:
   • what is involved in the pedicure treatment
   • how long it takes
   • expected treatment benefits
   • relevant home advice requirements

3. Welcome any questions to ensure client understanding

4. Sanitise the hands prior to client preparation for treatment

5. Select suitable pedicure preparations, equipment and materials for the treatment plan

6. Protect any clothing that may come into contact with pedicure products to avoid accidental spillage/damage

7. Ask the client to remove any jewellery from the treatment area

8. Place jewellery in view of client or requesting her to take possession of removed jewellery. Follow salon procedure

9. Invite the client to ask questions. The client should fully understand what the pedicure involves

Treatment plan

After analysing the client's nails and adjacent skin, a treatment plan should be considered. In order to correct any problems the client should attend the salon weekly. They should also be advised of the appropriate treatment preparations to use at home, so as to support the salon treatment.

- **Revitalising foot spa agents** These may be in tablet form or as a foaming soak. They are dissolved in warm water, in which the feet are then immersed.
- **Exfoliator** This is used following immersion of the feet in the foot spa. It removes surface dead skin cells, preventing the formation of callus tissue.
- **Massage lotion** This is a massage preparation which includes refreshing essential oils such as peppermint. It is recommended for the relief of tired, aching feet.
- **Foot mask** A mask may be applied to cool and to refresh the feet. Booties may be worn while the mask penetrates the epidermis.
- **Foot gel or spray** This may be applied to create an immediate cooling effect.

Whilst assessing the client's feet for treatment, you should also be looking for any contra-indications to treatment.

PROVIDING PEDICURE TREATMENTS

Outcome 4: Improve the appearance of the natural nails and cuticles

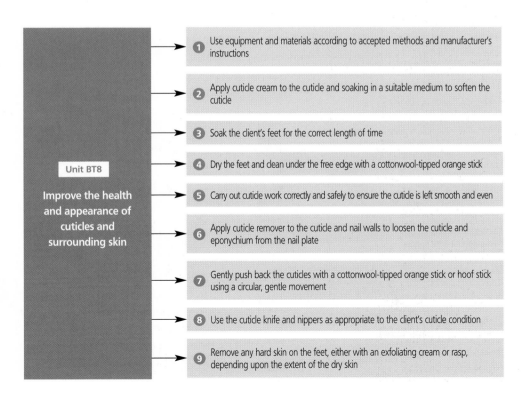

Unit BT8

Improve the health and appearance of cuticles and surrounding skin

1. Use equipment and materials according to accepted methods and manufacturer's instructions

2. Apply cuticle cream to the cuticle and soaking in a suitable medium to soften the cuticle

3. Soak the client's feet for the correct length of time

4. Dry the feet and clean under the free edge with a cottonwool-tipped orange stick

5. Carry out cuticle work correctly and safely to ensure the cuticle is left smooth and even

6. Apply cuticle remover to the cuticle and nail walls to loosen the cuticle and eponychium from the nail plate

7. Gently push back the cuticles with a cottonwool-tipped orange stick or hoof stick using a circular, gentle movement

8. Use the cuticle knife and nippers as appropriate to the client's cuticle condition

9. Remove any hard skin on the feet, either with an exfoliating cream or rasp, depending upon the extent of the dry skin

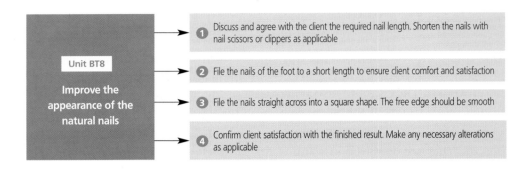

Unit BT8

Improve the appearance of the natural nails

1. Discuss and agree with the client the required nail length. Shorten the nails with nail scissors or clippers as applicable

2. File the nails of the foot to a short length to ensure client comfort and satisfaction

3. File the nails straight across into a square shape. The free edge should be smooth

4. Confirm client satisfaction with the finished result. Make any necessary alterations as applicable

Step by step: Pedicure procedure

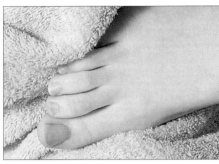

1 Wash your hands.

2 Wipe both feet including between the toes with cottonwool soaked in antiseptic or a specialised hygiene spray for the feet. Use separate pieces of cottonwool for each foot (shown).

3 Soak both feet in warm water to which a mild antiseptic liquid soap has been added.

4 Take out the left foot and towel-dry it.

5 Remove any existing nail polish, and check again for contra-indications below the nail plate. (If a nail contra-indication is present treatment must not continue. Tactfully explain why and give appropriate referral advice.)

6 Cut the toenails straight across, using toenail clippers or scissors.

7 File the nails smooth with the coarse side of the emery board.

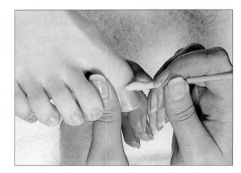

8 Apply cuticle massage cream.

9 Place the foot back in the water.

10 Remove the right foot and repeat procedures 4–9.

11 Dry the right foot and apply cuticle remover.

12 Push back the cuticles with a cottonwool-tipped orange stick, hoof stick or cuticle pusher.

13 Clean under the free edge with a separate tipped orange stick.

14 Use the cuticle knife and nippers where indicated.

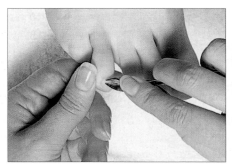

15 Using cuticle nippers.

16 Wipe off the remaining cuticle remover with cottonwool, and file the nails again if necessary. Apply cuticle oil.

17 Remove any hard skin. This may be done with exfoliating cream or a rasp, depending on the severity of the condition.

18 Wrap the foot in a dry towel and place it on the floor.

19 Repeat procedures **11–18** for the left foot.

20 Remove the foot bowl from the working area.

21 Perform a foot and lower leg massage.

22 Remove any grease from the nail plates with nail polish remover on cottonwool.

23 Place tissue between the toes to separate them and facilitate polish application.

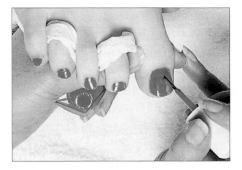

24 Apply the polish: base coat (once), polish (twice) and top coat (once) where indicated. If a pearlised polish is used a top coat is not required and a third coat of polish may be applied.

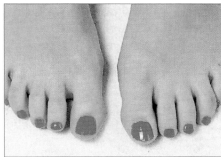

25 The completed pedicure

Cuticle work

Cuticle work is carried out to keep the cuticle area attractive and also to prevent cuticles from adhering to the nail plate, which could lead to splitting of the cuticle as the nail grows forward, and subsequently to infection of the area.

The work is carried out after soaking the feet in warm soapy water. This step loosens dirty particles from the free edge and softens the skin in the cuticle area.

How to provide cuticle work

1 Take the feet from the soapy water and pat them dry with a soft towel.

2 Apply cuticle remover to the cuticle and nail walls, using the applicator brush. (**Cuticle remover** is a slightly caustic solution that helps soften and loosen the cuticles and the eponychium from the nail plate.)

3 Gently push back the cuticle with a cottonwool-tipped orange stick. This is tipped with cottonwool to avoid splinters from the wood, and also so that the cottonwool may be replaced if necessary.) Use a gentle, circular motion to push back the cuticle, holding the orange stick like a pen.

Use a fresh orange stick for each part of the pedicure treatment, and when working on different hands, to prevent cross-infection.

4 Hold the cuticle knife at 45° to the nail plate and stroke it in one direction only, gently loosening any eponychium that has adhered to the nail plate: do not scratch it backwards and forwards. The cuticle knife should have a fine-ground flat blade which can be resharpened when necessary. Dampen it regularly in the pedicure bowl to prevent scratches occurring on the nail plate.

5 Hold the nippers comfortably in the palm of the hand, with the thumb resting just above the blades – this gives firm control over what can be a dangerous instrument. Use the cuticle nippers to remove any loose or torn pieces of cuticle, and to trim excess dead cuticle. *Do not cut into live cuticle*: if you do, it will bleed profusely and will be very uncomfortable for the client. Not every client will require the use of cuticle nippers – use them only when needed. (Cuticle nippers should have finely ground cutting blades to give a clean cut and to avoid tearing the cuticle.)

Pushing back the cuticles

Using a cuticle knife

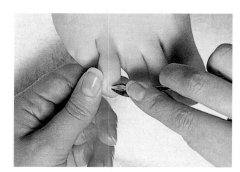

Using cuticle nippers

Cutting toenails

Cutting and filing toenails

Toenails should be cut straight across, using nail clippers or strong sharp scissors, then filed smooth using the coarse side of the emery board.

Removing hard skin

Hard skin develops on the feet as a form of protection, either from friction from footwear or from standing for long periods of time.

It is therefore not advisable to remove *all* the hard skin from an area, as this would remove the protective pad. Hard skin should be removed only to improve the appearance of the feet. Hard-skin build-up that causes pain or discomfort should be referred to a chiropodist for treatment.

Excess hard skin may be removed from the feet in a number of ways, including exfoliators, pumice stones, callus files, chiropody sponges, and corn planes. Exfoliators should be used with a deep circular massage movement: they are ideal when only a very small build-up of hard skin is present. Files, pumice stones and the rest should be used with a swift stroking movement in one direction only (similar to buffing). Sawing back and forth would lead to friction, and discomfort for the client.

Always finish off a hard-skin removal procedure with the application of a specialised foot moisturiser or lotion, to soften the newly exposed skin.

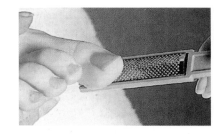

Removing hard skin with a rasp

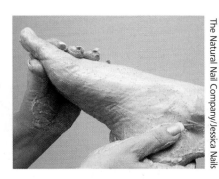

Courtesy Creative Nail Design

Retail exfoliation and foot masks

FOOT TREATMENTS

In addition to the pedicure, further treatments may be added as appropriate. Here are some examples:

- **Exfoliating treatment** is carried out prior to massage or as part of the massage routine. An abrasive massage cream is massaged over the skin of the foot in circular movements, concentrating over the ball and heel of the foot. Exfoliation has the following effects: it removes dead skin, increases blood circulation and improves the condition and appearance of the skin and the absorption of further treatment products.

- **Foot treatment mask** is applied according to the client's treatment requirements. The mask is applied to the skin and the feet can then be wrapped in warm thermal booties to aid the absorption of the mask. The mask removes dead skin cells, improves blood circulation and improves the condition of the skin of the feet.

- **Paraffin wax treatment** – this wax is heated in a special bath to a temperature of 50–55°C. It is then applied to the feet with a brush and left to set for 10–15 minutes. The heating effect stimulates the blood circulation, eases the discomfort of arthritic and rheumatic conditions, and softens the skin, improving the appearance and condition of dry skin. After use the wax is disposed of.

- **Thermal booties** are electrically heated booties. They are used to stimulate, rejuvenate and moisturise the skin of the feet. The feet are prepared with the application of a foot treatment mask, protected in a film wrap and placed inside warm booties for ten minutes to enable the mask to penetrate the skin of the epidermis.

The Natural Nail Company/Jessica Nails

Exfoliating treatment

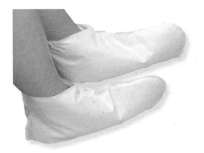

Courtesy Creative Nail Design

Foot treatment mask

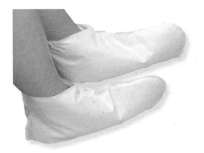

Ellisons

Thermal booties

TIP	✔

Paraffin wax
Heat the wax at least half an hour before the client arrives to ensure it has melted properly. Paraffin wax may have essential oils added to enhance the therapeutic effects.

Step by step: Specialist foot and leg treatment

Specialist treatments should be offered to your client when there is a specific need or if they feel they would like to benefit from such a treatment. Specialist treatment training in these advanced techniques is usually offered by major product companies.

The model for this specialist foot and leg treatment is a client who regularly visits the gym and wished to benefit from a spa-therapy revitalising treatment following a workout.

The following foot and leg treatment will:

- stimulate the blood circulation;
- aid with the removal of toxins and waste products;
- have a skin-cleansing action;
- remove dead skin cells (desquamation);
- improve the moisture content of the skin;
- relax tense/stiff muscles in the foot and leg.

Your treatments should be adapted the meet the treatment objectives for the client. Allow 30 minutes for the specialist foot and leg treatment below.

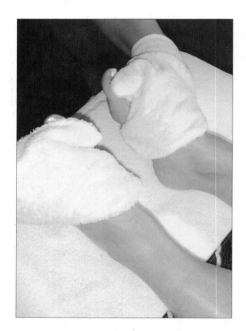 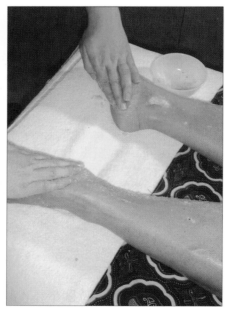 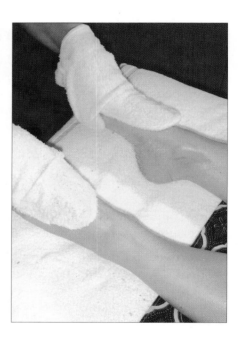

1 The skin of the feet and legs is cleansed using warm towelling mitts infused with lime oil for its therapeutic refreshing and energising properties.

2 The feet and legs are exfoliated to remove all dead skin cells and brighten the skin.

A sea salt-based preparation with emollient, skin softening ingredients is applied to each foot and leg.

3 Towelling mitts are used to remove the exfoliating treatment. These have been steamed and are warm when used.

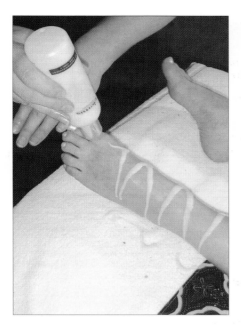

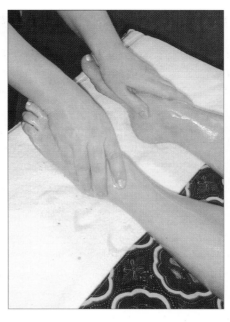

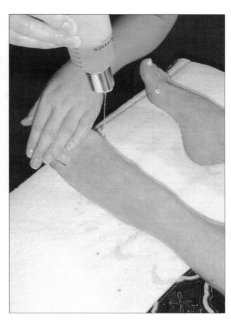

4 A skin-nourishing milk lotion is applied to each foot and leg using a 'drizzling' technique. The milk is particularly beneficial for dry skin.

5 Massage movements are applied using effleurage and petrissage manipulations to introduce the massage medium into the skin.

6 A further skin-treatment product oil is applied and massaged into the skin. This will act as a treatment mask for the skin to soften and condition.

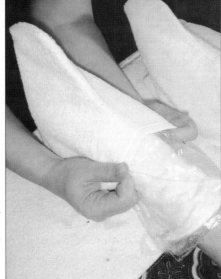

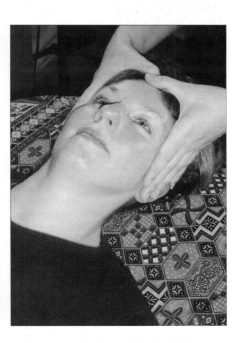

7 The feet are then placed in steamed towels, encased in a plastic bag and dry towelling foot mitten for 10–15 minutes.

8 When the treatment mask is applied, a scalp massage is applied to induce client relaxation.

FOOT MASSAGE

Outcome 5: Massage the foot and lower leg

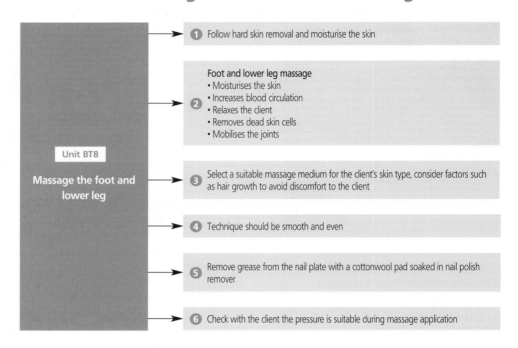

Unit BT8

Massage the foot and lower leg

1. Follow hard skin removal and moisturise the skin

2. **Foot and lower leg massage**
   • Moisturises the skin
   • Increases blood circulation
   • Relaxes the client
   • Removes dead skin cells
   • Mobilises the joints

3. Select a suitable massage medium for the client's skin type, consider factors such as hair growth to avoid discomfort to the client

4. Technique should be smooth and even

5. Remove grease from the nail plate with a cottonwool pad soaked in nail polish remover

6. Check with the client the pressure is suitable during massage application

As with a manicure massage, the pedicure massage is carried out near the end of the treatment, prior to nail polishing. The pedicure massage includes the foot and the lower leg, and offers the following benefits to the client as follows:

● moisturises the skin with the massage medium, cream, lotion or oil;

● increases blood circulation to the lower leg and foot;

● helps maintain joint mobility;

● eases discomfort from arthritis or rheumatism;

● relaxes the client;

● muscle tone is improved as the muscles receive an improved supply of oxygenated blood, essential for cell growth;

● lymphatic circulation is improved aiding the removal of waste products from the body

● to help remove any dead skin cells (desquamation).

The massage incorporates classic massage movements, each with different effects:

● **Effleurage** – a stroking movement, used to begin the massage as a link manipulation, and to complete the massage sequence.

● **Petrissage** – movements, including *kneading*, where the tissues are lifted away from the underlying structures and compressed. Pressure is intermittent, and should be light yet firm.

- **Tapotement**, also known as *percussion*, may be included – movements are performed in a brisk, stimulating manner to increase blood supply and improve tone of the skin and muscles. Movements include clapping and tapping.

The therapist can adapt the massage application according to the needs of the client. Either the *speed of application* or *depth of pressure* can be altered.

Step by step: Foot massage

1 **Effleurage from the foot to the knee** Use long sweeping strokes from the toes to the knee, moving on both the back and the front of the leg.

   Repeat step 1 a further 5 times.

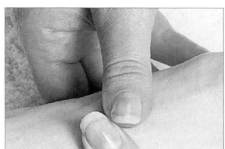

2 **Thumb frictions to the dorsal aspect of the foot** Use the thumbs, one in front of the other, and move backwards and forwards in a gentle sawing action. Move from the toes to the ankle, then slide back down to the toes.

   Repeat step 2 a further 2 times.

3 **Thumb frictions to the plantar aspect of the foot** Use the same movement as in step 2, but on the sole of the foot, moving from the toes to the heel.

   Repeat step 3 a further 2 times.

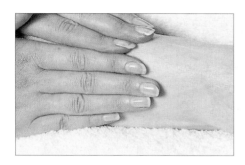

4 **Toe circling** Supporting the base of the toes with one hand, hold the toes individually with the other and move them through their full range of movement, first clockwise and then anticlockwise.

   Repeat step 4 a further 2 times.

5 **Palm kneading to the plantar surface of the foot** Place the heel of the hand into the arch of the foot and massage with deep circular movements.

   Repeat step 5 a further 5 times.

6 **Finger kneading around the ankle (malleolus) bone** Using two fingers of each hand, use small circular movements to knead around the ankle bone. Massage both sides of the ankle bone at the same time.

   Repeat step 6 a further 2 times.

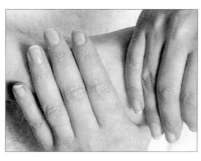 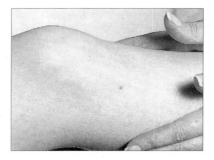

7 Deep stroking to the top and bottom of the foot simultaneously Cup the foot with the whole of the hand, so that the thumb is on the sole of the foot and the fingers on top of the foot. Firmly stroke the foot from toe to ankle, using alternate hands.
Repeat step 7 a further 5 times.

8 Effleurage from the foot to the knee Use the same movement as in step 1.
Repeat step 8 a further 5 times.

Outcome 6: Provide nail polish treatment

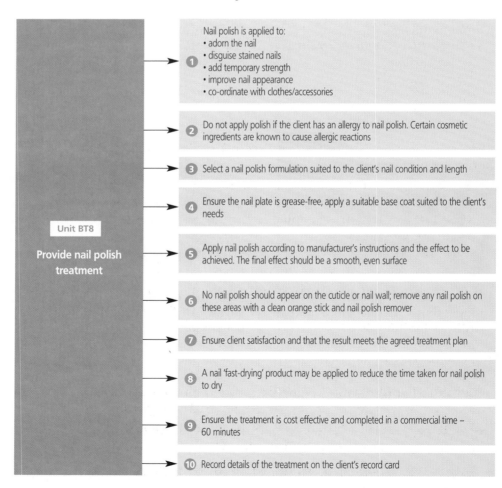

Unit BT8

Provide nail polish treatment

1 Nail polish is applied to:
• adorn the nail
• disguise stained nails
• add temporary strength
• improve nail appearance
• co-ordinate with clothes/accessories

2 Do not apply polish if the client has an allergy to nail polish. Certain cosmetic ingredients are known to cause allergic reactions

3 Select a nail polish formulation suited to the client's nail condition and length

4 Ensure the nail plate is grease-free, apply a suitable base coat suited to the client's needs

5 Apply nail polish according to manufacturer's instructions and the effect to be achieved. The final effect should be a smooth, even surface

6 No nail polish should appear on the cuticle or nail wall; remove any nail polish on these areas with a clean orange stick and nail polish remover

7 Ensure client satisfaction and that the result meets the agreed treatment plan

8 A nail 'fast-drying' product may be applied to reduce the time taken for nail polish to dry

9 Ensure the treatment is cost effective and completed in a commercial time – 60 minutes

10 Record details of the treatment on the client's record card

Nail polish application

Nail polish is applied to coat the nail plate for a numbers of reasons:

- to adorn the nail;
- to disguise stained toenails;
- to improve the condition and appearance of the nail;
- to co-ordinate with clothes;
- to create designs and effects called 'nail art'.

Types of polish

- **Cream** – this has a matt finish, and requires a top coat application to give a sheen.
- **Pearlised** – this has a frosted, shimmery appearance by the addition of natural fish scales or synthetic ingredients such as bismuth oxychloride.
- **Base coat** – this protects the nail from staining by a strong coloured nail polish; it also gives a good grip to polish, and smoothes out minor surface irregularities.
- **Top coat** – this gives a sheen to cream polish, and adds longer wear as it helps to prevent chipping.

Contra-indication to nail polish

- if there are diseases and disorders of the nail plate and surrounding skin;
- if the client is allergic to nail polish.

How to apply nail polish

Before nail polish is applied any jewellery worn in the area may replaced to avoid smudging afterwards.

1 Separate the toes using a hygienic method as discussed in pedicure procedure page 358.
2 After ensuring that the nail plate is free from oil, start with the big toe. Apply three to four brush strokes down the length of the nail from the cuticle to the free edge, beginning in the centre, then down either side close to the nail wall.

   Take care to avoid touching the cuticle or nail wall. If flooding occurs, remove the polish immediately with an orange stick and nail polish remover.
3 Apply one base coat, two coats of coloured polish and one top coat. Top coat is required only after using cream polish; pearl polish does not need a top coat but a third coat of polish may be applied.

Applying polish to the toenails

Styles of application

- **Traditional application** – This style is one of the most commonly requested by clients: the entire plate is covered with polish.
- **French application** – This style involves painting the nail plate of the nail be pink or pale beige, and the free edge white.

See page 338 for information about nail polish, including why it may chip or peel, and how to store.

Contra-actions

The client – or the pedicurist – may at some time develop an allergy to a pedicure product that has been successfully used previously. This could be for a number of reasons, including new medication being taken or illness.

The symptoms of an allergic reaction could be as follows:

- redness of the skin;
- swelling;
- itching;
- raised blisters.

The symptoms do not necessarily appear on the feet. In the case of nail polish allergy, the symptoms often show up on the face.

In the case of an allergic reaction:

- Remove the offending product immediately, using water or, in the case of polish, solvent.
- If symptoms persist, seek medical advice.

Always record any allergies on the client's record card, so that the offending product may be avoided in future.

COMPLETING THE PEDICURE TREATMENT

Outcome 7: Complete the treatment

Ready for the holidays

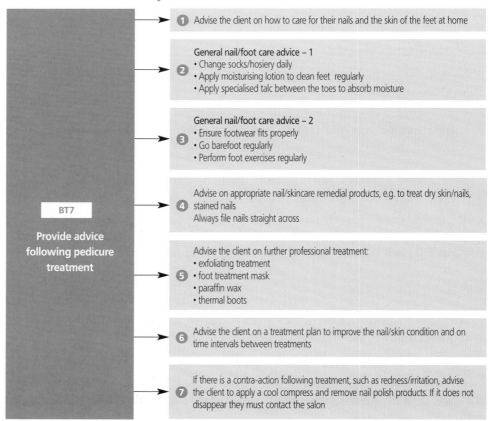

BT7

Provide advice following pedicure treatment

1 Advise the client on how to care for their nails and the skin of the feet at home

2 General nail/foot care advice – 1
• Change socks/hosiery daily
• Apply moisturising lotion to clean feet regularly
• Apply specialised talc between the toes to absorb moisture

3 General nail/foot care advice – 2
• Ensure footwear fits properly
• Go barefoot regularly
• Perform foot exercises regularly

4 Advise on appropriate nail/skincare remedial products, e.g. to treat dry skin/nails, stained nails
Always file nails straight across

5 Advise the client on further professional treatment:
• exfoliating treatment
• foot treatment mask
• paraffin wax
• thermal boots

6 Advise the client on a treatment plan to improve the nail/skin condition and on time intervals between treatments

7 If there is a contra-action following treatment, such as redness/irritation, advise the client to apply a cool compress and remove nail polish products. If it does not disappear they must contact the salon

The Natural Nail Company/Jessica Nails

Aftercare and advice

Offering aftercare advice at the end of a pedicure treatment will help the client to look after their feet between salon visits, and is also an ideal opportunity to recommend retail products.

Aftercare advice will differ slightly for each client, but it will basically be as follows:

- Change socks or tights daily.
- Apply moisturising lotion daily to the feet after bathing.
- Ensure that the feet are thoroughly dry after washing, especially between the toes.
- Apply talc or a special foot powder between the toes to help absorb moisture.
- Foot sprays containing peppermint or citrus oil to cleanse and refresh are useful to refresh the feet during the day.
- Go barefoot wherever it is safe and practical to do so.
- Ensure that footwear fits properly. Foot problems such as bunions can be aggravated by incorrect footwear.
- Avoid wearing high heels for long periods of time. They can cause postural problems and increase hard skin callus formation.
- Advise on appropriate nail/skin-care products to remedy the problems present, e.g. dry skin, nails, stained nails.
- Advise the client of any other professional treatments you could recommend.
- Advise the client on a treatment plan to improve the nail/skin condition and the time intervals recommended between each treatment.
- Always file the nails straight across.
- If any pain is felt in the feet, visit a chiropodist.

It is also advisable to advise the client what to do in the event of a contra-action.

Retail products

Exercises for the feet and ankles

As part of the homecare advice given to a pedicure client, **foot exercises** should be mentioned – these can play a very important role in keeping the client's feet healthy. They help:

- to stimulate circulation;
- to keep joints mobilised, allowing a greater range of movement in the toes and ankles;
- to keep muscles strong, reducing the chance of fallen arches (flat feet).

Here are some examples of exercises:

1 Sitting on a chair with the feet flat on the floor, raise the toes upwards and then relax.
2 Stand on tiptoes, and relax down again.
3 Sitting on a chair with the feet flat on the floor, lift one leg slightly and draw a circle with the toes so that the ankle moves through its full range of movement.

Dorsiflexion

Plantar flexion

Inversion

Eversion

4 **Dorsiflexion**: bending the foot backwards towards the body.

5 **Plantar flexion**: pointing the foot down towards the ground.

6 **Inversion**: moving the foot inwards towards the middle of the body.

7 **Eversion**: moving the foot out towards the side of the body.

GLOSSARY OF KEY WORDS

Aftercare advice recommendations given to the client following treatment to continue the benefits of the treatment.

Base coat a nail polish product applied to protect the natural nail and prevent staining from coloured nail polish.

Bevelling a nail filing technique used at the free edge of the nail to ensure it is smooth.

Blue nail nail condition where the nail bed has a blue tinge rather than a healthy pink colour due to poor blood circulation in the area.

Bruised nail nail condition where the nail appears blue/black in colour where bleeding has occurred on the nail bed following injury.

Bunion a foot condition. The large joint at the base of the big toe protrudes, forcing the big toe inwards towards the other toes.

Callus foot condition, displaying thick, yellowish hardened skin, usually found on prominent areas of the foot such as the heel.

Chillblains poor blood supply where the toes become red, blue or purple in colour and the area may become painful and itchy; aggravated in cold weather.

Chiropodist a person who is trained and qualified to treat minor foot complaints.

Consultation assessment of client's needs using different assessment techniques, including questioning and natural observation.

Contra-action an unwanted reaction occurring during or after treatment application.

Contra-indication a problematic symptom that indicates that the treatment may not proceed.

Corn small areas of thickened skin on the foot. Often white in appearance.

Cuticle cream or oil a cosmetic preparation used to condition the skin of the cuticle.

Cuticle knife a metal tool used on the nail to remove excess eponychium (the extension of the skin of the cuticle at the base of the nail).

Cuticle remover a cosmetic preparation used to soften and loosen the skin cells and cuticle from the nail.

Diabetes a disease that prevents sufferers breaking down glucose in their cells.

Eczema of the nail inflammation of the skin; different changes to the nail may occur including ridges, pitting, nail separation and nail thickening.

Effleurage a stroking massage movement, used to begin the massage, as a link manipulation and to complete the massage sequence.

Emery board a nail file used to shape the free edge of the nail.

Exfoliant a mild abrasive cream applied and massaged over the skin's surface to remove dead skin cells and improve the appearance and texture of the skin.

Foot cream/oil a cosmetic mixture of waxes and oils applied to soften the skin of the feet and cuticles.

Foot rasp a pedicure tool used to remove excess dead skin from the foot.

Foot spa a foot bath incorporating massage and water aeration, creating a bubbling effect to cleanse and relax the feet.

Hoof stick a nail tool used to gently push back the cuticles when softened.

Ingrowing toenails nail condition where the side of the nail penetrates the nail wall; redness, inflammation and pus may be present.

Mask a treatment mask applied to the skin of the feet to treat and improve the condition of the skin; this may include stimulating, rejuvenating or moisturising properties.

Nail polish a clear or coloured nail product that adds colour/protection to the nail. Cream polish has a matt finish and requires a top coat application. Pearlised polish produces a frosted, shimmery appearance and top coat is not required.

Nail polish drier an aerosol or oil preparation applied following nail polish application to increase the speed at which the polish hardens.

Nail polish remover a solvent used to remove nail polish and grease from the nails prior to applying polish.

Nail polish solvent used to thin nail polish and restore its consistency.

Onycholysis nail condition where the nail plate separates from the nail bed.

Orange stick a disposable wooden tool used around the cuticle and free edge of the nail and to apply products to the nail.

Paraffin wax paraffin wax is heated and applied to the skin of the feet to provide a heating effect. This improves skin functioning, aids the absorption of treatment products and is beneficial to ease the discomfort of arthritic and rheumatic conditions.

Paronychia bacterial infection where swelling, redness and pus appears in the cuticle area of the nail wall.

Pedicure a treatment to care for and improve the condition and appearance of the skin and nails of the feet.

Petrissage massage movements, including *kneading*, where the tissues are lifted away from the underlying structures and compressed. Pressure is intermittent, and should be light yet firm.

Psoriasis of the nail an inflammatory condition where there is an increased production of cells in the upper part of the skin. Pitting occurs on the surface of the nail.

Scissors nail tools used to shorten the length of the nail before filing.

Tapotement, also known as *percussion*, massage movements performed in a brisk, stimulating manner to increase blood supply and improve tone of the skin and muscles. Movements include clapping and tapping.

Tinea corporis or body ringworm fungal infection of the skin where small scaly red patches, which spread outwards and then heal from the centre, leave a ring.

Tinea pedis or athlete's foot fungal infection of the foot occurring in the webs of the skin between the toes. Small blisters form, which later burst. The skin in the area can become dry with a scaly appearance.

Tinea unguium fungal infection of the nails. The nail is yellowish-grey in colour.

Thermal booties electrically heated boots in which the feet are placed following the application of a skin treatment product such as a mask. The heat aids the absorption of the product and improves skin functioning.

Treatment plan after the consultation, suitable treatment objectives are established to treat the client's conditions and needs.

Top coat a nail polish product applied over another nail polish to provide additional strength and durability to the finish.

Verrucae or plantar wart a viral infection where small epidermal skin growths, either raised or flat depending upon their location, and with a rough surface, appear.

Assessment of knowledge and understanding

You have now learnt about the different pedicure treatments available to improve the condition of the feet, nails and surrounding skin. These skills will enable you to professionally provide pedicure treatment.

To test your level of knowledge, answer the following short questions. These will prepare you for your summative (final) assessment.

Additional anatomy and physiology questions required for this unit are found on pages 146–8.

Anatomy and physiology

1 How many bones form the foot? Name them.
2 Name the bones of the lower leg.
3 Name the main arteries of the lower leg.
4 Name the two muscles of the foot.
5 Name two muscles of the lower leg.

Consult with the client

1 What is the purpose of the client consultation?
2 Why is it important to assess the condition of the client's foot and nail condition before treatment commences?
3 Name three contra-indications observed at consultation that would prevent treatment being carried out.
4 What conditions, if present, would restrict your treatment application?
5 Why is diabetes considered a contra-indication to pedicure treatment?

Prepare for the treatment

1 Taking into account client comfort and modesty, why is it important that the client is correctly prepared for treatment?

2 How can you ensure that the position of the client for pedicure minimises potential risk of injury to yourself?

3 How can cross-infection be prevented when performing pedicure treatment? State three examples.

4 Why is it important to sanitise your hands effectively before treatment commences?

Plan the treatment

1 When would you choose to include the following foot and nail treatments in your treatment plan?
- heat treatments
- skin conditioners

2 What is the commercially acceptable time for a pedicure treatment?

3 What should be considered when designing a pedicure treatment plan for a client?

4 Why is it important to complete your treatment plan in the allocated time?

Improve the appearance of the natural nails

1 With regard to the nails, what should be agreed with the client before the nails are shaped?

2 Why should toenails be cut straight across, and not oval like fingernails?

Improve the health and appearance of the cuticles and surrounding skin

1 What is the purpose of the soaking medium usually added to the warm water to soak the client's feet?

2 Describe the methods available for removing hard skin from the feet.

3 How should the skin be left following hard skin removal?

4 Name three treatment products used in pedicure and their effect on the nail, cuticle or skin of the foot as applicable.

5 What do you understand by the term 'erythema', and its cause?

6 Give three effects on the nail and skin of the incorrect use of pedicure tools.

Massage the foot and lower leg

1 How is the quantity and type of massage medium selected for each client?

2 How and why should massage technique be adapted for each client?

3 State four benefits of foot and lower leg massage.

4 What are the terms used for the different types of massage applied in a pedicure?

Provide nail polishing treatment

1 Why should grease be removed from the nail plate prior to nail polish application?

2 How is the type of base coat selected for a client?

3 How many coats of coloured polish are usually applied with:
- cream polish?
- pearlised polish?

4 Following nail polish application, how should the painted nail and cuticle appear?

5 Why should client records be up to date following treatment?

Complete the treatment

1 State the general aftercare advice that you would give to a pedicure client.

2 List three retail products that you would recommend to a pedicure client.

3 What possible contra-action could occur during or after a pedicure treatment? What advice would you give to a client with regard to a contra-action occurring?

4 How can foot exercises be of benefit to a pedicure client?

5 How often would you recommend a pedicure to maintain the condition and appearance of the nails and feet?

6 For each of the clients below suggest a treatment routine. Detail the treatment plan to include the cause of the condition, aims of the treatment, products used, treatments recommended, relevant retail sales and homecare advice:
   - a middle-aged retail worker who has very hard, cracked skin on the soles of her feet around both heels;
   - an elderly man who has little movement in his ankle joints and slightly distorted joints in his toes;
   - a pregnant client who has tired, aching feet and swollen ankles.

chapter 11

BT9 Provide make-up treatment

BT10 Plan and promote make-up activities

Learning objectives

These units describe how to provide make-up for a variety of occasions including day, evening, special occasions and photographic work. The choice and application of make-up will be applied to suit the client's skin type, colouring and condition.

Also covered is **how to plan and promote make-up activities**.

In addition the techniques of **false lash application** to enhance the client's natural lashes or change the look of the eye area, are discussed. For further information on eye treatments, refer to Chapter 7: Provide eyelash and eyebrow treatments.

This chapter describes the competencies to enable you to:

- **consult with the client**
- **prepare for the treatment**
- **plan the treatment**
- **apply make-up products**
- **complete the treatment**

When providing make-up treatment it is important to use the skills you have learnt in the following core mandatory units:

UNIT G1 Ensure your own actions reduce risks to health and safety

UNIT G6 Promote additional products or services to clients

UNIT G8 Develop and maintain your effectiveness at work

Essential anatomy and physiology knowledge requirements for these units, BT9 and BT10, are identified on the checklist chart in Chapter 5, page 101.

RVB/Depilex

Lipstick

MAKE-UP SERVICES

Make-up is used to enhance and accentuate the facial features to make us appear more attractive – which in turn makes us feel more confident. Make-up is used to create balance in the face, by skilful application of different cosmetic products to reduce or to emphasise facial features.

Each client is unique, so each requires an individual approach for their make-up. The overall effect should be attractive, complementing the client's personality, lifestyle, and the context for which the make-up is to be worn.

PLAN AND PREPARE FOR MAKE-UP APPLICATION

Outcome 1: Consult with the client

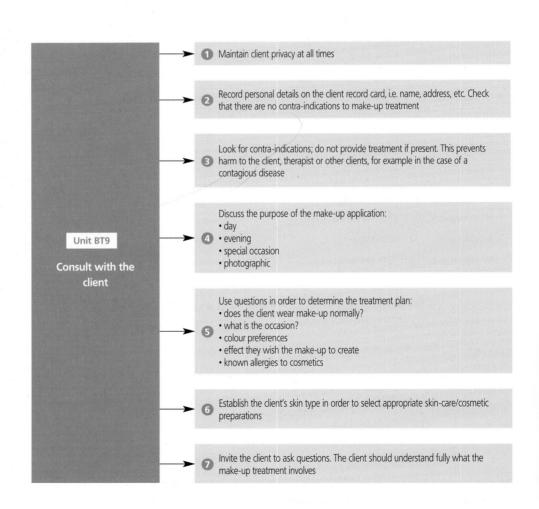

Unit BT9

Consult with the client

1. Maintain client privacy at all times

2. Record personal details on the client record card, i.e. name, address, etc. Check that there are no contra-indications to make-up treatment

3. Look for contra-indications; do not provide treatment if present. This prevents harm to the client, therapist or other clients, for example in the case of a contagious disease

4. Discuss the purpose of the make-up application:
   • day
   • evening
   • special occasion
   • photographic

5. Use questions in order to determine the treatment plan:
   • does the client wear make-up normally?
   • what is the occasion?
   • colour preferences
   • effect they wish the make-up to create
   • known allergies to cosmetics

6. Establish the client's skin type in order to select appropriate skin-care/cosmetic preparations

7. Invite the client to ask questions. The client should understand fully what the make-up treatment involves

Reception

Make-up application is offered for different purposes.

- *A make-up lesson*: a chance for the client to learn from a professional how to apply make-up that suits them.
- *Special occasion make-up*: that is applied by a specialist to suit the occasion for which it is to be worn, such as a wedding. If the make-up is for a bride, advise the client to visit the salon for a consultation and a practice session so that you can decide together on appropriate make-up. Ask the client if possible to bring a swatch of the dress material with her, so that you can select colours to complement this and to co-ordinate with the accessories.
- *Evening make-up* will be seen under artificial lighting. The effect this has on the appearance of the make-up will depend upon the source, which must be considered when applying evening make-up. Generally evening make-up is heavier in application and stronger colours may be applied. Products to emphasise and highlight, such as frosted eyeshadows and lip-glosses, may be introduced.
- *Remedial make-up* may be applied for remedial purposes, to cover facial disfigurements or birthmarks, and the client can be taught how to do this themself.
- *Photographic make-up* is applied for many reasons including magazine shoots, portrait work and fashion shows. Make-up application must be skilful to achieve the right end-result as the location may be a photographic studio or outdoors on location.
- *A professional job*: some clients simply wish to have their make-up professionally applied.

As always, you need to know how long each service will take. Here are some suggested times:

- make-up lesson: 1 hour;
- special occasion, evening and photographic make-up: 45 minutes–1 hour;
- straight make-up: 45 minutes.

In the salon advise the client that if they intend to have their hair washed and styled, this should be done before they have the make-up applied.

If a client requests a deep cleansing facial followed by make-up application, suggest that they have the facial at least five days prior to the make-up. The facial will stimulate the skin, increasing its normal physiological functioning. This will affect how long the make-up lasts; it may even cause the colour of the foundation to change.

Do not reshape the eyebrows at the same treatment as make-up application – secondary infection could occur; also the skin in the area will be very pink, altering the colour and thus the effect of eyeshadow.

The consultation

If the client is new, complete a record card noting the client's personal details. An example record card for make-up is found on page 382.

> **TIP**
>
> **Effective communication**
> When applying make-up it is important that you fully understand the effect to be achieved. Good communication is essential. Ask the client/photographer what the final result should look like.
>
> It is also important that you check that the client does not have allergies to any products to avoid a contra-action.

> **TIP**
>
> **Treatment timings**
> Make-up lesson: allow 1 hour.
> Special occasion make-up: allow 45 mins–1 hour.
> Straight make-up: allow 45 minutes.

BEAUTY WORKS

Date	Therapist name	
Client name		Date of birth (identifying client age group)
Address		Postcode

Evening phone number	Day phone number

Name of doctor	Doctor's address and phone number

Related medical history (conditions that may restrict or prohibit treatment application)

Are you taking any medication? (this may affect skin sensitivity)

CONTRA-INDICATIONS REQUIRING MEDICAL REFERRAL
(Preventing the application of make-up)

- ☐ bacterial infections (e.g. impetigo, conjunctivitis)
- ☐ viral infections (e.g. herpes simplex)
- ☐ fungal infections (e.g. tinea corporis)
- ☐ parasitic infestations (e.g. pediculosis and scabies)
- ☐ watery eyes

SKIN TYPE

- ☐ oily
- ☐ dry
- ☐ combination

FOUNDATION

- ☐ liquid
- ☐ cream
- ☐ compact
- ☐ mousse

POWDER

- ☐ loose
- ☐ compact

EYE PRODUCTS FOR EYE AREA

- ☐ cream eyeshadow
- ☐ liquid eyeliner
- ☐ pencil eyeliner
- ☐ powder eyeshadow

EYE PRODUCTS FOR BROW AREA

- ☐ pencil
- ☐ liquid
- ☐ shadow
- ☐ eyebrow mascara

EYE PRODUCTS FOR EYELASHES

- ☐ mascara
- ☐ false lashes
- ☐ lash curling

CONTRA-INDICATIONS WHICH RESTRICT TREATMENT
(Treatment may require adaptation)

- ☐ cuts and abrasions
- ☐ bruising and swelling
- ☐ recent scar tissue
- ☐ eczema
- ☐ skin allergies
- ☐ vitiligo
- ☐ styes

MAKE-UP CONTEXT

- ☐ day
- ☐ evening
- ☐ special occasion

CHEEK PRODUCTS

- ☐ highlighter
- ☐ shader
- ☐ blusher

LIP PRODUCTS

- ☐ pencil lipliner
- ☐ lipgloss
- ☐ lipstick

Foundation
Powder
Eyebrow colour
Browbone
Socket
Eyelid
Blusher
Contour
Mascara
Eyeliner
Lip pencil
Lip product

Therapist signature (for reference)

Client signature (confirmation of details)

BEAUTY WORKS *(continued)*

TREATMENT ADVICE

 Make-up treatment – *allow 45 minutes*

TREATMENT PLAN

Record relevant details of your treatment and advice provided for future reference.

Ensure the client's records are up to date, accurate and fully completed following treatment. Non-compliance may invalidate insurance.

DURING

Find out:

- what products the client is currently using to cleanse and care for the skin of the face and neck.

Discuss:

- the importance of a good skin-care routine in relation to make-up application;
- current satisfaction with the client's make-up technique;
- tips and explain each stage of the make-up application to enhance the client's understanding.

Note:

- any adverse reaction, if any occur.

AFTER

Record:

- any modification to make-up treatment application that has occurred;
- what products have been used in the make-up treatment;
- the effectiveness of the make-up result;
- any samples provided (review their success at the next appointment).

Advise on:

- how to reapply products to achieve/maintain the result;
- correct make-up removal technique.

RETAIL OPPORTUNITIES

Advise on:

- products that would be suitable for the client to use at home to care for their skin;
- the benefits of each make-up product clearly and logically during application;
- recommendations for further make-up treatments;
- further products or services that the client may or may not have received before.

Note:

- any purchase made by the client.

EVALUATION

Record:

- comments on the client's satisfaction with the treatment;
- if poor results are achieved, the reasons why.

HEALTH AND SAFETY

Advise on:

- appropriate action to be taken in the event of an unwanted skin reaction.

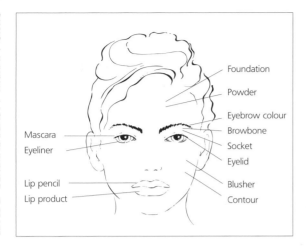

Foundation
Powder
Eyebrow colour
Browbone
Socket
Eyelid
Blusher
Contour

Mascara
Eyeliner
Lip pencil
Lip product

Retail advice make-up record card – this records the product type and colour applied

Discuss your make-up plan with the client to ensure that the make-up will meet their requirements. You may need to ask questions such as those that follow, but of course the questions depend on the purpose of the make-up application.

- 'Do you normally wear make-up?'
- 'For what occasion is the make-up to be worn?'
- 'What colour are the clothing and accessories to be worn on this occasion?'
- 'Are there any colours that you particularly like or dislike?'
- 'What effect would you like the make-up to create?' (This question may be asked in many contexts – the client/photographer may wish to achieve a natural or a glamorous effect, or to emphasise or diminish certain facial features.)

Contra-indications

Certain contra-indications prevent make-up application. Check for these at the consultation, and if any of the following are present on inspection of the skin, do not proceed with make-up application.

Remember that not all contra-indications are visible – a current bone fracture, for example would not be. Refer to the checklist of contra-indications on the client's record card.

Name	Description
Peducolsis capitis (head lice) 	Head and body lice are conditions where small parasites live and feed on the skin. The condition is highly infectious. The parasites bite the skin to draw nourishment from the blood; this creates irritation of the skin, which may lead to bacterial infection.
Pediculosis corporis (body lice) 	

Wellcome Photo Library

Wellcome Photo Library

Name	Description
Acne vulgaris (active) 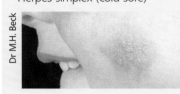 *Dr M.H. Beck*	A non-contagious skin disorder of the sebaceous gland, causing an increased production of sebum. The sebum may be retained in the sebaceous ducts, causing congestion and bacterial infection of the surrounding skin.
Herpes simplex (cold sore) 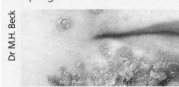 *Dr M.H. Beck*	A recurring infectious viral skin condition. The skin becomes inflamed locally. Small vesicles, a type of blister, appear, followed by a crust which may crack and weep tissue fluid. Common sites include the mucous membranes of the lips and nose.
Impetigo  *Dr M.H. Beck*	An inflammatory infectious bacterial skin condition. The skin becomes red, and this is followed by the appearance of small blisters that burst and form crusts. Common sites include the nose and mouth.
Styes or hordeola  *Wellcome Photo Library*	Infectious bacterial infection of the sebaceous glands of the eyelash hair follicles. Small lumps containing pus appear on the inner rim of the eyelid.
Conjunctivitis (pink eye) 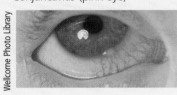 *Wellcome Photo Library*	Infectious bacterial infection. Inflammation of the mucous membrane that covers the eye and lines the eyelid. The skin of the inner conjunctiva of the eye becomes very red, itchy and sore; pus may exude from the eye area.
Watery eye or epiphora 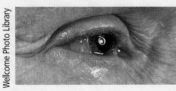 *Wellcome Photo Library*	The eye over-secretes tears, which would normally drain into the nasal cavity.
Blepharitis  *Wellcome Photo Library*	Inflammation of the eyelid caused by infection or an allergic reaction.

The following conditions also contra-indicate make-up application:

- *Skin disorders* including those not listed in the above chart, such as bacterial infections (e.g. boils), viral infections, and fungal infections (e.g. tinea corporis).
- *Active psoriasis and eczema.*
- *Bruising* in the area.
- *Recent haemorrhage.*
- *Swelling and inflammation* in the area.
- *Recent scar tissue.*
- *Sensory nerve disorders.*
- *Cuts or abrasions* in the area.
- *A recent operation* in the area.
- *Eye disorders* including those not listed in the chart.
- *Parasitic infestation* such as peducolosis and scabies.

Ask the client whether they have any known allergies to cosmetic preparations. Note the answer on the record card. Care must be taken to avoid contact with an allergen.

Refer to pages 25–37, where skin diseases and disorders are dealt with in more detail.

Outcome 2: Prepare for the treatment

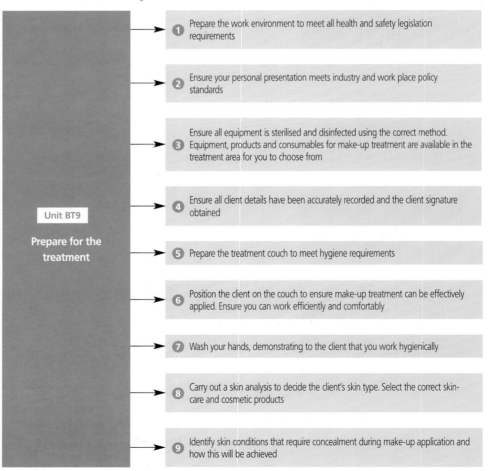

Unit BT9

Prepare for the treatment

1. Prepare the work environment to meet all health and safety legislation requirements

2. Ensure your personal presentation meets industry and work place policy standards

3. Ensure all equipment is sterilised and disinfected using the correct method. Equipment, products and consumables for make-up treatment are available in the treatment area for you to choose from

4. Ensure all client details have been accurately recorded and the client signature obtained

5. Prepare the treatment couch to meet hygiene requirements

6. Position the client on the couch to ensure make-up treatment can be effectively applied. Ensure you can work efficiently and comfortably

7. Wash your hands, demonstrating to the client that you work hygienically

8. Carry out a skin analysis to decide the client's skin type. Select the correct skin-care and cosmetic products

9. Identify skin conditions that require concealment during make-up application and how this will be achieved

ACTIVITY

The record card

Why is it important to complete a record card? What information should be recorded on it?

TIP

Contra-indications

Remember – never name a contra-indication, you may be wrong. Refer the client to their GP, this is their role.

In the case of the skin disorder herpes simplex, the make-up treatment may be received when the skin is healed and clear.

Equipment and materials

Before beginning the make-up, check that you have to hand the necessary equipment and materials.

EQUIPMENT LIST

 Couch or beauty chair with a reclining back, a head rest and an easy-to-clean surface
Trolley or other surface on which to place everything

 Headband (clean) to protect the client's hair whilst cleansing the skin

 Cleansing lotion to prepare the skin
Eye make-up remover to prepare the skin
Toning lotion to prepare the skin
Moisturiser (lightweight) to facilitate make-up application and create a barrier between the skin and make-up

 Dry cottonwool stored in a covered jar, to apply loose face powder

 Large white facial tissues to blot the skin after facial toning, and to protect the skin during make-up application

 Make-up (a range)

 Bright lighting and magnifying lamp to inspect the skin after cleansing and check for areas requiring special attention, e.g. broken capillaries that need concealer

 Make-up brushes (assorted) at least three sets, to allow for disinfection after use

 Disposable applicators and brushes where possible for example for mascara and the application of eyeshadow

 Cosmetic sponges for applying foundation

 Make-up palette for preparing cosmetic products prior to application

 Pencil sharpener for cosmetic pencils
Eyelash curlers

 Artificial eyelashes

 Spatulas (several)

 Orange sticks (several) for removing make-up products from their containers

YOU WILL ALSO NEED:

Disposable tissue (such as bedroll) to cover the work surface and the couch or beauty chair

Towels (2) freshly laundered for each client – one to be placed over the head of the couch or chair, the other over the client's chest and shoulders to protect their clothing

Hairclips to protect the client's hair during make-up application

Damp cottonwool prepared for each client and used during skin cleansing

Bowls to hold the prepared cottonwool

Bowls or lined pedal bin for waste materials

Hand mirror (clean) to show client results

Client record card – confidential card recording details of each client registered at the salon

Ellisons

Make-up products

TIP

As an alternative to a headband, you may wish simply to clip the hair out of the way with hairclips.

TIP

As an alternative to a towel, a make-up cape may be used to protect the client's clothing.

TIP

The chair must offer head support, or the client's neck will become strained during the make-up; also the head needs support if it is to be steady during the application of eye and lip make-up.

TIP

Positive promotion
Where possible, use make-up that you also sell in the salon, so that the client can buy the products for home use if they wish.

You will need to have to hand a good range of make-up, suitable for clients with known skin allergies to cosmetics, for contact-lens wearers, for different skin types and skin colours, including:

- concealing and contouring cosmetics (shaders, highlighters and blushers);
- foundations;
- translucent powders;
- eyeshadows;
- eyeliners;
- browliners;
- mascara;
- lipsticks;
- lipglosses;
- lipliners.

Make-up brushes

These are prepared from different fibres, which may be synthetic or animal including camel, sable, ox, pony and goat.

Powder and blusher brushes may be produced from softer hair, but for the purpose of contouring and blending brushes must be firmer.

Name	Description
Large face powder dusting brush	To remove excess face powder or to apply specialised powders
Foundation brush	To apply foundation to specific areas

Name	Description
Contouring blush brush 	To apply facial contouring products to highlight and shade areas of the face
Blusher brush (large to medium)	To apply powder colour to the face and for blending
Small flat angle-edged eyeshadow brush	To apply and blend powder eye make-up products in the socket area of the eye
Small rounded-edged eyeshadow brush	To apply eyeshadow, blend and shade
Medium firm eyeshadow blending brush	To blend powder eye colours and soften harsh lines and colour
Small concealer brush	For exact placement of concealing product
Eyebrow brush	To remove excess make-up from the brow hair and to add colour, blend eyebrow pencil and groom the brow hair into shape
Eyeliner brush	A fine brush used to apply make-up colour to contour the eyes, creating a precise line
Mascara wand/comb	To apply mascara and remove excess mascara to separate the lashes
Lip brush	To apply lip products and ensure a definite, balanced outline to the lips

Photographs courtesy Beauty Express Ltd.

Ellisons

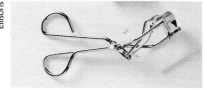

Eyelash curler

HEALTH AND SAFETY

Transporting make-up
If you are transporting your make-up in a box, keep the box clean. Clients won't be impressed if they see soiled, dirty make-up containers.

HEALTH AND SAFETY

Avoiding cross-infection
To avoid cross-infection, don't use the applicators supplied with cosmetic products directly on a client.

TIP

Make-up sponges
Keep a store of spare make-up sponges – they soon crumble with repeated cleaning.

HEALTH AND SAFETY

Hygiene at home
Advise clients to keep their own make-up clean. Dirty brushes spoil effective make-up application, and offer breeding grounds for bacteria.

Make-up sponges

TIP

Make-up case
If you intend to apply make-up at different locations, buy a large make-up case so that you can transport the make-up easily and hygienically.

Sterilisation and disinfection

Where possible, use disposable applicators during make-up application, costing these into the treatment price. Disinfect make-up brushes after each use: wash them in warm water and detergent, rinse them thoroughly in a disinfecting solution and then rinse in clean water, and allow them to dry naturally. Once dry, place the brushes in an ultra-violet light cabinet ready for use.

TIP

An *alcohol-based cleanser* may be used to clean make-up brushes. The brushes are first cleaned with a solution of warm water and detergent, then thoroughly rinsed in clean water and allowed to dry. They are then briefly immersed in the alcohol solution and again allowed to dry.

All cosmetic products should be removed from their containers using a clean spatula or orange stick, and placed on the clean plastic make-up palette before application. (This avoids contamination of the make-up with bacteria from unclean make-up applicators.)

The make-up palette should be cleaned with warm water and detergent, then wiped with a disinfectant solution applied using clean cottonwool. It should be stored in the ultra-violet cabinet.

Mascara should be applied using a disposable brush applicator, fresh for each client.

Sharpen cosmetic pencils with a pencil sharpener before each use.

Make-up sponges should be disposed of after use, or washed in warm water and detergent; then placed in a disinfectant solution and rinsed. Allow them to dry, then place them in the ultra-violet cabinet, with each side being exposed for at least 20 minutes.

HEALTH AND SAFETY

Maintaining hygiene
If you drop a make-up tool on the floor, discard it – don't use it again until it has been disinfected and sterilised.

Preparing the treatment area

The make-up room should be decorated in light, neutral colours to avoid the creation of unnecessary shadows. The area where the make-up is to be applied should be well lit, ideally with the same kind of light as that in which the make-up will be seen.

Place all the equipment and materials required on the trolley or work surface, in front of a make-up mirror. If you are displaying the make-up on a trolley, place the cosmetic products on a lower shelf until required, when they can be moved to the top shelf. This avoids cluttering the working area.

Lighting

You need to know the *type* of light in which the proposed make-up will be seen: this is important when deciding upon the correct choice of make-up colours, because the appearance of colours may change according to the type of light. Is the make-up to be seen in daylight, in a fluorescent-lit office, or a softly lit restaurant?

White light (natural daylight) contains all the colours of the rainbow. When white light falls on an object, it absorbs some colours and reflects others: it is the *reflected* colour that we see. Thus, an object that we see as red is an object that absorbs the colours in white light *except* red. A *white* object reflects most of the light that falls upon it; a *black* object absorbs most of the light that falls on it.

If the make-up is to be worn in natural light, choose subtle make-up products as daylight intensifies colours.

If the make-up is to be worn in the office, it will probably be seen under **fluorescent light**. This contains an excess of blue and green, which have a 'cool' effect on the make-up: the red in the face does not show up and the face can look drained of colour. Reds and yellows should be avoided, as these will not show up; blue-toned colours will. Don't apply dark colours, as fluorescent light intensifies these.

Evening make-up is usually seen in **incandescent light** – light produced by a filament lamp. This produces an excess of red and yellow light, which creates a warm, flattering effect. Almost all colours can be used in this light, except that browns and purples will appear darker. Choose a lighter foundation than normal to reflect the light, and use frosted highlighting products where possible for the same reason.

Because it is necessary to choose brighter colours and to emphasise facial features using contouring cosmetics, evening make-up will appear very obvious and dramatic in daylight. Explain to the client the reasons for the effect created, so that when she leaves the salon in daylight she won't feel that the make-up is inappropriate.

HEALTH AND SAFETY
Ventilation Good ventilation is important so that the client's skin does not become too warm. It is easier to apply make-up effectively to cool skin, and the make-up will be more durable.

TIP ✔
Lighting If working under artificial light, use warm white fluorescent light for day make-up, as this closely resembles natural light.   A diffuser may be used to cover the fluorescent tube. This softens the cool effect on the make-up and reduces the effects of shadows.

Outcome 3: Plan the treatment

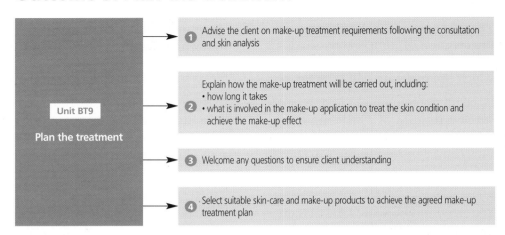

Preparing the client

Take the client through to the treatment area. Make-up application may take place either at the make-up chair, in front of a mirror, or at the treatment couch. Before you start the make-up, discuss and plan the make-up with the client, recording significant details on their record card.

Before preparing the client for the treatment, wash your hands. The client need remove only their upper outer clothing, to their underwear. Offer the client a gown, or drape a clean towel or make-up cape across their chest and shoulders. Place a headband or hairclip around the hairline, to protect the hair and keep it away from the face. Any jewellery in the treatment area should be removed. Refer to the record card to check for any known allergies to cosmetic products.

> **TIP**
>
> **Headbands**
> If a headband is used, remove it directly after the facial cleanse so that it doesn't flatten and spoil the hair.

> **HEALTH AND SAFETY**
>
> **Contact lenses**
> If the client wears contact lenses, ask them whether they wish to remove them before the skin is cleansed. (The need for this will depend on the sensitivity of the eyes.)

> **TIP**
>
> **Removing eyeliner**
> Existing cosmetic eyeliner is sometimes difficult to remove. Use a cotton bud soaked in eye make-up remover: gently stroke this along the base of the lower eyelashes, in towards the nose.

After preparing the client, and before touching the skin, wash your hands again. Now cleanse and tone the skin, using products appropriate to their skin type. Just as skin-care products vary in their formulation to suit the various skin types, so make-up products are designed for different skins. Record all relevant details on the record card.

Inspect the skin using a magnifying lamp. Identify any areas that require specific attention.

Apply a light-textured moisturiser before make-up application. This has the following benefits:

- it prevents the natural secretions of the skin changing the colour of the foundation;

- it seals the surface of the skin, and prevents absorption of the foundation into the skin;
- it facilitates make-up application by providing a smooth base.

Remove excess moisturiser by blotting the skin with a facial tissue.

APPLYING THE MAKE-UP

Outcome 4: Apply make-up products

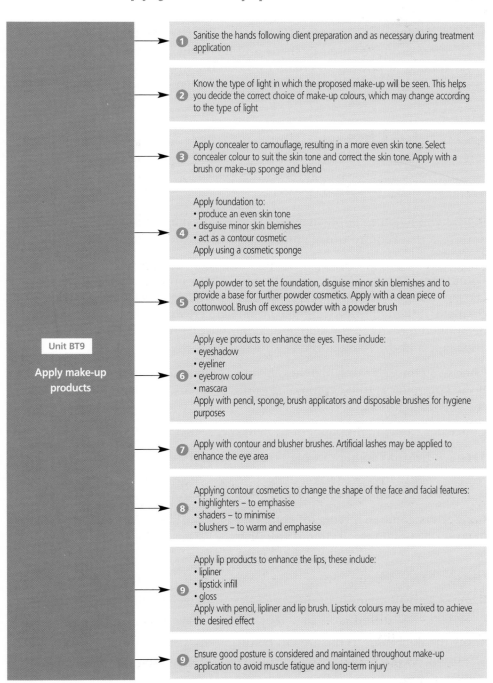

Unit BT9

Apply make-up products

1. Sanitise the hands following client preparation and as necessary during treatment application

2. Know the type of light in which the proposed make-up will be seen. This helps you decide the correct choice of make-up colours, which may change according to the type of light

3. Apply concealer to camouflage, resulting in a more even skin tone. Select concealer colour to suit the skin tone and correct the skin tone. Apply with a brush or make-up sponge and blend

4. Apply foundation to:
   • produce an even skin tone
   • disguise minor skin blemishes
   • act as a contour cosmetic
   Apply using a cosmetic sponge

5. Apply powder to set the foundation, disguise minor skin blemishes and to provide a base for further powder cosmetics. Apply with a clean piece of cottonwool. Brush off excess powder with a powder brush

6. Apply eye products to enhance the eyes. These include:
   • eyeshadow
   • eyeliner
   • eyebrow colour
   • mascara
   Apply with pencil, sponge, brush applicators and disposable brushes for hygiene purposes

7. Apply with contour and blusher brushes. Artificial lashes may be applied to enhance the eye area

8. Applying contour cosmetics to change the shape of the face and facial features:
   • highlighters – to emphasise
   • shaders – to minimise
   • blushers – to warm and emphasise

9. Apply lip products to enhance the lips, these include:
   • lipliner
   • lipstick infill
   • gloss
   Apply with pencil, lipliner and lip brush. Lipstick colours may be mixed to achieve the desired effect

9. Ensure good posture is considered and maintained throughout make-up application to avoid muscle fatigue and long-term injury

TIP

Asian clients very often have darker skin underneath the eye area, and this may require concealing.

TIP

Concealing may be completed before or after foundation application.

Applying concealer

Concealing products

TIP

Avoid rubbing the product whilst blending it, or it will wipe off.

The make-up sequence

- Conceal any blemishes.
- Apply foundation.
- Contour the face (with cream liquid products).
- Apply powder.
- Contour the face (with powder products).
- Apply blusher.
- Apply eyeshadow.
- Make up the eyebrows.
- Apply mascara.
- Make up the lips.
- Contour products, used to shade and highlight the face and features, can be applied in powder or cream formulation. Application sequence for contouring will depend upon product formulation chosen.

CONCEALER

Concealing blemishes

Before you begin to apply make-up to the face, inspect the skin and identify any areas that require concealing, such as blemishes, uneven skin colour or shadows.

Foundation may be used to disguise minor skin imperfections, but where extra coverage is required it is necessary to apply a special **concealer**, a cosmetic designed to provide maximum skin coverage. The concealer may be applied directly to the skin after skin moisturising, or following application of the foundation.

Choose a concealer that matches the client's skin tone as closely as possible. If the concealer is to be applied *after* the foundation, it should match the colour of the *foundation*.

Concealer can contain pigment to help correct skin tone.

- *Green* helps to counteract high colouring, and to conceal dilated capillaries.
- *Lilac* counteracts a sallow skin colour.
- *White or cream* helps to correct unevenness in the skin pigmentation.

Concealers come in a range of colours, to suit all skins. Mix different colours together to obtain the required colour.

Applying concealer

Remove a small quantity of the concealer from its container, using a clean disposable spatula.

Apply the concealer to the area to be disguised, using either a clean make-up sponge or a soft make-up brush. Blend the concealer to achieve a realistic effect.

> **TIP** ✔
>
> **Common racial skin problems:**
> - Caucasian – easily damaged by exposure to high temperatures and ultra-violet light, leading to broken veins and pigmentation disorders.
> - Oriental – prone to uneven pigmentation on ultra-violet light exposure.
> - Asian – often has uneven pigmentation skin tones; darker skin is often found around the eyes.
> - African-Caribbean – greater protection against ultra-violet light as melanin is present in all layers of the epidermis; tends to scar easily, possibly leading to uneven pigmentation, vitiligo and keloids.

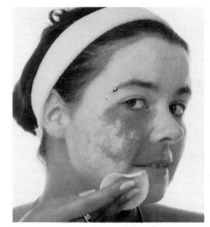

Vitiligo

Using concealer to camouflage

Specialist techniques are required to conceal problem areas; this technique is called *camouflage*. Areas that may be required to be camouflaged include:

- *Scars*: caused by injury, post-operative, keloids (lumpy scar tissue forming at the site of wounds), acne vulgaris, burns which can cause the skin to become ridged or discoloured.
- *Birthmarks*: darker pigmented areas.
- *Pigment disorders*: hypopigmentation (reduced melanin production, e.g. vitiligo) and hyperpigmentation (increased melanin production), e.g. chloasmata (brown patches), moles, dermatosis papulosa nigra, (a benign (non-malignant) skin condition common among adult black-skinned people characterised by multiple small, hyperpigmented (dark brown to black) papules on the face, neck, upper back and chest).
- *Vascular disorders*: Rosacea (chronic inflammation of the skin on the nose and cheeks caused by the dilation of the blood capillaries) and telangiectasia (dilated capillaries appearing on the face).

> **TIP** ✔
>
> It is preferable to build up several layers to achieve the desired effect, rather than applying a thick layer.

How to apply concealer to camouflage

Always check the manufacturer's instructions on how to apply the camouflage/concealing product. Brands vary and some may require different preparation and setting techniques.

This type of concealer is thick and it is preferable to build up several layers to achieve the desired effect, rather than applying a thick layer.

1 Select the chosen colour or colour mixture that best matches the skin tone surrounding the area to be treated.

2 Using your ring and middle fingers in a patting motion, or using a dry sponge, blend the make-up thinly over the problem area, extending it approximately two cm past the edge. If disguising scars, a brush may be used to feather the make-up at the edges to create a natural effect. The sponge may be dampened if needed to facilitate extra blending.

3 Build up the colour depth to ensure the blemish is completely covered, thinning the colour at the edge to blend in. A small make-up brush can be used to blend in the edges of the make-up.

Covering a deep red mark

HEALTH AND SAFETY

Medicated concealers

Advise clients to avoid medicated 'lipstick'-type concealers – these are too thick for general concealing. They are also unhygienic, as they are designed to be directly applied to a blemish: this means that the product becomes a breeding ground for bacteria.

Foundation products

TIP ✔

To achieve a light, healthy, natural appearance, the client may apply a tinted moisturiser.

TIP ✔

Cream and cake foundation can settle in creases and accentuate wrinkles. Apply only a very fine film of such foundations over these areas.

4 Once the required result has been achieved, apply the fixing powder generously with a large powder puff.

5 Leave the make-up to set for five to ten minutes.

6 Gently brush off any excess fixing powder with a large, soft make-up brush, e.g. blusher/powder brush. Blot off excess powder if required with damp cottonwool. The make-up is now waterproof and rub resistant, and should not be detectable.

7 If the camouflage has been applied to the face, full make-up may now be applied. The foundation colour selected should match the colour of the camouflage make-up.

8 Apply foundation up to the area of camouflage make-up and blend so that an invisible finish is created. Putting an oily cream foundation over the camouflage make-up will move or remove the camouflage make-up; it is best to use a non-oily or liquid foundation.

9 Record on the client record card the make-up products selected and application technique used.

● *Covering a deep red mark*: use a green pigmented make-up first, then apply make-up which matches the skin tone over the top

● *Covering a dark brown mark*: use white, opaque make-up first, then apply make-up which matches the skin tone over the top.

● *Covering a lighter mark*: commence with a darker foundation and apply make-up which matches the skin tone over the top.

FOUNDATION

Foundation is applied to produce an even skin tone, to disguise minor skin blemishes, and as a contour cosmetic. Black skin in particular often has an uneven skin tone, requiring certain parts of the face to be lightened and others darkened to produce an even skin tone.

Foundation is available as cream, liquid, gel, cake or mousse. It is composed of water, powder, oil, humectant (such as glycerol), inorganic pigments, and additives that protect the skin from the environment (such as sunscreens and moisturisers).

Some foundations contain **'anti-ageing' ingredients** such as vitamin E. These are to neutralise **free radicals**, natural chemicals thought to be responsible for damaging the skin and producing the signs of ageing – the lines and wrinkles!

ACTIVITY

Comparing foundations

Compare the proportions of ingredients contained in foundations for each skin type. How, and why, are they different?

Kinds of foundations

Each foundation differs in its formulation to suit a particular skin type. The correct choice will guarantee that the foundation lasts throughout the day.

Cream foundations are oil-based and blend easily on application. They provide a heavy coverage, and have these specific treatment uses:

- dry skin;
- normal skin;
- mature skin.

Liquid foundations are oil- or water-based, providing light to medium coverage. Oil-based liquid foundations have these specific treatment uses:

- dry skin;
- normal skin;
- mature skin;
- combination skin (apply the foundation to the *dry* areas).

Water-based liquid foundations have the following uses:

- normal skin;
- oily skin;
- combination skin (apply the foundation to the *oily* areas).

Water-based foundations do not spread very easily because the water content rapidly evaporates, so these foundations must be applied quickly.

Gel foundations provide sheer, non-greasy coverage. They have these specific treatment uses:

- black, unblemished skin;
- tanned skin;
- skin on which a natural effect is required.

Compact or cake foundations may have an oil, wax or powder base. They give a heavy coverage, and have these specific treatment uses:

- dry skin;
- normal skin;
- badly blemished or scarred skin.

Mousse foundations provide light to medium coverage depending on application technique. They have a mineral oil base. Their specific treatment uses are:

- normal skin;
- combination skin.

Care must be taken to apply the mousse foundation to an area of the skin and blend quickly or it may start to dry on the face, creating a chalky appearance.

TIP ✓

Using a palette
The make-up palette is useful when mixing foundations to match the colour of your client's skin.

Foundation colour

The colour of the foundation should match the client's natural skin colour. Test the foundation for compatibility on the client's jawline or forehead. If an incorrect colour is selected, or if the foundation is insufficiently blended on application, there will be a noticeable **demarcation line**.

Skin colour	Foundation colour
Fair	Ivory or light beige, with warm tones of pink or peach
Olive	Dark beige or bronze
Suntanned	Bronze
Florid	Matt beige with a green tint
Sallow	Beige with a pink tint
Light brown	Light brown foundation with a warm tone
Medium brown	Light brown with an orange tone
Dark brown	Deep bronze foundation with an orange tone
Black	Dark golden bronze (usually a gel)

Applying foundation

Applying the foundation

If the foundation is in a jar, remove some from its container using a clean disposable spatula. Put it on a clean make-up palette.

Foundation may be applied using either a large soft brush, which is stroked over the surface of the skin, or a cosmetic sponge. It should be applied to one area of the face at a time, with an outward stroking movement.

Use a cosmetic sponge to blend the foundation. Take care that you blend it at the hairline and at the jawline. Avoid clogging the eyebrows with foundation. The **cosmetic make-up wedge** is designed to apply varying amounts of pressure to the different areas of the face, and to ensure even coverage of the foundation.

When applying foundation around the eye area, use a small soft brush or the angular edge of a cosmetic sponge. This will help you achieve accuracy in application.

The extent of coverage can be controlled by the method of application. If the cosmetic sponge is damp, coverage is light and sheer. To achieve a heavier coverage, use a dry latex sponge.

Apply foundation to cover the entire face, including the lips and the eyelids. Do not extend the make-up past the jawline unless the occasion requires this – for example, if a bride's dress exposes part of the upper chest – because the foundation will mark clothes at the neckline.

TIP ✓

Avoid applying foundation with the fingers. Apart from being less hygienic, with this method the warmth of your hands may cause streaking.

CONTOURING

Contour cosmetics

Changing the shape of the face and the facial features can be achieved with the careful application of **contour cosmetics**. These products draw attention either towards or away from facial features, and can create the optical illusion of perfection.

Contour cosmetics include **highlighters**, **shaders** and **blushers**. They are available in powder, liquid and cream forms.

- Highlighters draw attention towards – they emphasise.
- Shaders draw attention away – they minimise.
- Blushers add warmth to the face and emphasise the facial contours.

Each face differs in shape and size, so each requires a different application technique.

Some blushers appear very vibrant in the container, yet when they are applied to the skin they are subtle.

Beauty Express Ltd.

Beauty Express Ltd.

Contour cosmetics

How to apply powder blushers

1 Stroke the contour brush over the powder blusher. Tap the brush gently to dislodge excess blusher.
2 Apply the blusher to the cheek area, carefully placing the product according to the effect you wish to create. The direction of brush strokes should be upwards and outwards, towards the hairline. Keep the blusher away from the nose, and avoid applying blusher too near the outer eye.
3 Apply more blusher if necessary. The key to successful blusher application is to build up colour slowly until you have achieved the optimum effect.

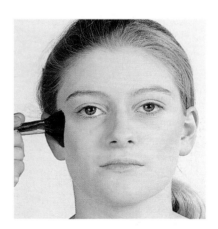

Applying blusher

How to apply cream blushers

Apply the cream blusher after foundation application, then place a loose translucent powder over the cream blusher.

If liquid or cream cosmetics are used, these must be applied on top of a liquid or cream foundation *before* powder application. (If powder contour products are used, these should be applied *after* the application of the loose face powder. The rule of contour cosmetic application is: powder on powder; cream on cream.)

Before applying these products, decide on the effect you wish to achieve. Study the client's face from the front and side profiles, and determine what facial corrective work is necessary.

> **TIP**
>
> Remember – it is easier to apply more blusher than to remove excess, which disturbs the foundation!

> **TIP**
>
> Foundation may be suitable as a contour cosmetic. Choose a foundation either two shades lighter (as a highlighter) or two shades darker (as a shader) than the base foundation.

Oval

Round

Facial bone structure
Draw and label the main facial bones. It is the differing sizes and proportions of these bones that give us our individual features.

To discover the size of each facial feature, feel the bony prominences of your own face with your fingers.

Face shapes

To assess the client's face shape, take the hair away from the face – hairstyles often disguise the face shape. Study the size and shape of the facial bone structure. Consider the amount of excess fat and the muscle tone.

Oval

This is regarded as the perfect face shape. Corrective make-up application usually attempts to create the *appearance* of an oval face shape.

Draw attention to the cheekbones by applying shader beneath the cheekbone, and highlighter above. Blusher should be drawn along the cheekbone and blended up towards the temples.

Round

Bone structure Broad and short.

Corrective make-up Apply highlighter in a thin band down the central portion of the face to create the illusion of length. Shader may be applied over the angle of the jaw to the temples. Apply blusher in a triangular shape, with the base of the triangle running parallel to the ear.

Square

Bone structure A broad forehead and a broad, angular jawline.

Corrective make-up Shade the angles of the jawbone, up and towards the cheekbone. Apply blusher in a circular pattern on the cheekbones, taking it towards the temples.

Heart

Bone structure A wide forehead, with the face tapering to a narrow, pointed chin, like an inverted triangle.

Corrective make-up Highlight the angles of the jawbone and shade the point of the chin, the temples and the sides of the forehead. Apply blusher under the cheekbones, in an upward and outward direction towards the temples.

Square

TIP

Blusher
Keep blusher away from the centre of the face to avoid accentuating the breadth of the face.

Heart   Diamond

Diamond

Bone structure A narrow forehead, with wide cheekbones tapering to a narrow chin.

Corrective make-up Apply shader to the tip of the chin and the height of the forehead, to reduce length. Highlight the narrow sides of the temples and the lower jaw. Apply blusher to the fullness of the cheekbones to draw attention to the centre of the face.

Oblong

Bone structure Long and narrow, tapering to a pointed chin.

Corrective make-up Apply shader to the hairline and the point of the chin to reduce the length of the face. Highlight the angle of the jawbone and the temples to create width. Blend blusher along the cheekbones, outwards towards the ears.

Pear

Bone structure A wide jawline, tapering to a narrow forehead.

Corrective make-up Highlight the forehead and shade the sides of the chin and the angle of the jaw. Apply blusher to the fullness of the cheeks, or blend it along the cheekbones, up towards the temples.

Oblong

Pear

ACTIVITY

Contouring
Study three different clients or colleagues. Identify their face shapes. Where would you apply the contouring cosmetics for each face shape, and why?

TIP

An Asian face may appear as a flat plane: the skillful application of shading and highlighting products can create highs and lows.

Features

Noses

- *If the nose is too broad*: apply shader to the sides of the nose.
- *If the nose is too short*: apply highlighter down the length of the nose, from the bridge to the tip.
- *If the nose is too long*: apply shader to the tip of the nose.
- *If there is a bump on the nose*: apply shader over the area.
- *If there is a hollow along the bridge of the nose*: apply highlighter over the hollow area.
- *If the nose is crooked*: apply shader over the crooked side.

ACTIVITY

Correcting nose shapes
Think of the different nose shapes you may encounter, such as Roman, turned up, bulbous, or with a long tip. Which contour cosmetics would you select to correct each? Where would you apply them?

TIP

Foreheads
Foreheads can be improved by a flattering hairstyle:
- Prominent forehead: choose soft, flat, textured fringes.
- Shallow forehead: choose a shorter, soft fringe. Height will make the forehead appear longer.
- Deep forehead: choose a longer, soft fringe

Foreheads

- *If the forehead is prominent*: apply shader centrally over the prominent area, blending it outwards toward the temples.
- *If the forehead is shallow*: apply highlighter in a narrow band below the hairline.
- *If the forehead is deep*: apply shader in a narrow band below the hairline.

Chins

- *If the jaw is too wide*: apply shader from beneath the cheekbones and along the jawline, blending it at the neck.
- *If the chin is double*: apply shader to the centre of the chin, blending it outwards along the jawbone and under the chin.
- *If the chin is prominent*: apply foundation to the tip of the chin.
- *If the chin is long*: apply shader over the prominent area.
- *If the chin recedes*: apply highlighter along the jawline and at the centre of the chin.

Necks

- *If the neck is thin*: apply highlighter down each side of the neck.
- *If the neck is thick*: apply shader to both sides of the neck.

FACE POWDER

Face powder is applied to set the foundation, disguising minor blemishes and making the skin appear smooth and oil-free. It also protects the skin from the environment by acting as a barrier.

Most powders are based on **talc** as the main ingredient, but talc particles are of uneven size, and substitutes such as **mica** are now becoming popular. These give a more natural, flattering appearance to the skin.

Powder adheres to the foundation through the addition of **zinc**, **magnesium stearate** or **fatty esters**. These chemicals set the make-up and remove tackiness. Further powder products can then be applied to the skin.

Face powder contains absorbent materials such as **precipitated chalk** or **nylon derivatives**. These absorb sweat and sebum throughout the day, reducing shine and giving the foundation greater durability.

During manufacture, the insoluble substances in face powder go through a process called **micronisation** in which the particles are finely ground to make a powder, which is then thoroughly blended. Colour pigment may be added to produce different shades and effects.

Beauty Express Ltd.

Face powders

Kinds of face powders

There are two basic products: loose powders and compact powders.

Loose powders

Loose powders do not contain any oils or gums to bind the powder together. They are available in a range of shades, with different pastel pigments added to counteract skin imperfections. Colours include pink and lilac, which are flattering when viewed under artificial lights; yellow, which enhances a tanned skin; and green, which counteracts a red skin. Iridescent ingredients may be included to produce shimmering and highlighting effects.

Many cosmetic products contain **titanium dioxide**, an opaque white pigment, to provide coverage. When applied to black skin, this can give the skin a chalky appearance. When selecting products for black skin, bear in mind not just the shade but also the ingredients.

Compact powders

Compact powders contain a gum, mixed with the ingredients to bind them together. These powders provide a greater coverage, especially if they contain titanium dioxide. Pressed powders should be recommended only for a client's personal use, and then only to remove shine from the skin during the day, as required.

> **HEALTH AND SAFETY**
>
> **Avoiding contamination**
> Before application, always remove sufficient loose powder from the container. This minimises the chances of bacteria entering the powder.

> **HEALTH AND SAFETY**
>
> **Home use**
> If the client uses a pressed powder, advise them to wash the powder applicator regularly to minimise the reproduction of bacteria.

> **TIP** ✓
>
> **Powders**
> Some powders reflect light whilst appearing subtle and non-shiny. These are most flattering for mature skin, as wrinkles appear less obvious.

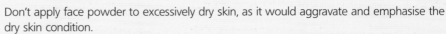

TIP

Don't apply face powder to excessively dry skin, as it would aggravate and emphasise the dry skin condition.

Beware of applying powder if a client has superfluous facial hair, as it may emphasise this.

How to apply powder

Face powder is applied *after* the foundation, unless a water-based foundation or a combination powder foundation has been selected. Select a matt powder for a daytime make-up, and an iridescent powder for an evening make-up.

1 Remove the loose powder from its container, using a clean spatula or, if the powder is in a shaker, by sprinkling it out. Place the powder on a clean facial tissue.

2 Ask the client to keep their eyes closed. Using a clean piece of cottonwool, press the cottonwool into the powder and then press the powder all over the face.

3 Remove excess powder using a large, disinfected facial powder brush. Direct the brush strokes first up the face, which dislodges the powder, then down the face, which flattens the facial hair and removes the final residue of excess powder.

Facial contouring using powder products may now be carried out.

THE EYES

Make-up is applied to the eye area to complement the natural eye colour, to give definition to the eye area, and to enhance the natural shape of the eye.

Eyeshadow

Eyeshadow adds colour and definition to the eye area. The different types include matt, pearlised, metallic and pastel. They are available in cream, crayon or powder form. Eyeshadows are composed of either oil-and-water emulsions or waxes containing inorganic pigments to give colour.

- **Cream eyeshadows** contain wax and oil.
- **Crayon eyeshadows** are composed of wax and oil, and are similar in appearance and application to an eyepencil.
- **Powder eyeshadows** have a talc base, mixed with oils to facilitate application. Lighter shades are produced by the addition of **titanium dioxide** – avoid these on dark skin as they contrast too harshly with the natural skin colour.

Pearlised eyeshadows are created by the addition of **bismuth oxychloride** or **mica**; a *metallic* effect is created by the addition of fine particles of **gold leaf**, **aluminium** or **bronze**.

Applying powder

HEALTH AND SAFETY +

Eye cosmetics
The eye tissue is particularly sensitive. Eye cosmetic products should be of the highest quality, and be permitted for use according to the Cosmetics Products (Safety) Regulations 1989.

Eyeshadows

TIP ✔

Cream eyeshadows
Cream eyeshadows are not very popular – they are difficult to blend and quickly settle into creases. They are usually used by clients who have dry, mature skin.

How to apply eyeshadow

Eyeshadow application will differ according to the eye shape of the client.

1 Protect the skin beneath the eye with a clean tissue – this is to collect small particles of eyeshadow that may fall during application.

2 Lift the skin at the brow slightly to keep the eye tissue taut, enabling you to reach the skin near to the base of the eyelashes.

3 Apply the selected eyeshadow to the eyelid, using a sponge or a brush applicator.

4 Highlight beneath the browbone.

5 Using a brush, apply a darker eyeshadow to the socket area, beginning at the outer corner of the eye. Blend the colour evenly, to avoid harsh lines.

> **TIP** ✔
>
> When applying powder colours, always tap the brush before application to remove excess eyeshadow. If too much colour is deposited on the applicator, stroke it over a clean tissue to remove the excess.

Applying eyeshadow

Eyeliner

Eyeliner defines and emphasises the eye area. It is available in pencil, liquid or powder form.

- **Eyepencil** – made of wax and oil, and contains different pigments which give it its colour.
- **Liquid eyeliner** – a gum solution, in which the pigment is suspended.
- **Powder eyeliner** – a powder base with the addition of mineral oil.

> **HEALTH AND SAFETY** ✚
>
> Eyepencil
> A good-quality eyepencil will be quite soft when applied to the skin, to avoid dragging the delicate eye tissue.

Powder eyeliner is the most suitable choice for a client who lives in a hot country, as it will not smudge.

How to apply eyeliner

If you are using a powder or liquid eyeliner, apply it with a clean eyeliner brush.

1 Lift the skin gently upwards at the eyebrows, to keep the eyelid firm and make application easier.

2 Draw a fine line along the base of the eyelashes, as required.

3 Lightly smudge the eyeliner to soften the effect of the line.

Eyeliners

Beauty Express Ltd.

> **TIP** ✔
>
> Have a clean cotton bud available so that you can remove the powder from any minor mistakes during application.

Applying eyeliner to the upper lashline

Applying eyeliner to the base lashline

Applying eyebrow colour

Beauty Express Ltd.

Mascara

Eyebrow colour

Eyebrow colour emphasises the eyebrow, alter their shape, and can make sparse eyebrows look thicker. It is available in pencil or powder form.

- **Eyebrow pencil** – firmer than an eyepencil, and is composed of waxes that hold the inorganic pigments.
- **Powder brow colour** – composed of a talc base, mixed with mineral oil and pigments.
- **Liquid eyebrow** – a fluid, quick-drying eyebrow colour to define the brows.
- **Eyebrow mascara** – composed of mineral oil and waxes with pigment suspended in it. The mascara defines the brows and controls and shapes them.

How to apply eyebrow colour

1 Select an appropriate colour of powder or eyebrow pencil. Brush the eyebrows with a clean brow brush to remove excess face powder and eyeshadow.

2 Simulate the appearance of brow hair by using fine strokes of colour, or disguise bald patches with a denser application.

3 Brush the eyebrows into shape.

Mascara

Mascara enhances the natural eyelashes, making them appear longer, changed in colour and thicker. It is available in liquid, cream and block-cake forms. It is composed of waxes or an oil-and-water emulsion, and contains pigments which give it its colour.

Mascara

Mascara when purchased is usually provided with a brush applicator. This applicator cannot be effectively cleaned and disinfected, however, so it should not be used. Instead use a disposable mascara brush for each client.

- **Liquid mascara** – a mixture of gum in water or alcohol; the pigment is suspended in this. It may also contain short textile filaments that adhere to the lashes and have a thickening, lengthening effect. Water-resistant mascara contains resin instead of gum, so that it will not run or smudge.
- **Cream mascara** – an emulsion of oil and water, with the pigment suspended in this.
- **Block mascara** – composed of mineral oil, lanolin and waxes, which are melted together to form a block on setting. It must be dampened with water before application.

HEALTH AND SAFETY

Allergies

If the client has hypersensitive eyes or skin, use hypoallergenic cosmetics that contain no known sensitisers.

HEALTH AND SAFETY

Contact lenses

If the client wears contact lenses, don't use either lash-building filament mascaras or loose-particled eyeshadows, which have a tendency to flake and may enter the eye.

How to apply mascara

Using a disposable mascara brush, apply mascara to the eyelashes:

1 Hold the brush horizontally to apply colour to the length of the lashes. Where the lashes are short and curly, or difficult to reach, hold the brush vertically and use the point of the brush.
2 Place a clean tissue underneath the base of the lower eyelashes, and stroke the brush down the length of the lashes from the base to the tips.
3 Lift the eyelid at the browbone. Ask the client to look down slightly whilst keeping their eyes open. From above, stroke down the length of the lashes from the base to the tips.
4 Using a zigzag motion, draw the brush upwards through the upper and lower surfaces of the lashes, from the base to the tips.
5 Finally, separate the eyelashes with a clean brush or lash comb.

ACTIVITY

Choosing mascara

What colour mascara should be applied if the client has the following hair colouring: brown, auburn, black or grey?

TIP

Clear mascara makes the lashes appear thicker, whilst appearing very natural.

TIP

Never pump the mascara wand when loading it with mascara. This encourages air to enter and makes the mascara dry out.

Applying mascara

TIP

Curly lashes will require brushing, using a clean brush, both before mascara application and after each coat, to separate the lashes.

Eye make-up for the client who wears glasses

If the client wears glasses, check the function of the lens, as this can alter the appearance and effect of the eye make-up.

- *If the client is short-sighted, the lens makes the eye appear smaller.* Draw attention to the eyes by selecting brighter, lighter colours. When applying eyeshadow and eyeliner, use the corrective techniques for small eyes. Apply mascara to emphasise the eyelashes.
- *If the client is long-sighted, the lens will magnify the eye.* Make-up should therefore be subtle, avoiding frosted colours and lash-building mascaras. Careful blending is important, as any mistakes will be magnified!

How to apply corrective eye make-up

Dark circles

Dark circles

1 Minimise the circles by applying a concealing product.

Wide-set eyes

Wide-set eyes

1 Apply a darker eye colour to the inner portion of the upper eyelid.
2 Apply lighter eyeshadow to the outer portion of the eyelid.
3 Apply eyeliner in a darker colour to the inner half of the upper eyelid.
4 Eyebrow pencil may be applied to extend the inner browline.

Close-set eyes

Close-set eyes

1 Lighten the inner portion of the upper eyelid.
2 Use a darker colour at the outer eye.
3 Apply eyeliner to the outer corner of the upper eyelid.
4 Pluck brow hairs at the inner eyebrow – this helps to create the illusion of the eyes being further apart.

Round eyes

Round eyes

1 Apply a darker colour over the prominent central upper-lid area.
2 Elongate the eyes by applying eyeliner to the outer corners of the upper and lower eyelids.

Prominent eyes

Prominent eyes

1 Apply dark matt eyeshadow over the prominent upper eyelid.
2 Apply a darker shade to the outer portion of the eyelid, and blend it upwards and outwards.
3 Highlight the browbone, drawing attention to this area.
4 Eyeliner may be applied to the inner lower eyelid.

TIP	
To make the eyes appear less prominent, select matt eyeshadows – pearlised and frosted eyeshadows will highlight and emphasise the eye.	

Overhanging lids

1 Apply a pale highlighter to the middle of the eyelid.
2 Apply a darker eyeshadow to contour the socket area, creating a higher crease (which disguises the hooded appearance).

Overhanging lids

Deep-set eyes

1 Use light-coloured eyeshadows.
2 Eyeshadow may also be applied in a fine line to the inner half of the lower eyelid, beneath the lashes.
3 Apply eyeliner to the outer halves of the upper and lower eyelids, broadening the line as you extend outwards.

Deep-set eyes

Downward-slanting eyes

1 Create lift by applying the eyeshadow upwards and outwards at the outer corners of the upper eyelid.
2 Apply eyeliner to the upper eyelid, applying it upwards at the outer corner.
3 Confine mascara to the outer lashes.

Downward-slanting eyes

Small eyes

1 Choose a light colour for the upper eyelid.
2 Highlight under the brow, to open up the eye area.
3 Curl the lashes before applying mascara.
4 Apply a light-coloured eyeliner to the outer third of the lower eyelid.
5 A white eyeliner may be applied to the inner lid, to make the eye appear larger.

Small eyes

Narrow eyes

1 Apply a lighter colour in the centre of the eyelid, to open up the eye.
2 Apply a shader to the inner and outer portions of the eyelid.

Narrow eyes

Oriental eyes

1 Divide the upper eyelid in two vertically. Place a lighter colour over the inner half of the eyelid and a darker colour at the outer half.
2 Apply a highlighter under the eyebrow.
3 White eyeliner may be applied at the base of the lashline, on the lower inner eyelid.

Oriental eyes

TIP	✔
False eyelashes may be effective in enhancing the eye's natural shape.	

Salon System

The eyelashes

To emphasise the eyelashes, making them appear longer temporarily, curl them using **eyelash curlers**.

How to curl the eyelashes

1 Rest the upper lashes between the upper and lower portions of the eyelash curlers.
2 Bring the two portions gently together with a squeezing action.
3 Hold the lashes in the curlers for approximately ten seconds, then release them.
4 If the lashes are not sufficiently curled, repeat the action.

HEALTH AND SAFETY

Eyelash curling
Repeated eyelash curling can lead to breakage. The technique should therefore be used only for special occasions.

False eyelashes

ARTIFICIAL EYELASHES

False eyelashes are made from small threads of nylon fibre or real hair. They are attached to the client's natural lash hair imitating the natural eyelashes and making the lashes appear longer and thicker, and thereby drawing attention to the eye. There are two main types: **semi-permanent individual lashes** and **strip lashes**.

False lashes are applied for the following reasons:

● to create shape and depth in the eye area, when completing corrective eye make-up;
● simply to add definition to the eye area;
● to enhance evening or fantasy make-up;
● to provide thick long lashes for photographic make-up;
● to provide an alternative eyelash-enhancing effect for a client who is allergic to mascara.

Reception

When making an appointment for false-eyelash application, find out why the client wants false lashes and determine which type would be most appropriate.

Strip lashes

Artificial **strip lashes** are designed to be worn for a short period, either for a day or an evening. They are attached to the natural eyelashes with a soft,

Strip lashes

weak adhesive. After removal the strip must be cleaned before re-application. Allow 20 minutes for the application of strip lashes; if applying them in conjunction with a make-up, allow an additional 45 minutes for the make-up.

Individual lashes

Artificial *individual* lashes are attached to the natural lashes with a strong adhesive. They may be worn for approximately four to six weeks, and are therefore known as **semi-permanent lashes**. Allow 20 minutes for the application of individual eyelashes; and again allow a further 45 minutes if applying them in conjunction with a make-up.

Although individual lashes can be worn for up to six weeks they look effective only for approximately three weeks. After this time, the appearance of the artificial lashes begins to deteriorate, the lash adhesive becomes brittle, and the eyelash area may become irritated.

Due to the cyclic nature of hair replacement some individual lashes will be lost when the natural lash falls out. These lashes may be replaced each week, as necessary; the client is usually charged a price for each individual lash replaced. The client must be told of this service as part of the aftercare advice.

Booking the treatment

When a client makes an appointment for an artificial lash treatment, they should be asked the following questions:

- *Have they had a similar treatment before in this salon?* If they have not, they should visit the salon beforehand for a skin test to assess any sensitivity to the adhesive (see page 53).
- *Are they having the false eyelashes applied for any particular reason, such as a holiday or a special occasion?* In deciding which type of false eyelash would be most appropriate, take into consideration the effect required and for how long the lashes are to be worn.

If the client wears glasses, the artificial lashes must not be so long as to touch the lenses. Also, if the lens magnifies the eye, this must be taken into account. Ask the client to bring their glasses with them to the salon.

Contra-indications

If following completion of the record card or inspection of the eye area you have found any of the following, do not apply false eyelashes:

- *Skin disease*.
- *Skin disorder* in the eye area, such as psoriasis or eczema.
- *Inflammation or swelling* around the eye.
- *Hypersensitive skin*.
- *Any eye disorder*, such as styes or hordeola, conjunctivitis, blepharitis, watery eye, or cysts.
- *A positive (allergic) reaction* to the adhesive skin test.
- *Contact lenses* (unless removed).

TIP

Treatment timing
False lash application: allow 20 minutes.

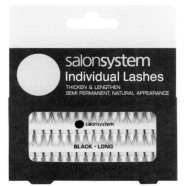

Salon System

Individual lashes

TIP

Fair lashes
If the client has fair lashes you could promote an eyelash tint service before false eyelash application to achieve a more natural, realistic effect.

An unduly nervous client with a tendency to blink could prove hard to treat in this way. Use your discretion in deciding on the suitability of a client for treatment.

Equipment and materials

To apply the false eyelashes you will need the following equipment and materials:

EQUIPMENT LIST

 Couch or beauty chair with sit-up and lie-down positions and an easy-to-clean surface
Trolley on which to display everything

 Headband freshly laundered for each client.

 Eye make-up remover (non-oily)

 Facial tissues (white) – for blotting the eyelashes dry

 Disposable mascara brush to avoid cross-contamination

 Manual tweezers (2 pairs, sterilised) – special tweezers are available, designed specifically to assist in attaching individual eyelashes

 Strip eyelash lengths (a selection) in a choice of colours

Eyelash adhesive for individual lashes

 Individual eyelash lengths (a selection) in a choice of colours

Eyelash adhesive solvent for removing and cleaning artificial lashes

 Sterilised scissors (1 pair) used for trimming the length of strip lashes

YOU WILL ALSO NEED:

Towels (2, medium-sized) freshly laundered for each client

Disposable tissue roll for example, bedroll

Cleansing milk used to remove facial make-up in the eye area

Damp cottonwool for removing cleansing product from the eye area

Surgical spirit for wiping the points of the tweezers to remove adhesive

Plastic palette (disinfected) on which to place the artificial lashes prior to application

Eyelash adhesive for strip lashes

Sterilised dish (small) lined with foil, in which to place the eyelash adhesive during lash application

Hand mirrors (clean) to show client results

Client record card – confidential card recording the details of each client registered at the salon

TIP

In order that you can effectively clean the dish after the treatment, you need to line the dish with a disposable lining.

Sterilisation and disinfection

When preparing to apply artificial *strip* lashes, clean the surface of the palette onto which you will stick the lashes once you have removed them from their packet. Use surgical spirit, applied with clean cottonwool. The palette may be stored in the ultra-violet light cabinet until ready for use. *Individual* lashes come in a special 'contoured' package: you can hold this securely whilst removing individual lashes, so the lashes can be kept hygienically until required.

Always have a spare pair of tweezers available during application of the individual or strip false lashes. Should you accidentally drop the tweezers with which you are working, you will need a clean, sterile pair available.

Scissors, used to trim strip lashes, should be sterilised before use.

Preparing the treatment area

Before the client is shown through to the treatment area, check it to ensure that the required equipment and materials are available and the area is clean and tidy. The plastic-covered couch should be clean, having been thoroughly washed with hot, soapy water, or wiped thoroughly with surgical spirit or a professional alcohol-based cleaner. The couch or chair should be protected with a long strip of disposable tissue-paper bedroll, or a freshly laundered sheet and a bath towel. A small towel should be placed neatly at the head of the couch, ready to be draped across the client's chest for protection during treatment. (The paper tissue will need changing and the towels will need to be laundered for each client.)

The couch or beauty chair should be in a slightly elevated position, to give the optimum position for the therapist when applying the false lashes. In this position, too, the client will not be staring into the overhead light (which might cause the eyes to water).

ACTIVITY

Position of client
Can you think of further disadvantages of having the client lying flat when applying false lashes?

Planning the treatment

A variety of false lashes is available, including lashes intended for corrective work as well as those simply intended to enhance the natural lashes. Lash length may be short, medium or long; their texture may be fine, medium or thick, with some having a feathered effect. Strips designed for use on the lower lashes are called **partial lashes**: here small groups of hairs are placed intermittently along the length of the false-lash base.

In a commercial salon, the most popular colours are usually black and brown. For special effects, however; strip lashes are available in fantasy colours, complete with glitter and jewels!

Factors when choosing false eyelashes

Before applying artificial lashes the beauty therapist should consider the following points, and advise the client accordingly.

TIP

In America streaked lashes are available, to give a more subtle effect for the mature client.

The client's age Artificial lashes create a very bold, dramatic effect, which can make an older client look too hard. Remember that the skin colour and the natural hair colour change with age: the lash chosen must enhance the client's appearance.

The client's natural lashes Does the client have short or long, sparse or thick, very curly or straight lashes? Choose an artificial lash to complement the natural lash. Here are some guidelines:

Short and stubby lashes

- *Short and stubby lashes* These are commonly seen on older clients who have overhanging eyelids. Choose a medium lash length in a medium thickness at the outer corner of the eyelid; the lashes should become gradually shorter from the centre of the eyelid to the inner corner. Brush the artificial and natural lashes together after application to ensure that they blend.

Sparse lashes

- *Sparse lashes* Place individual short lashes along the natural lashline; or, to give a more natural appearance, you may wish to apply partial strip lashes to the upper eyelid.

Curly lashes

- *Curly eyelashes* These are very common on African-Caribbean clients. Choose a longer, sweeping strip or individual false lashes, in black. The chosen lashes and colour should give emphasis and depth to the eye.

The natural eyelash colour Select false lashes that complement the hair and skin tone. Natural-hair false eyelashes offer the greatest choice of colour, but these are expensive and may be difficult to purchase.

False eyelashes

ACTIVITY

Choosing eyelash colours
Suggest a choice of false eyelash colour for the clients below:
- a mature grey-haired client;
- a young red-haired client;
- a mature client with bleached hair;
- a mature African-Caribbean client.

Using false eyelashes for corrective purposes

Here are some outlines of corrective techniques for various eye shapes.

Eye shape	Corrective steps
Small eyes 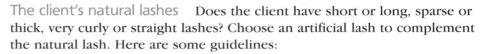	Place false lashes at the outer corners of the upper eyelid. These should be longer than the natural lashes.
Close-set eyes	Place fine, long, individual or partial lashes at the outer third of the eye. They may be applied to the lower lashes as well as to the upper.

Eye shape	Corrective steps
Wide-set eyes	Apply medium-length lashes at the inner corner of the eye and to the centre, becoming slightly shorter towards the outer corner of the upper eyelid. This may be repeated on the lower lash also.
Downward-slanting eyes	Apply longer lashes (individual or partial strip lashes) to the outer corners of the upper eyelid.
Round eyes	Individual or strip lashes should be used to lengthen the lashline. Apply the false lashes from the centre of the upper eyelid outwards.
Deep-set eyes	Apply fine lashes to the upper and lower lashes. The upper-lid false lashes should be longer, to draw attention to the eye.
Overhanging lids	Apply longer lashes to the upper eyelid, from the outer corner and tapering to a shorter length at the centre of the lid and toward the inner corner.

How to prepare the client

Show the client through to the prepared treatment area after filling in the record card at reception.

1 Position the client comfortably on the treatment couch or beauty chair (which should be slightly elevated). If the client wears contact lenses, these must be removed before the treatment begins.

2 Drape a clean towel across the client's chest and shoulders. Protect their hair with a clean headband.

3 Wash your hands, which indicates to the client that treatment is beginning and in a hygienic and professional manner.

4 Consult the client's record card, then check the treatment area for visible contra-indications or abnormalities before proceeding.

5 It is usual to carry out a full facial cleanse (rather than cleansing only the eye area), as make-up is usually applied to complement the false eyelashes. Use a cleansing milk to dissolve facial make-up, followed by a non-oily eye make-up remover to cleanse the eye area. Both products should be removed with clean, damp cottonwool.

6 To ensure that the eye tissue and eyelashes are thoroughly clean and grease-free, apply a mild oil-free toning lotion: stroke this over the skin using clean, damp cottonwool.

7   Blot the lashes dry, using a fresh facial tissue for each eye. (Any moisture left on the natural lashes will reduce the effectiveness of the eyelash adhesive.)

8   Brush the natural lashes to separate them before application.

How to apply semi-permanent lashes

1   Check that everything you need is on the trolley.

2   Check that the back of the couch or beauty chair is slightly raised, at a height that is comfortable for you.

3   Discuss the treatment procedure with the client. Explain that she will be required to keep her eyes open during the treatment. Reassure her that she may blink during application. Very often clients feel that they shouldn't, and their eyes begin to water.

4   Ask her to tilt her head downwards very slightly. This tends to lower the upper eyelids, making application easier.

5   Depending on the effect required, you may start application of the individual lashes at different positions along the natural lashline. In general, apply shorter lashes to the inner corners of the eyelid, and longer lashes to the outer corners; this creates a realistic effect and ensures client comfort. If you are applying individual lashes to the entire upper lid, it is practical to start application at the inner corner of the eyelid and work outwards: this follows the natural contour of the eye.

6   With the sterile tweezers, select a lash from the package, holding it near its centre. Brush the underside of the individual lash, at the root, through the adhesive. The adhesive should extend slightly beyond the root. You need sufficient adhesive, but not too much – excess adhesive should be removed by wiping the lash against the inside of the adhesive container.

7   Working from behind the client, hold the tweezers at the angle at which the false lash will be applied to the natural lashline. Hold the brow tissue with your other hand to steady the eyelid.

> **TIP** ✔
>
> Positioning the individual lashes correctly requires experience. It is a good idea initially to practise application without adhesive.

Using a stroking movement, place the underside of the false lash on top of the natural lash. Stroke the adhesive along the length of the natural eyelash. Guide the false lash towards the base of the natural lash, so that the false lash rests along the length of the natural lash. Wait a few seconds to allow the adhesive to dry (to prevent the lashes from sticking together). Continue placing further false lashes side by side until the desired effect is achieved.

During application, keep checking your work. If a lash is out of line, remove it while the adhesive is still soft. If the adhesive has set, the lash will need to be removed using adhesive solvent – see illustration on page 420.

8   Apply the false lashes one at a time, to each eye alternately. This avoids sensitising the eye, and makes it easier for you to create a balanced effect.

> **TIP** ✔
>
> Do not prepare the lash adhesive until you are ready to use it. It tends to dry on contact with air.

> **TIP** ✔
>
> When applying the individual lashes to the inner portion of the eyelid, hold the skin taut, stretching the skin slightly. This will enable you to position the false lash more easily.

> **TIP** ✔
>
> Use a clean pair of tweezers to remove the individual lashes from their container when required. Holding the tweezers firmly, grip each lash near its base (this avoids misshaping the outer lash hairs).

> **TIP** ✔
>
> To ensure efficient application, don't get adhesive on the points of the tweezers.

Salon System

The natural lashes

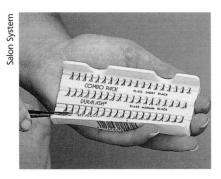

Salon System

Selecting a lash

Brushing through the adhesive

Salon System

Applying a lash to the upper lid

Salon System

The completed effect

9 If the client requires false lashes to be applied to the *lower* lid, the application technique is slightly different.

Work facing the client, with the client looking upwards, her eyes slightly open. Follow the same general procedure for applying the false eyelashes; here, however, the lashes curve downwards and the adhesive is applied to the *upper* surface of the lash.

Lashes applied to the lower eyelid are usually shorter than those chosen for the upper lid, and more adhesive is required for the lashes to be secure and have maximum durability.

10 When you have completed the lash application, ask the client to sit up, and show her the completed effect.

11 If the client is satisfied with the result, you can apply a water- or powder-based eye make-up if desired. Do not apply mascara, as this will reduce the adhesion to the natural lash. Mascara also clogs the lashes together; and is difficult to remove without affecting the eyelash adhesive. On completion, the lashes can be gently brushed – using a disposable brush – to remove particles of eyeshadow.

How to apply strip lashes

Strip false eyelashes are applied *before* carrying out the eye make-up – this avoids the eye make-up being spoilt if the eyes water slightly during application.

1 Carefully apply moisturiser and foundation, taking care not to get any cosmetic products on the lashes. (If you do, gently wipe over the lashes with the non-oily eye make-up remover, and blot the eyelashes dry again with a clean facial tissue.)

2 Brush the lashes to separate them, using a clean disposable mascara brush. This makes false-lash application easier, and removes any fine particles of loose powder.

3 Remove the strip lashes from their container; and place them on a clean, disinfected palette. Each strip is designed to fit either the left or the right eye: remember which is which when placing them on the palette.

4 Check the length of the strip against the client's eyelid. The strip should never be applied directly from one corner of the eyelid to the other; but should start about two mm from the inner corner of the eye, and end two mm from the outer corner. This ensures a natural effect and maximises the durability of the false lash.

> **TIP**
>
> Tell the client that artificial lashes applied to the lower lashes tend to fall off after one week. (This is probably due to the natural watering of the eye affecting the adhesive.)

> **TIP**
>
> Do not apply adhesive directly from the tube to the eyelash base – you would apply too much adhesive.

HEALTH AND SAFETY ✚

Lash length

If the lashes were not shorter at the inner corner of the eyelid, they would irritate the client's eye.

TIP ✓

If a client has straight eyelashes that grow downwards, curl them slightly using eyelash curlers (page 410). If you don't, a gap will be visible between the real lashes and the false strip lash.

Removing the strip lashes from their container using tweezers

Trimming the lashes

Positioning the lash on the base of the natural lashline

When you remove the strip lash from the package you will find that there is adhesive on the backing strip, which fixes the lash in the container: this adhesive is sufficient to hold the lash onto the client's natural lash while you measure the length.

5   To trim the false lashes you require a sharp pair of scissors. First correct the length of the *strip* if necessary. Hold the lashes securely with one hand, and then trim the strip at the outer edge.

Then trim the lashes themselves, if necessary. Never reduce the length of the lashes by cutting straight across them: the result would not look natural. Natural eyelashes are of varying lengths, due to the nature of the hair growth cycle; it is this effect that you must simulate. To shorten the lash, 'chip' into the lash. Use the *points* of the scissors to shorten the lash length. Cut the lashes so that the shorter lashes are at the inner corner of the eyelid, gradually increasing toward the outer corner.

6   Check that everything required for the false eyelash application is available on your trolley.

7   The couch or beauty chair should be in a slightly raised position. During the treatment you will be working from behind the client: the height must be comfortable for you.

8   Discuss the treatment procedure with the client. Explain to her that she will be required to keep her eyes open during the application. Ask her to tilt her head downwards very slightly – this lowers the upper eyelids, making application easier.

9   Using the sterile tweezers, remove one of the eyelash strips from the palette. Handle it very carefully, as it can easily become misshapen.

Remembering that the strip is designed to fit either the right or the left eye, place it against the appropriate eyelid and check the length (with the client's eyes closed).

10 Once satisfied that the length of the strip lash is correct, remove the adhesive tape used to hold it in the container.

11 Place a small quantity of strip lash adhesive on the disinfected palette.

12 Ask the client to look down slightly, with her eyes half open. With one hand lift her brow to steady the upper eyelid.

Holding the strip lash with the sterile tweezers at its centre, drag it at its base through the adhesive. (The adhesive must be moist.) It is usually white, but when it dries it becomes colourless.

Position the base of the strip lash as close as possible to the base of the natural eyelash, ensuring that it is about two mm in from the inner and outer corners of the eye. *Gently* press the false and natural eyelashes together with your fingertips, along the length of the lash and at the outer corners.

13 When you are sure that the first strip lash is secure, apply the second in the same way.

TIP ✓

Extra glue (although not excessive) may be applied to the ends of the lashes to prevent lifting whilst wearing them.

14 If strip lashes are to be applied to the bottom lashes also, apply these now, in the same way as the upper lashes. (Strip lashes for the lower lids are fine, with an extremely thin base. These lashes should be trimmed as before to ensure comfort and durability in wear.)

15 Allow three to five minutes for the adhesive to dry.

16 Gently brush the lashes from underneath the natural lashline, using a clean disposable mascara brush. This will blend the natural and false lashes together Check that both sets of lashes are correctly positioned, and that a balanced look has been achieved.

17 Artificial lashes look more realistic if eyeliner is applied to the client's eyelid: this disguises the base of the strip lash.

Pressing the strip lash and the natural lash together

Contra-actions

If during application of false lashes the eye starts to water, blot the tears with the corner of a clean tissue. The tears can cause the adhesive to take on an unsightly white crystallised appearance. Any possible irritation of the eyes should therefore be avoided, during both preparation of the eye area and application itself.

Never place eyelashes *underneath* the natural eyelashes – eye irritation would occur.

While practising individual eyelash application you may find at some point that you have accidentally glued a couple of the lower and upper natural lashes together. Apply adhesive solvent to a cottonwool-tipped orange stick, and gently roll this over the lash length to dissolve the adhesive.

If solvent or adhesive should accidentally enter the eye, rinse the eye thoroughly and immediately, using clean water. Repeat this until discomfort is no longer experienced.

Salon System

The completed effect

HEALTH AND SAFETY

Client comfort
Check the eyelash application as you work. Ensure that the lower and upper lashes are not stuck together, and that the eyelashes are accurately and evenly applied.

Aftercare and advice

The following aftercare instructions should be given to the client after false eyelash application:

- Avoid rubbing the eyes, or the lashes may become loosened.
- Do not use an oil-based eye make-up remover as its cosmetic constituents will dissolve the adhesive.
- Use only dry or water-based eye make-up (as these may readily be removed with a non-oily eye make-up remover).
- If the lashes are made of a synthetic material, heat will cause them to become frizzy. Advise the client to avoid extremes of temperature, such as a hot sauna.
- Do not touch the eyes for $1\frac{1}{2}$ hours after application, while the adhesive dries thoroughly.

If the client has had *individual* artificial lashes applied, the following homecare advice should be given on caring for the lashes:

- Use a non-oily eye make-up remover daily to cleanse the eyelids and eyelashes. Avoid contact with oil-based preparations in the eye area, such as moisturisers and cleansers – the oil content will dissolve the adhesive, and the lashes would become detached.
- Do not attempt to remove the artificial lashes – pulling at the artificial lash will also pull out the natural eyelashes.
- After bathing, gently *pat* the eye area dry with a clean towel.

Clients with individual false eyelashes should have the false lashes maintained by regular visits to the salon. Lost individual lashes can be replaced as necessary; this is often described as an eyelash **infill** service.

If the client wishes to have the individual false lashes removed, this should be done professionally.

How to remove individual eyelashes

1 Position the client lying on the couch.
2 Wash your hands.
3 Remove make-up from the eye area, cleansing the skin with a suitable eye make-up remover.
4 While the client's eyes are open, place a pre-shaped eyeshield underneath the lower lashes of each eye. (This will protect the eye tissue from the solvent.) Position the eyeshields so that they fit snugly to the base of the lower lashes.
5 Ask the client to close her eyes gently, and not to open them again until you tell her to do so.
6 Prepare a new disposable orange stick by covering it at the pointed end with clean, dry cottonwool.
7 Moisten the cottonwool with the artificial eyelash adhesive solvent.

> **HEALTH AND SAFETY**
>
> **Eye care**
> Do not allow eyelash adhesive solvent to come into excessive contact with the eye tissue – it could cause irritation of the skin. Ensure that there is sufficient solvent only on the cottonwool: it should be moist but not dripping wet or the solvent might enter the eye.

8 Treating one eye at a time, gently stroke down the false eyelashes with the adhesive solvent until the adhesive dissolves and the false eyelash begins to loosen.
9 When you are satisfied that the eyelash adhesive has dissolved, gently attempt to remove the false eyelash. Support the upper eyelid with the fingers of one hand, using the other hand to remove the eyelash with a sterile pair of manual tweezers. If the adhesive has been adequately dissolved, the eyelash will lift away easily from the natural eyelash. If there is any resistance, repeat the solvent application until the eyelash comes away readily.
10 As the artificial eyelashes are removed, collect them on a clean white facial tissue or a clean pad of cottonwool.

> **HEALTH AND SAFETY** +
>
> **Solvents**
> Although solvents are formulated to remove artificial lashes from the natural lash, great care must be taken to avoid skin/eye irritation. Ideally this solution should be used to clean the artificial lashes after removal. Removal of artificial lashes should be with an oil-based eye make-up remover product.

> **TIP** ✔
>
> Disposable cotton buds may be used to apply eyelash adhesive solvent.

Applying adhesive solvent to remove false eyelashes

HEALTH AND SAFETY +

Client comfort

Never attempt to remove the artificial eyelashes until they have begun to loosen – if you do, the client's natural eyelashes will also be removed, causing them discomfort.

---

11 Having removed all of the artificial eyelashes from one eye, soothe the area by applying damp cottonwool pads soaked in cool water. (This will also remove any remaining solvent.) A damp cottonwool pad may be placed over the eye, while you remove the false lashes from the other eye.

How to remove strip lashes

If a client wears strip eyelashes they will need instructions on how to remove and care for the false lashes themself.

1 Use the fingertips of one hand to support the eyelid at the outer corner. With the other hand, lift the lash strip base at the outer corner of the eye. Gently peel the strip away from the natural lash, from the outer edge towards the centre of the eyelid.

2 Peel the adhesive from the backing strip, using a clean pair of manual tweezers. Take care to avoid stretching the strip lash.

3 Clean the strip lash in the appropriate way.

- *Strips made from human hair* Clean with a commercial lash cleaner or 70% alcohol. This removes the remaining adhesive and the eye make-up.

- *Synthetic strips* Place in warm, soapy water for a few minutes, to clean the lashes and remove the remaining adhesive. Rinse in tepid water.

4 After cleaning the strip lashes should be recurled.

How to recurl strip lashes

For reasons of hygiene and because of the time involved, this service will not be offered by the salon. The client, however; will need advice on how to recurl the lashes at home.

1 On removal from the water, place the lashes side by side, ensuring that the inner edges are together inside a clean facial tissue.

2 Wrap a tissue around an even, barrel-shaped object such as a felt-tip pen, and secure it with an elastic band.

3 The false lashes, inside the facial tissue, should then be rolled around this object. Keep the base of the lash straight, so that the whole lash length curls around the object.

Once recurled, the strip lashes can be returned to the contoured shelves in their original container and stored for further use.

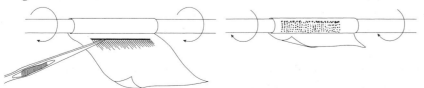

Soothing the eye area after removal of the lashes

HEALTH AND SAFETY +

Client comfort

When removing the strip lash, avoid pulling the natural lashes with the false lashes.

Removing strip eyelashes

HEALTH AND SAFETY +

Semi-permanent lashes

The client should be advised to return to the salon for semi-permanent lashes to be removed professionally.

Recurling strip lashes

THE LIPS

Lip cosmetics add colour and draw attention to the lips. As the lips have no protective sebum, the use of lip cosmetics also helps to prevent them from drying and becoming chapped.

It is not uncommon for the lips to be out of proportion in some way. Using lip cosmetics and corrective techniques, symmetrical lips can be created. A careful choice of product and accurate application are required to achieve a professional effect.

The main lip cosmetics are lipliner, lipsticks and lipglosses. Sometimes the lips may be unevenly pigmented. The application of a lip toner or foundation over the lips corrects this.

Beauty Express Ltd.

Lip cosmetics

Lipliner

Lipliner is used to define the lips, creating a perfectly symmetrical outline. This is coloured in with another lip cosmetic, either a lipstick or a lipgloss. The lipliner also helps to prevent the lipstick from 'bleeding' into lines around the lips.

Lipliner has a wax base which does not melt and can be applied easily. It contains pigments which give the pencil its colour.

When choosing a lipliner, select one that is the same colour as, or slightly darker than, the lipstick to be used with it.

Beauty Express Ltd.

Lipliners

HEALTH AND SAFETY

Lip pencils
Always sharpen the lip pencil before use on each client, to provide a clean, uncontaminated cosmetic surface.

RVB/Depilex

Lip pencil

Lipstick

HEALTH AND SAFETY

Lipstick
For reasons of hygiene, remove a small quantity of lipstick by scraping the stick with a clean spatula – don't apply the lipstick directly.

Lipstick contains a blend of oils and waxes, which give it its firmness, and silicone, essential for easy application. It also contains pigment, to add colour, an emollient moisturiser, to keep the lips soft and supple and perfume, to improve its appeal. In addition it may include vitamins, to condition the lips, or sunscreens, to protect the lips from ultra-violet rays. Some lipsticks contain a relatively large proportion of water – these moisturise the lips and provide a natural look. The coverage provided by a lipstick depends on its formulation.

Lipsticks are available in the following forms: cream, matt, frosted and translucent. Frosted lipstick has good durability, as it is very dry. Some other lipsticks also offer extended durability, and are suitable for clients who are unable to renew their lipstick regularly.

When choosing the colour of lipstick, take into account the natural colour of the client's lips, the skin and hair colours, and the colours selected for the rest of the make-up.

Lipgloss

Lipgloss provides a moist, shiny look to the lips. It may be worn alone, or applied on top of a lipstick. Its effect is short-lived. Lipgloss is made of mineral oils, with pigment suspended in the oil.

Note that mature clients often have creases on the lips that extend to the surrounding skin. If lipgloss is used it will often bleed into these lines.

Dry lips

Sometimes the lips become dry and chapped. Recommend that the client keeps them moisturised at all times, especially in extremes of heat, cold or wind. Some facial exfoliants can be professionally applied over the lips to remove dead skin.

If the client does not like to wear make-up during the day, or if the client is male, recommend that the lips be protected with a lip-care product.

How to apply corrective lip make-up

Thick lips

Select natural colours and darker shades, avoiding bright, glossy colours.

1 Blend foundation over the lips to disguise the natural lip line.
2 Apply a darker lipliner inside the natural lip line to create a new line.

Thicker upper or lower lip

1 Use the technique described above to make the larger lip appear smaller.
2 Apply a slightly darker lipstick to the larger lip.
3 If the lips droop at the corners, raise the corners by applying lipliner to the corners of the upper lip, to turn them upwards.

Thin lips

Select brighter, pearlised colours. Avoid darker lipsticks, which will make the mouth appear smaller.

1 Apply a neutral lipliner just outside the natural lip line.

Small mouth

1 Extend the line slightly at the corners of the mouth, with both the upper and the lower lips.

Thick lips

Thicker upper lip

Thicker lower lip

Thin lips

Small mouth

Uneven lips

Lines around the mouth

Uneven lips

1 Use a lipliner to draw in a new line.
2 Apply lipstick to the area.

Lines around the mouth

1 Apply lipliner around the natural lip line.
2 Apply a matt cream lipstick to the lips. (Don't use gloss, which might bleed into the lines around the mouth.)

How to apply lipstick

1 Select a lip pencil and lipstick to complement the client's colouring and the colour theme of the make-up.
2 Using a pencil sharpener, sharpen the lip pencil to expose a clean surface.
3 Ask the client to open her mouth slightly.
4 Outline the lips, carrying out lip correction as necessary. Begin the lip line at the outer corner of the mouth, and continue it to the centre of the lips. Repeat the process on the other side of the lip, commencing at the outer corner of the mouth.
5 Remove sufficient lipstick using a clean spatula.
6 Using a disinfected lipbrush, apply the lipstick to the lips.
7 Apply a clean facial tissue over the lip area, and *gently* press it onto the lips. This process, known as **blotting**, removes excess lipstick and fixes the colour on the lips.
8 A second light application of lipstick may then be applied.
9 If desired, lipgloss may be applied over the lipstick to add sheen, again using a disinfected lipbrush.

Applying lipliner

Applying lipstick

WHEN YOU HAVE FINISHED . . .

Outcome 5: Complete the treatment

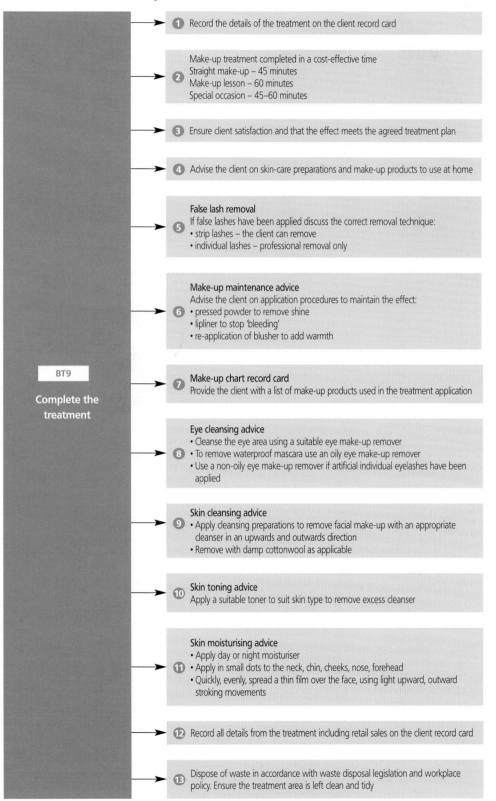

BT9

Complete the treatment

1. Record the details of the treatment on the client record card

2. Make-up treatment completed in a cost-effective time
   Straight make-up – 45 minutes
   Make-up lesson – 60 minutes
   Special occasion – 45–60 minutes

3. Ensure client satisfaction and that the effect meets the agreed treatment plan

4. Advise the client on skin-care preparations and make-up products to use at home

5. **False lash removal**
   If false lashes have been applied discuss the correct removal technique:
   • strip lashes – the client can remove
   • individual lashes – professional removal only

6. **Make-up maintenance advice**
   Advise the client on application procedures to maintain the effect:
   • pressed powder to remove shine
   • lipliner to stop 'bleeding'
   • re-application of blusher to add warmth

7. **Make-up chart record card**
   Provide the client with a list of make-up products used in the treatment application

8. **Eye cleansing advice**
   • Cleanse the eye area using a suitable eye make-up remover
   • To remove waterproof mascara use an oily eye make-up remover
   • Use a non-oily eye make-up remover if artificial individual eyelashes have been applied

9. **Skin cleansing advice**
   • Apply cleansing preparations to remove facial make-up with an appropriate cleanser in an upwards and outwards direction
   • Remove with damp cottonwool as applicable

10. **Skin toning advice**
    Apply a suitable toner to suit skin type to remove excess cleanser

11. **Skin moisturising advice**
    • Apply day or night moisturiser
    • Apply in small dots to the neck, chin, cheeks, nose, forehead
    • Quickly, evenly, spread a thin film over the face, using light upward, outward stroking movements

12. Record all details from the treatment including retail sales on the client record card

13. Dispose of waste in accordance with waste disposal legislation and workplace policy. Ensure the treatment area is left clean and tidy

After applying the make-up, fix the client's hair and then discuss the finished result in front of the make-up mirror.

Wash your hands. Record details of the treatment on the client's record card.

The completed make-up

Contra-actions

Certain cosmetic ingredients are known to provoke allergic reactions in some people. These allergens may cause irritation, excessive erythema, inflammation and swelling.

Known cosmetic allergens include the following:

- *Lanolin* This is similar to sebum, and is obtained from sheep's wool. It is added to many cosmetics as an emollient.
- *Mineral oils* Examples are oleic acid and butyl stearate.
- *Eosin (bromo-acid dye)* A staining pigment, used in some lip cosmetics and perfumes.
- *Paraben* An antiseptic ingredient, used as a preservative in facial cosmetics.
- *Certain colourants* One example is carmine.
- *Perfume* This is added to most cosmetics, and is a common sensitiser.

Other contra-actions include:

- *Watery eyes* The client's eyes water excessively. If the client has watery eyes a tissue may be placed at the corners until the irritation has ceased. If the client's eyes continue to water, remove eye make-up and discontinue treatment.
- *Excessive perspiration* Some clients may perspire, which will affect adherence of the make-up and its finished result. Blot the skin with soft facial tissue and apply more loose face powder to absorb perspiration. If the client continues to perspire, discontinue treatment.

External contact with an allergen may cause urticaria (hives or nettle rash), eczema or dermatitis. If an allergy occurs, the product should be removed from the skin and a soothing substance applied. The client should be advised not to use the product again.

Aftercare and advice

Following make-up application, recommend the correct skin-care products to remove the products you have applied. If false lashes have been applied their removal must also be discussed (see page 420).

Advise the client on application procedures to maintain the effect, e.g. removal of facial shine from the face with pressed powder.

Explain to the client that you can offer a make-up lesson in which you would discuss the reason for the selection of make-up products and colours, and the techniques for applying them. Recommend the correct skin-care products to remove the products you have applied.

PLANNING AND PROMOTING MAKE-UP ACTIVITIES

When correctly applied, make-up increases a person's confidence whilst accentuating their best features and correcting their worst. Professional make-up lessons or demonstrations can be applied in an individual or group context. Promotions are a useful method to generate further business through promotion of make-up products and other related services.

Outcome 1: Prepare and plan for the make-up activity

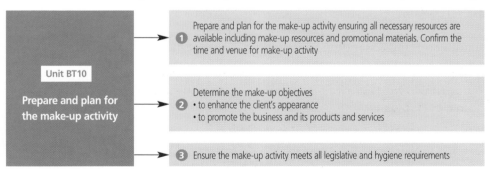

Unit BT10	
Prepare and plan for the make-up activity	**1** Prepare and plan for the make-up activity ensuring all necessary resources are available including make-up resources and promotional materials. Confirm the time and venue for make-up activity
	2 Determine the make-up objectives • to enhance the client's appearance • to promote the business and its products and services
	3 Ensure the make-up activity meets all legislative and hygiene requirements

Make-up being applied

Before performing an individual or group make-up demonstration ensure that you are familiar with the products that you will be using. Compile a checklist of all resources you will need and have them to hand during the demonstration. Finally remember that your own personal appearance is also important to gain client confidence in you and the product!

Planning a group make-up demonstration

Consider what you hope the demonstration will achieve – what is the objective?

If you are working in collaboration with others at an event, it is a good idea to hold a planning meeting with key people.

When setting the date, be realistic in the time required to plan it properly. Detailed planning is important to promote the activity to its best effect and ensure the objectives are met. Do you need to provide invitations? Do you need to know numbers attending? Do you require sponsorship? Will you need to book a venue? Do you have a budget to work within? Will staff need to be available outside their normal working hours?

Poor planning could lead to a potential good publicity opportunity instead becoming bad publicity!

Good time management is important. Plan a time schedule for the activities and keep to it. This will avoid audience irritation and boredom; remember you want to create a fun, sociable atmosphere.

For a group demonstration, allow sufficient time for client questioning during the demonstration and ensure you have available all the make-up resources required.

Consultation for make-up

At consultation, identify what effect the client wishes to achieve – client preference must *always* be considered. Many clients requesting a make-up lesson have tired of their usual make-up application and require inspiration; some are unaccustomed to wearing make-up but recognise its potential to enhance. Other clients will request the service for personal special occasions.

Make-up presentations are a great way to launch a company's new season colours. It is exciting for others to see the transformation of the client before and after. If you have a quiet period you can perform a make-up application for other clients to see.

Achieving the look

Gaining an understanding of the client's requirements is important to achieve a finished result that the client will feel comfortable to wear. Engage the client in conversation to establish their needs, likes and dislikes.

An effective consultation will have gathered important information such as:

- Is the client used to wearing make-up?
- What effect does the client wish to achieve?
- Does the client normally wear make-up? (If not, a more subtle effect should be aimed for.)
- Consider client preferences with regard to colours selected and the overall effect to be achieved.
- Does the client have any known allergies?

Use open questions which may not be answered with yes or no, during the consultation. Open questions usually start with *why*, *how*, *when*, *what* and *which*.

Agree all details of the make-up plan with the client.

During a make-up lesson or presentation ensure the lighting is adequate to show each stage of make-up application effectively. If you have not visited the venue before it is important to check this information in advance as you may need to request or obtain additional lighting.

Consider all related health and safety issues for the promotion, including any potential hazards. A **hazard** is something with potential to cause harm; this may range from using a product on a client who has an allergy to an ingredient, to having a trailing electrical lead that somebody could trip on.

In compliance with the Management of Health and Safety at Work Regulations 1999, complete a risk assessment. This will include identification of:

- any potential hazards;
- who is at risk from the hazard;
- how the risk can be minimised or eliminated;
- training staff to control the risks.

Outcome 2: Carry out the make-up activity

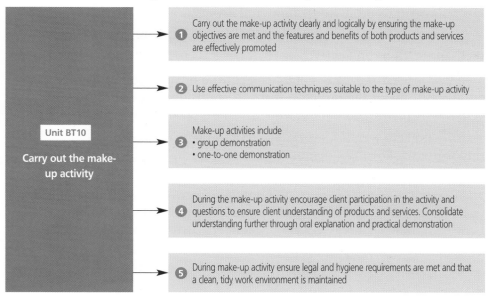

Unit BT10

Carry out the make-up activity

1. Carry out the make-up activity clearly and logically by ensuring the make-up objectives are met and the features and benefits of both products and services are effectively promoted

2. Use effective communication techniques suitable to the type of make-up activity

3. Make-up activities include
   - group demonstration
   - one-to-one demonstration

4. During the make-up activity encourage client participation in the activity and questions to ensure client understanding of products and services. Consolidate understanding further through oral explanation and practical demonstration

5. During make-up activity ensure legal and hygiene requirements are met and that a clean, tidy work environment is maintained

Gaining client satisfaction

Make-up application should be demonstrated in such a way that it enhances client understanding, showing cost-effectiveness. For a make-up lesson this will normally require that the make-up is completed in front of a mirror and the client has the opportunity to perform the application technique that you have demonstrated on them. For example, you demonstrate eye make-up application and then the client applies the make-up to the other eye following the same technique.

Tools of the trade are important, and the client must be shown which make-up tool/brush is selected and used to achieve a particular result. Supportive advice should be given to the client during this process, whilst responding positively to any questions with recommendations.

HEALTH AND SAFETY

Compliance with legislation
You will not be insured to provide your own electrical equipment at a venue.

TIP

Group demonstration of make-up activity
It is important that the audience can see and hear all stages of the make-up and product application. A large screen and a microphone that does not restrict your movement (such as a headpiece microphone) may be useful. Adequate time must be allocated to prepare the equipment for use.

Recording the demonstration is a useful marketing tool to present in the future and to evaluate for effectiveness.

TIP

Presentation confidence
- Be organised.
- Find out who our audience will be.
- Look your best.
- Practise your presentation and time yourself.

Ellisons

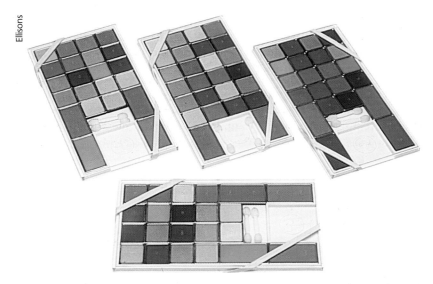

A make-up palette

During the demonstration keep the work area organised, clean and tidy.

Make-up demonstrations can be an ideal opportunity to promote and achieve a retail sale of the products that you have selected to use. Remember it is important to promote *features* and *benefits*.

A *feature* is the make-up product's specialist ingredients and the effects that their application can achieve.

A *benefit* is what the client could expect from buying the product. Be enthusiastic about the products that you are using: this will inspire the client. Knowledge will sell not only your products but yourself as well!

To further client interest, encourage trial of the product. Provide the opportunity following a demonstration to look and handle the products or give the client a complimentary gift of samples and information.

A successful demonstration should differentiate to the needs of your clients. Each client will be enthusiastic about the products and services offered for their own individual reasons. If the client chooses to purchase a product or book a service it is because they want to or feel they need to.

Outcome 3: Complete the make-up activity

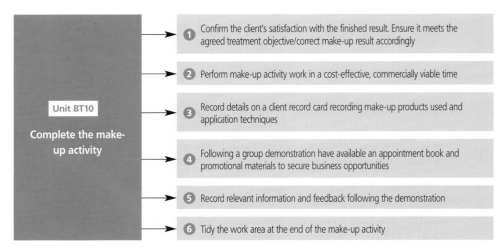

Unit BT10

Complete the make-up activity

1 Confirm the client's satisfaction with the finished result. Ensure it meets the agreed treatment objective/correct make-up result accordingly

2 Perform make-up activity work in a cost-effective, commercially viable time

3 Record details on a client record card recording make-up products used and application techniques

4 Following a group demonstration have available an appointment book and promotional materials to secure business opportunities

5 Record relevant information and feedback following the demonstration

6 Tidy the work area at the end of the make-up activity

Aftercare and advice

Ensure that the finished result is to the client's satisfaction. This is the opportunity to demonstrate to the client how to make any necessary changes to achieve the desired result. Allow time for the client to ask further questions about the products selected and applied. The make-up record card is useful to list products used and the make-up effect achieved (as is a before-and-after photograph for reference). A make-up chart can be given to the client to reinforce the discussion that has taken place during any make-up lesson; it will also be invaluable if the client returns wishing to purchase any of the make-up cosmetics you have used. Following a group demonstration you may wish to make your business card or service menu available for the client's future reference. You may even wish to enable the clients to book appointments. Ensure you have enough qualified staff available to answer client questions competently and thoroughly.

Promote additional services, professionally answer further questions following the make-up application and give additional tips on make-up technique as applicable – this will show your professional knowledge. Post promotion, keep in contact with your client to make them aware of future product promotions.

Following the make-up activity, seek client/audience feedback. If there was any criticism over the organisation or a group make-up activity, evaluate this and consider any recommendations in future planning.

Further guidance on promoting products and services can be found in Chapter 3, pages 67–73.

> **TIP**
>
> **Client motivation**
> A free prize draw could be held at the group make-up activity promotion to create interest in the event.
> Discounted prices could be offered for clients who book a make-up or other salon service at the demonstration.

THE CLIENT'S NEEDS

Day make-up

The effect should be natural. Any corrective work carried out should be very subtle and kept to the minimum, as natural light makes any imperfections appear obvious.

Select a foundation the same colour as the skin – aim to even out the skin tone. Set the foundation with a translucent face powder.

Apply a subtle, warm blusher to add colour to the face. Avoid strong colours of cosmetics, especially on the eyes. The mascara colour should be chosen to complement the client's natural lash and skin colours. Mascara should be used to emphasise, but not exaggerate, the length and thickness of the eyelashes. Eyeliner may be used, but it should be carefully placed and blended.

Line the lips in a colour that will coordinate with the lipstick to be applied, which again should be quite natural.

Evening make-up

This should be applied bearing in mind the type of lighting in which the client will be seen. Artificial light dulls the effect, and changes the colour of

> **TIP**
>
> In poor lighting, face shading should be subtle as it makes shadows appear darker.

RVB/Depilex

Evening make-up

the make-up: dark shades lose their brilliance, appearing 'muddy', so you need to use brighter colours. Emphasise the facial features with the careful placement of contouring cosmetics.

Areas where shadows may be created, such as the eyes, should be emphasised using light, bright and highlighting cosmetic products. Add warmth to the face with an intense colour of blusher placed on the cheekbones. A highlighting powder in a pearlised or metallic shade may be applied directly on top of or over the blusher. The client may like to try adventurous cosmetics such as metallics and frosted eye products.

Curl the eyelashes with eyelash curlers or apply false eyelashes to emphasise the eyes. Fashion shades of mascara may be selected, in purples, greens and blues, to complement the make-up and produce the effect required. Light shades of eyeliner may be used to frame the eyes and to 'open' them up.

Add a lipgloss to the lips, or apply a frosted lipstick to emphasise the mouth.

Colour the eyebrows, and carefully groom them to frame the eye area.

Special occasion make-up

A special occasion is usually an important event such as a wedding, day at the races, graduation ceremony or New Year's Eve party.

Whatever the occasion, whether daytime or evening, indoors or outdoors, you will need to consider the type of lighting the make-up will be viewed in – natural or artificial – and any other factors, such as how long it is to be worn for.

The selection of colours should co-ordinate with what the client will be wearing, and finally you need to know the effect they wish the make-up to create – should it be subtle or glamorous? Make-up products can then be selected and appropriately applied to suit the occasion.

Special occasion make-up

Photographic make-up

If applying make-up for photographic purposes, it is important to consider the effect to be created. This should be planned with the photographer in advance of the make-up application.

Consider the brightness of the lighting used. The brighter the lighting is the lighter the make-up pigment will appear. Make-up will therefore need to be applied more strongly. Lighting can be hot and may affect the make-up application making it melt, especially with oil-based make-up. Therefore, avoid oily make-up and regularly apply powder to remove shine.

Generally, matt colours are used, as the lighting will emphasise any shine.

For black and white photography remember dark colours will appear darker when photographed. Therefore, it may be necessary to apply lighter shades in preference to dark – for example, a dark shade of cheek colour would create a dark shadow.

Photographic make-up

Avoid lipgloss unless you wish the lips to appear full.

It is important to define facial features using shading and highlighting techniques, as photographic make-up removes natural shades and highlights.

Care should be taken to blend all make-up to avoid any demarcation lines, which will be emphasised in the photograph.

Make-up to suit skin and hair colouring

Fair skin and blonde hair

If the client has fair hair and fair skin, keep the skin colour natural. Apply a blusher in rose pink or beige.

Define the eyes with soft tones of browns and pinks. Apply a brown-black mascara.

Colour the lips with a rose-pink or peach lip-colour. Avoid lip colours lighter than the natural skin tone.

Caucasian client

Oriental skin and black hair

For creamy, sallow skin with dark hair, use blusher to add warmth and to brighten the skin, in either pink or brown.

The eyes are dark, with a prominent browbone. Emphasise the socket of the eye with careful shading; extend this upwards and outwards. Place highlighter along the browbone.

Pastel colours complement the eye colour. Select black mascara to emphasise the eyes. Deep pinks and orangey-reds suit the lips.

Fair skin and red hair

Redheads usually have fair skin with freckles. The skin will flush and colour easily, probably requiring the application of a green-tinted moisturiser, concealer or face powder. Apply blusher in a warm rose or peach colour. Browns, rusts, greens and peach eyeshadow colours suit this skin and complement the eyes. Brown mascara is preferable, to avoid making the eyes appear hard.

Philippine client

For the lips, select a lipstick in peach, golden rust or pink.

African-Caribbean client

Indian client

Mexican client

Black skin and black hair

A yellow-toned foundation is required: it may be necessary to blend foundations to obtain the correct colour. Avoid pink-toned foundations, which make the skin appear chalky.

Women with dark skin tend to have dark brown to brown-black eyes, and can use a wide range of heavily pigmented colours, especially browns and bronzes. Dark shades of blusher in red and plum may be chosen; eyeliner and mascara can be black, or any other dark shade.

Avoid lip colours lighter than the skin tone. A lipliner darker than the lip colour may be used.

Olive or fair skin and dark hair

Select a foundation to suit the basic skin tone. If the skin is fair, choose an ivory base; if it is sallow, select a foundation with a rusty, yellow tone. (With a sallow skin, avoid the use of pinks on the eyes – they make the eyes look sore.)

A beige blusher suits this skin colour, and is complemented by the selection of brown or green shades for the eyes. Black mascara should be used for the eyelashes.

For the lips, choose warm reds or beige.

Make-up for the mature skin

As the skin ages it becomes sallow in colour and appears thinner. Small capillaries can be seen, commonly on the cheek area, and small veins may appear around the eyes. Pigment changes in the skin become obvious, and remain permanently.

At the make-up consultation, discuss your ideas with your client. Very often a mature client will have been using the same colours and the same cosmetics for many years, and they may not even be complementary. You will need to advise them tactfully on a fresh approach.

Select a foundation that matches the skin colour yet enhances the skin's appearance. An oil-based foundation is appropriate for use on mature skin: it keeps the skin supple and prevents the foundation from settling into the creases and emphasising the lines and wrinkles.

A concealer may be applied to cover obvious capillaries and small veins, or a foundation may be selected which provides adequate coverage.

A lighter foundation may be applied over wrinkled areas, to make them less obvious. These areas include:

- around the eyes (crow's feet);
- between the brows;
- across the forehead;
- between the nose and the mouth (naso-labial folds);
- around the mouth (the lipline).

With age, the contours of the face lose their firmness as the fat cells that plump the face reduce, and the facial muscles lose tone and sag. Poor muscle tone can be seen in the following areas:

- the cheek area;
- loose skin along the jawline;
- loose skin under the brow and overhanging the lid;
- loose skin on the neck.

TIP

Dark circles under eyes
Dark circles under the eyes can be minimised with concealer. Select a concealer lighter than the foundation to be applied.

ACTIVITY

Shading
Where would you place the shading product in order to correct poor muscle tone in the areas discussed opposite?

The application of a shader, subtly blended, can improve the appearance of such areas.

Apply translucent powder. It may be preferable to avoid doing so in the eye area as it can emphasise lines around the eyes. To reduce the powdery effect, which may make the skin appear dry, you may direct a fine water spray from a suitable distance to set the make-up.

Apply a blusher with a warm tone – avoid harsh, bright shades. A cream blusher may be applied after the foundation. Place it high on the cheekbone and blend it upwards at the temples, drawing attention upwards rather than downwards.

Step by step: Special occasion make-up application

Make-up applied to a Caucasian, fair skinned, normal skin type to achieve a glamorous evening make-up and enhance the eyes.

At consultation the client identified that normally she wears little make-up, usually mascara, blusher and lipgloss. This is taken into account when considering choice of colours, products and application technique. We allowed 45 minutes to create this look.

The client has recently had UV exposure, which has increased pigmentation of the skin.

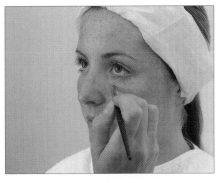

1   The client's skin has been cleansed, toned, moisturised and blotted to remove excess moisturiser.

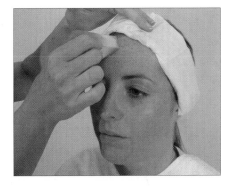

2   Concealer is applied using a brush for accuracy to disguise darkness under the lower eyelid. Pressure is light to avoid excessive drag around this delicate area.

3   Foundation is selected to match the client's skin tone. As the client does not normally wear make-up a light liquid foundation formulation is selected. The foundation is applied and blended with a cosmetic sponge all over the face, over the jawline, blended into the neck and over the eyelids and lips.

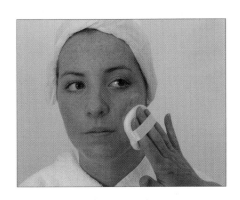

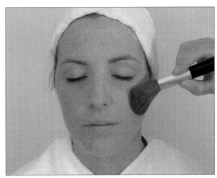

4   A translucent loose powder is used to set the foundation and remove any stickiness. This facilitates the application of further powder cosmetics and gives durability to the foundation.

5   A large powder brush is used to remove excess powder, and brushed in an upward and outwards direction.

6   An ivory pearlised eyeshadow is applied over the entire eyelid using a sponge disposable applicator.

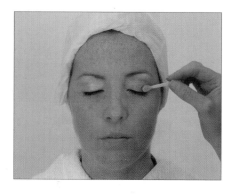

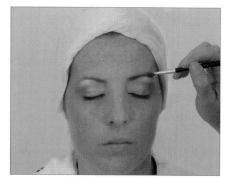

7 A bronze coloured metallic eye shadow is applied at the outer corners of the eyelid and blended upwards and outwards.

8 A matt black eye shadow is lightly applied at the corner of the eyes and blended into the eye socket. This draws attention to the eyes. A shading brush is used to soften and blend the colour, creating a smoky look.

9 Colour is applied to the brows. Brow pencil or powder eyeshadow may be used to define the shape of the brows. The brows are groomed following colour application by brushing them with an eyebrow brush in the direction of hair growth. This also ensures all eyebrow colour is blended evenly.

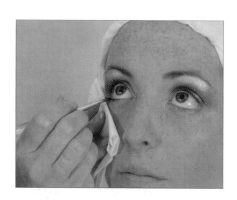

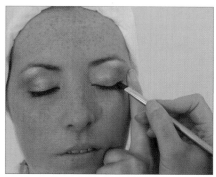

10 Eyeliner is applied using a dark grey colour to the outer corners of the lower and upper eyelids, just above and below the eyelashes using an eyeliner brush. This application opens the eyes.

11 Mascara in black is applied using a disposable mascara brush. Additional coats have been applied on the lashes at the outer corners of the eyes to lengthen the eyelashes and create a vibrant look.

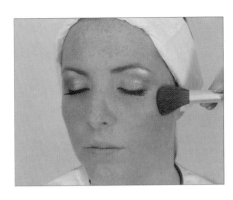

12 Colour is added to the face using a rust coloured blusher. This also accentuates the cheekbone area. The colour is stroked along the cheekbone towards the hairline.

13 The lips have been outlined using a sharpened lipliner pencil. A neutral colour, which complements the lipstick, has been chosen. This allows for subtle correction to balance the lip shape. The lipstick chosen is a light coloured matt brown, which is enhanced by the application of lipgloss. Lip colour is chosen to complement the eyeshadow.

14 The finished result – make-up for a special occasion.

Step by step: Mature client special occasion make-up application

Make-up is to be applied to a Caucasian client to achieve a glamorous appearance for a social evening. We allowed 45 minutes to achieve this look.

The client has dry skin as the sebaceous and suderiferous glands have become less active as part of the ageing process. Noticeable facial characteristics include:

- Dark circles appear around the eyes area.
- Thin, delicate tissue is found around the eyes with small veins and capillaries showing through the skin.
- Habitual frown lines occur.
- Poor muscle tone has resulted in dropped facial contours, i.e. double chin.
- Poor skin tone exists because the skin loses its elasticity, resulting in wrinkling and loss of firmness.
- Sallow skin colour is due to poor blood circulation.

1 The client's skin has been cleansed, toned, moisturised and blotted to remove excess moisturiser.

2   The finished special occasion make-up

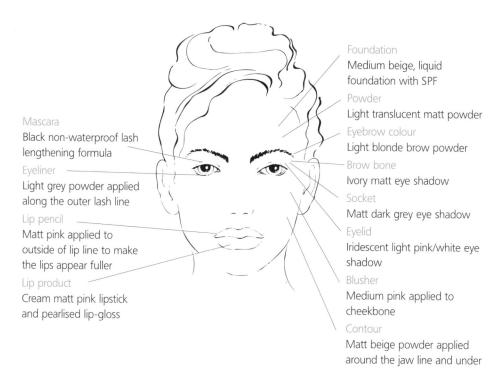

Mascara
Black non-waterproof lash lengthening formula

Eyeliner
Light grey powder applied along the outer lash line

Lip pencil
Matt pink applied to outside of lip line to make the lips appear fuller

Lip product
Cream matt pink lipstick and pearlised lip-gloss

Foundation
Medium beige, liquid foundation with SPF

Powder
Light translucent matt powder

Eyebrow colour
Light blonde brow powder

Brow bone
Ivory matt eye shadow

Socket
Matt dark grey eye shadow

Eyelid
Iridescent light pink/white eye shadow

Blusher
Medium pink applied to cheekbone

Contour
Matt beige powder applied around the jaw line and under the cheekbones

Mature client special occasion retail advice make-up record card

Step by step: Asian client day make-up application

Corrective work completed is subtle, as natural daylight makes any imperfections seem more obvious.

The client's skin has been cleansed, toned, moisturised and blotted to remove excess moisturiser. 30 minutes was allowed to achieve the look.

This is an oily skin type, where over-activity of the sebaceous glands in the skin is creating a shiny, sallow appearance.

Other noticeable facial characteristics include:

- Darker skin underneath the eye area requires concealer correction.

  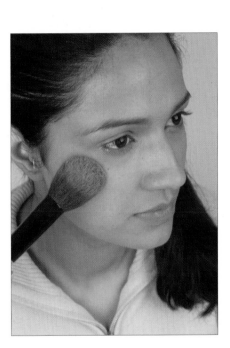

1 A concealer is applied with a brush underneath the eyes to disguise the darker skin tone.

2 A liquid foundation matched to the client's skin tone is applied. Application is over the whole face, including the eyelids and lips, as this gives an even skin tone.

3 Following the application of loose powder, again matched to the client's skin tone, excess powder is removed using a large powder brush. Application is upwards and outwards.

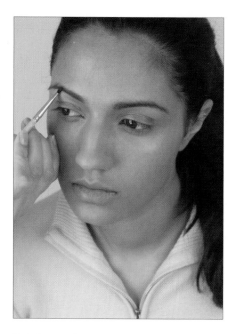

4 Blusher colour is applied to accentuate the cheek area and add colour to the face.

5 Colour applied to the eye emphasises the eye area. We used complementary colours in a purple range. A highlighting colour accentuates the brow-bone.

6 The eyebrows are accentuated using a dark matt brown colour applied with a stiff eyebrow brush. This gives definition to the eyebrow, disguising sparse hair and gaps.

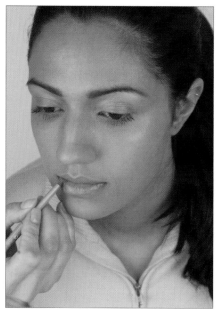

7 The lashes are lengthened using a lash-building mascara in black.

8 Lipliner colour is applied to define the desired lip contour. A co-ordinating lip colour is selected to match the lipliner and complement the eye make-up colour.

9 The lip colour is applied using a lipbrush.

10 The final day make-up look.

Step by step: African-Caribbean client evening make-up application

Make-up which will be seen under artificial lighting is applied. Stronger pigmented make-up colours have been selected, and the make-up effect emphasises facial features through the choice and application of make-up products. 45 minutes was allowed to achieve the look.

The client's skin has been cleansed, toned, moisturised and blotted to remove excess moisturiser.

This is a combination skin type and the sebaceous glands are overactive in the 'T' zone – forehead, nose and chin – and the pores appear larger in this area. The sebaceous glands are less active in the cheek, which results in dry skin with tight pores.

Other noticeable facial characteristics include:

- The skin tone of the face has uneven pigmentation.
- The face shape requires balance, which can be achieved using shaded contour colour.

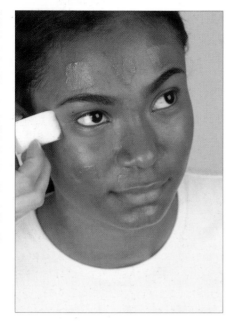

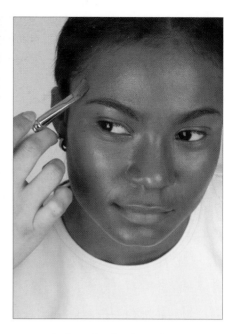

1 Foundation is selected to match the client's skin type and even the skin tone. A mousse foundation has been used to provide a medium coverage and has been blended quickly to avoid a chalky appearance.

2 A cream formulation shading product, in a darker shade than the foundation, is applied underneath the cheekbone and at the temples to accentuate the cheekbones and reduce the width of the face at the temples.

3 Loose powder matching the client's skin tone is applied to set the foundation and facilitate application of further powder products. Powder blusher is applied to the cheekbone.

4 Following application of a neutral eye shadow matt colour, a darker shading product is used to emphasise the eye socket.

5 The natural lash line is accentuated by eyeliner application. A steady hand is required!

6 The brows are defined.

7 Mascara application draws attention to the eyes.

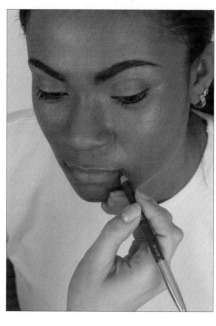

8 Lipliner is applied to define the perfect lip line.

9 The lips are coloured in using a matt lipstick co-ordinated to suit the lipliner. Lip gloss achieves a final touch which will focus attention and add emphasis in darker lighting.

10 The final evening make-up look.

GLOSSARY OF KEY WORDS

Aftercare advice recommendations given to the client following treatment to continue the benefits of the treatment.

Blusher cosmetic applied to add warmth to the face and emphasise the facial contours.

Cleanser a skin-care preparation that removes dead skin cells, excess sweat and sebum, make-up and dirt from the skin's surface to maintain a healthy skin complexion. These are formulated to treat the different skin types, skin characteristics and facial areas.

Concealer cosmetic product used to disguise minor skin imperfections such as blemishes, uneven skin colour or shadows.

Consultation assessment of client's needs using different assessment techniques, including questioning and natural observation.

Contour cosmetics applied to cosmetically change and enhance the shape of the face and facial features.

Contra-action an unwanted reaction occurring during or after treatment application.

Contra-indication a problematic symptom that indicates that the treatment may not proceed or may restrict treatment application. Contra-indications identified for facial treatments are discussed in more detail in Chapter 1.

Eyebrow colour cosmetic applied to emphasise the eyebrows, alter their shape, and which can make sparse eyebrows look thicker.

Eyeliner cosmetic applied to define and emphasise the eye area.

Eyeshadow cosmetic applied to the eye to complement the natural eye colour, to give definition to the eye area and enhance the natural shape of the eye.

Face shape the size and shape of the facial bone structure. Face shapes include oval, round, square, heart, diamond, oblong and pear.

Facial features the size of a person's nose, eyes, forehead, chin, neck, etc. When applying make-up products, make-up application can emphasise or minimise the appearance of facial features.

False eyelashes threads of nylon fibre or real hair attached to the natural eyelash hair. There are two main types: individual or strip.

Foundation a make-up product applied to produce an even skin tone, to disguise minor skin blemishes and as a contour cosmetic.

Highlighter a make-up product that draws attention to and emphasises features.

Hyperpigmentation increased pigment production.

Hypopigmentation loss of pigmentation.

Lipliner cosmetic used to define the lips, creating a perfectly symmetrical outline.

Lipgloss cosmetic applied to the lips to provide a moist, shiny look.

Lipstick cosmetic applied to the lips to add colour and keep the lips soft and supple.

Make-up cosmetics applied to the skin of the face to enhance and accentuate, or to minimise facial features. Make-up products create balance in the face.

Make-up products different cosmetics available to suit skin type, colour and condition, i.e. sensitive or mature. Make-up products include concealing and contour cosmetics, foundations, translucent powders, eyeshadows, eyeliners, browliners, mascaras, lipsticks, lip glosses, lipliners, etc.

Mascara cosmetic that enhances the natural eyelashes, making them appear longer, changed in colour and/or thicker.

Moisturiser a skin-care preparation whose formulation of oil and water helps maintain the skin's natural moisture by locking in moisture, offering protection and hydration. The formulation is selected to suit the skin type, facial characteristics and facial area.

Pigment the colour of skin and hair, called melanin. The amount of pigment varies for each client, resulting in different skin and hair colour.

Powder cosmetic applied to set the foundation, disguise minor skin blemishes and make the skin appear smoother and oil-free.

Promotion ways of communicating products or services to clients to increase sales.

Record cards confidential records recording personal details of each client registered at the salon.

Shader a make-up product that draws attention away from and minimises certain facial features.

Skin analysis assessment of client's skin type and condition.

Skin characteristics whilst looking at the skin type, additional characteristics may be seen. These include skin that may be sensitive, dehydrated, moist or oedematous (puffy), in addition to dry, oily or combination.

Skin tone the strength and elasticity of the skin.

Skin type the different physiological functioning of each person's skin dictates their skin type. There are four main skin types normal (balanced), dry (lack of oil), oily (excessive oil) and combination (a mixture of two skin types, i.e. dry and oily).

Toning lotion a skin-care preparation formulated to treat the different skin types and facial characteristics. It is applied to remove all traces of cleanser from the skin. It produces cooling and skin-tightening effects.

Treatment plan after the consultation, suitable treatment objectives are established to treat the client's conditions and needs.

Assessment of knowledge and understanding

You have now learnt about the different make-up application techniques and how to adapt these to suit the client's skin type, colouring and condition. These skills will enable you to professionally provide make-up treatment.

To test your level of knowledge, answer the following short questions. These will prepare you for your summative (final) assessment.

Anatomy and physiology questions required for this unit are found on pages 146, 149–53.

Consult with the client

1 How can you ensure that you fully understand the effect to be achieved with the make-up application?

2 In order to select the correct skin-care and make-up products to complement the client's skin, it is necessary to identify the skin type. What are the facial characteristics for the following skin types:

- oily
- dry
- combination?

3 Name three skin, and three eye, disorders that would contra-indicate make-up application.

4 Why is it important that you never diagnose a contra-indication?

5 What product ingredients are known to cause allergic reactions, and should therefore not be used on a client with sensitive skin?

Prepare for the treatment

1 How can you ensure that the treatment environment is suitable for the application of make-up?

2 How should the make-up brushes be prepared for each client in order to avoid cross-infection?

3 Why is it important to have a variety of make-up products available?

4 How should the skin be prepared before the application of make-up?

Plan the treatment

1 What should be considered when planning make-up with a client?

2 How should the client be positioned when applying make-up?

3 What is the difference in application technique for the following make-up contexts:
- day
- evening
- special occasion?

4 How is the correct colour of foundation selected for your client?

5 Why is it important to match lighting with the occasion for which the make-up is to be worn?

6 What planning is necessary when preparing for a group make-up activity?

Apply make-up products

1 Why is it important that make-up is applied in a suitable sequence?

2 How can you ensure hygienic practice when applying the following products:
- foundation
- face powder
- mascara
- lipstick?

3 For what purposes would you apply a concealer?

4 Describe how a minor skin imperfection may be disguised with make-up application.

5 How and why would you curl the natural lashes?

6 What is the purpose of:
- shader
- highlighter?

7 What corrective make-up techniques should be applied for each of the following?
- square face
- high forehead
- narrow eyes
- hyperpigmentation
- hypopigmentation?

8 Below is a picture of a client with a mature skin. Looking at the facial characteristics, what corrective work would be required?

9 False lashes may be applied to enhance the eyes. What is the difference in each type in terms of:
- application
- how long they may be worn for
- removal?

Complete the treatment

1 What aftercare advice should be given to a client following make-up application?

2 If a client has received a make-up lesson, what should they be provided with?

3 Name three contra-actions that could occur during or after make-up application. What action should be taken?

4 How can you promote the sale of skin-care and make-up products during make-up application?

5 What advice would you give with regard to the type of make-up products and application for a client who is not used to wearing make-up and is getting married abroad?

6 From a magazine, collect a photographic image from the client group below:
- African-Carribean
- Asian
- Caucasian
- Oriental.

Describe how each look has been created, explaining the make-up application and products used.

chapter 12

Extend and maintain nails

Learning objectives

This unit describes how to extend and maintain nails. It describes the competencies to enable you to:

- **consult with the client**
- **prepare for the treatment**
- **plan the treatment**
- **repair natural nails to improve condition and appearance**
- **apply artificial nail using the wrap system**
- **maintain and repair artificial nail structures (discussed in each nail system)**
- **complete the treatment**

When performing extending and maintaining nail treatments, it is important to use the skills you have learnt in the following core mandatory units:

UNIT G1 Ensure your own actions reduce risks to health and safety

UNIT G6 Promote additional products or services to clients

UNIT G8 Develop and maintain your effectiveness at work

Ellisons

Nail extensions

Essential anatomy and physiology knowledge requirements for this unit, BT44, are identified on the checklist chart in Chapter 5, page 101.

TYPES OF NAIL EXTENSIONS

Nail extensions are a rapidly growing area in the beauty industry and it is the duty of the professional beauty therapist to be aware of current trends. There are many professional methods available to enhance the length, strength, appearance or repair of the nail. These include sculptured nails, nail tips, tips and overlays and pre-formed 'stick-on' nails. To achieve sculptured nails, tips and overlays there is a choice of materials to select

TIP ✓

Electric nail drills
Electric nail drills are becoming more commonly used to save time when shaping, buffing nail product and preparing the smile line when performing a backfill.
 Training is necessary before the purchase and use of a drill; damage can occur in unskilled hands!

Applying sculptured nails

from including liquid/powder acrylic; fibreglass/silk wrapping systems; UV gel and UV liquid/powder acrylic.

- **Sculptured nails** These can be achieved using a liquid and powder system or gel. The mixture is 'sculpted', built up over the natural nail plate and extended past the free edge on a nail form.

Nail tips

- **Nail tips** This method uses nail tips commonly made from plastic or nylon, applied to the natural nail tip only to add length. The seam area where the nail tip is attached to the natural nail plate is buffed so there is no visible line.

- **Tips and overlays** A nail tip is applied, blended to remove the visible line and is then overlaid with acrylic, gel or fibreglass. This extends the length of the nail and increases the strength of the structure.

Tips and overlays

- **Pre-formed 'stick-on' nails** A plastic nail is applied to cover the whole natural nail plate, therefore no buffing is required. These are also available painted.

- **Nail repairs** When a nail that has been extended requires repair, it should be repaired using the relevant method. This is discussed in the section on maintenance for each nail system.
    To repair a natural nail in the case of flaking or free-edge break the beauty therapist can use a *nail wrap*.

- **Nail wraps** Material such as silk or fibreglass is attached to the nail using an adhesive and adhesive dryer. They are used to strengthen the natural nails or nail tips. Wraps are made either from tissue or fabric such as linen, silk or fibreglass.

Clients demand a high level of service when they attend a salon for nail treatments, so thorough knowledge is essential. A good trade supplier will usually offer training courses to ensure current product knowledge and full back-up support.

Due to the vast number of products available, however, specific application techniques may vary. To ensure a completely safe and professional-looking application, always follow the manufacturer's instructions.

Pre-formed 'stick-on' nails

Nail extension and maintenance service

These services offer the following benefits:

- improve the appearance of short, stubby fingers by lengthening the free edge;
- improve the appearance of the natural nail shape;
- strengthen the natural nail;
- can motivate a nail-biter to break the habit – an acrylic/gel overlay or nail wrap will strengthen the nail and improve its appearance;

Applying fibreglass mesh

- provide temporary length to the nails in the case of application for a special occasion but the client does not want the nails to be permanent – tips may be applied for this effect;
- repairs, in the case of flaking nails, free edge or flesh line break or severed free edge – the client can have the nail appearance balanced using the most appropriate nail system;
- disguises a disfigured nail that is not contra-indicated to treat – a nail system can be applied for corrective purposes;
- an overlay placed over nail polish extends its durability.

PLAN AND PREPARE FOR NAIL EXTENSION SERVICES

Outcome 1: Consult with the client

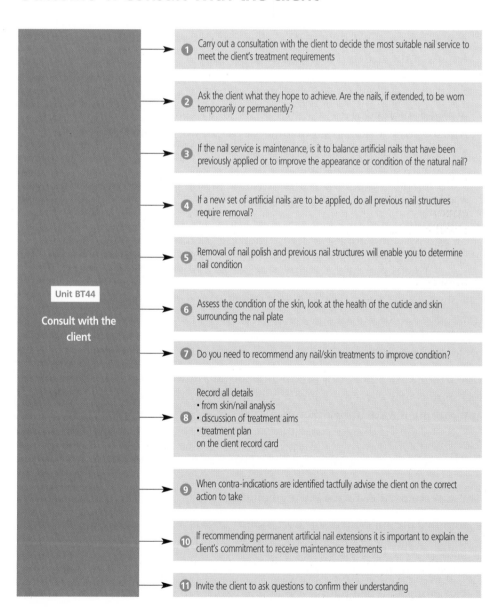

Unit BT44

Consult with the client

1. Carry out a consultation with the client to decide the most suitable nail service to meet the client's treatment requirements

2. Ask the client what they hope to achieve. Are the nails, if extended, to be worn temporarily or permanently?

3. If the nail service is maintenance, is it to balance artificial nails that have been previously applied or to improve the appearance or condition of the natural nail?

4. If a new set of artificial nails are to be applied, do all previous nail structures require removal?

5. Removal of nail polish and previous nail structures will enable you to determine nail condition

6. Assess the condition of the skin, look at the health of the cuticle and skin surrounding the nail plate

7. Do you need to recommend any nail/skin treatments to improve condition?

8. Record all details
   • from skin/nail analysis
   • discussion of treatment aims
   • treatment plan
   on the client record card

9. When contra-indications are identified tactfully advise the client on the correct action to take

10. If recommending permanent artificial nail extensions it is important to explain the client's commitment to receive maintenance treatments

11. Invite the client to ask questions to confirm their understanding

Reception

It is important that treatments are received in the given time to ensure client satisfaction, to ensure the efficiency of the reception area, and that expected income targets are met. A client who is kept waiting or finds the treatment time excessive will probably go to an alternative nail technician/salon next time.

When a client makes an appointment for a nail-extension service, the receptionist should ask a few simple questions in order to ascertain their needs. Information obtained from the client will help the nail technician to set up the working area with the appropriate equipment and materials, and will save time when the client arrives for treatment. The basic questions that the receptionist should ask are these:

- Why do they want a nail-extension treatment – is it for a special occasion, for example, or to help stop nail biting?
- Have they had nail extensions applied before?
- Do they want a temporary or permanent result?

Effective communication and questioning techniques are important to ensure that you fully understand the client's treatment requirements. A professional, friendly approach will give the client confidence in you and their expectation of the level of service they can expect.

All data on the client relating to their treatment should be recorded on the client's record card. This should be stored confidentially and accessed only by those with authority to do so to comply with the Data Protection Act 1998.

As with all beauty treatments, accurate record cards must be kept for clients having nail-extension services. If a client has had such services before, the receptionist should consult the card and tell the nail technician about these. This will give the nail technician a good idea of what to expect when the client arrives. For example, if the client has not attended for over three weeks, their nails may need a lot of maintenance work and extra time could be booked to allow for this.

> **TIP**
>
> **Booking appointments**
> Because of the maintenance procedures with nail-extension treatments, clients' appointments should be booked in advance. This ensures that maintenance can be carried out as required.

> **TIP** ✓
>
> **Treatment timings**
> The following time should be allocated for nail extension and maintenance services:
> - Sculptured nails: approximately 1 hour and 20 minutes full set
> - Nail tips: approximately 45 minutes
> - Tips and overlays: approximately 1 hour and 30 minutes
> - Pre-formed stick-on nails: approximately 30 minutes
> - Nail repair and natural nail wraps: approximately 10 minutes per nail

Information recorded on the client's record card will include the following.

Occupation/lifestyle

The client's occupation/lifestyle will help the nail technician to decide which type of nail system to use, and how long to leave the free edge. A client with a very physically demanding occupation, for example, will need a very strong

BEAUTY WORKS

Date	Therapist name	
Client name		Date of birth (identifying client age group)
Address		Postcode

Evening phone number	Day phone number

Name of doctor	Doctor's address and phone number

Related medical history (conditions that may restrict or prohibit treatment application)

Are you taking any medication? (this may affect skin sensitivity to the treatment or client suitability)

CONTRA-INDICATIONS REQUIRING MEDICAL REFERRAL
(Preventing nail extension or maintenance treatment)

- ☐ bacterial infections (e.g. paronychia/impetigo)
- ☐ viral infections (e.g. warts)
- ☐ fungal infections (e.g. onychomycosis)
- ☐ onycholysis (nail separation from nail bed)
- ☐ nail/skin disorders　　☐ nail/skin disease
- ☐ severe bruising　　☐ severe cuts and abrasions
- ☐ medical conditions　　☐ recent scar tissue
- ☐ allergic reaction to products　☐ diabetes
- ☐ loss of sensation in the fingers/hands
- ☐ extreme nail curvature

NAIL TREATMENTS ARE

- ☐ repairs
- ☐ replacement of overlay　☐ finishing　☐ balancing
- ☐ tips and overlays
- ☐ natural nail overlays

NAIL SHAPE AND NAIL/SKIN CONDITION

- ☐ nail shape e.g. round, oval, square
- ☐ natural nail shape e.g. claw, spoon, fan (this will guide your application technique)
- ☐ nail condition e.g. dry, damaged
- ☐ skin type e.g. dry/sensitive, moist
- ☐ cuticle condition e.g. normal, overgrown (a pre-treatment service may be necessary to improve nail/skin condition)

PRODUCTS USED

- ☐ adhesives　　☐ artificial nail products
- ☐ cuticle oils　　☐ dehydrators
- ☐ primers

CONTRA-INDICATIONS WHICH RESTRICT TREATMENT
(Treatment may require adaptation)

- ☐ cuts and abrasions
- ☐ bruising and swelling of nail/skin
- ☐ recent scar tissue in area (avoid area)
- ☐ eczema　　☐ onychopagy (severely bitten nails)
- ☐ undiagnosed lumps, bumps, swellings
- ☐ recent injuries to the treatment area
- ☐ medication　　☐ mild psoriasis/eczema

CONSULTATION TECHNIQUES

- ☐ questioning, including:
  - • reasons for treatment　• previous nail treatments received
  - • occupation　　• hobbies
  - • condition of skin and nails
- ☐ visual　　☐ manual
- ☐ reference to client records

OBJECTIVES OF TREATMENT

- ☐ nail length　　☐ nail shape
- ☐ nail finish, natural/polish

RECOMMENDATIONS

- ☐ from the client's expectations, record recommendations; nail system/nail length, shape and finish

EQUIPMENT AND MATERIALS

- ☐ nail and skin treatment tools
- ☐ nail and skin products
- ☐ consumables　　☐ tips
- ☐ wraps fibreglass/silk　☐ setting agents
- ☐ forms

Therapist signature (for reference)

Client signature (confirmation of details)

BEAUTY WORKS *(continued)*

TREATMENT ADVICE

 Nail tips – *allow 45 minutes*
Nail tips and overlays – *allow up to 60 minutes*

Nail repair and natural nail wraps – *allow 10 minutes per nail*

TREATMENT PLAN

Record relevant details of your treatment and advice provided for future reference.

Ensure the client's records are up to date, accurate and fully completed following treatment. Non-compliance may invalidate insurance.

DURING

Discuss:

- the products the client is currently using to care for the skin of the hands and nails;
- the client's satisfaction with these products;
- occupation/lifestyle considerations in terms of nail length and type of nail extension service.

Note:

- any adverse reaction, if any occur.

AFTER

Record:

- results of treatment;
- any modification to treatment application that has occurred;
- the products used in the nail extension/maintenance treatment;
- the effectiveness of treatment;
- any samples provided (review their success at the next appointment).

Advise on:

- product application in order to gain maximum benefit from product use;
- products following nail treatment for homecare use (e.g., non-acetone nail polish remover, recommended nail files to file the nails);
- general nail care and maintenance advice including how to deal with accidental damage and to return to the salon for any repairs;
- the recommended time intervals between treatments and the importance of keeping to this schedule.

RETAIL OPPORTUNITIES

Advise on:

- products that would be suitable for the client to use at home to care for the skin of the hands and nail area;
- how to gain maximum benefit from product use;
- recommendations for further treatments;
- further products or services that the client may or may not have received before.

Note:

- any purchases made by the client.

EVALUATION

Record:

- comments on the client's satisfaction with the treatment;
- if poor results are achieved, the reasons why;
- how you may alter the treatment plan to achieve the required treatment results in the future, if applicable.

HEALTH AND SAFETY

Advise on:

- appropriate action to be taken in the event of an unwanted skin or nail reaction;
- action to take in the event of a poor nail result, e.g., premature loss of nail extension or lifting of nail products.

> **TIP**
>
> Examples of treatment modifications to extend and maintain nails include:
> - adaption of application to suit the client's nail shape and condition;
> - length of artificial nail to suit the client hands/lifestyle considerations.

nail extension with a medium-to-short free edge. Other things to consider include any hobbies or interests the client may have that may affect the nail system chosen, for example swimming or gardening.

Condition of natural nails and cuticles

The condition prior to nail extension will be relevant later when the nail extensions are removed. The client cannot expect their nails to be in perfect condition later if they were not so at the outset.

If the client's nails or skin are in poor condition this may mean that alternative nail services, such as manicure or nail/skin conditioning treatments, should be carried out.

If the client has excessively overgrown cuticles, a manicure must be performed before nail extensions are applied. This must be carried out at a previous appointment because the nail plate will be too moist following the cuticle treatment, which will affect the adherence of the material used to the nail plate.

Type of nail system used

Should the nail technician be away for any reason, other technicians must know what type of nail system to apply. The record card will tell assisting staff which products to set out at the working area.

Size of nail tips (if used)

A record of the size of tip used will save time during repairs and maintenance – the technician will know which tip size to use, and won't have to measure each time to get the right size.

Allergies to products

Knowing which products (if any) the client is allergic to is crucial so that these products can be avoided. An allergy to a product may cause discomfort at the nail or surrounding skin. This can result in dryness, cracking, redness and swelling.

Reason for having nail extensions

This information helps the technician to assess whether to recommend temporary or permanent extensions. It is important that the correct service is chosen for the client to ensure client satisfaction. Explain why the service is best suited to the client.

Client signature

The client must confirm that they have been informed of the treatment details and possible contra-actions.

Contra-indications

Question the client to check for contra-indications. If, whilst completing the record card or on visual inspection of the skin or nail, you find the client to have any of the following nail conditions, services should not be carried out. Treating a client with a contra-indication may lead to cross-infection or a worsening of the client's condition.

Below is a chart of common disorders that may be seen on the hands. Refer to Chapter 9 Provide manicure treatment pages 315–19 for further hand/nail contra-indications.

Name	Description
Paronychia 	Infectious bacterial infection. Swelling, redness and pus appears in the cuticle area of the nail wall. Discomfort would be caused to the client during application and the product might irritate the condition.
Tinea unguium 	Fungal infection of the fingernails. The nail plate is yellowish-grey. Eventually the nail plate becomes brittle and separates from the nail bed. This condition can spread unnoticed beneath the artificial nail. As it is contagious, it may also infect the nail technician as well as the nail tools.
Cuts or abrasions 	Broken skin. Applying nail extensions near a cut or abrasion will cause discomfort and could lead to secondary infection. The area should not be treated until healed.
Severe nail separation (onycholysis) 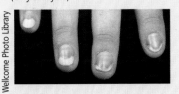	Lifting of the nail plate from the nail bed. May be caused by trauma or infection to the nail or surrounding area. Where separation has occurred, it appears as a greyish-white area on the nail and the pink undertone of the nail bed does not show. Further trauma would be caused to the natural nail during artificial nail application.
Severely bitten nails (onychopagy) 	Very little nail plate; bulbous skin at the fingertip; nail walls often red and swollen due to biting skin around the nails. There is insufficient nail plate for adhesion of a nail tip. Also the bulbous skin at the fingertip would cause the result to be spoon shaped.
Split, flaking nails (onychorrhexis) 	The condition of the nails does not provide a secure enough base for nail extensions.

Wellcome Photo Library

Dr A.L. Wright

HEALTH AND SAFETY

Nail health
If the client has inflammation, redness and swelling or infection, or if pus is present, **never treat the client**. Refer them to their GP.

HEALTH AND SAFETY

Treating a diabetic client
Great care should be taken when performing nail services on a diabetic client. This is because the skin has slow healing and if the skin was accidentally broken with cuticle nippers or a file, infection could occur. It is best not to nip the cuticles on this client.

TIP

Nail extension to the toenails
The contra-indications to pedicure (pages 353–6) apply to nail extension application to the toes. Check during consultation.

ACTIVITY

Contra-indications
Using your knowledge of nail diseases and disorders (Chapter 9), write down any other contra-indications to nail-extension application that you can think of.

HEALTH AND SAFETY

Nail fungal infection

If a fungal infection occurs while the client is wearing extensions, it may appear as a yellowy-green colour on the nail plate below the extension that later turns to black. This is usually because moisture has gained entrance between the free edge of the natural nail and the artificial nail. The extension must be removed and the nail disinfected. Extensions can be worn when the fungus has gone. The client should be referred to their GP if the disorder persists. Fungus colour and appearance vary depending on the type.

The following conditions also contra-indicate artificial nail application without permission from the client's GP (the GP's note should be kept with the client's record card).

- *Severe psoriasis or eczema of the nail plate.*
- *Broken bones.*
- *Bruised nail* A blood clot forms under the nail plate caused by injury.
- *Atrophy of the nail* The nail wastes away. Caused by injury or by poor health.
- *Onychocryptosis* Ingrowing fingernail where the nail grows into the tissue of the surrounding nail. This commonly occurs where there has been damage to the nail resulting in deformity.
- *Warts* Raised horny skin tissue with a rough surface; caused by a virus.
- *Extreme curvature of the natural nail* For nail extensions, as effective adherence would not occur.
- *Certain occupations* Some heavy manual occupations, such as those involving lifting, preclude nail extensions: the nails would be too easily broken. However, application in such cases would not actually be detrimental to the client's well-being, so it is at the discretion of the nail technician.

Outcome 2: Prepare for the treatment

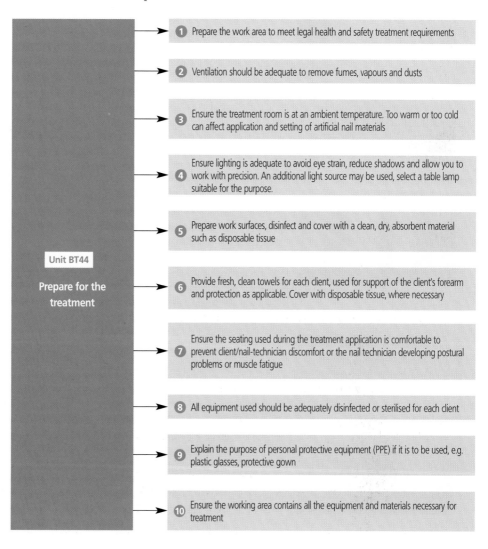

Equipment and materials

The equipment and materials listed below are general to all applications of nail extensions, maintenance and natural nail repair. Additional specialised items are listed with the individual techniques.

EQUIPMENT LIST

 Nail workstation

 Lamp for workstation use

 Waste bin (with lid)

Plastic glasses to protect the eyes

 Manicure pads or disposable tissue

 Cottonwool discs

 Tissues

 Orange sticks to loosen the cuticle at the base of the nail

Cuticle knife and cuticle nippers to trim excess cuticle

 Dappen dish small glass or plastic dishes to hold products during treatment application

 Scissors used to cut wrap material to size, often referred to as stork scissors

 Coarse file (100-grit) for reducing and shaping the length of the artificial free edge

Medium file (180-grit) for blending in the seam areas and shaping the artificial free edge

Fine file (240-grit) to smooth the nail and remove any scratches from the nail surface

1000–2000 grit file termed *micro-abrasive* and used to buff and shape the nail

 Medium-sized towels (3)

 Acetone remover to remove nail polish

Non-acetone remover and products to remove nail extensions for clients with artificial nails or nail wraps

YOU WILL ALSO NEED:

Seating for technician and client

Safety mask to avoid the inhalation of dust

Nail preparation products to prepare the nails before repair/enhancement with artificial nail products

Nail wipes lint-free pads used to remove dust created during treatment

Cotton buds

Glass bowl to immerse the client's nails, for general cleansing of skin/nails, and removal of artificial nail products

Tip cutters to cut the artificial nail structure

Four-sided buffer to bring the nail surface to a shine

Disinfectant fluid (in a jar)

Spray disinfectant for small pieces of equipment

Nail disinfectant alcohol-based disinfecting agent used to prevent bacterial and fungal growth

Cuticle oil to condition the cuticles following application of the artificial nail structure

Mild antiseptic cleanser for hands or an antibacterial soap and water

Aftercare leaflets – recommended advice for the client to refer to following treatment to care for the nails

Client record card – confidential card recording details of each client registered at the salon

Dappen dishes

Ellisons

TIP

The lower the number of grit, the coarser the file. Thus a 100-grit file is coarse; a 240-grit file is smooth.

Sterilisation and disinfection

For the health and safety of both the nail technician and the client, and to uphold the standards of the profession, you should ensure that all tools and materials are sterilised or disinfected prior to use. Disposable items should be used where applicable.

Prior to treatment both the client and the technician should wash their hands with a mild antiseptic cleanser and dry them on soft disposable paper towels. This will help to prevent cross-infection, and make the working area pleasant for both.

Before artificial nails are applied, the natural nail should be sanitised using an appropriate solution such as **isopropyl alcohol**. This reduces the risk of infection from bacteria and fungi.

Allow the client to see the cleaning and sterilising procedures taking place: they will instil in them confidence in your work and professional competence as well as reassure them about their own safety.

Preparing the working area

The working area should contain all the equipment and materials necessary for the treatment: this avoids unnecessary disturbance to the client during treatment. It should be well ventilated, warm, and with a good source of light. The bulb used in the workstation lamp should be 40 watts. This will avoid excessive heat production, which affects product consistency when sculpting during nail extension treatment.

A ventilation system is required to remove fumes, vapours and dusts that could lead to eye and respiratory problems. The system used must ensure effective ventilation, taking into account the number of nail technicians working in the area.

In the case of a freelance nail technician, a desktop extractor may be purchased. Temperatures must not be too warm as this can affect the application and setting properties of nail materials. When carrying out nail services you will need a lamp on the work surface, in addition to general room lighting. This reduces shadows and allows you to work with precise detail.

Work surfaces should be covered with a clean, dry material capable of absorbing liquid if spilt. The material should be disposable or capable of being disinfected. Ideal materials are towels or disposable tissue.

If blood is spilt (this is often caused by using a new file) the contaminated waste should be placed in a sealed bag and incinerated and the area cleaned using a disinfectant cleaner. Wear gloves when using disinfectants and handling contaminated waste.

TIP

Brush cleaner is available to place the brushes in immediately following their use. This prevents brushes becoming hard and retains their shape.

HEALTH AND SAFETY

Smoking
Due to the flammable nature of the products used, clients should be advised not to smoke during treatment. Also warn them that the artificial nail products will be damaged if care is not taken lighting a cigarette.

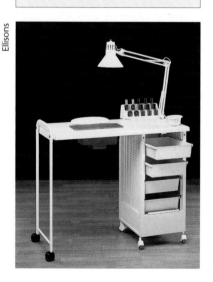

A manicure and nail extension station

Towels must be clean, dry and soft to ensure client comfort. Fresh towels must be used for each client. Place one towel flat to cover the work surface; fold the other towel into a small pad and place it beneath the client's forearm. This supports the client's arm during treatment and helps to keep them comfortable.

Disposable tissue should be placed over the top of the towel. It should be changed two or three times during treatment, to keep the dust from filing to a minimum.

The chairs for both the client and nail technician should be comfortable – they will be in use for approximately one and a half hours. The client will not be happy with their nails if they have had to sit in discomfort whilst they were being applied.

Preparing the client

The client may be given a light protective gown to wear during treatment. This will protect their clothes from the dust created during filing and from accidental spillages.

When artificial nails are cut they occasionally flick towards the client's face. This could prove to be uncomfortable or dangerous should clippings get into the client's eyes, so **plastic glasses** should be available to the client whilst nail clipping is taking place. Advising the client to wear the glasses also assures them that you are taking all possible precautions to safeguard their health.

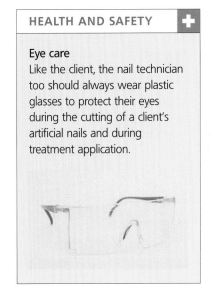

Outcome 3: Plan the treatment

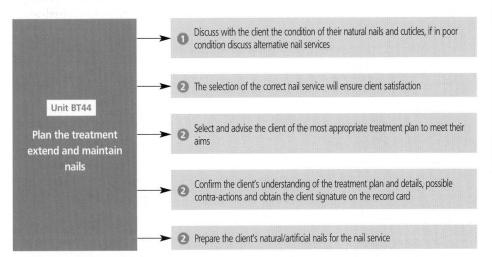

Unit BT44

Plan the treatment extend and maintain nails

1. Discuss with the client the condition of their natural nails and cuticles, if in poor condition discuss alternative nail services

2. The selection of the correct nail service will ensure client satisfaction

2. Select and advise the client of the most appropriate treatment plan to meet their aims

2. Confirm the client's understanding of the treatment plan and details, possible contra-actions and obtain the client signature on the record card

2. Prepare the client's natural/artificial nails for the nail service

Before applying nail services for a client, you should first discuss what they require. This will help you to decide which nail service best matches their needs. Points to discuss include:

- Is the client's lifestyle/occupation very physical? If so they will need their nails to be shorter and very strong.
- Is the client's hand in water a great deal?
- Are they allowed to wear nail polish at work? If not they will need a nail system that looks natural without nail polish.

> **TIP** ✓
>
> **Nail length**
> To ensure durability of the artificial nail, the length of the artificial nail free edge must not be longer than the length of the client's nail bed.

- How long do they want the nails to last? Temporarily or semi-permanently?
- What nail length does the client want?

Discovering your client's treatment requirements will help you to offer them the best possible service to meet their needs.

Explain in full why the service is recommended, what is involved and what realistic results they can expect. Invite the client to ask questions, as this will help confirm their understanding of the treatment.

Explain the importance of maintenance requirements for the nail service. Record details on the client record card.

Aftercare and advice

Maintenance and advice is provided with each nail system discussed.

Outcome 6: Maintain and repair artificial nail structures

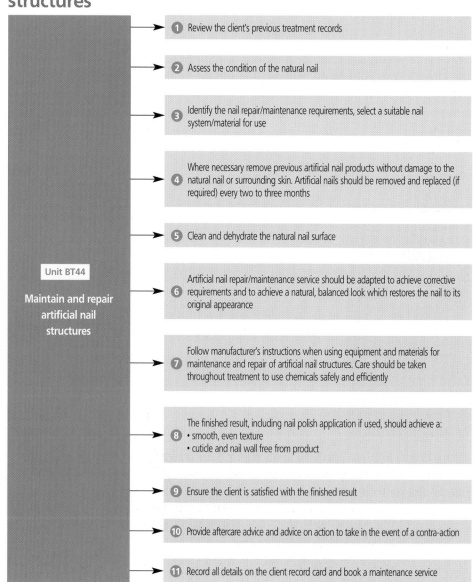

Unit BT44

Maintain and repair artificial nail structures

1. Review the client's previous treatment records

2. Assess the condition of the natural nail

3. Identify the nail repair/maintenance requirements, select a suitable nail system/material for use

4. Where necessary remove previous artificial nail products without damage to the natural nail or surrounding skin. Artificial nails should be removed and replaced (if required) every two to three months

5. Clean and dehydrate the natural nail surface

6. Artificial nail repair/maintenance service should be adapted to achieve corrective requirements and to achieve a natural, balanced look which restores the nail to its original appearance

7. Follow manufacturer's instructions when using equipment and materials for maintenance and repair of artificial nail structures. Care should be taken throughout treatment to use chemicals safely and efficiently

8. The finished result, including nail polish application if used, should achieve a:
   - smooth, even texture
   - cuticle and nail wall free from product

9. Ensure the client is satisfied with the finished result

10. Provide aftercare advice and advice on action to take in the event of a contra-action

11. Record all details on the client record card and book a maintenance service

PRE-FORMED NAILS

Pre-formed nails are only a temporary way of producing attractive nails as they are designed to last only 7–14 days. Made of plastic, these nails come in many shapes and sizes, and are also available in colours to eliminate the need for nail polish.

Advantages	Disadvantages
1 Quick to apply.	1 The least natural-looking of all types of nail extension.
2 Ideal as a temporary measure for nail-biters who have insufficient nail plate for a semi-permanent nail extension.	2 Only last 7–14 days.
3 Ideal for special occasions.	3 Not suitable for matching odd broken nails, due to their own unnatural appearance.
4 Inexpensive to apply.	4 Nail polish is required to give a more natural appearance.
5 The procedure is easy to learn.	

Equipment and materials

In addition to the basic equipment and materials (page 459), you will need the following:

EQUIPMENT LIST

Nail tips assorted styles and sizes

Resin and nozzle

Polishes a selection, including base coat and top coat

How to apply pre-formed nails

1 Wash your hands, and ask your client to wash theirs. Dry thoroughly.

2 Remove any existing nail polish and check for contra-indications.

3 Spray or wipe the nails with a sanitising product and allow to dry. Wipe from the free edge towards the cuticle to avoid body oils coming into contact with the nail plate. The nail may be sanitised with isopropyl alcohol or a proprietary product designed for this purpose. Do not use surgical spirit as this would leave an oily film on the nail plate, preventing proper adhesion of the artificial nail.

4 Remove any excess cuticle with cuticle nippers. Remove excess cuticle on the nail plate with a cuticle knife.

5 Choose the style and shape of tip appropriate to the needs of the client. Measure the pre-formed nail against the natural nail. If the exact size cannot be found, choose a nail that is slightly too big and file it to the correct size with a medium-grit file.

Check the sizes of the pre-formed nails in relation to the natural nails. Shape the base of the artificial nail with a fine-grit file until it matches the shape of the cuticle. This gives a better fit and a more natural-looking result.

6 Dehydrate the nails to remove any oil or moisture. Use a cotton bud, cottonwool-tipped orange stick or spray. Attention should be paid to the side of the nail and cuticle and under the free edge.

7 Start at the little finger and work across to the thumb. Apply a line of adhesive down the centre of the natural nail plate, and spread it over the whole nail using the applicator nozzle. Leave a small gap around the edges to allow for spreading when the artificial nail is applied.

8 Holding the free edge of the pre-formed nail, apply it to the natural nail by gently sliding it towards the cuticle. Hold it in place for a few seconds with your thumb to allow the adhesive to set. Do not push the pre-formed nail *under* the cuticle area as this might cause permanent damage to the matrix and subsequent growth of the nail. If air bubbles appear under the nail, remove the nail quickly, before the adhesive begins to set, and re-apply it.

9 Repeat steps 7 and 8 for the other nails.

10 Cut the nails to the desired length with scissors or tip cutters. File them into shape, first with a coarse-grit file to reduce bulk, then with a fine-grit file to give a smooth finish. Cut the free edge with scissors *from the side to the centre*. (Cutting straight across may result in the nail splitting or cracking.) Specially-designed clippers are available to cut artificial nails: they save time by cutting the nail in one movement, and leave the free edge with little filing to be carried out.

11 Apply polish as usual.

12 Make another appointment for the client.

13 Dispose of used materials, clean the workstation and equipment using effective sterilisation and disinfection procedures.

TIP

Length

The artificial free edge should be no longer than the nail plate from the cuticle to the flesh line. This will ensure that the nail is balanced, and reduces the chance of the nail coming off.

HEALTH AND SAFETY

Adhesives

Artificial nail adhesives will bond skin in seconds. If this happens, use a cotton bud to apply acetone to the bonded area to dissolve the resin, and gently ease the skin apart. If this does not work, or if the skin is sore, seek medical attention immediately.

Always read manufacturers' instructions, and follow them carefully.

Aftercare and advice

Give your client the following instructions:

- Use rubber gloves when immersing the hand in water.
- Do not use the fingernails as tools!
- Use only non-acetone nail polish removers. Acetone will soften the artificial nails and lead to lifting.
- Caution should be exercised when near any naked flame, including cigarettes, as nail adhesives are flammable and plastic nails can melt.
- Advise on retail products including non-acetone polish remover.
- Contact the salon if any problems occur.

Maintenance

This type of nail extension is only temporary – it is not designed to stay on for long. The client should return to the salon after one week to allow you to check for signs of lifting: as soon as these appear, the nails should be removed. Pre-formed nails should be removed after two weeks in any case, as after this time regrowth will have caused a noticeable gap between the cuticle and the pre-formed nail.

If the client desires artificial nails that will last longer, they should be advised on the application of semi-permanent extensions such as acrylic, fibreglass or gel.

NAIL TIPS

Nail tips are a very natural-looking type of nail extension, but they are also very weak. As the name suggests, nail tips are applied only to the tip of the natural nail – approximately halfway down the natural nail – and this leaves the cuticle area free.

Nail tips can be strengthened by the overlay application of gel, fibreglass or acrylic.

Advantages	Disadvantages
1 Very natural-looking.	1 The weakest form of nail extension.
2 Ideal for special occasions such as weddings where the hands are on show.	2 Only last 7–10 days.
3 Easy to remove.	3 Easily broken.
4 Ideal for matching odd broken nails.	
5 Odourless during application.	

Kinds of nail tips

There are many different styles of nail tip, but generally they fall into two categories: *cut-out tips* and *full tips*. **Cut-out tips** are used for a client:

- with a small nail plate area;
- with an exaggerated transverse arch of the nail plate;
- who only desires short nail extensions.

Full tips are used for a client:

- who desires long nail extensions;
- who has a medium-to-large nail plate area;
- who has a regular transverse arch to the nail plate.

Equipment and materials

In addition to the basic equipment and materials (page 459), you will need the following:

EQUIPMENT LIST

 Nail tips assorted styles and sizes

 Resin and nozzle

 Polishes a selection, including base coat and top coat

How to apply nail tips

Nail tips

1 Wash your hands, and ask your client to wash theirs. Dry thoroughly.

2 Remove any nail polish and check for contra-indications.

3 Disinfect the nail plate. (Wiping or spraying the nails with an appropriate nail disinfectant will help to inhibit the growth of bacterial and fungal infections.)

4 Check the size of the nail tips. Tips are curved in their design to suit different nail plate shapes – this is the 'C' curve. The tip should be selected to suit the shape of the natural nail. The tip is also arched, and again the shape should be selected to suit the nail arch. The sidewalls of the tip are also important and should match the client's nail shape, tapered or straight, and fit snugly into the nail grooves. It may be necessary to file the nail tip to achieve the correct fit. Incorrect selection will result in weakness and lifting. Place the tip against the client's nail to select the correct tip. When the nail tips have been sized correctly, lay them out on the work surface in order of application. For clients with very small nail plates (such as nail-biters), use a tip with a cut-out well area.

5 Dehydrate the nails to remove surface oils and moisture.

6 Lightly buff the distal end of the natural nail, where the tip is to be applied, with a medium-grade file (e.g. 180-grit). Buff the nail surface gently with the file to remove remaining surface oils: this promotes better adhesion of the nail tip.

7 Apply a small amount of adhesive to the *natural* nail tip. Adhesive should be applied only in the area that the well of the nail tip is to cover.

8 Apply a small amount of adhesive to the well of the tip. Apply the nail tip at a 45° angle to the natural nail. Hold the edge of the well against the free edge, then gently press down and rock the tip into position, squeezing out all air bubbles until the tip is flat against the nail surface. Hold the tip in place for a few seconds. Firm pressure is required to ensure effective adhesion.

   If air bubbles appear or if the nail tip is not straight, remove it immediately before the adhesive starts to set; then re-apply. If the adhesive has already set, the nail will have to be carefully removed and then reapplied.

9 Remove excess adhesive from surrounding tissue. Apply a small amount of adhesive to the seam area and allow this to set. (This is to ensure that the edge of the tip is securely bonded; it also allows blending to be done more quickly.)

10 Blend the seam area. Blending can be achieved manually using a file, or chemically using acetone or tip-blender agent. Begin with a fine 240-grit file to blend the tip to the natural nail. Hold the board at a slight angle, and blend the seam area without touching the nail plate excessively. If you are using a chemical blender, it dissolves the plastic tip. This should be applied with a cotton bud or brush to the area to be blended. Apply to each nail and after a few minutes the plastic will soften. A fine file is then used to remove any excess and blend the line by removing the excess plastic. Further chemical blender may be applied if necessary. Excess plastic *must* be removed.

11 Buff the nail to a shine with a four-sided buffer, using the coarse side first and working through to the smooth side. The tip must look like a natural nail.

12 Cut the nail tip to the desired length with tip cutters and file to shape. The client's choice must always be taken into consideration, but remember to *advise* about length.

13 Apply cuticle oil to soften the cuticles and surrounding skin.

14 Ask the client to wash their hands to remove the cuticle oil and dust particles. Wash your own hands. Change the towel on the work surface for a fresh one at this stage. This keeps dust to a minimum and prevents dust particles from spoiling the nail polish application.

15 Apply base coat over the entire nail plate.

16 Nails may be left to appear natural or painted with a coloured polish, as desired.

17 Make another appointment for the client.

18 Dispose of used materials, clean the workstation and equipment using effective sterilisation and disinfection procedures.

Applying adhesive to the seam area

HEALTH AND SAFETY

Blending
Care should be taken when blending.
Chemical blending – excessive use can cause dehydration of the natural nail.
Manual blending – a coarse file, or excessive blending in an area can cause nail thinning.

Electric nail drills may be used only by a trained competent nail technician.

Aftercare and advice

These are the same as for pre-formed nails – see page 464. However, extra care must be taken when removing nail polish. Use non-acetone remover *only,* as acetone will dissolve the nail tips.

Also see Outcome 6: Maintain and repair artificial nail structures, page 462.

Maintenance of nail tips

Clients wearing nail tips will need to return for maintenance treatment each week. Nail tips are temporary and will require replacement, re-gluing and rebuffing. Glue is applied to the seam area.

NAIL WRAPS

Material is attached to the natural nail, or over the nail tip to provide strength. Wraps are also popular where nail repair is required.

Advantages	Disadvantages
1 The natural nail is not damaged.	1 Paper wraps are less expensive but are temporary and can be removed with acetone.
2 Provides strength and protection whilst growing the natural nails.	2 Fibreglass is more durable but more expensive.
3 Easy to remove.	3 The thinness of the product makes it unsuitable for certain nail conditions such as bitten nails.

Outcome 4: Repair natural nail to improve condition and appearance

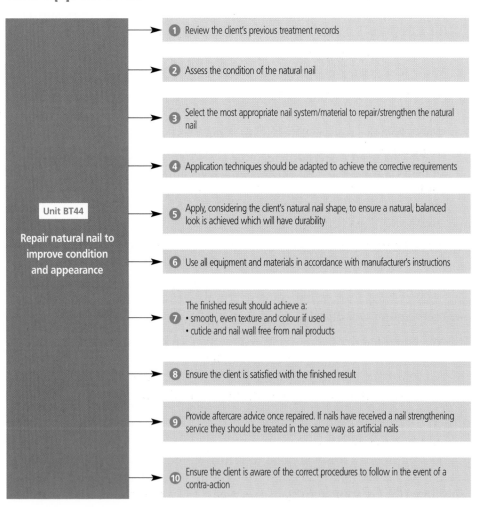

Unit BT44

Repair natural nail to improve condition and appearance

1 Review the client's previous treatment records

2 Assess the condition of the natural nail

3 Select the most appropriate nail system/material to repair/strengthen the natural nail

4 Application techniques should be adapted to achieve the corrective requirements

5 Apply, considering the client's natural nail shape, to ensure a natural, balanced look is achieved which will have durability

6 Use all equipment and materials in accordance with manufacturer's instructions

7 The finished result should achieve a:
• smooth, even texture and colour if used
• cuticle and nail wall free from nail products

8 Ensure the client is satisfied with the finished result

9 Provide aftercare advice once repaired. If nails have received a nail strengthening service they should be treated in the same way as artificial nails

10 Ensure the client is aware of the correct procedures to follow in the event of a contra-action

Equipment and materials

In addition to the equipment and materials listed on page 459, you will also need:

- Fabric or tissue
- Resin
- Resin activator
- If tissue wrap is used, mending liquid is required to strengthen the tissue.

How to apply nail wraps

1 Wash your hands, and ask your client to wash theirs. Dry thoroughly.

2 Remove any nail polish and check for contra-indications.

3 Sanitise the natural nail plate. Wiping or spraying the nails with an appropriate nail sanitiser will inhibit the growth of bacterial and fungal infections.

4 File the nails to shape and push back the cuticles gently with a cottonwool-tipped orange stick or hoof stick. This is to ensure that as much of the nail plate as possible is uncovered to allow optimum adhesion of the nail wrap. Using cuticle nippers, remove excess cuticle.

5 Lightly buff the nail surface to remove shine using a fine-grit file.

6 Use a dehydrator to remove excess oil and moisture.

7 Cut fabric to the size of the nail using very sharp scissors to avoid fraying. Fibreglass mesh usually has an adhesive backing. Attach this to the nail plate leaving a 3 mm gap round the edges, this prevents lifting.

8 If your wrap is non-adhesive, apply adhesive to the nail plate first.

9 Apply a layer of resin over the material, and allow this to dry. Apply a resin activator to speed the drying process.

10 Repeat stage 9, applying a further coat of resin. Allow the resin to soak into the fibreglass wrap for a few seconds before spraying with activator.

11 Buff the surface of the nail to remove shine and blend the nail wrap seam area into the natural nail. Avoid excessive buffing or the fibreglass mesh will show through.

12 Gently buff the surface of the nail to create shine, using a four-sided buffer.

13 Apply cuticle oil.

14 Ask the client to wash their hands to remove dust and oil.

15 Wipe over with non-acetone nail polish remover, then nail polish may be applied.

16 Make another appointment for the client.

17 Dispose of used materials, clean the workstation and equipment using effective sterilisation and disinfection procedures.

> **TIP**
>
> Resin *wets* the wrap material, helping to disguise it, whilst also providing strength and flexibility.
> **Application**
> Too much will prevent effective adhesion and could result in lifting.

Aftercare and advice

These are the same as for pre-formed nails – see page 464. Also see Outcome 6: Maintain and repair artificial nail structures, page 462.

Maintenance

Fabric wraps area maintained following the two-week and four-week maintenance plan listed on pages 476–7.

Further information on repairing and strengthening the natural nail is found on pages 491–3.

Fabric wraps area maintained following the two-week and four-week maintenance plan listed on pages 476–7.

Further information on repairing and strengthening the natural nail is found on pages 491–3.

> **TIP**
>
> **Maintenance**
> Maintenance requirements of the client's nails will depend upon growth rate and how the nails have been cared for.

FIBREGLASS NAIL EXTENSIONS

Fibreglass nail extensions are the most natural-looking nail-extension system: the finished nail is transparent over the nail bed, allowing the natural pink colour to show through. The nails look very thin and flexible, similar to natural nails.

Fibreglass nails are also the least damaging to the natural nails, because no primer is needed during application. This makes them an ideal choice as a temporary measure for clients who wish to grow their own nails to wear without artificial products.

Advantages	*Disadvantages*
1 Very natural-looking.	1 Not suitable for clients with very little nail plate (principally nail-biters), as not enough nail plate is available for adequate adhesion of the nail tip and the fibreglass overlays.
2 Ideal for matching odd broken nails.	
3 Very strong and flexible.	
4 Not porous, so do not stain.	2 More expensive to apply than other nail systems.
5 Easy and quick to remove.	
	3 The shape of the finished nail relies on the shape of the tip. Additional curves can be created with thicker overlay systems which can balance the nail's appearance.

> **TIP**
>
> As with gel and acrylic nail extensions, fibreglass nails may go yellow after sunbed use or after long periods in the sun, such as on holiday. The yellowing is only temporary and will fade once exposure has ceased. Discoloration can be stopped by covering the nails with coloured nail polish during exposure to the sun.

Outcome 5: Apply artificial nails using the wrap system

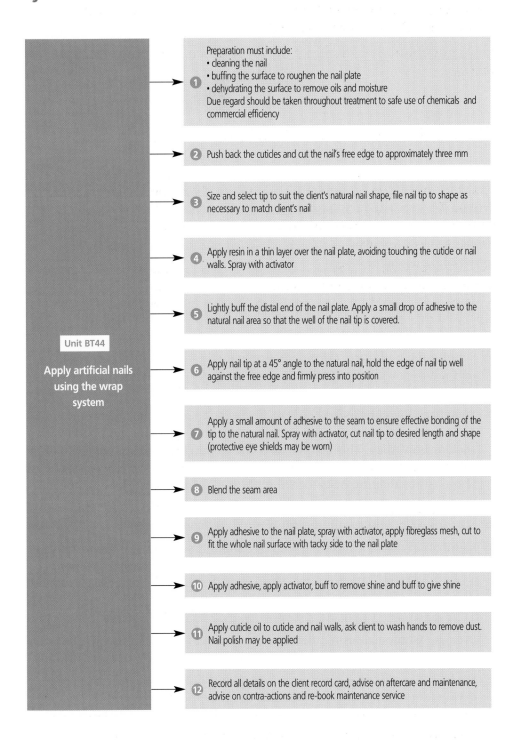

Unit BT44

Apply artificial nails using the wrap system

1. Preparation must include:
   - cleaning the nail
   - buffing the surface to roughen the nail plate
   - dehydrating the surface to remove oils and moisture
   Due regard should be taken throughout treatment to safe use of chemicals and commercial efficiency

2. Push back the cuticles and cut the nail's free edge to approximately three mm

3. Size and select tip to suit the client's natural nail shape, file nail tip to shape as necessary to match client's nail

4. Apply resin in a thin layer over the nail plate, avoiding touching the cuticle or nail walls. Spray with activator

5. Lightly buff the distal end of the nail plate. Apply a small drop of adhesive to the natural nail area so that the well of the nail tip is covered.

6. Apply nail tip at a 45° angle to the natural nail, hold the edge of nail tip well against the free edge and firmly press into position

7. Apply a small amount of adhesive to the seam to ensure effective bonding of the tip to the natural nail. Spray with activator, cut nail tip to desired length and shape (protective eye shields may be worn)

8. Blend the seam area

9. Apply adhesive to the nail plate, spray with activator, apply fibreglass mesh, cut to fit the whole nail surface with tacky side to the nail plate

10. Apply adhesive, apply activator, buff to remove shine and buff to give shine

11. Apply cuticle oil to cuticle and nail walls, ask client to wash hands to remove dust. Nail polish may be applied

12. Record all details on the client record card, advise on aftercare and maintenance, advise on contra-actions and re-book maintenance service

Equipment and materials

In addition to the basic equipment and materials (page 459), you will need the following:

EQUIPMENT LIST

 Nail tips in assorted styles and sizes

 Scissors for fibreglass. The scissors should be fine and sharp bladed

 Resin and nozzle

 Resin activator to speed the drying time

 Fibreglass mesh

 Polishes a selection, including base coat and top coat

TIP ✔

Use nail wipes or tissues during treatment, not cottonwool. Cottonwool may shed its fibres onto the nail extension, spoiling the finished result.

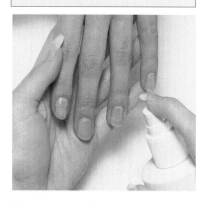

Sanitising the nail

Buffing the nail to remove shine

Applying resin

How to apply fibreglass nail extensions

In the procedure below, each step is carried out for all ten nails before proceeding to the next step.

Approximate application time: 1–1½ hours.

1 Wash your hands, and ask your client to wash theirs. Dry thoroughly.

2 Remove any nail polish and check for contra-indications.

3 Sanitise the nail plate. (Wiping or spraying the nails with an appropriate nail sanitiser will help to inhibit the growth of bacterial and fungal infections.)

4 Push back the cuticles and cut the free edge to approximately three mm. The cuticles must be pushed back gently with a cottonwool-tipped orange stick or hoof stick. This is to ensure that as much as possible of the nail plate is uncovered to allow optimum adhesion of the nail extension. It also ensures that the nails look their best after treatment. Using cuticle nippers, remove excess cuticle.

5 Size and select tip to suit the client's natural nail shape.

6 Lightly buff the nail surface to remove shine. Use a fine-grit file to remove any surface oils and to roughen the nail plate slightly. This allows better adhesion of the nail extension. Use a dehydrator to remove excess oil and moisture.

7 Apply resin down the centre of the nail plate, and spread it in a thin layer over the whole nail using the extender nozzle. Leave a small gap all around the nail plate, to avoid resin touching the cuticle or the nail walls.

8 Spray with activator. An activator is used not only to speed up the drying time of the adhesive, but also to make the surface non-porous. This helps to prevent staining from nail polish or other dyes. Activator must be sprayed from at least 40–45 cm away to ensure even application and client comfort. A mask may be worn to avoid respiratory problems.

   Depress the pump fully to ensure a fine mist of activator. (Failure to do so will result in large droplets of activator falling on the nail plate. This could cause a heat reaction, making application uncomfortable for the client and pitting the resin, which would prevent even application.)

9 Lightly buff the distal end of the nail plate.

Buffing the nail tip

Applying the nail tip

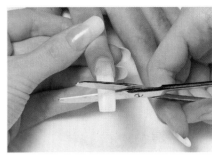

Cutting the nail tip

10 Apply a small drop of adhesive to the natural nail tip. Adhesive should be applied only in the area that the well of the nail tip is to cover.

11 Apply the nail tip, at a 45° angle to the natural nail. Hold the edge of the well against the free edge, then gently press and rock it into position, squeezing out all air bubbles until the tip is flat against the nail surface.

12 Apply a small amount of adhesive to the seam. (This is to ensure that the edge of the tip is securely bonded; it also allows blending to be done more quickly.)

13 Spray with activator.

HEALTH AND SAFETY ✚

Fibreglass systems
Some fibreglass nail systems may use an ultra-violet light or brush-on activator to set the resin. Always follow the manufacturer's instructions carefully.

---

14 Cut the nail tip to the desired length, and file it to shape.

15 Blend the seam area. Do not buff to a shine as this would prevent further resin from adhering properly.

Blending the seam

HEALTH AND SAFETY ✚

Cleaning the nail
Remove excessive dust from the nail plate using a dry tissue or nail wipe. Do not use a brush: brushes are difficult to disinfect and may encourage cross-infection.

---

16 Apply adhesive to the nail plate and spread it over the nail. This must be done carefully, to avoid touching the cuticle and surrounding skin. Any product that touches the skin will allow natural oils to get underneath, resulting in lifting later.

17 Spray with activator.

TIP ✔

After each use, the sides of the resin bottle should be squeezed to allow any resin in the applicator nozzle to flow back into the bottle. A 'burping' sound will be heard from the bottle if this has been done correctly. (Failure to do this will result in the nozzle becoming blocked, making application difficult.)

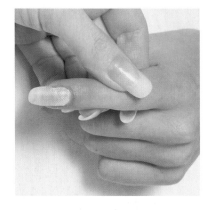

Applying fibreglass mesh

18 Apply fibreglass mesh. Very sharp scissors must be used to cut the mesh, or fraying will result. Cut the fibreglass to fit the whole nail surface, leaving approximately three mm gap around the edges. Avoid over-handling the fibreglass mesh to prevent contamination which could affect adhesion.

Apply the mesh with the tacky side to the nail plate, and ensure that it is completely smooth with no frayed edges.

19 Repeat steps 16 and 17 twice. Allow the resin to soak into the fibreglass mesh for a few seconds before spraying with activator. This reduces the chance of the mesh showing through the finished application.

Applying resin over the fibreglass

HEALTH AND SAFETY

Resin

If resin flows onto the skin, wipe it off immediately, before it dries, with the corner of a tissue or nail wipe soaked in acetone. Allowing the resin to dry on the skin will irritate the client's skin and may cause the nail to lift later.

20 Gently buff the surface to remove shine. This allows step 21 to be carried out effectively. If the surface is buffed too much the fibreglass mesh will show through. If this happens, repeat steps 16 and 17 twice before continuing as usual.

21 Buff the surface to a shine. Using a four-sided buffer, bring the now dull surface to a shine. Begin with the coarsest side of the buffer and work down to the smooth.

22 Apply cuticle oil. This is to reintroduce moisture to the area, which may have become dehydrated with all the buffing and filing. It also gives a luxurious glossy finish. Apply oil to the cuticle and the nail walls then massage in with thumbs.

23 Ask the client to wash her hands, to remove all dust particles and leave the hands feeling fresh and comfortable.

24 Nail polish may be applied, if required. Treat the nails as if they were natural: apply a base coat to avoid staining from dark colours.

Remember that only *acetone-free* nail polish remover may be used. Acetone nail polish remover will result in softening of the nails.

Buffing the nail to a shine

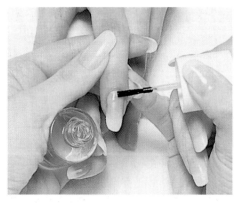

Applying cuticle oil

25 Make another appointment for the client.

26 Dispose of used materials. Clean the workstation and equipment using effective sterilisation and disinfection procedures.

> **TIP** ✔
>
> **Base coat**
> Fibreglass nails are not porous and therefore do not need a base coat under coloured polish. It is a good idea to advise the client to use it anyway, however, as this gets them into a good habit for the future when they are applying nail polish to their natural nails.

> **TIP** ✔
>
> **Activator**
> Do not spray activator towards the adhesive bottle as it might set inside.

Completed fibreglass nail extensions

Stress strip application

A **stress strip** is simply a narrow piece of fibreglass mesh, placed across the nail where the nail tip is blended into the natural nail. This is the weakest area of the nail extension and is usually where breaks will occur if the client is careless with their nails.

Stress strips should be used on the nails of clients:

- who desire very long nail extensions;
- who are quite physical with their hands.

To apply a stress strip, simply apply the nails in the usual way but stop prior to the application of the fibreglass mesh (i.e. before step 18). Now apply the stress strip across the nail, and coat with a layer of resin and spray activator. Then continue in the usual way, applying mesh over the whole nail plate without touching the cuticle or nail walls:

18a Apply the fibreglass stress strip.

18b Apply resin over the whole nail, and spray with activator.

18c Apply fibreglass mesh over the whole nail, without touching the cuticle or nail walls.

18d Proceed with application in the usual way.

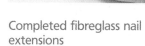

A fibreglass stress strip

Fibreglass mesh over the whole nail

Aftercare and advice

These are the same as for pre-formed nails – page 464. See also Outcome 6: Maintain and repair artificial nail structures, page 462.

Maintenance

Two weeks after the initial application

1 Cleanse the hands and nails and check that the client has been satisfied with their nails. If not, explore why.

2 Remove any nail polish with acetone-free polish remover, and check for any signs of infection. If infection is present, remove the nails immediately and advise the client to see their GP.

3 If the nails are healthy push back the cuticles with a cottonwool-tipped orange stick or hoof stick.

4 Buff the seam area using a fine 240-grit file to remove any loose or lifting fibreglass, then buff with a fine-grit file until the seam becomes invisible. Buff the whole nail plate with a fine-grit file to remove shine.

   Do not use cuticle nippers to remove loose or lifting fibreglass: these cause discomfort to the client and will damage the natural nail.

5 Cleanse and dehydrate the nail's new growth area.

6 Apply a small amount of resin to the regrowth area and spread it with the nozzle to cover the whole regrowth area.

7 Spray with activator from at least 40–45 cm away.

8 Apply resin to the whole nail surface, including the regrowth area.

9 Spray with activator.

10 Buff gently with a fine-grit file to remove shine.

11 With a four-sided buffer, bring the nails to a shine.

12 Apply cuticle oil.

TIP

Clients can still have a regular manicure whilst they are wearing nail extensions. Recommending a regular manicure will help to keep the client's skin and cuticles in good condition, whilst allowing you to keep a check on the condition of the nail extensions.

Four weeks after the initial application

1 Cleanse the hands and nails and check that the client has been satisfied with their nails. If not, explore why.

2 Remove any nail polish with acetone-free polish remover, and check for any signs of infection. If infection is present, remove the nails immediately and advise the client to see their GP.

3 If the nails are healthy push back the cuticles with a cottonwool-tipped orange stick or hoof stick.

4 Buff the seam area using a fine 240-grit file to remove any loose or lifting fibreglass, then buff with a fine-grit file until the seam becomes invisible. Buff the whole nail plate with a fine-grit file to remove shine.

   Do not use cuticle nippers to remove loose or lifting fibreglass: these cause discomfort to the client and will damage the natural nail.

5 Cleanse and dehydrate the nail's new growth area.

6 Apply a small amount of adhesive to the regrowth area and spread it with the nozzle to cover the whole regrowth area.

7 Spray with activator from at least 40–45 cm away.

8 Apply a small piece of fibreglass to the regrowth area, slightly overlapping the old application.

9 Apply resin over the new fibreglass.

10 Spray with activator.

11 Repeat steps 8 and 9.

12 Apply adhesive to the whole nail surface, including the regrowth area.

13 Spray with activator from at least 40–45 cm away.

14 Buff gently with a fine-grit file to remove shine.

15 With a four-sided buffer, bring the nails to a shine.

16 Apply cuticle oil.

Problem solving

- *White areas under the nail tip* This could be due to air bubbles trapped during application of the nail tip. Remove the tip and start again. Use slightly more adhesive, to give more time before the nail bonds.

- *Fibreglass mesh shows through the finished nail* This can happen if the first coat of adhesive did not soak through properly before the activator was sprayed, or if the fibreglass was handled too much prior to application.

- *Lifting of the fibreglass overlay* This may be due to products touching the cuticle or nail wall. Too much adhesive, or not enough, may also cause this problem.

- *Burning* If the client complains of a burning sensation, hold the activator further away to avoid this heat reaction.

- *Frayed fibreglass mesh* If the mesh has frayed through the adhesive, it could be that the scissors were not sharp enough, or that the fibreglass was not pressed smooth to the nail before the adhesive was applied.

SCULPTURED ACRYLIC NAILS

Liquid and **powder acrylic** can be used in two ways to produce strong, natural-looking nail extensions: they can be sculpted over a nail form, or they can be sculpted over a nail tip. Which method is used depends on the client's needs and the therapist's preference. With nail tips:

- application takes longer, as time is needed to apply and blend in the tips;

- less sculpting skill is required, as the tip provides the basis of a natural shape;

- the method is more expensive, due to the use of tips;

- less filing is required, as the need for sculpting is minimal.

With nail forms:

TIP

Alternate maintenance procedures so that one maintenance is with fibreglass, the next without. This avoids unnecessary use of fibreglass and build-up of product around the cuticle area.

HEALTH AND SAFETY

Acrylic products
Products are available which can be added to acrylic liquids to eliminate the unpleasant odour. This makes the treatment much more pleasant for both the client and the nail technician.

- once the application skill has been mastered, sculpting over a form is quicker than with application of a tip;
- the method is cheaper, as no nail tips are required;
- the technique is more difficult to learn;
- if the form is incorrectly applied or is moved during application, extensive filing is required to achieve a natural shape.
- it is easy to replace a broken nail to create a balanced look during a manicure.

Acrylic nails are very strong and durable, and are therefore ideal for clients who are very physical with their hands.

Advantages	Disadvantages
1 Very strong. 2 Suitable for nail-biters, due to the strong adhesive qualities of acrylic and the fact that a large nail plate is not needed. 3 The moulding qualities of acrylic allow sculpting to be adapted to any size or shape of natural nail.	1 The need for primer means that the natural nails are weaker when acrylic nails are removed. However, this weakness is not permanent and will grow out as the nails grow forward. 2 Acrylic nails are not suitable for clients who wish to grow their own nails without artificial products to strengthen them. 3 Products have a strong, unpleasant odour.

Equipment and materials

In addition to the basic equipment and materials (page 459), you will need the following:

EQUIPMENT LIST

 Acrylic powder in a variety of colours, including white, pink and clear – often referred to as a *polymer*

Acrylic liquid often referred to as a *monomer*

Primer methocrylate acid, which aids the adhesion of the acrylic to the natural nail

 Nail forms available in metal, plastic or paper

 Brush for use with acrylics; the best brushes are sable

 Polishes a selection, including base coat and top coat

TIP	

Polymerisation
When liquid monomer and powder polymer are mixed, a chemical reaction called *polymerisation* occurs and concludes with setting.

HEALTH AND SAFETY

Personal protective equipment (PPE)
To prevent harm to yourself or the client you may choose to wear PPE during nail services. This includes:
Glasses to prevent chemical splashes and dust entering the eyes.
Dust masks to prevent inhalation of dust, especially when filing.
Gloves to prevent absorption of chemicals through the skin or nail plate. Regular contact with skin irritants can result in irritant contact dermatitis, where the skin becomes allergic to the product.

How to apply sculptured acrylic nail extensions

Approximate application time: $1\frac{1}{2}$ hours.

1 Wash your hands, and ask your client to wash theirs. Dry thoroughly.
2 Remove any nail polish and check for contra-indications.
3 Push back the cuticles with a cottonwool-tipped orange stick or hoof stick. Remove any excess cuticle with cuticle nippers.
4 Sanitise the natural nail plate. (This prevents the growth of bacterial and fungal infections beneath the artificial nail.)
5 Lightly buff the nail plate with a fine-grit board, to remove shine.
6 Apply primer to the nail plate and allow this to dry. Do not allow primer to touch the cuticle or the nail walls. Avoid over-use or the nail plate will become too smooth and the acrylic will lift.
7 Apply the nail form to the fingertip, beneath the free edge of the natural nail. This is the base for the extended acrylic tip. Check from all angles that the form is in the most natural position.

HEALTH AND SAFETY

Ventilation
Because of the volatile nature of acrylic liquids and the dust created from filing, you must always work in a well-ventilated room. Specially designed extractor fans are available for use at the workstation.

---

8 To achieve a natural look when applying acrylic nails using the two-colour acrylic method, use pink or white acrylic for clients with light skin, and ivory or peach acrylic for clients with dark skin.

   Dip the brush in the liquid rotating the brush slightly, then in acrylic powder to form a ball of medium-dry consistency the size of a small pea. Apply this to the nail form to create a free edge. Smooth and shape the acrylic using the middle and side of the brush to flatten and press the acrylic into place.
9 Dip the brush in liquid, then in powder, as before, and apply to the middle of the nail plate. Use the sides of the brush to blend the acrylic towards the free edge and the sides of the nail.

10 Dip the brush in liquid, then powder, and apply the acrylic near the cuticle. This should be a wetter, thinner application to avoid a ridge and give a more natural-looking application.

11 When the desired shape has been created, allow it to set hard. To check whether the acrylic has set, tap it with an orange stick: listen for an audible click rather than a dull sound.

   Once set, remove the nail form and shape the free edge with a coarse/medium-grit file.

12 Using a four-sided buffer, smooth the nail surface to a shine.

13 Apply cuticle oil.

14 Wash your hands, and the client should wash theirs. This step is very important: you both need to remove any acrylic dust that might otherwise irritate the skin.

   Remove the towel from the workstation and replace it with a clean one. This prevents dust particles from ruining the nail enamel application, and makes the working environment more pleasant. Dust can also lead to irritant contact dermatitis.

15 Polish the nails as usual. Always use a base coat, as acrylic is a porous substance and nail polish might stain it.

16 Make another appointment for the client.

17 Dispose of used materials. Clean the workstation and equipment using effective sanitisation and disinfection procedures.

Aftercare and advice

These are the same as for nail extensions on page 464. See also Outcome 6: Maintain and repair artificial nail structures, page 462.

> **TIP**
>
> **Consistency control**
> To achieve a medium consistency of acrylic liquid (monomer) and powder (polymer), mix 1.5 parts monomer to one part polymer.
>   To achieve a wet consistency mix two parts liquid to one part powder.

> **TIP**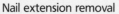
>
> **Nail extension removal**
> Every two to three months the nails should be removed and a new set applied. This allows the new nail growth to be properly dehydrated with acetone. Failure to due this will result in repeated problems with nails lifting in the cuticle area.

How to apply nail tips with acrylic overlay

Follow the instructions for nail-tip application up to and including step 12 (pages 466–7). Then follow this procedure:

13 Apply primer to the natural nail area only.

14 Dip the brush in liquid, then in clear powder, to form a ball the size of a large pea.

15 Apply the acrylic ball to the centre of the nail plate. Use the sides of the brush to blend acrylic over the entire nail plate, ensuring that application is thinner at the cuticle, the nail wall and the free edge areas, to give a natural appearance. Acrylic applied too thickly near the cuticle will cause lifting.

16 Re-apply acrylic if necessary to ensure adequate coverage of the nail plate.

17 Check the nail from all angles to ensure that the shape is natural.

18 Once the desired shape has been created, allow the product to set hard.

19 Remove any surface irregularities using a coarse/medium-grit file.

20 Buff the surface to a shine with a four-sided buffer.

21 Apply cuticle oil to the skin around the nail.

22 Wash your hands, and your client should wash theirs.

23 Apply nail polish as desired.

24 Make another appointment for the client.

25 Dispose of used materials. Clean the workstation and equipment using effective sterilisation and disinfection procedures.

Aftercare and advice

These are the same as for nail extensions – see page 464. See also Outcome 6: Maintain and repair artificial nail structures, page 462.

Maintenance: sculptured acrylic nail extensions

Maintenance should be carried out approximately every two weeks after the initial application. This keeps the nails strong, balanced, attractive and healthy.

1 Wash your hands, and ask your client to wash theirs. Refer to the client's record card for details of previous nail-extension applications.

2 Remove any nail polish with acetone-free nail polish remover, and check for any signs of infection. If infection is present remove the extensions immediately and advise the client to see their GP.

3 If the nails are healthy push back the cuticles with a cottonwool-tipped orange stick or hoof stick. Use cuticle nippers to remove excess cuticle.

4 Lightly buff the seam area with a medium-grit file to remove any loose or lifting acrylic, then buff with a fine-grit file until the seam becomes invisible. Buff the whole nail plate with a medium-grit file to remove the shine. Do not try to cut off loose acrylic with cuticle nippers: this damages the natural nail plate and is extremely uncomfortable for the client.

5 Lightly buff the new nail regrowth with a fine-grit file, and apply primer to this area only. Avoid contact with previously applied acrylic as it will weaken and discolour it.

6 Apply a small ball of pink or clear acrylic near the cuticle. This should be a thin application, to avoid a ridge and to give a more natural-looking finish.

Blend in the new application by brushing the acrylic down towards the free edge.

Dip the brush into liquid and wipe it clean on a tissue regularly throughout the application. This will prevent the acrylic from setting on the brush.

7 When the infill is finished, allow it to set hard.

8 Using a four-sided buffer, smooth the nail surface to a shine.

9 Apply cuticle oil.

10 Both of you should now wash your hands.

11 Polish the nails as usual.

12 Make another appointment for the client.

13 Dispose of used materials. Clean the workstation and equipment using effective sterilisation and disinfection procedures.

Maintenance: tips with acrylic overlay

This procedure is carried out using exactly the same method as for sculptured acrylic nails (pages 481–2).

TIP	

The white free edge moves forward with the growing nail, and soon the natural nail's free edge can be seen through the acrylic. To disguise this, file the surface of the artificial free edge to form a step at the natural flesh line. Be careful not to file it right through. Fill in this step with white acrylic. Use a fine layer of clear acrylic to strengthen the join.

HEALTH AND SAFETY	

Working with acrylic
The dust created during the filing of acrylic nails can lead to skin allergies and respiratory problems. Keep dust to a minimum by using an extractor fan near the workstation and changing the towels on the workstation during treatment.

Repairing acrylic nails

Due to the strength of a correctly applied acrylic nail, repairs are seldom necessary. If nails are cracked, chipped or broken, however, repairs may be carried out using the following methods.

Lifting or cracking of the product around the cuticle area

1 Repair using the general maintenance procedure.

Chip or crack in the free edge

1 Use the edge of a coarse-grit file to widen and roughen the crack. (This makes filling it in easier.)

2 Place a nail form beneath the free edge and 'fill in' the chip or crack with matching coloured acrylic. Wetting the old acrylic nail with acrylic liquid will improve adhesion.

3 File and buff the new acrylic as in original application.

HEALTH AND SAFETY	

Lifting acrylic
Do not use nippers to clip away lifting acrylic. To do so is extremely uncomfortable for the client, and may cause bruising to the nail plate and further lifting of the existing acrylic.

Free edge broken off

1 Roughen the nail surface with a medium-grit file.

2 Place a nail form beneath the free edge. Dampen the free edge with acrylic liquid, and sculpt the free edge with white powder as in original application. Secure free edge with a thin layer of clear acrylic over the entire nail.

3 Finish off as in the original application.

Problem solving

- *Acrylic overlay lifting from the natural nail* This is probably due to incorrect preparation of the natural nail plate. Alternative reasons are that too much or too little product was used, or that the product was touching the skin.

- *Infills are obvious* Ensure a thorough blending-in of the previous application before applying new acrylic.

- *Nails break at the flesh line* Not enough product was applied in the area, or it was over-buffed.

- *Acrylic liquid is solid in the bottle* The liquid has been contaminated with powder. Never pour products back into the bottle, or put the brush in the bottle.

- *Acrylic appears frosty when set* The room is too cold. The room should be quite warm if the product is to set correctly.

- *The finished nail points upwards or downwards* This results from incorrect placing of the nail form or incorrect application of the nail tip. Check regularly from all angles during application.

- *The transverse arch of the nail is irregular* The acrylic was applied unevenly:
- too much product at the sides of the nail;
- too much product on the middle of the nail;
- too much product at one side – the client's fingers were tilted before the product set, or the application was too wet (causing the product to run).

- *The longitudinal arch of the nail is irregular* The acrylic was applied unevenly:
- too much product at the cuticle area;
- too much product in the centre of the nail;
- too much product at the free edge.

If you make a mistake, remove the nail using the correct procedure and re-apply it.

Nail pointing up

Nail pointing down

Too much product in the cuticle area

Too much product in the middle

Too much product at the free edge

Too much product at the sides

Too much product in the middle

Too much product at one side

GEL NAIL EXTENSIONS

Gel can be applied over a tip or can be sculpted over a nail form, as with acrylic. Application methods are very similar to those with acrylic, but due to the self-levelling nature of the gel, the procedure is easier. Because gel is clear, the finished nail is very natural-looking and does not require nail polish. Coloured gels are also available: these give a permanently polished look which doesn't chip or fade, but clients may get bored with the colour.

Some gel systems require the use of an ultra-violet light to set the gel, others use a spray activator similar to that used in fibreglass application.

Advantages	*Disadvantages*
1 Very natural-looking and retain their surface shine.	1 Not as strong as acrylic or fibreglass.
2 Easier to apply than acrylic or fibreglass.	2 Methods using ultra-violet light are more expensive than other systems.
3 Self-levelling gel means less filing.	3 Light must penetrate the gel to harden the oligomers. The products must be thin in application and exposed to the correct UV light or uncured product will remain.
4 Less filing means less dust, so the environment is more pleasant for the client and the nail technician.	

HEALTH AND SAFETY

UV light
The light in nail lamps used to cure the nails is UVA. The wattage of the equipment is between 38-45 watts, and is not considered harmful to skin. Too high a wattage will cause heat reactions on the nail bed.

Equipment and materials

In addition to the basic equipment and materials (page 459), you will need the following:

EQUIPMENT LIST

 Gel usually oligomers, semi-liquid in consistency, similar to monomer and polymer system

 Gel-setting spray or ultra-violet light to harden and cure the gel nail

 Primer

Nail forms

 Nail tips

 Adhesive

Brushes a synthetic brush may be used as it holds the gel and spreads it evenly

 Polishes a selection, including base coat and top coat

How to apply gel extensions using the tip and overlay method

Approximate application time: 1–1½ hours.

1 Wash your hands, and ask your client to wash theirs. Dry thoroughly.

2 Remove any nail polish and check for contra-indications.

3 Sanitise the natural nail plate. This prevents the growth of bacterial and fungal infections beneath the artificial nail.

4 If the nails are healthy push back the cuticles and cut the free edge to approximately three mm.

5 Size up the nail tips.

6 Lightly buff the natural nail to remove shine.

7 Apply a small drop of adhesive to the tip of the natural nail.

8 Apply the nail tip.

9 Cut the nail tip to the desired length, and file it to shape.

10 Blend the seam area.

11 Apply primer to the natural nail plate area.

12 Apply gel according to the manufacturer's instructions. Some gels need an ultra-violet light source to cure them; others may be set with an activator spray or brush-on setting liquid.

13 Oxygen inhibits polymerisation, the chemical reaction of the gel on the nail surface, leaving a sticky layer. This usually requires the application of a base coat gel, which is cured. Followed by a building gel which again is cured. Ensure the client places the fingers and thumbs correctly when the gel is being cured.

14 Buff the nail's surface.

15 Remove any dust and finally apply a top coat from the cuticle to the free edge, which is cured.

16 Remove any sticky residue with a nail-wipe soaked in non-acetone nail polish remover.

17 Buff the surface of the nail vigorously to a shine.

18 Apply cuticle oil.

19 Ask the client to wash her hands.

20 Apply nail polish if desired.

21 Make another appointment for the client.

22 Dispose of used materials, clean the workstation and equipment using effective sterilisation and disinfection procedures.

TIP

Gel

Because gel is semi-liquid, ask the client to keep their fingers flat until the gel is set, otherwise the gel will slide to one side of the nail, resulting in an uneven application. Apply gel to the fingers and thumbs separately, so that the client can keep them level.

How to apply sculptured gel nail extensions

Approximate application time: 1–1½ hours.

1 Wash your hands, and ask your client to wash theirs. Dry thoroughly.

2 Remove any nail polish and check for contra-indications.

3 Sanitise the natural nail plate. (This prevents the growths of bacterial and fungal infections beneath the artificial nail.)

4 Lightly buff the nail plate with a fine-grit board, to remove the shine.

5 Apply primer to the nail plate and allow it to dry. Do not allow primer to touch the cuticle or the nail walls.

6 Apply a nail form to the fingertip, beneath the free edge of the natural nail: this is the base for the extended gel tip. Check from all angles that the form is in the most natural position.

7 Dip the brush in gel to form a ball the size of a small pea. Apply this to the nail plate near the cuticle, and pull the gel towards the free edge using the brush. (Do not apply like nail polish, as this would result in too thin an application of gel.) Gel is self-levelling: push it over the nail plate, avoiding the cuticle and nail walls. Shape the gel over the nail form to create the free edge.

8 When you have created the desired shape, allow the gel to set hard. Gel may be set with an activator spray, a brush-on activator, or with an ultra-violet light, according to the manufacturer's instructions.

9 Once set, remove the nail form and shape the free edge with a coarse-grit file.

10 Remove any sticky residue on the gel with a nail wipe soaked in non-acetone nail polish remover.

11 Using a four-sided buffer, smooth the nail surface to a shine.

12 Apply cuticle oil.

13 You and your client should now wash your hands. This step is very important: it removes any dust or gel residue that might otherwise irritate the skin.

   Remove the towel from the workstation and replace it with a clean one. This prevents dust particles from ruining the nail polish application, and makes the working environment more pleasant.

14 Apply polish to the nails as usual. Always use a base coat to prevent the polish staining the gel.

TIP

Every two to three months the nails should be removed and a new set applied. This allows the new nail growth to be properly dehydrated with acetone. (Failure to do this will result in repeated problems with nails lifting in the cuticle area.)

Sanitising the nail plate

Buffing the nail plate to remove shine

Fitting the nail forms

Applying the base coat gel

Curing the gel

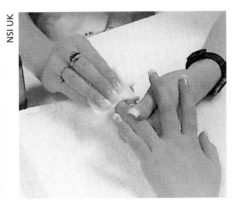

Wiping with acetone

Smoothing the nail plate

Applying the cuticle oil

TIP ✔

Some systems use three different gels, others only one. Always read the manufacturer's instructions carefully.

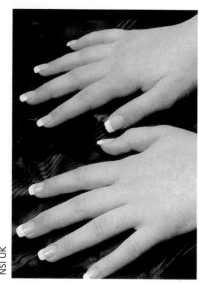

Completed sculptured gel nail extensions

Aftercare and advice

Maintenance to the nail extensions should be carried out approximately every two weeks after the initial application. This keeps the nails strong, balanced and attractive.

Maintenance

1 Wash your hands, and ask your client to wash theirs. Refer to the client's record card for details of previous nail extension applications.

2 Remove any nail polish with acetone-free nail polish remover and check for any signs of infection. If infection is present, remove the extensions immediately and advise the client to see their doctor.

3 Push back the cuticles with a cottonwool-tipped orange stick or hoof stick.

4 Buff the seam area with a medium-grit file to remove any loose or lifting gel, then buff with a fine-grit file until the seam becomes invisible. Buff the whole nail plate with a medium-grit file to remove the shine and to avoid build-up of product. Do not try to cut off loose gel with cuticle nippers: this damages the natural nail plate and is extremely uncomfortable for the client.

5 Lightly buff nail regrowth with a fine-grit file, and apply primer to this area only.

6 Apply a small ball of gel near the cuticle. This should be a thin application to avoid a ridge and to give a more natural-looking finish. Blend in the new application by brushing the gel down towards the free edge.

7 When the infill is finished, cure it with ultra-violet light or activator spray.

8 Remove any sticky residue with non-acetone polish remover.

9 Using a four-sided buffer, smooth the nail surface to a shine.

10 Apply cuticle oil.

11 You and your client should now wash your hands.

12 Apply polish to the nails as usual.

CONTRA-ACTIONS TO ARTIFICIAL NAIL APPLICATION

A contra-action to artificial nail application is an adverse condition that appears after nails have been applied. Examples are:

- thinning of the natural nail plate;
- allergies;
- infection (such as paronychia, tinea unguium or onychomycosis);
- softening of the nail plate;

- physical trauma to the nail plate, bed or cuticle;
- lifting of the nail extension product.

Thinning of the natural nail plate

Appearance

When artificial nails are removed, the natural free edge is very thin. It can easily be bent or torn using very light pressure.

Causes

- Excessive filing of the nail plate during preparation.
- Excessive filing whilst blending in nail tip.
- Incorrect removal of the nails.

Treatment

1 Keep the free edge short.
2 Allow the thin nail plate to grow out.
3 Apply nail strengthener to the nails.
4 Do not re-apply artificial nails until the thin nails have grown out.

Allergies

Appearance

Redness, blisters, inflammation and itching. These may appear on the cuticle or skin around the nails, or on the face and neck, which the nails regularly touch.

Cause

- Exposure to a product to which the client is allergic. Allergies are specific to individual people, so what may irritate one client may prove harmless to another.

Treatment

1 Remove the artificial nails immediately, using the correct procedure. If the allergic reaction is severe, advise the client to seek medical attention.
2 Once the allergy has cleared alternative nail systems may be applied to single nails to test the client's tolerance. Do not test products on the client's skin: they are not designed for such use, and will cause an allergic response in many clients and therefore give misleading results.

HEALTH AND SAFETY

Allergenic products
There are many suppliers of nail-extension products. If a product regularly causes allergies among clients when being used correctly, inform the manufacturer and try alternative products to discover one that is less irritating.

Infection

Appearance

Redness, inflammation and pus in the cuticle area and surrounding skin; separation of the nail plate from the nail bed at the flesh line; or dark spots between the artificial nail and the natural nail plate.

Causes

- Lack of hygiene in the salon during application.
- Incorrect homecare.

Treatment

1 Remove the nails immediately, using the correct method.
2 Advise the client to seek medical attention.

HEALTH AND SAFETY

Lifting nails
If nails start to lift, moisture will get underneath: this creates an ideal breeding ground for bacteria. Always advise clients to return to the salon immediately the nails start to lift, so that the appropriate treatment can be carried out at once to avoid infection.

Softening of the natural nail plate

Appearance

When nails are removed, the natural nail plate is very soft and easily torn at the free edge.

Cause

- Prolonged exposure to the products used in artificial nail application, particularly primer.

Treatment

1 Allow the softened nail to grow out, keeping the free edge short. Apply nail strengthener, and do not re-apply artificial nails until soft nails have grown out.

Physical trauma

Appearance

Bruising, ridges in the nail plate and cuts and abrasions to cuticle and surrounding skin.

Causes

- *Bruising* Too much pressure applied to nails during treatment.
- *Ridges* Excessive filing in one place, causing thinning of the nail plate.
- *Cuts and abrasions* Careless use of files and buffers.

Treatment

1 Apply antiseptic to cuts and abrasions. Allow bruises and ridges to grow out.

Extreme care should be taken during application. Use tools correctly and do not apply too much pressure. Ensure that tools are of a high quality, with no rough or sharp edges.

Lifting of the nail extension product

Appearance

The products applied to the nail lift away from the natural nail plate.

Causes

- Incorrect nail preparation.
- Incorrect application of nail products/materials.
- Incorrect mixture of nail products.
- Nail extension length too long.
- Maintenance treatment schedule not followed.

Treatment

1 Ensure the natural nail is prepared adequately before application of artificial nail products.

2 Use product as recommended by the manufacturer. Attend manufacturer training update workshops to ensure professional competence in product use.

3 Ensure a realistic length is agreed for the client at consultation.

HEALTH AND SAFETY

Files
If the sides of files are rough or sharp, use a fine-grit file to gently smooth them down. This will reduce the risk of cutting clients' cuticles, and will also make the files more pleasant for the nail technician to work with.

REPAIRING AND STRENGTHENING THE NATURAL NAIL

If a natural nail is broken, split or cracked, it is sometimes possible to repair and strengthen the damage so that the client doesn't lose the free edge of their nail. Repairs and strengthening can be done with different types of materials, the strongest being silk, fibreglass, linen and acrylic. Once repaired, nails should be treated in the same way as artificial nails – for example, non-acetone nail polish remover must be used.

Types of nail damage that can be repaired are:

- brittle nails;
- flaking nails;
- free edge or flesh-line break;
- severed free edge.

Brittle nails

Brittle nails may be protected with a gel overlay. This will provide additional protection as the natural nail grows, whilst providing a natural appearance. A thin protective coating of a nail system is applied to the natural nail over the nail plate.

1 Remove any nail polish, and dehydrate the nail plate by wiping it with a cotton bud soaked in acetone. Check that there are no contra-indications.
2 Following manufacturer's instructions, prepare the natural nail.
3 Apply base coat gel and cure, remove tackiness.
4 Apply building gel and cure, remove tackiness.
5 File the nail to shape including the nail walls and free edge.
6 Buff and dust.
7 Apply top coat gel and cure, remove tackiness.
8 Apply cuticle oil.
9 Clean the hands and nails.
10 Apply polish if required.

> **TIP** ✔
>
> Coating the whole nail with any of the materials used in repairs or extensions is known as capping. This service can be offered to clients who don't want artificial nails but who need something to keep their own nails from breaking. Capping needs to be maintained in the same ways as semi-permanent nails.

Flaking nails

1 Remove any nail polish, and dehydrate the nail plate by wiping it with a cotton bud soaked in acetone. Check that there are no contra-indications.
2 Place a piece of mending material over the whole nail plate, extending over the free edge.
3 Apply a layer of resin over the material and allow this to dry. Use a resin activator, if available, to reduce the drying time. If using acrylic, allow it to dry before proceeding to step 5.
4 Repeat step 3.
5 Use a four-sided buffer to bring the nails to a shine.

Free edge or flesh-line break

1 Remove any nail polish, and dehydrate the nail plate by wiping it with a cotton bud soaked in acetone. Check that there are no contra-indications.
2 Place a small piece of mending material over the break.
3 Apply a layer of resin over the material and allow this to dry. Use a resin activator, if available, to reduce the drying time.
4 Repeat step 3.
5 Use a four-sided buffer to smooth the repair application and bring the nails to a shine.

Severed free edge

1 Place the severed free edge into a bowl of hot water, to soften the nail. Soak for approximately three minutes, then dry with a tissue.

2 Remove any nail polish, and dehydrate the nail plate by wiping it with a cotton bud soaked in acetone. Check that there are no contra-indications.

3 Lightly buff the whole nail plate to remove the shine.

4 Place a small drop of resin close to the free edge.

5 Apply the severed nail tip to the nail plate, overlapping it slightly.

6 Blend the join with a medium-grit file.

7 Place a small piece of mending material over the join.

8 Apply a layer of resin over the material and allow this to dry. Use a resin activator, if available, to reduce the drying time.

9 Apply mending material to the whole nail plate.

10 Repeat step 8 twice.

11 Use a four-sided buffer to smooth the repair application and bring the nails to a shine.

If the client did not keep their severed free edge, the broken fingernail could be matched to the others by applying a nail extension.

ACTIVITY

Nail services
List the different types of nail service that could be offered using the procedures detailed in this chapter.

AFTERCARE AND ADVICE FOR ARTIFICIAL NAILS

Outcome 7: Complete the treatment

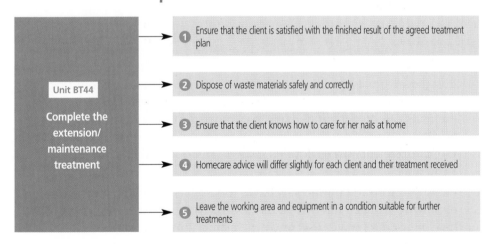

Unit BT44

Complete the extension/ maintenance treatment

1 Ensure that the client is satisfied with the finished result of the agreed treatment plan

2 Dispose of waste materials safely and correctly

3 Ensure that the client knows how to care for her nails at home

4 Homecare advice will differ slightly for each client and their treatment received

5 Leave the working area and equipment in a condition suitable for further treatments

After confirming that the finished nail shape and length is suitable for the client it is important that thorough aftercare advice is provided.

It is important when carrying out nail treatments that the client knows how to care for their nails at home. It is up to you to give them the correct advice, otherwise they may unwittingly undo the work done during treatment.

When you give homecare advice you can also recommend products such as nail polish or handcream and specialised nail treatments, enhancing retail sales and your profits.

Homecare advice will differ sightly for each client, but basically it will be as follows for nail extensions:

- Use only non-acetone nail polish remover, to avoid softening the nails.
- Have the nails regularly maintained (infilled), to keep them attractive and strong.
- Always use a base coat under nail polish, to avoid yellowing.
- Do not pull the nails off if they start to lift: have them removed professionally and safely.
- Use a pen when dialling a telephone number on a rotary phone to avoid stress to the free edge.
- Use a nail brush to gently remove dirt from underneath the free edge.
- Contact the salon if there is any indication of infection, such as swelling, discoloration or inflammation.
- Return for nail extension maintenance treatment as advised for the nail system.

REMOVING ARTIFICIAL NAILS

TIP

Every two to three months the nails should be removed and a new set applied. This allows the new nail growth to be properly dehydrated with acetone. (Failure to do this will result in repeated problems with nails lifting in the cuticle area.)

HEALTH AND SAFETY

Loosening nails
Never try to re-stick nails that are coming loose by applying adhesive under the false nail – this could trap bacteria beneath the nail, leading to infection.

1 The client should wash their hands.

2 Remove any existing nail polish.

3 Cut off the artificial free edge, being careful not to cut the natural free edge.

4 Slightly roughen the surface of the nail with a medium-grit file, to encourage absorption of the solvent by the nail.

5 Place the fingertips in a glass bowl containing a solvent such as acetone to a depth of two to three cm. To ensure client comfort, place the hands in separate bowls. Leave to soak for 15–20 minutes. Care should be taken when using acetone. It is extremely drying to the natural nails and the nails can be dehydrated and weakened resulting in splitting and peeling. Fibreglass is the easiest nail system to remove, whilst UV gel is the hardest. This strength differs due to the bonds that form the structures.

6 Every two to three minutes, remove the fingers and wipe away the dissolving artificial nail with a tissue soaked in acetone. An orange stick may be used to gently buff away the artificial nail structure.

7 When the nail has completely dissolved, a full manicure, including the application of a nail strengthener, should be carried out to ensure that the client leaves the salon with their nails in the best possible condition.

8 Make another appointment for a nail service to improve the condition of the natural nail or nail extension replacement.

TIP

Retail advice
Always recommend after nail extension removal that the client purchase a nail-strengthener for home use.

GLOSSARY OF KEY WORDS

Acrylic sculptured nails use powder and liquid to make a strong acrylic from which to form artificial nail structures.

Aftercare advice recommendations given to the client following treatment to continue the benefits of the treatment.

Bacteria minute, single-celled organisms of various shapes. Large numbers live on the skin's surface and are not harmful (non-pathogenic). Others, however, are harmful (pathogenic) and can cause skin diseases.

Buffer a manicure tool used on the nail to smooth surface irregularities and to give sheen to the nail surface.

Consultation assessment of client's needs using different assessment techniques, including questioning and natural observation.

Contra-action an unwanted reaction occurring during or after treatment application.

Contra-indication a problematic symptom which indicates that the treatment may not proceed or may restrict treatment application. Contra-indications identified for nail/hand treatments are discussed in more detail in Chapter1 and Chapter 9.

Dehydrate remove moisture and oil from the natural nail plate – necessary to ensure the effective application of the artificial nail product.

Fungi microscopic plants, which are parasites. Fungal diseases of the skin feed off the waste products of the skin. They are found on the skin's surface or they can attack deeper tissues.

Gel nail product that can be applied over a tip or sculpted over a nail form, as with acrylic. Some gel systems require the use of ultra-violet light to set the gel; others use a spray activator.

Maintenance scheduled treatments necessary following the application of artificial nails to repair any damage and maintain their appearance as the natural nail grows underneath.

Nail file tool used to shape, reduce the length, blend the nail surface to create balance and impart shine. The surface texture, referred to as 'grit', is numbered and varies according to its purpose. The lower the grit number, the coarser the file.

Nail forms made of paper or metal. These are placed at the end of the nail. The natural nail is lengthened onto the nail form using nail extension product.

Nail tips plastic nail tips used to extend the length of the natural nail.

Nail wrap a material such as silk or fibreglass is attached to the nail to repair or strengthen the natural nail.

Onycholysis nail condition where the nail plate separates from the nail bed.

Onychopagy nail condition where a person bites their nails excessively.

Onychorrhexis nail condition split, flaking nails.

Paronychia bacterial infection. Swelling, redness and pus appears in the cuticle area of the nail wall.

Personal Protective Equipment (PPE) at Work Regulations 1992 this legislation requires employers to identify, through a risk assessment, those activities that require special protective equipment to be worn or used.

Polymerisation a chemical reaction that occurs when using liquid monomer and powder polymer during acrylic nail application, and which concludes with hardening.

Resin an adhesive used in the fibreglass artificial nail system.

Sculptured nails artificial nail system using a liquid and powder or gel system. The mixture is sculpted, built up over the natural nail plate and extended past the free edge onto a nail form.

Stress strip a narrow piece of fibreglass mesh, placed across the nail where the nail tip is blended into the natural nail. This is a weak area and the stress strip provides additional strength.

Tinea unguium fungal infection of the nails. The nail is yellowish-grey in colour.

Tips and overlays a nail tip is applied, blended to remove the visible line, and is overlaid with acrylic, gel or fibreglass.

Treatment plan after the consultation, suitable treatment objectives are established to treat the client's conditions and needs.

Wrap a fibreglass or silk nail system to overlay natural nails or artificial tips.

Assessment of knowledge and understanding

You have now learnt about the different nail extension and maintenance services available. To be effective in your role you must be able to consult with the client and select the most appropriate nail service to meet her treatment requirements. This skill enables you to effectively extend and maintain nails.

To test your level of knowledge, answer the following short questions. These will prepare you for your summative (final) assessment.

Additional anatomy and physiology questions are found on page 148.

Structure and growth of the nails

1 What are the functions of the following nail parts:
   - nail groove
   - free edge
   - matrix?
2 What factors affect the growth rate of the nail?
3 How can damage to the nail bed or matrix be recognised?
4 Name four functions of the skin.

Consult with the client

1 How can you ensure that you comply with the requirements of the Data Protection Act 1998?
2 Name three contra-indications to nail extension services.
3 Why is it important not to name specific contra-indications but to refer the client to their GP?
4 Why must an accurate record be kept for clients receiving nail extension and maintenance services?
5 How will the following information discussed and recorded on the record card help you to decide on the nail service to apply?
   - occupation
   - condition of the client's natural nails and cuticles
   - reasons for having nail extensions.
6 Why is it important to fully explain the treatment service recommended, and what results the client can expect to achieve?

Prepare for the treatment

1 What Health and Safety legislation states how chemicals required for nail extension services should be stored and used?

2 Why is good ventilation important in the working area?

3 What other environmental conditions are important to ensure that your treatment is effective and comfortable for your client and yourself?

4 How may the client's clothing be protected during treatment?

5 What personal protective equipment may the client wear during the trimming of nail tip length?

6 Why should the client's nail plate be free of oil and moisture prior to the application of natural nail wraps and extensions?

7 Why is your working position important when performing nail services?

8 What equipment should be sterilised before treatment?

9 What does the term 'sterilisation' mean?

Plan the treatment

1 Name four different nail shapes that you may expect to see.

2 Why must natural nail shape be considered during extension treatment application?

3 Why is it important to treat overgrown cuticles before nail extension treatment?

4 How could nail extension materials be used to improve the quality or appearance of the following nail conditions:
- brittle nails
- flaking/peeling nails?

5 Why is it important to spend time sizing the nail tip to match the client's natural nail shape and size?

6 Why are the nails dehydrated before wrap system treatment?

Repair natural nails to improve condition and appearance

1 If the skin is accidentally broken during treatment, how would you deal with this to ensure the safety of yourself, the client and others?

2 Why should a margin be left around the edge of the nail when applying artificial nail products to lengthen or strengthen?

3 How is the nail system for natural nail repair chosen?

4 What are the different overlay systems available?

5 How would you repair the following:
- free edge broken at flesh line
- flaking nails
- brittle nails?

Apply artificial nail using the wrap system

1 Why is the nail plate dehydrated before treatment?

2 How is the nail tip selected for the client?

3 How can damage to the natural nail be avoided when blending the nail tip?

4 Why is a free margin left around the cuticle and side of the nail wall area?

5 How would excessive resin application affect the durability of the nail?

6 What are the advantages of artificial nail application using the wrap system?

Maintain and repair artificial nail structures

1 What is the recommended time following application for a maintenance treatment for:
- natural nail wraps
- tip and overlay nail extensions?

2 What do you understand by the term *achieving* balance when applying artificial nail materials to the nails?

3 What is the purpose of nail maintenance treatment:
- two weeks after the initial application
- four weeks after the initial application?

4 Before application of repair materials how should the new natural nail be prepared?

Complete the treatment

1 How can you ensure that client satisfaction is achieved both during treatment and following nail extension treatment application?

2 What advice should be given to a client with regards to care for their nails?

3 If accidental damage occurs what actions should the client be advised to take?

4 What information should be recorded following a treatment application?

5 What do you understand by the term 'contra-action'?

6 State the possible cause and action to take for the following contra-actions:
- allergic reaction
- onycholysis (nail separation)
- lifting of the nail extension product?

chapter 13

BT13 Provide nail art service

This unit describes how to provide a variety of nail art techniques for clients. It describes the competencies to enable you to:

- **consult with the client**
- **prepare for the service**
- **plan the service**
- **provide nail art service to clients**
- **complete the service**

When providing nail art service it is important to use the skills you have learnt in the following core mandatory units:

UNIT G1 Ensure your own actions reduce risks to health and safety

UNIT G6 Promote additional products or services to clients

UNIT G8 Develop and maintain your effectiveness at work

Nail art

Essential anatomy and physiology knowledge requirements for this unit, BT13, are identified on the checklist chart in Chapter 5, page 101.

TIP

Being creative
There are increasing opportunities for you to compete with other skilled operatives in nail art competitions. These usually occur at beauty exhibitions.

Nail trade magazines are extremely useful to keep you updated on the latest colours, nail products and designs, as many nail artists display their creations.

INTRODUCTION TO NAIL ART

Nail art is an exciting and elaborate form of nail decoration, which may be applied to the hands or feet.

As the nail industry grows, nail art is becoming increasing popular, especially for special occasions, and designs are limited only by the manicurist's imagination. The artwork can be as simple as a single stripe across a painted nail, or as intricate as a detailed desert island scene.

PLAN AND PREPARE FOR NAIL ART SERVICES

Outcome 1: Consult with the client

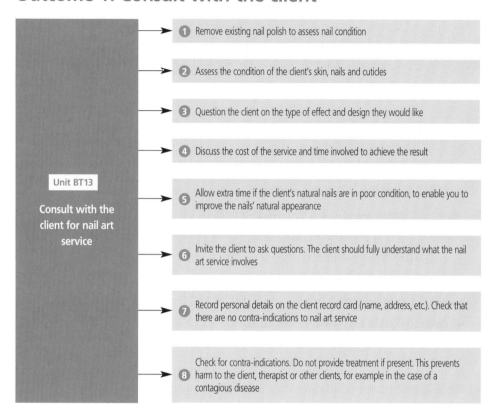

Unit BT13

Consult with the client for nail art service

1 Remove existing nail polish to assess nail condition

2 Assess the condition of the client's skin, nails and cuticles

3 Question the client on the type of effect and design they would like

4 Discuss the cost of the service and time involved to achieve the result

5 Allow extra time if the client's natural nails are in poor condition, to enable you to improve the nails' natural appearance

6 Invite the client to ask questions. The client should fully understand what the nail art service involves

7 Record personal details on the client record card (name, address, etc.). Check that there are no contra-indications to nail art service

8 Check for contra-indications. Do not provide treatment if present. This prevents harm to the client, therapist or other clients, for example in the case of a contagious disease

Reception

When a client makes an appointment for nail art, question the client on the type of effect and design they would like. Discuss the cost of the service; prices will vary depending on the materials used, or the time involved to create the design. If the client's natural nails are in poor condition it will be necessary to allow extra time to perform a simple nail treatment, to improve the nails' natural appearance, and facilitate application. Allow extra time accordingly when booking the treatment.

The client must be aware that it takes 20–30 minutes for the polish to harden. It is also a good idea if the client pays *before* the service to prevent spoiling their painted nails.

Allow 5–10 minutes for each nail.

Nail Art

Christmas designs

TIP ✓

Nail art designs
Nail art designs can be prepared ahead of time and displayed to show your clients.

Client consultation

Before carrying out the nail art service, it is necessary to assess the condition of the client's nails and cuticles. This is done to see if it is necessary to carry out a simple nail treatment, including file and cuticle work, beforehand.

BEAUTY WORKS

Date		Therapist name	
Client name		Date of birth	
Address		Postcode	
Evening phone number		Day phone number	
Name of doctor		Doctor's address and phone number	
Related medical history (conditions that may restrict or prohibit treatment application)			
Are you taking any medication? (this may affect skin sensitivity and reaction to the treatment or client suitability)			

CONTRA-INDICATIONS REQUIRING MEDICAL REFERRAL
(Preventing nail art service application)

- ☐ bacterial infections (e.g. paronychia)
- ☐ viral infections (e.g. plane or plantar warts)
- ☐ fungal infections (e.g. tinea ungium)
- ☐ severe nail separation
- ☐ severe eczema and psoriasis
- ☐ severe bruising

EQUIPMENT AND MATERIALS
- ☐ nail and skin treatment tools
- ☐ nail and skin products
- ☐ consumables

PRODUCTS
- ☐ nail conditioners e.g. cuticle cream
- ☐ skin conditioners e.g. hand cream
- ☐ nail, skin and cuticle corrective treatments e.g. paraffin wax
- ☐ nail polish

NAIL ART MATERIALS
- ☐ polishes
- ☐ flatstones
- ☐ paints
- ☐ glitters
- ☐ self-adhesive transfers
- ☐ topcoats
- ☐ foiling
- ☐ rhinestones
- ☐ polish secures
- ☐ basecoats
- ☐ blending
- ☐ water release transfers
- ☐ marbling
- ☐ striping

CONTRA-INDICATIONS WHICH RESTRICT TREATMENT
(Treatment may require adaptation)

- ☐ minor nail separation
- ☐ minor eczema and psoriasis
- ☐ severely bitten nails
- ☐ severely damaged nails
- ☐ broken bones
- ☐ minor cuts or abrasions
- ☐ minor bruising or swelling

Therapist signature (for reference)

Client signature (confirmation of details)

TREATMENT ADVICE

 Nail art – *allow 5–10 minutes per nail*

TREATMENT PLAN

Record relevant details of your treatment and advice provided for future reference.

Ensure the client's records are up to date, accurate and fully completed following treatment. Non-compliance may invalidate insurance.

DURING

Discuss:

- details that may influence the client's nail condition, such as occupation or lifestyle;
- the products the client is currently using to care for the skin of the hands and nails, and regularity of their use;
- the client's satisfaction with these products;
- relevant manicure procedures (e.g., how to file the nails correctly).

Note:

- any adverse reaction, if any occur.

AFTER

Record:

- results of treatment;
- any modification to treatment application that has occurred;
- what products have been used in the nail art treatment;
- the effectiveness of treatment;
- any samples provided (review their success at the next appointment).

Advise on:

- product application in order to gain maximum benefit from product use;
- specialised products following nail art treatment for homecare use (e.g., top coat polish application to maintain the nail art result);
- general hand/nail care and maintenance advice;
- the recommended time intervals between nail art treatments.

RETAIL OPPORTUNITIES

Advise on:

- products that would be suitable for the client to use at home to care for the skin of the hands and nails;
- recommendations for further treatments;
- further products or services that the client may or may not have received before.

Note:

- any purchases made by the client.

EVALUATION

Record:

- comments on the client's satisfaction with the treatment;
- if poor results are achieved, the reasons why;
- how you may alter the treatment plan to achieve the required treatment results in the future, if applicable.

HEALTH AND SAFETY

Advise on:

- appropriate action to be taken in the event of an unwanted skin or nail reaction.

> **TIP** ✓
>
> **Examples of nail art treatment modification include:**
> - choice of nail art products to complement the client's nail condition and appearance;
> - choice of nail art service to accommodate the client's occupation/lifestyle factors;
> - nail tips/overlay nail products are applied because the client's natural nails are too short or in poor condition to show the nail art to its best effect.

Whilst assessing the client's hands/feet you should also be looking for any *contra-indications* to treatment.

Discuss the nail art requirements. Question the client on what type of result they wish to achieve – are the nails to match a special outfit? If so, what colour would be most suitable, or is it for a special occasion where the nail art could match the theme!

It is a good idea to prepare a number of nail art designs to show the client. These may be applied to artificial nails, or they may be images of nail art designs that you have created and photographed.

If the client's expectations are unsuitable because of the client's natural nail shape or size, offer a suitable alternative. For example, if the client's nails were too short you could apply plastic nail tips, secured to the natural nail with nail adhesive, blend flush to the natural nail and paint these.

Allow 45 minutes extra in your treatment timing to add nail tips.

Decide upon the nail shape and length. It is important that the nail shape and length selected suits the client's hands and fingers. Nail shapes include:

> **TIP** ✓
>
> **Colour choice**
> Choice of nail polish should suit the client's skin colouring and tone. Hold the bottle against the skin for compatibility.

| Oval | Square | Pointed | Squoval | Round | Fan |

> **TIP** ✓
>
> **Squoval nail shape**
> Squoval is a term used in the nail industry to describe a square nail shape which is slightly rounded at the free edge!

Nail polishes

Record all details on the client treatment record card. This will be useful if the client returns for this service, also it is important in the event of a contra-action such as an allergic reaction. It will inform you of those products that were used which may have caused the contra-action.

Contra-indications

The consultation will draw any contra-indications to your attention. If the client has any of the following conditions, nail art service must not be carried out. Chapter 1 provides further guidance on contra-indications – see pages 25–30.

Name	Description
Tinea unguium Wellcome Photo Library	Ringworm infection of the fingernails. The nail plate is yellowish-grey. Eventually the nail plate becomes brittle and separates from the nail bed.
Tinea pedis (athletes' foot) Dr A.L. Wright	A common fungal foot condition. Small blisters form, which later burst. The skin in the area can then become dry, giving a scaly appearance.
Paronychia Wellcome Photo Library	Bacterial infection of the tissue surrounding the nail. The area appears red and swollen, with pus present in the cuticle area of the nail wall.
Cuts or abrasions on the hands or feet Wellcome Photo Library	Any cut or abrasion in the area could lead to secondary infection and the area should not be treated until it has healed.
Infectious disease	Infectious conditions include bacterial, viral and fungal disease and infestations. These are highly contagious.
Verrucae or warts on the hands or feet Plane wart – found on the fingers or surface of the hand Dr M.H. Beck	A viral infection. Small epidermal skin growths. Warts may be raised or flat, depending upon their position. Warts vary in size, shape, texture and colour. Usually they have a rough surface and are raised. If the wart occurs on the sole of the foot it grows inwards, due to the pressure of body weight.

Name	Description
Plantar wart – found on the sole of the foot 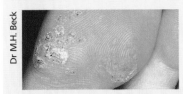	
Severe nail separation (onycholysis) 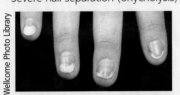	Lifting of the nail plate from the nail bed, may be caused by trauma or infection to the nail or surrounding area. Where separation has occurred this appears as a greyish-white are on the nail as the pink undertone of the nail bed does not show.
Severe psoriasis of the nail 	An inflammatory skin condition where there is an increased production of cells in the upper part of the skin. Pitting occurs over the surface of the nail plate. Separation (onycholysis) may also occur.
Severe eczema of the nail 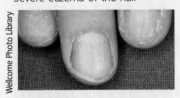	Inflammation of the skin occurs. Differing changes to the nail may occur including the appearance of ridges, pitting, onycholysis and nail thickening (hypertrophy).
Broken bones 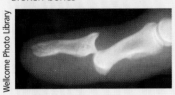	Injury resulting in a broken bone can often not be seen. Confirm at consultation that there is no injury in the treatment area.
Severely bitten nails (onychopagy) 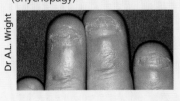	Very little nail plate; bulbous skin at the fingertip; nails walls often red and swollen due to biting skin around the nails.

Dr M.H. Beck

Wellcome Photo Library

Wellcome Photo Library

Wellcome Photo Library

Wellcome Photo Library

Dr A.L. Wright

HEALTH AND SAFETY

Dealing with a contra-indication

Remember never advise a client as to what the contra-indication may be: you are not qualified to do so. Always refer the client to their GP if you are at all unsure. Never treat the client.

Outcome 2: Prepare for the service

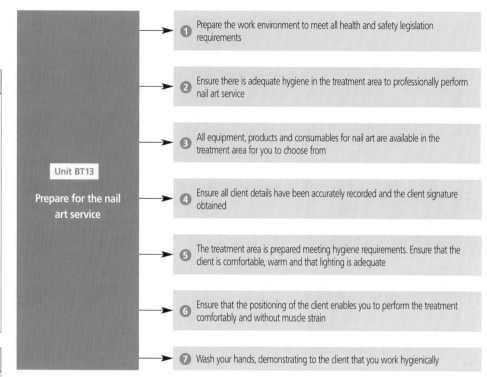

Unit BT13

Prepare for the nail art service

1 Prepare the work environment to meet all health and safety legislation requirements

2 Ensure there is adequate hygiene in the treatment area to professionally perform nail art service

3 All equipment, products and consumables for nail art are available in the treatment area for you to choose from

4 Ensure all client details have been accurately recorded and the client signature obtained

5 The treatment area is prepared meeting hygiene requirements. Ensure that the client is comfortable, warm and that lighting is adequate

6 Ensure that the positioning of the client enables you to perform the treatment comfortably and without muscle strain

7 Wash your hands, demonstrating to the client that you work hygienically

Equipment and materials

Below is a list of equipment and materials that you may require when offering nail art service.

EQUIPMENT LIST

 Manicure trolley or other surface on which to place everything

 Dry cottonwool

 Tissues

 Emery board

 Orange sticks these may be used to apply nail art materials or polish remover to remove excess nail polish

 Base coat

 Top coat or specialised nail art sealer, which is thicker in consistency

 Coloured nail polish a selection for the client to choose from

 Nail scissors to trim the nails and cut nail art materials

 Nail polish remover

 Nail art materials – see list below

 Tweezers to place and fix decorations to the nail surface

YOU WILL ALSO NEED:

Medium-sized clean towels freshly laundered for each client

Paper tissue disposable bedroll for hygiene and to protect the work area from accidental spillage

Skin-cleansing agent such as witchhazel or eau de cologne

Dotting/marbling tool this has a small round metal head used to apply dots of colour to the nail, called 'dotting' and to mix colours, called 'marbling'

A selection of prepared nail designs to show the client. These are applied to artificial nails

Nail polish solvent to restore the fluid consistency of nail polish

Nail art materials:

- paints – specialist water-based acrylic paints;
- glitters;
- glitter dust and mixer, to add shimmer to a design;
- transfers – these may be either water release or self adhesive;
- foil strips, strips of metallic foil in various colours and designs, secured with foil adhesive;
- striping tape;
- polish secures – jewellery and tiny gems;
- gem stones such as rhine stones and flat stones;
- jewellery – this includes sterling silver or 9ct gold nail studs, charms and initials;
- any other item you choose!

Nail polish drier to increase the speed of the polish hardening process

Bowls or lined pedal bin for waste materials

Client record card – confidential record of details of all clients registered at the salon

---

TIP ✔

Starting off
Initially, purchase basic colours of nail paint that can be mixed to create other colours. These include black, red, white, blue, green and yellow.

TIP ✔

Nail charms
Reusable nail charms are available, and applied to the nail with adhesive.

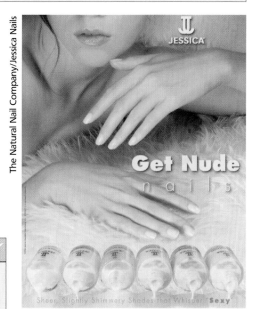

The Natural Nail Company/Jessica Nails

JESSICA

Get Nude n a i l s

Sheer, Slightly Shimmery Shades that Whisper **Sexy**

Selection of nail polish products to achieve a French polish application

TIP ✔

Nail studs
Nail piercing is used to attach nail jewellery to the free edge. A small hole is made using nail tools, a drill and wrench. Posted nail jewellery such as a nail stud or ring may then be fixed, similarly to an earring.

Nail studs must only be applied to artificial nail structures not the natural nail plate to avoid damage.

Air brushing

Air brushing is a further popular method of applying nail art. This uses a mechanical tool that applies the paint, mixed with air, onto the nail's surface through a nozzle. This speeds application time, and is also very hygienic as there is no physical contact with the client.

Jefford and Swain

Nail art pens

Pens that provide a nail striping brush or dotter in their own bottle of paint polish are available. These are known as *flexi brushes* and are available in a choice of nail polish colours and effects such as glitter.

Millennium Nails

Maintaining your nail art brushes

Clean your brushes thoroughly after use.

Nylon brushes may be cleaned safely in acetone or washed in detergents as applicable. Brushes should be cleaned to remove nail art material used.

Where adhesive has been used, it is necessary to use solvent such as nail polish remover to clean them effectively.

Brushes made of animal hair are delicate so harsh detergents and acetone should be avoided. Clean in water temperature 45–55°C.

Always reshape the brushes before drying at room temperature.

Dry upright to retain the brush shape.

Only use brushes for their intended use.

Replace brushes when quality deteriorates as poor quality brushes will affect the end result!

Stencils

Simple nail art designs can be created using stencils. Paint the nail with the chosen colour, and then when dry, place a stencil over the nail and apply further polish or nail paint to create the design. Remove the stencil when the paint/polish is dry to reveal the image. Apply a top coat to seal the design.

Nail art brushes

Brush	Description
Fine brush	Fine, pointed brush
	Used where detail is required
Liner brush	Medium-length liner brush
	For creating thick, straight lines
Fan brush	Fan-shaped brush
	To sweep nail art products across the nail and create a fan effect; also used to blend colours
Shading brush	Flat, square-headed brush
	To create shades and filling

Brush	Description
Glitter dust brush	Short, fine-pointed brush To add glitter, creating a sparkle effect on the nails
Striping brush	Long length, thin brush To create thin and narrow and long, straight lines

Jefford and Swain

Millennium Nails

Sterilisation and disinfection

Hygiene must be maintained in a number of ways to prevent secondary and cross-infection:

- ensure that tools and equipment are clean and, where applicable, sterile before use;
- disinfect work surfaces after each client;
- always follow hygienic working practices;
- clear discarded waste after each client;
- maintain a high standard of personal hygiene.

Preparing the treatment area

Ensure that the area is well ventilated to avoid inhalation of excessive fumes. Ensure that all products are stable to avoid products being knocked over and spilt.

The area must be free of any other previous materials, such as dust created from the application of artificial nails. Dust could spoil the effect of a client's newly painted nails.

Lighting should be good, to enable you to avoid eyestrain, especially when performing intricate artwork. It is a good idea to use a table lamp.

Preparation of the therapist

Sitting properly is important. Ideally sit on a properly designed manicure stool or chair which offers adequate back support.

When performing the treatment it is important to sit upright with both feet flat on the floor.

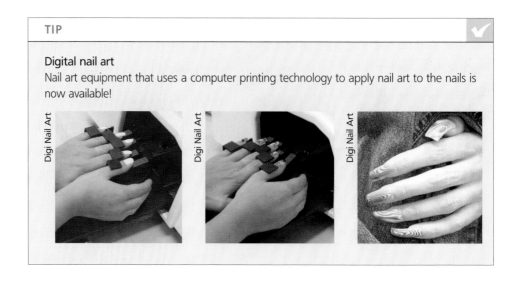

TIP	✔

Digital nail art

Nail art equipment that uses a computer printing technology to apply nail art to the nails is now available!

Digi Nail Art

Digi Nail Art

Digi Nail Art

Outcome 3: Plan the service

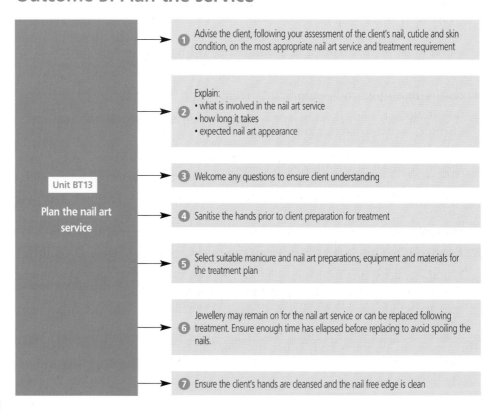

Unit BT13

Plan the nail art service

1 Advise the client, following your assessment of the client's nail, cuticle and skin condition, on the most appropriate nail art service and treatment requirement

2 Explain:
• what is involved in the nail art service
• how long it takes
• expected nail art appearance

3 Welcome any questions to ensure client understanding

4 Sanitise the hands prior to client preparation for treatment

5 Select suitable manicure and nail art preparations, equipment and materials for the treatment plan

6 Jewellery may remain on for the nail art service or can be replaced following treatment. Ensure enough time has ellapsed before replacing to avoid spoiling the nails.

7 Ensure the client's hands are cleansed and the nail free edge is clean

Preparing the client

1 Confirm the client's choice of nail art.
2 File the nails to achieve the desired shape and length. Ensure the free edge is clean.
3 The cuticles should be neat and smooth. Use the cuticle nippers to trim any uneven, excess cuticle.
4 Ensure the surface of the nail plate is clean and grease-free. Wipe with a non-acetone polish remover to prepare the nail. Use a lint-free pad as

Nail Art

Lint-free pads

> **TIP**
>
> **Corrective base coats**
> If a corrective base coat is used, such as a nail ridge filler, these have a longer drying time because they are thicker.

cottonwool may leave fibres, which may spoil the application of nail polish.

5 Apply the required nail art base. Usually this is a good quality base coat.

GENERAL TECHNIQUE

Tips for nail painting

- Ensure the surface of the nail is grease-free. If grease is present this will result in nail polish peeling or chipping. Also nail art materials such as foil will not attach securely.
- Select colours that suit the client's nail length and skin colour.
- Dark colours will draw attention to the nails, and will make small/short nails appear smaller/shorter.
- If the nails are very broad leave a margin at the sides of the nail wall free of polish, this will help them to appear slimmer.
- Avoid pearlised polish if the client's nail surface is uneven or ridged. The polish will emphasise the imperfection.
- Always apply a good quality base coat suited to the client's nail condition. This helps to prevent staining from pigment in the polish, and may strengthen the nail or smooth ridges depending on its formulation.
- Apply the base nail polish in strokes, usually three as shown opposite.
- When applying nail polish colour, apply two coats, allowing the nails to dry between each coat to prevent the appearance of brush marks.
- Ensure good colour coverage.
- Allow nail polish to dry before top coat application.
- Apply top coat to seal the polish and to protect and provide durability to the nail art design.

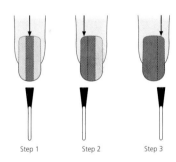

Step 1   Step 2   Step 3

Nail polish application

> **TIP**
>
> **Nail polish application**
> Keep nail polish clear of the cuticle area and surrounding skin to ensure a clean, professional finish and avoid skin irritation.
>   Always clean the neck of the bottle after use to prevent the polish becoming thick, as solvent used to keep the polish fluid evaporates. It is important that the nail polish is not too thick. This will result in brush marks, the nail polish will not dry evenly and is easily smudged.
>   Add solvent according to the manufacturer's instructions to return the polish to the correct consistency.

FREEHAND NAIL ART TECHNIQUES

Outcome 4: Provide nail art service to clients

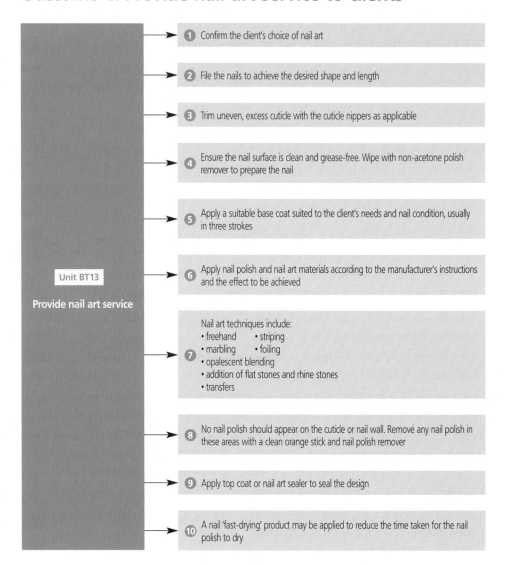

Unit BT13

Provide nail art service

1. Confirm the client's choice of nail art

2. File the nails to achieve the desired shape and length

3. Trim uneven, excess cuticle with the cuticle nippers as applicable

4. Ensure the nail surface is clean and grease-free. Wipe with non-acetone polish remover to prepare the nail

5. Apply a suitable base coat suited to the client's needs and nail condition, usually in three strokes

6. Apply nail polish and nail art materials according to the manufacturer's instructions and the effect to be achieved

7. Nail art techniques include:
   - freehand   • striping
   - marbling   • foiling
   - opalescent blending
   - addition of flat stones and rhine stones
   - transfers

8. No nail polish should appear on the cuticle or nail wall. Remove any nail polish in these areas with a clean orange stick and nail polish remover

9. Apply top coat or nail art sealer to seal the design

10. A nail 'fast-drying' product may be applied to reduce the time taken for the nail polish to dry

Using your imagination, you can apply different designs and illustrations freehand to the nail using the variety of nail art materials available. For freehand techniques you will need to be able to handle your nail art tools and materials confidently. It is important that you support and hold the client's hand, which is at a height and position to ensure that your hand is steady. Posture is also important to avoid muscle strain and future postural problems. The angle of your brush, and pressure of application will influence the result achieved.

Examples of freehand techniques follow.

Step by step: French manicure

This is simple nail art, enhancing the natural appearance of the nails. It is particularly suitable to disguise stained nails. If the free edge is too short then this technique cannot be applied. This is a simple freehand technique.

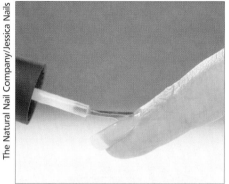

1 Apply base coat.

2 Paint the free edge white, ensuring that the line is even. If the nails are particularly stained you may wish to paint the reverse of the free edge also.

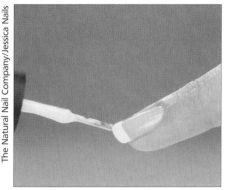

3 Apply a neutral nail polish, suited to your client's nail and skin, in soft beige, pink or clear to evenly cover the nail surface.

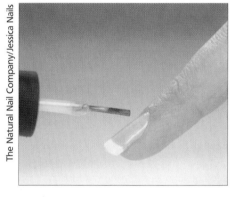

4 Apply a further coat of neutral polish to soften the white, or simply apply top coat.

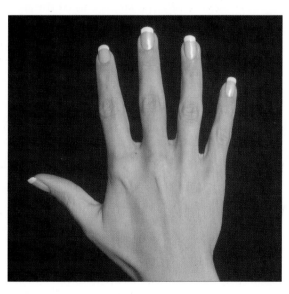

5 The finished look.

How to create a Japanese symbol

This is an example of freehand technique which has been created using a fine detail brush.

1 Apply base coat and two coats of nail polish to each nail, allow to dry.

2 Select a bold contrasting paint, ensure that there is not excessive paint on the brush or 'blobbing' will occur.

3 Apply the symbol of your choice in stages, using light pressure to achieve a fine line and heavier pressure to achieve a thicker line.

4 When dry apply a top coat or nail art sealer to seal the design.

Japanese symbol design

Marbling design

Dotting design

How to create a marbling effect

Coloured paints are applied using a marbling tool, creating a marbled effect.

Select two or three nail paint colours and a nail polish that complement each other.

1 Apply base coat and two coats of coloured nail polish to each nail.

2 Next, using the large end of the marbling tool, place small drops of nail paint onto the polished nail.

3 Clean the marbling tool, and then use it to mix the colours together, creating swirls of colour to achieve a 'marbled' effect.

4 Add more colour using the marbling tool as necessary, until the desired effect and colour is achieved.

5 When dry, apply top coat or nail art sealer.

Dotting

The marbling tool may also be used to apply small dots of paint, called 'dotting', creating designs such as a dog's paw or flowers etc.

1 Apply base coat and two coats of nail polish to each nail.

2 Next, using the small end of the marbling tool place small dots to create different designs.

3 When dry, apply top coat or nail art sealer.

TIP
Dotting application To keep dots to a uniform size, place marbling/dotting tool in the nail art product for each application. 　To create varying sizes, use the remaining product to continue to apply the product on the tool, which will create smaller and smaller dots.

Jefford and Swain

How to create an opalescent blending effect

Opalescent paints are applied over the base nail polish colour, creating an iridescent effect on the nails.

1 Apply base coat and two coats of the selected coloured nail polish to the nails. This technique is particularly effective when a dark colour is chosen.

2 Apply the opalescent paint in dots down either side of the nail using a marbling tool.

3 Using a fan brush, sweep the colours from side to side. This blends the colours and achieves the iridescent effect.

4 Apply top coat or nail art sealer when the paint and polish has hardened.

Opalescent blending

How to create a striping design with dotting

Different brush sizes make stripes of colour in varying widths.

1 Apply base coat and two coats of the selected nail polish colour to the nails.

2 Using a striping brush, apply stripes of paint to the nails, in one or several colours, using the sides of the brush not the point.

3 Work across the nails from one side to the other, making some stripes thicker than others. Polish secures or rhinestones can be added to enhance the effect.

4 Apply top coat or nail art sealer when the paint and polish has hardened.

Jefford and Swain

Striping design with dotting

How to use striping tape

Self-adhesive striping tape is applied to create or enhance a design on the nail.

1 Apply base coat and two coats of the selected nail polish colour to the nails.

2 When dry, apply the striping tape across the nail. Apply gentle pressure and secure the tape to the nail. Trim off any excess tape using nail scissors.

3 A rhine stone may be applied to enhance the effect.

4 Cover the nail with top coat or nail art sealer to seal the design.

Nail Art

Striping tape

How to use flat stones and rhine stones

These are tiny stones and gems available in differing colours, size and shapes which are secured to the nail polish whilst it is still wet.

1 Apply base coat and two coats of the selected nail polish colour to the nails.

2 Select a flat stone or rhine stone. Use the end of an orange stick that has been dampened with water to pick it up. Secure the flat stone to the polish. As the polish dries the stone will set in place.

3 Apply top coat or nail art sealer to seal the design. Flat stones and rhine stones may be used to create a design such as a straight line, or alternatively they can be used to enhance a design.

French manicure with rhine stone

How to create a striping design with rhine stones

1 Apply base coat and two coats of the chosen nail polish. Allow to dry.

2 Apply a small dot of top coat and attach rhine stones to the nail, to create the design required.

3 Using a striping brush, apply lines of paint, feathering out from the corner of the bottom of the nail to enhance the effect.

4 Apply top coat or nail art sealer to seal the design.

Jefford and Swain

Striping and rhine stone design

TIP ✔

Stained glass effect
Apply the glitter, allowing the base polish colour to show through, creating a stained glass effect.

How to use glitter dust (and mixer)

This is a fine sparkly powder available in different colours, applied with a brush.

1 Apply base coat and two coats of the selected nail polish colour to the nails.

2 Dip a glitter brush in to the glitter mixer, forming a ball.

3 Dip the end of the brush into the glitter.

4 Apply the tip of the brush to the nail surface and position the glitter. This is achieved by gently moving the glitter over the nail surface using the brush. Apply gentle pressure with the brush to position and flatten the glitter.

5 Further colours may be applied. Clean the brush using nail polish remover before each application.

6 Apply top coat or nail art sealer when the paint and polish has hardened to seal the design.

TIP ✔

Glitter polish
When glitter is suspended in translucent polish, this may be used as a top coat, applied over a coloured polish, creating a simple, eye catching effect.

How to use transfers

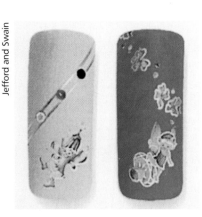

Transfers

These are images that can be secured to the nail, creating an instant design. They are available in two forms: *water release* and *self adhesive*.

- **Water release transfers**, also known as decals, are dampened using water applied with a damp cottonwool bud on the reverse of the transfer. When dampened sufficiently (approximately 30 seconds), the transfer may be removed from its backing, using your thumb to position it on the nail.

- **Self-adhesive transfers** have a backing that is removed, to provide a sticky surface that adheres to the nail.

1 Apply base coat and two coats of the selected nail polish colour to the nails.

2 Prepare the transfer, according to which form is chosen.

3 Position in place on the nail, ensuring it is flat, and apply gentle pressure.

4 Apply top coat or nail art sealer to seal the design.

How to use foil

Foiling

1 Apply two coats of the selected nail polish colour to the nails and allow to dry.

2 Apply foil adhesive: this is placed where you wish to apply the foil. The adhesive is white on application and becomes clear as it dries.

3 Once clear apply the foil securely to the adhesive with the pattern facing upwards to the nail.

4 Rub the foil carefully with a cottonbud and lift the foil off the nail leaving the required design on the nail.

5 Apply top coat or nail art sealer to seal the design.

COMPLETING THE NAIL ART SERVICE

Outcome 5: Complete the service

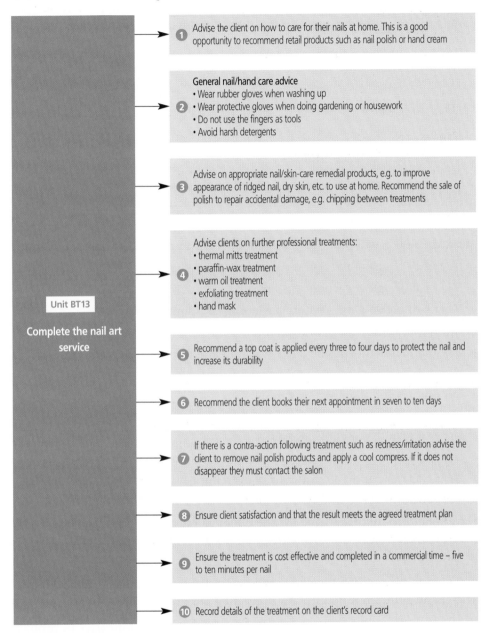

Unit BT13

Complete the nail art service

1. Advise the client on how to care for their nails at home. This is a good opportunity to recommend retail products such as nail polish or hand cream

2. General nail/hand care advice
   • Wear rubber gloves when washing up
   • Wear protective gloves when doing gardening or housework
   • Do not use the fingers as tools
   • Avoid harsh detergents

3. Advise on appropriate nail/skin-care remedial products, e.g. to improve appearance of ridged nail, dry skin, etc. to use at home. Recommend the sale of polish to repair accidental damage, e.g. chipping between treatments

4. Advise clients on further professional treatments:
   • thermal mitts treatment
   • paraffin-wax treatment
   • warm oil treatment
   • exfoliating treatment
   • hand mask

5. Recommend a top coat is applied every three to four days to protect the nail and increase its durability

6. Recommend the client books their next appointment in seven to ten days

7. If there is a contra-action following treatment such as redness/irritation advise the client to remove nail polish products and apply a cool compress. If it does not disappear they must contact the salon

8. Ensure client satisfaction and that the result meets the agreed treatment plan

9. Ensure the treatment is cost effective and completed in a commercial time – five to ten minutes per nail

10. Record details of the treatment on the client's record card

Confirm with the client that the finished result is to their satisfaction.

Complete details of the nail art service on the client's record card.

Clear instructions should be provided on how to care for their nails and also what action to take in the event of a contra-action.

Contra-actions to nail art

A contra-action is an unwanted reaction to the service. An unwanted reaction to nail art service might include an *allergic reaction*. This occurs

HEALTH AND SAFETY

Avoiding a contra-action
Always check at the consultation for any known allergies to substances or ingredients. *Formaldehyde* is used in some base coats to strengthen the nail plate and it can cause an allergic reaction in some people. Always follow the manufacturer's instructions to ensure that products are used correctly and safely.

HEALTH AND SAFETY ✚

Nail tips

If the client has had artificial nail tips applied which have been painted, they may be advised to return to the salon to have them removed, or to soak the nails in acetone-based polish remover, which softens the artificial nail – *never* pull these off as this will result in damage to the natural nail.

Retail products

when a person becomes sensitised to a product ingredient. It is possible to become allergic to a product after having been in contact with it for years. The reaction would be recognised if the skin becomes red, itchy and inflamed.

If an allergic reaction occurs, remove all nail products and apply a cool compress and soothing agent to the skin to reduce skin redness and irritation.

Aftercare and advice

It is important when carrying out a nail service that the client knows how to care for their nails at home.

When giving aftercare advice it is a good opportunity to recommend retail products, such as nail polish or handcream, thereby enhancing retail sales and the salon's profits.

Aftercare advice will differ for each client according to individual needs, but generally it will be as follows:

- Wear rubber gloves when washing up.
- Wear protective gloves when gardening or doing housework.
- Always wear gloves in cold weather.
- Dry the hands thoroughly after washing and apply handcream.
- Avoid harsh soaps when washing the hands.
- Do not use the fingernails as tools.
- Advise on appropriate nail/skin-care products to remedy the problems present, e.g. dry skin, weak nails.
- Advise the client on other professional treatments that are suitable.
- Advise the client on a treatment plan to improve the nail/skin condition and on the time interval recommended between each treatment.

Have retail products available for the client to purchase. These include coloured nail polish, emery boards, nail polish remover and nail/skin treatment products.

It is a good idea to have available the nail polish colours that you have used. The client can then touch up any accidental chip themself.

Recommend the use of a top coat applied every three to four days to protect the nail polish, increase its durability and impart shine.

Nail art will last approximately ten days, so recommend the client books their next appointment after this.

Advise the client as to what to do in the event of a contra-action (see above).

GLOSSARY OF KEY WORDS

Acrylic paints specialist water-based acrylic paints, which can be diluted and mixed together to create new colours.

Aftercare advice recommendations given to the client following treatment to continue the benefits of the treatment.

Base coat clear polish applied to the nail, formulated to provide a base for the nail art. It helps to prevent nail staining from the nail art and provides durability to the design.

Coloured polishes these are used to provide a base colour on the nail or to add colour to the nail art design.

Consultation assessment of client's needs using different assessment techniques, including questioning and natural observation.

Contra-action an unwanted reaction occurring during or after treatment application.

Contra-indication a problematic symptom that indicates that the treatment may not proceed.

Dotting technique application of dots of nail paint/polish using a marbling/dotting tool to create or enhance a design.

Flat stones small polish-secured gems.

Flat stone/rhine stone technique polish-secured gems are applied to create or enhance a .nail art design.

Foiling metallic foil, available in various colours and designs, is secured to the nail using foil adhesive.

Freehand technique handling and applying nail art materials to create different designs and illustrations on the nail plate.

Glitter sparkly powder applied to add shimmer to a design.

Glitter dust technique fine, sparkly powder is applied with a glitter mixer and positioned on the nail.

Marbling technique dots of different nail paint/polish colours are mixed together using a marbling tool to create a marbled effect.

Nail art nail decoration applied to the nails of the hands or feet.

Opalescent blending technique opalescent paints applied over a base nail polish colour creating an iridescent effect on the nails.

Polish secures jewellery and tiny gems that are placed in the wet nail polish and become 'secured' when the polish dries.

Rhine stones polish-secured gems.

Striping tape coloured self-adhesive tape applied to create a striping effect.

Striping technique stripes of colour are applied in varying widths using a striping brush.

Top coat clear polish, applied to seal the nail polish and to protect and provide durability to the nail art design.

Transfers water-release (decals) and self-adhesive transfers secured to the nail, creating an instant design.

Treatment plan after the consultation, suitable treatment objectives are established to treat the client's conditions and needs.

Assessment of knowledge and understanding

You have now learnt about the different nail art techniques available to enhance the nails. These skills will enable you to professionally provide nail art service.

To test your level of knowledge, answer the following short questions. These will prepare you for your summative (final) assessment.

 Anatomy and physiology questions required for this unit are found on pages 146–8, 151–3.

Consult with the client

1 Why is it important to discuss and agree the nail art service and outcomes with your client at consultation?

2 What is the benefit of having pre-prepared designs available for the client to view?

3 When deciding on the colour of polish, what should you consider?

4 If nail art service is unrealistic because the client has badly bitten nails, what alternative could you offer them?

Prepare for the service

1 Why is good lighting important?

2 How can you ensure that you have a professional appearance that complies with organisational standards?

3 What different brushes are required for nail art? When are each used?

4 What is the purpose of a marbling tool?

5 How is cross-infection prevented when applying nail art?

6 Name three contra-indications observed at consultation that would prevent treatment being carried out. (Remember these may be on the hands or the feet.)

Plan for the service

1 Describe how you and the client should be positioned when performing nail art. Why is this important?

2 How would you decide upon the recommended nail art for a client?

3 How does the condition of the client's nails influence timing and the choice of nail art?

4 Why is it important to complete the nail art service in the allocated time?

5 What is the commercially acceptable time for nail art?

6 How should the nails be prepared for nail art?

Provide nail art service

1 Name three different nail shapes.

2 Name four nail art techniques.

3 What is the purpose of a nail art base?

4 Why should the cuticle and surrounding skin be kept free of nail polish?

5 How can the quality of nail polish be maintained?

6 Why is it important to confirm that the client is satisfied with the finished result?

7 Why is it important to record all details of the service on the client record card?

Complete the service

1 What aftercare advice should be given to a client following nail art service?

2 What could occur if clients did not receive this specific advice?

3 What is a contra-action? What could be a contra-action to a nail art service?

4 How often should the clients receive this service if they wish to maintain the effect?

5 What retail products could be recommended to a client to care for the appearance of their nails and maintain the result?

chapter 14

BT14 Pierce ears

Learning objectives

This unit describes how to provide the service skin piercing of the earlobe. It describes the competencies to enable you to:

- **consult with the client**
- **prepare for earlobe piercing**
- **carry out earlobe piercing**
- **complete the treatment**

When providing ear piercing treatment it is important to use the skills you have learnt in the following core mandatory units:

UNIT G1 Ensure your own actions reduce risks to health and safety

UNIT G6 Promote additional products or services to clients

UNIT G8 Develop and maintain your effectiveness at work

> **TIP** ✔
>
> **Cosmetic piercing**
> Skin piercing of the earlobe and cosmetic body piercing are classified in the single term *cosmetic piercing*.

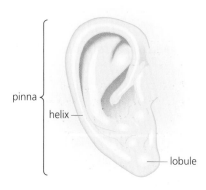

The earlobe

THE EARS

Ear piercing is the perforation of the skin and underlying tissue of the ear to create a hole in the skin where jewellery is inserted. It is a quick, profitable and popular salon service, which also has the potential to generate further custom. This may be the client's first visit to a beauty salon, and the service they receive may encourage them to return for further treatments.

The structure and function of the earlobe

The external ear collects sound waves and directs these to the inner ear. The part of the ear that is commonly seen pierced is called the **pinna**, which comprises the **helix** and **lobule**. The helix is composed of cartilage, which does not heal quickly and can form lumpy scar tissue; it is therefore considered unsuitable for piercing. The lobule, in contrast, consists of fibrous and fatty tissue with no cartilage, and is therefore suitable for piercing.

PREPARE FOR EARLOBE PIERCING

Outcome 1: Consult with the client

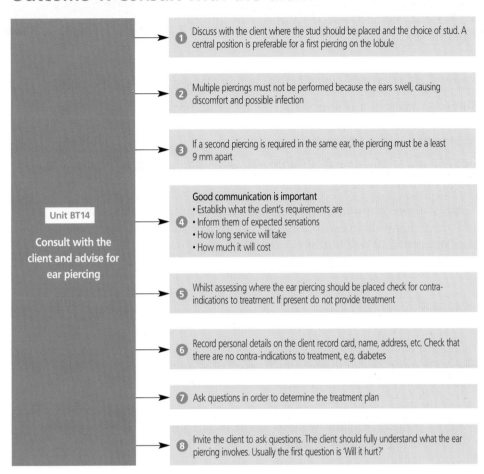

Unit BT14

Consult with the client and advise for ear piercing

1 Discuss with the client where the stud should be placed and the choice of stud. A central position is preferable for a first piercing on the lobule

2 Multiple piercings must not be performed because the ears swell, causing discomfort and possible infection

3 If a second piercing is required in the same ear, the piercing must be a least 9 mm apart

4 Good communication is important
• Establish what the client's requirements are
• Inform them of expected sensations
• How long service will take
• How much it will cost

5 Whilst assessing where the ear piercing should be placed check for contra-indications to treatment. If present do not provide treatment

6 Record personal details on the client record card, name, address, etc. Check that there are no contra-indications to treatment, e.g. diabetes

7 Ask questions in order to determine the treatment plan

8 Invite the client to ask questions. The client should fully understand what the ear piercing involves. Usually the first question is 'Will it hurt?'

Reception

When making an appointment for this service, allow 15 minutes. Although ear piercing is completed quickly, time must be allowed to complete the client's record card, determine the client's treatment plan and give clear concise aftercare instructions. Good communication is important. Speak clearly, establish what the client's requirements are and listen to ensure communication is effective and that a professional relationship is developed with the client, gaining client confidence.

A record card should be prepared for the client, recording just the information that is relevant to the ear-piercing treatment. Record keeping protects both the therapist and client. Whilst completing the record card you will be able to ascertain whether the client is suited to this treatment – if the client is under 16 years of age, for example, it is necessary for a parent or guardian to accompany them and sign a **consent form** containing a disclaimer in the event of contra-indications.

Contra-indications to ear piercing should be checked for. If the area for piercing is unsuitable, politely explain to the client why this is so. All details

TIP

The earring industry is worth £50 million annually in the UK alone.

ACTIVITY

Research ear piercing treatment in three local salons. These may include hairdressing salons as it is a popular treatment to perform in the hair salon.
 What is the cost of this service?

recorded on the client record card are confidential and should be stored in a secure area following treatment. Access to this information will require written consent from the client. This is enforced through the Data Protection Act 1998 – legislation designed to protect the client's privacy and confidentiality. These records should be kept for at least three years, and be available for inspection as required. This may be by an authorised officer from the local health authority.

Explain the simple treatment procedure. Most clients will be interested to know what to expect – usually the client's first question is 'Will it hurt?'

Discuss aftercare. It is important to check that the client does not have any known allergies that may be contained in products to be used in the treatment, i.e. the aftercare lotion.

Prepare the equipment required for ear piercing, and show the client the range of studs available.

Some salon receptionists are trained to carry out this service. This is practical: many clients will be acting on impulse in deciding to have their ears pierced, and will not have made an appointment.

Contra-indications

In certain circumstances you should not carry out the ear-piercing treatment. Use your professional judgement to assess the suitability of each client. The consultation will draw any contra-indications to your attention.

- *If a client is particularly nervous* it would be inadvisable to pierce their ears – they might faint or jump whilst the treatment was being carried out, causing incorrect placement of the earring.

- *Do not pierce the ears of a client who may have allergies* to the metal used for the jewellery stud.

HEALTH AND SAFETY

Recommended metals for ear piercing
Certain metals may cause an allergy. These include nickel, poor quality gold-plated metals and 9ct gold.
The use of nickel-containing jewellery is subject to the Dangerous Substances and Preparations (Nickel) (Safety) Regulations 2000.
Recommended metals are surgical stainless steel, titanium (6AL4V) and 14ct gold.
Check what metal is used for your ear jewellery with your supplier, and that it complies with the Regulations.

If any of the following are present, do not proceed with ear piercing:

- *Diabetes* – the skin is very slow to heal, so infection of the area would be a strong possibility.

- *Epilepsy* – the stress before the treatment and the possible shock incurred during it might induce a fit.

BEAUTY WORKS

Date	Therapist name	
Client name		Date of birth (identifying client age group)
Address		Postcode
Evening phone number	Day phone number	
Name of doctor	Doctor's address and phone number	

Related medical history (conditions that may restrict or prohibit treatment application)

Are you taking any medication? (e.g. anti-coagulant drugs may affect the sensitivity of the skin and reaction to the treatment)

CONTRA-INDICATIONS REQUIRING MEDICAL REFERRAL
(Preventing ear piercing treatment)

- ☐ bacterial infection
- ☐ viral infection
- ☐ fungal infection
- ☐ severe skin conditions
- ☐ diabetes
- ☐ ear infections
- ☐ cardiovascular problems
- ☐ dysfunction of the nervous system
- ☐ allergies to metals
- ☐ epilepsy
- ☐ anti-coagulant drugs

EQUIPMENT, MATERIALS AND PRODUCTS
- ☐ ear-piercing gun
- ☐ surgical skin marker pen
- ☐ sterile pre-packed alcohol skin-cleansing wipes
- ☐ personal protective equipment
- ☐ sterile pre-packed ear studs (metal type identified)
- ☐ consumables
- ☐ aftercare products
- ☐ mirror
- ☐ sharps disposal box (for use in the event of disposing of a contaminated ear stud)
- ☐ waste bin (with disposable liner)

CONTRA-INDICATIONS WHICH RESTRICT TREATMENT
(Treatment may require adaptation)

- ☐ cuts and abrasions
- ☐ bruising and swelling
- ☐ recent scar tissue
- ☐ skin disorders
- ☐ moles
- ☐ skin inflammation
- ☐ keloid scar tissue

AREA TREATED
- ☐ earlobe

Therapist signature (for reference)

Client signature (confirmation of details)

BEAUTY WORKS *(continued)*

TREATMENT ADVICE

 Ear piercing – *allow 15 minutes*

TREATMENT PLAN

Record relevant details of your treatment and advice provided for future reference.

Ensure the client's records are up to date, accurate and fully completed following treatment. Non-compliance may invalidate insurance.

DURING

Discuss:

- details that may influence the client's ear piercing treatment (e.g., thickness of earlobes).

Note:

- any adverse reaction, if any occur.

AFTER

Record:

- results of treatment;
- any modification to treatment application that has occurred;
- what type of ear studs have been used in the ear piercing treatment;
- the effectiveness of treatment.

Advise on:

- use of specialised aftercare products following ear piercing treatment for homecare use to promote skin healing and prevent contra-actions from occurring;
- aftercare product application in order to gain maximum benefit from their use;
- general ear piercing and maintenance advice;
- the recommended time interval before removal of the stud;
- the recommended time interval between ear piercing treatments.

RETAIL OPPORTUNITIES

Advise on:

- recommendations for further ear piercing treatments;
- products that would be suitable for the client to use at home to care for the pierced skin;
- further products or services that the client may or may not have received before.

Note:

- any purchases made by the client.

EVALUATION

Record:

- comments on the client's satisfaction with the treatment;
- if poor results are achieved, the reasons why;
- how you may alter the treatment plan to achieve the required treatment results in the future, if applicable.

HEALTH AND SAFETY

Advise on:

- how and when to turn the ear stud;
- how and when to remove the ear stud;
- recommended replacement of the ear stud used for piercing;
- appropriate action to be taken in the event of an unwanted reaction to the treatment.

TIP

Examples of ear piercing treatment modification include:
- if a second piercing is requested, ensure the first stud is placed to accommodate leaving a 9mm distance for the second piercing;
- if the client has fat lobes, adjust the tightness following piercing.

- *Skin disease or disorder*.

- *Hepatitis B or HIV (Human Immunodeficiency Syndrome)* – though the client may not know that they are a carrier, or may choose not to disclose the fact if they do (hygienic practice is vital, for this reason).

- *Inflammation of the ear*.

- *Open wounds, cuts or abrasions* in the area.

- *Moles or warts* in the area.

- *Circulatory disorders*, such as high or low blood pressure.

- *A predisposition to keloid scarring* – lumpy scar tissue (black skin often forms keloid scar tissue following skin healing).

- *Following an operation* – piercing must not be carried out at the site of a recent operation.

- *Anti-coagulant drugs* – individuals are likely to bleed persistently.

- *Inflammation of the ear* – the skin in the area appears red, swollen and pus a sign of infection may be present.

- *Keloid scarring* – keloids occur following skin injury and are overgrown abnormal scar tissue which spreads, characterised by excess deposits of collagen. The skin tends to be red, raised and ridged at the site of the wound.

Where there is any contra-indication to ear piercing, the client must seek written permission from their GP before treatment can be carried out.

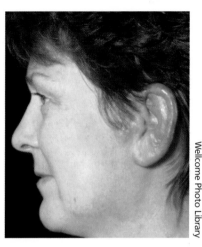

Inflammation of the ear

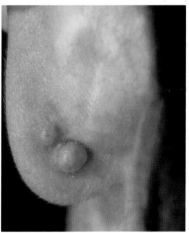

Keloid scarring on the ear

ACTIVITY

Safety and hygiene
Research the ear-piercing systems available. Which ones are designed to protect the client's ear, and the gun, from contamination?

Display the literature you have collected in your log book, explaining the various systems' safety features.

Outcome 2: Prepare for earlobe piercing

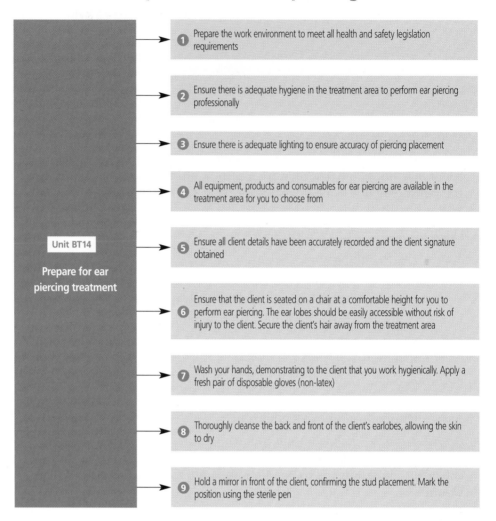

Unit BT14

Prepare for ear piercing treatment

1. Prepare the work environment to meet all health and safety legislation requirements

2. Ensure there is adequate hygiene in the treatment area to perform ear piercing professionally

3. Ensure there is adequate lighting to ensure accuracy of piercing placement

4. All equipment, products and consumables for ear piercing are available in the treatment area for you to choose from

5. Ensure all client details have been accurately recorded and the client signature obtained

6. Ensure that the client is seated on a chair at a comfortable height for you to perform ear piercing. The ear lobes should be easily accessible without risk of injury to the client. Secure the client's hair away from the treatment area

7. Wash your hands, demonstrating to the client that you work hygienically. Apply a fresh pair of disposable gloves (non-latex)

8. Thoroughly cleanse the back and front of the client's earlobes, allowing the skin to dry

9. Hold a mirror in front of the client, confirming the stud placement. Mark the position using the sterile pen

Equipment and materials

You will need the following equipment and materials:

EQUIPMENT LIST

 Ear-piercing gun one that complies with current health and safety legislation

 Pre-packed alcohol-based sterile tissues (2) or manufacturer's cleansing solution used to cleanse the ear area

YOU WILL ALSO NEED:

Studs a variety of styles and designs to accommodate differing client preferences. Preferably of hypo-allergenic metal to minimise allergic reactions in people with metal allergies, e.g. nickel

Surgical skin-marker pen to mark where the piercing will be

Surgical spirit for cleaning the gun after use

Clean cottonwool to apply the surgical spirit

Single use disposable nitryl/vinyl gloves to ensure a high standard of hygiene and to reduce the possibility of contamination

Disposable tissue roll, such as bedroll

Waste bin (with yellow coloured waste liner) to collect waste

Sharps box to dispose of studs

Headband (clean) or clip to hold the hair away from the ear during ear piercing

Hand mirror (clean) to show the client the proposed placement of the earrings, after marking and after the ear piercing

Client record card – confidential card recording details of each client registered at the salon

Aftercare solution either to offer for sale or to include as part of the cost of the service

Aftercare instruction leaflet instructions for the client to keep to minimise healing times and reduce the risk of secondary infection

Ultra-violet light cabinet to store the ear-piercing gun between piercing treatments; helps avoid the risk of contamination

Hand disinfectant containing chlorhexidine

Ellisons

Medi swabs (sterile tissues)

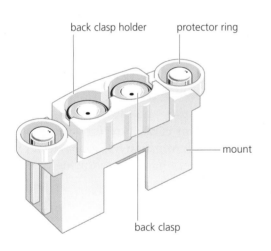

back clasp holder   protector ring

mount

back clasp

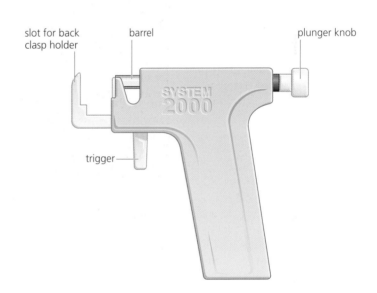

slot for back clasp holder   barrel   plunger knob

trigger

System 2000 cassette and instrument

Sterilisation and disinfection

The premises should be kept clean and hygienic. The floor covering should be such that the surface can be cleaned with a disinfectant and hot soapy water; work surfaces likewise should be washed regularly with detergent and wiped with a disinfectant. Hypochlorite solutions (bleach) are recommended for disinfecting work surfaces.

Some salons that offer the ear-piercing service also sell earrings. Those designed for pierced ears should not be tried on by a client, in the interest of health and hygiene. (Although there have been no reported cases of transmission of hepatitis B or HIV in this way, all possible risks should be avoided.) Such earrings may instead be attached to a special clear acrylic slide that can be held against the ear to assist in selection.

HEALTH AND SAFETY

Cross-infection

If you have any cuts on your hands or fingers, these should be covered with a clean dressing before you treat the client. It is essential to wear disposable gloves.

HEALTH AND SAFETY

Ear-piercing guidelines
The Chartered Institute of Environmental Health has developed useful best practice guidance for those employed as operators in body art, cosmetic therapies and other special treatments.

TIP

Disposable ear-piercing gun
Available for ear piercing is a sterile disposable ear gun. This ensures a sterile gun with pre-loaded ear studs and clasp.

HEALTH AND SAFETY

The Control of Substances Hazardous to Health (COSHH) Act 2002 – including biological agents
These regulations require employers and the self employed to prevent or control the exposure of employees and clients to hazardous substances. This includes exposure to biological agents such as bacteria, fungi and viruses and chemical cleaning/sterilising agents. Records of the COSHH assessment must be available for inspection.

A COSHH essential information document is available for cosmetic piercers at www.coshh-essentials.org.uk.

The gun approved for ear piercing is designed so that it does not come into contact with the client's skin, and is used with pre-sterilised ear studs and ear clasps.

The studs are provided in sterile packs. Many give a date after which their sterility can no longer be assumed; others have a seal that changes colour when the expiry date has been reached. Only use studs that come from a sealed package.

The **Local Government (Miscellaneous Provisions) Act 1982** requires that salons offering any form of skin piercing be registered with the local health authority. This registration includes both the operators who will be carrying out the treatment and the salon premises where the treatment will be carried out.

The Local Government Act 2003 (section 120 and schedule 6) has amended the 1982 Act to enable each local authority to regulate businesses providing cosmetic body piercing. Each local authority can introduce its own bye-laws to set the standards as required for cosmetic piercing.

Premises are inspected by a local authority enforcement officer, who checks that relevant local bye-laws are being followed. (The bye-laws are to ensure that treatment is carried out in a healthy, safe and hygienic manner.)

If the inspector is satisfied, the salon will be issued with a **certificate of registration**; this should be displayed in the reception area. Any breach of the Act or the bye-laws could result in a fine, and permission to carry out the treatment could be withdrawn.

The Greater London Council (General Powers) Act 1981 covers the London boroughs and relates to cosmetic piercing. It provides that no person can carry out cosmetic piercing unless they and the business are registered. Records are required to be kept. This is essential for a business with five employees or more. A business with fewer than five employees requires minimal records but it is best practice to have the following available for inspection relating to cosmetic piercing:

* COSHH assessment records;
* dated client treatment plan records;
* sterilisation methods and records.

The London Local Authorities Act, 1991 states that no person shall carry out cosmetic piercing at an establishment without obtaining a licence from a participating council. Conditions can be attached to the licence such as hygiene practices, age limits, etc.

ACTIVITY

Personal cleanliness
Personal cleanliness is a fundamental requirement of the Local Government (Miscellaneous Provisions) Act 1982 and its amendments. Discuss how a high standard of personal cleanliness can be guaranteed. It is important to check any updates to the Act on a regular basis to ensure compliance.

Preparing the cubicle

Ear piercing can be carried out either in a private cubicle or at reception. Use your discretion to decide which would be more appropriate.

Good ventilation and lighting is important – some clients may feel faint following the treatment. The client should sit on a chair at a comfortable height for you.

All furniture and fittings in the treatment area should be kept clean and in good repair so that they can be cleaned effectively.

The surface that the ear-piercing equipment is to be placed on should be cleaned immediately prior to treatment with detergent. It should then be covered with disposable tissue roll, which is disposed of immediately following treatment.

Check the positioning of the client when performing the treatment. The earlobe should be easily accessible without risk of injury to the client.

How to prepare the client

If the position of the stud has not already been marked, do this now with the surgical skin-marker pen.

1 Wash your hands using a hand disinfectant that contains chlorhexidine as an active ingredient and apply a fresh pair of disposable gloves.

2 Place paper tissue roll over customer's shoulder.

3 Thoroughly cleanse the back and the front of the client's earlobes. Allow the skin to dry. (If moisture is present, the mark will blur.)

4 Holding a mirror in front of the client, discuss with them where the stud should be placed. Mark the position using the sterile pen.

Remember that the ears are not at the same level on each side of the head, and may protrude at different angles. Take time when marking the position of the studs, to ensure that the final appearance is balanced.

Marking the ear prior to piercing

HEALTH AND SAFETY

Secondary infection
As you cleanse the client's earlobes, you may notice that their skin, ear or hair is dirty. You may proceed, but when giving her the aftercare instructions politely and tactfully point out the importance of cleanliness in preventing secondary infection.

HEALTH AND SAFETY

Piercing ears
Never perform multiple piercing in each ear. The ears will swell, causing discomfort and possible infection.
If more than one hole is required in the same ear, the piecing must be at least 9mm apart.

TIP

If the client has fat lobes explain that the studs may feel a little tight.
Adjust tightness of stud in each ear using a clean tissue to hold the stud.

Placement
Try to aim for a central position on the earlobe – this will achieve the best result.

HEALTH AND SAFETY

Ear studs
Studs are preferable to hooped earrings or sleepers, as dirt is less likely to cling to the stud and infect the ear. Select studs that are manufactured from hypo-allergenic material.

PIERCING THE EARS

Outcome 3: Carry out the earlobe piercing

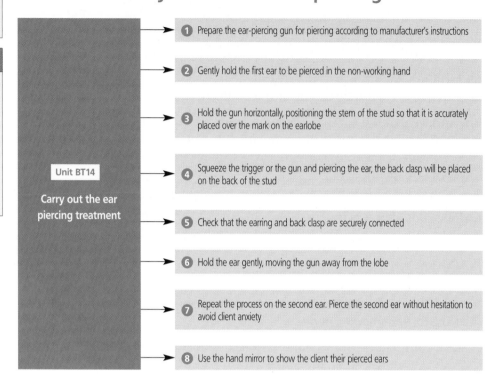

Unit BT14

Carry out the ear piercing treatment

1 Prepare the ear-piercing gun for piercing according to manufacturer's instructions

2 Gently hold the first ear to be pierced in the non-working hand

3 Hold the gun horizontally, positioning the stem of the stud so that it is accurately placed over the mark on the earlobe

4 Squeeze the trigger or the gun and piercing the ear, the back clasp will be placed on the back of the stud

5 Check that the earring and back clasp are securely connected

6 Hold the ear gently, moving the gun away from the lobe

7 Repeat the process on the second ear. Pierce the second ear without hesitation to avoid client anxiety

8 Use the hand mirror to show the client their pierced ears

Step by step: Piercing the ears

The following procedure illustrates the general technique, with the therapist wearing transparent blue gloves. The details differ according to the ear-piercing gun you are using. Always follow the manufacturer's instructions.

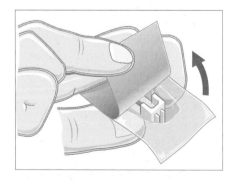

1 Holding the stud pack firmly, remove the backing paper. Take care not to drop the cartridge on the floor! (If you do drop it you will have to throw it away.)

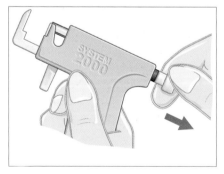

2 Pull back the plunger knob on the back of the gun, until it is fully extended – you will hear it click.

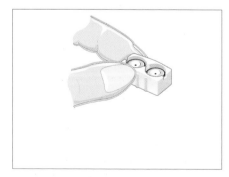

3 Remove the plastic cartridge from the package, holding it by the plastic mount. To avoid contamination, make sure that you do not touch the stud or backing clasp.

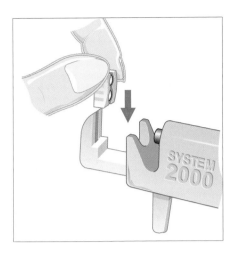

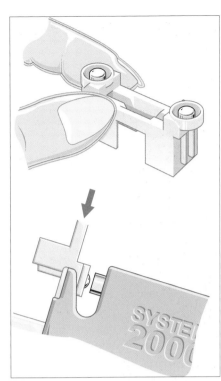

4 There are two parts, which must be separated. One part holds the back clasps: this is positioned in the slot. Push the cartridge down until it will go no further. The second holds the studs: position this against the stud barrel of the gun, which places a protective plastic ring around the barrel of the gun and stud.

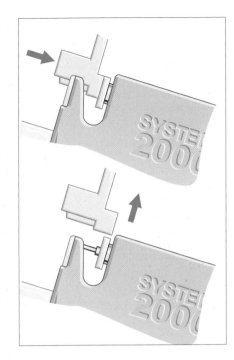

5 Gently pull the holder upwards, away from the barrel: this will deposit the stud in the barrel.

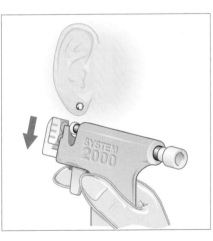

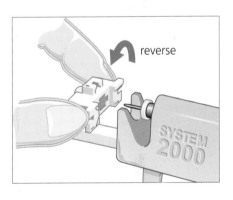

reverse

6 Gently hold the first ear to be pierced in the non-working hand.
   Holding the gun horizontally, position the stem of the stud so that it is accurately placed over the mark on the earlobe.
   Gently squeeze the trigger until it stops. Check that the point of the stud is still in the correct position. If it is, squeeze the trigger again. The ear will be pierced, with the back clasp placed onto the back of the stud.
   Check that the earring and back clasp are securely connected.

7 Holding the ear gently, move the gun down from the lobe. Hold the gun upside down and discard the plastic ring into the waste bin. Pull back the plunger knob and insert the next stud and protective ring.

8 Holding the gun in one hand, grip the back-clasp holder (using the mount in the other hand) and remove the holder from the gun. Invert the holder and place it back into the gun, with the remaining clasp in the top position.

9 Now pierce the second ear, repeating stage 6. If only one piercing is required where double packs of studs are used, the other stud should be discarded.

10 Using the hand mirror, show the client her pierced ears and check that the result is to the client's satisfaction.

HEALTH AND SAFETY ✚

Do not handle studs with your bare hands
Follow the manufacturer's instructions for correct loading. There should not be a need to touch the studs or stud-holding devices.

TIP ✓

Technique
Always hold the gun either horizontally or upwards. Never point the gun downwards once it has been loaded – if you do, the studs will fall out.

TIP ✓

Gun malfunction
If the piercing is successful but the clasp fails to attach to the post, firmly attach this manually without causing the client unnecessary distress.

If the ear stud needs adjustment following piercing, rewash your hands and apply a fresh pair of gloves before touching the pierced ear.

TIP ✓

Technique
To avoid anxiety to the client, pierce the second ear without hesitation, yet safely.

TIP ✓

Client comfort
Allow the client to sit still for a few minutes following the treatment. Offer them tea or coffee. Some clients may be very anxious and need time to relax.

TIP ✓

Technique
The gun should not point down or up when piercing. If the angle of piercing is incorrect, the earring will hang forward, sideways or backwards.

Even simple studs add to the glamour

Outcome 4: Complete the treatment

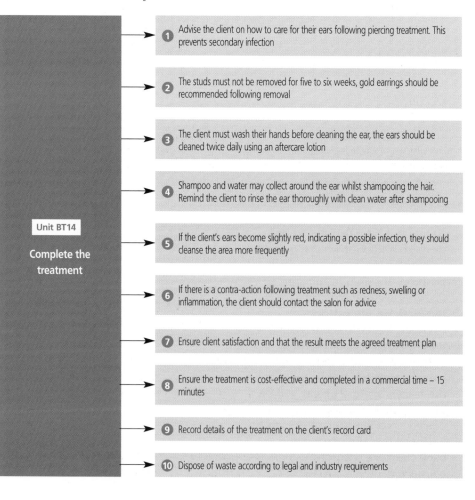

Unit BT14

Complete the treatment

1. Advise the client on how to care for their ears following piercing treatment. This prevents secondary infection

2. The studs must not be removed for five to six weeks, gold earrings should be recommended following removal

3. The client must wash their hands before cleaning the ear, the ears should be cleaned twice daily using an aftercare lotion

4. Shampoo and water may collect around the ear whilst shampooing the hair. Remind the client to rinse the ear thoroughly with clean water after shampooing

5. If the client's ears become slightly red, indicating a possible infection, they should cleanse the area more frequently

6. If there is a contra-action following treatment such as redness, swelling or inflammation, the client should contact the salon for advice

7. Ensure client satisfaction and that the result meets the agreed treatment plan

8. Ensure the treatment is cost-effective and completed in a commercial time – 15 minutes

9. Record details of the treatment on the client's record card

10. Dispose of waste according to legal and industry requirements

Beauty Express Ltd.

How to complete the treatment

1 Discuss the aftercare instructions with the client (see page 536).

2 When the service has been completed, invert the gun, eject the protective ring, and remove the empty back-clasp holder. Dispose of the plastic cartridges into the waste bin.

3 Clean the gun using clean cottonwool and surgical spirit, and place it in the ultra-violet sterilising cabinet.

4 Dispose of all used products in the covered lined waste bin.

HEALTH AND SAFETY

Disposal of waste
Waste from skin-piercing procedures is classed as clinical waste.

All consumable materials used during the ear-piercing treatment should be placed in a covered, lined waste bin, and disposed of in a sealed bag.

Waste materials that have come into contact with body fluids must be collected and disposed of by special arrangement.

The disposal of clinical waste is controlled by the Environment Agency. **The Environment Protection Act (1990): Waste Management: The Duty of Care, A Code of Practice** (ISBN 011 752577 X) provides further information on this subject.

Sharps box

5 Any article that has been used on a client must be sterilised before use on another client to prevent *secondary*, or *cross-infection*.

Any article that has penetrated the skin must be disposed of hygienically immediately in a sharps box and should be disposed of safely in compliance with clinical waste procedures.

ACTIVITY

Differing procedures
The procedure for loading the different ear-piercing guns varies. The procedure given above is one example. Referring to the literature you have collected on the different guns, note ways in which the various treatment procedures differ.

Contra-actions

Infection

Redness, swelling, inflammation and the exudation (oozing) of serum (weeping) all signify that the ear is infected. If this occurs, the client should contact the salon. Depending on what they describe, it may be possible to give them adequate instructions over the telephone, or it may be necessary to make an appointment for the therapist to look at the ear. If, following action by the therapist, the infection persists, the client should be advised to contact their GP. Infection usually results from incorrect aftercare, removing the studs too early, or wearing cheap earrings.

Closed holes are caused by removing the studs too early, or by not continuing to wear earrings after the removal of the original studs.

HEALTH AND SAFETY

Secondary infection
If the client's ears become slightly red, indicating a possible infection, they should cleanse the area more frequently.

Jewellery embedding

This occurs when the ear jewellery descends beneath the skin's surface. This is usually a sign of infection or rejection or allergy to the ear jewellery. The client should contact the salon for advice. If, following action by the therapist, the jewellery remains embedded, the client should be advised to visit their GP.

Keloids – overgrowths of scar tissue – sometimes occur at the site of ear piercing. If a client suffers from keloids, advise them not to have their ears pierced more than once – further keloid tissue could develop, giving an unsightly appearance.

Fainting may occur if the client was particularly nervous beforehand. The shock of the ear-piercing treatment may cause a short period of unconciousness due to insufficient blood flow to the brain.

Allergy to the aftercare lotion

The client may be allergic to the aftercare lotion. Check for known allergies to products at the client consultation.

Aftercare and advice

After the ear piercing, complete details of the treatment on the client's record card. The client should be given clear instructions on how to care for their ears to prevent secondary infection. The studs must not be removed for five to six weeks to enable effective skin healing and prevent infection. Invite the client to return to the salon after this period for you to remove the studs.

Remind the client always to wash their hands before cleaning the ear area. (If someone else is going to clean the ears, they also must wash their hands with soap and warm water before touching the client's ears.) The ears should be cleaned twice daily, using an **aftercare lotion**. The lotion must be applied as directed by the manufacturer. It should be applied to clean cottonwool, and the cottonwool squeezed to allow the lotion to run around the stud, at the front of the ear and then at the back. Whilst the ears are being bathed with the cleansing solution, the stud should be rotated by holding it firmly at the front.

Even if the client cleanses their ears effectively, infection could still occur in other ways. These include the following:

- Long nails harbour germs. Infection of the ear can occur whilst the client is turning the stud.
- The client may touch the stud and ear at times other than when cleaning the ear.
- Shampoo and dirty water may collect around the ear whilst shampooing the hair. Remind the client to rinse the ear thoroughly with clean water after shampooing.

HEALTH AND SAFETY

If a client faints
Loosen any restrictive clothing. Reassure the client, and position them lying flat with their feet raised higher than their head, or sat with their head bent forwards between their knees. Instruct them to breathe deeply and slowly. Increase ventilation in the area.

HEALTH AND SAFETY

Aftercare lotion
Following an ear piercing, a professional manufacturer's aftercare lotion should be provided for each client, which is protected by the manufacturer's product liability insurance.

- Dry the area with a clean tissue if the area is wet, i.e., after showering.
- The client should protect their ears when applying hair lacquer or perfume, to avoid sensitising the ear.
- Following the removal of the studs, the client should only wear gold earrings. Cheap fashion earrings should be worn only for short periods of time, or allergic reactions and ear infections may occur.

After oral instructions have been given, the client should be provided with an aftercare leaflet containing these instructions.

HEALTH AND SAFETY

Antiseptic lotions
Remind the client that if an antiseptic lotion is applied to the ear area, it must be diluted as directed or skin burning may occur.

BODY PIERCING

Body piercing is currently very fashionable. Common areas for piercing include the nipples, the eyebrows, the nose and the navel. Note that body piercing is inappropriate for clients under 17 years of age, as the body is still growing.

Beauty therapy salons that offer ear piercing are often also asked for body piercing. Body piercing should be undertaken only if you have had thorough training, however, and only if you have the necessary specialised equipment and appropriate insurance cover.

TIP

Legal requirements
Always check with your insurance company which areas of the body you are able to pierce.

Equipment

The equipment for piercing is either a **body-piercing gun**, which inserts a hollow reed, or the **needle and clamp** method. With the latter, the clamp reduces circulation in the area, thereby anaesthetising it, and the needle is inserted into the skin. The opening made by the needle is then filled with a ring of high-quality non-reactive surgical steel or gold (above 16 carat).

Aftercare and advice

Special care should be taken of the area for one month following piercing. Ideally the jewellery must not be changed for four to six months to avoid tissue damage and possible infection. If infection occurs, causing excessive redness, swelling or a discharge, the client should return to the salon.

HEALTH AND SAFETY

Body piercing
Before performing body piercing, approval is required from your local environmental health authority and registration is required.

Age and consent issues can be confirmed with your local authority who may have used licensing powers to impose licensing conditions relating to the age of the client.

GLOSSARY OF KEY WORDS

Aftercare advice recommendations given to the client following treatment to continue the benefits of the treatment.

Certificate of registration awarded when the premises have been successfully inspected to ensure that the local bye-laws are being followed in relation to cosmetic piercing.

Clinical waste waste from ear piercing is classed as clinical waste. The disposal of clinical waste is controlled by the Environment Agency. Waste materials that have come into contact with body fluids must be collected and disposed of by special arrangements. The Environment Protection Act (1990): Waste Management: The Duty of Care, A Code of Practice (ISBN 011 752577 X) provides further information on this subject.

Consent form written permission obtained from a parent or guardian to perform a treatment on a client under 16 years of age.

Consultation assessment of client's needs using different assessment techniques, including questioning and natural observation.

Contra-action an unwanted reaction occurring during or after treatment application.

Contra-indication a problematic symptom that indicates that the treatment may not proceed.

Control of Substances Hazardous to Health (COSHH) 2002 (Including Biological Agents) Regulations legislation that requires employers and the self employed to prevent or control the exposure of employees and clients to hazardous substances. This includes exposure to biological agents such as bacteria, fungi and viruses and chemical cleaning/sterilising agents. Records of the COSHH assessment must be available for inspection.

Dangerous Substances and Preparations (Nickel) (Safety) Regulations 2000 the use of nickel has been found to cause allergies. Check what metal is used for your supplier's ear-piercing jewellery and that it complies with the Regulations.

Ear piercing the perforation of the skin and underlying tissue of the earlobe to create a hole in the skin where jewellery is inserted.

Greater London Council (General Powers) Act 1981 this act covers the London boroughs and relates to cosmetic piercing. It provides that no person can carry out cosmetic piercing unless they and the business are registered. It also states what records are required to be kept.

Keloids overgrowths of scar tissue, occurring at the site of the ear-piercing.

Local Government Act 2003 (section 120 and schedule 6) has amended the Local Government (Miscellaneous Provisions) Act 1982 to enable each authority to regulate businesses providing cosmetic body piercing. Each local authority can introduce its own bye-laws to set the standards for cosmetic piercing.

Local Government (Miscellaneous Provisions) Act 1982 requires that salons offering any form of skin piercing be registered with the local health authority. This registration includes the operators who will be carrying out the treatment and the salon premises where the treatment will be carried out.

London Local Authorities Act, 1991 this Act states that no person shall carry out cosmetic piercing at an establishment without obtaining a licence from a participating council. Conditions can be attached to the licence, such as hygiene practices, age restrictions, etc.

Treatment plan after the consultation, suitable treatment objectives are established to treat the client's conditions and needs.

Assessment of knowledge and understanding

You have now learnt about the service skin piercing of the earlobe. This will enable you to professionally pierce ears.

To test your level of knowledge, answer the following short questions. These will prepare you for your summative (final) assessment.

Consult with the client

1 Which part of the ear is recommended for ear piercing?

2 Which parts of the earlobe are considered unsuitable and why?

3 How would you describe the procedure of ear piercing to ensure a client was confident both about the procedure and your expertise?

4 Why is it necessary to obtain parental/guardian consent for children under the age of 16 years?

5 How long should be allowed when booking for this treatment?

6 Why should only one pair of studs be fitted at once?

Prepare for earlobe piercing

1 What does the Local Government Miscellaneous Provisions Act 1982 and its amendments require of those who perform ear piercing?

2 What personal protective equipment must be worn when carrying out the ear-piercing treatment?

3 What conditions would contra-indicate an ear-piercing treatment?

4 How should the client be positioned for ear-piercing treatment? Why is this important?

5 What factors should be considered when piercing the earlobes of the following clients?
- a client who has previously suffered from keloid scarring
- a particularly nervous client
- a client with fat earlobes
- a client with diabetes
- a client who is allergic to nickel
- a client who has had their earlobes pierced previously, and this is a second piercing.

6 How can you ensure that the position of the ear stud will be correct?

7 How is the ear sanitised for treatment?

8 What salon environmental factors should be considered to ensure that the piercing is carried out competently?

Carry out earlobe piercing

1 How can you prevent infection when carrying out an ear-piercing treatment?

2 What is the normal reaction following ear-piercing treatment? You may wish to discuss this with the client at consultation

3 What should be recorded on the client's record card following the ear-piercing treatment, and is this of importance?

4 If the ear-piercing gun malfunctioned, what action should be taken?

5 How should waste be disposed of safely and correctly?

Complete the treatment

1 What aftercare instructions should be given following ear-piercing?

2 If the client failed to follow the aftercare instructions, what complications could occur?

3 How would infection of the earlobe be recognised?

4 If an infection of the earlobe were to occur, what action should a client take?

5 If a second piercing to the lobe was requested, when would you recommend this take place?

BT15   Assist with spa treatments

 Essential anatomy and physiology knowledge requirements for this unit, BT15, are identified on the checklist chart in Chapter 5, page 101.

INTRODUCTION TO SPA TREATMENTS

Spa treatments are used for their beneficial effects upon the whole body. The spa environment and spa treatments induce a physical and mental sense of wellbeing.

The term 'spa' is said to be derived from a village near Liege, in Belgium called *Spau*. It had mineral hot springs that people would visit to improve their health and ailments.

The choice of spa treatments offered in the workplace will depend on the space available and the nature of other treatment services offered. Health farms commonly offer a comprehensive range of spa treatments whereas leisure centres and gyms popularly offer heat treatments such as sauna, steam and spa pools.

TIP

Before adding spa treatments to the services available, consider client usage and profitability. If you do not have a shower facility you will be limited in the range of spa services you can offer.

> **TIP** ✓
>
> **Spa treatments as a preparatory service**
> Spa treatments are beneficial when applied before other body treatments as they make the body tissues and systems more receptive.
>
> **Spa treatments as a rehabilitation service**
> Water is used for the treatment of medical conditions such as rheumatism and rehabilitation after injury.

Spa treatments include:

- **sauna** – a dry heat treatment where air is heated;
- **relaxation room** – sometimes referred to by the Latin name *tepidarium*, a room of ambient temperature (close to body temperature);
- **steam** – a wet heat treatment where water is heated;
- **hydrotherapy** – where water is used for its therapeutic effect;
- **flotation** – the body is suspended (wet flotation), or supported (dry flotation), inducing relaxation;
- **body wrapping** – the body is wrapped in bandages, plastic sheets or thermal blankets for different therapeutic effects.

Ingredients such as marine minerals or clay are applied to the bandages or directly to the skin to achieve different results.

> **TIP** ✓
>
> **History of spa treatments**
> The therapeutic effects of spa treatments including steam, sauna and spa pools have been recognised throughout the ages.
>
> During the Roman Empire baths were used for their healing, health benefits and as a social meeting place. Examples of these original bath houses can still be seen today in the city of Bath, England.
>
> For thousands of years people from all cultures including Europe, Russia, the Middle East and India have used steam baths, and the medical benefits of the Turkish or Middle Eastern *hamman* steam baths date back to 200 BC. Hippocrates, the founder of Western medicine more than 2000 years ago said, '*Give me the power to create a fever and I will cure any disease*'.
>
> Water is still used in medicine today for the treatment of sport injuries, rehabilitation and rheumatic disease.

EzFlow

The therapeutic effects of spa treatments go beyond the body

General effects of spa therapy treatments

Spa heat treatments and therapeutic skin-conditioning treatments have the following effects.

- Relaxation is induced through treatments that raise the body temperature, increasing the blood circulation generally, which soothes sensory nerve endings and causes muscle relaxation. Heat therapy is a popular de-stressing treatment.
- Blood pressure falls as the superficial capillaries and vessels dilate.
- Heart rate and pulse rate increase.
- Blood circulation is improved. Vasodilation occurs, which increases the blood flow through the area, supplying oxygen and nutrients to the cells.
- Lymphatic circulation is increased, assisting with the elimination of toxins and waste materials.
- Desquamation – the removal of surface dead skin cells from the stratum corneum is increased.

- Increased activity of the sebaceous and sudoriferous glands improves skin condition. This also creates a deep-cleaning action.
- Metabolism may be increased or decreased depending upon the treatment received.
- Flotation treatment causes a fall in heart and pulse rate due to its relaxation effect.
- Body wrapping treatments cause a rise in pulse rate due to an increase in body temperature.

ANATOMY AND PHYSIOLOGY

Heat treatments: sauna, steam and relaxation room

When heat treatments are applied, there is an increase in body temperature generally of about 1–2°C. Vasodilation of the blood capillaries occurs, lowering the body temperature by increasing heat loss. This vasodilation effect causes erythema, where the skin becomes reddened. This effect soon subsides after application.

The increase in body temperature causes a corresponding increase in the heart and pulse rates. There is a fall in blood pressure as the resistance of the capillary walls is reduced when the capillaries dilate.

The dilation of the blood capillaries enables the blood to transport increased nutrients to the skin, enhancing its function and appearance.

The maximum temperature that the body can tolerate varies according to the type of treatment – dry or wet. Dry air holds less heat than water vapour, and body sweat is able to evaporate in dry heat, thus cooling the skin. This enables the body to tolerate a higher temperature.

Air that is saturated with water vapour is able to hold more heat, and body sweat is unable to evaporate so the body cannot cool itself. The body therefore cannot tolerate very high temperatures in wet heat.

HEALTH AND SAFETY

Sweat loss during heat treatments
The amount of sweat lost during heat treatments can vary from 0.15 to 1.5 litres.

It is important that the client is given water during and after heat treatment as necessary to rehydrate.

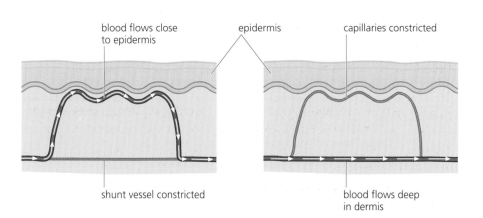

blood flows close to epidermis

epidermis

capillaries constricted

shunt vessel constricted

blood flows deep in dermis

Vasodilation and vasoconstriction

Hydrotherapy treatment

Hydrotherapy uses water to induce physical and mental well-being.

Hydrotherapy treatments include:

- spa pools;
- hydro baths and foam baths.

Spa pool

Also known as a whirlpool or Jacuzzi bath, a spa pool will increase blood and lymphatic circulation due to the thermal and mechanical stimulating effect of the water. The rise in body temperature causes the pulse to increase.

Air is forced by a compressor through the water, passed through small openings in the bath. Water jets striking the skin's surface create a skin toning effect. Muscular pain and fatigue is reduced as accumulated toxins and waste are dispersed in the improved lymphatic circulation.

Hydro bath

The hydro bath is fitted with air and water jets that massage the tissues of the body as an air compressor aerates the water. These can be pressure controlled to achieve different effects. A hose may also be used to manually direct air over the body. This can be used to improve the skin tone in specific areas and can relieve muscular aches and pains by the heating effect and improved circulation.

Body temperature is increased which causes muscles to be relaxed due to increased blood circulation. Metabolism is increased.

Foam bath

An air compressor creates foam when air is passed through a shallow bath of water containing a foaming agent. The foam surrounds the body of the client and has a thermal effect, insulating the body and keeping it warm. The heating effect on the body induces perspiration but this cannot evaporate as the surrounding air is saturated with water vapour.

Increased perspiration aids elimination of waste products and toxins from the skin. Muscles are relaxed due to the rise in body temperature and increased blood circulation.

Flotation treatments

During flotation treatment total relaxation occurs and this affects the autonomic nervous system. It has two divisions: the *parasympathetic* and the *sympathetic*.

- The parasympathetic division is stimulated in periods of relaxation.
- The sympathetic division is stimulated in periods of stress.

During flotation treatment, the sympathetic system is deactivated and the parasympathetic division is stimulated. A calming effect on the body occurs as pulse rate slows, metabolism reduces, and muscles relax.

Aquasun

Hydrotherapy bath

> **TIP** ✓
>
> **Metabolism**
> Metabolism is a series of chemical reactions which utilises the nutrients required for growth and body repair.

Floataway

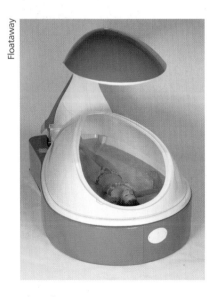

Flotation treatment

Body wrapping

Body wrapping results in an increase in body temperature, blood circulation generally and pulse rate.

The dilation of the blood capillaries enables the blood to transport increased nutrients to the skin, enhancing its function and appearance. As the skin warms, therapeutic ingredients are absorbed by the skin and have a skin-conditioning effect. They are absorbed through the pores, hair follicles and the epidermis (stratum corneum).

The increase in body temperature also increases perspiration and waste elimination. Ingredients such as clay are used to help to draw out toxins.

The lymphatic circulation increases, which aids the elimination of excess fluid and toxins in the improved circulation.

Where heating is an effect of the body wrap, this helps to relax tense muscles.

SPA OPERATION

Sauna – dry heat treatment

Sauna is a dry heat treatment. There are alternative methods of sauna including traditional Finnish or Tyrolean sauna, and the Laconium sauna.

Finnish or Tyrolean sauna

The sauna is usually a timber construction, often made from pine, which is a porous wood. This allows the condensation created to be absorbed and the internal furnishing walls to breathe. The sauna air is usually heated by an electric stove to between 70°–110°C.

The sauna is heated by a stove that contains coals. The coals get very hot and steam is created by pouring water onto them. An air inlet is situated at floor level and an outlet is found near the top of the cabin.

This high temperature is tolerable because the heat is reduced on contact with the skin and the sweat induced rapidly reduces the skin temperature.

Laconium sauna

This sauna creates an evenly distributed mild dry heat. The temperature in the laconium sauna is approximately 55°C, generated by underfloor heating as opposed to heat created from a stove.

Laconium is suitable for gently heating the skin for the purpose of cleansing and purifying. Some clients will prefer this sauna type as the heat is less intense.

Electricity is used to produce the heat and a sauna is operated by the mains supply because of the high power rating used.

Additional therapeutic effects of dry heat:

TIP

Sauna history
Saunas were used in Scandinavia as part of ancient historical religious ceremonies to cleanse physically, mentally and spiritually.

Sauna (traditional wood)

 HEALTH AND SAFETY

Sauna temperature
High temperatures are only recommended in larger saunas where there is a greater volume of air.

TIP

Infrared sauna
An infrared sauna heats the body directly, rather than heating the air which in turn heats the body. Infrared radiators penetrate the body tissues to a depth of 45mm and this stimulates the cardio-vascular system which improves cellular metabolism and improves muscular fatigue and tension.

The positive effect of colour as a therapy – called *phototherapy* – can be combined with this treatment.

Courtesy of the Detox Box

HEALTH AND SAFETY

Humidity in the sauna
Water can be sprinkled onto the stones in the sauna to raise moisture content (humidity).

- elimination of metabolic waste is increased;
- skin cleansing occurs as the pores dilate, secreting sweat onto the skin's surface, thereby eliminating waste products;
- respiratory congestion can be relieved;
- increased sweating can cause temporary weight loss. However, this loss is quickly replaced with fluids consumed following treatment;
- muscles are relaxed due to the rise in body temperature and increased blood circulation.

Relaxation room

The relaxation room enables the client to rest between experiencing different spa treatments, allowing the body temperature and blood pressure to lower. The air is ambient, the same as the body's temperature. The air in the room is dry to enhance the body's immune system and relieve stress. It is important that this area is very quiet to induce relaxation. Heated couches warmed by a heat-conducting hot mortar may be found in this room. These are ideal for clients unsuitable to receive heat treatment, which significantly increases blood circulation, e.g. sauna treatment.

Additional therapeutic effects of the relaxation room:

- heating effect soothes the sensory nerve endings;
- relieves muscular aches and pains;
- increases blood flow and removes waste products;
- the relaxing environment reduces stress and tension.

Electricity is used to produce the heat. The room is operated by the mains supply because of the high power rating used.

Steam – a wet heat treatment

Steam treatment can be received individually in a steam bath, or communally in a steam room. To produce steam, water is heated to 100°C. This then mixes with air to produce water vapour.

Steam bath

This is constructed from fibreglass. A hinged door allows access and encloses the client; an opening at the top of the bath exposes the client's head. The client sits on a seat inside the bath that is adjustable for the height of each client and for their comfort.

Water is heated in a small tank inside the bath, situated underneath the seat. On boiling, the water produces steam. The steam mixes with the air in the bath and produces water vapour, which circulates inside the cabinet. The temperature inside the cabinet is most comfortable at between 45°–50°C.

Steam room

To provide steam for a room, the water is heated in a boiler. The steam created is passed through tubes and the water vapour created circulates inside the room.

The *caldarium* is a steam room that uses natural herbal essences to create an aromatic steam room.

The *hamman* is a communal steam bath with a hot, moist aromatic atmosphere to purify and detox. The hamman bath traditionally has a dome-shaped central chamber with further chambers, of differing temperatures, leading from it. The hottest room is heated from the floor.

Additional therapeutic effects of steam heat:

- Muscles are relaxed due to the rise in body temperature and increased blood circulation.

HEALTH AND SAFETY

Temperature in the steam room
The air in the steam bath/room is saturated with water vapour (that is, it is unable to hold more water) and sweat on the skin's surface is unable to evaporate to create the skin-cooling effect. For this reason, the temperature for steam treatment is lower than that for sauna to avoid the body overheating.

Hydrotherapy

In hydrotherapy, water is used for its therapeutic effect.

Spa pool

A spa pool is full of heated warm water in which the client sits. It is constructed from shaped, durable acrylic, or tiled concrete. Provided with an electric power supply, air is forced through small openings and jets of air pass through the water, creating bubbles. These bubbles massage the surface of the skin from all directions, which has a stimulating effect.

The pool may incorporate features such as jets placed to massage different body parts, for example the lower back, and water fountains which can massage the neck with the power of the water flow.

Hydro baths and foam baths

The hydro bath is usually made of acrylic and is filled with warm water. Operated by electricity, an air compressor provides underwater massage through high-powered jets. The air is forced through perforations in a duckboard or through outlet holes in the bath. A hose can also be used to manually direct water to stimulate circulation in specific areas.

The bath may be used to maintain wellbeing or as a rehabilitation treatment. Features include preset massage programmes to achieve different effects.

Foam baths are usually made of acrylic. A plastic duckboard perforated with small holes is located at the bottom of the bath. Operated by electricity, an air compressor forces air through the holes which mixes with water and a foam agent to create the foam bath.

TIP

Steam cubicles
These are filled with steam and offer an alternative to the steam bath. The air is gently heated to 45°C and usually infused with herbal aromatic oils for their therapeutic effect.

Caldarium

Courtesy of Dale Sauna Ltd

TIP

Bath houses have been used for thousands of years – the ancient Romans had hot rooms.

TIP

Hydrotherapy
Hydrotherapy bath water may have seaweed, sea salt or essential oils added to enhance its therapeutic effect.

TIP

Hydrotherapy pool – weighing less

When in water the human body weighs 10 times less than normal.

TIP

Natural spas

Natural spas are swimming pools filled with mineral water and are considered to have therapeutic effects.

TIP

Hydro-oxygen baths

This is a bath-type cabinet. A compressor aerates hot water which strikes the body; the cabinet is also diffused with oxygen which is extremely stimulating to the skin. It is important for the client to relax following treatment.

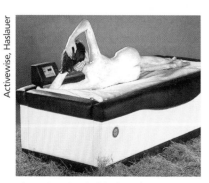

Flotation bath (wet)

Flotation bath (dry)

Additional therapeutic effects of hydrotherapy treatment:

- relaxation – the body weight is supported by the warm water and gently massaged;
- skin cleansing – as the water massages the skin's surface, desquamation is increased;
- skin toning when using jets of water to massage the body tissues;
- muscle fatigue and joint pain can be relieved by the increased blood and lymph circulation and increased cellular metabolism.

Flotation, wet and dry

The body is suspended, floats or is supported, inducing physical and mental relaxation.

Wet flotation in a bath or tank

Flotation baths or tanks are commonly capsule-shaped and constructed from fibreglass. The inside is lined with plastic resin.

Flotation pools are also available.

The treatment uses epsom salts diluted in water at high concentration which enables the body to float, and be suspended in the water. Approximately 280 kilogrammes of epsom salts are diluted in 500 litres of water, which is maintained at body temperature. This is approximately 570g of epsom salts to 1 litre of water.

Due to the high salt content, the skin does not lose body salts, and does not wrinkle, as would commonly occur when exposed to warm water for long periods of time.

Dry flotation

Here the client lies on a warmed tank of water, protected by a polymer flexible membrane covering protected by paper roll. The client lies on a bench that is lowered by the therapist so that the client is suspended by the water but has no direct contact with it.

The client may have specific therapeutic skin-care products applied to the skin to nourish or purify and detoxify. The body is then wrapped to maintain heat and absorb the products.

Additional therapeutic effects of flotation treatment:

- stress is reduced as blood pressure is lowered;
- skin conditioning occurs as circulation is increased, or in dry flotation the skin benefits from the therapeutic skin products applied;
- beneficial to those with back injuries, as the water supports the body and takes pressure off the back;
- rheumatic conditions are relieved as there is improved blood circulation between the affected joints and relief of muscular tension;
- slower brain wave patterns, known as theta waves, occur in wet flotation.

Body wrapping

A manual treatment. A small electrical heater may be used to heat the towels before use.

Additional therapeutic effects of body wrapping treatment:

- cellular regeneration is increased;
- waste products and toxins are eliminated;
- temporary weight loss through increased sweating and increased loss of body fluids;
- the therapeutic effect of body products helps balance the skin and body by skin stimulation caused by the cleansing, heating action.

PLANNING FOR SPA TREATMENTS

Reception

Heat treatments can be offered as individual treatments, but are also beneficial when given before other body treatments to increase their therapeutic effects. If you offer communal sauna, steam or other spa treatments, there will be a recommended number of clients who can use these facilities at once. Make sure you are aware of this to avoid overbooking.

For the client's first heat treatment, treatment time is shorter to monitor their physiological and psychological response to treatment.

Facility	Treatment time
Sauna	Treatment may be received 2–3 times per week Treatment duration 15–20 minutes
Relaxation room	Treatment may be received 2–3 times per week Treatment duration 30 minutes
Steam room	Treatment may be received 2–3 times per week Treatment duration 10–15 minutes
Steam bath	Treatment may be received 2–3 times per week Treatment duration 10–20 minutes
Hydrotherapy spa pool	Treatment may be received daily Treatment duration 10–15 minutes.
Hydrotherapy/foam bath	Treatment may be received 2–3 times per week Treatment duration 15–20 minutes
Flotation	Treatment may be received 1–2 times per week Wet flotation treatment duration 20–60 minutes Dry flotation treatment duration 40 minutes
Body wrap	Treatment may be received 2–3 times per week Treatment time 45–60 minutes, depending on the technique used

B E A U T Y   W O R K S

Date	Therapist name	
Client name		Date of birth
Address		Postcode
Evening phone number	Day phone number	
Name of doctor	Doctor's address and phone number	
Related medical history (conditions that may restrict or prohibit treatment application)		
Are you taking any medication? (this may affect the sensitivity of the skin and reaction to the treatment)		

CONTRA-INDICATIONS REQUIRING MEDICAL REFERRAL
(Preventing spa treatment application)
(Temporary CI are indicated*)

☐ bacterial infection, e.g. impetigo*
☐ viral infection, e.g. verruca*
☐ fungal infection, e.g. tinea corporis/pedis*
☐ skin disorders
☐ skin disease, e.g. malignant melanoma
☐ high or low blood pressure
☐ heart disease/disorder
☐ medical conditions under supervision
☐ history of thrombosis/embolism
☐ recent scar tissue
☐ dysfunction of the nervous system
☐ epilepsy   ☐ respiratory conditions
☐ liver/kidney or pancreatic conditions
☐ lymphatic disorders   ☐ recent alcohol consumption*
☐ recent heavy meal – temporary*
☐ recent UVL exposure – temporary*

LIFESTYLE
☐ dietary and fluid intake   ☐ exercise habits
☐ smoking habits   ☐ sleep patterns
☐ hobbies, interests, means of relaxation

EQUIPMENT
☐ sauna
☐ steam room   ☐ steam cabinet
☐ flotation bath   ☐ flotation pool – dry/wet
☐ body wrapping
☐ relaxation room

CONTRA-INDICATIONS WHICH RESTRICT TREATMENT
(Treatment may require adaptation)
(Temporary CI are indicated*)

☐ cuts and abrasions*
☐ bruising and swelling*
☐ recent scar tissue (avoid area)
☐ undiagnosed lumps, bumps, swellings
☐ recent injuries to the treatment area*
☐ mild psoriasis/eczema   ☐ medication
☐ high/low blood pressure ☐ pregnancy*
☐ body piercings   ☐ highly anxious client
☐ allergies   ☐ claustrophobia
☐ menstruation   ☐ migraine

TREATMENT OBJECTIVES
☐ improved skin and body condition
☐ lymphatic drainage
☐ slimming – improved contours
☐ relaxation

TREATMENT AREAS
☐ trunk – body wrap   ☐ limbs – body wrap
☐ body – general

CLIENT PREPARATION
☐ exfoliation   ☐ skin cleansing
☐ showering

PREPARATION FOR AND MONITORING OF TREATMENT ENVIRONMENT
☐ heat   ☐ humidity
☐ water levels   ☐ chemical concentrations
☐ treatment time   ☐ ventilation
☐ consumables   ☐ ambience of environment

Therapist signature (for reference)
Client signature (confirmation of details)

BEAUTY WORKS (continued)

TREATMENT ADVICE

Sauna – *allow 30 minutes*
Steam – *allow 15–20 minutes*
Hydrotherapy pool – *allow 15–20 minutes*
Hydrobaths – *allow 15–20 minutes*

Foambath – *allow 15–20 minutes*
Flotation treatment (wet/dry) – *allow 20–60 minutes*
Body wrap – *allow 60 minutes*

TREATMENT PLAN

Record relevant details of your treatment and advice provided for future reference.
Ensure the client's records are up to date, accurate and fully completed following treatment. Non-compliance may invalidate insurance.

DURING

Discuss:

- relevant spa treatment products the client is currently using and regularity of their use;
- satisfaction with these products;
- how to gain maximum benefit from product use;
- relevant spa products and procedures.

Monitor:

- client's reaction to treatment to confirm suitability.

Note:

- any adverse reaction, if any occur.

AFTER

Record:

- results of treatment;
- any modification to treatment application that has occurred;
- what products have been used in the spa treatment;
- the effectiveness of treatment;
- any samples provided (review their success at the next appointment).

Advise on:

- product application in order to gain maximum benefit from product use;
- use of specialised spa products following treatment for homecare use;
- general aftercare and maintenance advice (e.g., rest and relaxation, exercise and diet);
- avoidance of certain treatments following treatment, which may sensitise the skin;
- the recommended time intervals between treatments;
- the importance of a course of treatment to achieve and maintain the treatment objectives.

RETAIL OPPORTUNITIES

Advise on:

- progression of the treatment plan for future appointments;
- products that would be suitable for the client to use at home;
- further spa products or services that the client may or may not have received before.

Note:

- any purchases made by the client.

EVALUATION

Record:

- comments on the client's satisfaction with the treatment;
- if treatment plan results are not achieved, the reasons why;
- how you may alter the treatment plan to achieve the required treatment results in the future, if applicable.

HEALTH AND SAFETY

Advise on:

- appropriate action to be taken in the event of an unwanted reaction;
- avoidance of stimulants;
- suitable rest period following treatment;
- general advice re food and fluid intake;
- recommended time intervals between treatments.

HEALTH AND SAFETY

Patch test for allergies

If a client has allergies or hypersensitive skin, assess skin tolerance by applying a small amount of the treatment product to the skin behind the ear or at the inner elbow.

Skin allergy will be recognised by skin irritation itching, redness and swelling.

Record this on the client's record card and do not perform the treatment.

TIP

Data Protection Act 1998

Remember client records should be stored securely and viewed only by those authorised to do so.

Consultation

At the consultation identify what the client wishes to achieve from the spa treatment – their treatment needs. From this you will be able to select a suitable treatment plan of relevant spa treatments. Discuss why these would be most suitable for the client.

Advise the client that a bathing costume may be worn if preferred for heat treatments. Inform the client beforehand that jewellery should not be worn during heat treatments and may have to be removed for body wrapping. They may prefer to not wear it for the appointment for reasons of security.

If the client is attending for a body wrap that contains iodine, check that the client does not have an allergy to it. If unsure the client may receive a patch test to assess skin reaction before treatment.

Heat and hydrotherapy treatments generally may be received two to three times per week.

Body wraps should be recommended as a course if the client's aim is slimming; these may be received twice a week. Otherwise once a week would be appropriate. Advise the client that the slimming effect lasts four to five days.

Allow time for client questions when booking or advising on any spa treatment. It is important that the client has a thorough understanding of the treatment plan.

Complete personal details on the client's record card. Question the client to check for contra-indications.

Contra-indications

If whilst completing the record card or on visual inspection of the skin you find the client to have any of the following, heat treatment may not be carried out:

- Severe skin conditions, e.g. acute eczema.
- Systemic medical conditions:
  - high/low blood pressure;
  - thrombosis, a clot in the blood vessel or heart;

- phlebitis, inflammation of the vein;
- lymphatic disorders such as medical oedema;
- epilepsy, a disorder of the nervous system;
- respiratory conditions i.e. bronchitis/asthma;
- diabetes, decreased insulin secretion which causes excess glucose (sugar) to accumulate in the bloodstream. Increased urination occurs to excrete the excess glucose;
- liver, kidney or pancreatic conditions;
- viral, bacterial or fungal skin disorders such as verrucas and athlete's foot;
- disorders requiring medication;
- allergy to iodine, found in seaweed-based skin preparations: this must be checked when performing body wraps;
- severe varicose veins (avoid heat treatment, massage and body wrapping on the lower limbs);
- claustrophobia – unsuitable treatments for clients with a fear of being in a confined area include flotation treatment and heat treatments such as the sauna and steam room.

HEALTH AND SAFETY

Preventing cross-infection
Disposable paper slippers may be worn to prevent cross-infection for spa therapy treatments such as body wrapping.
  Verruca socks may be worn for hydrotherapy treatments.

- Other contra-indications may be temporary and include:
  - pregnancy;
  - menstruation, first days;
  - not having eaten for several hours – fainting may occur;
  - a recent heavy meal;
  - recent active exercise – wait approximately 20–30 minutes;
  - recent alcohol consumption;
  - recent drug use;
  - recent over-exposure to UV light;
  - recent wax depilation, electrical epilation treatment (24–48 hours before a spa treatment) to avoid skin sensitivity and possible secondary infection;
  - migraine;
  - severe bruising;
  - high body temperature with infections such as influenza.

HEALTH AND SAFETY

Treating a client with a contra-indication
Certain contra-indications, if mild or under GP control, may be treated. A GP's permission must be sought before a contra-indicated treatment can be given.

HEALTH AND SAFETY

Flotation treatment and skin disorders
Some skin disorders can become aggravated by the salt used in wet flotation treatment. If unsure refer your client to their GP for approval to treat.
Alternatively, if available, dry flotation treatment may be offered.

HEALTH AND SAFETY

Increase in pulse
The heart works much faster during heat treatments. It needs to pump the blood to the surface of the skin to regulate body temperature and can increase from 72 beats per minute to 150 beats per minute.
  Because there is an increase in pulse rate with a body wrap it is necessary to gain a GP's permission to treat if the client has high or low blood pressure.

TIP ✔

Claustrophobia
To enable clients to become accustomed to the enclosed environment of the flotation bath, some models have a door which may be kept open during treatment.

TIP ✔

Your work role
Your role is to assist with spa treatments and you must work within your job responsibilities. However, it is important to respond courteously to requests for assistance from colleagues and anticipate their needs to ensure the smooth running of the spa.

Outcome 1: Prepare work areas for water, temperature and spa treatments

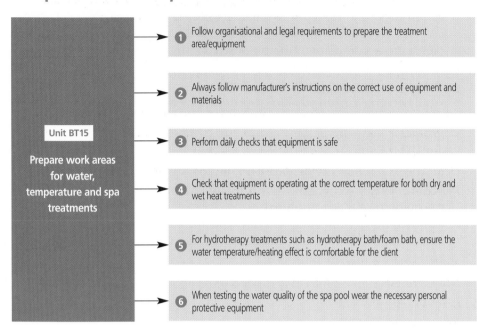

Unit BT15

Prepare work areas for water, temperature and spa treatments

1. Follow organisational and legal requirements to prepare the treatment area/equipment

2. Always follow manufacturer's instructions on the correct use of equipment and materials

3. Perform daily checks that equipment is safe

4. Check that equipment is operating at the correct temperature for both dry and wet heat treatments

5. For hydrotherapy treatments such as hydrotherapy bath/foam bath, ensure the water temperature/heating effect is comfortable for the client

6. When testing the water quality of the spa pool wear the necessary personal protective equipment

Spa equipment and materials

Sauna treatment

- *Sauna* – there must be adequate space for the air to circulate around the sauna.
- *Client record card* – to assess client and record details of treatment.
- *Client guidance instructions* – clearly sited.
- *Appropriate ventilation*.
- *Shower* – to cleanse the skin and regulate body temperature; body and hair shampoos may be provided.
- *Protective footwear* – to avoid cross-infection, e.g. disposable paper slippers.
- *Clean towels for each client* – to drape the body after showering and to protect the hair.
- *A wooden pail containing purified water to ladle over the coals* – the water boils when poured onto the heated coals which increases the humidity (water vapour content of the air), cooling the air and making breathing more comfortable. This raising of humidity also makes the sauna feel hotter.

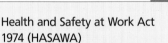

HEALTH AND SAFETY

Health and Safety at Work Act 1974 (HASAWA)
This Act is the main legislation covering employer's responsibilities to a variety of healthy, safe, working practices and associated regulations.

Chemicals used in the spa and to clean and maintain the spa must be stored, handled and used correctly – see the **Control of Substances Hazardous to Health Regulations (COSHH) 1999.**

If necessary protective clothing may have to be worn – see the **Personal Protective Equipment (PPE) at Work Regulations 1992.**

HEALTH AND SAFETY

For safety the relative humidity of the air should be between 60–70 per cent

$$\text{Relative humidity (per cent)} = \frac{\text{Actual water vapour content of the air}}{\text{Maximum it can hold at that temperature}}$$

Essential oils may be added to the purified water. When poured over the coals, the steam produced has therapeutic inhalation properties. Typical oils include eucalyptus.

- *Temperature gauge* – to record the heat of the sauna, 70°C for a mild sauna, 110°C for a hot sauna.
- *An electric stove* – which heats the stones or coals, protected by a guard.
- *Hygrometer* – an instrument to measure relative humidity – generally the reading should be between 45–50 per cent.
- *Drinking water* – to rehydrate following treatment.
- *Relaxation area* – to use following treatment.

Steam treatment

- *Steam bath or steam room.*
- *Distilled water* – to fill the water tank.
- *Essence* – to introduce into the steam room, e.g. pine.
- *Appropriate ventilation.*
- *Client guidance instructions* – clearly sited.
- *Client record card* – to assess client and record details of treatment.
- *Shower* – to cleanse the skin and regulate body temperature.
- *Body and hair shampoos* – may be provided.
- *Protective footwear* – to avoid cross-infection e.g. disposable paper slippers.
- *Clean towels for each client* – to drape over the seat and over the floor to protect the back of the client's legs from scalding by the steam, to provide modesty, dry the body after showering and to protect the hair. Also a small towel may be draped around the opening of the cabinet during treatment to prevent moist heat escaping.
- *Drinking water* – to rehydrate following treatment.
- *Relaxation area* – to use following treatment.

Spa pool

- *Spa pool* – with filtration system to maintain water quality; the floor area must be reinforced to withstand the weight of the water.
- *Plant room* – within five metres of the pool with appropriate power supply and ventilation.
- *A heavy-duty control panel* – all fittings should be strong, safe and reliable.
- *Water testing equipment* – the pH should read 7.2–7.8.
- *Water temperature should be between 37–40°C.*
- *Client guidance instructions* – clearly sited.
- *Client record card* – to assess client and record details of treatment.
- *Shower* – to cleanse the skin and regulate body temperature.
- *Body and hair shampoos* – may be provided.

Sauna coals
Sauna coals should be replaced every six months depending upon use, as they lose their capacity to absorb and retain heat. The larger coals should be placed beneath the smaller ones.

Steam room
The relative humidity in a steam room is probably 95 per cent as the air is saturated with water vapour. The temperature for steam treatment must therefore be lower than that for sauna treatment.

Showers
The shower should be separate from the treatment room. This will avoid time wastage as the therapist can proceed with other treatments. The shower may also form part of the treatment, for example an affusion shower.

- *Protective footwear* – to avoid cross-infection, e.g. disposable paper slippers.
- *Drinking water* – to rehydrate following treatment.
- *Clean towels* – for each client to dry the body after showering.
- *Relaxation area* – to use following treatment.

Hydro bath

- *Water temperature should be between 34–38°C.*
- *Position duckboard* (if used).
- *Client record card* – to assess client and record details of treatment.
- *Shower* – to cleanse the skin and regulate body temperature.
- *Body and hair shampoos* – may be provided.
- *Protective footwear* – to avoid cross-infection, e.g. disposable paper slippers.
- *Clean towels* – for each client to dry the body after showering.
- *Drinking water* – to rehydrate following treatment.
- *Relaxation area* – to use following treatment.

Foam bath

- *Water temperature should be between 37–40°C.*
- *Foam agent* – to add to the water.
- *Position duckboard.*
- *Client record card* – to assess client and record details of treatment.
- *Shower* – to cleanse the skin and regulate body temperature.
- *Body and hair shampoos* – may be provided.
- *Protective footwear* – to avoid cross-infection, e.g. disposable paper slippers.
- *Clean towels* – for each client to dry the body after showering.
- *Drinking water* – to rehydrate following treatment.
- *Relaxation area* – to use following treatment.

Flotation – wet

- *Flotation tank/pool.*
- *Epsom salts.*
- *Chemicals* – to maintain water cleanliness.
- *Client record card* – to assess client and record details of treatment.
- *Client guidance instructions* – clearly sited.
- *Water temperature preheated to 33°C.*
- *Shower* – to cleanse the skin.
- *Petroleum jelly* – to cover any small abrasions.
- *Ear plugs* – to prevent water entering the ears.
- *Neck support* – if required.
- *Clean towels* – for each client to dry the body after showering.
- *Treatment gown* – for client modesty.
- *Protective footwear* – to avoid cross-infection, e.g. disposable slippers.

> **TIP**
>
> **Body temperature**
> The temperature of the skin's surface is 33°C.
> Temperatures above 33°C heat the body – the *hyperthermal effect*. Temperatures below 33°C reduce body temperature – the *hypothermal effect*.

- *Shower facility* – to use following treatment.
- *Drinking water* – to rehydrate following treatment.
- *Relaxation area* – to use following treatment.

Flotation – dry

- *Flotation bed.*
- *Paper roll* – to cover the polymer membrane covering.
- *Treatment product* – to apply to the skin during dry flotation if required.
- *Clean towels* – for the client to dry the body after showering to cleanse the skin.
- *Client record card* – to assess client and record details of treatment.
- *Client guidance instructions* – clearly sited.
- *Clean towels* – for each client to dry the body after showering.
- *Treatment gown* – for client modesty.
- *Protective footwear* – to avoid cross-infection, e.g. disposable slippers.
- *Shower facility* – to remove treatment product.
- *Steamed towels* – should be used to cleanse the skin if there is no shower facility.
- *Drinking water* – to rehydrate following treatment.
- *Relaxation area* – to use following treatment.

Body wrapping

There are various treatment techniques used in body wrapping according to the effect to be achieved or the treatment product used. Always refer to manufacturer's instructions.

The skin may be prepared for treatment by applying an exfoliating treatment or by body brushing, which stimulates both blood and lymphatic circulation.

The body may be wrapped in hot linen bandages that have been soaked in therapeutic ingredients.

Alternatively treatment products using ingredients such as marine minerals or clay may be applied to the skin to achieve different skin conditioning results, including detoxification.

The body can then be wrapped in a thermal blanket, foil, plastic or bandages to maintain and increase body heat which increases lymphatic circulation and fluid loss, achieving a slimming effect.

- *Treatment couch.*
- *Paper briefs* – for the client to wear.
- *Treatment gown* – for client modesty.
- *Headband* – to protect the hair.
- *Clean bandages, plastic, metallic spa sheet* – (dependent upon system used). There must be sufficient bandages available for demand.
- *Bowls* – to mix products as applicable.
- *Water* – used to mix with powder mask ingredients (as applicable).

TIP

Flotation treatment environment
The treatment may be received in silence or meditation/relaxation tapes may be played according to client choice.

TIP

Spa products
Seaweed is particularly high in minerals and is a key ingredient of many spa products. Sea water can be used on its own or mixed with seaweeds, muds and essential oils. Marine minerals include sodium, copper, magnesium, zinc, potassium and iron.

TIP

Headband
The headband may be removed following treatment product application, especially if a scalp massage is to be given whilst the treatment takes effect.

- *Treatment products* – herbal; essential oils; sea clay; marine algae; seaweed.
- *Spatulas/brushes* – to apply treatment products.
- *Thermal blankets* – to maintain heat (if required).
- *Tape measure* – to measure the client before and after treatment if performing a slimming body wrap.
- *Client record card* – to assess client and record details of treatment.
- *Shower facility* – to cleanse the skin before treatment and remove treatment products following treatment.
- *Hot, steamed towels* – may be used to remove product if the workplace does not have a shower facility.

Relaxation room

- *Neutral, calm decor.*
- *Seating* – to allow the client to sit or lie down.
- *Treatment gown* – for client modesty and to maintain warmth.
- *Water facility* – to rehydrate.

Babor

Relaxation room

CLEANING AND MONITORING THE SPA ENVIRONMENT

Outcome 2: Clean, maintain and monitor the spa environment

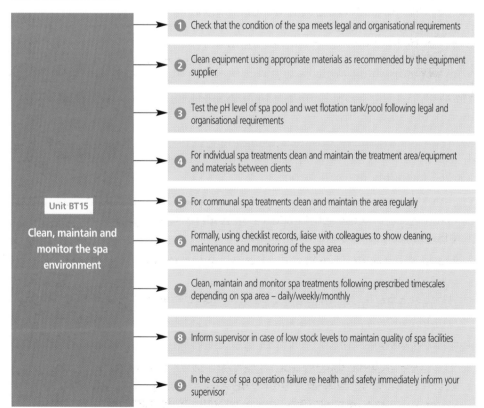

Unit BT15

Clean, maintain and monitor the spa environment

1. Check that the condition of the spa meets legal and organisational requirements

2. Clean equipment using appropriate materials as recommended by the equipment supplier

3. Test the pH level of spa pool and wet flotation tank/pool following legal and organisational requirements

4. For individual spa treatments clean and maintain the treatment area/equipment and materials between clients

5. For communal spa treatments clean and maintain the area regularly

6. Formally, using checklist records, liaise with colleagues to show cleaning, maintenance and monitoring of the spa area

7. Clean, maintain and monitor spa treatments following prescribed timescales depending on spa area – daily/weekly/monthly

8. Inform supervisor in case of low stock levels to maintain quality of spa facilities

9. In the case of spa operation failure re health and safety immediately inform your supervisor

Sterilisation and disinfection

Where the spa treatments are communal and involve heat and moisture they provide ideal breeding conditions for harmful micro-organisms. It is important that all furnishings are regularly cleaned and disinfected as recommended by the manufacturers. This will also avoid stale smells occurring.

A plentiful supply of towels and robes is required. Towels should be boil washed at 60°C to ensure effective laundering and prevent cross-infection.

Written instructions should be displayed in the treatment area and hygiene practice brought to the attention of the client, e.g. showering thoroughly before using the spa pool, etc.

Staff should make regular safety checks to ensure that the facilities are clean, safe and hygienic. These checks may need to be made on a daily, weekly or monthly basis. Sample checklist records follow.

HEALTH AND SAFETY

- All chemical storage areas should be clearly identified and accessible to authorised persons
- Keep all chemicals stored as directed
- Handle the chemicals wearing protective clothing to avoid skin contact and potential injury. Protective eye goggles which conform to the relevant British Safety Standard may also be a requirement
- Follow manufacturer's instructions when carrying out sterilisation and disinfection procedures
- Emergency first aid procedures must be operative and adequate
- First aid resources must be readily available in a designated place
- Fire alarm systems may be available depending upon legal requirements and fire-fighting equipment should be available. Regular training is important to ensure staff are familiar with evacuation procedures

---

Sauna

- Clean the sauna furnishings and floor regularly with a disinfectant.
- Check that the internal shelving is smooth to avoid splinters entering the skin and also harbouring germs.
- Empty the wooden bucket of water when not in use to avoid mould formation.
- When not in use, keep the sauna door open to allow fresh air to enter.

Steam cabinet/room

- Clean the steam cabinet/room internal walls and floor furnishings regularly with a disinfectant that removes surface grease. This also prevents unpleasant smells created by stale body odours.

DAILY SAFETY CHECKS

CLUB: _____   DATE: Mon ____ to Sun ____ of ____ 20 ____

AREA	CONTROL MEASURES/ OBSERVATION POINTS	INITIALS AS CHECKED Please link to action required with an *							ACTION REQUIRED	URGENT YES/NO	DATE ACTIONED
		M	T	W	T	F	S	S			
Spa pool	No surround slip/trip hazards										
	No damaged surfaces										
	Access ladder/handrail secure										
	Air temperature and environment satisfactory										
	Water temperature set to appropriate level with temperature details on display										
	Emergency call button working/tested										
	Water test carried out every 2 hours										
Plant room	Doors kept locked										
	Hazardous substances stored in correct areas										
	Pool dosing controls working and set to correct levels										
	Pool pumps operating correctly										
	Chemical dosing tanks full										
	Chemical injectors not blocked										
	No leaks evident										
	Emergency call button working/tested										
	Evacuation routes/Fire exits clear and freely opening										

DATE	NUMBER OF WASTE BAGS TAKEN OUT DAILY	NAME OF STAFF MEMBER WHO TOOK OUT THE WASTE	DATE	NUMBER OF WASTE BAGS TAKEN OUT DAILY	NAME OF STAFF MEMBER WHO TOOK OUT THE WASTE
M			F		
T			S		
W			S		
T					

DAILY SAFETY CHECKS

CLUB: _____   DATE: Mon ____ to Sun ____ of ____ 20 ____

AREA	CONTROL MEASURES/ OBSERVATION POINTS	INITIALS AS CHECKED Please link to action required with an *							ACTION REQUIRED	URGENT YES/NO	DATE ACTIONED
		M	T	W	T	F	S	S			
Steam room	No slip/trip hazards										
	No damaged floors										
	Door in safe condition, including hinges										
	Light working and in safe condition										
	Wall thermostat in safe condition										
	Steam outlet cover secure, in place/properly guarded										
	Temperature set to appropriate level										
	Seating in safe condition										
	Guidance notes on display in the area										
	Emergency call button working/tested										
	Plant room door locked										
Office	No trip hazard from trailing cables										
	No damaged floor surfaces										
	Air temperature satisfactory										
	Equipment/files/stationery stored safely										
	Evacuation routes/Fire exits clear and freely opening										
	Waste bins emptied										

Daily safety checks courtesy of Spirit Health Club, Holiday Inn Hotel, Newton-le-Willows

DAILY SAFETY CHECKS

CLUB: _____   DATE: Mon ____ to Sun ____ of ____ 20 ____

AREA	CONTROL MEASURES/ OBSERVATION POINTS	INITIALS AS CHECKED Please link to action required with an *							ACTION REQUIRED	URGENT YES/NO	DATE ACTIONED
		M	T	W	T	F	S	S			
Reception and foyer area	No slip/trip hazards										
	No damaged floor surfaces										
	Hazardous substances stored in secure locations										
	Furniture in safe condition										
	Electrical sockets covered										
	Glazing in safe condition										
	Air temperature satisfactory										
	Waste bins emptied										
	Emergency call button working/tested										
	Evacuation routes/Fire exits clear and opening freely										
Sauna	No slip/trip hazards										
	No damaged floor surfaces										
	Evacuation routes/Fire exits clear and freely opening										
	Walls and benches free from damage										
	Stove guarded and secure										
	Light working, in safe condition and properly guarded										
	Benches secure and stable										
	Door in safe condition, including hinges										
	Temperature set to appropriate level 80–100										
	Emergency call button working/tested										
	Guidance notes on display in area										

DAILY SAFETY CHECKS

CLUB: _____   DATE: Mon ____ to Sun ____ of ____ 20 ____

AREA	CONTROL MEASURES/ OBSERVATION POINTS	INITIALS AS CHECKED Please link to action required with an *							ACTION REQUIRED	URGENT YES/NO	DATE ACTIONED
		M	T	W	T	F	S	S			
Female changing rooms and toilets	Hairdryers in safe condition										
	Storerooms locked										
	No hazardous substances left out/unattended										
	No slip/trip hazards										
	No damaged floor surfaces										
	All mirrors in safe condition										
	No damaged lockers										
	No damaged benches										
	No damaged wash basins										
	No damaged toilets										
	No damaged showers/shower areas										
	Temperature of showers/hot water taps not scalding										
	Waste bins emptied										
	Evacuation routes/Fire exits clear and freely opening										
Male changing rooms and toilets	Hairdryers in safe condition										
	Storerooms locked										
	No hazardous substances left out/unattended										
	No slip/trip hazards										
	No damaged floor surfaces										
	All mirrors in safe condition										
	No damaged lockers										
	No damaged benches										
	No damaged wash basins										
	No damaged toilets										
	No damaged showers/shower areas										
	Temperature of showers/hot water taps not scalding										
	Waste bins emptied										
	Evacuation routes/Fire exits clear and freely opening										

Daily safety checks courtesy of Spirit Health Club, Holiday Inn Hotel, Newton-le-Willows

DAILY SAFETY CHECKS

CLUB: _____   DATE: Mon ____ to Sun ____ of ____ 20 ___

AREA	CONTROL MEASURES/ OBSERVATION POINTS	M	T	W	T	F	S	S	ACTION REQUIRED	URGENT YES/NO	DATE ACTIONED
Children's playroom/ crèche	No slip/trip hazards										
	No damaged floor surfaces										
	No hazardous substances in the area										
	Furniture in safe condition and appropriate to children										
	Electrical items in safe condition/out of childs reach										
	Electrical sockets covered										
	Mirrors in safe condition										
	Air temperature satisfactory										
	Toilets clean, safe and undamaged										
	Wash basins clean, safe and undamaged										
	Temperature of hot water not scalding										
	Toys clean and in safe condition										
	Waste bins emptied										
	Emergency call button working/tested										
	Evacuation routes/Fire exits clear and freely opening										
Outside areas	Emergency access routes/Fire exits clear										
	Waste stored in containers										
	Chemical storage secure										
Other											

*Initials as checked — Please link to action required with an ***

WEEKLY SAFETY CHECKS

CLUB: _____   DATE: _____

AREA	CONTROL MEASURES/ OBSERVATION POINTS	DATE CHECKED	INITIALS AS CHECKED	ACTION REQUIRED	URGENT YES/NO	DATE ACTIONED
Office	Wall surfaces in safe condition					
	Ceilings free from leaks or damage					
	Light fittings secure and working					
	Electrical sockets and wiring safe and undamaged					
	Electrical equipment safe and undamaged					
	All equipment used as intended and correctly stored					
Plant room	Wall surfaces in safe condition					
	Ceilings free from leaks or damage					
	Light fittings secure and working					
	Electrical sockets secure, not exposed to water					
	All glazing undamaged					
	All cables and wires not exposed					
	All electrical distribution boards locked					
	Area clean, tidy and secure					
	Day tanks sufficiently apart or partition separation is in place					
Reception and foyer area	Wall surfaces in safe condition					
	Ceilings free from leaks or damage					
	Light fittings secure and working					
	Electrical sockets secure					
	Reception/foyer furniture in safe condition					
	Sufficient supply of sunbed goggles or winkies					

Daily and weekly safety checks courtesy of Spirit Health Club, Holiday Inn Hotel, Newton-le-Willows

WEEKLY SAFETY CHECKS

CLUB: _____   DATE: _____

AREA	CONTROL MEASURES/ OBSERVATION POINTS	DATE CHECKED	INITIALS AS CHECKED	ACTION REQUIRED	URGENT YES/NO	DATE ACTIONED
Outside areas	Walkways around Club are safe and free from potholes					
	Lighting sufficient, secure and working					
	Area around Club free from debris					
	External cables, wires or power sources safe, not dangerous					
Spa pool	Light fittings secure and working					
	All jets working properly					
Children's playroom/ crèche	Procedure in place to protect the children					
	All paperwork in place for each child					
General	First Aid boxes checked and recorded					
	Check waste collection has been carried out					
	Fire alarm test carried out and recorded					
Circulation areas	Wall surfaces in safe condition					
	Ceilings free from leaks or damage					
	Light fittings secure and working					
	Glazing/mirrors secure and safe					
	Electrical sockets safe and covered					
	Notice boards secure and safe					
	Furniture safe and free from damage					

WEEKLY SAFETY CHECKS

CLUB: _____   DATE: _____

AREA	CONTROL MEASURES/ OBSERVATION POINTS	DATE CHECKED	INITIALS AS CHECKED	ACTION REQUIRED	URGENT YES/NO	DATE ACTIONED
Female changing rooms and toilets	Wall surfaces in safe condition					
	Ceilings free from leaks or damage					
	Light fittings secure and working					
	Lockers in working condition					
	Cubicles, benches and vanity units undamaged					
Male changing rooms and toilets	Wall surfaces in safe condition					
	Ceilings free from leaks or damage					
	Light fittings secure and working					
	Lockers in working condition					
	Cubicles, benches and vanity units undamaged					
Relaxation/ lounge areas	Wall surfaces in safe condition					
	Ceilings free from leaks or damage					
	Furniture in safe condition					
	Electrical sockets covered					
	Light fittings secure and working					
Sauna	Walls and benches free from damage					
	Light fitting secure and undamaged					
	Door in safe condition					
Steam room	Walls and benches undamaged, all areas sealed					
	Ceilings free from damage					
	Light fitting secure and undamaged					
	Essence tank full					

Weekly safety checks courtesy of Spirit Health Club, Holiday Inn Hotel, Newton-le-Willows

WEEKLY SAFETY CHECKS

CLUB: _____   DATE: _____

AREA	CONTROL MEASURES/ OBSERVATION POINTS	DATE CHECKED	INITIALS AS CHECKED	ACTION REQUIRED	URGENT YES/NO	DATE ACTIONED
Treatment/ beauty rooms	Wall surfaces in safe condition					
	Ceilings free from leaks or damage					
	Light fittings secure and working					
	Sharps disposal containers provided for the disposal of sharps (if applicable)					
Storage rooms	Wall surfaces in safe condition					
	Ceilings free from leaks or damage					
	No damaged floor surfaces					
	Light fittings secure and working					
	Electrical sockets safe and covered					
	Items in area stored in a safe location					
	Chemicals stored safely					
Others						

MONTHLY SAFETY CHECKS

CLUB: _____   DATE: _____

AREA	CONTROL MEASURES/ OBSERVATION POINTS	DATE CHECKED	INITIALS AS CHECKED	ACTION REQUIRED	URGENT YES/NO	DATE ACTIONED
General	Emergency lighting tested and recorded					
	Fire extinguishers checked and recorded					
	Personal protective equipment checked and recorded					
	Monthly eye wash station checked and recorded					
	Monthly ladder/stepladder checked and recorded					
	Monthly water analysis samples taken for pool/spa					
Female changing rooms and toilets	Monthly showerhead descale					
	Sanitary bins changed by contractor					
Male changing rooms and toilets	Monthly showerhead descale					
Plant room	Plant room safety signage in place					
	PPE available in area for use					
Sauna	Sauna guidance notices in place					
	Check temperature settings					
Steam room	Steam room guidance notices in place					
	Check temperature settings					
Outside areas	Check for damage/deterioration to perimeter walls/ fences					
Spa pool	Guidance notes on display					
	Handrails free from excessive movement					
	Check temperature settings					

Weekly and monthly safety checks courtesy of Spirit Health Club, Holiday Inn Hotel, Newton-le-Willows

Shower

- Check after each client use, clean to remove residue body skin treatment products such as marine clay, etc.
- Ensure there are adequate consumables, body shampoo, etc.

Hydrotherapy spa pool

- The spa is not drained and filled after every use, but relies on the water being continually filtered and chemically treated.
- The edge of the spa pool should be cleaned daily to remove body oils and dead skin cells, which would otherwise form a scum.

HEALTH AND SAFETY

Electrical equipment
All electrical equipment must be protected from contact with water. There should be sufficient drainage around the spa to avoid flooding.

Water testing

It is essential in the spa to ensure that this damp and warm environment is as free from contamination as possible. Diseases such as Legionellosis (Legionnaires' Disease) could prove fatal. This is controlled by following stringent cleaning and water tests to check for water balance.

Backwashing is important to filter out harmful organisms not killed by disinfectant.

An integral strainer removes hair and other debris such as skin flakes and plasters from the water and this should be routinely cleaned to maintain its efficiency.

Water is kept free from potential hazard by the use of chemical disinfectants such as sodium and calcium hypochlorite. The normal operating range of the chemical will depend upon the disinfectants used. The water is tested according to the chemical disinfectant selected to ensure it is safe, effective and balanced. This will also assess the water to prevent water corrosion, staining and scaling.

Water is regularly tested for the following:

- pH (acidity/alkalinity)
- hardness (calcium content)
- temperature

Regular testing of water and maintenance of records is an essential part of spa operation.

These measurements are known as **Langelier index** or **Palintest balanced water index**. Water samples are compared against acceptable operating levels. The quantity of disinfectant agents required will depend upon the hydrotherapy pool usage and the results of the water testing.

The amount of available free chlorine (that available to neutralise contaminants in the water) and the pH value need to be controlled and the amount and the effectiveness of the sterilising agent determined. Further chemicals may also need to be added to raise or lower alkalinity or calcium levels. Chemicals used to control the pH of water include sodium bicarbonate and carbon dioxide (CO_2).

TIP

Backwashing requirement
An electronic meter is available which shows the total dissolved particles in the water. A reading of over 1500 requires a backwash of the water.

HEALTH AND SAFETY

Chemicals
Because of lower water levels in the spa pool it is important to avoid introducing high chemical levels.

The pH of water will be affected by any substance introduced into it. Above pH 7 skin and eye irritation occurs.

Step by step: Water testing

 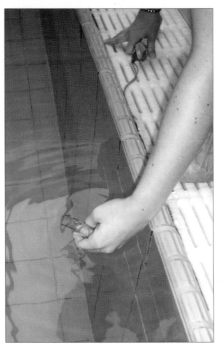

1 Using a thermometer to check the temperature of the water

2 A spa pool water sample is taken. A phenol red tablet is added to the water which develops in colour according to the chemical content. The resulting colour is compared against the colour metric system to identify the reading for pH. This indicates pH chemical level, which should read between 7.2–7.8.

3 Calculate free chlorine level by adding DPD1 tablet to a pool sample.

Rotate disc until a colour match is found, then record the reading.

A total chlorine reading is taken by the addition of a DPD3 tablet to the coloured DPD1 sample. The tablet should be crushed and stirred into the water sample thoroughly.

Wait two minutes for the colour to develop.

Rotate disc until a colour match is found then record the reading.

4 When performing water testing ensure your hands are clean and always avoid touching the tablets.

Outdoor shoes must not be worn beside the pool, protective coverings must be worn.

To calculate the combined chlorine levels subtract the reading using the DPD1 tablet from the reading obtained from the DPD3 tablet.

Ideally, the free chlorine reading should be twice as much as combined chlorine.

A record of tests carried out by an authorised person must be kept for inspection by the local health authority. Failure to carry out this legally required duty by a responsible staff member can result in disciplinary action being taken. The Environmental Health Officer (EHO) will make regular checks to ensure that effective maintenance/hygiene is being enforced and will check standards.

Ventilation

The spa pool will create heat, humidity and chemical smells. Adequate ventilation is necessary. High levels of humidity can cause discomfort because the body cannot cool and becomes overheated but on contact with colder surfaces condensation occurs. This may result in a corrosive action as chemicals are deposited in the air. A relative humidity of 50–70 per cent is recommended. Air must be transported into the area through fan units fitted with filters and then heated.

HEALTH AND SAFETY

pH levels in the water affect the efficiency of disinfection. The pH should always be at a level which renders the water safe. Risks to bathers from chemicals used in disinfection include sore eyes and skin irritation. All bathers must be instructed to have a thorough pre-pool shower to cleanse the skin and avoid water contamination which will affect the pH level.

TIP

Ozone water treatment
Ozone systems may be used as a water treatment for the maintenance of the spa, destroying harmful bacteria and viruses.

HEALTH AND SAFETY

The Environmental Health Authority
Heat treatments for use by the public are subject to inspection by the Environmental Health Authority. In spa treatment, the water is checked for safe bacterial levels and the presence of *E.coli* and coliform organisms.

Cleaning and maintaining specific spa facilities

Hydro baths and foam baths

- These should be drained and cleaned after each client use.
- Specialised cleaning agents should be used as directed by the manufacturer. These will help prevent discolouration, algae formation and limescale build-up.
- The surrounding floor should be dry.
- Dirty towels in the area should be removed.
- All waste should be disposed of in a covered, lined waste bin.

Flotation – wet

- The water should be checked to see that it looks clear; hair, etc. should be removed.
- The surface of the flotation tank should be cleaned regularly to remove body oils and dead skin cells, which would otherwise form a scum. Use sodium hypochlorite solution mixed as per manufacturer's instructions.
- Chemicals are added to maintain water cleanliness.
- The pH of the water is tested daily – a pH of 7.2–7.4 is normal.
- The water is filtered between each session.
- All waste should be disposed of in a covered, lined waste bin.
- The water depth should be 25cm.
- Epsom salts need to be added regularly to maintain water density. Add these as guided by the manufacturer.

Flotation – dry

- Wipe the vinyl surface of the flotation bed with a proprietary disinfectant cleaner following the manufacturer's instructions.
- Ensure the floor area is clean and dry.
- All waste should be disposed of in a covered, lined waste bin.

Body wrapping

- Wipe the surface of the treatment couch with a proprietary disinfectant cleaner following manufacturer's instructions.
- Boil wash the bandages at 60°C using a detergent or as directed by manufacturer's instructions.
- Thoroughly clean bowls used to mix treatment products.
- Brushes used to apply products should be washed in warm soapy water, rinsed, dried and disinfected, e.g. placed in the ultra-violet cabinet.
- All waste should be disposed of in a covered, lined waste bin.

Relaxation room

- Seating should be cleaned regularly.
- Used towels should be collected.
- Ensure there are no spillages from drinks, etc.
- Replenish drinking cups and maintain water facility to rehydrate.
- Empty waste bins.

Outcome 3: Assist with monitoring water, temperature and spa treatments

Unit BT15

Assist with monitoring water, temperature and spa treatment

1. Monitor the spa treatment area and equipment at regular levels to maintain safety and hygiene

2. Check clients at regular intervals to ensure their comfort and wellbeing

3. Observe and advise supervisor of overcrowding in spa areas

4. Monitor clients to ensure they receive treatments for the recommended time. This will reduce the possibility of contra-action

5. Ensure written instructions, re safe equipment use, are displayed where clients are left to use equipment themselves such as the spa pool, sauna and steam. Draw client attention to the notices

6. Provide clear instructions on treatment procedures to enable the client to relax and gain maximum benefit from the spa treatment

7. Provide large towels or bath robes to ensure client privacy and modesty is respected

8. When performing a body wrap service ensure the area is private and screened adequately

9. Observe clients regularly to check for contra-actions such as fainting, nausea and skin irritation. Take necessary action if this occurs

10. When dealing with a client contra-action work within your responsibility, inform the relevant qualified person as necessary

In many cases the spa treatments such as sauna, steam and hydrotherapy and relaxation room will be used on a continuous basis.

Ensure the area is hygienically maintained, any waste such as disposable paper drinking cups removed, floor areas cleaned regularly and any water spillage dealt with to prevent slippage and accidents.

There are checks to be made on a daily, weekly and monthly basis. These ensure that the condition of the spa meets legal and organisational requirements.

Everyday consumables should be checked and replenished daily. Shortages should be reported to the supervisor.

HEALTH AND SAFETY

All equipment should be serviced as recommended by the manufacturers. A trained member of staff should regularly check all electrical equipment for safety, usually on a weekly basis, although daily safety checks occur.

This will follow compliance with the **Electricity at Work Regulation 1989**.

PREPARING FOR SPA TREATMENTS

Preparing the treatment areas

Sauna

- Switch the sauna on at the mains.
- Heat the sauna adequately before use to allow the heat to evenly penetrate the timber surfaces. This will be between 1 hour and 1 hour 30 minutes depending on the size of the sauna.
- Select the preferred temperature – 70–110°C for a Finnish/Tyrolean sauna, 55°C for a Laconium sauna.
- Ensure air vents are open and clear from obstruction.
- Ensure that there is no metal exposed, which would burn the client's skin on contact.
- Fill the wooden bucket with water (if used). Water poured on the sauna coals raises the humidity of the sauna atmosphere.
- Clean towels may be provided for the client to place over the seating.

Steam bath

- Drape clean towels over the seat of the bath and the floor.
- Fill the tank with water to cover the heating element. There should be at least five cm of water above the heating element.
- Cover the opening of the bath with a clean towel to prevent heat loss.
- Switch the machine on at the mains.
- Set the temperature of the bath with the temperature dial and set the control for 15 minutes to preheat the cabinet.

Steam room

- The preheating time will depend on the size of the steam room.
- The recommended temperature is 40°C.
- Provide water for the clients to pour over their skin in the hamman steam room.

Hydrotherapy spa pool

- The water in the spa should be regularly tested to ensure that it has a balanced pH of 7.2–7.8.
- The operating temperature is usually 36–40°C.
- Check the water levels at the beginning of each day and regularly throughout the day.

Hydrobath

- Fill the bath with warm water; ensure the water level covers all jets before operation but will be no higher than the client's shoulders.

TIP

The steam bath is less claustrophobic for clients than a steam room, as the head remains exposed. It also offers a more private treatment and the temperature may be adjusted to suit the client.

- Add ingredients to the bath for their therapeutic properties as the bath is filling.
- The operating temperature is usually 36–40°C.
- Switch the compressor on after the client has got into the bath. Air aerates the bath water creating bubbles through the duckboards' perforated holes, or jets situated in the bath.

Foam bath

- Cover the duckboard with hot water, approximately 38–43°C, to a depth of approximately 10–15 cm.
- Add a foam ingredient to the water in the quantity directed by the cosmetic manufacturer.
- Switch on the compressor, which aerates the water causing the foam to rise. When near the top of the bath, approximately 15 cm, the compressor is switched off.

Flotation – wet

- The water should be filtered between each use and the level checked daily
- The temperature should be checked and maintained at surface body temperature (34.5–35.5°C).
- The condition of the water should be regularly monitored and should be clear at all times.
- The water should be regularly tested to ensure it has a balanced pH of 7.2–7.4.
- Test the alkalinity and free chlorine as per manufacturer's guidelines for usage.
- Ensure the lighting is working in the room.
- Gentle meditation music may be played.
- Check the panic alarm is working.

Flotation – dry

- Heat the water to the correct temperature as advised by the manufacturer.
- Atmospheric mood music may be played to relax the client.
- Raise the board to the top of the tank. Protect the polymer membrane covering with paper roll.
- Ensure the floor is protected adequately to avoid marking from the skin treatment product mask if used.

Body wrapping

- Ensure the room is warm, clean and aromatic to enhance the sensory experience.
- Atmospheric mood music may be played to relax the client.
- Prepare the bandages, if used, as appropriate. This may include soaking the bandages in the treatment product.
- Ensure there are sufficient bandages to cover the body treatment area adequately.

HEALTH AND SAFETY

Underwater massage
The hose attachment, when used, should be kept under water at all times to prevent injury and unnecessary water spillage.

TIP

Music
Music selection is important for inducing the relaxation atmosphere of the spa. Meditational, peaceful background music is an appropriate choice.

TIP

Fibre-optic lighting
Colour influences the senses through the autonomic nervous system. This can affect the client's mental and physical state. Importantly it reinforces the effects of the spa treatment, inducing relaxation and a feeling of wellbeing.

Relaxation room

- Ensure the room is at an ambient temperature (close to body temperature) of 30–40°C.
- Ensure that any waste is removed on a regular basis.

Preparation of the therapist

Ensure that all equipment and materials are regularly maintained. Prepare equipment and materials for specific treatments as required, e.g. foam baths, body wrapping. Ensure operating temperatures of heat and flotation treatments are correct.

Hair, if long, should be secured for reasons of hygiene.

For body wrapping a protective apron may be worn to prevent the treatment mask marking the protective workwear.

Protective clothing may need to be worn when performing tasks such as water testing.

Preparation of the client

Complete a consultation explaining the treatment thoroughly. This will enable the client to gain maximum relaxation from the treatment.

- Complete the client record card and check for contra-indications.
- Explain the treatment procedure to the client, its effects and use of equipment as applicable.
- Explain expected skin sensations, treatment effects and contra-actions that they must inform you of as necessary.
- Long hair should be secured and protected. If chemically treated it is advisable to protect the hair with a towel when receiving heat treatments or with a bathing cap for hydrotherapy.
- The client should remove all outside clothing in a private changing area.
- A secure area should be provided for the client to store clothing and personal possessions.
- Contact lenses, glasses and jewellery should be removed.
- Provide the client with clean towels and disposable slippers.
- Paper briefs may be provided to the client receiving body wrapping or dry flotation body mask treatment.
- It is important to encourage the client to ask questions; allow time for this.
- Encourage the client to visit the toilet before treatment as spa treatments may have a diuretic effect.
- Instruct the client to shower before treatment to remove any cosmetics from the skin's surface. Shower facilities are essential in the spa to cleanse before, during and after spa therapy treatments to remove exfoliating products and body masks from the skin such as those with a mud, marine algae or seaweed base.

HEALTH AND SAFETY

Jewellery will become hot during a heat treatment such as sauna, as will any exposed metal. It is important that the client's skin is not in contact with any metal as this could cause burns.

TIP

Therapeutic showers
Showers may be offered as a therapeutic treatment in itself.
   Multi-sensory showers offer different experiences in temperature and sensation where the shower simulates rain. Certain showers provide water massage therapy. These may be used after each spa experience to revitalise the body.

- Ensure that the shower is at a comfortable temperature and instruct on shower operation. A non-slip mat must be placed in the shower to prevent the client slipping.
- Pre-treatment the client may receive an exfoliating treatment such as a salt, herb or enzyme scrub. This removes dead skin cells, increases blood and lymph circulation and increases cellular metabolism.

PROVIDING SPA TREATMENTS

Sauna

1 Before the client enters the sauna:
   - check the temperature of the sauna by reading the thermometer;
   - check the relative humidity by reading the hygrometer.

2 The client then enters the sauna. New clients should be advised to sit on the lower benches where the air temperature is cooler. Existing clients may move to higher positions.

3 Check client comfort and close the sauna door.

4 After a 10–12 minute period the client should take a shower to cool the skin.

5 The client may return to the sauna for a further 10 minutes. During this time water may be poured onto the coals. The client then takes a final shower.

6 Treatment time is approximately 30 minutes.

7 Record details of the treatment on the client record card.

8 The client should rest after the final shower to allow the blood pressure to return to normal.

Steam bath/room

1 Treatment time is normally 15–20 minutes.

2 Check the temperature in the steam/cabinet room.

3 In the steam bath, adjust the seating height for the height of the client. Close the hinged door.
   - In the *steam room* the client sits in the steam atmosphere.
   - In the *hamman steam room* the client must acclimatise to the heat in different chambers before entering the hottest room.

4 Drape a towel around the neck of the steam bath to avoid loss of steam.

5 The client should be supervised at all times in the steam bath.

6 A shower should be taken at the end of the treatment to cleanse and cool the skin.

7 Record details of the treatment on the client record card.

HEALTH AND SAFETY

Sauna safety
The sauna door has a glass window that enables you to check the client without opening the door. This attention will reassure the client if it is their first sauna session. Check the temperature of the sauna on a regular basis: it may be necessary to record these temperatures.

TIP

Cooling the skin
Cold plunge pools and ice showers offer a stimulating alternative to showers, increasing the metabolic rate and blood pressure slightly.

TIP

Hamman steam room
Traditionally hamman steam treatment is followed by a body exfoliation and massage.

Hydrotherapy spa pool

1 A bathing time of 15–20 minutes is recommended.

2 The client should be monitored during treatment.

3 A shower should be taken at the end of the treatment.

4 Provide the client with water for rehydration.

5 Allow the client to rest following treatment.

6 Record details of the treatment on the client record card and provide aftercare advice.

Hydrobaths

1 The client may be advised to hold onto the handles for balance and support during the underwater massage.

2 The therapist may use the hose feature to direct water over the muscle groups. This helps improve muscle tone. It also helps improve the appearance of soft fat.

3 At conclusion of treatment – 15–20 minutes – switch the compressor off.

4 Assist the client from the bath if required.

5 Provide the client with water for rehydration.

6 Allow the client to rest following treatment.

7 Record details of the treatment on the client record card and provide aftercare advice.

Foam bath

1 The client should lie in the shallow water with their head exposed and their body covered with foam.

2 The client should be allowed to relax but monitored regularly.

3 At the end of the treatments – approximately 15–20 minutes – assist the client from the bath if required.

4 A shower should be taken at the end of the treatment.

5 Provide the client with water for rehydration.

6 Allow the client to relax.

7 Record details of the treatment on the client record card and provide aftercare advice.

Flotation – wet

1 The client should take a cleansing shower and make-up, if used, should have been removed, as it will contaminate the water.

2 Advise the client on how long they will be in the flotation room.

3 Explain how to operate the door, demonstrate this and then observe them to confirm understanding.

4 Explain how to alter the lighting level, adjust the audio level, operate the panic alarm.

5 Explain how they should position themselves in the water. These procedures will facilitate relaxation.

6 The client may then apply the earplugs to prevent water entering the ears.

7 A neck cushion may be provided to support the client's neck.

8 Check on the client during treatment as necessary. If the client is enclosed in a room or capsule this may be through the intercom system. This is an important feature to reassure a highly nervous/anxious client.

9 Following treatment the client should shower to remove excess salt and toxins from the skin's surface.

10 Provide the client with water for rehydration.

11 The client should take time to relax following treatment. A suitable area should be provided for this purpose.

12 Record details of the treatment on the client record card and provide aftercare advice.

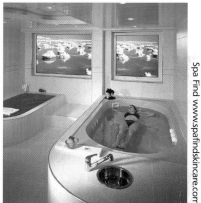

Spa Find www.spafindskincare.com

Wet flotation

Flotation – dry

1 The client should take a cleansing shower and make-up, if used, should have been removed.

2 A body spa treatment product may be applied before the treatment is received.

3 Advise the client on how long the flotation treatment will take.

4 The client lies on top of the board, which is then lowered, controlled by the therapist.

5 A head and scalp massage may be offered whilst the client relaxes.

6 At the end of the treatment the board is raised.

7 The client may shower, specifically if a treatment product has been applied.

8 Provide the client with water for rehydration.

9 The client should take time to relax following treatment. A suitable area should be provided for this purpose.

10 Record details of the treatment on the client record card and provide aftercare advice.

HEALTH AND SAFETY

Client care
During treatment it is important to check the client at regular intervals. This reassures the client and ensures that the client is not suffering from a contra-action.

TIP

Body wraps

Body wraps may be applied to specific body parts only such as the foot and lower leg.

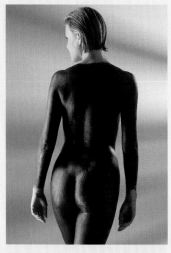

Images courtesy of Spa Find
www.spafindskincare.com

TIP

Foot massage

With some body wrap systems a foot massage is given to the client whilst the body wrapping treatment takes effect.

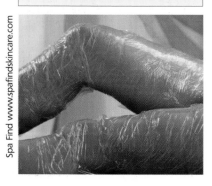

Body wrap for slimming effect

Body wrapping

Ensure the room is warm, clean and aromatic to enhance the sensory experience. Atmospheric mood music may be played to relax the client.

Treatment will vary depending upon the body wrapping system used. The client may receive a pre-treatment before the body wrap such as a heat treatment, shower and exfoliation or dry body brush.

How to provide body wrapping using bandages to induce a slimming, detoxification effect

1 Measure the client from specific areas and record these measurements on the client record card.

2 a. Apply the treatment product to the skin and then unfold and wrap the bandages around the body part.
   or
   b. Unfold and wrap the bandages around the body part that have already been soaked in active treatment ingredients.

3 The client lies on the treatment couch, covered by a thermal blanket to maintain heat.

4 After the recommended treatment time, dependent upon the treatment system but usually 60 minutes, remove the bandages and excess treatment product.

5 Re-measure the client and advise them of inch loss. Record the results on the record card. When the client re-dresses they will usually find their clothes much looser.

6 Provide the client with water for rehydration.

7 Provide aftercare advice and re-book the client if part of a slimming course.

How to provide body wrapping to induce a skin conditioning/detoxification effect

1 Apply a specialist treatment product to body parts to intensify the effect.

2 Mix and apply the treatment product to the skin using a brush.

3 The body may then be wrapped in plastic film and foil or blanket to induce a heating effect depending on the system used.

4 After the recommended time (usually 20 minutes), remove any coverings and treatment product.

5 Further treatment may follow such as massage to the area.

6 Provide the client with water for rehydration.

7 Provide aftercare advice.

HEALTH AND SAFETY

Ensure that the bandage application is not too tight or circulation will be poor in the area, resulting in loss of skin sensation and discomfort.

Relaxation room

1 Guide the client on facilities and use of the room.

2 Explain the importance of drinking water to rehydrate.

3 Check on the client's wellbeing at regular intervals.

TIP	

Body brushing
Body brushing may be provided before a body treatment mask. This will remove dead skin cells, stimulate lymphatic circulation and aid the absorption of the product.

HEALTH AND SAFETY	

Spa cosmetic products
Always check to ensure that you are storing spa products correctly and that the use by date is clearly identified.

COMPLETING THE SPA TREATMENT

Aftercare and advice

- Heat treatments and body wraps cause a loss of body fluids through perspiration. Clients must be provided with still water or fruit juices to rehydrate following treatment. Water imbalances of only one to two per cent can lead to ill health. Increased water consumption aids toxin elimination.

- Following heat treatments and those that induce relaxation, such as flotation treatment, the client should rest for 20–30 minutes. In the case of heat treatments this is to allow body temperatures and blood pressure to return to normal. Sudden movements can cause dizziness and fainting. Monitor the client's reactions during the rest period to check for any contra-action that may occur.

- Avoid infrared or ultra-violet light treatments following heat treatments as the skin will be sensitised.

- Other treatments may follow the service, such as exfoliation and body massage, depending on the service that has been received.

- If the client's aim is weight reduction, give advice on healthy eating habits and increased, regular exercise to raise metabolism, increase fitness and muscle tone. An aftercare leaflet may be given to your client suggesting health advice tips.

- Advise the client about other treatments that can be given. Provide literature or a treatment plan for the client to refer to.

- The client may be encouraged to recreate the benefits of spa mineral treatments at home through the sale of retail products. These contain ingredients such as seaweed, sea salts, algae and mud.

Client resting

Scott and Harrison, Spa: The Official Guide to Spa Therapy at Levels 2 & 3

Contra-actions to heat treatments

In the case of any contra-action to treatment it is important to discontinue treatment if it occurs while the client is receiving the treatment. You should take the appropriate remedial action or contact the relevant member of staff trained to deal with the situation.

Aftercare advice should always be given to the client in the case of a contra-action occurring following the treatment.

Treatment duration too long.

- Low blood pressure and loss of water from the body. Dehydration will occur, causing the cells to absorb fluid from other organs in the body. This may also cause the client to feel faint.

Sauna treatments – relative humidity too low.

- Excessive water loss may occur, leading to dehydration. Also, breathing difficulties may be experienced due to lack of moisture in the air. The temperature of the air will also be higher, causing discomfort when breathing.
- Nausea and dizziness caused by heat exhaustion. This can also be caused by the heat and motion in the spa pool.

Action

- The client should lie down and rest. Raise the legs to avoid fainting.
- Water should be given to rehydrate.
- Seek medical attention if necessary.

Heat exhaustion caused by loss of fluids and sodium chloride (body salt).

This results in symptoms such as dizziness, sickness, headaches and fainting.

Action

- The client should lie down and rest, raise legs to avoid fainting.
- Fruit juices or sports drinks may be taken.
- Seek medical attention if necessary.
- Salt tablets may be recommended by the GP to replace lost salts.

Cramp caused by excessive perspiration.

Action

- Stretch the muscle and massage the area.
- Encourage the client to drink water. Salts may be added to replace lost body salts.

Burning/scalding the skin.

- Through not ladling the water over the coals in the sauna with an outstretched arm, causing the skin to come into contact with the rising steam.
- Skin contact with the heated metal in the sauna.

Action

- Cool the area with cold water immediately.
- Apply a dry dressing, which will not stick to the skin injury. This will protect the skin against infection.
- Medical treatment may be advisable dependent upon the severity of the burn.

Nosebleed due to irritation of the mucous membranes and the effect of the high temperature upon the circulatory system.

Action

- Bend the head forwards. The client should breathe through their mouth.
- The nose should be gently but firmly pinched for about ten minutes.
- If the bleeding does not cease after 30 minutes seek medical attention.

Skin reaction.

- Skin irritation due to chemicals in the spa pool.
- Skin irritation due to high temperatures in the steam or sauna room and irritant effect of the dry heat in the sauna room.

Action

- The client should take a cool shower to remove the products/chemicals from the skin or lower skin temperature.
- Apply a soothing cream to reduce irritation.
- Medical treatment may be advisable if skin irritation continues.

HEALTH AND SAFETY

Heat therapy should not be taken together with ultraviolet treatment to avoid further stimulation of blood in the area.

Respiratory disorders may be aggravated due to the heat of the sauna or steam room.

Clients with respiratory disorders should avoid heat treatments where they have to breathe hot air directly.

Action

- Sit the client down, and if they have medication with them, allow them to use it.
- Seek medical assistance if necessary.

Outcome 4: Assist with the shutdown of treatment areas

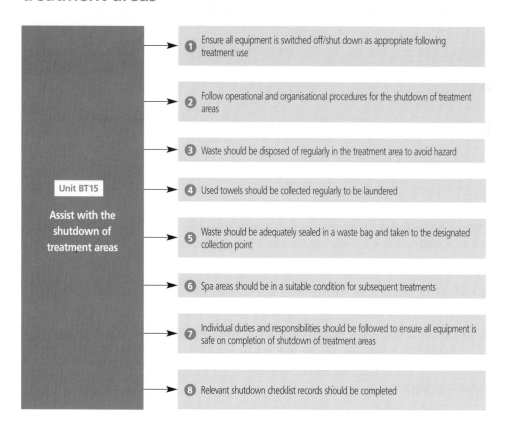

Unit BT15

Assist with the shutdown of treatment areas

1. Ensure all equipment is switched off/shut down as appropriate following treatment use

2. Follow operational and organisational procedures for the shutdown of treatment areas

3. Waste should be disposed of regularly in the treatment area to avoid hazard

4. Used towels should be collected regularly to be laundered

5. Waste should be adequately sealed in a waste bag and taken to the designated collection point

6. Spa areas should be in a suitable condition for subsequent treatments

7. Individual duties and responsibilities should be followed to ensure all equipment is safe on completion of shutdown of treatment areas

8. Relevant shutdown checklist records should be completed

When you have been using the spa for treatments it is important that it is prepared for subsequent treatments.

Hygiene and cleaning of the spa areas should occur following legal and organisational procedures.

Treatment areas should be shut down in accordance with manufacturer's instructions and legal and organisational procedures.

Following treatments such as a hydrotherapy bath or foam bath, equipment, water supplies and electricity at the mains should be switched off.

Following flotation treatment and heat therapy treatments switch off the equipments at the mains.

The spa boosters that create the aeration of the spa pool are switched off at the end of the working day (the switch is located in the plant room). The pump which circulates the water is left on. A back wash, which reverses the flow of water through the filter removing waste particles and debris, may occur.

A final water test is recommended before pool shutdown in order that any problems with water quality can be rectified before the next working day. Regular testing and the maintenance of records is an essential part of spa plant operation and health and safety maintenance.

All waste must be removed in accordance with workplace policy. The spa and all areas of the working environment should be left clean and tidy ready for the next working day. Remember many spas have early opening times so the spa on opening must be ready for use.

It is important to work within your responsibilities when operating shutdown of the spa area.

GLOSSARY OF KEY WORDS

Aftercare advice recommendations given to the client following treatment to continue the benefits of the treatment.

Body wrapping a treatment where the body is wrapped in bandages, plastic sheets or thermal blankets to achieve different therapeutic effects including skin toning and weight loss.

Consultation assessment of client's needs using different assessment techniques, including questioning and natural observation.

Contra-action an unwanted reaction occurring during or after treatment application.

Contra-indication a problematic symptom that indicates that the treatment may not proceed or may restrict treatment application. Further contra-indications identified for spa treatments are discussed in more detail in Chapter 1.

Flotation a spa treatment where the body is suspended (wet flotation) or supported (dry flotation), inducing relaxation.

Foam bath a shallow bath of water containing a foaming agent surrounds the body, achieving a thermal effect. Increased perspiration caused by this effect aids the elimination of wastes and toxins.

Heat treatments these include sauna, steam and the relaxation room. When heat treatments are applied, there is an increase in body temperature of about 1–2°C.

Humidity moisture content of the air.

Hydrotherapy spa treatments where water is used for its therapeutic effect.

Palintest balanced water index the method of regular testing and maintenance of water quality in the spa whirlpools/swimming pool.

pH the degree of acidity or alkalinity measured on a pH scale. This scale goes from 0–14. In the range of 0–6.9 the lower the pH value, the greater the acidity. Above 7, the greater the pH value, the greater the alkalinity. A pH of 7 is neutral – it is neither acid or alkaline. Spa pool water is regularly tested for its pH.

Relaxation room a room of ambient temperature (close to the body's own temperature) and often referred to by the Latin name tepidarium.

Sauna a treatment room of timber construction where the air inside is heated to produce a therapeutic effect on the body.

Spa pool a pool of warm water in which the client sits with jets of air passing through to create bubbles which massage the skin.

Spa treatments treatments used to induce a physical and mental sense of wellbeing. The term 'spa' is said to be derived from a village near Liege in Belgium called Spau. It had mineral hot springs which people could visit to improve their health and ailments.

Steam treatment water is heated to create steam, which is applied to the body for its therapeutic purposes.

Systematic medical condition a medical condition caused by a defect in one of the body's organs, e.g. the heart.

Thermometer equipment used to measure temperature.

Treatment plan after the consultation, suitable treatment objectives are established to treat the client's conditions and needs.

Ventilation the transport of fresh air into an area. The spa pool will create heat, humidity and chemical smells. Adequate ventilation is necessary.

Assessment of knowledge and understanding

You have now learnt about the different spa treatments that are available. To be effective in your role it is necessary for you to be able to prepare, monitor, maintain and assist with the shutdown of the different spa areas. This enables you to effectively assist with spa treatments.

To test your level of knowledge and understanding, answer the following short questions. These will prepare you for your summative (final) assessment.

Prepare work areas for water, temperature and spa treatments

1 Who enforces and monitors local bye-laws with regard to water, temperature and quality for spa treatments?

2 How can cross-infection be avoided in the spa area? State three examples of cross-infections and what can be done to avoid them.

3 What health and safety legislation should be complied with in the spa environment?

4 Where and why should written instructions about treatment usage be displayed?

5 For each of the following treatments explain how you would ensure the spa equipment was safe, clean and hygienic for each client:
  - wet flotation
  - sauna
  - foam bath
  - steam cabinet.

6 How is humidity measured in the sauna room?

Clean and maintain spa environment

1 How are water and chemical concentrations checked for the spa pool?

2 What Health and Safety legislation states how chemicals required for spas should be stored and used?

3 Which treatments are referred to as dry heat?

4 Which treatments are referred to as wet heat?

5 Why should up-to-date records be kept for clients receiving spa treatments?

6 Why should a client shower before entering the spa pool area?

7 Which heat treatment would be most suitable for a client with dry, mature skin? Discuss the reasons for your choice.

8 When planning a slimming treatment, what advice would you give to a client requiring a body wrap?

9 If a client was suffering from stress, what benefits would heat therapy have? Discuss how you would design a treatment plan for such a client. Explain the spa treatment selected, its benefits, and what other treatment could be received by the client.

10 How would you ensure the client's understanding of spa treatment at the consultation?

11 Name six contra-indications to heat therapy treatments.

Assist with monitoring water, temperature and spa treatments

1 What are the recommended operating temperatures of a:
- spa pool
- hydrotherapy bath
- wet flotation
- mild sauna
- steam cabinet treatment?

2 What is the recommended pH level for a:
- spa pool
- wet flotation.

3 What information should be recorded following a body wrap treatment?

4 What dangers can occur if the chemical pH concentrations in the spa pool are not checked regularly?

5 Why must you check a client regularly when they are receiving spa treatments?

6 What should be checked on a daily basis in the spa environment? How is this check recorded?

7 How often should electrical equipment be serviced?

8 What Health and Safety legislation does this comply with?

9 How often may heat treatment be received per week?

10 How long is allowed for the following treatments:
- dry flotation
- body wrap
- spa pool
- hydrotherapy bath?

11 Why is it important for the client to relax following treatment?

12 How can you ensure the client's modesty and privacy is respected when receiving spa treatment?

13 How would you deal with the following contra-actions:
- fainting
- allergic reactions
- breathing difficulties?

14 Give three examples of aftercare advice that may be given following spa treatment.

Assist with the shutdown of spa areas

1 How are the following treatments shut down at the end of the working day?
- spa pool
- sauna room
- steam room?

2 Why is it important to follow organisational procedures for assisting with shutdown of the treatment areas?

3 How are the bandages used in the body wrap cleaned and prepared for the next client?

4 How should waste be disposed of?

glossary

Accident book a written record of any accident occurring in the workplace. Incidents in the accident book should be reviewed to see where improvements to safe working practice could be made.

Accident form a detailed report from to be completed following any accident in the workplace.

Acid mantle the combination of sweat and sebum on the skin's surface, creating an acid film. The acid mantle is protective and discourages the growth of bacteria and fungi. The pH scale is used to measure the alkalinity of a substance using a numbered scale. The skin's pH is 5.5–6.5.

Acrylic paints specialist water-based acrylic paints, which can be diluted and mixed together to create new colours.

Acrylic sculptured nails use powder and liquid to make a strong acrylic from which to form artificial nail structures.

Aftercare advice recommendations given to the client following treatment to continue the benefits of the treatment.

After-wax lotion a product applied to the skin following hair removal to reduce redness and promote skin healing.

Allergen a substance that the skin is sensitive to, and which causes an allergic reaction.

Anagen the active growth stage of the hair growth cycle.

Antioxidant properties of some foods that maintain the health of the skin fighting the damaging effects of free radicals (unstable molecules which can cause skin cells to degenerate) in the body. Antioxidant ingredients are increasingly being included in skin-care preparations to neutralise free radicals or repel them from the skin.

Antiseptic a chemical agent that prevents the multiplication of micro-organisms. It has a limited action and does not kill all micro-organisms.

Appointment arrangement made for a client to receive a service on a particular date and time.

Appraisal a process whereby a supervisor identifies and discusses with an individual their performance and achievements in their job role, against previously set targets.

Arrector pili a small muscle attached to the hair follicle and base of the epidermis. When the muscles contracts (shortens) it causes the hair to stand upright in the hair follicle.

Autoclave an effective method of sterilisation, suitable for small metal objects and beauty therapy tools, where water is boiled under increased pressure and reaches temperatures of 121–134°C.

Bacteria minute single-celled organisms of various shapes. Large numbers live on the skin's surface and are not harmful (non-pathogenic). Others, however, are harmful (pathogenic) and can cause skin diseases.

Base coat a nail polish product applied to protect the natural nail and prevent staining from coloured nail polish.

Bevelling a nail filing technique used at the free edge of the nail to ensure it is smooth.

Blepharitis inflammation of the eyelid caused by an infection or an allergic reaction.

Blood nutritive liquid circulating through the blood vessels. It transports essential nutrients to the cells and removes waste products. It also transports other important substances such as oxygen and hormones.

Blue nail condition where the nail bed has a blue tinge rather than a healthy pink colour due to poor blood circulation in the area.

Blusher cosmetic applied to add warmth to the face and emphasise the facial contours.

Body language communication involving the body.

Body wrapping a treatment where the body is wrapped in bandages, plastic sheets or thermal blankets to achieve different therapeutic effects including skin toning and weight loss.

Bone the hardest structure in the body. It protects the underlying structures, gives shape to the body and provides an attachment point for muscles.

Bruised nail nail condition where the nail appears blue/black in colour where bleeding has occurred on the nail bed following injury.

Buffer a manicure tool with a handle made of plastic and a pad with a replaceable cover. Used on the nail to give a sheen, increase blood supply to the area, and if used with the gritty cream buffing paste, to help smooth out nail surface irregularities.

Bunion a foot condition. The large joint at the base of the big toe protrudes, forcing the big toe inwards towards the other toes.

Burn injury to the skin caused by excess heat, the skin appears red and may blister.

Callus a foot condition displaying thick, yellowish hardened skin, usually found on prominent areas of the foot such as the heel.

Cash float a small sum of money to provide change at the beginning of each day.

Catagen the stage of the hair growth cycle where the hair becomes detached from its source of nourishment, the dermal papilla, and stops growing.

Cell the smallest and simplest unit capable of life.

Certificate of registration awarded when the premises have been successfully inspected to ensure that the local bye-laws are being followed in relation to cosmetic piercing.

Charge card an alternative form of payment where the complete amount of credit spent must be repaid each month to the card company.

Cheque an alternative form of payment to that of using cash. A cheque must be accompanied by a cheque-guarantee card.

Chilblains poor blood supply where the toes become red, blue or purple in colour and the area may become painful and itchy; aggravated in cold weather.

Chiropodist A chiropodist is a person who is trained and qualified to treat minor foot complaints.

Circulatory system transports material around the body.

Cleanser a skin-care preparation that removes dead skin cells, excess sweat and sebum, make-up and dirt from the skin's surface to maintain a healthy skin complexion. These are formulated to treat the different skin types, skin characteristics and facial areas.

Clinical waste materials that have come into contact with body fluids, classed as clinical waste, must be collected and disposed of by special arrangements. The disposal of clinical waste is controlled by the Environment Agency.

Code of conduct workplace service standards with regard to appearance and behaviour whilst in the working environment.

Code of practice the expected standards and behaviour for the professional beauty therapist to follow, which will uphold the reputation of the industry and ensure best working practice for the industry and protect members of the public. Beauty therapy professional bodies produce codes of practice for their members. A business may have its own code of practice.

Cold wax a wax used straight from its container or mildly heated. Cold waxes are often natural rubber substances in a volatile solvent. The solvent evaporates to leave a rubber film with the hairs embedded in it: this is removed with a wax removal strip.

Coloured polishes used to provide a base colour on the nail or to add colour to the nail art design.

Comedone removal facial techniques used to extract comedones (blackheads) from the skin. A small tool called a comedone extractor is used for this purpose.

Communication the exchange of information and the establishment of understanding between people.

Complaint procedure a formal, standardised approach adopted by the organisation to handle any complaints.

Concealer cosmetic product used to disguise minor skin imperfections such as blemishes, uneven skin colour or shadows.

Conjunctivitis a bacterial infection. Inflammation of the mucous membrane that covers the eye and lines the eyelid. The skin of the inner conjunctiva of the eye becomes inflamed, the eye becomes very red, itchy and sore, and pus may exude from the eye area.

Consent form written permission obtained from a parent or guardian to perform a treatment on a client under 16 years of age.

Consultation assessment of client's needs using different assessment techniques, including questioning and natural observation.

Consumer Protection (Distance Selling) Regulations 2000 these regulations are derived from a European Union Directive and cover the supply of goods/services made between suppliers acting in a commercial capacity and consumers. They are concerned with purchases made by telephone, fax, internet, digital television and mail order.

Consumer Protection Act 1987 this act follows European Union (EU) Directives to protect the customer from unsafe, defective services and products that do not reach safety standards.

Consumer Safety Act 1978 this act aims to reduce risks to consumers from potentially dangerous products.

Continuous Professional Development (CPD) activities undertaken to develop technical skill and expertise to ensure current, professional experience in the beauty industry is maintained.

Contra-action an unwanted reaction occurring during or after a treatment application.

Contra-indication a problematic symptom that indicates that treatment may not proceed.

Control of Substances Hazardous to Health (COSHH) Regulations 2002 these regulations require employers to identify hazardous substances used in the workplace and state how they should be stored and handled.

Contour cosmetics applied to cosmetically change and enhance the shape of the face and facial features.

Controlled Waste Regulation 1992 categorises waste types. The Local Authority provides advice on how to dispose of waste types in compliance with the law.

Corn small areas of thickened skin on the foot. Often white in appearance.

Cortex the thickest layer of the hair structure.

Cosmetic Products (Safety) Regulations 2004 part of Consumer Protection legislation that requires cosmetics and toiletries be safe in their formulation and safe for use for their intended purpose as a cosmetic and comply with labelling requirements.

Credit card an alternative form of payment to that of using cash. These cards are held by those who have a credit account, where there is a pre-arranged borrowing limit. These can only be used if your business has an arrangement to deal with the relevant credit-card company.

Cross-infection the transfer of contagious micro-organisms.

Customer care statement defined customer service standards that are expected.

Cuticle cream or oil a cosmetic preparation used to condition the skin of the cuticle.

Cuticle knife a metal tool used on the nail to remove excess *eponychium* (the extension of the skin of the cuticle at the base of the nail).

Cuticle remover a cosmetic preparation used to soften and loosen the skin cells and cuticle from the nail.

Cyst localised pocket of sebum that forms in the hair follicle or under the sebaceous glands in the skin. Semi-globular in shape, either raised or flat, and hard or soft. Cysts are the same colour as the skin, or red if bacterial infection occurs.

Dangerous Substances and Preparations (Nickel) (Safety) Regulations 2000 the use of nickel has been found to cause allergies. Check that the metal used for your ear piercing jewellery complies with the Regulations.

Data Protection Act 1998 legislation designed to protect client privacy and confidentiality.

Debit card an alternative method of payment where the card authorises immediate debit of the cash amount from the client's account.

Dehydrate removal of moisture and oil from the natural nail plate necessary to ensure the effective application of the artificial nail product.

Dermal papilla an organ that provides the hair with blood, necessary for hair growth.

Dermis the inner portion of the skin, situated underneath the epidermis.

Diabetes a disease that prevents sufferers breaking down glucose in their cells.

Disability Discrimination Act 1995 implemented to prevent disabled persons being discriminated against during recruitment and employment. Employers have a responsibility to remove physical barriers and to adjust working conditions to prevent discrimination on the basis of having a disability.

Disinfectant a chemical agent that destroys most micro-organisms when cleaning non-metallic tools, equipment and work areas.

Disulphide bonds two chemical sulphur bonds joined together forming a chemical bond in the cortex of the hair.

Dotting technique application of dots of nail paint/polish using a marbling/dotting tool to create a design or enhance a design on the nail plate.

Ear piercing is the piercing of the lobule part of the ear, which is composed of fibrous, fatty tissues. An ear-piercing system is used to pierce the ear and insert a stud to adorn the ear.

Eczema of the nail inflammation of the skin, differing changes to the nail may occur including ridges, pitting, nail separation and thickening of the nail.

Effleurage a stroking massage manipulation used to begin the massage, as a link manipulation, and to complete the massage sequence. Applied in a rhythmic, continuous manner, it induces relaxation.

Eggshell nail condition where thin, fragile white nails curve under at the free edge.

Electrical current hair removal techniques, galvanic electrolysis, electrical epilation and the blend epilation are permanent hair removal techniques that use an electrical current. The current is passed to the hair root via a fine needle inserted into the hair follicle. The current destroys the hair root, preventing hair regrowth.

Electricity at Work Regulations 1989 these regulations state that every piece of equipment in the workplace should be tested every 12 months by a qualified electrician. It is the responsibility of the employer to keep records of the equipment tested and the date it was checked.

Emery board a nail file used to shape the free edge of the nail.

Employers' Liability (Compulsory Insurance) Act 1969 this provides financial compensation to an employee should they be injured as a result of an accident in the workplace. A certificate indicating that a policy of insurance has been purchased should be displayed.

Epidermis the outer layer of the skin.

Equal opportunity non-discrimination on the basis of sex, race, disability, age, etc.

Equal opportunities policy the Equal Opportunities Commission (EOC) states it is best practice for the workplace to have a written equal opportunities policy. This will include a statement of the commitment to equal opportunities by the employer and the structure for implementing the policy.

Erythema reddening of the skin caused by increased blood circulation to the area.

Exfoliant a treatment used to remove excess dead skin cells from the surface of the skin, which has a skin cleansing, cell rejuvenating action. This process can be achieved using a specialised cosmetic, or mechanically by using facial equipment where a brush is rotated over the skin's surface.

Exfoliation a salon treatment used to remove excess dead skin cells from the surface of the skin, which has a skin cleansing action. This process can be achieved using a specialised cosmetic, or mechanically by using facial equipment where a brush is rotated over the skin surface.

Eyebrow colour cosmetic applied to emphasise the eyebrows, alter their shape and can make sparse eyebrows look thicker.

Eyebrow shaping involves the removal of eyebrow hair to create a new shape or to remove stray hairs to maintain the existing brow shape. Small metal tools called tweezers are used to remove the hairs, or alternatively wax depilation may be used.

Eyelash and eyebrow tinting definition of the brow and lash hair, achieved by the application of a permanent dye, especially formulated for use around the delicate eye area.

Eyelash adhesive an adhesive used during perming eyelash treatment to secure the eye lashes to the curlers.

Eyelash curlers small flexible rods around which the natural eyelashes are curled during eyelash perming treatment.

Eyelash perming a chemical treatment applied to the eyelashes to permanently curl the lashes, which enhances the appearance of the eyes.

Eyeliner cosmetic applied to define and emphasise the eye area.

Eyeshadow cosmetic applied to the eye to complement the natural eye colour, to give definition to the eye area and enhance the natural shape of the eye.

Face shape the size and shape of the client's facial bone structure. Face shapes include: oval, round, square, heart, diamond, oblong and pear.

Facial a treatment to improve the appearance, condition and functioning of the skin and underlying structures.

Facial features the size and shape of a person's nose, eyes, forehead, chin, neck, etc. When applying make-up products, make-up application can emphasise or minimise the facial features.

False eyelashes threads of nylon fibre or real hair attached to the client's natural eyelash hair. There are two main types: individual or strip.

Fibreglass nail extensions a nail extension system using fibreglass in conjunction with a nail tip.

Fire Precautions Act 1971 legislation that states that all staff must be familiar with and trained in fire and emergency evacuation procedures for their workplace.

Fire Precautions (Workplace) Regulations 1997 this legislation requires that every employer must carry out a risk assessment for the premises in relation to fire evacuation practice and procedures, under the Management of Health and Safety Regulations 1999.

Fixing/neutralising lotion usually containing sodium bromate, which makes the curl produced during eyelash perming permanent.

Flat stone small polish-secure gems.

Flat stone/rhine stone technique polish-secure gems are applied to create or enhance a nail art design.

Flotation a spa treatment where the body is suspended (wet flotation) or supported (dry flotation), inducing relaxation.

Foam bath a shallow bath of water containing a foaming agent surrounding the body achieving a thermal effect. Increased perspiration caused by this effect aids the elimination of waste and toxins.

Foiling metallic foil, available in various colours and designs, is secured to the nail using foil adhesive.

Folliculitis a bacterial infection where pustules develop in the skin tissue around the hair follicle.

Foot cream/oil a cosmetic mixture of waxes and oils applied to soften the skin of the feet and cuticles.

Foot rasp a pedicure tool used to remove excess dead skin from the foot.

Foot spa a foot bath incorporating massage and water aeration, creating a bubbling effect to cleanse and relax the feet.

Foundation a make-up product applied to produce an even skin tone, to disguise minor skin blemishes and as a contour cosmetic.

Freehand technique handling and applying nail art materials to create different designs and illustrations upon the nail plate.

Fungi microscopic plants that are parasites. Fungal diseases of the skin feed off the waste products of the skin. They are found on the skin's surface or they can attack deeper tissues.

Gel nail product that can be applied over a tip or sculpted over a nail form, as with acrylic. Some gel systems require the use of ultra-violet light to set the gel; others use a spray activator.

Gift voucher a pre-payment method for beauty therapy services or retail sales.

Glitter sparkly powder applied to add shimmer to a nail art design.

Glitter dust technique fine, sparkly powder is applied with a glitter mixer and positioned on the nail.

Greater London Council (General Powers) Act 1981 this act covers the London boroughs and relates to cosmetic piercing. It provides that no person can carry out cosmetic piercing unless they and the business are registered. It also states what records are required to be kept.

Grievance a cause for concern or complaint.

Hair a long slender structure that grows out of, and is part of the skin. Each hair is made up of dead skin cells, which contain the protein called keratin.

Hair follicle an appendage (structure) in the skin formed from epidermal tissue. Cells move up the hair follicle from the bottom (the hair bulb), changing in structure, to form the hair.

Hair growth cycle the cyclical pattern of hair growth, which can be divided into three phases: anagen, catagen and telogen.

Hairy moles moles exhibiting coarse hairs from their surface.

Hand cream/oil a cosmetic mixture of waxes and oils applied to soften the skin of the hands and cuticles.

Hangnail nail condition where small pieces of epidermal skin protrude between the nail plate and nail wall, accompanying a dry cuticle condition.

Hazard something with potential to cause harm.

Health and Safety at Work Act 1974 legislation that lays down the minimum standards of health, safety and welfare requirements in each workplace.

Health and Safety (Display Screen Equipment) Regulations 1992 these regulations cover the use of visual display units (VDUs) and computer screens. They specify acceptable levels of radiation emissions from the screen and identify correct working posture, seating position, permitted working heights and rest periods.

Health and Safety (First Aid) Regulations 1981 legislation that states that workplaces must have first aid provision.

Health and safety policy each employer of more than five employees must formulate a written health and safety policy issued to their employees outlining their health and safety responsibilities.

Heat rash a reaction to heat exposure where the sweat ducts become blocked and sweat escapes into the epidermis. Red pimples occur and the skin becomes itchy.

Heat treatments these include sauna, steam and the relaxation room. When heat treatments are applied, there is an increase in body temperature of about 1–2°C.

Highlighter a make-up product that draws attention to or emphasises features.

Hirsutism a term used to describe a pattern of growth that is abnormal for a person's sex, such as when a woman's hair follows a male growth pattern.

Histamine a chemical released when the skin comes into contact with a substance that it is allergic to. Cells called 'mast cells' burst, releasing histamine into the tissues. This causes the blood capillaries to dilate, which increases blood flow to limit skin damage and begin repair.

Hoof stick a nail tool used to gently push back the softened cuticles.

Hot wax a system of wax depilation used to remove hair from the skin. Hot wax cools and sets on contact with the skin. They contain a blend of waxes, such as beeswax and resins, which keep the wax flexible. Soothing ingredients are often included to avoid skin irritation.

Humidity moisture content of the air.

Hydrogen peroxide (H_2O_2) an oxidant, a chemical that contains available oxygen atoms and encourages chemical reactions.

Hydrotherapy spa treatments where water is used for its therapeutic effect.

Hygiene the recommended standard of cleanliness necessary in the salon to prevent cross-infection and secondary infection.

Hyperpigmentation increased pigment production.

Hypertrichosis abnormal excessive hair growth. It is usually due to abnormal conditions in the body caused by disease or injury.

Hypopigmentation loss of pigmentation.

Infestation a condition where animal parasites invade and live off a host.

Ingrowing hair a build-up of skin occurs over the hair follicle causing the hair to grow under the skin.

Job description written details of a person's specific work role, duties and responsibilities.

Keloids overgrowths of scar tissue, occurring at the site of the ear-piercing.

Keratin protein produced by cells in the epidermis called keratinocytes. Keratin makes the skin tough and reduces the passage of substances into our bodies. Each hair and nail contains keratin.

Laser hair removal a technique of permanent hair removal. Laser energy is passed through the skin which stops the activity of the hair follicle creating hair growth through a process called photothermolysis.

Legislation laws affecting the workplace in relation to treatments and services, systems and procedures, the premises, employers and employees.

Leuconychia nail condition where white spots or marks appear on the nail plate.

Lipgloss cosmetic applied to the lips to provide a moist, shiny look to the lips.

Lipliner cosmetic used to define the lips, creating a perfectly symmetrical outline.

Lipstick cosmetic applied to the lips to add colour and keep the lips soft and supple.

Local Government Act 2003 (section 120 and schedule 6) amends the 1982 act; enables each Local Authority to regulate businesses providing cosmetic body piercing. Each Local Authority can introduce its own bye-laws to set the standards for cosmetic piercing.

Local Government (Miscellaneous Provisions) Act 1982 legislation that requires that salons offering any form of skin piercing be registered with the local health authority. This registration includes both the operators who will be carrying out the treatment and the salon premises where the treatment will be carried out.

London Local Authorities Act, 1991 this Act states that no person shall carry out cosmetic piercing at an establishment without obtaining a licence from a participating council. Conditions can be attached to the licence such as hygiene practices, age restrictions, etc.

Longitudinal ridges nail condition where grooves appear in the nail plate, running along the length of the nail from the cuticle to the free edge.

Lymph a clear, straw-coloured liquid circulating in the lymph vessels and lymphatics of the body, filtered out of the blood plasma.

Lymphatic system closely connected to the blood system. Its primary function is defensive: to remove bacteria and foreign materials to prevent infection.

Maintenance scheduled treatments necessary following the application of artificial nails to repair any damage and maintain appearance as the natural nail grows underneath.

Make-up cosmetics applied to the skin of the face to enhance and accentuate or de-emphasise certain facial features. Make-up products create balance in the face to reduce or emphasise.

Make-up products different cosmetics available to suit skin type, colour and condition, i.e. sensitive or mature. Make-up products include: concealing and contour cosmetics, foundations, translucent powders, eyeshadows, eyeliners, brow liners, mascaras, lipsticks, lipglosses, lipliners.

Management of Health and Safety at Work Regulations 1999 this legislation provides the employer with an approved code of practice for maintaining a safe, secure working environment.

Manicure a treatment to improve the appearance and condition of the skin and nails of the hands.

Manual Handling Operations Regulations 1992 legislation that requires the employer to carry out a risk assessment of all activities undertaken which involve manual handling (lifting and moving objects).

Marbling technique dots of different nail paint/polish colours are mixed together using a 'marbling tool' to create a marbled effect on the nail plate.

Mascara cosmetic that enhances the natural eyelashes, making them appear longer, changed in colour and/or thicker.

Mask a skin-cleansing treatment preparation applied to the skin which may contain different ingredients. It can have a deep cleansing, toning, nourishing or refreshing effect. It may be applied to the hands, feet and face.

Massage manipulation of the soft tissues of the body, producing heat and stimulating the muscular, circulatory and nervous system.

Massage manipulations movements which are selected and applied according to the desired effect, which may be stimulating, relaxing or toning. Massage manipulations include effleurage, petrissage, percussion (also known as tapotement) and vibration.

Melanin a pigment in the skin and hair that contributes to skin and hair colour.

Melanocytes cells that produce the skin pigment melanin that contributes to skin colour.

Messages communication of information to another person in written or verbal form.

Milium extraction facial technique used to extract milia (whiteheads) from the skin. A small tool called a milia extractor is used for this purpose, which superficially pierces the epidermis allowing effective removal of the milia.

Moisturiser a skin-care preparation whose formulation of oil and water helps maintain the skin's natural moisture by locking in moisture, offering protection and hydration. The formulation is selected to suit the skin type, facial characteristics and facial areas.

Muscle contractile tissue responsible for movement of the body.

Muscle tone the normal degree of tension in healthy muscle.

Nail art nail decoration applied to the natural nail plate or artificial nail, using nail art materials including nail polish, transfers, gemstones, glitter and foil.

Nail file tool used to shape, reduce the length, blend the nail surface to create balance and impart shine. The surface texture, referred to as 'grit', is numbered and varies according to its purpose. The lower the number of grit, the coarser the file.

Nail forms made of paper or metal, these are placed at the end of the nail. The natural nail is lengthened onto the nail form using nail extension product.

Nail polish a clear or coloured nail product that adds colour/protection to the nail. Cream polish has a matt finish and requires a top coat application. Pearlised polish produces a frosted, shimmery appearance and top coat is not required.

Nail polish drier an aerosol or oil preparation applied following nail polish application to increase the speed at which the polish hardens.

Nail polish remover a solvent used to remove nail polish and grease from the nails prior to applying polish.

Nail polish solvent used to thin nail polish and restore its consistency.

Nail strengthener a nail polish product that strengthens the nail plate, which has a tendency to split.

Nail tips plastic nail tips used to extend the length of the natural nail.

Nail wrap a material such as silk or fibreglass is attached to the nail to repair or strengthen the natural nail.

Nails hard, horny epidermal cells that protect the living nail bed of the fingers and toes.

National Occupational Standards for Beauty Therapy Standards that set the relevant performance objectives, range statements and knowledge specifications to support performance. These can be obtained from the Hairdressing and Beauty Industry Authority (Habia) website: www.habia.org.uk.

Nerve a collection of single neurones surrounded by a protective sheath through which impulses are transmitted between the brain or spinal cord and another part of the body.

Nervous system co-ordinates the activities of the body by responding to stimuli received by sense organs.

Neurones nerve cells which make up nervous tissue.

Non-verbal communication communicating using body language, i.e. using your eyes, face and body to transmit your feelings.

Nutrition the process of nourishment derived from food, required for the body's growth, energy, repair and production.

Oedema extra fluid in an area, causing swelling.

Onycholysis nail condition where the nail plate separates from the nail bed.

Onychopagy nail condition where a person bites their nails excessively.

Onychorrhexis nail condition where a person has split, flaking nails.

Opalescent blending technique opalescent paints applied over a base nail polish colour creating an iridescent effect on the nails.

Orange stick a disposable wooden tool used around the cuticle and free edge of the nail and to apply products to the nail.

Overlay a thin coating applied to the natural nail or an application over the natural nail and tip.

Palintest balanced water index the method of regular testing and maintenance of water quality in the spa whirlpool/swimming pool.

Paraffin wax paraffin wax is heated and applied to the skin of the hands to provide a warming effect. This improves skin functioning, aids the absorption of treatment products and is beneficial to ease the discomfort of arthritic and rheumatic conditions.

Paronychia a bacterial infection where swelling, redness and pus appears in the cuticle area of the nail wall.

Patch test a.k.a. skin text – a method used to assess skin tolerance to substances.

Pedicure a treatment to improve the appearance and condition of the skin and nails of the feet.

Perm solution usually containing 6% thioglycollate, which when applied to the eyelash hair softens and curls the hair into its new shape.

Personal Protective Equipment (PPE) at Work Regulations 1992 this legislation requires managers to identify, through a risk assessment, those activities that require special protective equipment to be worn.

Petrissage massage manipulation which applies intermittent pressure to the tissues of the skin, lifting them away from the underlying structures. Often known as compression movements.

pH the degree of acidity or alkalinity measured on a pH scale. This scale goes from 1-14. In the range of 0-6.9 the lower the pH value, the greater the acidity. Above 7, the greater the pH value, the greater the alkalinity. A pH of 7 is neutral – neither acid nor alkaline. Spa water is regularly tested for its pH.

Photothermolysis an effect created when using a laser for hair removal. The melanin pigment that provides hair colour absorbs the laser energy, which is converted to heat, and at a sufficient temperature destroys the part of the hair follicle where the cells divide to create the hair.

Pigment the skin's and hair's colour, called melanin. The amount of pigment varies for each client, resulting in different skin/hair colour.

Polish secures jewellery and tiny gems.

Polymerisation a chemical reaction that occurs when using liquid monomer and powder polymer during acrylic nail application, and which concludes with hardening.

Positive skin sensitivity test an allergic reaction to the skin test. The skin appears red, swollen and feels itchy.

Posture the position of the body, which varies from person to person. Good posture is when the body is in alignment. Correct posture enables you to work longer without becoming tired. It prevents muscle fatigue, stiff joints and repetitive strain injury (RSI).

Powder cosmetic applied to set the foundation, disguise minor skin blemishes and make the skin appear smoother and oil-free.

Pre-wax lotion an antibacterial skin cleanser to clean the skin before wax application.

Prices Act 1974 this act states that the price of products has to be displayed in order to prevent the buyer being misguided.

Promotion ways of communicating products or services to clients to increase sales.

Provision and Use of Work Equipment Regulations (PUWER) 1998 the regulations lay down important health and safety controls on the provision and use of equipment.

Psoriasis of the nail an inflammatory condition where there is an increased production of cells in the upper part of the skin. Pitting occurs on the surface of the nail.

Pterygium nail condition where the cuticle is thickened and overgrown.

Public Liability Insurance protects employers and employees against the consequences of death or injury to a third party while on the premises.

Punctuality arriving at the correct time.

Reception the area where clients are received.

Receptionist person responsible for maintaining the reception area, scheduling appointments and handling payments.

Record cards confidential cards recording personal details of each client registered at the business. This information may be stored electronically on the salon's computer.

Relaxation room a room of ambient temperature (close to the body's temperature) often referred to by the Latin name *tepidarium*.

Reporting of Injuries, Diseases and Dangerous Occurences Regulations (RIDDOR) 1995 RIDDOR requires the employer to notify the local enforcement officer in writing in cases where employees or trainees suffer personal injury at work.

Resale Prices Act 1964 and 1976 this act states that the manufacturer can supply a recommended price (MRRP), but the seller is not obliged to sell at the recommended price.

Resin an adhesive used in the fibreglass artificial nail system.

Rhine stones polish-secure gems.

Ridge-filler a nail product used on ridged nails that improves the nails appearance and provide a more even surface.

Roller wax a warm wax system used to remove hair from the skin. The wax is contained in a cartridge container with a disposable applicator, which rolls the wax onto the skin's surface. The applicator is renewed for each client.

Sales and Supply of Goods Act 1994 goods must be as described, of merchantable quality and fit for their intended purpose.

Sanitisation the destruction of some, but not all, living micro-organisms when cleansing the skin.

Sauna spa treatment room of timber construction where the air inside is heated to produce a therapeutic effect on the body.

Scissors nail tools used to shorten the length of the nail before filing.

Sculptured nails artificial nails formed using a liquid and powder system or a gel. The mixture is sculpted and built up over the natural nail plate and extends past the end of the nail onto a nail form.

Sebaceous gland a minute sac-like organ usually associated with the hair follicle. The cells of the gland decompose and produce the skin's natural oil sebum. Found all over the body, except for the soles of the feet and the palms of the hands.

Sebum the skin's natural oil which keeps the skin supple.

Secondary infection bacterial penetration into the skin causing infection occurring as a result of injury to the client during treament, or if the client already has an open cut.

Shader a make-up product that draws attention away – minimises.

Skin allergy if the skin is sensitive to a particular substance an allergic skin reaction will occur. This is recognised by irritation, swelling and inflammation.

Skin analysis assessment of the client's skin type and condition.

Skin appendages structures within the skin including sweat glands (that excrete sweat), hair follicles (that produce hair), sebaceous glands (produce the skin's natural oil sebum) and nails (a horny substance that protects the ends of the fingers/toes).

Skin characteristics whilst looking at the skin type of the skin additional characteristics may be seen. These include skin that may be sensitive, dehydrated, moist or oedematous (puffy).

Skin removal accidental removal of the upper, dead, protective cornified layer of the skin, leaving the granular layer exposed.

Skin sensitivity (patch) test method used to assess skin tolerance/sensitivity to a particular substance or treatment.

Skin tags skin-coloured threads of skin 3–6mm long, projecting from the skin's surface.

Skin tone the strength and elasticity of the skin.

Skin type the different physiological functioning of each person's skin dictates their skin type. There are four main skin types: normal (balanced), dry (lacking in oil), oily (excessive oil) and combination (a mixture of two skin types, e.g., dry and oily).

Spa pool a pool of warm water in which the client sits with jets of air passing through to create bubbles, which massage the skin.

Spa treatments treatments used to induce a physical and mental state of wellbeing. The term 'spa' is said to be derived from a village near Liege in

Belgium called *Spau*. It had mineral hot springs which people could visit to improve their health and ailments.

Specialist skin-care treatment products additional skin-care preparations available to target improvement. These products include eye gels, throat creams and ampoule treatments.

Steam treatment a warming effect created by boiling water, which is then vapourised and used on the skin to achieve both cleansing and stimulation.

Sterilisation the total destruction of all micro-organisms in metal tools/objects.

Stress strip a narrow piece of fibreglass mesh, placed across the nail where the nail tip is blended into the natural nail. This is a weak area and the stress strip provides additional strength.

Strip sugar a system of wax depilation similar to warm wax technique, used to remove hair from the skin. Made from sugar, lemons and water, the paste is applied to embed the hair, which is then removed from the skin using a wax removal strip.

Striping tape coloured self-adhesive tape applied to create a striping effect in nail art.

Striping technique stripes of colour are applied in varying widths using a striping brush on the nail plate.

Stye bacterial infection. Infection of the sebaceous glands of the eyelash hair follicles. Small lumps appear on the inner rim of the eyelid and contain pus.

Subcutaneous tissue a layer of fatty tissue situated below the epidermis and dermis.

Sugar paste a system of wax depilation used to remove hair from the skin. An organic paste made from sugar, lemons and water is used to embed the hair, which is then removed in the paste from the skin.

Sugaring an ancient popular method of hair removal using organic substances, sugar and lemon.

Superfluous hair (excess hair) this hair growth is perfectly normal at certain parts in a woman's life, such as puberty and pregnancy, when there is a hormone disturbance in the body. New hairs, which grow at these times, usually disappear once hormone balance returns.

Systemic medical condition a medical condition caused by a defect in one of the body's organs e.g. the heart.

Tapotement also known as percussion. A massage manipulation which is used for its general toning and stimulating effect.

Target a goal or objective to achieve, usually set within a timescale.

Teamwork supportive work by a team.

Telogen the resting stage of the hair growth cycle, when the hair is finally shed.

Terminal hair deep-rooted, thick, coarse, pigmented hair found on the scalp, underarms, pubic region, eyelash and brow areas.

Thermal booties electrically heated boots in which the feet are placed following the application of a skin treatment product such as a mask. The heat aids the absorption of the product and improves skin functioning.

Thermal mitts electrically heated gloves in which the hands are placed following the application of a skin treatment product such as a mask. The heat aids the absorption of the product and improves skin functioning.

Thermal sensitivity test a test performed before wax application to check that the temperature of the wax is not too warm. The wax is tested by the therapist on themselves, usually on the inner wrist, and then on the client on a small visible area such as the inside of the ankle.

Thermometer equipment used to measure temperature.

Thioglycollate the active ingredient in perm solution.

Tinea corporis or body ringworm fungal infection of the skin where small scaly red patches, which spread outwards and then heal from the centre, leave a ring.

Tinea unguium a fungal infection of the nails. The nail is yellowish-grey in colour.

Tips and overlays a nail tip is applied, blended to remove the visible line, and is overlaid by acrylic, gel or fibreglass.

Toluenediamine small molecules of permanent dye used in tinting treatment.

Toning lotion a skin-care preparation to remove all traces of cleanser from the skin. It produces a cooling effect on the skin and has a skin-tightening effect.

Top coat a nail polish product applied over another nail polish to provide additional strength and durability to the finish.

Towel steaming an alternative to facial steaming using an electrical vapour unit. Small, clean facial towels are heated in a bowl of warm water or specialised heater, before application to the face to warm, cleanse and stimulate the skin.

Trades Description Act 1968 and 1972 legislation that states that information when selling products both in written and verbal form should be accurate.

Transfers water release (decals) and self-adhesive transfers secured to the nail, creating an instant design.

Transverse furrows nail condition where grooves appear on the nail running from side to side.

Travellers' cheques alternative form of payment used when travelling abroad and must be compared with the client's passport.

Treatment plan after the consultation, suitable treatment objectives are established to treat the client's conditions and needs.

Tweezers small metal tools used to remove body hair, by pulling it from the bottom of the hair follicle (small openings in the skin where the hair grows from). There are two types: *automatic,* designed to remove the bulk of the hair; and *manual,* designed to remove stray hairs.

Ultra-violet light invisible rays of the light spectrum with a wavelength shorter than visible light rays.

Ultra-violet light (UVL) cabinet a unit which uses UVL to *disinfect* small objects. Objects need to be clean before being placed in the cabinet, and must be turned, in order that the UVL rays effectively strike each surface of the object.

Vapour unit an electrical unit that heats water to produce steam, which is applied to the skin of the face and neck, to warm, cleanse and stimulate the skin.

Varicose veins veins whose valves have become weak and lost their elasticity. The area appears knotted, swollen and bluish/purple in colour.

Vellus hair hair which is fine, downy and soft – found on the face and body.

Ventilation the transport of fresh air into an area. The spa pool, for example, will create heat, humidity and chemical smells. Adequate ventilation is necessary for spa and other treatments.

Verbal communication occurs when you talk directly to another person, either face to face or over the telephone.

Verrucae or wart a viral infection. Small epidermal skin growths either raised or flat depending upon their location, and have a rough surface.

Vibrations massage manipulation applied on a nerve centre. They stimulate the nerves and can produce a relaxation effect. The movements are firm and trembling, performed with one or both hands.

Viruses the smallest living bodies, too small to see under an ordinary microscope. They are considered to be *parasites*, as they require living tissue to survive. Viruses invade healthy body cells and multiply within the cell. Eventually the cell walls break down and the virus particles are freed to attack further cells.

Warm oil treatment involves gently heating a small amount of treatment oil and soaking the nails and cuticles in it to nourish the nails and soften the cuticles and surrounding skin.

Warm wax a system of wax depilation used to remove hair from the skin. Warm wax remains soft at body temperatures. It is frequently made of mixtures of glucose syrup and zinc oxide. Honey can be used instead of glucose syrup – referred to as honey wax.

Watery eye over-secretion of tears from the eyes, which would normally drain into the nasal cavity.

Wax depilation the temporary removal of excess hair from a body part using wax.

Workplace (Health, Safety and Welfare) Regulations 1992 these regulations provide the employer with an approved code of practice for maintaining a safe, secure working environment.

Wrap a fibreglass or silk nail system to overlay natural nails.

index